05 06 07 08 09
15 16 17 18 19
25 26 27 28 29
35 36 37 38 39
45 46 47 48 49

GUINNESS MILLENNIUM EDITION
BOOK OF THE
20th CENTURY

GUINNESS
WORLD RECORDS

World Copyright Reserved
Copyright© 1997, 1999
and 2000 Guinness World
Records Ltd

Published in Great Britain by
Guinness World Records Ltd,
338 Euston Road,
London NW1 3BD

British Library Cataloguing in
Publication Data A catalogue
record for this book is available
from the British Library
ISBN 1-892051-05-2

Managing Editors
David Gould
Karen O'Brien

Editor
Kirsty Seymour-Ure

Assistant Editors
Emma Dixon
Tim Footman
Gill Moodie
Trevor Morris
Naomi Peck

Writers
Steven Armstrong
David Baker
Ariane Bankes
Peter Bently
Clifford Bishop
Deborah Chancellor
Ian Chilvers
Charlotte Evans
Robert Hanks
Nigel Hawkes
Nic Kynaston
Charles Phillips
Christina Rodenbeck
Robert Stewart
Lisle Turner
Iain Zaczek

Editorial Research
Mark Featherstone
Lorna Matthews
Jeff Evans
Dave McAleer

Proofreading and Index
Laura Hicks
Essi Berelian

Creative Director
Ian Castello-Cortes

Art Director
Peter Jackson

Picture Editor
Richard Philpott

Page Make-up
Keith Bambury
Robert Hackett
Paul Kime

Picture Research
Laura Jackson
Sophie Spencer-Wood
Yannick Yago

Production Manager
Patricia Langton

Thanks to
A C Nielsen ratings

Cover Design
Ron Callow at Design 23

Colour Origination
Graphic Facilities, London
Colour Systems, UK

Printing and Binding
Printer Industria Grafica SA,
Barcelona

Paper
Printed on wood-free, chlorine-
free and acid-free paper

GUINNESS BOOK OF THE
MILLENNIUM EDITION
20th CENTURY

GUINNESS
WORLD RECORDS

··· A CENTURY OF CONTRASTS ···

Future historians might see this as the century of extremes, full of highs and lows: kindness and cruelty, creation and destruction, freedom and enslavement. Or they might call it the century of paradox, as many of our achievements have been turned, by a series of oddly unpredictable consequences, into setbacks. Breakthroughs in civil rights have been matched by new abuses in human rights; advances in technology have given us ever-higher living standards and weapons of mass destruction. On the other hand, some ostensibly disastrous developments have brought unexpected benefits – from the debris of two world wars there emerged freedom for most of the world's colonies and a new mood of international cooperation.

As the century comes to an end, local religious and cultural traditions are rising to meet the march of Western culture. Instantaneous communication across massive distances is taken for granted. Meanwhile, advances in public health have generated a massive population boom. The next century will begin with a very different set of challenges from its predecessor.

HISTORY REPEATS In the 1930s, the 'scat' singing of Cab Calloway (left) was condemned as wild, debauched and corrupting. In the 1990s, Calloway's distant heir, the Prodigy's Keith Flint (right), met similar criticism.

FROM TINY ACORNS Robert Goddard's experiments with rocket propulsion (left) in the 1920s were the first steps in a programme that sent us into space (Hubble telescope, right) and changed forever the way we saw the Earth.

··· HARD NEWS, QUIRKY FACTS ···

The *Guinness Book of the 20th Century* tells the fast-moving story of the last 100 years, tracking the major news events – from the optimistic early years of the century, through the central decades of war and political tension and into the closing period of relative stability – in a way that will inform the curious and engross the browser. We also cover the popular events that defined the times – the scandals, the stars, the television shows – and the people who gave each year its flavour, from Charlie Chaplin to the Spice Girls. This unique combination of serious history with quirkier items adds up to a fascinating chronicle of a dynamic century.

··· HOW TO USE THIS BOOK ···

The *Guinness Book of the 20th Century* covers events on a chronological basis, and is organised year by year. Each year opens with a calendar page which gives information at a glance. Key developments are covered in news articles, while in-depth features give the background detail to the year's events, inventions, styles and cultural trends. Extra features cover cinema, pop and TV hits of the year, while 'newsflashes' pepper the pages of the book with extra facts. A full index makes it easy to track down information.

CALENDAR PAGE
Every year opens with a large number like this, using a different typeface for each decade. Underneath is a selective calendar of the year's events

BIRTHS AND DEATHS
We track the births and deaths of significant people

PICTURES
Selected entries are given a fuller treatment with pictures and extended captions

MILESTONES
Important or unusual events are grouped in date order under themed headings

NEW WORDS
New dictionary entries give vital insights into social and cultural trends

FEATURES
Special articles survey long-term developments and give background information

NEWS PAGE
The year's major events are covered in fresh, live reportage – as if they were taking place today

NEWSFLASH
Special boxes highlight fascinating facts, bizarre events and amazing statistics

SPORTING TRIUMPHS
We focus on the great athletic feats of the century. The Olympic Games are covered in full

WORLD NEWS
Full coverage of the great stories of the century – political turning-points, natural disasters, or momentous events in people's lives

ART AND ARTEFACTS
We cover the most influential artists and movements of the century, and look at the everyday objects that changed our lives

THE YEAR IN CINEMA
Revisit the great movies as they hit the silver screen

HITS OF THE YEAR
From 1956, we track the best-selling songs; from 1960, we also feature the most-watched TV shows of the year

00 10

1900

1916

20 30 40

1920

1931

1948

50 60 70

1955

1960

1976

80 90

1985

1993

The 20th century

1900

BORN

22 Feb: Luis Buñuel, Spanish film director
2 Mar: Kurt Weill, German-American composer
5 Apr: Spencer Tracy, US actor

Sigmund Freud publishes The Interpretation of Dreams, *which presents new views on the human mind. Freud's theories of psychoanalysis treat mental and emotional disorders by examining the subconscious.*

4 July: Louis Armstrong, US jazz trumpeter and singer
14 Nov: Aaron Copland, US composer

DIED

20 Jan: John Ruskin, British writer and art critic
6 Mar: Gottlieb Daimler, German designer and manufacturer of cars
30 Apr: Casey Jones, US train engineer
25 Aug: Friedrich Nietzsche, German philosopher

ATTACKED

4 Apr, Brussels: the Prince of Wales, shot at by a 16-year-old anarchist; the Prince is unhurt

30 July, Monza: King Umberto I of Italy, shot and killed by anarchist Angelo Bresci
2 Aug, Paris: the Shah of Persia, by anarchist François Salsou; the Shah survives
16 Nov, Germany: Kaiser Wilhelm, by woman with axe; the Kaiser is unhurt

FOUNDED

27 Feb, London: the Labour Representation Committee, foundation of the Labour Party

FASTEST

13 Aug, Plymouth: Hamburg-American liner *Deutschland* sets new record for transatlantic crossing from New York: five days, 19 hours and 45 minutes

On 2 July, German Count Ferdinand von Zeppelin launches the first trial flight of his airship LZ1. Flying by Lake Constance, the hydrogen-filled airship travels at a speed of 22.5 km/h (14 mph). Zeppelin began designing airships in 1891.

DISCOVERED

Cuba: yellow fever is transmitted by a variety of mosquito, by US army surgeon and bacteriologist Walter Reed

Vienna: three types of human blood (groups A, B and C), by Austrian pathologist Dr Karl Landsteiner

OPENED

19 July, Paris: the Métro underground railway system

FIRST

Woman to win Olympic gold medal: British tennis player Charlotte Cooper

FIRST NIGHTS

14 Jan, Rome: *Tosca*, opera by Italian composer Giacomo Puccini
4 June, Paris: French artist Auguste Rodin's sculpture *The Kiss* first exhibited publicly
3 Oct, Birmingham: *The Dream of Gerontius*, oratorio by Edward Elgar

SIGNED

20 Oct: Lord Salisbury and Baron von Hatzfelt sign agreement between Germany and Britain to keep China's ports open to international trade

On 30 November, writer Oscar Wilde dies a poor man in exile. A scandal destroyed Wilde's career after his homosexual relationship with Lord Alfred Douglas was made public. Wilde is best remembered for The Importance of Being Earnest *(1895).*

ON SALE

31 Aug, Britain: Coca-Cola introduced; launched in USA 14 years ago

SEIZED

1 Sept, South Africa: the Boer republic of the Transvaal, by British General Roberts

POISONED

1 Dec, Liverpool, Manchester: beer drinkers, by chemicals used in brewing process

INVENTED

Escalator, by Charles Seeberger, shown at the Paris Exhibition

PUBLISHED

Joseph Conrad, *Lord Jim*

NEW WORDS

concentration camp *n*: fortified area in which a regime's political enemies or prisoners of war are detained
brunch *n*: meal eaten late in morning; breakfast and lunch combined

Rebels driven out

14 AUGUST, BEIJING
Beijing has been liberated from its Chinese rebel captors by a 10 000-strong international armed force. The siege of the British Embassy, where European women and children took refuge, has been lifted after 56 days; they had just one week's food left.

The rebels are members of a patriotic mystical martial-arts society, and have been dubbed 'Boxers' because they practise a form of shadowboxing that they believe makes them immune to bullets. They inflicted three months of terror on Europeans in China in a protest against 'foreign devils' in the country.

The uprising began in May in southern China when the Boxers defeated imperial Chinese government troops before moving northward to take control of Tientsin and Beijing. Foreign governments determined to protect the lives of diplomats, business-men and missionaries mobilised a joint army including Japanese, French, British, American and German soldiers.

When the rebels murdered the German ambassador on 16 June, the stakes were raised. The Boxers were driven out of Tientsin in July – but only after killing 1500 Europeans. The failure of the imperial government to impose order forced foreign intervention, and when the Europeans reached Beijing its ruling Dowager Empress fled.

BANNER PROTEST A Chinese rebel shows his opposition to foreigners.

··· MAX PLANCK DISCOVERS ENERGY COMES IN PACKETS CALLED 'QUANTA', GIVING BIRTH TO QUANTUM THEORY ···

Tide turns against Boers

18 MAY, MAFEKING, SOUTHERN AFRICA
The seven-month siege of British troops in a southern African railway town has been lifted. The retreat of Boer soldiers besieging Mafeking, on 16 May, coming six weeks after the relief of another British garrison at Ladysmith, suggests that the British army has recovered from its disastrous start to the war. Britons will greet the news with jubilation.

Attempts to force the southern African Boer republics to join the British Empire provoked a war in 1880–81 that was won by the Boers, but tension remained. Fighting broke out again in October 1899, and at the turn of the year things looked grim for the British. The Boers won three major battles in one December week, and besieged the British-held rail junctions of Mafeking, Ladysmith and Kimberley.

The tide turned in January, when Field Marshal Lord Roberts arrived to take charge of the British army, and the siege of Kimberley was lifted in early February. The Boers were at their best fighting in small mobile groups, and their decision to mount long sieges was a mistake.

AGE NO BARRIER Three generations of grim Boer fighters.

USA wins Davis Cup

TEAM PRIDE US captain Dwight Davis is the first holder of the trophy to which he gives his name.

10 AUGUST, BOSTON

The game of lawn tennis has taken on a new international dimension, with the USA trouncing Britain 3–0 in the first contest for the Davis Cup.

Dwight Davis won his singles match against the British captain Arthur Gore, and teamed up with Holcombe Ward to win the doubles. Absent from the British team were the stars of Wimbledon, the Doherty brothers, and without them the British players were unable to cope with the high-kicking 'American twist' serves of their opponents.

London welcomes opening of the 'twopenny tube'

27 JUNE, LONDON

The Prince of Wales today opened the Central London Railway, an electrified line running nearly 10 kilometres (nearly 6 miles) across the capital between Shepherds Bush in west London and the Bank in the east.

Competition is growing among London's railway companies to provide fast, comfortable and efficient underground services. The first electrified railway, the City and South London, opened in 1890, but the Central line is much grander, with luxurious cars and a single class. It also has a single fare of twopence whatever the length of the journey.

The Central's electric trains are much cleaner than the steam trains that are still operating on the Metropolitan and District systems, and it is envisaged that the 'twopenny tube' will be an enormous success.

HELPING HAND The Scarecrow and the Tin Man, as seen in an early stage version of the book.

Wizardry is a hit

'A modernised fairy tale' called *The Wonderful Wizard of Oz,* by American author L Frank Baum, was published this year. The enchanting story relates the strange adventures of Dorothy, whisked away by a cyclone to a magical country. The book's first print run sold out within weeks, partly due to W W Denselow's much praised whimsical illustrations of the book's characters.

··· WORLD'S FIRST TAPE RECORDER, THE TELEGRAPHONE, IS INVENTED BY VALDEMAR POULSEN ···

Giant exhibition shows off genius of the French

SPLENDID PAVILIONS Almost 40 million people flock to see the world's latest wonders.

15 APRIL, PARIS

The greatest exhibition Europe has ever seen opened its doors today. The Paris International Exhibition occupies almost 220 hectares (545 acres) of space in seven separate sites across the city.

The greatest impressions of the show are the magnificent effects produced by electric lighting in the halls, while the industrial exhibits include some of the first motor cars.

Most of the objects are displayed in halls devoted to a particular subject. In each of these France has more than half the space, enabling it to overwhelm rivals. But national pavilions have also been built along the Quai d'Orsay, including – for the first time since the war of 1870 – a German pavilion. The president of France, M Loubet, declared that this meeting of the peoples of the world 'would not remain without fruit'.

Paris itself has gained two permanent galleries, the Grand and Petit Palais in the Champs Elysées, and a new bridge over the river Seine.

Dancing – for cake

The dancehalls of Europe have been swept by a new craze from America this year: the cake walk. The dance is thought to have started as a slaves' parody of their masters' grand manners and probably takes its name from graceful walking or dance competitions with a cake as the prize. It was popularised by the vaudeville partnership of Bert Williams and George Walker.

The dance's centrepiece is a high-kicking parade down the dance-floor, with the dancing couple, arm in arm, bowing and waving to spectators.

WALKOVER The cake walk is fun as a solo dance, but really takes off when partners join in.

··· JOHN BROOKS, USA, DESIGNS THE BUTTON-DOWN COLLAR 'POLO' SHIRT, INSPIRED BY BRITISH POLO PLAYERS ···

Tiny clip set to be next big thing

Johann Waaler, a Norwegian inventor based in Germany, has patented a tiny device made of bent wire for keeping papers together. He intends his new paperclip to replace pins in doing this job – providing a safer and more effective solution.

INGENIOUS TWIST Small but perfectly formed.

SNAP BOX The camera that brought photography to the people.

Eastman launches people's camera

This year has seen the introduction of the 'Brownie' camera, invented by George Eastman. Made out of stiff cardboard, with no viewfinder – just a V marked on top to show where to aim – the Brownie is on sale in the USA for $1. It is billed as the first camera that anyone can use, and it certainly makes taking a snapshot very simple. You just point it and click the shutter.

Dig reveals ancient bull-leaping culture

APRIL, CRETE
Some of the marvels of a previously unknown prehistoric civilisation have been revealed by British archaeologist Arthur Evans at an ancient Greek site at Knossos in Crete.

Perhaps most exciting for Evans is the discovery of fragments of inscribed pottery – vital evidence proving that, as he suspected, the culture that lived here was a literate one. Furthermore, Evans identifies the culture as 'pre-Mycenaean' – older than the ancient Homeric civilisation (16th century BC) discovered by Heinrich Schliemann some years earlier at Mycenae.

From the discovery of a gypsum throne, Evans surmises that the complex was a vast palace, perhaps that of the legendary King Minos of Crete, leading him to term the civilisation 'Minoan'. The mazelike plan of the palace may even have given rise to the legend of the Minotaur – the half-man, half-bull monster of the labyrinth – a theory supported by Evans's discovery of numerous signs of a bull-worshipping cult and frescoes depicting 'bull-leaping'.

1901

DIED
27 Jan: Giuseppe Verdi, Italian composer
9 Sept: Henri de Toulouse-Lautrec, French painter

On 24 June, Pablo Picasso, aged 19, from Barcelona, impresses critics with his first exhibition in Paris, which includes Harlequin and his Companion. *Picasso takes inspiration from the cabaret night-life in Paris.*

BORN
1 Feb: Clark Gable, US film star
7 May: Gary Cooper, US film star
5 Dec: Walt Disney, US producer of cartoon films
18 Nov: George Gallup, US statistician
27 Dec: Marlene Dietrich (born Magdalena von Losch), US film star

DENOUNCED
17 June, London: conditions endured by Boers in concentration camps, by Liberal politician David Lloyd George

ARRESTED
31 Mar, Russia: 72 revolutionaries, following recent riots

14 Apr, New York City: actors at the Academy of Music, for wearing costumes on a Sunday

WRECKED
22 Feb, San Francisco: Pacific mail steamer; 128 die
22 May, Isle of Wight: Racing yacht, *Shamrock II*, with King Edward VII on board; no one is hurt

EXECUTED
26 Feb, Beijing: Chi-hsui and Hsu-cheng-yu, leaders of the failed Boxer Rebellion
29 Oct, US: Leon Czolgosz, anarchist assassin of US President McKinley

FLED
18 Dec, Birmingham: politician David Lloyd George, from pro-Boer public meeting, when crowd riots

SOLD
9 Aug, Oklahoma: American Indian land to settlers, by lottery

FOUNDED
1 Jan: Commonwealth of Australia
12 Mar, New York City: public library system; US businessman Andrew Carnegie provides funds of $2.5 million
29 July, Indianapolis: the Socialist Party of America
21 Aug, Detroit: the Cadillac Motor Company
24 Oct, New Jersey: the Eastman Kodak Company, international company, following success of $1 Brownie camera launched in 1900

FIRST NIGHTS
31 Jan, Moscow: *Three Sisters*, play by Anton Chekhov

FIRSTS
Facelift: performed by Eugene Hollander in Berlin on a Polish aristocrat, using detailed drawings she supplied
Getaway car: used by three bandits who raided a bank in Paris
Mercedes motor car: made by the Daimler Motor Co for Austrian diplomat Emile Jellinek, and named after his daughter, Mercedes
6 Feb, Paris: public telephones at railway stations
16 Oct: black man invited to the White House, Booker T Washington
10 Dec, Oslo: Nobel Prizes awarded: for literature, peace, medicine, chemistry and physics

INVENTIONS
30 Nov, USA: first hearing aid, designed by Miller Reese Hutchinson
Christmas tree lights: developed by Edison General Electric Co, USA

SIGNED
7 Sept, Beijing: treaty to end Boxer Rebellion; China must pay reparations
18 Nov, USA: Hay-Pauncefote Act by USA and Britain, gives USA the right to build a canal in Panama, central America

FASTEST
16 Nov, New York: French driver Henri Fournier, one mile in 52 seconds in a motor car
26 Aug, New York: US cyclist Robert Walthour, one mile in 1 minute 37.4 seconds on a bicycle

DISCOVERED
10 Jan, Beaumont: first oil in Texas; the first well, Spindletop, sends out an oil gusher 61 m (200 ft) high

Hormone adrenalin: by Japanese chemist Jokichi Takamine & US physicist John Jacob Abel

INTRODUCED
Netball: by Adair Roberts at Dartford Physical Training College, Kent

The decorative influence of Art Nouveau is apparent everywhere, even in cigarette advertising. This advertisement draws on the style of the French painter Henri de Toulouse-Lautrec, who developed the poster as an art form.

RECOGNISED
Boxing: as a legal sport, under Queensberry rules, but not in USA and many other countries

INSTALLED
Peanut vending machines: at the Pan-American Exhibition, Buffalo, New York, by Mills Novelty Company

NEW WORDS
fetishism *n*: a condition in which an inanimate object or part of the body causes sexual arousal
accessories *n*: small accompanying items of dress, eg gloves, handbag

NATION MOURNS QUEEN VICTORIA

ROYAL FAMILY The Queen with her granddaughter by marriage Mary of Teck (left) and her daughter-in-law Alexandra (right) cradles her great-granddaughter Mary.

4 FEBRUARY, WINDSOR

Queen Victoria, the longest-reigning monarch in British history, was laid to rest in the family mausoleum at Windsor, two weeks after her death on 22 January, aged 81. Four years ago throngs of supporters lined the streets of London to mark her Diamond Jubilee, celebrating 60 years on the throne; today the crowds watched in solemn silence as her funeral procession passed by.

The Queen's last days were spent at Osborne House on the Isle of Wight. Her son and heir, 'Bertie', now the new King Edward VII, was at her deathbed.

The Queen's body lay in state for ten days at Osborne before being carried to the mainland by the royal yacht *Alberta*. The funeral train then made its stately progress to London. By Victoria's own instruction the colour black was banned from her funeral and the hangings in London's streets were purple cashmere with white satin bows. An 81-gun salute was sounded – one for every year of her life – and a simple service was read before a small congregation.

Queen Victoria, the Empress of India, presided over a momentous era of British power and security. She ascended the throne in 1837 aged 18, and married Prince Albert from the German duchy of Saxe-Coburg-Gotha in 1840. Her reign lasted 63 years. In her lifetime Britain reaped the benefits of the Industrial Revolution, becoming the leading industrial nation of the world. At its height, the Empire over which 'the sun never sets' stretched across five continents. The Indian Empire alone encompassed some 250 million people. Australia, New Zealand and British Canada were brought under the umbrella of the Empire, as were many parts of Africa.

Recent stirrings in the Empire point to a growing desire for independence, raising the spectre of unrest in parts of the empire. The death of the Queen leaves Britain pondering the close of a great chapter in its history, and an uncertain future.

··· INSTANT COFFEE IS FIRST SOLD AT THE PAN-AMERICAN EXHIBITION, BUFFALO, NEW YORK ···

President assassinated by Polish anarchist

14 SEPTEMBER, USA

The United States is in shock after the death of President William McKinley, from wounds suffered when he was shot last week in Buffalo, New York. McKinley is the third US President to be assassinated.

The fatal incident occurred at the Pan-American Exhibition in Buffalo. As the President greeted admirers he was shot at point-blank range by Leon Czolgosz, the son of Polish immigrants. Czolgosz, a well-dressed 28-year-old, blended easily into the crowd. In the searing heat of late summer, with fluttering handkerchiefs everywhere, the revolver that he hid in a handkerchief went unnoticed.

The outrage has appalled the nation, which two days earlier had warmed to the President's call for the United States to abandon isolationism and enter fully into international affairs.

Doctors initially hoped that the President would survive, but the bullet that ripped through his abdomen did such extensive damage that his heart eventually gave way. The mantle of the presidency has passed to the vice-president, Theodore Roosevelt.

SURPRISE ATTACK Czolgosz, his weapon concealed in a handkerchief, shoots McKinley.

Cossacks disperse student strikers

17 MARCH, ST PETERSBURG
Students interrupted services at Kazan Cathedral today,
agitating for the removal of the Tsar – but they were pushed
back into the streets and scattered by charging Cossack
cavalry. The riot followed a week of unrest in several Russian
cities including Kiev and Moscow, where striking workers and
students together set up street barricades.

The students were protesting against new rules governing
student life, introduced by the Interior Ministry. Matters were
inflamed by the decision of the Orthodox Church to
excommunicate the writer Leo Tolstoy because of his
pronouncements against the Church.

Russian Jews have repeatedly taken the blame for outbreaks
of lawlessness. Anti-Semitism thrives under Tsar Nicholas II –
officials believe allegations that Jewish agitation is behind
strikes and riots. The five million Russian Jews are the first
target for random violence among peasants and poor city-
dwellers. Police are known to encourage anti-Jewish violence.

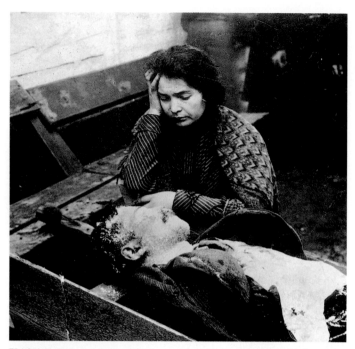
TRAGIC END Increasingly, violent unrest is ending in injury and death.

··· LONDON'S POPULATION REACHES 6.6 MILLION; PARIS HAS 2.7 MILLION, BERLIN 1.9 MILLION ···

You can throw this blade away

A razor that is thrown away
after one use was launched
this year in Boston. King
Camp Gillette had the idea
six years ago when he
realised how little of his
'cutthroat' razor was actually
used for shaving. His
assistant, William Nickerson,
found a way to make thin
steel blades with a keen
edge, so that Gillette could
finally file his patent.

Wireless message crosses Atlantic

RADIO DAYS Guglielmo Marconi at St Johns, Newfoundland, with some of
his wireless broadcasting and receiving apparatus.

12 DECEMBER, ST JOHNS,
NEWFOUNDLAND
The Italian inventor
Guglielmo Marconi has
astonished scientific experts
by transmitting a wireless
message from Poldhu in
Cornwall to Signal Hill in
Newfoundland, a distance of

more than 3200 kilometres
(2000 miles).

The signals, a series of
three dots – the letter S in
Morse code – were
transmitted from Cornwall
from a 50-metre (164-ft)
aerial, at 6.00 pm, a time
fixed in advance. Across the

Atlantic, where an aerial was
taken high into the sky by a
kite, Marconi crouched over
his receiving apparatus. The
signals, although faint, were
received clearly and almost
immediately.

Marconi, who settled in
England in 1896 after failing
to gain support for his
pioneering work in Italy, has
until now been almost alone
in believing that radio signals
could travel so far, although
in 1899 he succeeded in
sending a message across the
English Channel.

Nobody knows how
radio waves, which travel in
straight lines, are able to
follow the curvature of the
Earth over such a large
distance. Marconi's successful
experiment proves that they
can, and opens up immense
possibilities for global
communications.

Good sounds on disc

A new recording format is bringing new heights of fidelity to the growing market for recorded music. Single-sided 24-centimetre (10-in) discs, introduced this year, can record up to three minutes of music on each record. They produce a far better sound than the wax cylinders of Thomas Edison's phonograph, and threaten to replace both them and the old 16-centimetre (7-in) format. The Consolidated Talking Machine Company, of Camden, New Jersey, is making shellac discs with a circular title label pressed into them – a valuable help to those who are now storing their discs in albums.

THAT'S ENTERTAINMENT The cylinder disc could soon be a thing of the past.

A new art for a new era

The Art Nouveau style, with its sinuous, curving, naturalistically inspired forms, has flourished in the decorative arts and architecture all across Europe.

In Paris the new signs for the Métro station entrances have been cast as flamboyant scrolls and twining tendrils; in Spain, architect Antonio Gaudì designs buildings with flowing curves and organic forms. The curvaceous, plantlike shapes of Art Nouveau, so well suited to sculpture, have inspired the stunning jewellery of René Lalique and been taken up by London's famous Liberty department store.

In northern Europe, Art Nouveau is epitomised by the furniture of Scottish architect Charles Rennie Mackintosh, who uses intricate linear designs and geometric patterns.

GRACEFUL CURVES Developing out of the Arts and Crafts Movement, Art Nouveau uses highly stylised natural forms worked into strong, often asymmetric patterns.

··· 24 OCTOBER: ANNA TAYLOR, AGED 43, SAILS OVER NIAGARA FALLS IN A BARREL AND SURVIVES ···

Fingertip control for criminals

The world's first fingerprint file was installed in London this year, at New Scotland Yard, the headquarters of the Metropolitan Police.

No two fingerprints are the same – every person's are completely unique and remain unchanged from birth to death. Sir Edward Henry, the Assistant Commissioner of the Metropolitan Police, has worked out a system of classifying fingerprints according to their distinctive whorls and loops. The police hope that this will prove a valuable way to trace and identify criminals.

UNIQUE SIGNATURE
Every fingerprint tells a tale.

Commonwealth of Australia

1 JANUARY, SYDNEY
Australia today enters a new century with bright hopes for the future as a united commonwealth. By the act of parliament which received British approval and the royal assent last year, the six formerly independent states of the colony have been joined together.

The selling-points of the advocates of union have been the benefits of internal free trade, a common defence against external threat, and control of immigration. Despite strong opposition in New South Wales, the union was approved by the people in referendums held in each of the six states. Elections to the federal parliament will be held this year. Edmund Barton is the favourite to become prime minister.

1902

DIED

26 Mar: Cecil Rhodes, British statesman
18 June: Samuel Butler, British writer
29 Sept: Emile Zola, French writer
22 Nov: Friedrich Krupp, German industrialist

The teddy bear is invented in the United States. The creator, a Russian immigrant, made the toy after seeing a newspaper cartoon depicting President Theodore 'Teddy' Roosevelt on a bear hunt.

BORN

4 Feb: Charles Lindbergh, US aviator
27 Feb: John Steinbeck, US novelist

BESTSELLERS

12 Nov: *Vesti La Gubbia*, record by Italian tenor Enrico Caruso, sells 1 million copies
Beatrix Potter *The Tale of Peter Rabbit*
Arthur Conan Doyle *The Hound of the Baskervilles*

PUBLISHED

Joseph Conrad, *Heart of Darkness*
Owen Wister, *The Virginian: A Horseman of the Plains*
Rudyard Kipling *Just So Stories*
Helen Keller *The Story of My Life*
William James *The Varieties of Religious Experience*

BANNED

1 Feb, China: binding of women's feet, by imperial decree
3 Mar, USA: dealing in financial 'futures', by Supreme Court
5 May, Germany: women's political groups, by Prussian government

FOUNDED

4 Jan, Washington DC: Carnegie Institute
4 Mar, USA: American Automobile Association
7 Apr, USA: Texas Oil Company (Texaco)
29 May, London: London School of Economics and Political Science

FIRST NIGHT

20 Apr, Paris: Art Nouveau exhibition opens, at Société Nationale des Beaux-Arts

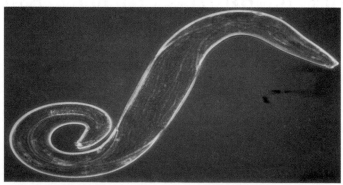

Sir Ronald Ross, the British bacteriologist, is awarded the Nobel Prize for his discovery of how malaria is transmitted. Ross demonstrates that the disease is transmitted via a parasitic organism called plasmodium (above) contained in the bite of the female Anopheles mosquito. Most of Ross's groundbreaking research was completed while he was working in the Indian Medical Service.

ON STRIKE

4 Feb, Russia: 30 000 students as part of political campaign against Tsar
14 Feb, Italy: workers calling for shorter working days
5 Mar, Paris: French miners, calling for eight-hour day
2 May, Pennsylvania: 200 000 miners, for union recognition and pay rise

INVENTIONS

28 May, USA: electrical storage battery, lighter and longer-lasting than existing lead-acid batteries, by US inventor Thomas Edison
9 June, Philadelphia: 'Automat', coin-operated automatic vending machine

FED

5 July, London: 456 000 poor Londoners, at dinners to mark King Edward VII's coronation

RETIRED

12 July: Lord Salisbury as British prime minister (Tory); Arthur James Balfour succeeds him

SURRENDERED

10 Apr, South Africa: Boers, to the British

FIRSTS

3 Aug: parcel mail from Britain to the USA, on the liner *Teutonic*
17 Oct: Cadillac motor car sold

ATTACKED

15 Nov, Belgium: King Leopold II by anarchist Genaro Rubbino

On 9 August, King Edward VII is crowned at Westminster Abbey following the death of his mother, Queen Victoria. King Edward and Queen Alexandra, a member of the Danish royal family, have six children.

DESTROYED

14 July, Venice: 10th-century Gothic belltower of St Mark's Cathedral
22 Nov, New York City: Williamsburg Bridge over the East River, by fire

NEW WORDS

curriculum vitae *n*: an outline of a person's professional and educational history, usually prepared for job applications
electronic *adj*: equipment controlled by devices or special circuits in which electrons are conducted

A trip to the Moon

MAY, PARIS
Crowds have flocked to see the new moving picture from Georges Méliès which opened this week in Paris. In *A Trip to the Moon* Méliès creates genuine magic. Using daring special effects, this Jules Verne-inspired tale of a rocket voyage in outer space takes the medium of cinema to a new level of sophistication.

MOON MAN *A Trip to the Moon* uses 'special effects' to depict fabulous life on other planets.

With this film it is as if Méliès, a former magician, has invented moving pictures all over again. For the pioneering Lumière brothers, film had been a way of recording reality; now Méliès has shown that it can be a vehicle for dreams and fantasy.

SKY HIGH One man said that the Flat Iron is to America what the Parthenon was to Greece.

Triangular edifice is the toast of NY

The Flat Iron Building – whose construction New Yorkers have been observing attentively for some years – was finally completed this year in New York City. Other skyscrapers may be bigger, but none symbolises the daring of modern architecture better than this 20-storey limestone wedge with its six new Otis elevators. Its remarkable shape – a slender triangle – fills an odd plot of land where Broadway joins Fifth Avenue, at 23rd Street.

Rumours abound of strange wind patterns caused by its triangular form – a young messenger boy is said to have been blown off the pavement and killed. But the building's grand profile, likened to 'a ship sailing up the avenue', is sure to make it one of New York's most popular landmarks.

Aswan Dam opens

10 DECEMBER, EGYPT
Egypt's new dam was unveiled today at Aswan, 950 kilometres (590 miles) south of Cairo. The 40-metre (130 ft) high Aswan Dam, designed to control the Nile flood waters, is 2 kilometres (1¼ miles) long – the result of four years' labour by 11 000 workers. It is hoped that modern irrigation methods will help the region's farmers.

··· DURING THE BOER WAR IN SOUTH AFRICA, MORE SOLDIERS DIE OF DISEASE THAN BY ENEMY ACTION ···

1903

BORN

13 Feb: Georges Simenon, Belgian crime writer

25 June: George Orwell (born Eric Arthur Blair), British novelist

25 Sept: Mark Rothko, US artist

17 Oct: Nathanael West, US author

28 Oct: Evelyn Waugh, British novelist

On **13 December**, *Italo Marcioni of New Jersey, USA, registers a patent for his mould for the first ice-cream cone. Although other inventors are laying claim to the cone, the ice-cream salesman Marcioni is the first to patent his idea.*

DIED

25 Feb: Richard Gatling, US inventor of the rapid-fire gun

8 May: Paul Gauguin, French painter

17 July: James McNeill Whistler, US painter

20 July: Pope Leo XIII

22 Aug: Robert Cecil, Third Marquess of Salisbury, British statesman

12 Nov: Camille Pissarro, French artist

8 Dec: Herbert Spencer, British philosopher

PUBLISHED

Jack London, *The Call of the Wild*

Kate Douglas Wiggin, *Rebecca of Sunnybrook Farm*

FIRSTS

22 Feb: newspaper published at sea, on board transatlantic liner *Etruria*; news was broadcast from Britain by wireless, and the paper was delivered in New York at end of crossing

KILLED

14 Apr, Macedonia: 165 Muslims by Bulgarian mob. As Turkish government weakens, violence between Turks, Bulgarians and Albanians grows

16 Apr, Russia: Jews by Russian mob in Kishinev, Bessarabia. Anti-Jewish feeling is running high, apparently encouraged by the Tsar

8 Sept, Macedonia: 50000 Bulgarians by Turkish troops; every Bulgarian village in Monastir area is destroyed

LINKED

29 Mar: New York City and London, by news service using Marconi wireless

FIRST NIGHTS

20 Jan, New York City: *The Wizard of Oz*, play adapted from Frank Baum's bestselling book

23 Nov, New York City: Italian tenor Enrico Caruso debuts at the Metropolitan Opera in Verdi's *Rigoletto*

CLOSED

2 Jan, Missouri: a post office that refused to employ a black woman as postmistress, by US President Roosevelt

IN BUSINESS

23 July, Detroit: Ford Motor Company sells its first motor car; the Ford Model A costs $850 and can reach a speed of 48 km/h (30mph)

16 June, USA: Pepsi Cola Company registers trade name 'Pepsi Cola'

CHAMPIONS

2 July, Ireland: Belgian Camille Jenatzki, winner of Gordon Bennett motor race

14 Dec, Sydney: English amateur cricketer 'Tip' Foster, scorer of 287, highest ever individual Test Match score, on his England debut; England rack up 577 against Australia

DISCOVERED

8 Aug, India: new operation to combat cataracts – opacity of lenses in human eye - by Indian Medical Service doctor Lieutenant-Colonel Henry Smith

2 Oct, London: part of Roman city wall, while other buildings are being demolished

3 Nov, Holland: electro-cardiograph, new machine to monitor heartbeat, by Willem Einthoven

DONATED

15 Aug, New York City: $2 million to fund journalism school, by Hungarian-born American journalist Joseph Pulitzer

RAZED

9 June, Germany: Daimler Motor Company factory at Cannstadt, by fire

30 Dec, Chicago: Iroquois Theatre, by fire; 578 die, and tragedy sparks campaign to bring in stricter safety laws

NEW WORDS

clone *n*: genetic material that has been isolated and reproduced by laboratory manipulation

déjà vu *n*: the experience of perceiving a new situation as if it had occurred before

The Thermos vacuum flask is patented in Germany by Reinhold Burger. The flask was invented in 1892 by Scottish scientist James Dewar; however, Dewar did not have the foresight to patent his invention.

MOMENT OF TRUTH Having run alongside the aircraft as it gathered speed, holding the wing to steady it, Wilbur Wright watches as brother Orville takes off.

At last, man can fly

17 DECEMBER, NORTH CAROLINA
At 10.35 this morning the 'Flyer', a
contraption of wood, wire and fabric,
rose from a wooden rail in the blustery
sand dunes of Kitty Hawk. Its pilot,
Orville Wright, flew it for 12 seconds,
for a distance of 36 metres (120 ft) – the
first controlled, powered flight in history.

This is the fourth autumn that
Orville and his brother Wilbur, bicycle-
makers from Dayton, Ohio, have spent
experimenting with flying machines at
Kitty Hawk. The Wrights' methodical
approach and firm grasp of aeronautical
theory has set them apart from many
other would-be aviators; in their
workshop they have carefully analysed
their rivals' experiments and tested their
own theories before conducting further
trials on the beach. Last year they
perfected a system of 'warping' the wings

of their biplane gliders to achieve an
unprecedented degree of control over
their flight. This year they added a
lightweight engine and pair of propellers
to their successful glider design. The
pilot has to lie in a precarious harness on
the lower wing, moving his body to
control the rudder and warp the wings
via a complex system of wires and
pulleys which leaves his hands free to
make other adjustments.

The Flyer was first tested three days
ago, with Wilbur at the controls. He
pulled too sharply on the aircraft's
elevator, and it nosedived into the sand.
Today the brothers made four successful
trials, culminating in a 59-second flight
before a gust of wind caught the
machine and damaged it. A new chapter
in human achievement has opened: man
can fly.

Turks massacre Bulgarian rebels

8 SEPTEMBER, MACEDONIA
Troops of the Ottoman Empire
have killed an estimated 50 000
Bulgarian rebels in a savage move to
crush a planned uprising against Turkish
rule in Macedonia. Bulgarians fled for
their lives as Turkish soldiers razed
villages around the town of Monastir.
Some victims hid in the countryside but
were shot after being forced into the
open by fires.

Turkish authority in the Balkans has
been in danger of dissolving altogether.
Bulgarians in the Monastir area were
the aggressors in April, destroying a
Muslim village and killing 165 people.
The Turks, hearing of plans for an
August revolt, sent 300 000 men to
Macedonia. The brutal show of force
will only make further rebellion certain.

TIRELESS WORKER Marie toiled for long hours in her laboratory in search of new radioactive materials.

Prize solves Curies' cash crisis

10 DECEMBER, PARIS
The French scientists Pierre and Marie Curie have been awarded the Nobel Prize for physics for their investigations into radioactivity. The prize is shared with Henri Becquerel, who discovered the ability of uranium rays to fog photographic plates.

Inspired by Becquerel's discovery, the Curies set out to discover the cause of what Marie termed 'radioactivity'. She was sure that uranium was not the only radioactive element, and together with Pierre set out to prove her theory. In their primitive laboratory at the Sorbonne the Curies had to purify several tons of the uranium-bearing ore pitchblende in order to isolate two new elements: polonium (named after Marie's country of birth) and radium.

Last year they ran out of money. The Nobel Prize, worth 70000 francs, not only makes them famous but also solves their financial crisis.

Prophet says people will travel in space

A pioneering Russian research physicist published a series of papers this year prophesying rocket travel in space. Konstantin Tsiolkovsky, little known even in his own country, backs his extraordinary claim with complex mathematical theories and practical experiments. A schoolteacher near Moscow, he spent years investigating aerodynamics using a wind tunnel that he invented and built himself. In a series of scholarly articles, Tsiolkovsky has shown himself to be far ahead of his time, predicting the invention of satellites, space-suits, liquid fuel propellants and space stations. He even says that we will one day colonise other parts of the solar system.

ROCKET MAN Tsiolkovsky: prophet or crank?

··· HARLEY-DAVIDSON MOTORCYCLE COMPANY FOUNDED BY WILLIAM HARLEY AND ARTHUR DAVIDSON ···

Tour de France defeats two-thirds of field

19 JULY, PARIS
The French cyclist Maurice Garin has won the first ever Tour de France, 19 days after setting out with 59 other competitors. One of only 20 racers to complete the gruelling six-stage course, he finished nearly three hours ahead of the rest, covering the 2428-mile (3907-kilometre) course in 19 days and nights of hard pedalling.

With cycling now well established as a mass hobby, the race was the brainchild of the newspaper editor Henri Desgrange. It began and ended in Paris, reaching Marseilles on the Mediterranean coast and looping back via Toulouse, Bordeaux and Nantes. Mountain stages will be added in the next year or two to what is certain to become a popular annual event.

First 'western' film

An 11-minute film, *The Great Train Robbery*, has taken US audiences by storm. Edwin S Porter's 'western' has a simple yet gripping plot, but it is a huge leap forward for cinema. Longer and faster-moving than any previous film, it boasts a sustained, logical narrative and bold camerawork − including the startling closing shot of a bandit firing his gun straight at the audience.

Heroes' welcome for coast-to-coast drivers

23 JUNE, NEW YORK CITY
Nelson Jackson and Sewall Crocker have completed an epoch-making journey from coast to coast in a car named after its designer, Alexander Winton. It is the first time that anyone has completed the transcontinental drive.

Jackson and Crocker set out from San Francisco in their 20-horsepower, two-cylinder Winton loaded with so much food, fuel supplies and spares that it looked more like a vehicle on military duty than a family saloon. It lurched and rolled its way across uncharted terrain – over the towering sierras and across the scorching, inhospitable sands of Nevada. But the Winton survived every test and brought its drivers – after 65 gruelling days – a heroes' welcome in New York. There will be no stopping the American demand for the motor car now.

DRIVING FORCE British rally driver Charles Rolls poses in a current model.

··· 24 MAY: PARIS–MADRID ROAD RACE IS ABANDONED AFTER SIX DRIVERS ARE KILLED ON FIRST DAY ···

Triumph of vaudeville

ACTING FUNNY 'King Booriaboola' entertains.

WORLD CLASS After the National League's defeat, the World Series was not staged again until 1905.

In the United States this year the variety shows known as vaudeville continue to be virtually synonymous with entertainment. The pattern of each show is traditional, incorporating a dozen acts or so, including a singer, a comedian, animals, acrobats, magicians and dancers, each act being announced by a sign at the side of the stage. The business is dominated by giant booking agencies, which place acts in more than 10000 theatres across the USA.

Red Sox beat Pirates in first World Series

13 OCTOBER, BOSTON
The Boston Red Sox have made baseball history, inspired by the mean pitching of Cy Young and Bill Dineen. By beating the Pittsburgh Pirates five games to three they have won the first World Series, in which the champions of the two major leagues play a series of championship matches after the end of the baseball season.

The Pirates were let down by their outstanding shortstop Honus Wagner, the National League batting champion, who had a miserable series at the plate and in the field.

The American League, formed three years ago, was only this year recognised as a 'major' league, and by turning the tables on its senior rivals it has left the National League somewhat redfaced.

1904

BORN

18 Jan: Cary Grant (born Archibald Leach), British-born film star

1 Mar: Glenn Miller, US bandleader, trombonist and composer

2 May: Bing Crosby (born Harry L Crosby), US singer

26 June: Peter Lorre, German-born film star

2 Oct: Graham Greene, British novelist

DIED

24 Apr: Friedrich Siemens, German industrialist

9 May: Sir Henry Morton Stanley, British explorer who tracked down Dr David Livingstone in Africa

14 July: Paul Kruger, South African leader of Boers

15 July: Anton Chekhov, Russian playwright and short-story writer

4 Oct: Frédéric-Auguste Bartholdi, French sculptor who carved Statue of Liberty that stands in New York City

FIRST NIGHTS

17 Jan, Moscow: *The Cherry Orchard*, play by Anton Chekhov

17 Feb, Milan: *Madama Butterfly*, opera by Giacomo Puccini

PUBLISHED

Joseph Conrad, *Nostromo*

GK Chesterton, *The Napoleon of Notting Hill*

Henry James, *The Golden Bowl*

Jack London, *The Sea-Wolf*

OPENED

29 Mar, London: Richmond Park

26 Dec, Dublin: the Abbey Theatre, with a double bill

Ritz Hotel, London: first building built on a steel frame

LINKED

21 July, Russia: Chelyabinsk and Vladivostok, after completion of 7312-km (4570-mile) Trans-Siberian Railway

INVENTED

Teabags: by US businessman Thomas Sullivan

The Gibson Girl, created by US artist Charles Dana Gibson, features often in the New York periodicals. Gibson created the character as a model of 'perfect femininity', and his cartoons strike a chord with high society.

FIRSTS

22 Mar: colour photographs published in a newspaper – the US *Daily Illustrated Mirror*

17 Nov: underwater journey by a submarine – from Portsmouth to Isle of Wight

BANNED

8 Jan: women's low-cut gowns at parties when leading Catholic churchmen are present, by Pope Pius X

ARRESTED

28 Sept, New York City: woman for smoking in open-top car – although smoking in public is not illegal

MASSACRED

18 Feb, Macedonia: 800 Albanians, by Turks besieging Shemsi Pasha

3 Apr, East Indies: 541 locals during revolt in Sumatra, by Dutch

CHAMPIONS

12 Jan, Michigan: car manufacturer Henry Ford, holder of new world land speed record; he reaches 146 km/h (91 mph) in his car '999' on frozen Lake St Clare

27 Aug, San Francisco: Jim Jeffries, heavyweight boxing champion of the world; he beats Jack Munroe in just two rounds

NEW WORDS

paranoid *adj*: suffering from false sense of persecution

hangover *n:* the after-effects of drinking too much alcohol

On 26 December, Peter Pan - or the Boy Who Wouldn't Grow Up premieres on the stage in London. The show, written for children by Scottish playwright and novelist James Barrie, is well received and looks set to become a theatre classic.

On 27 October, *a new subway system is opened in New York City. The first run is from Broadway to 145th Street, and the electric-powered carriages can reach 40 km/h (25 mph). New York's mayor drove the first train, marking the completion of a four-year project. The New York subway is the second such system to be built in the USA; the first was in Boston.*

British fishing trawlers caught up in foreign war

FAR AWAY BATTLE A Japanese lithograph depicts victory at Fort Urlungshan, captured from its Russian garrison.

22 OCTOBER, NORTH SEA
Two British fishing trawlers from Hull were sunk near the North Sea's Dogger sandbank in an unprovoked attack by a Russian fleet sailing for Japan. It seems that the Russians mistook them for Japanese warships.

Russia and Japan have been at war since February, when Japanese torpedo boats attacked the Russian fleet at Port Arthur in China and occupied Seoul. Sparked by conflict over Manchuria and Korea, the conflict has been a disaster for Russia, whose forces have been routed on land and at sea. This incident is a further setback.

··· 4 MAY: CHARLES ROLLS AND HENRY ROYCE BECOME PARTNERS IN THE MOTOR CAR BUSINESS ···

New deal seals peace in Europe

8 APRIL, PARIS
Britain and France today signed a historic treaty designed to end all conflict between the two countries. The 'Entente Cordiale' settles long-standing disputes and confirms the status of both nations' colonies. France has first call on Morocco, in exhange for respecting British claims in Egypt; French ships' fishing rights off Newfoundland are guaranteed, while France gives up its claims there.

The accord stems partly from King Edward VII's visit to Paris last year, and follows months of intense diplomatic negotiations.

Immigrants flock to the USA

A surge of immigration into the United States from eastern Europe is changing the face of the nation.

By 1900 non-Anglo-Saxon immigrants made up most of the urban working class. Huge numbers of Italians have come over in recent years, and now peasants from Russia, Poland and other eastern European countries are flooding into the factory towns of industrial America – determined to make a better life for themselves and their children in the flourishing American economy.

Hungry Hollow, for example, a steel town in Illinois, has become home to 15000 Bulgarians; but the

NEW BEGINNINGS Russian exiles arrive in New York with all they possess.

greatest impact is on New York City, where the majority of the Jews fleeing persecution in the Baltic and eastern Europe have taken up residence. It is predicted that this influx will soon make

New York the world's leading Jewish city. The new citizens, many of them from an artistic background, are already invigorating the cultural life – and the diet – of the metropolis.

1905

BORN

16 May: Henry Fonda, US actor
29 May: Bob Hope, UK-born comedian and actor
21 June: Jean-Paul Sartre, French philosopher, playwright and novelist
18 Sept: Greta Garbo, Swedish-born film star
24 Dec: Howard Hughes, US businessman

DIED

24 Mar: Jules Verne, French science-fiction writer
19 Sept: Thomas John Barnardo, Irish-born doctor, founder of Barnardo's Children's Homes
13 Oct: Sir Henry Irving, English actor

KILLED

22 Jan, St Petersburg: more than 500 striking Russian workers, during protest march, by Tsar's troops.
17 Feb, Moscow: Grand Duke Sergei, adviser to Tsar Nicholas of Russia, by assassin's bomb

Lawn tennis takes off as a popular sport, becoming a favourite middle-class pastime. As sport opens up to women, tennis is one of the acceptable forms of sporting activity for ladies. At Wimbledon the ladies' singles winner is Dorothea Douglass.

10 Mar, Manchuria: bulk of 200000-strong Russian army in Manchuria, by Japanese army
4 Apr, India: more than 10000 people, in Lahore earthquake
1 May, Poland: 100 people celebrating May Day, when troops open fire

BANNED

31 Oct, New York City: *Mrs Warren's Profession* by George Bernard Shaw, closed by police after single performance; the play is about a prostitute

This year sees a surge in the number of picture-postcards sent in Britain, while at the same time the number of letters declines. Scenes depicting the idylls of rustic life, like this one, are especially popular.

INVENTED

Intelligence tests, by French scientist Alfred Binet

BESTSELLERS

Sir Arthur Conan Doyle, *The Return of Sherlock Holmes*
Baroness Orczy (Hungarian-born Mrs Montague Barstow), *The Scarlet Pimpernel*

FOUNDED

23 Feb, Chicago: Rotary Club, businessmen's group, where members meet in each other's offices on a rota

The telephone, although expensive, is becoming ever more popular and widespread. Recent developments include the invention of both the automatic telephone exchange and the triode amplifier.

7 June, Dresden: 'Die Brücke' ('The Bridge') group of expressionist artists
13 July, Ontario: Niagara Movement of US blacks calling for civil rights
26 Oct, St Petersburg: the first workers' council or *soviet,* by typographers; Leon Trotsky is its vice-president

SOLD

7 June, New York City: 113 square metre (1250 sq ft) plot on Wall St, for $700000
30 Oct, Britain: aspirin, for the first time

DISCOVERED

Magnetic north pole, by Norwegian Arctic explorer Roald Amundsen

PUBLISHED

E M Forster, *Where Angels Fear to Tread*
George Santayana, *The Life of Reason*
Edith Wharton, *The House of Mirth*
Oscar Wilde (posthumously), *De Profundis*

REJECTED

12 May, London: parliamentary bill to give women the vote

OPENED

Belmont Park, Long Island, biggest race track in the world

Robert Koch, German bacteriologist, is awarded the Nobel Prize for medicine for his pioneering work on tuberculosis. Koch discovered the bacillus that causes tuberculosis in 1882 and has since also discovered the bacillus that causes cholera.

NEW WORDS

depression *n*: mental disorder characterised by feelings of gloom
smog *n*: thick fog over cities and towns, caused by chimney smoke; blend of the words smoke and fog

WORKERS DEFEAT RUSSIA'S TSAR

30 OCTOBER, ST PETERSBURG
Tsar Nicholas II has yielded to demands for reform, promising an elected parliament, or *duma*. The move comes at the end of a year of growing popular agitation, crowned by a ten-day general strike.

On 22 January, 500 demonstrators were shot by imperial troops, sparking off a wave of revulsion at the Tsar's policies. Defeat in the war with Japan in May further fuelled anti-government feeling, especially in the armed forces.

On 27 June, sailors raised the revolutionary red flag on the *Potemkin*, Russia's biggest battleship, hurling their commander overboard. The mutiny began when a sailor complained about bad food and the first lieutenant shot him. Eight officers backed the rebels.

The mutiny made a big impact during a summer of unrest in Russia. Rebellion spread to other ships in the fleet. In the Black Sea port of Odessa, where the *Potemkin* was anchored offshore, rioters took to the streets. Elsewhere workers show their support by building barricades.

This month has seen the first establishment of a *soviet*, or council of workers' delegates. The people have now forced the Tsar to listen to their demands for a greater say.

SEEDS OF REVOLUTION Mutinous seamen throng the deck of the mighty battleship *Potemkin*.

··· *THE PREACHER AND THE BEAR* IS FIRST GRAMOPHONE RECORD TO SELL OVER A MILLION COPIES ···

Time is relative, says scientist

26 SEPTEMBER, BERNE, SWITZERLAND
A young physicist, Albert Einstein, has published a daring new theory which overturns all accepted ideas about the laws of physics. The 'special theory of relativity' defies the commonsense view of the world. Instead of mass and time being fixed, Einstein asserts that they can alter; at speeds approaching that of light, mass increases, objects shrink, and time slows down — so that a clock moving fast enough would not only get heavier but also run more slowly. Nothing can go faster than the speed of light — the only absolute in the universe.

Einstein's theory, which transforms our conception of the universe, declares that all measurements of space and time depend on the motion of the observer. A moving object at close to light speed would appear to a stationary observer to be half its actual length, but to the person moving at the same speed it would not change.

SCIENTIFIC GENIUS Einstein, theorist of time.

Russian navy reels under onslaught

28 MAY, JAPAN
The Russian navy has been crushed in a sea battle with Admiral Togo's Japanese fleet in the Tsushima Straits between Japan and Korea. Just three out of 38 Russian ships have survived the onslaught, which must effectively bring an end to the bruising Russo-Japanese War.

The ships of the Russian Baltic fleet had carried out their plan of sailing halfway round the world from western Russia, with the intention of striking a decisive blow against the Japanese. But Admiral Togo surprised them in foggy conditions when he ordered his ships to turn sharply and attack. The overwhelming defeat at sea follows the annihilation of the Russian army in Manchuria at the Battle of Mukden in March.

··· 30 JANUARY: BIGGEST DIAMOND EVER, THE CULLINAN DIAMOND, DISCOVERED IN TRANSVAAL ···

PROTEST BUS Men are astonished as 'Votes for Women' magazine takes to the streets in a specially decorated cart.

Pavlova dances the dying swan

Greeted by ecstatic audiences in St Petersburg, the Russian ballet dancer Anna Pavlovna Pavlova this year performed a ballet solo created specially for her by the choreographer Michel Fokine, with music by the French composer Camille Saint-Saëns. In *Le Cygne* (*The Dying Swan*) she mimed the dying bird's struggle for life. The dancer's lightness, grace and poetry were seen at their height in what must become one of the most famous of all ballet solos.

Pavlova has helped to make the world aware of ballet, beginning to become a legend in the process.

Women's suffrage campaign gains new stridency

14 OCTOBER, MANCHESTER
Two young women have chosen to go to prison rather than pay a fine for causing a disturbance. Christabel Pankhurst and Annie Kenney are the first women to be imprisoned for demanding the vote.

Uproar broke out at Manchester's Free Trade Hall when Pankhurst and Kenney demanded to know if a Liberal government would give women the vote. Their protest came at the end of an election address by the leading Liberal politician Sir Edward Grey, when they stood up and unfurled their 'Votes for Women' banner.

Their behaviour provoked an angry reaction from the crowd. The women were dragged from the hall and thrown into the street, where they were arrested by police officers.

In 1903 Christabel Pankhurst founded the Women's Political and Social Union with her mother, Emmeline Pankhurst, the pioneer of women's suffrage. The arrest of the two women marks a new militancy in what had been a peaceful and law-abiding campaign.

SAD SWAN Pavlova in the stunning costume she wears for the dance.

FAST FEAST
Quick to make, easy
to eat, pizza is an ideal
food for busy city workers.

Tenor of the century

The career of the young Italian tenor Enrico Caruso reached a new peak this year. On his first tour of the USA he sang to packed houses from Boston to Los Angeles. The public greeted him rapturously, while the critics praised his charisma and his voice of 'exceptional resonance and power'. Such verdicts were echoed in Europe during the summer. His year ended back in New York, where he is singing 14 different parts and has become a star.

VELVET VOICED Enrico Caruso as Pierrot.

Americans discover obscure Neapolitan dish

The pizza has crossed the Atlantic, with the establishment of Lombardi's in Spring Street, New York: America's first pizzeria. Pizza is virtually unknown outside Naples, where it is eaten mainly by the poorer classes; it is a cheap, tasty dish of crisp baked bread dough, topped with tomato sauce and mozzarella cheese. The American pizza, with its thick crust and variety of toppings, is a richer version of its Italian cousin.

··· THERE ARE 78 000 CARS IN THE USA, COMPARED WITH 300 IN 1895 ···

Drivers club together

26 JUNE, LONDON
Fifty motorists, impelled by a recent upsurge of prejudice against motoring, have founded Britain's Automobile Association. The organisation aims to combat police hostility to motorists, protesting against measures such as the use of stopwatches to estimate a car's speed, and the arrest of any driver exceeding 32 kilometres per hour (20 mph). The AA has pledged to send out patrolmen on bicycles to help drivers avoid such inaccurate speed-traps.

HELPING HAND AA scouts roam the highways,
looking for ways to help motorists.

Sinn Fein founded

DECEMBER, DUBLIN
Printer Arthur Griffith has set up a political party to campaign for Irish independence from Britain. A committed Irish nationalist, Griffith founded an earlier form of the party Sinn Fein (Gaelic for 'Ourselves Alone') in 1900. He also founded a newspaper, *The United Irishman*, to publicise the nationalist cause. Griffith argues that British withdrawal from Ireland could be a natural result of the creation of an Irish government in Dublin.

1906

BORN

15 Jan: Aristotle Onassis, Greek shipping tycoon
13 Apr: Samuel Beckett, Franco-Irish playwright
3 June: Josephine Baker, US-born French dancer and jazz singer
25 Sept: Dmitri Shostakovich, Russian composer
19 Dec: Leonid Brezhnev, Soviet leader

DIED

19 Apr: Pierre Curie, Nobel Prize-winning French physicist
3 May: Henrik Ibsen, Norwegian dramatist
22 Oct: Paul Cézanne, French painter

FIRSTS

22 Mar: international Rugby Union match – England beat France in Paris, 35–8
10 May: *Duma,* Russian parliament, meets in St Petersburg
30 Sept: international hot-air balloon race, won by US Army Lt Frank Lahm, landing in Yorkshire
Oct: SOS message becomes international distress signal
17 Oct: picture transmitted by telegraph over 1600 km (1000 miles), by Professor Arthur Korn
14 Dec: a submarine, U1, enters German navy

RECORD

2 Jan: new French Darracq racing car breaks record at 173 km/h (108 mph)

DEVASTATED

8 Feb: Tahiti and the Cook Islands hit by cyclone; 192 km/h (120 mph) winds killed 10000

On 26 June, *the first motor-racing Grand Prix is held at Le Mans in France. The two-day event is won by Romanian driver Ferenc Szisz who drives a Renault AK at an average speed of 101 km/h (63 mph). The drivers complete 12 laps of a 102-km (64-mile) circuit, and the contest is open to all-comers.*

7 Apr: the town of Ottaviano, destroyed by an eruption of Vesuvius
18 Aug: Valparaiso, Chile, struck by earthquake, leaving hundreds dead and destroying two thirds of the city

PROPOSED

14 June: Bill to ban women from dangerous sports, after the death of a female parachutist

LAUNCHED

June: *Lusitania*, the world's largest liner, in Glasgow
15 Nov: *Satsuma*, the world's largest battleship, in Japan

ELECTED

7 Feb: Liberals, in landslide victory in British General Election
12 Feb: James Keir Hardie, leader of Labour MPs in House of Commons

INVENTED

19 Feb: cornflakes, by William Kellogg
26 May: sonar, by Lewis Nixon
electric washing machine, sold by Hurley Machine Co

MARRIED

17 Feb: Alice Roosevelt, daughter of President Theodore Roosevelt, to Ohio Congressman Nicholas Longworth
31 May: King Alfonso XIII of Spain to Princess Victoria (Ena) of Battenberg, narrowly escaping an assassin's bomb thrown at the wedding

AWARDED

17 July: the French Legion of Honour, to Captain Alfred Dreyfus in vindication of his innocence
10 Dec: the Nobel Peace Prize, to President Theodore Roosevelt for his mediation in the Russo-Japanese war
10 Dec: the Nobel Prize to physicist J J Thomson for his work on ions

EXILED

2 Nov: Bolshevik Leon Trotsky to Siberia, along with 1000 prisoners a day

ARRESTED

17 Nov, New York City: Enrico Caruso, for sexual harassment (touching a woman's arm) and fined $10

JAILED

24 Oct: 11 British suffragettes, after their protests disrupt the State Opening of Parliament

EXECUTED

23 Feb, USA: Johann Koch, known as the 'Bluebeard' of Chicago, for the murder of at least one of his 50 wives

KILLED

14 Apr: two blacks burnt to death in front of cheering crowds at Springfield, Ohio
21 June: hundreds of Jews massacred in planned pogrom at Bielostock, western Russia

VISITED

15 Aug: Kaiser Wilhelm, by Edward VII at Kronberg in an attempt to ease deteriorating Anglo-German relations
The United States, by Russian writer Maxim Gorky in an attempt to raise support for the revolution of 1905 in Russia

FOUNDED

19 Feb, Michigan, Kellogg's cereal company, by William Kellogg

PUBLISHED

John Galsworthy, *The Man of Property*, first volume of *The Forsyte Saga*

NEW WORDS

suffragette *n*: female political activist who demands equal voting rights for women
hot dog *n*: sausage, especially frankfurter, served hot in a long bread roll; named after a newspaper cartoon showing a dachshund in a frankfurter bun

Quake rocks San Francisco

18 APRIL, CALIFORNIA

At 5.18 this morning, a devastating earthquake rocked the city of San Francisco on the western US coast – so powerful that shock waves registered on seismographs as far away as Australia. The main quake lasted a full three minutes, and was followed by a series of aftershocks.

The city has been reduced to chaos. Buildings everywhere collapsed into the streets, and fires broke out as lamps and stoves were overturned. Within three hours these fires were raging out of control, with firefighters unable to get access to damaged water mains. Buildings that survived the quake are succumbing to the blaze, which, according to firefighters, may take days to bring under control.

Thousands of San Franciscans have fled their homes and left the city, packing into trains and ferries. Parks and squares are crowded with thousands more homeless people, without access to food or water. Martial law has been declared in an attempt to keep order.

A thousand or more lives are believed to have been lost, and 250 000 people made homeless – two-thirds of San Francisco's population. A total of 28 000 buildings have been destroyed over a huge area, causing estimated damage of up to $200 million.

SHATTERED STONES The ruins of San Francisco City Hall still stand tall in a city reduced to rubble.

··· THE 'PERMANENT WAVE' IS LAUNCHED IN A LONDON SALON BY GERMAN-BORN HAIRDRESSER KARL NESSLER ···

Nobel prize for Pavlov

10 DECEMBER, STOCKHOLM
The Russian scientist Ivan Pavlov has received the Nobel prize for physiology for his research on the digestive system. His experiments showed that even when a dog's gullet had been severed, gastric juices were still released into the stomach when the dog was fed. The brain, triggered by messages sent by

PRIZE CANINE Pavlov's digestive experiment.

nerve endings in the mouth, caused digestive juices to flow even though no food had reached the stomach.

Pavlov has also investigated what he terms 'conditioned reflexes'. Every time he fed his laboratory dogs, he rang a bell. After a time, when the dogs had become used to the bell ringing, he noticed that the dogs dribbled when the bell rang – even if no food was offered. Pavlov thus proved that it is possible to 'condition' the dribbling reflex, and believes that his discovery might help the understanding of how we learn.

1907

BORN

28 Feb: W H Auden, British poet
13 May: Daphne du Maurier, British writer
22 May: Laurence Olivier, British actor
22 May: Georges Rémi, alias Hergé, creator of cartoon character 'Tintin'

DIED

10 Feb: Sir William Howard Russell, first great war correspondent
4 Sept: Edvard Grieg, Norwegian composer
1 Nov: Alfred Jarry, French writer

AWARDED

26 July: honorary Doctorate of Letters to US author Mark Twain by Oxford University
29 Nov: Order of Merit to 87-year-old Florence Nightingale

Les Demoiselles d'Avignon *by Pablo Picasso is hung in the Museum of Modern Art, New York. The painting marks a radical departure for the art world, introducing a new geometric and multi-perspectived approach to painting, called Cubism.*

LAUNCHED

1 Mar: suicide counselling service in New York, by Salvation Army

16 Mar: HMS *Indomitable*, the world's largest cruiser, in Glasgow
29 July: the Boy Scout Movement, by Robert Baden-Powell
18 Oct: proposal for an International Court of Justice, in The Hague

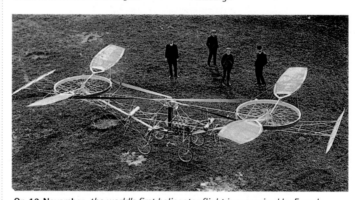

On 13 November, *the world's first helicopter flight is supervised by French designer Paul Cornu. Cornu, who designs bicycles for a living, created an aircraft that could take off vertically, powered by two rotors. However, the flight lasts only a few seconds as there are problems with control and direction.*

23 Nov: the Rockefeller Institute, founded with a $2.5 million gift from John Rockefeller

INVENTED

Chemotherapy, by Dr Paul Erlich of Frankfurt, to combat syphilis
Blood transfusion, following classification of blood groups in 1901
Colour screening process, capable, they claim, of making colour photography 'commonplace', by Auguste and Louis Lumière

DEVASTATED

14 Jan: massive earthquake hits Kingston, Jamaica, killing hundreds and flattening much of the city
22 Jan: Dutch East Indies swept by tidal wave, killing 1500

OPENED

27 Feb: Criminal Courts of Justice at the Old Bailey, opened by Edward VII and Queen Alexandra
11 Apr: the Carnegie Institute, Pittsburgh

DEFEATED

8 Mar: Keir Hardie's Women's Enfranchisement Bill
3 June: the Irish Council Bill, giving a measure of self-government to Ireland

PROTECTED

28 July: seals and sea-lions from culling, by Russo-Japanese treaty

TRIUMPHANT

10 Aug: Prince Borghese, on winning the Beijing–Paris motor race, 12800 km (8000 miles) of rugged terrain, in 62 days

RECORD

13 Sept: the liner *Lusitania*, reaching New York after 4½-day voyage averaging 24 knots

FIRST NIGHTS

22 Jan: *Salome* by Richard Strauss opens at the Metropolitan Opera House, New York, and is soon to be banned
26 Jan: *The Playboy of the Western World* opens at the Abbey Theatre, Dublin, causing a riot
16 Aug: *Madam Butterfly* first performed in English at the Lyric Theatre, London

TRIED

20 August, St Petersburg: 18 revolutionaries accused of plotting the death of Tsar Nicholas II

NEW WORD

racialist *adj:* abusive or aggressive behaviour towards another person on the grounds of race

On 10 December, *Rudyard Kipling becomes the first British writer to be awarded the Nobel prize for literature. Born in Bombay and educated in England, Kipling has been publishing short stories, novels, and poetry for more than 20 years. Much of his work is written for children.*

HUDDLED MASSES Hopeful immigrants en route from Bremen to New York cram every inch of a passenger ship.

Record immigration into the USA

This has been a record year for immigrants to the United States, with more than a million new Americans. On some days officials have processed nearly 5000 arrivals, refusing entrance to only 2 per cent of the hopefuls – mainly carriers of contagious disease.

Immigrants who arrive as steerage passengers have to pass through the special immigration centre at Ellis Island to have their admissions processed. The building provides an impressive introduction to the land of the free: the registration hall has Italian tiles and brass chandeliers, while a roof garden has commanding views of Manhattan.

Since 1840 more than 16 million immigrants, mostly Irish, Scandinavian, German and Italian, have answered the call inscribed on the Statue of Liberty in New York harbour – 'Give me your tired, your poor, your huddled masses yearning to breathe free' – doubling America's population.

The new arrivals are assimilating themselves to the American way of life with an eagerness matched only by an impressive speed.

Women MPs come to Finnish parliament

15 MARCH, FINLAND Finnish women are today savouring the taste of political power, winning their first seats in the Finnish Diet (parliament).

As a result of a strong women's movement, backed by the Social Democratic party, Finland stands out among the rest of the Europe in its decision to elect the first women members of parliament.

Last year Finland was the first country in Europe to grant women the vote as part of a complete reform of the parliamentary system. It was only the third country in the world to do so – after New Zealand in 1893, and Australia almost a decade later, in 1902.

Women elsewhere in Europe and in North America continue to press for the right to vote, and hope that today's events will give their campaigns a boost.

··· 31 DECEMBER: 167 OF 169 MEMBERS OF RUSSIAN PARLIAMENT ARE SENT TO PRISON FOR TREASON ···

TYPHOID MARY ARRESTED

**MARCH, NEW YORK CITY
A medical mystery that has haunted New York since 1900 has been solved.** At least 51 people in the city have been infected with typhoid fever, which is spread through contaminated food and water. The source of the epidemic, which killed three people, puzzled the authorities. However, it has now been traced to Mary Mallon, an Irish cook who has the dubious distinction of

being the USA's first known carrier of typhoid. All the sufferers had eaten food that she had prepared in households across New York State.

'Typhoid Mary', as she has been dubbed, was apprehended in Manhattan after careful detective work by the health authorities. She has been detained to protect public health, and isolated on North Brother Island off the Bronx to prevent the spread of infection.

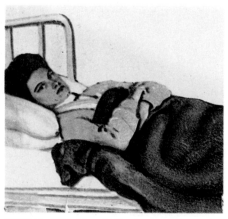

ISOLATED CASE Mary Mallon in a hospital ward.

1908

BORN

9 Jan: Simone de Beauvoir, French feminist writer
5 Apr: Bette Davis, US actress
20 May: Ian Fleming, British writer
26 July: Salvador Allende Gossens, Chilean president
27 Aug: Lyndon B Johnson, US president

LEGALISED

6 June, France: divorce after three years' separation

BANNED

1 Jan: alcohol, by the state of Georgia, USA, followed by North Carolina on 26 May
29 Sept: working night shifts for children in Switzerland

PROPOSED

14 Nov, Berne: the quantum theory of light, by German-born mathematical physicist Professor Albert Einstein

The Wind in the Willows, a children's idyllic countryside tale, is published. The animal characters, such as Ratty, Toad of Toad Hall and Mole, are sure to become great favourites. The author, Kenneth Grahame, worked in the banking trade until last year but is now a full-time writer.

MARRIED

12 Sept: Winston Churchill, President of the Board of Trade, to Clementine Hozier, after less than a month's engagement

On **16 October,** *the first flight on British soil takes place at Farnborough. US pilot Samuel Cody flies the British Army Aeroplane No 1, with its 50 hp engine, at a height of 424 m (1390 ft) before crash-landing. He has no injuries.*

LAUNCHED

7 Mar: *Nassau,* first German Dreadnought battleship, supremely armed with heavy guns
1 Apr: British Territorial Army, by Liberal War Secretary Haldane
14 May: Franco-British Exhibition at White City, the largest yet
16 Sept: General Motors, formed by a merger of Buick and Oldsmobile

ADOPTED

22 Jan: Socialism, by the British Labour Party in Hull

PROTESTED

21 June: 200 000 British suffragettes on 'Women's Sunday'

PATENTED

22 May: the Wright Brothers' flying machine, leading to a spate of new flight records

DESTROYED

13 Sept, France: Champagne harvest, reducing the region's annual production to the yield of a single vineyard

28 Dec, Sicily: Messina, by biggest earthquake recorded in Europe
15 May: £20 000 worth of his own paintings by Claude Monet, who thought them 'unsatisfactory'

ASSASSINATED

1 Feb: King Carlos and Crown Prince, in Portugal

FREED

30 Jan: Mahatma Gandhi, from prison in Johannesburg

ANNEXED

27 Feb: Oklahoma, which becomes the 46th state of the United States
19 Aug: the Congo, ruled hitherto as a private estate by King Leopold II of the Belgians, ceded to Belgium for £5 million
5 Oct: Bosnia and Herzegovina, by Austria, with Russian approval

ESCAPED

28 Feb: the Shah of Persia, who survived an assassination attempt
4 June: Alfred Dreyfus, scapegoat of notorious French espionage case, from murder attempt; Dreyfus was at a ceremony to honour writer Emile Zola, who supported him publicly

OPENED

27 Apr, Salzburg: the first International Congress of Psychoanalysis
11 June, London: the Rotherhithe Tunnel under the River Thames
27 July, London: the fourth modern Olympic Games, at White City

INDEPENDENT

5 Oct: Bulgaria, proclaiming independence from Ottoman Empire

TRIUMPHANT

July: Ray C Ewry, taking two gold medals at the Olympics, bringing his total to a record ten
30 July: US team, winning the round-the-world automobile race

INVENTED

Paper cups, by International Paper Company, New York

COMPLETED

Singer Building, New York City: the world's tallest skyscraper, 47 storeys tall and 187 m (612 ft) high

NEW WORDS

haute couture *n*: high-fashion designing and dressmaking, especially for women
Africana *n*: objects of cultural or historical interest of sub-Saharan African origin

Boy emperor to rule China

CHILD'S PLAY China's new emperor (pictured later in his reign) faces an uncertain future.

15 NOVEMBER, BEIJING
The youngest-ever emperor of China has succeeded to the throne, aged just two years old.

The succession follows the death of Dowager Empress Cixi, who for decades has been the manipulative power behind the Chinese throne. Rumours of foul play surround her death – further fuelled by the announcement that the Emperor, Guangxu, had died shortly before her. The Emperor had been in good health, and the cause of his death is not known.

The new ruler, Pu Yi, is the nephew of the late Emperor, and is the ninth emperor of the Manchu (Qing) Dynasty which has ruled China in an unbroken line since 1644. The infant's father, Prince Chun, has been made regent and will take practical control of the Chinese government, ruling in his son's name.

The crisis of imperial authority can only enhance the revolutionary republican movement in China which for some time has been pressing for progressive reforms.

Ford unveils Model T

12 AUGUST, DETROIT
The first Model T Ford motor car rolled out of the factory in Detroit today. Costing just $900, the Model T brings its maker, Henry Ford, one step nearer to fulfilling his dream of a popular vehicle that everyone can afford.

The Model T owes its low cost to new techniques of mass production – breaking down the complex job of building a car into a succession of simple operations. Ford intends to introduce even greater efficiency by introducing a moving assembly line. The car is assembled so fast that it is currently available only in black – because black enamel is the only paint that dries fast enough.

Known affectionately as 'Tin Lizzy', the Model T Ford will be an immediate success; the next few years will see 16.5 million Model Ts on the road.

TIN LIZZY Henry Ford said the Model T was 'a motor car for the great multitude'.

··· 30 JUNE: HUGE METEORITE HITS SIBERIA, CAUSING LARGEST-EVER RECORDED EXPLOSION ···

Victory snatched from brave marathon runner

30 JULY, LONDON
Italian runner Dorado Pietri has seen the gold medal for the marathon cruelly snatched away from him at the last gasp, in the most moving episode of this summer's Olympic Games at the spanking new White City stadium in London.

Pietri, visibly suffering from dehydration and cramp, entered the

NO CONSOLATION Pietri staggers to the end.

stadium in the lead for the final lap. He collapsed four times, but, roared on by the crowd, managed to stagger to his feet. He was the first to cross the line, but was disqualified for accepting the assistance of track officials over the last few yards. The gold medal went to the American John Hayes, who covered the 26 miles and 385 yards (about 42 km) in 2 hours, 55 minutes and 18 seconds.

Italian quake kills thousands

28 DECEMBER, MESSINA, SICILY
A devastating earthquake has brought the Christmas season to a horrific end for the Sicilian city of Messina. Around 80 000 of its citizens have been killed, and the city itself has been almost completely razed to the ground. Local troops are desperately searching through the rubble for survivors.

Thousands more are believed to have perished in surrounding villages and on the mainland of Calabria, the 'toe' of Italy. Martial law was declared as the scale of the disaster became known, and a massive international relief operation has been mounted. The city's inhabitants – those that have survived – have been left dazed and homeless. Much-needed temporary shelters have been set up and emergency supplies of food, clothing and medicine brought in.

Messina's heritage of ancient buildings has been almost entirely destroyed in Europe's worst ever earthquake. Along with many other medieval churches, the cathedral – already ravaged by previous earthquakes – is now just a pile of dust and crumbled bricks.

DESPERATE WORK Italian sailors rushed from ships berthed at Messina to help search for survivors.

··· CELLOPHANE IS INVENTED BY SWISS CHEMIST JACQUES BRANDENBERGER ···

Radioactivity counter invented

NUCLEAR MEASURE A modern geiger counter.

7 NOVEMBER, MANCHESTER
A new instrument to measure radioactivity has been developed by German nuclear physicist Hans Geiger, working with Ernest Rutherford. Geiger's device monitors the electrical changes produced by the 'alpha' (positively charged) particles given off by radioactive substances as they decay, and is able to count them. It has shown that 1 gram of the element radium emits more than 30 billion alpha particles every second, and that each carries a double charge.

Instant success for much-rejected novel

A previously unknown Canadian writer, Lucy Maud Montgomery, published her first novel, *Anne of Green Gables*, to enormous success this year. It was rejected by several publishers before being eventually accepted.

The story involves a young orphan girl who is sent to live with an elderly couple in rural Canada. Many people believe that the character of the sensitive and outspoken young heroine is based on the author herself.

Johnson is the new heavyweight champ

26 DECEMBER, SYDNEY
Jack Johnson, the heavyweight boxer from Texas, has finally caught up with Tommy Burns and wrested the world title from him in Australia.

Constantly taunting the Canadian, and baffling him with superb feinting moves and lightning-quick counter-punching, Johnson so overpowered his opponent that the police had to step in and put an end to the contest in the fourteenth round. Johnson won on a technical knock out.

Johnson, who ran away from home at the age of 12 to become a stable-boy and then a sparring partner, is the first black boxer to wear the heavyweight belt. His arrogant manner has earned him unpopularity, and already the search is on for a 'great white hope' to take the title from him. Even his detractors, however, allow that he is a superb athlete – destined to be recognised as one of the very greatest of boxing champions.

CHAMPION IN ACTION Johnson went on to defeat Jim Jeffries at Reno in 1910. 'Mister Jeff, you ain't showed me nothin' yet,' he taunted.

··· GIDEON BIBLE COMPANY STARTS ITS MISSION TO LEAVE A BIBLE IN EVERY HOTEL ROOM ···

Taft wins the race for the presidency

3 NOVEMBER, WASHINGTON
William 'Big Bill' Taft has retained the American presidency for the Republicans by roundly defeating his Democratic opponent, William Jennings Bryan, by 7.7 million votes to 6.3 million. His party has retained control of the Senate and increased its majority in the House of Representatives.

It was the third time that Bryan, an impassioned orator, had tried to capture the White House, setting a new American record for political failure. He stood little chance, however, against Taft, the favoured choice of the incumbent president, the combative but popular Theodore Roosevelt.

Taft's mild manners and conciliatory approach will bring a change of political style to Washington. But there are signs that if – as many commentators predict – he proves unable to honour his campaign pledge to lower protective tariffs, or to respond to growing public calls to conserve the natural resources of the United States, his presidency may split the Republican Party into conservative and progressive factions.

BIG BILL America's 27th President.

1909

BORN

28 Feb: Stephen Spender, British poet and critic
30 Apr: Queen Juliana of the Netherlands
30 May: Benny Goodman, US jazzman
8 Nov: Katharine Hepburn, US stage and film actress

DIED

24 Mar: J M Synge, Irish playwright
10 Apr: Algernon Charles Swinburne, British poet and critic
17 Dec: King Leopold II of the Belgians

FIRSTS

1 Jan: payment of old age pensions in Britain to all over 70

On 17 February, Geronimo, Apache Indian chief, dies aged 80. From 1875 to 1885 he led Apaches from Arizona and New Mexico in the fight against federal troops and settlers encroaching on tribal lands.

9 Apr: double-decker bus appears on British streets
Apr: wireless transmission sent from New York to Chicago

15 July: organ transplants on animals, performed by French biologist Dr Alexis Carrel
23 Aug, London: British counter-espionage unit formed, later to become MI5

On June 1, a conference in New York City marks the birth of the National Association for the Advancement of Colored People. The Association, founded by W E B DuBois, is comprised of African-American radicals and liberals who will address equal rights issues through political action.

OPENED

Glasgow School of Art, designed by Charles Rennie Mackintosh
26 June, London: the Victoria and Albert Museum, opened by King Edward VII

ELECTED

24 July: Aristide Briand as premier of France
21 Dec: Dr José Madriz as president of Nicaragua

AWARDED

10 Dec: the Nobel Prize for physics to Guglielmo Marconi, Italian inventor, for his contribution to the the invention of the wireless

ARRESTED

25 Mar: Madame Popova, for 300 murders in Russia

DISGRACED

21 Dec: Dr Frederick Cook, whose claim to have beaten Robert Peary to the North Pole is shown to be fraudulent, along with several other extravagant claims

BEATIFIED

18 Apr: Joan of Arc, 478 years after being burnt at the stake by the English

BANNED

Opium imports by US Congress for anything but medical use

PROPOSED

7 July: £120 million worth of new ships for the French navy, to enable France to enter the European arms race
14 Nov: a naval base at Pearl Harbor for the USA, to protect America from Japanese attack

PREMIERED

18 May: Diaghilev's Ballets Russes in Paris, starring Nijinsky and Anna Pavlova

DISCOVERED

Typhus is spread by the human body louse, by French bacteriologist Charles Nicolle, proving that good hygiene helps prevent disease

COMPLETED

The Robie House in Chicago, by architect Frank Lloyd Wright: modernist design characterised by horizontal lines
Manhattan Bridge over East River, New York, by US engineer O F Nichols

INVENTED

Bakelite, a plastic that sets hard after moulding, by Belgian chemist Leo Baekeland
Motion pictures, the first commercially made colour films, by George Smith of Brighton, Sussex

On 15 March, Selfridge's department store opens in Oxford Street, London. Harry G Selfridge started his career as a messenger boy in Wisconsin, United States, and moved to London in 1906.

NEW WORDS

gene n: a unit of heredity, comprised of DNA transmitted from parent to offspring during reproduction
camp adj: effeminate, affected in mannerisms, dress, etc.; homosexual

North Pole reached by intrepid Peary

6 APRIL, THE ARCTIC
One of the most inhospitable terrains in the world has been conquered by the explorer Robert Peary, who reached the North Pole today. The American naval commander is triumphant at last, having persevered through five previous unsuccessful attempts, dating back over seven years, to reach his goal. These expeditions all foundered in the icy seas of the Arctic.

Peary's successful assault on the Pole began on the *Roosevelt*, a ship specially designed to withstand Arctic ice, which sailed north from the USA to Greenland. Then followed a gruelling 145-kilometre (90-mile) trek, in preparation for the final 36-day push towards the Pole. The party dwindled in size as the expedition progressed, with exhausted members turning back. Peary shared his triumph with the four remaining Inuit team members and his African-American assistant, Matthew Hensen.

WELL INSULATED A close-fitting fur coat keeps Peary warm in freezing conditions.

··· FIRST ELECTRIC TOASTER IS SOLD IN THE UNITED STATES BY THF GENERAL ELECTRIC COMPANY ···

Blériot flies the Channel

25 JULY, DOVER
French aviator Louis Blériot was greeted by cheering crowds this morning as he landed at Dover Castle – the first person to fly across the English Channel. His aircraft was a wooden monoplane tied together with piano strings, weighing only 20 kilos (45 lb).

The 36-year-old airman took off at 5.00 am from Sangatte, near Calais, and landed 43 minutes later, guided in to land by a journalist waving a French tricolour. Blériot confessed that he had set his course by following the ships

TOP FLIGHT Blériot averaged 64 km/h (40 mph).

below, having no compass on board. He can now claim the £1000 prize money offered by the *Daily Mail* for this feat.

Dictator challenged

DECEMBER, MEXICO
Pro-democracy leader Francisco Madero has announced that he will take on the dictator Porfirio Díaz in a presidential head-to-head.

General Díaz seized power in 1876 and was made president the next year. He took a firm grip on the country and created wealth, but his brutal rule has won him enemies. Madero stands as an anti-Díaz candidate with the slogan 'Effective suffrage – no re-election!'. His challenge has made Mexicans believe that change is possible, and will be the spark that ignites the revolution.

1910

BORN

13 June: Jean Anouilh, French playwright

3 Sept: Samuel Barber, US composer

13 Oct: Art Tatum, US jazz pianist

DIED

21 Apr: Mark Twain, US author

6 May: Albert Edward of Saxe-Coburg-Gotha, King Edward VII

2 Sept: Henri 'Le Douanier' Rousseau, French painter

7 Sept: William Holman Hunt, British painter

30 Oct: Jean Henri Dunant, Swiss founder of the Red Cross

10 Nov: Count Leo Tolstoy, Russian author

The Earth passes through the tail of Halley's comet as it makes one of its periodic appearances. Named after Sir Edmond Halley, the British astronomer who observed it in 1682, the comet returns every 76 years. Many people fear that the comet will cause weather disturbances.

EMBARKED

1 June: Captain Robert Falcon Scott for Antarctica, aboard the *Terra Nova*

FIRSTS

8 Mar: woman pilot's licence given to the French Baroness de Laroche

10 Mar: Hollywood film, *In Old California,* made by D W Griffith

2 July: Arctic crossing by automobile, made by American Oscar Tamm

OPENED

29 Mar, Monaco: the world's largest oceanographic museum

ERUPTED

27 Mar: Mount Etna in Sicily, causing widespread devastation

ASSASSINATED

21 Feb: Boutros Pasha Ghali, Christian prime minister of Egypt, by radical Egyptian nationalist

ANNEXED

22 Aug: Korea, by Japan, after a treaty brokered in secret

DISCOVERED

2 June: Pygmies in the mountains of Dutch New Guinea, by British explorers

On October 5, a new republic of Portugal is declared. Revolutionary troops such as the soldiers and sailor pictured above staged a coup and overthrew King Manuel II, who fled to Gibraltar. The revolutionaries have chosen a professor of literature, Theophilo Braga, to head the new government.

9 July: a tablet describing the fall of Jerusalem, in Egypt

7 Sept: the first pure sample of radium, isolated by Marie Curie

INVENTED

Neon lighting, by French physicist Georges Claude

28 Mar, Martigues: the seaplane, given its maiden flight by French aviator Henri Fabre

16 June, USA: Father's Day, by Mrs John B Dodd

27 Aug, New Jersey: talking motion pictures, demonstrated by Thomas Edison

Artificial silk stockings, using viscose rayon, at Bamberg, Germany

Colt .45 semi-automatic handgun, by American John Moses Browning

RECORDS

Land speed, Florida: by Barney Oldfield, driving a 'Blitzen' Benz at 211 km/h (132 mph) at Daytona Beach

The tango, a sensual new dance from South America, is catching on quickly among young people. However, some quarters of society have denounced the dance as immoral because of its daring poses and the close physical contact it allows between couples.

7 July, Rheims: French aviator Hubert Lathan reaches 305 m (1000 ft)

ABOLISHED

10 Mar: slavery, by the imperial government in China

19 June: the transport of women across US state boundaries for 'immoral purposes', by the Mann Act signed by President Taft

ROUTED

23 Feb: the Dalai Lama, forced to flee Tibet for India as Chinese troops invade Lhasa

PUBLISHED

E M Forster, *Howard's End*

NEW WORD

intelligentsia *n:* the educated or intellectual people in a society or community

Radio catches a killer

31 JULY, CANADA

In the first instance of a criminal being brought to justice by wireless, Dr Hawley Harvey Crippen has been arrested aboard the liner *Montrose* off the coast of Canada, on suspicion of murdering his wife in London.

Crippen and his mistress fled London for Belgium on 9 July, and 11 days later boarded the *Montrose* disguised as 'Mr Robinson and son'. Meanwhile, police were searching his home in north London, where they discovered the dismembered and badly mutilated body of his wife buried in the cellar.

Before leaving port Captain Henry Kendall read a newspaper description of the pair which aroused his suspicions. He noticed that 'Mr Robinson' had recently shaved off a moustache, and a surreptitious search of their cabin revealed a woman's bodice. Kendall wired England, and two Scotland Yard officers were dispatched on the *Laurentic*, a faster ship. Disguised as St Lawrence River pilots, the policemen came aboard. 'Robinson' was sent for. 'Good morning, Dr Crippen,' said one officer. 'Inspector Dew from Scotland Yard.' The wireless message sent that day read: 'Crippen and Le Neve arrested.'

CAUGHT OUT British police make a maritime arrest of Crippen and his 'son'.

··· 1 JULY: DUNCAN BLACK AND ALONZO DECKER FOUND A TOOL COMPANY IN BALTIMORE, USA ···

Russian painter turns his back on representation

NEW LOOK Wassily Kandinsky's daring *Kirche in Murnau*, an early example of abstract art.

Established traditions in art were overturned this year by Wassily Kandinsky, who has produced the first abstract painting. The Russian-born painter, a leader of the German avant garde, has declared that art no longer depends upon subject matter.

Kandinsky's first entirely 'abstract' work is an oil painting in which daubs of colour and random brushstrokes are intended to convey meaning to the viewer through their direct emotional effect. The artist reveals that the turning point for him came when he caught sight of 'a picture of indescribable incandescent loveliness … [which] depicted no recognisable subject and was entirely composed of bright patches of colour'. This extraordinary picture turned out to be one of Kandinsky's own landscapes, standing on its side.

Wishing his work to speak directly to the human soul, Kandinsky has developed his art accordingly, relying on colour, line and form to create a powerful emotional impact. He builds upon the techniques of artists such as Van Gogh and Matisse who 'liberated' colour by, for example, painting grass red. In an increasingly materialistic society, Kandinsky and his associates, such as Franz Marc and Paul Klee, are using abstraction as a means of appealing to a more spiritual side of humanity.

1911

BORN
6 Feb: Ronald Reagan, US actor and President
26 Mar: Tennessee Williams, US author
6 Aug: Lucille Ball, US actress and television star

DIED
18 May: Gustav Mahler, Austrian composer
9 June: Carrie Nation, US anti-alcohol campaigner
29 Oct: Joseph Pulitzer, US journalist

BROKEN UP
15 May, Washington: Rockefeller's Standard Oil Company, by order of Supreme Court, under anti-trust legislation

MURDERED
18 Sept, Russia: Russian premier Peter Stolypin, shot during interval at Kiev Opera House

On 22 June, King George V is crowned at Westminster Abbey, London. He succeeds his father, Edward VII, who died last year. The new king married Princess Mary of Teck in 1893. They have four sons and one daughter.

Machu Picchu, an ancient Inca town in Peru, is discovered by US archaeologist Hiram Bingham. The architecture and location of the ruined town, carved out of the mountainside, suggest that it was a religious site or a military outpost.

FIRSTS
1 Nov: air raid; Italian Giulio Gavotti drops bombs on Turkish troops in Libya from his Blériot aircraft
23 Oct, Manchester: Ford car built outside USA, a Model T
9 Sept: airmail, carried by Gustav Hamel in a Blériot aeroplane, from London to Berkshire

MARCHED
17 June, London: supporters of campaign to win vote for women; around 60000 walk through London to rally at Albert Hall

ON STRIKE
11 July, Paris: 60000 stonemasons
18 Aug, Britain: 200000 including railway workers, carters and stevedores, in sympathy with striking Liverpool seamen

18 Sept, Valencia: all workers on general strike
2 Nov, London: 6000 cabbies

BANNED
24 Mar, Denmark: corporal punishment
6 Nov, USA: alcohol, in Maine

CHAMPION
30 May, Indianapolis: Ray Harroun, winner of first Indianapolis 500-mile track car race

DISPATCHED
2 July: German gunboat to port of Agadir, in Morocco; Kaiser Wilhelm claims German firms in Morocco need protection

PUBLISHED
D H Lawrence, *The White Peacock*

Frances Hodgson Burnett, *The Secret Garden*
Rupert Brooke, *Poems, 1911*

FOUNDED
15 Nov, Detroit: Chevrolet Motor Car Company
10 Nov, New York City: Carnegie Foundation, educational body; funded by US industrialist Andrew Carnegie
First Hollywood film studios

On 25 March, 146 employees die in the Triangle Shirtwaist factory fire in Manhattan. Although the building was a fire hazard, the owners were not held responsible in court. Afterwards, fire prevention measures were enforced in factories across the USA.

SIGNED
4 Nov: treaty ending French–German clashes over Morocco; France will take Morocco, and give French lands in Congo to Germany

NEW WORD
jinx *n*: an unlucky force, person or thing

SOUTH POLE TRIUMPH FOR AMUNDSEN

14 DECEMBER, OSLO
Norwegian explorer Roald Amundsen has beaten a rival British team to the South Pole. He and his four companions used sleds drawn by teams of husky dogs to cross the Antarctic's vast mountain ranges and icy windswept plains.

The British, led by Captain Robert Falcon Scott, set out in November but have not been heard from since.

According to Amundsen, the toughest part of the Norwegians' journey was crossing a vast glacier pockmarked with crevasses, dubbed the 'devil's dancing room'. The rest of the trip went 'like a dance,' Amundsen said. The Norwegian explorer attributes his success to the years he spent living with the Inuit people. They taught him the skills he needed to survive, including how to handle a team of huskies. Amundsen brought his own dog teams all the way from the Arctic for his South Pole attempt.

POLE POSITION Amundsen takes a sighting at the Norwegian flag planted to mark his conquest of the Pole.

··· THE WORD 'VITAMIN' IS FIRST USED TO DESCRIBE THE CHEMICALS NECESSARY TO HUMAN AND ANIMAL DIETS ···

Mona Lisa is missing from Louvre

22 AUGUST, PARIS
The world's most famous portrait, Leonardo da Vinci's *Mona Lisa*, has been stolen from the Louvre in Paris.

The hunt for the thieves began in the early hours of this morning. A museum spokesman said that only a madman could have committed the crime – no one could hope to sell such a well-known image. The Paris police are keeping an open mind, but already a crack team is at work. Not the least of the mystery is how the thief managed to get in and out of the museum without being noticed.

Leonardo painted this portrait, also known as *La Giaconda*, around 1503 when he was working in Florence. The French King François I purchased it soon after, and since then the painting has always hung in one of the French royal palaces.

THE LADY VANISHES The stolen *Mona Lisa*.

Republic of China founded

10 OCTOBER, CHINA
Revolution has erupted in China, triggered by an explosion yesterday at the offices of a group of republican sympathisers in the town of Hankow.

As police rounded up the rebels local soldiers mutinied, taking control of the, nearby city of Wuchang. From there the unrest spread rapidly. Responding to the revolutionary call of the republican politician Sun Yat-sen, who has directed a number of previous unsuccessful uprisings, citizens in 13 central and southern provinces rose up against the corrupt Manchu Dynasty. Sun Yat-sen lays the blame for China's weakness with its imperial overlords, and their overthrow by the people will end more than 2000 years of imperial rule.

1912

BORN

11 May: Phil Silvers, US actor, famous as 'Sergeant Bilko'
28 May: Patrick White, British-born Australian novelist
23 Aug: Gene Kelly, US singer and dancer

DIED

10 Feb: Joseph Lister, pioneer of antiseptic medical methods
20 Aug: William Booth, British founder of the Salvation Army

PUBLISHED

Karl Jung, *The Psychology of the Unconscious*
Thomas Mann, *Death in Venice*

On **18 December**, *'Piltdown Man'*, *supposed human remains found on Piltdown Common in Sussex, is declared the evolutionary 'missing link' that Charles Darwin wrote about. Years later, in 1953, the claim was shown to be an elaborate hoax.*

PROTESTED

28 Sept, Belfast: 471 414 people, against Home Rule for Ireland, by signing a covenant to defeat the introduction of an Irish Parliament

INVENTED

Electric cooker, by British engineer Charles Belling

WRECKED

23 June, USA: bridge over Niagara Falls; 47 die when it collapses
4 Oct, UK: submarine B2, after colliding with the German liner *Amerika*; 14 die

JOINED

6 Jan: New Mexico, to United States, as the 47th state; Arizona follows as the 48th on 14 February

FIRST NIGHTS

5 May, Munich: second show by 'Der Blaue Reiter' group of artists; works by Swiss artist Paul Klee and German Emil Nolde on show
23 Sept, USA: first movies from Keystone Films – *Cohen Collects a Debt* and *The Water Nymph*

LAUNCHED

15 Apr, London: Socialist newspaper the *Daily Herald*
5 May, Russia: *Pravda* (*Truth*), journal of the illegal Bolshevik Central Committee, by Joseph Stalin

SNUBBED

18 Feb, Berlin: socialist winners of German general election, by Kaiser Wilhelm

FOUNDED

13 Apr: British armed forces' Royal Flying Corps
1 July: French protectorate in Morocco
11 Sept, UK: Barbour Clothing Co, makers of waterproof clothes
1 Oct: German Military Aviation Service
Board of Film Censors, Britain
International Lawn Tennis Association, Paris

VICTORIOUS

13 Mar, Boston: textile workers, after two-month struggle for pay rise

SIGNED

18 Oct, Switzerland: peace treaty between Italy and Turkey; Italy gains control of Libya
30 Nov, Balkans: armistice between Bulgaria, Turkey, Montenegro and Serbia after Balkan war in which Turkish forces have been routed

DENOUNCED

Cocaine, chloroform and ether: by US surgeons, who recommend nitrous oxide gas instead

ELECTED

5 Nov: Woodrow Wilson, Democrat, as US President

ATTACKED

14 Oct, Milwaukee: Theodore Roosevelt, campaigning for US presidency for the Progressive Party, shot by gunman John Chrank
23 Dec, Delhi: Lord Hardinge, governor-general of India, after a bomb explodes inside the 'howdah' where he sits on elephant back; he is badly injured

FIRSTS

Mar 7, Missouri: parachute jump from an aeroplane, by Albert Berry
Dec 7, Chicago: diagnosis of a heart attack in a living person, by physician James B Herrick
Air race in Australia: won by William Hart in a Bristol Boxkite
Fashion salon, opened by designer Coco Chanel in Deauville, France
Neon advertising sign, for Cinzano, displayed in Paris

DISCOVERED

13 Aug, Paris: cancer microbe, by Dr Gaston Odin; he predicts that his finding may lead to a cancer vaccine
7 Dec, Egypt: bust of Queen Nefertiti, by German archaeologist Ludwig Borchardt – bust dates from the 14th century BC

BESTSELLER

Zane Gray, *Riders of the Purple Sage*

On **31 March**, *both boats in the annual Oxford and Cambridge boat race sink in choppy conditions. The umpire orders a re-race a few days later, when Oxford wins easily. This photograph shows the Oxford boat just before it was swamped.*

RECALLED

22 July: British Royal Navy ships in the Mediterranean, to patrol the North Sea

NEW WORDS

blues *n*: African-American folk music usually built around a 12-bar structure with frequent minor intervals and sad lyrics
floozy *n*: slang term used to describe a disreputable woman, usually gaudily dressed; a prostitute

DISASTER AT SEA The *Titanic* sinks into the dark waters of the Atlantic after colliding with an iceberg.

LUXURY PLATTER Much later, divers retrieved fine dishes bearing the crest of the White Star Line.

GREAT LINER GOES DOWN

15 APRIL, NORTH ATLANTIC
The world's largest ocean liner, the White Star Line's Titanic, sank in the the Atlantic early this morning, with the loss of more than 1500 lives. She was on her maiden voyage from Southampton to New York when she grazed an iceberg at 20 minutes before midnight last night.

Declared unsinkable before she sailed, the *Titanic* took just two and a half hours to slip beneath the surface. Her captain, Edward Smith, was an experienced mariner of 62 who had enjoyed an uneventful career. The night of 14 April was clear, with a flat, calm

sea. At about 9.00 pm, Smith agreed with the officer of the watch that even if an iceberg should appear they would have time to avoid it. In fact, the *Titanic* had received six messages warning of a great belt of ice stretching across her path.

The liner carried enough lifeboats for about half those on board. Even so, many boats left the ship only half filled. The *Titanic* had never had a boat drill, and few of the crew knew how to handle the davits from which the boats were lowered. But there was no panic.

Survivors related how the band played on as the *Titanic* began to tilt. The last tune they played was the jaunty hit

Autumn; all players perished. Captain Smith went down with his ship, and many passengers showed equal gallantry. Colonel John Astor helped his wife into a boat saying: 'Goodbye dearie, I will join you later.' He never did. Mrs Isidore Strauss would not leave her husband, declaring: 'We have lived 40 years together, and we will not part now in old age.' The couple were last seen in each other's arms.

But the chairman of White Star Line, Bruce Ismay, did survive, earning criticism from those who believe that he should have gone down along with his unsinkable ship.

··· FIRST EVER CROSSWORD PUZZLE PUBLISHED IN *NEW YORK JOURNAL* ···

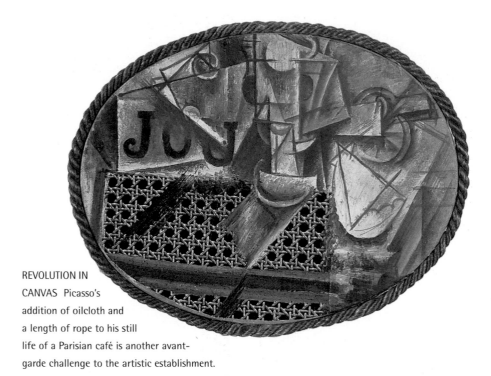

REVOLUTION IN CANVAS Picasso's addition of oilcloth and a length of rope to his still life of a Parisian café is another avant-garde challenge to the artistic establishment.

Art: it's a stick-up

SEPTEMBER, PARIS
These days, a painter does not even have to paint in order to call himself an artist. The young Spaniard Pablo Picasso has developed a technique that he calls *collage*, from the French 'to glue'. In his latest piece, *Still Life with Cane Chair*, he has stuck patterned oilcloth to his canvas instead of drawing the caning.

Picasso's work has already stimulated his friend and colleague, the Frenchman Georges Braque, to new heights of invention. His technique of *papier collé* (glued paper), can be seen in his latest still life, *Fruit, Dish and Glass,* where he uses real pieces of wallpaper.

The artistic partnership of these two young painters has enthralled the art world ever since the pair developed the Cubist style of painting in 1907.

Balkan states throw off Turkish yoke

4 DECEMBER, ISTANBUL
The 'sick man of Europe' took a lurch towards the grave today when Turkey surrendered to the Balkan states of Bulgaria and Serbia ending the period of Ottoman rule.

In March the Balkan states of Greece, Serbia and Bulgaria decided to put aside their rivalries and sign a secret treaty to unite in the attempt to oust the Ottoman Turks. After Montenegro joined, just over two months ago, the so-called Balkan League launched an attack on its overlords in support of its neighbour Macedonia's bid for independence. Last month, at the battle of Lule Burgas, Balkan League troops inflicted a crushing defeat on the Turks, whose resistance had been weakened by their 1908 revolution and the recent Italian offensive in Libya.

Greece is fighting on, but there is no doubt that the map of Europe has already been redrawn. A new country, Albania, has declared independence; Serbia and Montenegro have both enlarged their territory, and Turkey has lost its access to the Adriatic.

··· 8 JANUARY, BLOEMFONTEIN: AFRICAN NATIONAL CONGRESS FOUNDED WITH AIM TO END COLONIAL RULE ···

Houdini escapes death nightly

Tightly bound and shackled upside down in a tank full of water, Harry Houdini, the world's greatest escapologist, seems to have no way out.

In his latest illusion, the 'water torture cell trick', the 38-year-old performs one of his most spectacular escapes. With his ankles secured in stocks and padlocked to the metal frame of the tank, and his body confined in a steel grille, Houdini is lowered upside down into the water. The cell is then covered and the audience holds their breath. Minutes later, Houdini emerges triumphantly to a gasp of disbelief.

Over the past few years Houdini, the Hungarian-born magician and master of illusion, has become famous all over the world. He is reputedly able to wriggle out of any kind of bond or container – from a prison cell to a straitjacket suspended in mid-air.

His latest escape is one of his cleverest tricks. After being immersed he uses the grille as a ladder to clamber to the top of the tank, where his body will have displaced enough water to allow him to breathe. Bent double, he undoes the false rivets that hold him in place, after which escaping from the tank is easy.

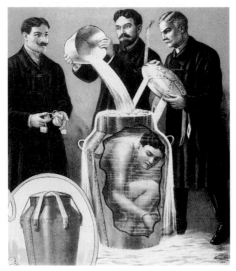

NO WAY OUT In another death-defying exploit, Houdini is placed in a hermetically sealed iron can.

AMERICAN HERO The indomitable Jim Thorpe, winner of six events, including the shot put, in Stockholm.

Double Olympic victory for Thorpe

JULY, STOCKHOLM

Spectators at the fifth modern Olympic Games were awed by the performance of Native American athlete Jim Thorpe.

He broke all records to claim the gold in both the decathlon, a competition that comprises ten gruelling events and the pentathlon, a new contest. Based on a competition held in the ancient Greek Olympics which consisted of five events, the pentathlon tests long-distance running, shooting, riding, swimming and wrestling. Thorpe also won the 200-metre dash and the 1500 metres, and came fourth in the individual high jump and seventh in the long jump. Thorpe's rivals declared him unbeatable.

Presenting him with his gold medal in that event, King Gustav V of Sweden, a keen tennis-player himself, reportedly said: 'Sir, you are the world's greatest athlete.' Thorpe replied: 'Thanks, King.'

The laconic 24-year-old hails from the small town of Prague, Oklahoma, where neighbours will undoubtedly be celebrating his amazing double victory. Partly of European ancestry, Thorpe is mostly Native American and the first of his people to claim an Olympic victory.

These Games were also notable for the increased participation of women (in swimming and diving competitions), and for the first use of electric timing equipment used in the running events.

Continents are drifting apart

Scientists have ridiculed the cranky theories of German geologist Alfred Wegener. In a recent paper, Wegener claims that the world's continents were once joined together in a giant landmass, which broke up into pieces that gradually drifted apart.

Wegener calls this super-continent Pangaea. Over many millennia, Pangaea disintegrated and the giant pieces began to drift like flotsam on the huge sea of

TALL STORY The new theory suggests that the Alps and other mountain ranges were formed by the collision of continents over aeons of time.

molten rock that lies beneath the surface of the earth. He has named this process 'continental drift', and bases his proposal on similarities in the flora and fauna and rock formations of continents that are now separated by thousands of miles. Furthermore, Wegener claims that on a map the current shapes of our continents can be seen to fit together like a gigantic jigsaw puzzle. For example, South America would tuck neatly into Africa.

But most scientists have dismissed Wegener's theory as nonsense. The idea of continents moving, they say, is simply laughable. The timescale involved would have to be unimaginably long.

··· FIRST EVER SELF-SERVICE FOOD STORE OPENS, IN CALIFORNIA ···

1913

DIED
10 Mar: Harriet Tubman, US campaigner against slavery
29 Sept: Rudolf Diesel, German inventor of the diesel engine

BORN
9 Jan: Richard M Nixon, US politician and President
12 Sept: Jesse Owens, US athlete
5 Nov: Vivien Leigh, British actress
7 Nov: Albert Camus, French philosopher, playwright and novelist

PUBLISHED
Marcel Proust, first volume of *Remembrance of Times Past*
D H Lawrence, *Sons and Lovers*

MUSIC HALL HIT
It's a Long Way to Tipperary, as sung by Florrie Forde

PROTESTED
3 Mar, Washington DC: 5000 women demanding the right to vote
3 Aug, California: hop ranch workers, over attempt to arrest union leader Blackie Ford; four die in riots

INVENTED
23 May: telephone recorder, by Thomas Edison

FLOODED
26 Mar: large parts of Ohio and Indiana, after Ohio River floods; 200 000 lose their homes and 467 die

REJECTED
6 May, London: bill to give women the vote, by House of Commons
15 July, London: Irish Home Rule Bill, for second time this year, by House of Lords

ON SALE
28 Mar, Oxford: the Morris Oxford motor car, costs £175

FIRST NIGHT
17 Feb, New York City: opening night of the Armory Show, featuring work by Kandinsky, Rodin and Duchamp, causes public outcry

FOUNDED
5 Mar, Texas: US Army's first air squadron
14 May, New York City: Rockefeller Foundation, by US industrialist John D Rockefeller; it aims to work for 'the well-being of mankind throughout the world'
23 Dec, USA: 12 Federal Reserve banks, under control of Federal Reserve Board

APPOINTED
26 May: Emily Duncan, first woman magistrate in England

Carter's potato crisps go on sale in London, after trial runs in Paris. The crisp was created in 1853, when a New York hotel customer complained that his french fries were too thick. The chef angrily sliced his potatoes as thinly as possible.

On **29 May**, *Russian dancer Vaclav Nijinsky performs in the avant-garde ballet* The Rite of Spring, *which he also choreographed. The music is composed by Russian Igor Stravinsky. The show's admirers and detractors cause uproar in the auditorium.*

FOUND
10 Feb, Antarctica: bodies of Captain Robert Falcon Scott and two companions; the men died returning from the South Pole in January 1912, after being beaten to the Pole by Roald Amundsen
12 Dec, Florence: Leonardo da Vinci's painting *Mona Lisa*, stolen from the Louvre in 1911; the thief, painter Vincenzo Perugia, is arrested

BANNED
15 Apr, London: public meetings held by suffragettes, by the British home secretary, on the grounds of the danger of public disorder
17 Nov, Berlin: the tango dance, for German army and navy, by Kaiser Wilhelm

STRUCK OFF
27 Jan: US athlete Jim Thorpe, as Olympic pentathlon and decathlon gold medallist; discovered to have been paid for playing minor league baseball in 1909–10

JAILED
3 Apr, London: Emmeline Pankhurst, suffragette leader, for inciting her followers to bomb David Lloyd George's home
11 Nov, South Africa: Mahatma Gandhi, for leading Indian passive resistance movement to British rule

EXPLODED
17 Oct, Germany: Zeppelin L2, world's largest airship; all 28 on board die

LEGALISED
25 Feb, Washington DC: income tax, by new 16th Amendment to US Constitution; in 1895 the Supreme Court had ruled that tax on income was unconstitutional

FIRST
21 June, Los Angeles: woman to make a parachute jump, Georgia 'Tiny' Broadwick

ARRESTED
27 Aug, Kiev: Russian Air Service Lieutenant Pyotr Nikolaevich Nesterov, for 'looping the loop' in his aeroplane – the first pilot in the world to do so

NEW WORD
isotope *n*: a chemical term describing any of two or more forms of a chemical element

VOTE CAMPAIGN GAINS A MARTYR

14 JUNE, LONDON

Thousands of people have attended the funeral procession of Emily Davison, who died after throwing herself in front of the King's horse at the Derby ten days ago.

The tragedy happened as the field thundered around Tattenham Corner, when Miss Davison darted out from the crowd and flung herself at Anmer, King George V's horse. She was knocked to the ground, and died four days afterwards from her injuries. The police found a return ticket to the racecourse in her handbag, suggesting that she had not intended to die but only to make the horse shy up.

A guard of suffragettes dressed in white with black sashes escorted Miss Davison's coffin as it was drawn through the streets of London by four black horses. At King's Cross station the mourners paid their final respects as the coffin was loaded on to a train bound for Northumberland, where Miss Davison was laid to rest in her home town of Morpeth.

Described by many as an act of crazed sacrifice, Miss Davison's dramatic action has focused public attention on the Votes for Women campaign. There have been many violent clashes between suffragettes and the forces of law and order in

SOLEMN VIGIL Suffragettes stand guard over Emily Davison's coffin.

recent months. Members of the Women's Social and Political Union have staged noisy, disruptive protests at many public meetings. They have marched, shouted, chained themselves to railings and smashed the windows of government buildings. Suffragettes have refused to pay taxes and to recognise the authority of the courts.

··· STAINLESS STEEL, AN ALLOY OF STEEL AND CHROME, IS INVENTED IN SHEFFIELD BY HENRY BREARLY ···

Manhattan gains two new architectural wonders

FEBRUARY, NEW YORK
Two new buildings, monumental in scale, have opened in New York this month. Grand Central Station, New York's new rail terminal, is the largest railway station in the world. With a vaulted ceiling dominated by enormous arched windows, this Beaux-Arts building is more reminiscent of a cathedral than a station.

Meanwhile Cass Gilbert's Woolworth building, with its pinnacles modelled on Europe's Gothic architecture, has set the standard for skyscrapers. At 60 storeys high, the Woolworth company's new headquarters is the world's tallest building.

TRULY GRAND Slanting sunbeams add drama to the cavernous ticket hall.

Ford's cars get much cheaper

Thanks to improved production methods, the price of a Model T has dropped from $850 in 1908 to around $500 today. Manufacturer Henry Ford has perfected his famous assembly line at Highland Park, Michigan, with the introduction this October of a 76-metre (250-ft) nonstop conveyor belt.

Workers no longer move around the shop floor; the work, in the form of a vehicle chassis, now comes to them. The moving assembly line means that employees are up to four times more productive than under the old system.

1914

BORN
27 Oct: Dylan Thomas, Welsh poet and playwright
25 Nov: Joe DiMaggio, US baseball star

DIED
25 Feb: Sir John Tenniel, British illustrator of *Alice's Adventures in Wonderland* and *Through the Looking Glass*

On **12 April**, Pygmalion *by George Bernard Shaw opens on stage at Her Majesty's Theatre, London. The comedy centres on Eliza Doolittle, a cockney girl, who is transformed into a gentrified lady by Professor Higgins.*

DAMAGED
10 Mar, London: Velázquez's *Rokeby Venus* painting, by suffragette Mary Richardson with a knife; damage costs £15000 to repair

ON STRIKE
30 Mar, Yorkshire: 100000 miners, calling for minimum wage to be introduced
1 Apr, London: electricians, calling for shorter working hours
1 Apr, Russia: 10000 workers in St Petersburg
4 June: British railway and mine workers, in support of builders and other striking workers

US author Edgar Rice Burroughs publishes Tarzan of the Apes, *the story of a British aristocrat raised in the jungle by apes. The Tarzan stories, and their cartoon and film spin-offs, would provide Burroughs with a steady income for the rest of his life.*

PUBLISHED
James Joyce, *Dubliners*

KILLED
16 Mar, Paris: Gaston Calmette, editor of newspaper *Le Figaro*, by wife of finance minister Joseph Caillaux, after Calmette threatens to publish embarrassing letters
20 Apr, Colorado: three striking mine workers, two women and 13 children; they are shot by National Guard troops and security men

WAR DECLARED
28 July: by Austria-Hungary, on Serbia
1 Aug: by Germany, on Russia
3 Aug: by Germany, on France
4 Aug: by Britain, on Germany
12 Aug: by Britain, on Austria-Hungary
2 Nov: by Russia, on Turkey
5 Nov: by Britain and France, on Turkey

RENAMED
1 Sept, Russia: city of St Petersburg, as Petrograd

APPOINTED
6 Aug: Lord Kitchener, as British secretary of state for war

FLED
15 July: President Huerta of Mexico, following US seaborne invasion
20 Oct: US birth control advocate Margaret Sanger, to Canada

POSTPONED
16 Sept: plans for Irish Home Rule, because of war

On **15 August**, *the Panama Canal opens to commercial shipping, and the first vessel to pass through is the* Cristobal. *The canal offers a passage between the Atlantic and Pacific oceans across the narrow Isthmus of Panama. It took the US Corps of Engineers a decade to build, and claimed the lives of many workers.*

FIRSTS
1 Jan: commercial airline, flying a round trip service from Tampa to St Petersburg in Florida
8 Jan, London: treatment of cancer with radium, at Middlesex Hospital
5 Oct, France: aerial dogfight; Sgt Joseph Frantz and Corporal Louis Quénault in a Voisin aircraft shoot down a German Aviatik

9 Dec: first custom-built aircraft carrier, the Royal Navy's HMS *Ark Royal* – holds up to 10 aircraft

INVENTED
Electric safety lantern for miners, developed and patented by Thomas Edison, USA
Colour photographic process, by the Eastman Kodak Company, USA

ELECTED
3 Sept, Rome: Pope Benedict XV

PROTESTED
4 Apr, London: opponents of Irish Home Rule, about threatened use of troops in Ulster

NEW WORD
birth control *n:* deliberate control or prevention of conception through artificial or natural means; term publicised by Margaret Sanger

GUNSHOTS SHATTER PEACE

STATELY PROGRESS Austria's archduke and duchess descend to their car.

KILLER HELD Moments after their murder, officials arrest the assassin.

28 JUNE, SARAJEVO

The heir to the Habsburg throne and his wife were shot dead in the streets of Bosnia's capital today. The murderer was arrested on the spot.

Archduke Franz Ferdinand and his wife, the Duchess of Hohenberg, were on an official visit to this tiny Balkan state, a small part of the vast Austro-Hungarian empire. As they drove down a narrow street, two loud shots rang out. One hit the archduke in the neck, and the other struck his wife in the stomach. The duchess died almost instantly, and the archduke some ten minutes later at 11.00 am.

The assassin, 19-year-old Gavrilo Princip, surrendered immediately. A member of a nationalist group from neighbouring Serbia, Princip said that he was revenging the oppression of the Serbian people. His action will bring into play the complex network of Europe's alliances and oppositions.

··· FIRST PASSENGER MEAL SERVED ON AN AEROPLANE IN FLIGHT, FROM RUSSIA TO UKRAINE; WINE IS PROVIDED ···

Europe slides into war

4 AUGUST, LONDON

Britain has declared war on Germany. Excited Londoners sang the national anthem outside 10 Downing Street, the home of Prime Minister Herbert Asquith, and swarmed around Buckingham Palace to cheer the King.

Europe is now embroiled in what looks set to be the biggest conflagration for more than 100 years. The key players are the Allied Powers – Britain, France and Russia – on one side and the Central Powers – Germany, Austro-Hungary and Turkey – on the other.

On 1 August, Kaiser Wilhelm II announced that Germany was at war with Russia. 'Let your hearts beat for God and your fists on the enemy,' he exhorted. Tsar Nicholas, the Kaiser's cousin, wasted no time and sent troops into eastern Germany the following day. The first shots of the war were fired near the little town of Eydtkuhnen. On 3 August, Germany declared war on France, and today German troops invaded neutral Belgium. Britain's declaration of war came soon afterwards.

Germany intends to use the plan devised by Count Alfred von Schlieffen for a war on two fronts. This involves fending off Russia with a minimum of troops, while throwing as much

FATAL ANNOUNCEMENT The Kaiser's proclamation of war is read out in Berlin.

manpower as possible into an invasion of France via Belgium. The Allies are optimistic. The commander of the British Expeditionary Force, General Sir John French, has already declared that the war 'will be over by Christmas'.

Armies dig themselves into trenches

READY FOR ACTION On their arrival in France, British troops pause to sample the local bread.

NOVEMBER, WESTERN FRONT
The war has reached a stalemate since the German advance on Paris was stopped at the river Marne. Battle-weary troops have dug hundreds of kilometres of defensive trenches which stretch across Europe from the North Sea to Switzerland.

Enemy trenches are separated by a muddy no-man's-land strewn with water-filled shell craters, barbed wire and unclaimed bodies. Forays by either side have so far simply added to the lengthy casualty lists. Commanders have yet to find a way to break the deadlock.

Meanwhile, life in the trenches has become nightmarishly monotonous. Most of the soldiers' time is spent waiting – either to be sent 'over the top' to attack enemy lines, a task likely to end in injury or death, or for the next enemy assault.

The trenches are warrens of slippery mud, populated by rats. It is almost impossible to stay dry and some soldiers have developed 'trench foot', a fungal disease caused by permanently wet feet. Men pass the time by writing letters home, mending their clothes, telling jokes – and digging more trenches.

Conditions are so bad that a rota system has developed. Soldiers spend about one week in every four on the front line. The rest of their time is spent in the reserves.

DEFENSIVE BEHAVIOUR German infantrymen on the Marne front take shelter in hastily-dug trenches.

KEEPING UP APPEARANCES Even in the front line, officers enjoy reasonably comfortable conditions.

··· WORLD'S FIRST TRAFFIC LIGHTS INSTALLED IN FRONT OF BRITISH HOUSE OF COMMONS ···

Military fastens on to zippy invention

The zip fastener, a device that binds and unbinds material quickly and easily, was launched this year, to an almost universal lack of interest.

Designed by engineer Gideon Sundback, the unassuming but practical little device is used by the United States armed forces to fasten overalls and pockets. The zip fastener's unique rows of interlocking identical teeth, pulled together by a moving slide, will stay securely together even under the most adverse conditions.

However, the makers and designers of clothes are not rushing to pick up on the zip's potential. For the time being, buttons and hooks are here to stay.

TOOTHSOME The slide pulls the zip together.

Liberating garment made from a couple of handkerchiefs

13 NOVEMBER, NEW YORK CITY
New York socialite Mary Phelps Jacob, fed up with the usual constricting and uncomfortable corsets, patented a revolutionary garment for woman – the 'backless brassiere'. It is a comfortable and lightweight alternative to the whalebone corsets that women are accustomed to enduring, and will enable them to take part in sports and strenuous activities with far greater freedom than before.

Jacobs told her maid to stitch together her original brassiere out of two handkerchiefs and a piece of pink ribbon. Her creation gently supported the bosom without squeezing it into an unnatural, constrictive shape – in fact, it minimised the bust, which suits current fashions.

When her friends started asking her to make brassieres for them, Jacobs realised that there was quite a demand for her invention. She intends to found a company to start manufacturing this innovative item of clothing.

Honour thy mother, urges US President

9 MAY, UNITED STATES
President Wilson has officially proclaimed today America's first Mother's Day - an occasion that owes much to the lobbying efforts of Anna Jarvis, whose mother started a 'mothers' friendship day' to bring families together after the Civil War. After her mother died, Jarvis – herself childless – started to campaign for a national day to honour the work done and love given by all mothers, so often taken for granted. Now the second Sunday of May has been set aside as their special day.

··· 25 DEC: GERMAN AND BRITISH SOLDIERS PLAY FOOTBALL AND EXCHANGE GIFTS DURING A ONE-DAY TRUCE ···

Short clubs and long drive propel golfer to triumph at the Open

SEPTEMBER, SCOTLAND
For a record-breaking sixth time, veteran British golfer Harry Vardon has won the British Open Golf championship, beating long-time rival John Henry Taylor by just three strokes at Prestwick, the home of the Open.

Vardon has been a master of the sport since the last century, winning his first open in 1896. The 44-year-old golfer has won numerous tournaments both in Europe and across the Atlantic, where he won the US Open in 1900 and was runner-up last year. According to golf enthusiasts, along with Taylor and James Braid, he is one of the Great Triumvirate – the finest players the sport has ever seen.

At the start of Vardon's career, his innovative approach to swing and stance gave him an edge over his rivals. Today many players, amateur and professional alike, have adopted his technique, including the famous overlapping 'Vardon grip'.

The secret of Vardon's success may lie in his choice of clubs. He plays with shorter, lighter clubs than most other golfers, and when he does not have his own he is apt to borrow a ladies' set.

CHAMPIONS ALL Harry Vardon (left) poses with fellow golfers Francis Ouimet and Ted Ray.

1915

BORN
7 Apr: Billie Holiday, US jazz singer
29 Aug: Ingrid Bergman, Swedish-born Hollywood actress
17 Oct: Arthur Miller, US playwright and novelist
19 Dec: Edith Piaf, French singer

DIED
23 Oct: W G Grace, British cricketer
14 Nov: Booker T Washington, black educationalist and cultural leader

PUBLISHED
John Buchan, *The Thirty-Nine Steps*
D H Lawrence, *The Rainbow*
Virginia Woolf, *The Voyage Out*

FOUNDED
28 Jan, Washington DC: US Coast Guard

SIGNED
9 Jan, Mexico: treaty between USA and revolutionary leader Pancho Villa, ending border disputes
26 Apr, London: secret treaty between Britain, France and Italy under which Italy will enter war in return for land concessions

DEFENDED
2 Feb, Suez Canal: British troops drive back Turkish soldiers

BOMBED
19 Jan, Norfolk: Great Yarmouth and King's Lynn in first Zeppelin raid
25 May, Italy: Venice, by Austrian aircraft, two days after Italy declares war on Austria

SUNK
19 Aug, Atlantic Ocean: White Star liner *Arabic;* 44 missing

BRITONS
"WANTS
YOU"
JOIN YOUR COUNTRY'S ARMY!
GOD SAVE THE KING

Lord Kitchener, British secretary of state for war, is featured on the most famous recruitment poster of World War I. Kitchener had huge popular appeal in Britain, and an estimated three million men responded to his call to arms. Alfred Leete designed the poster, which was one in a series.

KILLED
27 July, Haiti: Vilbrun Guillaume, president, by a mob
19 Nov, Utah: Joe Hill, composer of radical songs for US unionists; after being convicted of murder

FIRST
12 Dec, Germany: all-metal aeroplane, built by Hugo Junkers

WAR DECLARED
23 May: by Italy, on Austria-Hungary
25 Aug: by Italy, on Turkey
15 Oct: by Britain, on Bulgaria

SOLD
21 Sept, Salisbury: Stonehenge, at auction, for £6000

PROTESTED
7 Nov, Chicago: 40000 people at new law closing bars on Sundays

DISCOVERED
Dysentery bacillus, by British scientist James Kendall

RESIGNED
9 June, Washington DC: US secretary of state William Jennings Bryan, over President Wilson's movement away from neutrality in the European war

BESTSELLERS
Joseph Conrad, *Victory*
W Somerset Maugham, *Of Human Bondage*

CONVICTED
1 July, London: George Smith, of murder; he married three women at once and drowned each in the bath to claim life insurance or an inheritance

REVIVED
25 Nov, Georgia: racist organisation the Ku Klux Klan, by ex-preacher William J Simmons

NEW WORDS
abstract *adj*: denoting art characterised by geometric, formalised, or otherwise nonrepresentational qualities
sonar *n*: a location device used underwater; from so(und) na(vigation) and r(anging)

THE LUSITANIA IS LOST

7 MAY, IRELAND

The famous Cunard liner *Lusitania* was hit by a torpedo from a German U-boat off the coast of Ireland today and sank almost immediately, with the loss of more than 1000 lives.

The *Lusitania*, which had capacity for 3000 passengers and was capable of 24 knots, left New York a week ago, bound for Liverpool. She was unarmed, but was carrying a cargo of rifle ammunition and shells. Before she set off the German ambassador had published notices in New York warning of an attack. However, the threat was not considered serious, and 218 Americans were on board as she sailed away.

Owing to German submarine activity in Irish coastal waters, the British Admiralty had advised ships to steer a zigzag course as an evasive tactic, but the *Lusitania* appeared to be on a straight course. She was attacked suddenly at 2.15 pm and was struck amidships by a single torpedo which blew a hole in her side. This was followed minutes later by a second, heavier, explosion – possibly the ship's boilers, or a second torpedo. The 32000-ton liner went down in 94 metres (310 ft) of water in just 20 minutes, listing so steeply that it was impossible for many of the lifeboats to be launched.

Of the 1959 passengers and crew on board, 1198 have been lost, including 124 American citizens - among them the millionaire Alfred Gwynne Vanderbilt.

Germany has justified the action by claiming that the ship was armed and carrying contraband munitions, but condemnation by both Allied and neutral countries has been swift and unequivocal. US President Woodrow Wilson, although maintaining his country's neutrality, reacted strongly against the outrage; ex-President Theodore Roosevelt called it 'piracy on a vaster scale than the worst pirates of history'.

FACES OF SHOCK Crew members reflect on the tragedy they have witnessed.

··· JAMES LEWIS KRAFT LAUNCHES THE WORLD'S FIRST PROCESSED CHEESE IN CANADA ···

Poison gas used as weapon

23 APRIL, WESTERN FRONT

Allied lines north of Ypres, in Belgium, have been decimated by a deadly new weapon in the struggle for control of the Western Front.

The German army sprayed Allied troops with poisonous chlorine gas at dusk yesterday. The yellowish-green vapour sent men stumbling back from the front line, blinded and unable to breathe. Worst hit were the French Zouaves, who fled choking and panic-stricken. The damage might have been worse but for Canadian troops, whom the gas failed to reach.

German troops in gas masks quickly followed and claimed a 6.4-kilometre (4-mile) gap in the Allied front. Gas masks have yet to be issued as standard military gear for Allied troops. Until this happens, British commanders expect their men to go into battle clutching wet cloths to their faces. Whether this is an effective deterrent remains to be seen.

ALL KITTED OUT French troops don goggles and face masks in preparation for a gas attack.

Armenians killed

DECEMBER, ARMENIA

Reports of the murder and torture of Armenians by the Turks have filtered through to the West – some estimates put the number of Armenians dying every day at thousands.

Armenia – divided between Russia and the Ottoman Empire – has suffered before; between 1894 and 1896 the Muslim Turks massacred thousands of Christian Armenians. Despite hopes offered by the new Young Turk government of 1908, it became clear that such persecution would continue. With the outbreak of war Turkey allied itself with Germany against Russia and, fearing that its Armenian population would sympathise with Russia, used this as an excuse to begin the slaughter early this year. Armenian soldiers, leaders and 'subversives' were sent to labour camps and then executed.

Since April, Turkey has been deporting its Armenian population. Although ostensibly bound for Syria or Palestine, few reach their destination. Denied food, water and medicine, thousands die along the routes, of starvation, exhaustion and disease. Rape and torture are commonplace, and many are murdered outright.

Those who offer resistance are brutally punished. In the town of Zov they were locked in stables, doused in kerosene and set alight. In Bitlis, 4500 men were forced to dig their own graves before being slaughtered. Around Van, 24 000 Armenians were killed in three days.

MERCILESS ATTACK An artist's impression of Turkish pillage and murder.

Both Germany and the Allies sheltered Armenians and protested against Turkey's actions, but the tide of bloodshed appeared unstoppable. In what was described by one Armenian as a 'prolonged anguish of soul', up to 1.5 million people died.

··· PYREX, FIRST OVEN-PROOF GLASSWARE, INVENTED IN NEW YORK BY EUGENE SULLIVAN AND WILLIAM TAYLOR ···

NURSING HEROINE Edith Cavell, pictured before the war, helped Allied soldiers to flee.

Nurse shot for helping Allied soldiers escape

12 OCTOBER, BRUSSELS
The British nurse Edith Cavell was executed by a German firing squad at 2 am today

Cavell, the daughter of a Norfolk vicar, was appointed the first matron of the Berkendael Institute, Brussels, in 1907, and greatly improved the standard of care. After the German occupation of Belgium she ran her nursing institute in the Belgian capital as a Red Cross hospital, treating injured German and Allied soldiers alike. Cavell also became involved in an underground group formed to help Allied soldiers escape.

In August she and several others were arrested. Cavell was placed in solitary confinement, and charged with helping 130 British, French and Belgian soldiers escape across the border to the neutral Netherlands. She did not deny the accusation – and the true number was probably closer to 300.

While she made a full confession of her involvement, Cavell courageously stated that she had received letters of thanks from many of those she had helped to safety. After a trial lasting just two days, and despite the efforts of American and Spanish diplomats, the death sentence was passed.

Just hours before she faced the firing squad, the condemned woman was allowed to see a British chaplain. Edith Cavell's last words were reported as: 'I realise that patriotism is not enough. I must have no hatred or bitterness towards anyone.'

Chaplin stars as lovable tramp ...

The public queued to see Charlie Chaplin's latest film, *The Tramp*. Audiences warmed to the charming clown whom Chaplin introduced in his film debut, *Making A Living*. In *The Tramp*, however, audiences see a fully rounded character capable of arousing both laughter and tears, one moment acting with hilarious stupidity, the next with great courage or sensitivity. Chaplin's bowler-hatted tramp has become popular in both the United States and Great Britain, and the universal appeal of silent films means worldwide success cannot be far off. His versatile talent is evident everywhere in the film – Chaplin is not only its star but also its scriptwriter and director. *The Tramp*'s slapstick comedy and bitter-sweet ending will make it a cinema classic.

TALENTED SCRUFF Chaplin blends pathos, humour and sheer cheek.

... but Miss Pickford is a much bigger star

Mary Pickford and William S Hart are the leading lady and first man of the film industry. According to a new survey, these actors are attracting the largest cinema audiences. William S Hart is the serious face of the new film genre of Westerns – cowboy adventures. The actor has starred in 22 films so far, of which 18 were released this year.

Mary Pickford, who started her cinematic career aged 16, is now hot box-office property. She lies just two places behind Hart overall, and is the movies' most popular actress by far. Known as the 'Biograph girl', she started on $10 per day, but now earns $2000 a week. She was the subject of the first cinematic close-up, in *Friends,* released in 1912.

SCREEN BEAUTY Mary Pickford.

MOVIE HERO Rugged and good-looking William S Hart.

Poet dies going to war

23 APRIL, SKYROS, GREECE
Britain mourned the death of the young war poet Rupert Brooke, who died aged 27 while on active service.

He contracted blood poisoning en route to the Dardanelles, the channel connecting the Aegean and the Sea of Marmara, with his Royal Naval division. Brooke was buried on the island of Skyros.

The poet published his five *War Sonnets* at the beginning of this year to enormous acclaim. Along with his good looks and charm, these poems helped to establish him as a dashing – and now tragic – hero.

With Brooke's death, one of his most famous sonnets, 'The Soldier', in which he meditates sadly on the possibility of dying abroad, took on a prophetic poignancy:

If I should die, think only this of me:
That there's some corner of a foreign
field
That is forever England.

1916

DIED

20 Feb: Robert Peary, US explorer, first man to reach the North Pole
28 Feb: Henry James, US novelist
6 June: Yuan Shi-kai, Chinese politician
31 Oct: Charles Taze Russell, US founder of Jehovah's Witnesses
24 Nov: Sir Hiram Maxim, US-born designer of first machine-gun

SURRENDERED

29 Apr, Mesopotamia: British forces at Kut-el-Amara, to Turkish army after 143-day siege

REBELLED

21 June, Arabia: Tribes led by Hussein, grand sharif of Mecca, against Turkish rule

PROPOSED

27 May, USA: peacekeeping League of Nations, to be created at war's end

SIGNED

20 Mar: agreement between British and French to share out Turkish lands at end of war
6 July, Petrograd: peace treaty between Russia and Japan
1 Sept, Washington DC: child labour law; children under 16 may not work at night, more than eight hours a day or in mines

FOUNDED

18 Apr, France: all-US air squadron, made up of volunteer pilots under French captain Georges Thénault
15 July, Canada: aircraft construction company, by William Boeing
16 Oct, New York City: birth control information clinic, by Margaret Sanger and Ethel Byrne

DENOUNCED

21 Aug, New York City: movies, for 'immoral' stories and 'insidious attacks on Christianity', by the US Federation of Catholic Societies

CALLED UP

27 Jan, Britain: unmarried men between 18 and 41; and married men between 18 and 41 on 25 May

FOR SALE

19 Feb, Britain: first National Savings certificates

SHOWN

Blue Lines, by US painter Georgia O'Keefe

Field Marshal Douglas Haig was appointed British commander-in-chief on the Western Front last year. His previous positions include chief of general staff in India and head of military training in London.

EXECUTED

3 Aug, London: disgraced Irish-born British diplomat Roger Casement, for high treason; he tried to smuggle arms into Ireland for rebel use

KILLED

4 Feb, Turkey: Crown Prince Yussuf Izzedin, by assassin
9 Mar, New Mexico: 19 US citizens, by raiding Mexican rebels

On 15 September, the first tanks are used in warfare by the British Army at the Battle of the Somme. The armoured vehicles are shipped to France in crates marked 'water tanks' to confuse the enemy. The tanks are not as effective as expected owing to fuel shortages and mechanical breakdowns.

1 July, France: 20000 British soldiers in one day as the Battle of the Somme begins
2 July, Illinois: 39 in race riots

DISPATCHED

18 June, USA: 100000 US National Guards to Mexican border, by President Wilson; US warships are also sent to Mexican coasts

FIRSTS

7 Dec: woman elected to US Congress – Jeannette Rankin
28 Sept: dollar billionaire, John D Rockefeller, following US stock market boom

PROMISED

8 Sept, New Jersey: the vote for women 'in a little while', by US President Wilson

WAR DECLARED

27 Aug: by Romania, on Austria-Hungary
28 Aug: by Italy, on Germany

30 Aug: by Turkey, on Russia
27 Sept: by Greece, on Bulgaria

FIRST NIGHTS

Feb, Zurich: Dada performances at Cabaret Voltaire, by among others Romanian poet Tristan Tzara and German artist Max Ernst
Intolerance, epic movie directed by US director D W Griffith

RE-ELECTED

7 Nov: Woodrow Wilson, as US President (Democrat)

BANNED

21 Mar, London: import of pianos, spirits and motors
1 July, USA: alcohol, in states of Michigan, Montana, Nebraska and South Dakota
28 July, London: imports of cocaine and opium

APPOINTED

9 Feb, Africa: former Boer leader General Jan Smuts as commander of British and South African troops in East Africa
27 Aug, Germany: Field Marshal Paul von Hindenburg as German chief of general staff
7 Dec, London: David Lloyd George as British prime minister, after resignation of Herbert Asquith

NEW WORDS

intelligence quotient (IQ) *n*: a person's mental ability as shown on a numbered scale following tests
x-ray *n*: image of person's internal organs and bone structure created by passing electromagnetic radiation through body to photographic plate
backpack *n*: rucksack

SOMME OFFENSIVE TAKES HEAVY TOLL

OVER THE TOP The open, flat countryside of La Boiselle offers little cover to troops en route to another skirmish.

13 NOVEMBER, PICARDY, NORTHERN FRANCE
Wounded soldiers drowned in the battlefield mud as heavy rain brought an end to the five-month British–French offensive against German lines near the river Somme. It has won 8 kilometres (5 miles) from the Germans but at a devastating cost – around 420 000 British and 195 000 French lost their lives winning the land, and about 650 000 Germans died defending it.

The first day of the battle, 1 July, was the most appalling. After a week's bombardment of German lines by heavy guns, British and French soldiers were ordered 'over the top' – to clamber out of their trenches and attack the German lines – at 7.30 am. The British commander, Field Marshal Douglas Haig, thought the artillery would have cleared the German defences and that his soldiers would be able to go forward virtually unopposed. The reality was horribly different.

The artillery had merely warned the Germans of an impending attack, and they were ready and waiting. The British soldiers each carried some 30 kilos (70 lb) of equipment, including ammunition, wirecutters and tools for digging trenches. They could not move fast, especially as November rains had turned the battlefield into a swamp. As they went forward in waves they were cut down by German machine-gunners. In the first day 60 000 British soldiers were wounded and 20 000 killed – the British Army's worst ever losses in one day. The French attacked in an area where the Germans were not as strong, and took 4000 prisoners.

The Somme offensive was planned as part of a 'Big Push' to smash the German lines and end the war. It did not come off partly because the French could not lend as much weight as promised because they were trying to contain German attacks on Verdun further south. Haig pushed on with the Somme offensive and slowly won small amounts of enemy territory, but failed to build on these victories.

On 15 September the British unleashed a new weapon with a great future – the tank, an armoured vehicle with tracks that can go where wheels cannot, ploughing through the mud and gore of no-man's-land and over the trenches. In two hours the British took 2000 prisoners, but this brief breakthrough was not exploited. There were not enough tanks at the Somme to make a lasting difference – and too many of them broke down under the strain of battle.

This terrible campaign, which has cost so many lives, has had one good outcome for the Allies. By drawing the Germans into a prolonged slogging match it has prevented them from making a breakthrough elsewhere on the Western Front.

BEHIND THE BARRICADE Shattered trees overlook the vast and well-established subterranean city where Allied troops live between offensives.

North Sea battle leaves both navies shattered

1 JUNE, NORTH SEA

British and German fleets have torn pieces out of each other in the Battle of Jutland, the biggest naval battle of all time. It ended with both sides claiming victory, with the Germans forced to retreat to the safety of their coastal minefields, although the British have lost more ships. German losses are reported as one battleship, one battle cruiser, four cruisers and five destroyers, against three battle cruisers, three cruisers and eight destroyers for the British.

The battle started at 4.00 pm yesterday, when one section of the British fleet, under Sir David Beatty, encountered a German scout force. After an exchange of fire, Beatty drew the German ships to where he knew the British Grand Fleet under Sir John

FULL STEAM AHEAD Britain's Grand Fleet patrols the North Sea before its encounter with Germany.

Jellicoe was waiting. Battle was joined, and by dusk the British had gained the upper hand. As they turned to go home, the fleets passed each other, dealing out a further battering in a final skirmish. As dawn broke, it emerged that the German High Seas Fleet had retreated to the naval base at Wilhelmshaven.

··· 3 JULY, NEW YORK CITY: THE LOUDSPEAKER, INVENTED BY AT&T, IS FIRST USED AT A CONVENTION ···

Gallipoli campaign ends in humiliating withdrawal

8 JANUARY, GALLIPOLI

The last Allied soldiers were evacuated from the Gallipoli peninsula in north-west Turkey, finally ending the disastrous eight-month operation. Troops from Australia and New Zealand played a gritty role in the campaign, but despite their heroism it was a catastrophe – 250 000 out of 480 000 Allied troops have been killed and none of the strategic aims has been achieved.

The Gallipoli campaign was an attempt to find a way around the deadlock on the Western Front by knocking Turkey, Germany's backer, out of the war. The initial plan was for the Royal Navy to force its way through the Dardanelles straits to the south of Gallipoli, taking Constantinople and forging a supply route to Russian ports on the Black Sea. But on 18 March the

RETREAT UNDER FIRE As British troops prepare to embark, an enemy shell falls short into the sea.

British fleet lost six ships when it ran into mines strung across the Dardanelles, and the attempt was abandoned. Perhaps one of the war's great ironies was that the Allies abandoned their naval attack at the very moment when the Turkish ammunition was exhausted. A land assault was launched on 25 April when British, Australian, New Zealand and French troops came ashore from ships and took control of six Gallipoli beaches. Some were easily taken, but at others the Allied forces met a wall of Turkish fire, at a terrible cost in lives.

Once established, the Allied soldiers could make no progress against the well-fortified Turkish positions on the inland hills, even after a seond wave of landings on 6 August. The decision to withdraw came in December, and the campaign's one success was a daring night-time operation on 19 December in which ships evacuated most of the surviving troops without a single life being lost.

Stalemate on the Western Front

READY FOR BATTLE French machine-gunners at Fort Douaumont are poised to meet the next onslaught.

2 NOVEMBER, VERDUN
French troops have recaptured Fort Douaumont, wiping out gains made by the Germans in their bloody attempt to take the city of Verdun. German General Erich von Falkenhayn has failed in his grim ambition to sap France's will to win by draining its army of manpower.

The attack on defences around Verdun was launched at 7.15 am on 21 February with a devastating artillery bombardment that took the French by surprise, flattening their trenches. In the afternoon the Germans advanced, and over the next days they made easy progress, capturing Fort Douaumont on 25 February.

In March France's General Pétain came in with reinforcements to defend Verdun, and the battle became a terrible slogging match. By 23 June the Germans were nearing the city, but the French were saved by the launch of the Allies' Somme offensive on 1 July, after which the German onslaught on Verdun dried up. In the autumn, the French fought back.

In one of the war's longest and bitterest battles, the French lost around 400000 men, and the Germans about 350000. At the end the armies were in roughly the same places they had been when the bloodbath began.

Some artists record the war, others speak out against it

The destruction caused by the war is proving, paradoxically, to be a creative stimulus for a generation of young artists. This year Britain's Ministry for Information has even introduced an official war artists scheme, under which painters have been recruited to record the war for the purposes of information and propaganda.

The first such war artist was the distinguished etcher Muirhead Bone, who toured the battle zones of France in a chauffeur-driven car. Other official artists have less cushioned lives. Christopher Nevinson, for example, made a series of drawings from balloons. He has seen appalling suffering while serving in the army's medical corps, and some of his work has had to be censored.

Many of the war artists produced work of a quality that they were never to match in their postwar careers. Some women were employed as war artists, and several artists who were entirely unconnected with the official scheme drew inspiration from the conflict.

One of them is Londoner Mark Gertler, who painted *Merry-Go-Round* this year. Gertler, a committed pacifist, probably intended the picture as a satire on militarism. The puppet-like figures — some wearing uniform, others not — are carried around on an endless whirligig of war. Theirs is a heartless world in which normal moral values have been swept aside and people mechanically go on fighting and hating, without thought or feeling.

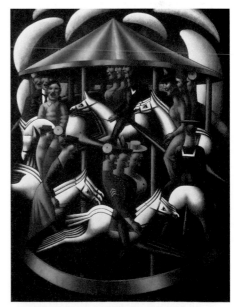

DEADLY GAME In Gertler's *Merry-Go-Round*, soldiers and civilians share the carousel of war.

··· THE FIRST FORTUNE COOKIES ARE PRODUCED IN LOS ANGELES BY GEORGE JUNG ···

Irish rebels seize GPO

25 APRIL, DUBLIN
Dublin remains in a state of emergency after yesterday's incident when armed rebels seized control of the General Post Office and other strategic buildings and declared an independent Irish republic.

The rebels are Irish nationalists mainly belonging to two radical groups, the Irish Volunteers and the Irish Republican Brotherhood. The move towards open rebellion had been simmering since the start of the war, when the Home Rule bill – which would have granted a degree of autonomy to Ireland – was put on hold until the end of hostilities. The radicals have looked to Germany to assist them in their cause, using Roger Casement, a former diplomat in the British Foreign Office, as go-between. Last week the British seized a ship carrying a consignment of arms from Germany for the rebels and arrested Casement after he landed near Tralee from a German submarine. He will be tried as a traitor.

GUARDIANS British forces patrol Dublin's gutted General Post Office.

Despite this setback the nationalists pressed ahead. Under the leadership of Pádraic Pearse and James Connolly the uprising began at around noon yesterday, Easter Monday, with an army of just over 2000 men. Soldiers were fired on at the British headquarters, Dublin Castle, and a number of buildings were set alight, including the law courts. A provisional government was set up, with Pearse as president, proclaiming equal rights and opportunities for all Irish citizens and his intention to 'pursue the happiness of the whole nation'.

Barricades have been erected in the streets of Dublin, and the Royal Navy has been bombarding the post office with shells. Britain will soon regain control of Dublin, but the struggle for independence will go on.

A new bottle for a brand leader

A curvaceous new bottle modelled on the cola nut has been unveiled by the Coca-Cola company in Atlanta, Georgia.

Coca-Cola's launch of its distinctive bottle has caught imitators on the hop. Many firms have sought to emulate the fizzy drink's runaway success by imitating its formula and bottle design, but the new patented bottle will assure that Coca-Cola, with its distinctive logo in flowing longhand, remains instantly recognisable.

The product started life being sold in the soda fountains of the American South, billed as an invigorating health tonic by its pharmacist inventor John Pemberton. The name came from two of the drink's constituents: cocaine from the coca leaf and cola from the cola nut (a plant rich in caffeine). After public pressure the cocaine content of the drink was dropped at the beginning of the 1900s, but the drink remained very popular all the same, and demand quickly spread overseas. The drink is made up of 15 special ingredients, of which one, code-named 7X, remains a closely guarded secret, known to no fewer than two and no more than three people at a time. As an extra precaution, these guardians of the recipe are never permitted to travel together.

THE REAL THING
Coca-Cola's new,
distinctive bottle.

Slow death for monk

CHARISMATIC CLERIC Rasputin's piercing gaze transfixed all who met him.

16 DECEMBER, PETROGRAD
Russian nobles led by Prince Felix Yusopov have murdered the Siberian monk Rasputin, notorious for drunkenness and his ravenous sexual appetite, and hated because of his intimacy with the Empress Alexandra. Grand Duke Dmitri Pavlovich and Yusopov, both relatives of Tsar Nicholas II, persuaded Rasputin to come to Yusopov's home – where they stabbed, poisoned and shot him. They then dumped his body from a bridge into the icy water of the river Neva.

Gregory Rasputin, born a peasant in the early 1870s, was a member of a religious sect which believed in flagellation. He came to Petrograd (then St Petersburg) in 1905 and won the hearts of Tsar Nicholas and his wife Alexandra by apparently using hypnotism to control the bleeding of their son Alexei, who suffers from haemophilia. But Russians resented his mysterious position at court. They blamed government incompetence on Rasputin's influence over appointments. Rumours of sexual scandal flew – not least after the Tsar, who made himself commander of Russian forces in 1915, left for the war front leaving Alexandra and Rasputin in Petrograd.

Rasputin had charisma and an air of mystery, and he was as strong as an ox. Before he died he was attacked in three different ways, each of which should have been enough to kill him, but the postmortem showed that he was still alive when he was thrown into the Neva. The news of Rasputin's murder has been greeted with delight among the middle classes, and in the face of such public approval Tsar Nicholas cannot demand the murderers' execution.

Irish author's autobiography stirs up trouble

29 DECEMBER, NEW YORK CITY
A Portrait of the Artist as a Young Man, **James Joyce's semi-autobiographical novel, has been published** in New York by B W Huebsch. No London printer would touch the book, deeming its passages about religion to be blasphemous.

The book has been surrounded by controversy; the story was first rejected by publishers because its style – with passages of 'stream of consciousness' prose echoing our internal dialogue with ourselves – was considered too unconventional. It has been published in Britain in serial form by Joyce's friend and supporter Harriet Shaw Weaver in her magazine *The Egoist.* A book edition is now planned.

The novel looks certain to continue to be the subject of much debate and is likely to confirm its Irish author, now working on a massive tome called *Ulysses,* as one of Europe's most original creative talents.

Guerrillas raid United States

9 MARCH, NEW MEXICO
The Mexican bandit and revolutionary Francisco 'Pancho' Villa launched a raid across the US border today, damaging property and killing several citizens in the town of Columbus. In response President Woodrow Wilson has despatched an expeditionary force, led by General John J 'Black Jack' Pershing, to hunt down the fugitive bandit.

PEOPLE'S HERO Leader of Mexico's Army of the Revolution, Pancho Villa.

Villa's motives are mainly political; he objects to the way that the US government has offered recognition and support to the regime of his former ally Venustiano Carranza, Mexico's conservative president. This attack, accompanied by the battle cry of 'Viva Villa' from the elite guerilla team, targeted the US garrison town of Columbus in the pre-dawn hours. Even though the Villistas lost over 100 men this latest foray, together with other similar raids, can be seen as a demonstration of the revolutionary leader's military strength.

The presence of US troops in Mexico will arouse great resentment, and will no doubt hasten the process of turning the elusive Pancho into a national hero.

1917

BORN

25 Feb: Anthony Burgess, British author
29 May: John F Kennedy, US President
21 Oct: Dizzy Gillespie, US jazz musician
19 Nov: Indira Gandhi (née Nehru), Indian prime minister

DIED

22 Sept: Frances X Cabrini, first US Catholic saint
26 Sept: Edgar Degas, French painter
17 Nov: Auguste Rodin, French sculptor

PURCHASED

31 Mar: the Virgin Islands, sold by Denmark to the USA for $25 million, to prevent their use as a German military base and to protect the Panama Canal

CAPTURED

11 Mar, Iraq: Baghdad, by the British
9 Dec, Palestine: Jerusalem, by Allied troops under General Edmund Allenby

DECLARED

6 Apr: war on Germany by the US; followed by Cuba (7 April) and Panama (8 April)
4 June: war on Germany, by Brazil
15 Sept: Russia as a republic, by Prime Minister Alexander Kerensky

EXPLODED

19 Jan, London: the Venesta munitions works, rocking the city and killing 80 people
6 Dec, Canada: munitions ship at Halifax, Nova Scotia, killing 2000 people

Leon Trotsky is second-in-command to Lenin in the October Revolution in Russia. Trotsky – born Lev Davidovich Bronstein – has spent most of the century on the run from the tsarist authorities. Now he has taken their place.

FIRST NIGHTS

18 Apr, Paris: the Ballets Russes present *Parade* by Jean Cocteau, with music by Erik Satie and sets and costumes by Picasso
17 June, USA: *The Immigrant*, starring Charlie Chaplin

FIRSTS

13 Feb, UK: women taxi-drivers in Britain
7 Mar, New York City: jazz recording, *The Darktown Strutters' Ball*, by the Original Dixieland Jazz Band
1 June: protected convoys of merchant ships, to counter German U-boats
20 Nov: Allied use of tanks in mass assault, at Battle of Cambrai, establishing a new form of warfare

Baseball game played on a Sunday, at the Polo grounds in New York
Pulitzer prizes in USA, for biography, history and journalism, awarded from bequest of US newspaper tycoon Joseph Pulitzer

FOUNDED

Bayerische Motoren Werke (BMW), car manufacturing firm in Germany

ADOPTED

Bobbed hair by women, initially as a safety measure for factory workers

BANNED

5 Feb, USA: Asian workers (except Japanese), vagrants, alcoholics, illiterates, and anyone of 'immoral purpose' from entering USA, under Immigration Act
15 June, USA: seditious materials, and any attempt to hinder US war effort, under Espionage Act

LAUNCHED

11 Apr: Allied offensive against the Hindenburg line at Arras; British take 11000 German prisoners
Liquid nail polish, manufactured by Cutex

DESTROYED

30 Dec: Guatemala City, by massive earthquake

SCREEN HITS

Cleopatra, starring a scantily clad Theda Bara as the seductress
The Little Princess, starring Mary Pickford

CLOSED

Storyville, quarter of New Orleans where jazz was born

SIGNED

25 Mar, San Antonio: record $50000 contract, by John McGraw, to manage the New York Giants baseball team for one year

PUBLISHED

Arthur Conan Doyle, *His Last Bow*
T S Eliot, *Prufrock and Other Observations*

NEW WORDS

camouflage *n:* the exploitation of natural surroundings or artificial aids to conceal or disguise the presence of military units
fighter *n:* a combat aircraft
jaywalk *vb:* to cross a street in a place other than the official crossing; to cross the street in a reckless fashion

On 10 January, Buffalo Bill (left), born William F Cody, died. He was the founder of the touring Wild West Show which created the popular image of 'cowboys and Indians'. Buffalo Bill's nickname dates from the days when he sold buffalo meat to railway workers.

BLOODY SLAUGHTER IN FRANCE

SHELLSHOCKED LANDSCAPE Allied soldiers cross a makeshift bridge over the waterlogged wasteland in the Château Woods region, near Ypres.

10 NOVEMBER, BELGIUM
The protracted campaign around the tiny village of Passchendaele has finally reached its bloody end. Canadian troops retook the ruined village four days ago and held their positions in the face of fierce German counterattacks. The campaign has produced one of the bloodiest encounters of the war. Allied forces have suffered huge casualties but made only marginal territorial gains.

The village is situated a few kilometres away from Ypres, a key location that guards the approaches to the English Channel. Passchendaele is the third major battle to have taken place in the region. The offensive was

launched in the summer by troops from Britain and the Empire, under the leadership of Field Marshal Haig. His initiative came at a time when Allied fortunes were badly in need of a boost.

Haig's plan was to clear a route through to the Belgian coast, and initially the strategy worked well. A preliminary assault on the ridge at Messines was successful, but there was a disastrous seven-week delay before the attack began in earnest on 31 July, allowing the enemy time to regroup. Haig's luck ran out.

Saturation bombing of the low-lying German positions wrecked the natural drainage system and turned the entire

area into a quagmire. Torrential rain added to the problem, and many of the casualties drowned in flooded shell craters. Others were killed by exposure to blistering, poisonous mustard gas.

Despite this, Haig's force continued its slow advance. In late September there were successes at the Menin Road ridge and Polygon Wood before rain halted proceedings again. It was only on 30 October that Canadian troops reached the edge of Passchendaele before being pushed back again, and not until today that the village was finally secured. The cost of the enterprise has been enormous on both sides, with losses estimated at around 300 000 men each.

··· CHARLIE CHAPLIN SIGNS THE FIRST MILLION-DOLLAR FILM CONTRACT, WITH FIRST NATIONAL FILM COMPANY ···

Russian revolts topple Tsar

15 MARCH, PETROGRAD
Tsar Nicholas II gave up his throne today, shocked by the Petrograd garrison's refusal to put down the wave of strikes and demonstrations that has swept the country over the past few weeks. Strikes sparked by food shortages began among women textile workers on 8 March and quickly spread to other sectors. Street riots erupted as crowds broke into bakeries, and bitterly cold weather increased people's desperation. The Tsar's authority finally disintegrated, and his abdication ends a thousand years of royal rule in Russia.

A provisional government was formed on 12 March, but it faces a struggle for power with the Petrograd *soviet*, a council of delegates chosen by workers and soldiers. Public feeling is now strongly against the war being fought with the Allied powers, in which the Russian army has lost millions of

HOLDING COURT The Tsar's former home, the Winter Palace – now the seat of the provisional government.

troops and suffered a series of humiliating defeats. However, the provisional government's foreign minister, Pavel Milyukov, has declared his commitment to fighting on.

Because the old-style Russian Julian calendar runs 13 days behind the generally accepted Gregorian calendar, the revolt has been dubbed the 'February Revolution'.

POWER TO THE PEOPLE One of Lenin's slogans was: 'All land to the peasants!'

A leader in waiting

Just before the Bolsheviks seized power, Vladimir Lenin told them: 'History will not forgive us if we do not take power now.' He had spent most of the previous 17 years in political exile, preparing for revolution. Now he was ready.

Born Vladimir Ilyich Ulyanov in 1870, Lenin was thrown out of university for subversive activity before qualifying as a lawyer in 1891. By this time his elder brother, Alexander, had already been executed for his part in a plot to assassinate the Tsar. Lenin was imprisoned from 1895 to 1897 and then spent three years exiled in Siberia. He used this time to study Marxism and to formulate his political ideas, and it was during this period that he began to use the pen-name 'Lenin'.

After agitating for a split in the Russian Social Democratic Party at its conference in London in 1903, Lenin came out leading the Bolshevik faction. He spent much of his exile in Switzerland, building up a following and publishing a radical newspaper called *Iskra* (*The Spark*). Lenin argued that, on their own, the workers could never attain political awareness – an educated elite was needed to lead them into revolution. One of the elite, Lenin bided his time until he was smuggled from Finland into Petrograd in a sealed train, just before the February Revolution.

SECOND UPRISING BRINGS SOCIALISTS TO POWER

7 NOVEMBER, PETROGRAD
In a swift and almost bloodless coup, Bolshevik revolutionaries have ousted the provisional government set up in March and seized power – completing Russia's second revolution in the space of nine months.

Bands of armed workers (known as Red Guards) and soldiers occupied centres of power in Petrograd, including railway stations, banks and post offices. Rebels swarmed into the Winter Palace, where most of the government had taken refuge, and arrested the ministers. A new socialist government, the Soviet (Council) of People's Commissars, has been proclaimed, with Vladimir Ilyich Lenin as its chairman.

Russia has been in a state of upheaval since the Tsar's abdication in March. The new government's

STORMING THE PALACE Woodcut by Vitali Lentshin.

determination to continue the hugely unpopular war with Germany provoked mass demonstrations in April. The Bolsheviks agitated for the overthrow of the government, winning popular support with their demand for 'peace, land and bread'.

In mid-July a revolt erupted in Petrograd, but the government crushed it and outlawed the Bolsheviks. Lenin fled to Finland. In August the army's commander-in-chief, General Lavr Kornilov, tried to launch a military coup, but it was defeated by troops loyal to the Petrograd soviet. The government lifted the ban on the Bolsheviks, only to see its support dwindle further and backing for the Bolsheviks rise.

In September the Bolsheviks won a clear majority on the Moscow and Petrograd *soviet*s. Lenin seized the opportunity and secretly returned to Petrograd, where he persuaded his party colleagues that the time was ripe for revolution. He has now become head of the world's first government by *soviet*, promising: 'We shall now proceed to construct the socialist order.'

··· 17 JULY: THE BRITISH ROYAL FAMILY CHANGES ITS NAME FROM SAXE-COBURG TO WINDSOR ···

Glamorous spy is executed

15 OCTOBER, VINCENNES, FRANCE
Mata Hari, celebrated dancer and mistress, was executed by firing squad at dawn today after being found guilty by the Allies of espionage.

Born in the Netherlands as Margaretha Gertrude Zelle, she shot to fame as an exotic dancer in the clubs of Europe. She became the lover of many rich and powerful men, including the French foreign secretary and the Dutch prime minister.

However, with the outbreak of the war, Mata Hari's friendships with leaders from both the Allies and the Central Powers made her an embarrassment. She was arrested by the French and brought before a court martial. It is rumoured that the documents used to condemn her were falsified, and secrecy continues to surround the details of both her life and her death.

COVER UP Mata Hari, known for her scantily clad dancing, dressed modestly for court appearances.

Italian front collapses

10 NOVEMBER, ITALY
Nearly half a million Italian soldiers are thought to have fled from an Austro-German onslaught at Caporetto, near Italy's border with Austria. Some 10 000 Italians have been killed and 30 000 wounded, and the Germans claim to have captured 293 000 men and 2000 guns.

Germany's attack on 23 October took the Italians by surprise. An intense artillery bombardment, accompanied by clouds of poison gas, was followed by an powerful infantry thrust. The Italian line broke, and German and Austrian troops poured into the gap.

Italy, hitherto a traditional ally of Austria and Germany, declared war in 1915 after Austria refused to hand over land in the Balkans claimed by Italy. Today Allied generals rushed British and French troops to the pressure-point at Montebello. They also agreed to coordinate future attacks on the Western and Italian fronts.

USA changes course and enters war

**6 APRIL, WASHINGTON
The United States Congress
has voted to take its country
into the war,** obeying the
exhortation of President
Wilson to 'make the world
safe for democracy'. After
announcing the decision just
after 1.00 pm today, the
President is said to have burst
into tears.

The decision represents
a reversal of the USA's
carefully guarded policy of
neutrality, but it is one that
observers have been
predicting for some time. The
sinking of the unarmed liner
Lusitania in 1915, with the
loss of more than 100
American lives, had already
brought the USA to the
brink of war; Germany's
announcement in February
this year of its intention to

WAVING FAREWELL The first US soldiers set out for the Western Front.

use its submarines against any
vessel entering the area
around the Mediterranean
and Britain hastened today's
declaration.

American public opinion
was also outraged by the
so-called 'Zimmerman
telegram', a secret message
intercepted by the British,

which raised the sinister
possibility of a German
alliance with Mexico.

The British prime
minister, David Lloyd
George, has greeted the
American declaration with
the comment that the
USA had 'with one bound
become a world power'.

US troops join British and French soldiers on the front line in Europe

American infantrymen have
been serving in Europe since
June, when the US Congress
voted in conscription. The
introduction of the draft
provoked heated debate, but
it was finally thought
necessary in order to build
up US military forces as
rapidly as possible.

'Doughboys', as the
soldiers are nicknamed, saw
their first major action in
November, when engineer
regiments fought in support
of British troops at Cambrai.
The aim is to have a total of
at least one million men,
under the command of
General John Pershing. There
are now five US divisions
stationed in France, with
50 000 more troops arriving
each month.

··· CANADIAN LEGISLATURE GRANTS WOMEN THE RIGHT TO VOTE ···

AERIAL TERROR The Gotha G.IV is a deadly new weapon.

German bombers wreak havoc

**25 MAY, KENT, ENGLAND
For the first time Germany
has used aeroplanes – Gotha
bombers – on a raid over**

**England, heralding a deadly
new form of warfare.**
Launched from airfields in
Belgium, the 23 aircraft

caused an estimated 300
casualties on their first
outing. Among the dead
were 16 Canadian soldiers
at a military camp in
Shorncliffe and some 70
civilians at Folkestone.

The Germans have
previously used Zeppelin
airships to carry out
bombing raids, but the
Gothas add a new dimension
in firepower. They are large
twin-engined biplanes, which
can carry almost half a ton
of explosives. They also have
the ability to fly at a height
of around 6000 metres
(20 000 ft), which, together
with their speed and agility,
takes them out of range of
most defensive batteries.

SMILING DOUGHBOYS The
nickname dates from the Civil War,
when buttons on army uniforms
resembled dumplings or 'doughboys'.

Cheeky iconoclasm sweeps art world

Even the most avant-garde collectors, connoisseurs and critics had their patience stretched to the limit this year. In the United States a piece called *Fountain* by French artist Marcel Duchamp shocked New York sophisticates. Duchamp simply took an ordinary white urinal, signed it 'R Mutt' and put it on show in a well-known art gallery. Duchamp, an iconoclast of the first order, is clearly thumbing his nose at the entire art establishment.

In the Netherlands, the journal *De Stijl* was launched, advocating a new, stripped-down approach to art, architecture and design. One of the contributors, Piet Mondrian, appears to have given up painting reality entirely. Mondrian claims he is engaged in reducing painting to its bare essentials. His pictures are simply arrangements of vertical or horizontal lines and rectangles of primary colour, grey, black or white. Whether anyone sees fit to buy his work is another matter.

In Russia, Kasimir Malevich went a step further and produced a painting that is just a white canvas. Without a hint of irony he calls his new style 'Suprematism'. Meanwhile the revolutionary government in Russia turned to its most modern artists, including Malevich and the sculptor Vladimir Tatlin, to lead the way in art and design. One leading artist, abstract painter Wassily Kandinsky, may yet be recalled from Germany and given an official role by the Communists.

Some artists still painted traditional subjects, staying closer to realist forms. Amedeo Modigliani produced more beautiful nudes and portraits of his mistress. Henri Matisse's move to the South of France has stimulated a delightful series of paintings of the interior of his room with its goldfish, shutters and wrought-iron balcony.

The impact of photography continued to make itself felt. This was largely the result of efforts by Alfred Stieglitz, owner of New York's 192 Gallery and himself a highly accomplished photographer. But one of Stieglitz's more interesting recent finds was the work of a young woman painter, Georgia O'Keefe.

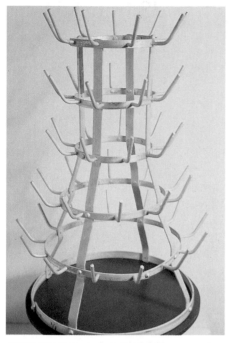

READY MADE Duchamp's *Bottlerack*, an everyday object ironically elevated to the status of art.

FROM THE LIFE The sensuous elongation of form is characteristic of Modigliani's nudes.

··· 22 OCT: TRANS-AUSTRALIAN RAILWAY OPENS, RUNNING BETWEEN KALGOORLIE AND PORT AUGUSTA ···

Britain pledges support for Jewish homeland

2 NOVEMBER, LONDON
Arthur Balfour, the British foreign secretary, has offered British support for the establishment of a Jewish homeland in Palestine.

The letter containing the pledge, written to Baron Rothschild, a British Jewish leader, already looks set to cause controversy. Some observers say that the declaration is deliberately ambiguous in order not to offend either Jewish or Arab allies, thus safeguarding Britain's commercial and political interests in the Middle East.

The declaration states that in the founding of a Jewish national home 'nothing shall be done which may prejudice the civil and religious rights of existing non-Jewish communities'. Surprisingly, the letter stops short of discussing independent statehood, preferring to use the word 'homeland'.

Implementing the declaration will prove difficult, as British politicians grapple to reconcile Zionist and Arab aspirations in Palestine.

1918

BORN

15 Jan: Gamal Abdel Nasser, Egyptian leader
25 Apr: Ella Fitzgerald, US jazz singer
25 Aug: Leonard Bernstein, US conductor and composer
11 Nov: Alexander Solzhenitsyn, Russian author

DIED

25 Mar: Claude Debussy, French composer
31 Oct: Egon Schiele, Austrian painter
11 Nov: Guillaume Apollinaire, French writer and critic

APPOINTED

11 Feb: Chaim Weizmann to head commission on Jewish colonies in Palestine
26 Mar: Marshal Ferdinand Foch as Allied commander-in-chief in France

AGREED

3 Mar: Treaty of Brest-Litovsk, settling peace terms between Russia and Germany

FOUNDED

1 Apr: the Royal British Air Force, from the merged Royal Flying Corps and Royal Naval Air Service, to counter German air raids
Nov: republics of Austria, Czechoslovakia and Germany
Warner Brothers Pictures: by Polish immigrants Harry, Albert, Jack and Sam Warner, in California

CLOSED

12 Feb, New York City: all Broadway theatres, to save coal for the American war effort

ATTACKED

24 Mar: Paris, by German 'Big Bertha' howitzer gun, positioned 120 km (75 miles) from the city
30 Aug: V I Lenin, wounded by revolutionary Fanya Dora-Kaplan

On 22 April, *German Manfred von Richthofen is shot down and killed during the second battle of the Somme. A legendary fighter pilot, he is said to have shot down 80 enemy planes during the war. Goering was a member of his squadron.*

LAST

Missouri: state to make school attendance compulsory

IMPOSED

22 Jan: food rationing in Britain

MUSIC HIT

Swanee, by 19-year-old George Gershwin

KILLED

27 Oct: 343 aboard the Canadian Pacific liner *Princess Sophia*, in one of the worst civilian maritime disasters in history

9 July: 101 at Nashville, Tennessee, in the worst US train accident

DISCOVERED

Milky Way, its size and shape, by US astronomer Harlow Shapley

On 14 November, *Josef Pilsudski is elected president of the newly declared republic of Poland. The republic was founded following the Allied victory and the collapse of the Habsburg empire. Pilsudski has been granted full dictatorial powers.*

ADOPTED

The Gregorian calendar by Russia – a solar dating system introduced in 1582 by Pope Gregory XIII, already used by most of the Western world

RELOCATED

5 Mar: capital of Russia, from Petrograd to Moscow

RENAMED

7 Mar: Bolsheviks become Russian Communist Party

FIRSTS

15 May: civilian airmail service, from New York City to Washington DC

'Believe it or not!' strip by Robert Ripley appears in *New York Globe*; eventually appears in 326 newspapers in 38 countries

RAISED

Britain: school leaving age from 10 to 14

INVENTED

Electric food mixer, manufactured by the American firm Universal Company

BANNED

21 Jan: all works by living German composers, by the New York Philharmonic Society
France: manufacture and sale of all cakes, puddings and sweets

ARRESTED

18 May: 500 members of Ireland's Sinn Fein, including their leader, Eamon de Valera

ELECTED

14 Nov: Tomàs Masaryk, first president of Czechoslovakia

RELEASED

27 Nov: more than 1.5 million Allied war prisoners, by Germany

ASSASSINATED

15 Dec: Portuguese President Sidonio Paes, after only one year in office

NEW WORDS

climax *n*: an orgasm, the most intense or highest part of a sexual experience
to go over the top *vb clause*: to go over the leading edge of a trench on the battlefield

Great War comes to an end

11 NOVEMBER, FRANCE
In the early hours of this morning, in a railway carriage in the forest of Compiègne, a defeated Germany surrendered to the Allies. At 11.00 am – the eleventh hour of the eleventh day of the eleventh month – the Great War came to an end.

The armistice negotiations began two days ago. German delegates wanted a ceasefire and a lifting of the Allied blockade while talks were in progress, but this was denied. Today the defeated Germans agreed to evacuate all territories occupied after 1 August 1914, to remove all military forces west of the Rhine and to repatriate Allied prisoners. Germany must hand over 2500 heavy guns, 25000 machine guns, 1700 aeroplanes, all its U–boats, 5000 trucks, 5000 locomotives and 150000 wagons.

After so many years of stalemate, the crucial push towards victory came in the summer. The Allied blockade on Germany was biting hard, and both food and military supplies were almost exhausted. The gradual build-up of fresh troops from America tilted the balance

GOOD NEWS The headlines proclaim Allied victory, and the 'war to end all wars' is over at last.

of power in the Allies' favour. With this in mind, General Erich von Ludendorff made a last desperate attempt to break through the enemy lines in the spring. When this offensive petered out in June, the Allied counterattack proved decisive. Beginning on 18 July, the combined armies made rapid gains, culminating in

a resounding victory at Amiens on 8 August, which von Ludendorff later described as 'Germany's black day'.

The German general advised the Kaiser to sue for peace, although he agreed to try to hold his positions on the Western Front while negotiations were in progress.

Germany's allies began to melt away. Bulgaria signed an armistice on 30 September, and Turkey followed suit a month later, after General Allenby's capture of both Damascus and Beirut. The old Habsburg empire began to break up; unable to contain the Czechs, Hungarians, Poles and Croats pressing for independence, Austria signed its armistice on 3 November.

In Germany itself, internal pressures hastened the end. Sailors mutinied at Kiel on 4 November, and similar revolts followed at Lübeck, Hamburg and Bremen. A Soviet-style republic was declared in Bavaria, and the red flag was raised over Cologne. Bowing to the inevitable, the Kaiser abdicated and fled into exile in Holland.

CELEBRATION News of the German surrender brought people onto the streets to express their relief.

··· MISS MARGARET OWEN SETS A NEW TYPEWRITING SPEED RECORD OF 170 WORDS PER MINUTE ···

President Wilson presents Fourteen Points for peace

AMBITIOUS PLANS Members of Congress listen as the President presents his programme for world peace.

8 JANUARY, WASHINGTON DC
President Woodrow Wilson presented his formula for peace before a joint session of Congress today. The plan – which consists of 14 main clauses – is, like its creator, idealistic: Wilson believes that it will be successful in bringing a fair and lasting peace to Europe.

The programme calls for a number of general points, such as an end to secret diplomacy, the removal of economic barriers, a reduction in the arms trade, the freedom of movement for all nations on the open seas, and a reassessment of the rights of citizens in colonial possessions. Several other, more specific points deal with the return of territories that have been seized by Germany and its allies, calling for the evacuation of all Russian territory, Belgium and the Balkan states, for the redrawing of Italy's frontiers, for the return of Alsace-Lorraine to France, and for an independent Polish state to be formed. Wilson's fourteenth – and perhaps most ambitious – point argues for the creation of 'a general association of nations to guarantee independence and territorial integrity' – a league of nations to uphold the peace.

The high moral tone of the plan is prompted by a fear that communism, which brought about the fall of the government in Russia, might soon spread to other countries. Wilson also hopes that his scheme might prove sufficiently attractive to bring about an early end to the war.

The Welshman who won the war

Recent British politics have been dominated by one man – David Lloyd George. Liberal Member of Parliament for Caernarfon, Wales, since 1890, he is renowned as a vigorous speaker. At the outset of the war Lloyd George was chancellor of the exchequer; he moved to the post of secretary of state for war in 1916 before taking over from Asquith as prime minister, heading a coalition with the Conservatives.

His leadership during the latter stages of the war was highly influential. In particular he did much to speed up US involvement, persuading a reluctant General Pershing that American troops should reinforce British and French divisions until sufficient numbers had arrived for a separate US force to be formed. Lloyd George was also instrumental in uniting the Allied armies under a single commander, Ferdinand Foch.

Over the coming months he will play a leading role at the Paris peace conference, mediating between the fiery demands of French premier Georges Clemenceau and the idealism of US President Woodrow Wilson.

TAKING WORK HOME Lloyd George studies political documents intently.

··· BRITISH BEER SUPPLIES RUN OUT COMPLETELY, DUE TO A SHORTAGE OF INGREDIENTS ···

TSAR NICHOLAS AND FAMILY MURDERED IN CELLAR

AUGUST, EKATERINBURG, RUSSIA
An investigation by the White Army has confirmed that Tsar Nicholas II and his family were murdered last month. The slaughter on 16 July by Bolshevik forces was a ruthless act fuelled as much by fears of the counter-revolutionary White Army advance as by the urge for revenge against the Tsar. In the middle of the night Nicholas, his wife Alexandra and their son and four daughters were taken down to a cellar and shot by members of the secret police. Two of the children survived the hail of bullets, only to be bayoneted to death. A number of their servants and their dog were also killed.

Following his abdication last year amid government disarray, the former ruler of Russia and his family were held in relative comfort as state prisoners at a mansion in the Urals. As the Whites moved towards Ekaterinburg – a hotbed of revolutionary Bolshevik activity – the Bolsheviks feared a rescue attempt. The Tsar and his family were told that they were being moved to a new location.

FINAL DAYS Tsar Nicholas and his family were confined on a country estate prior to their brutal murder.

Instead, they were hustled down into the cellar, where the cold-blooded killing took place. The bodies were then taken to a nearby forest and were dismembered and burned. The remains were dumped in a pool by a mineshaft.

The Russian authorities admitted to killing the Tsar but tried to conceal the fate of his family. When the White Army took control of Ekaterinburg, suspicions were aroused by bullet holes and bayonet marks in the cellar.

··· THE NATIVE AMERICAN CHURCH IS FOUNDED, COMBINING NATIVE AMERICAN AND CHRISTIAN BELIEFS ···

X MARKS THE SPOT A mother comes to vote, bringing her children with her.

British women vote for first time

28 DECEMBER, UNITED KINGDOM
In today's general election, called at the end of the war, women have turned out to exercise their new right to vote for the first time. In February an act granting suffrage to women property-owners over the age of 30 was passed. Today nearly 8½ million British women were eligible to vote in the election – although, since the total votes cast were only 11 million, many of them did not bother.

During the war, many supporters of women's suffrage agreed with the government to stop campaigning so that women could concentrate on essential wartime work. The extension of voting rights to women now is seen by some as a reward for this hard work and invaluable service. Others, however, point out that it has only come at a time when major reforms on voting rights for men were being considered as well. Whatever the reason, the fight is not yet over. Many suffragettes will continue to campaign until the voting age for women is lowered to 21, the same as it is for men.

SOCIAL ENGINEERING Despite initial resistance from employers, women eagerly tackled dirty, greasy jobs such as vehicle maintenance – and did them well.

New roles for women outside the home

Among its many effects on society, the war has transformed the lives of women. In 1915 few women worked; some found posts as teachers or nurses – jobs that were considered respectable – and working girls could find jobs in factories and shops or in domestic service as maids. Even at the start of the war the government did not want to employ women workers, but from 1915 onwards, as more and more men were called up, women were encouraged to take up jobs in large numbers. They were called on to take the place of men, and the idea that a mother's place is in the home was expediently forgotten.

By 1916 half a million British women were working in heavy industry, in iron, steel and chemical factories producing shells, bullets and other equipment for the army. Others found jobs in the civil service, banks and businesses. Women worked as plumbers, engineers, porters and electricians; public transport relied on women bus

drivers and conductors. Such jobs had formerly been considered unsuitable, and employers were often suspicious of women workers. But resistance to the idea of women going out to work grew less as the labour shortage became severe, and employers conceded that women were just as skilled as men. Working outdoors and in dirty factories also led women to start wearing trousers, previously almost unheard of.

HEAVY WORK Women delivering ice blocks.

Women's direct contributions to the war effort were equally important. Such jobs varied from voluntary part-time work knitting clothes for soldiers, to full-time work as nurses, or as volunteers in canteens or charity organisations. Well-paid war work was available in munitions factories where the work was hard and often dangerous. There were also opportunities for posts in the uniformed services, such as the police force, the Red Cross, the Women's Army Auxiliary Corps (WAAC) and the Women's Royal Naval Service (WRNS). Women in the WAAC worked behind the front lines, in the kitchens, stores and offices of army camps.

For many women the war brought a new independence and higher wages than they had ever known. Men returning from the war are unlikely to approve of these new roles. Women will be encouraged to give up the skills they have learned and to return to their more traditional roles at home.

Birth control pioneers weather storm of public criticism

FAMILY LAW Women and children greet Mrs Sanger and her sister Ethel Byrne after a court appearance.

The early years of this century saw not only women's demands for political rights but also a demand for social reforms, such as birth control and sex education. Two pioneers of this new way of thinking are Marie Stopes and Margaret Sanger.

Scottish-born Marie Stopes, acknowledged as a brilliant academic scientist, published two books this year, both of which caused an immediate furore. The first, *Married Love*, caused a sensation with its open discussion of sexual relationships in a straightforward manner and its assertion that both men and women could – and should – enjoy sex. This was followed by *Wise Parenthood*, which advocates birth control and sex education for women. Despite their controversial nature, millions of copies of the books were sold, and they were translated into 13 languages. Opposition to Stopes's campaign, in which she advocates cheap contraceptives for women overburdened by childbirth,

has been particularly strong from the medical profession and from the Catholic Church, which believes that making contraceptives freely available to

poor women will increase what it calls 'immoral behaviour'.

Margaret Sanger began working as a nurse in New York's Lower East Side in 1912, and became very concerned at the connections she saw between poverty, constant childbirth and backstreet abortions resulting in the death of infants and mothers. Her experiences led her to publish, in 1914, a pamphlet defending birth control, *Family Limitation*. For this Sanger was charged with disseminating obscene literature; two years later the proceedings were dropped, and that same year she and her sister, Ethel Byrne, opened America's first birth control clinic in Brooklyn, New York. However, the clinic was soon closed down for outraging public morals, and Sanger was sentenced to 30 days in the workhouse. The judge declared that birth control was against the law of the state and also the law of God. Like Marie Stopes, Margaret Sanger continues to work with women who she believes will benefit from birth control, and the whole issue is being forced into the area of public debate.

FIRM FIGHTER Marie Stopes believed that planned families were happy families.

1919

BORN

1 Jan: J D Salinger, US author
1 July: Iris Murdoch, British author
8 Oct: Pierre-Elliott Trudeau, Canadian statesman

DIED

6 Jan: Theodore Roosevelt, US statesman and former President
3 Dec: Auguste Renoir, French painter

ELECTED

28 Nov: Nancy Astor, MP for Plymouth, first woman to take her seat in the House of Commons

REINTERRED

15 May: British nurse Edith Cavell, whose body was brought back to Britain from Belgium where she was executed during the war

On 17 April, *United Artists Corporation* film company is founded in Hollywood by Douglas Fairbanks, Charlie Chaplin, Mary Pickford and producer D W Griffith. The new company will produce and distribute films starring the founding actors.

OCCUPIED

23 Sept: the Adriatic city of Fiume, by Italian poet-aviator Gabriele d'Annunzio and 2600 men, claiming it for Italy as a spoil of war

FOUNDED

5 Jan: National Socialist (Nazi) Party in Germany
23 Mar: Fascist Party in Italy, by Benito Mussolini
Bauhaus School of Art and Design in Weimar, by Walter Gropius

MASSACRED

2 Jan: 1.5 million Armenians in Turkey, by the Turks
10 Apr: 379 Indians in Amritsar, by British troops

MURDERED

10 Apr: Emiliano Zapata, Mexico's rebel leader, by government forces in an ambush

RECORDS

18 Sept: new altitude flight record of 34 610 feet attained by US aviator Roland Rohlfs
10 Dec: 135-hour flight to Australia completed by Britons Ross and Keith Smith in a Vickers Vimy

DISCOVERED

3 Jan: a means of splitting the atom, by New Zealand-born British physicist Professor Ernest Rutherford

VICTORIOUS

4 July: Jack Dempsey, beating Jess Willard in the world heavyweight championship

LANDED

27 Nov: meteor in Lake Michigan, causing tremors in nearby cities

OUSTED

1 Aug: Hungarian leader Bela Kun, after brief summer in power in newly declared Soviet Republic of Hungary

FIRSTS

3 Mar: international airmail run, from Seattle to Vancouver, by Boeing
13 July: British airship R-34 crosses Atlantic both ways in 13 days – with a stowaway on board

On 15 January, 'Bloody Rosa' – German revolutionary Rosa Luxemburg – and Karl Liebknecht, leaders of the radical Spartacist movement, are murdered by soldiers while in custody. They were arrested after the failure of their group to stage a communist coup in Berlin.

ESCAPED

10 Sept, Dublin: Michael Collins, Sinn Fein minister of finance, from the Irish parliament, which has been declared illegal by the British and surrounded by police

APPOINTED

Countess Markiewicz as minister for labour in Irish parliament; however, the parliament is banned by the British government

INVENTED

16 Mar: wireless telephone, enabling pilots to talk in-flight

LIBELLED

14 Aug: Henry Ford, labelled an anarchist by the *Chicago Tribune*

ATTACKED

19 Feb: French premier Georges Clemenceau, shot by an anarchist

RESCUED

25 May: Pilots Hanker and Grieve, 1370 km (850 miles) off Ireland, having failed to fly the Atlantic

US scientist Professor Robert Goddard develops the design of high-altitude rockets and announces his theory of rocket propulsion. However, Goddard's predictions of future travel to the Moon are not being taken seriously by the US government.

PUBLISHED

Sherwood Anderson, *Winesburg, Ohio*
Thomas Hardy, *Collected Poems*
Somerset Maugham, *The Moon and Sixpence*

NEW WORDS

airport *n*: landing and taking off area for civil aircraft
banger *n*: an old, worn-out or decrepit car
loony bin *n*: mental hospital, or asylum

Versailles: an angry peace

28 JUNE, PARIS, FRANCE
Exactly five years since the assassination of Archduke Ferdinand – the act that sparked the greatest conflagration the world has seen – the Treaty of Versailles has been signed, concluding the armistice between Germany and the Allied Powers. The signing of the document, signalled by a gunfire salute, was greeted by cheering crowds.

But the treaty, although designed to implement peace, continues to bring discord and controversy. The German government, appalled at the harshness of the conditions, has only signed at the last possible moment. It is outraged by the 'war guilt' clause, in which Germany takes full blame for the conflict, and by the 'reparations' clause, which forces Germany to pay compensation. The full amount of such compensation has yet to be decided, but it will amount to many millions of pounds – which the country insists it will not be able to pay. Other conditions include the division of the German empire between the Allies, the

SIGNED AND SEALED Allied officers strain their necks to witness the historic signing of the peace treaty.

disbanding of Germany's armed forces, and the paring down of its borders.

The treaty has been hammered out in Paris by the Allies over five months, complicated by the divergent agendas of the parties. Thirty nations were present, although the principal powers were France, Britain and the USA – the treaty was based on the 'Fourteen Points' drawn up by President Wilson last year. Germany was not permitted to attend and had to sign without negotiation,

despite the protests of the foreign secretary, Count Brockdorff-Rantzau, and the German parliament.

Even some of the Allies believe that the terms of the treaty are too harsh. The British prime minister, David Lloyd George, has said that they are merely sowing the seeds of another, greater, conflict to come, while the Allied commander-in-chief, Ferdinand Foch, stated: 'This isn't peace, but an armistice for 20 years.'

··· CONRAD HILTON BUYS A HOTEL IN CISCO, TEXAS, THE FIRST OF MANY ···

League of Nations brings world security one step nearer

PEACEFUL AGREEMENT Members of the 17 international delegations who are hoping to secure a safer world. Wilson had previously outlined his idea in his 1918 peace programme, the Fourteen Points.

14 FEBRUARY, PARIS
Seventeen nations voted at the Paris peace conference to accept US President Woodrow Wilson's proposal for a League of Nations – an international peacekeeping body.

The League is created in a spirit of immense optimism, in the hope that it will prevent further war. Its principles are contained in its covenant. Aiming for greater world security, this plans to stop disputes or swiftly settle them by peaceful means, promises collective action in the event of an attack on any member state, and tries to restrict the arms trade. The covenant will be incorporated into the Paris peace treaty.

GERMAN NAVY SCUTTLES ITS OWN FLEET

21 JUNE, SCOTLAND
A party of schoolchildren was vastly entertained at the sight of the entire German fleet sinking in the harbour at Scapa Flow in the Orkney Islands. Unfortunately this was no naval exercise but the final act of defiance by German seamen, who scuttled their own ships in order to avoid handing them over to the victorious Allies.

When Germany's forces surrendered last November the fleet was taken to the major British naval base at Scapa Flow. Since then the German officers and crews have been interned, awaiting the outcome of the Paris peace conference.

In protest at the severity of the conditions imposed by the Versailles Treaty, and at a five-day deadline for signing the revised version of the document, the commander of the German fleet, Rear-Admiral von Reuter, gave the order for his fleet to be destroyed. His seamen opened the ships' underwater valves, let in water and allowed them to sink. The process began, after a given signal at midday, with the sacrifice of the *Friedrich der Grosse*. Five hours later the battleship had been joined by a further 73 ships.

This embarrassing incident has taken the authorities completely by surprise. They opened fire on a few of the lifeboats, hoping to make the German crews return to their ships and stop them sinking, but to no avail. In the end only a few vessels were saved, dragged onto the shoreline by tugboats.

SINKING FEELING One of the last of the German fleet, the *Fandango*, sinks beneath the waves.

··· THE HIGH-FIBRE CEREAL ALL-BRAN IS LAUNCHED BY THE KELLOGG CEREAL COMPANY ···

Millions die in flu epidemic

A virulent influenza, the 'Spanish flu', claimed the lives of millions across the world this year. Worst hit were China and India, whose populations were decimated. In the United States one in four citizens was taken ill. Experts estimate that the death toll could reach 20 million – more people than were killed in the Great War.

The disease was first identified among troops, but it soon spread to the civilian population. Businesses ground to a halt due to unprecedented amounts of sick leave. In the USA, the Boston Stock Exchange was forced to close temporarily.

Quacks raked in money as desperate people tried anything to fight off the illness. Some believed that a poultice of cooked onion on the chest was effective, while in Philadelphia, where it was rumoured that whiskey could cure the flu, the price of spirits rocketed. A very few people have taken up the most bizarre 'remedy' of all: walking around outside in the nude.

UTMOST CAUTION Medical staff take essential measures against the flu.

BOLD PILOTS FLY THE ATLANTIC NONSTOP

15 JUNE, LONDON
Two veteran aviators completed the first nonstop flight across the Atlantic today when their plane crash-landed nose-first in an Irish bog. Both men climbed out unharmed.

The British pilot, Captain John Alcock, said that it had been 'a terrible journey', through fog and storms of sleet. The plane was forced to loop the loop and do some 'very comic stunts'. Alcock and his American navigator, Lieutenant Arthur Whitten Brown, sustained themselves on the gruelling flight with

coffee, beer, sandwiches and chocolate.

The Vickers Vimy biplane took off from Newfoundland yesterday and took 16 hours and 12 minutes to make the 3040-kilometre (1900-mile) journey – an average speed of about 160 kilometres per hour (100 mph).

The historic flight was successful thanks both to the steady nerves of Alcock and Brown and to the excellence of British engineering. Two Rolls-Royce engines powered the aeroplane, which was originally designed as a bomber – the

PIONEERS Alcock (r) and Brown opened the way for transatlantic air travel.

bombs were replaced by extra fuel tanks. Vickers will collect the £10000 prize

offered by the *Daily Mail* for the first nonstop flight across the Atlantic Ocean.

··· 17 OCT: KLM OF THE NETHERLANDS IS THE WORLD'S FIRST AIRLINE COMPANY ···

Blackout proves relativity correct

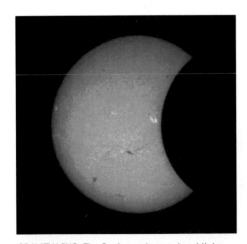

GRAVITY LENS The Sun's gravity can bend light, but this can only be observed during an eclipse.

30 MARCH, LONDON
Observation of a solar eclipse has proved a groundbreaking theory correct. Albert Einstein's general theory of relativity offers a radical answer to many scientific problems, but it had never been confirmed by observation.

Einstein suggested that Isaac Newton's explanation of gravity was only true within a certain range; on the minute scale of the atom or the giant scale of the universe, different rules must apply. According to Einstein, gravity is not a force, as Newtonian physics claims, but a curved field in what he calls 'space-time'. In 1911 he predicted the amount by which the light from a star passing the Sun should be deflected or bent by the Sun's gravitational field. This should, he asserted, be detectable during a solar eclipse.

The eclipse that took place yesterday was the first opportunity for scientists to discover whether Einstein's formula worked. London's Royal Astronomical Society sent two expeditions – one to Brazil and one to West Africa – to observe it. They found that a star's light was bent by the Sun's gravitational field exactly as predicted.

New German republic founded in Weimar

11 FEBRUARY, WEIMAR, GERMANY
Friedrich Ebert was elected today as the first president of the new German republic. Ebert, the Social Democrat leader, first took power last November after Emperor Wilhelm abdicated and a republic was declared. Swept to office in the Socialist revolution, Ebert has since identified himself as a moderate; he called in the army last month to suppress an uprising led by the Marxists Rosa Luxemburg and Karl Liebknecht.

The Social Democratic Party has shifted the seat of parliament from unstable Berlin to the smaller city of Weimar on the River Elbe. Just days ago the national assembly moved to Weimar to draw up a new democratic constitution. The Weimar administration will have to turn its immediate attention to the Versailles peace conference and the controversial issue of war reparations.

1920

BORN

20 Jan: Federico Fellini, Italian film director
3 May: Sugar Ray Robinson, US boxer
18 May: Karol Wojtyla (Pope John Paul II)
29 Aug: Charlie Parker, US jazz musician

DIED

25 Jan: Amedeo Modigliani, Italian painter
25 Oct: King Alexander I of Greece, from pet monkey bite

On 2 November, Warren Harding is swept to power as 29th President of the United States. The Republicans win with near-record majorities in many states. Harding, pictured giving the traditional front porch speech from the White House, is elected on his 55th birthday.

BANNED

The film *Holy Bible*, by Pope Benedict XV, for its portrayal of Adam and Eve naked

The Meccano Hornby Locomotive No 1 is launched this year. Although clockwork toy trains have been around for 30 years, Frank Hornby's stylish designs are the most popular. Made from pressed tin and run on custom-made tracks, Hornby toy trains are manufactured in Liverpool.

FIRSTS

American to win Wimbledon, 'Big Bill' Tilden
Appearance of Hercules Poirot, in Agatha Christie's detective story *The Mysterious Affair at Styles*
International Dada Fair, in Berlin – the largest 'anti-art' exhibition ever mounted
Electric hand-iron on sale in London, but without thermostat control
2 Nov, Pittsburgh: broadcast US presidential election, from KDKA radio station

INVENTED

Imitation coal fire, the Magicoal, by H H Berry
Tommy-gun, patented by John T Thompson

Fox's Glacier Mints
Boysenberries, hybrid of black-, logan- and raspberries, by Rudolph Boysen
Baby Ruth candy bar in the USA

INTRODUCED

26 Aug: the vote for all women over 21 in the USA

MARRIED

29 Mar: screen sweetheart Mary Pickford to Douglas Fairbanks

SIGNED

10 Aug: Treaty of Sèvres, between the Allies and Turkey, ceding 80 per cent of the Ottoman Empire's land to the Allies and bringing its rule to a close

FOUNDED

2 Feb, Ireland: the Black and Tans (Royal Irish Constabulary) to combat Sinn Fein
31 July: the British Communist Party
1 Sept: the state of Lebanon, with Beirut as its capital, declared by the British

AWARDED

Pulitzer Prize to Edith Wharton for *The Age of Innocence*

UNVEILED

11 Nov, London: the Cenotaph in Whitehall, designed by Edwin Lutyens, by George V

FIRST NIGHT

The Four Horsemen of the Apocalypse, starring screen heart-throb Rudolf Valentino

TRANSFERRED

5 Apr: Red Sox baseballer George Herman 'Babe' Ruth, to New York Yankees for record $125000

CANONISED

30 May: Joan of Arc, on anniversary of her death in 1431 – she was burned at the stake for heresy

OPENED

9 June, London: the Imperial War Museum, by George V
16 June, The Hague: the League of Nations Permanent Court of Justice
14 Aug, Antwerp: the sixth modern Olympic Games, by King Albert

NEW WORDS

deadline *n*: a time limit for any activity
gaga *n*: senile; slightly crazy

LAST ORDERS – AMERICA BANS ALCOHOL

IN THE BREWERY Beer spurts out as a federal agent turns the taps on a vat.

The 18th Amendment to the US Constitution went into effect on 16 January. The law deems the sale, manufacture and possession of alcohol a crime. However, while alcoholic consumption has declined in the 33 states that have already banned alcohol, increased crime and corruption as well as unsafe drinking practices are direct by-products of the law.

Prohibition has its roots in the American Midwest, where there is a strong tradition of temperance, and where, after a long and fierce campaign, the sale of alcohol was first banned. In recent years, demonstrations against alcohol have increased in number, often ending with the sound of shattering glass, as protesters caused disturbances in bars. Carrie Nation was a leading figure in this movement - with an army of 500 men and women behind her, she marched into towns and smashed up the saloons with her famous hatchet.

Accompanying Prohibition, however, is the rise of the 'speakeasy', an illegal bar where, once you have uttered the password and paid your money, the outside world of Prohibition does not exist. There is a vast selection of alcohol on sale, from home-made 'moonshine' to top-quality wines and spirits smuggled in from Canada and Europe.

Speakeasies, with their atmosphere of decadent hedonism, have become immensely popular, and there are an estimated 5000 in New York City alone. Venues such as New York's 21 Club are extremely fashionable with the urban middle classes who have little to lose by drinking there – after all, although the sale of alcohol has been made illegal, its consumption has not.

Ambitious individuals can make a fortune from Prohibition. Not only are the police and federal officials bribed to turn a blind eye, but also the importers of alcohol – the 'rum runners' dodging the US coastguard en route from the Caribbean – the bootleggers and the speakeasy owners are all profiting. And where money is to be made, the Mafia is sure to be found. Gangsters such as Al Capone and Dutch Schultz have been quick to add the importation and sale of alcohol to their list of illegal activities.

Prohibitionists say that the law is beneficial in many respects for America's poor – money that would have been spent on alcohol is going to food and clothing instead. However, there has been no decline in alcoholism, and there are also increasing reports of people dying after drinking poisoned home-made liquor.

IN THE STREET Agents smash kegs of alcohol, demonstrating government determination to stop alcohol consumption. A bemused public looks on.

··· THE FIRST ICE CREAM ON A STICK IS SOLD BY HARRY BURT AT HIS GOOD HUMOR BAR IN THE USA ···

SHOW OF STRENGTH British Army volunteers make their presence felt in the streets of east Belfast.

Tit-for-tat murders shock Dublin

21 NOVEMBER, DUBLIN
Thirty people were killed today in a series of murderous reprisals between the Irish Republican Army and the British authorities. The murders began at daybreak, when the IRA burst into the homes of 12 British intelligence agents in Dublin and shot them all dead.

The killings are part of the IRA's campaign of violence to secure an independent and united Ireland. In retaliation, the Black and Tans opened fire on the crowd at a Gaelic football match this afternoon. Twelve people died – either shot or trampled to death in the stampede that followed – and a further 60 were injured. Tonight the British Army rounded up two suspected Irish terrorists outside Dublin Castle and shot them dead.

White Sox players accused of fixing World Series

20 NOVEMBER, CHICAGO
Eight Chicago White Sox players, including one of baseball's finest batters, Joe Jackson, were today formally accused of playing to lose in the 1919 World Series. Players allegedly accepted bribes of up to $20000 each from a gambling syndicate. New baseball commissioner Judge Kenesaw Landis has banned the men from playing organised baseball until the case comes to court.

The White Sox play-off against the Cincinnati Reds was widely rumoured to be fixed before the game began. Thousands of dollars were bet on a Reds victory despite the superiority of the Chicago team's play.

The indictment of Joe Jackson, nicknamed 'Shoeless' because of his dirt-poor beginnings, is the biggest shock to the nation. His rise to the pantheon of baseball greats won him the hearts of millions. Jackson claims he tried his best to win the series. But although his batting was up to scratch, it appears his fielding may have been lacking.

··· BLOODY MARY COCKTAIL IS INVENTED BY A BARTENDER AT HARRY'S NEW YORK BAR IN PARIS ···

I believe in fairies, says Doyle

NOVEMBER, LONDON
The writer Arthur Conan Doyle, best known as the creator of Sherlock Holmes, has published an article declaring the existence of fairies – and supports his belief with photographs.

Doyle, a respected novelist, is also known for his interest in the spiritual and supernatural. When he heard of the photographs of fairies taken by two schoolgirls, Elsie Wright and Frances Griffiths, in the Yorkshire village of Cottingley, he used them to accompany his article in the *Strand* magazine under the headline 'An Epoch-Making Event – Fairies Photographed'. The photographs were taken three years ago, but were only authenticated recently.

However, many observers are saying that the 'Cottingley fairies' are no more than a schoolgirls' hoax, and Doyle is receiving more ridicule than praise for his discovery.

FAIRY FOLK Frances Griffiths, photographed with fairies by her cousin Elsie.

Inkblot test gives clues to unconscious

Swiss psychiatrist Hermann Rorschach has devised a controversial new method of delving into his patients' unconscious thoughts. The 'inkblot test', as he calls it, is causing a stir in the medical world.

During the test, patients are asked to look at symmetrical patterns made by ink on paper – some in black and white and some in colour. As the psychiatrist holds up each sheet of paper, he asks, 'What might this be?'

According to Rorschach, the patient's response will reveal personality traits and deep psychological motivations. Where a 'normal' person might see a butterfly in an inkblot, a mentally disturbed patient might see a bleeding heart. The more disturbed a patient, the more likely he or she is to perceive violence in the inkblot.

Gramophones are all the rage

The gramophone is fast becoming a familiar sight in many homes. No longer is it the preserve of wealthy households – lower prices are making Thomas Edison's invention affordable to everyone.

The replacement of the old expensive cylinders for more convenient and less costly records that are played on a rotating turntable has also popularised the machine. In fact, since it was invented in 1877 the gramophone has changed extensively. The familiar horn, used to magnify the records' sound, is no longer required, replaced by a tone-arm which opens into a metal shell and conducts the sound.

Nor are gramophones still housed in large wooden cabinets – instead they are lightweight and can be easily transported from place to place.

Nellie Melba sings live on wireless

15 JUNE, CHELMSFORD, ENGLAND Opera singer Nellie Melba made recording history today when she became the first professional singer to be paid to perform on radio. The Australian diva was paid £1000 for her live wireless broadcast, for which she sang 'Home Sweet Home', 'Addio' from Puccini's *La Bohème*, and the 'Chant Vénetien'.

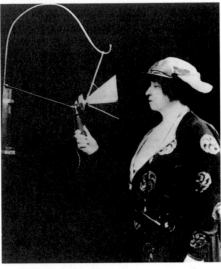

PRIMA DONNA Nellie Melba has performed all over the world since her debut in 1887.

The soprano was asked to perform by the *Daily Mail* newspaper after two amateur singers provoked public interest on the Marconi Company's Chelmsford wireless station. Until now broadcasting has been left to amateurs, but Melba's broadcast received immense public acclaim and marks a new move towards professionalism in radio.

OUT WITH THE OLD The phonograph was patented by Thomas Edison on 12 August 1877.

1921

BORN
31 Jan: Norman Mailer, US author and journalist
16 Apr: Peter Ustinov, British actor
18 July: John Glenn, US astronaut and politician

DIED
21 Sept: Engelbert Humperdinck, German composer
5 Nov: Rev Antoinette Brown Blackwell, first US woman ordained pastor

CROWNED
23 Aug: Emir Feisal, formerly King of Syria, crowned King of Iraq

ABOLISHED
8 May: capital punishment in Sweden

On 2 October, *baseball's brightest star George Herman 'Babe' Ruth hits his 59th home run to end the season for the New York Yankees. Ruth's career has soared since his transfer from the Red Sox last year.*

FIRSTS
Drive-in restaurant: J G Kirby's 'Pig Stand' in Dallas, Texas
Band-aid brand adhesive bandage, by Johnson and Johnson
Stiff but starchless collars, by clothing firm Van Heusen

Motorway, the Avus Autobahn, Berlin
18 July: tuberculosis vaccine, BCG, developed by French scientists Calmette and Guérin, given to children in France

ELECTED
8 Feb: Jan Smuts, as prime minister of South Africa
10 Apr: Sun Yat-sen, as president of China
29 July: Adolf Hitler, as president of National Socialist German Workers' Party

ANNOUNCED
12 Mar: Lenin's New Economic Policy (NEP) for Soviet recovery, permitting free enterprise

OPENED
17 Mar: Marie Stopes's first birth control clinic in London, strongly opposed by clergymen and doctors, who thought it would encourage immorality

INVENTED
The lie detector (polygraph), by Californian medical student John Larson

DISCOVERED
Insulin, isolated from the pancreas by Dr Frederic Banting and Charles Best, providing reprieve for millions with diabetes
Mysterious footprints in the Himalayas, giving rise to the legend of the Yeti

RECORDS
23 Mar, Illinois: parachute jump from 7315 m (24000 ft), by Arthur Hamilton

On 5 May, *one of the world's great perfumes, Chanel No 5, goes on sale. Created by French fashion designer Coco Chanel with chemist Ernest Beaux, the fragrance is called No 5 because it is launched on the fifth day of the fifth month.*

23 Apr, California: Charles Paddock, 'The World's Fastest Human', won the 100 metres in 10.4 seconds

CRUSHED
Anti-Bolshevik rebellion in Kronstadt, Russia, by Red Army troops

CONDEMNED
22 May, Chicago: rising hemlines – the city imposes fines on women with short skirts and bare arms

ADOPTED
Mahatma Gandhi's policy of non-violent non-cooperation with India's British rulers

ASSASSINATED
20 Oct: Portuguese premier Antonion Granjo, during military coup
4 Nov: Japanese premier Takashi Harakei

AFFLICTED
Franklin D Roosevelt, rising US politician, struck by polio

AWARDED
10 Dec: Nobel Prize to Anatole France (literature) and to Albert Einstein (physics)

APPOINTED
5 Aug: Mustafa Kemal made ruler of Turkey and supreme commander of the army
5 Nov: Crown Prince Hirohito named regent of Japan

PUBLISHED
D H Lawrence, *Women in Love*
Aldous Huxley, *Chrome Yellow*

NEW WORDS
cold turkey *n*: a method of curing drug addiction by abrupt withdrawal of all doses
junkie *n*: (slang) drug addict

The striking Einstein Observatory, designed by architect Erich Mendelsohn, is unveiled in Potsdam, Germany. The dynamic form of this bizarre building is characteristic of a growing move towards Expressionism in architecture, which reflects highly personal and often bold visions.

Irish Free State is founded

6 DECEMBER, LONDON

After more than 500 years of British rule, the Anglo-Irish Treaty today declared 26 counties of Ireland independent, marking the birth of the Irish Free State.

The treaty is the culmination of a series of rapid political changes which began with the 1918 general election, when a majority of Irish seats in the British parliament at Westminster was won by the nationalist Sinn Fein party. The Sinn Fein MPs, led by Eamon de Valera, refused to sit in the British House of Commons and in 1919 set up an independent Irish parliament, the Dáil Eireann, in Dublin.

The British government has always rejected the rebel parliament's declarations of independence. Last year Westminster introduced the idea of partition and limited self-rule in the Government of Ireland Act, but the Dáil has been relentless in its demand for a free and united Ireland. In today's treaty the British government made a major concession by setting up the Irish Free

STATE HANDOVER A month after the treaty, Free State troops take over Dublin Barracks.

State. The 26 Roman Catholic-dominated counties in the south now comprise a self-governing country with dominion status, while the six mainly Protestant counties of Ulster remain under British rule. It only remains to be seen whether de Valera's government will agree to ratify the treaty.

··· 7 SEPT, NEW JERSEY: THE FIRST MISS AMERICA BEAUTY PAGEANT IS HELD, WITH EIGHT CONTESTANTS ···

False allegations ruin Hollywood comedian

At the end of this year the career of Roscoe 'Fatty' Arbuckle – the cinema's greatest comedian – lies in tatters. His reputation, tainted by allegations of debauchery and rape, is ruined.

The scandal began in September, when Arbuckle and a group of friends checked into a hotel in San Francisco. They threw a party which turned into a bootleg liquor-fuelled orgy. One of the women, a 26-year old actress called Virginia Rappe, became ill and died a few days later of peritonitis. Arbuckle was accused of causing the fatal injury in a violent attack.

HOLLYWOOD DRAMA Arbuckle and a friend sit through the trial that gripped the showbiz world.

In November Arbuckle faced trial for manslaughter, and was acquitted by the jury. The publicity, however, has proved extremely damaging, making Arbuckle an early victim of what will later be known as 'trial by media'.

Electric chair for political dissidents

14 JULY, MASSACHUSETTS

Nicola Sacco and Bartolomeo Vanzetti, two Italians accused of murdering a paymaster and guard in the course of a $16 000 theft from a factory, have been found guilty and sentenced to death.

The trial has stirred up a storm of protest. Many observers claim that the prosecution was political, as both men are well-known radicals.

The judge, Webster Thayer, called the defendants 'anarchistic bastards' and allowed the prosecution to mount a case based on circumstantial evidence and the defendants' political beliefs.

1922

BORN

1 Mar: Yitzhak Rabin, Israeli general and statesman
12 Mar: Jack Kerouac, US writer of Beatnik generation
10 June: Judy Garland (born Frances Gumm), US film star

DIED

5 Jan: Sir Ernest Shackleton, British polar explorer
1 Aug: Alexander Graham Bell, inventor of the telephone
26 Oct: George Cadbury, British chocolate maker and philanthropist
18 Nov: Marcel Proust, French author

On 12 February, *Cardinal Achille Ratti (above) is elected Pope, taking the name Pius XI. He succeeds Pope Benedict XV who died last month. Pius XI, aged 65, has an outstanding scholarly background and has recently begun diplomatic work.*

FIRSTS

Woman to fly across USA: Lilian Gatlin
Baby food sold in cans: Clapp's Vegetable Soup
Suburban shopping mall: opened by National Department Stores in USA

Police car, designed especially for police work, in Denver; called a bandit-chaser, it used a Cadillac engine
3–D feature film: Nat Deverich's *Power of Love* premieres in Los Angeles
Snowmobile: built by 15-year-old Joseph Bombardier in Quebec, using a Model T Ford engine to drive a wooden propeller on family sleigh

CAPTURED

9 Sept: Smyrna (Izmir), by Turkey from Greece – completing Turkey's reconquest of land lost to Greece during World War I

On 5 February,
the first edition of The Reader's Digest is launched by husband-and-wife team De Witt Wallace and Lila Acheson. The pocket-sized magazine can be bought by subscription, and each issue features 30–31 articles, one for each day of the month.

NOBEL PRIZES

Physics: Niels Bohr, Denmark, modelling the atom
Chemistry: Francis Aston, UK, work on isotopes

Medicine: Archibald Hill, UK, and Otto Meyerhof, Germany
Literature: Jacinto Benavento, Spain
Peace: Fridtjof Nansen – explorer, scientist and humanitarian – Norway

US swimmer Johnny Weissmuller sets a new world record, becoming the first man to swim the 100 metres race in under a minute. At athletics contests Weissmuller is a huge hit with the crowds, entertaining them between races with comic diving routines.

MURDERED

21 June, London: British Field Marshal Sir Henry Wilson, by IRA gunmen
24 June, Berlin: foreign minister Walter Rathenau, by right-wing nationalist gunmen
9 Nov, London: Metropolitan Police Commissioner William Horton, poisoned by arsenic-filled chocolates

APPOINTED

23 Oct: Andrew Bonar Law, British prime minister (Conservative)

PROTECTED

Koala bears: Australia introduces legislation to protect the endangered marsupial; koala fur is being sold as wombat fur in North America

DISCOVERED

Toronto: a way to manufacture insulin for diabetic patients

ENDED

16 Mar, Cairo: British protection of Egypt – Sultan Ahmed Fuad Pasha proclaims himself King of Egypt

BANNED

6 Oct: alcohol on all US ships, public and private
24 Oct, Boston: dancer Isadora Duncan, after taking her clothes off on stage

English novelist and social theorist H G Wells produces the best-selling The Outline of History *in which he attempts to 'reform history teaching by replacing narrow nationalist history by a general review of the human record'. It marks a departure from his earlier science fiction work.*

NEW WORDS

bimbo *n*: an attractive but unintelligent young woman
broadcast *n*: a programme transmitted by radio; *vb*: to transmit such a programme
gigolo *n*: a man living off the earnings or gifts of a woman; a professional male dancer or escort (from *gigolette*, meaning female prostitute)

PHARAOH'S TOMB DISCOVERED INTACT

30 NOVEMBER, LUXOR
Earlier this month the British Egyptologist Howard Carter found a sunken staircase beneath the floor of an ancient builder's hut in the Valley of the Kings, the sacred burial place of the pharaohs of Egypt's New Kingdom. At the bottom was a sealed door, which was breached today to reveal the unrobbed tomb of Tutankhamun, who was pharaoh c1316–1322 BC.

Carter delayed opening the tomb until his sponsor, the Earl of Carnarvon, arrived from England. Together they made a hole in the door, and Carter gingerly thrust a candle into the chamber beyond. 'What can you see?' asked Carnarvon. 'Wonderful things,' answered Carter.

The 'things' – life-size golden statues, furniture inlaid with precious stones, lapis lazuli vases and sumptuous jewellery – are now starting to emerge from the tomb, which is situated next to the crypt of Rameses VI. The presence of an untouched sarcophagus believed to contain Tutankhamun's mummified body confirms that this is the most spectacular archaeological discovery ever.

EDGE OF DISCOVERY Carter and colleagues at the entrance to the tomb.

··· HOTTEST EVER TEMPERATURE RECORDED IN THE SHADE: 56° C (136° F) AT AL'AZIZIYAH, SAUDI ARABIA ···

Fascism comes to unruly Italy

30 OCTOBER, ROME
Black-shirted supporters of Benito Mussolini, a former schoolmaster and journalist, thronged the streets of Rome today to welcome their leader to the post of prime minister. King Victor Emmanuel sent for Mussolini – known to his followers as *Il Duce* ('the leader') – amid fears of civil war. The presence in the capital of 40000 unruly members of the Fascist Party, who had marched from Naples to Rome to demand strong government, no doubt greatly helped the King to make his decision.

Mussolini's dreams of restoring Rome's ancient position at the heart of a great empire have struck a chord with a wide range of people, from war veterans to students and professionals who feel discontented with Italy's politicians and international status. France and Britain, who promised so much in 1915 when Italy joined the Allies in the Great

VIOLENT MARCH Marchers wreaked havoc on the way, seizing government buildings and train stations.

War, failed to deliver in the post-war settlement. Italy's economy is in dire straits, with a soaring inflation rate that is second only to Germany's.

Although the electorate returned just 35 Fascists to the national assembly this year, voters are tired of Italy's ramshackle and corrupt parliamentary system. Judging by the wild displays of public support for Mussolini and his 'Blackshirts', voters are already embracing the Fascist promises for a brighter future.

Lincoln Memorial unveiled

30 MAY, WASHINGTON DC
Crowds thronged the city today for a typically American display of patriotism. The occasion, however, was anything but typical: the dedication of the Lincoln Memorial, a towering monument to Abraham Lincoln (President 1861–5). At the heart of the building, which is based on the Parthenon in Athens, is a 6-metre (19-ft) statue of Lincoln, designed by Daniel Chester French and carved by the Picirilli brothers.

TRIBUTE IN STONE Lincoln's gaze reminds every US President of the wisdom of 'Honest Abe'.

Wireless comes of age

15 NOVEMBER, LONDON
The first broadcast of the British Broadcasting Company, from Marconi House today, marked a milestone in the history of communications.

Today's transmission was a newscast read by Arthur Burrows, and more programmes are planned for the future. The setting up of the BBC marks the entry of the government into the broadcasting business.

Just two years ago the Australian diva Dame Nellie Melba made Europe's first advertised radio broadcast, and Station KDKA in Pittsburgh started weekly broadcasts to an audience of less than 1000, listening on the first affordable crystal sets.

··· 12 MAY: 20-TON METEOR GOUGES 387 SQ M (500 SQ FT) HOLE IN BLACKSTONE, VIRGINIA ···

Irish leader shot dead

22 AUGUST, CO CORK, IRELAND
Last year Michael Collins, the architect of Ireland's independence, muttered, 'I am signing my own death warrant', as he signed the treaty creating the Irish Free State. His prophecy has come true. His agreement to accept an Irish state in which six counties in Ulster remained under British rule sparked off a civil war, which led to his death today in an ambush mounted by an IRA splinter group near the remote settlement of Beal-na-Blath.

Collins was a rebel-turned-statesman, whose brief career – he was only 31 when he died – was packed with adventure. Born in West Cork, he was imprisoned for his part in the 1916 Easter Rising. The failure of the rebellion convinced Collins that the British could only be beaten by a new form of warfare, and so he became the first urban guerrilla. His elite team, 'The Squad', picked off policemen and organised large-scale arms smuggling. By the time of his death, Collins was not only the head of state but also the commander of the Irish National Army. He will become a legend in Ireland.

STREET-FIGHTING MAN There is speculation that Collins's murder was in retaliation for the killing of Harry Bolland, an opponent of the Irish Free State.

Women enjoy new freedoms

In 1912 few women worked, and none had the vote. The Great War of 1914–18 changed all that, and today's woman has a freedom that her ancestors would envy.

She can smoke and drink and even swear in public; she has opinions and expresses them freely. This new self-expression extends to fashion, and in many ways the look of the early 1920s is a self-conscious suppression of femininity. Hair is worn bobbed (short) and covered by a cloche hat. Instead of accentuating curves, clothing hides them – and many women bind their breasts to achieve a boyish silhouette.

Liberated by a war that decimated the male population, women are out to have fun. The press has coined a word for these happy-go-lucky women of the jazz age who make no secret of the fact that they enjoy sex: flappers.

COLD STORY IS A FAKE

In the film world, *Nanook of the North* looked like a documentary about the Inuit people of North America, but it was in fact completely staged by director Robert Flaherty. Buster Keaton took up the theme with *The Frozen North*. Chaplin waited for *Pay Day*, while Erich von Stroheim rebuilt Monte Carlo in Universal Studio's backlot for *Foolish Wives* (left).

THE FLAPPER Regarded as depraved and unfeminine by the media.

Joyce's epic *Ulysses* is banned

Swearwords and explicit, poetic descriptions of urination, defecation and genitalia have led British and US authorities to ban *Ulysses*, the latest novel by Irish exile James Joyce, on grounds of obscenity.

A bookshop owner and friend of Joyce, Sylvia Beach, printed 1000 copies of the book in Paris, where literati fought for a glimpse of the volume. T S Eliot and Ernest Hemingway applauded the novel, while Virginia Woolf dismissed it as 'the work of a queasy undergraduate scratching his pimples'.

Art world in ferment

NEW ART Malevich's painting shows the new preoccupation with purity of form and line.

The world is changing rapidly, and the art world is changing with it. New movements with dramatic names are born every day, it seems. One of the buzzwords of recent years is 'Constructivism' – a type of art that is designed to reveal the building blocks of forms, rather than to render an impression of reality. It is influenced by the Italian Futurist movement which focused on machines and dynamism.

Another trend gaining hold in the art world is 'Suprematism', an abstract movement led by the Russian painter Kasimir Malevich, who paints complex groups of over-lapping lines and geometric shapes. Malevich claims his paintings demonstrate 'the supremacy of pure feeling'.

Both movements began in Russia in the last six or seven years, and are now influential in the West.

1923

BORN

4 Oct: Charlton Heston, US actor
2 Dec: Maria Callas, Greek-American soprano

DIED

9 Jan: New Zealand-born writer Katherine Mansfield
29 Mar: Sarah Bernhardt, French actress
2 Aug: Warren Harding, US President
28 Dec: Gustave Eiffel, French engineer

P G Wodehouse's comic novel Very Good Jeeves *is published, featuring the already popular characters Bertie Wooster and his butler Jeeves. Wooster and Jeeves first appeared in a short-story collection in 1917.*

FIRSTS

6 Nov: commercially successful electric shaver, patented by Colonel Jacob Schick in the USA
5 Mar, USA: old-age pensions in Montana and Nevada
Records that can be played on both sides

16 mm home movie camera, the Kodak Model A, is launched in the USA

APPOINTED

3 Aug, Washington DC: Calvin Coolidge, sworn in as US President after death of President Harding
22 May, London: Stanley Baldwin, British prime minister (Conservative)

OCCUPIED

11 Jan, Germany: Ruhr Valley, by France and Belgium, angered by German failure to pay agreed war reparations
27 Oct, Germany: Bonn and Wiesbaden, by French troops

KILLED

20 July, Mexico: Pancho Villa, retired rebel leader

COUPS

9 June, Bulgaria: led by League of ex-Army Officers; successful
13 Sept, Spain: led by General Miguel Primo de Rivera; successful

TUMBLED

Germany: value of German mark, from 85 000 to £1 on 1 Jan to 10 000 million to £1 on 11 Oct

PROPOSED

21 Mar, Paris: that smoking is good for you because nicotine works against bacteria, by French scientists

'CENTURION'

8 May, Bath: cricketer Jack Hobbs scores 100 runs or more for the hundredth time; only W G Grace and Tom Hayward have previously achieved this

SPORTS FIRSTS

26–27 May, France: 24-hour Grand Prix in Le Mans; winners Frenchmen Lagache and Leonard in Chenard et Walcker car cover 2209 km (1373 miles) in 24 hours – average speed is 92 km/h (57 mph)

Harold Lloyd stars in Safety Last, *the comedy hit of the year. In this famous scene, Lloyd hangs on for real – he never used stuntmen. Lloyd's dangerous stunts, based on split-second timing, made him the highest-paid comedian in Hollywood in the 1920s, outstripping Buster Keaton and even Charlie Chaplin.*

28 Apr: FA Cup Final at Wembley stadium – Bolton Wanderers 2, West Ham United 1

DECLARED

15 Sept, Oklahoma: martial law, by Governor Walton, following racist attacks by Ku Klux Klan members

SET UP

Letters on hill above Los Angeles spelling HOLLYWOODLAND – they advertise a property development

FOUNDED

Interpol – the International Criminal Police Organisation
USA: *Time* magazine, by Henry Luce and Briton Hadden
Cotton Club in Harlem, New York City

BANNED

16 July, Italy: gambling, by Benito Mussolini
31 July, Britain: sale of alcohol to under-18s, under Liquor Bill

NEW WORDS

aerosol *n*: a substance such as paint or insecticide dispensed from a small metal container by a propellant under pressure
hijack *vb*: to seize or divert a vehicle while in transit

UNIVERSE CONTAINS OTHER GALAXIES

6 OCTOBER, CALIFORNIA
Using the 254-centimetre (100-in)
telescope at Pasadena's Mount Wilson
Observatory, astronomer Edwin Hubble
has focused on the nebula in the
constellation of Andromeda, and made
a discovery which is set to transform
our knowledge of the universe and our
place in it.

Nobody knows what nebulae, named
after their cloudy appearance, really are.
In 1755 the philosopher Kant suggested
they were 'island universes' – distant star
systems like our own galaxy, the Milky
Way – but his idea could not be proved.

In the Andromeda nebula, Hubble
noticed an object whose brightness
varied. He realised that it was a Cepheid
variable, a type of star that can be used
for calculating distances. He worked out
that the star was so far away that it was
beyond the limits of the Milky Way –
whch means that the Andromeda nebula
must be an entirely separate galaxy.
This would indicate that the universe

COSMIC GLOW The Andromeda nebula was the first galaxy to be identified outside our own galaxy, the Milky Way. Edwin Hubble's discovery revealed new possibilities for the study of space.

is far larger than anyone has supposed.

Hubble, a former lawyer, gave up his
practice for the stars. 'Even if I were
second-rate or third-rate, it was astronomy
that mattered,' he said. His recent
discovery amply justifies his decision.

··· 16 OCT: JOHN HARWOOD INVENTS THE SELF-WINDING WATCH IN SWITZERLAND ···

REFORMING ZEAL Kemal later became known as 'Atatürk', or 'Father of the Turks'.

Kemal drags Turkey into the modern age

29 OCTOBER, ANKARA
Turkish women can lift their veils and
wave goodbye to the harem if the
newly elected president of the Turkish
Republic, Mustafa Kemal, has his way.
Kemal plans to bring in swingeing
reforms that will force his country, the
rump of the Ottoman Empire, into the
modern world.

The young Turkish leader has turned
his back on his Muslim neighbours in
the Arab world and is looking towards
the West for inspiration on how to
govern his young country.

At the top of Kemal's agenda is
secularisation. His liberal attitudes
towards women have already shocked
fellow Muslims – but he has shown that
he means business by stripping religious

leaders of any political power. He also
plans to ban religious instruction in the
country, as well as the traditional
Muslim practice of polygamy.

Mustafa Kemal is a veteran of the
Great War, when he successfully
commanded the Turkish Ottoman army
at Gallipoli against the Allies. After the
war he joined the officers known as the
'Young Turks' who brought about the
end of the Ottoman Empire. He has
now abolished the sultanate, the
hereditary Ottoman rulership, and
moved the capital from Istanbul to
Ankara. Kemal himself wears only
Western dress and expects his people to
follow suit. He also intends to abolish
the use of the Arabic alphabet and adopt
the Roman one instead.

Germany reels under grip of hyperinflation

TOY MONEY Children play with bundles of German marks; these days, the notes are virtually worthless.

Unprecedented price rises in war-shattered Germany this year have rocked the fledgling Weimar Republic.

The German economy, struggling under the weight of huge reparation payments to the Allies and the loss of major industrial regions under the Treaty of Versailles, is reeling. At the beginning of this year, the mark stood at less than four to the US dollar; now, at the end of 1923, it has reached the dizzying figure of 4200 million to the dollar. In real terms this means that Germans are paying 250 billion marks for a pound of sugar and around 3000 million for a pound of meat. Paper mills and printing presses, working on 24-hour shifts, have struggled to keep pace with the demand for new paper currency – and the daily dollar quotation has replaced the weather as the topic of conversation.

Even the issue of a new mark by Germany's central bank has been unable to halt the country's currency chaos. In fact, it has created greater confusion, as there are now three currencies in circulation: the new *Rentenmark*, the old mark, and an even older gold mark.

··· 1 SEPT, JAPAN: HUGE EARTHQUAKE KILLS MORE THAN 300 000 PEOPLE IN TOKYO AND YOKOHAMA ···

ATTEMPTED COUP LANDS HITLER IN JAIL

NEW ORDER A unit of brown-shirted 'putschists' parades in the street.

BEER HALL BOYS Hitler (fourth from right) with supporters of the failed coup.

11 NOVEMBER, MUNICH

Adolf Hitler has been arrested after his attempt to gain power in Germany. Two days ago the charismatic newcomer on the German political stage dramatically failed to seize power in an abortive putsch, or coup, staged in Munich.

Hitler, an Austrian-born failed artist who served as a corporal in the German Army during World War I, is leader of the tiny National Socialist German Workers' Party, one of many separatist groups that emerged after the war. He was joined by General Erich von Ludendorff and others seeking to exploit public discontent amid rocketing inflation and French occupation of the Ruhr.

The strike against the Bavarian state, intended as a prelude to an assault on the federal government in Berlin – to be modelled on Mussolini's march on Rome – ended in fiasco almost before it began. Hitler decided to force the hand of the Bavarian leaders, who had agreed to the march but not to a date for it. On 8 November he and an armed escort burst in on a rally being held by the state commissioner, Ritter von Kahr, in the Bürgerbräu, a Munich beer hall.

Here he declared the Bavarian and national governments deposed and forced von Kahr and his colleagues to agree to join him in a coup; the next day, however, they said they had changed their minds. Undeterred, Hitler and von Ludendorff marched on the centre of Munich with 3000 stormtroopers. They looked a formidable force, but one whiff of grapeshot from the police was enough to scatter them without a struggle. Hitler, wounded in the shoulder, retired to a country house, where he was arrested the following day in his pyjamas.

Despite the plan's failure, Hitler has gained great publicity for his movement; overnight he has been transformed from the 'king of Munich' into a firebrand known throughout Germany.

Short runway plane takes off

9 JANUARY, MADRID

Today the 'autogiro' – an odd-looking craft with an unpowered rotor above it to add extra lift – proved its worth, flying a circuit of 4 kilometres (2½ miles) and reaching a height of 24 metres (80 ft) at Cuatro Vientos airfield.

Juan de la Cierva was inspired by the search for a machine that could land and take off from short runways. Like a conventional aeroplane, the autogiro is powered by an engine and propeller, but the four-blade rotor turns naturally in the flow of air around the aircraft's body.

The autogiro is similar to another fledgling flying machine with a rotor – the helicopter. But in helicopters the

UP AND AWAY Well-wishers crowd around the autogiro and its inventor after its maiden flight.

rotors are powered by a motor. Frenchman Etienne Oechmichen designed a helicopter that flew for a minute and a half and reached a height

of around 8 metres (25 ft) two years ago, but earlier helicopter designs such as that of French bicycle-maker Paul Cornu in 1907 only managed the shortest of hops.

Glamorous Lenglen's stylish fifth triumph

7 JULY, WIMBLEDON

The incomparable Suzanne Lenglen, known as the 'Pavlova of tennis' for her balletic movement on court, has won her fifth Wimbledon singles title in a row by beating the number one British player, Kitty McKane, 6–2, 6–2.

The French ace, relying more on the steadiness of her strokes than their speed, routinely hands out such drubbings to her opponents, to whom she rarely yields a set. Apart from her controversial retirement from a match against Molla Mallory at the United States championships in 1922, she has not lost a match since first winning Wimbledon in 1919. Yet, despite the uneven nature of her contests, the public flock to see her. In order to accommodate them, all her matches have had to be played on Centre Court. Glamorously dressed in a stylish chiffon bandeau and and a flimsy *toile de soie*

SMASH HIT Mlle Lenglen (left), one of tennis's most popular and glamorous players, in 1924.

frock that, shockingly, barely reaches the knee, the flamboyant Mademoiselle Lenglen is the first truly international superstar of tennis.

New craze of dancing until you drop

14 APRIL, HOUSTON, TEXAS

A couple have broken the world record for continuous dancing by a twosome. They were on the floor for more than 40 hours – afterwards he passed out and was rushed to a nearby Turkish bath.

A craze for marathon dancing has gripped America. Dancing used to be fun; now it looks like a chore. Exhausted couples cling to each other on the near-empty dance floor, wearily lifting one foot after the other, vaguely in rhythm with the band.

The task is to dance for longer than anyone else; the reward is money. It seems only a matter of time before someone dies dancing. In Baltimore the police stepped in and stopped a marathon that had been going some 53 hours. No one knows where it all began, but young people in towns and cities across the country are dancing until they collapse.

··· FRANK EPPERSON INVENTS THE POPSICLE WHEN HE LEAVES HIS LEMONADE MIX ON A WINDOWSILL OVERNIGHT ···

1924

BORN

3 Apr: Marlon Brando, US Hollywood actor and screen icon
16 Sept: Lauren Bacall, Hollywood actress
1 Oct: Jimmy Carter, US politician and President

DIED

21 Jan: Vladimir Ilyich Lenin, former Soviet leader
4 May: Edith Nesbit, British author of books for children
3 June: Franz Kafka, Czech writer
29 Nov: Giacomo Puccini, Italian composer
28 Dec: Leon Bakst, Russian artist

On 12 February, US composer George Gershwin's Rhapsody in Blue *premieres to a rapturous audience in New York City. Gershwin calls the piece 'symphonic jazz' – the orchestral sound is tempered by jazz-like instrumentation.*

INVENTED

4 July, Tijuana, Mexico: Caesar's salad, by Caesar Cardini, US owner of 'Caesar's Place' restaurant
USA: Kleenex; the spindryer

RENAMED

26 Jan, Soviet Union: Petrograd, as Leningrad, in honour of the late Soviet leader

ELECTED

4 Nov: Calvin Coolidge (Republican), US President

APPOINTED

10 Mar, Washington DC: J Edgar Hoover, acting director of Federal Bureau of Investigation

PUBLISHED

A A Milne, *When We Were Very Young*
E M Forster, *A Passage to India*

PRIZEWINNER

11 May, New York City: US poet Robert Frost, Pulitzer Prize (poetry) for *New Hampshire: A Poem with Notes and Grace Notes*

FALLEN

29 Oct, London: first ever Labour government; it loses vote of censure over its handling of charges against a communist journalist accused of inciting soldiers to mutiny; Conservatives are reinstated

FOUNDED

14 Feb, New York City: International Business Machines (IBM), new name for the Computing-Tabulating-Recording Co
16 Apr, USA: film company Metro-Goldwyn-Mayer (MGM)
USA: Columbia Pictures

AGREED

16 Aug: Dawes Plan, by Germany, to reorganise German economy

On November 23, this magnificent gold mask is recovered from the inner shrine in Tutankhamun's tomb by Howard Carter and his excavation team. The mask dates from c 1342 BC. The discovery of ancient treasures in the burial chamber continues.

FASTING

18 Sept, India: Mahatma Gandhi, on hunger strike in attempt to persuade clashing Hindus and Muslims to bury their differences

FIRSTS

25 Jan–4 Feb, Switzerland: Winter Olympics, at Chamonix
8 Feb, USA: gas-chamber execution for prisoners sentenced to death
1 Apr, Britain: national airline in Britain, Imperial Airways
4 Apr–28 Sept, USA: round-the-world flight, by US Army Air Service Douglas World Cruisers; the planes start and finish in Seattle
4 Nov, Texas: female state governor, Miriam Ferguson

Use of seeding at Wimbledon Tennis Championships
'Alice in Cartoonland' film by Walt Disney, called *Alice's Day at the Sea*

DENOUNCED

26 Nov, USSR: Leon Trotsky, by Communist Party
18 Dec, Rome: the Soviet Union, by Pope Pius XI

DONATED

29 Dec, New York City: $1 million to Metropolitan Museum of Art, by US industrialist John D Rockefeller

Silent-movie star Buster Keaton appears in Sherlock Jr; *musicians accompany this silent masterpiece with appropriate improvised music. Keaton's characteristic deadpan expression earned him the nickname 'the Great Stone Face'.*

CHAMPION

July, Paris Olympics: US swimmer Johnny Weissmuller, winner of three gold medals

NEW WORDS

left-wing *adj*: the radical or progressive wing of a party, group or organisation
superstar *n*: an extremely popular film star

WEALTHY TEENAGE MURDERERS KILL FOR THRILLS

31 MAY, CHICAGO
The American public has been outraged at the revelation that two wealthy teenagers murdered a young boy to show their own 'intellectual superiority'.

The two 19-year-olds, Nathan Leopold Jr and Richard Loeb, are the sons of prominent Chicago millionaires. Both are undergraduates at the University of Michigan, where they are said to be excellent students. Ten days ago, bored with their studies and their want-for-nothing lifestyles, the pair kidnapped their 14-year-old neighbour Bobby Franks and strangled him. Coldly and cynically, the two murderers then demanded $2000 ransom from the boy's parents, but Franks's naked body was found stuffed into a culvert before the

PARTNERS IN CRIME Leopold and Loeb.

money was to be delivered. Hydrochloric acid had been poured over his face. On confessing to this cold-blooded crime,

the young men told police that for a long time they had wanted to murder someone to see how the victim reacted. They were convinced that they were too clever to get caught and the police too stupid to connect them with the crime. It was, the boys believed, the 'perfect murder'.

Leopold's and Loeb's parents are said to be horrified at what their children have done. Their lawyer, Clarence Darrow, one of the nation's top defence lawyers, has advised the two to plead not guilty due to emotional illness. Although both boys are sane, he says that they have been damaged by heredity and environment. This plea will, he hopes, save them from almost certain execution.

··· FORD TURNS OUT ITS 10-MILLIONTH CAR – MORE THAN HALF THE CARS IN THE WORLD ARE MODEL T FORDS ···

Long-running Finn wins five gold medals

MAN OF PRINCIPLE Eric Liddell breasts the tape well ahead of his nearest rival in the 400 metres.

30 JULY, PARIS
Great Britain's athletes have scored a series of spectacular victories on the track at the Paris Olympics, upstaging the highly fancied Americans. Harold Abrahams outpaced the American

world-record-holder, Charles Paddock, to win the 100 metres in 10.6 seconds, thus equalling the Olympic record; and, Eric Liddell, the Scottish rugby international who withdrew from the 100 metres rather than race on a Sunday, has

taken the 400 metres in 47.6 seconds. A third Briton, Douglas Lowe, claimed the gold in the 800 metres, but a British sweep of the short distances was thwarted when Liddell finished third after two Americans in the 200 metres.

Proudly as Britain has hailed its heroes, the towering figure at the games has been the Finnish long-distance runner Paavo Nurmi. Nurmi, who trained from the age of 12 by running in his native forests and using trams as pacemakers, is the first athlete to win five gold medals at a single Olympics.

Mean-spirited Games officials tried to thwart Nurmi's chances by scheduling the 1500 metres and 5000 metres events within little more than an hour of each other, but he triumphed in both. By adding to his tally the cross-country gold in a race run in sweltering heat and two team golds – in the 3000 metres and the cross-country – Nurmi has carved out for himself an ineradicable niche in the pantheon of supreme athletics champions.

1925

BORN
26 Jan: Paul Newman, US actor
19 May: Malcolm Little (Malcolm X), US political leader
8 Sept: Peter Sellers, British actor
13 Oct: Margaret Thatcher, British politician and prime minister

DIED
12 Mar: Dr Sun Yat-sen, Chinese Nationalist leader
14 Apr: John Singer Sargent, US artist
14 May: H Rider Haggard, British writer

FOUNDED
21 Feb, USA: *New Yorker* magazine by Harold Ross
6 June, Detroit: Chrysler Motor Co, by Walter P Chrysler
5 Aug, Wales: Plaid Cymru, Welsh nationalist group

Professor Raymond Dart identifies the skull brought to him last year by one of his students, who found it in a lime quarry near Taung in South Africa. Dart demonstrates that the skull is a juvenile specimen of Australopithecus africanus, *an intermediate between hominids and humans.*

9 Nov, Germany: Nazi *Schutzstaffel* ('Protection Squad') – or SS
15 Nov, Dublin: the Legion of Mary, religious organisation to combat immorality

RENAMED
1 Jan, Norway: the capital city, Christiania, as Oslo

When German Oskar Barnack designed the Leica in 1913, it became the first commercially successful 35 mm camera. The Leica 1A, launched this year, will become a much-imitated standard model for the photographic industry.

PARADED
8 Aug, Washington DC: over 40000 Ku Klux Klan members, on day of the Klan's first national congress

INVENTED
Playing frisbee, by Yale University students, using empty pie plates – the plates originally held pies baked by Frisbie Baking Company of Bridgeport, Connecticut

ON SHOW
April–Oct, Paris: *Exposition des Arts Décoratifs* – new styles in fashion, design and architecture, nicknamed 'Art Deco'

FIRSTS
3 Jan: rugby player sent off for foul play in international match – Cyril Brownlie of the New Zealand All Blacks, against England; All Blacks win 17–11
In-flight movie, offered by German airline

COLONISED
1 May, Cyprus: by Britain – the island has been under British administration since 1878 and was annexed from Turkey in 1914

SIGNED
16 Oct, Locarno: security pact, agreed by Britain, Germany, France, Belgium and Italy; agreement reaffirms frontiers set out in Treaty of Versailles

DISCOVERED
19 Oct: ancient sea shells in the Sahara Desert – evidence that the area was once under water

PUBLISHED
Virginia Woolf, *Mrs Dalloway*
F Scott Fitzgerald, *The Great Gatsby*
Anita Loos, *Gentlemen Prefer Blondes*
Adolf Hitler, *Mein Kampf*

SCREEN HITS
The Phantom of the Opera, directed by Rupert Julian
Go West, starring Buster Keaton
The Gold Rush, starring and directed by Charlie Chaplin

BANNED
23 Mar, Tennessee: teaching the theory of evolution, in schools
5 Nov, Rome: left-wing political parties, by Benito Mussolini

CLAIMED
2 June, Ottawa: land from Alaska/Greenland to North Pole, as part of Canada, by Canadian government

BARRED
29 June, South Africa: blacks, 'coloureds' (those of mixed race) and Indians, from skilled and semi-skilled work

Irish playwright George Bernard Shaw is awarded the Nobel Prize for literature, but refuses it for political reasons. An important socialist thinker and critic, he is best known for dramas that explore political and class issues.

ELECTED
25 Apr, Germany: Field Marshal Paul von Hindenburg as president of Germany

NEW WORD
tabloid *n*: a newspaper with pages about 30 cm (12 in) by 40 cm (16 in), usually with many photographs and written in a concise and often sensationalist style

Darwin on trial: court rejects evolution

TRIAL AND ERROR Defence lawyer Clarence Darrow (seated on desk) ponders before a packed courtroom.

21 JULY, DAYTON, TENNESSEE
John Thomas Scopes, a high school biology teacher, was convicted today of the crime of teaching Darwin's theories of evolution to pupils at Rhea High School in Dayton. After a trial that pitted America's greatest lawyers against one another and held the country enthralled, Scopes was fined $100.

The moral victor, however, was not the Tennessee law that Scopes admitted violating, but his defence lawyer, Clarence Darrow. In sweltering heat, and in front of a crowd so large that the judge eventually moved proceedings out of doors, Darrow subjected the prosecution lawyer William Jennings Bryan to a ruthless cross-examination. Bryan, a Christian fundamentalist, was forced into admitting that perhaps Joshua had not made the Sun stand still, and that the creation of the world in six days by God did not necessarily mean six 24-hour days.

'The creation might have been going on for a long time?' asked Darrow.

'It might have continued for millions of years,' admitted Bryan.

Hundreds of fundamentalists cheered, sang hymns and prayed as the jury announced its verdict. An appeal to the state's supreme court is inevitable.

··· 2 OCT, LONDON: RED DOUBLE-DECKER BUSES ENTER SERVICE ···

Nepia takes All Blacks to victory

3 JANUARY, TWICKENHAM
The All Blacks of New Zealand, inspired by their great fullback, the Maori George Nepia, have ended their unbeaten tour of the British Isles by defeating England 17–11 at Twickenham before a full house which included the Prince of Wales and Stanley Baldwin, the prime minister. Nepia showed all the kicking prowess (with both feet), crisp tackling and sure passing that have already established him as a rugby union legend. Despite sharing the place-kicking duties with Mark Nicholls, he has ended the Kiwis' triumphant European tour – which finished with a victory over France – with 29 conversions and four other goals for a total of 70 points.

LIVING LEGEND George Nepia, aged 19, part of the greatest New Zealand side to tour Britain.

China on the brink of civil war

12 MARCH, CANTON
The reins of power in the Chinese Nationalist Party, the Guomindang, passed to military commander Chiang Kai-shek today on the death of party leader Sun Yat-sen. Chiang runs a military academy at Whampoa near the southern Chinese city of Canton, where the Nationalists run a separatist regime. He looks ready to lead his 40 000-strong Guomindang army against the Beijing government and the warlords who dominate northern China.

Two years ago Chiang visited the Soviet Union and studied the Red Army's organisation. He has applied what he learnt to his own troops.

1926

BORN

1 June: Marilyn Monroe (Norma Jean Baker), film actress
18 Oct: Chuck Berry, US singer

DIED

23 Aug: Rudolf Valentino, Italian-born Hollywood star
31 Oct: Harry Houdini (born Ernst Weiss), Hungarian-born escape performer
5 Dec: Claude Monet, French painter
29 Dec: Rainer Maria Rilke, Austrian poet

US star of silent cowboy films Tom Mix, with his horse Tony Jr, is one of the most popular Hollywood actors, having already made hundreds of westerns. Harold Lloyd is the only other actor who earns as much as Mix – a staggering £4000 per week.

PUBLISHED

T E Lawrence, *The Seven Pillars of Wisdom*
A A Milne, *Winnie-the-Pooh*

PROCLAIMED

8 Jan, Mecca: Arab leader Abdul Aziz ibn Saud as King of the Hejaz (later renamed Saudi Arabia)

4 Apr: martial law in India, following fighting between Hindus and Muslims

EXPELLED

23 Oct, Moscow: Leon Trotsky and Gregory Zinoviev, from Communist Party Central Committee

GRANTED EQUALITY

20 Nov, London: Canada, Australia, New Zealand, South Africa and Newfoundland, which become self-governing dominions with equal standing to Britain within the British Commonwealth

DISCOVERED

12 Jan, Paris: serum to combat tetanus, by Pasteur Institute
18 Feb, Mexico: five ancient Mayan cities, by archaeologists

FIRST

9 May: to fly over the North Pole, US Navy Lt-Col Richard E Byrd and pilot Floyd Bennett, in Fokker aircraft

FOUNDED

6 Jan, Germany: national airline Lufthansa, by merger of existing German airlines
24 Mar, USA: Safeway food stores in Maryland, by Marion B Skaggs
16 May, Dublin: Fianna Fáil ('soldiers of destiny'), Irish political party

ATTACKED

7 Apr: Italian prime minister Benito Mussolini, by Irishwoman the Hon Violet Gibson; her shot makes his nose bleed but does not kill him
May: French airmail pilot Jean Mermoz, tied up by Moroccan tribesmen after technical trouble forces him to land; Mermoz is ransomed for 1000 pesetas

SCREEN LANDMARKS

The Lodger, first British film directed by Alfred Hitchcock – he has previously directed two co-productions in Germany
Metropolis, expressionist epic, directed by German Fritz Lang

On 16 March, Professor Robert Goddard oversees the first flight of his liquid-fuelled rocket on his Massachusetts farm. The device, powered by gasoline and liquid oxygen, reaches a height of 12.5 m (41 ft) and travels 56 m (184 ft).

The Mother, directed by Soviet film-maker Vsevelod Pudovkin
Don Juan, starring John Barrymore, directed by Alan Crosland

ARRESTED

26 Apr, New York City: actress Mae West, for 'corrupting the morals of youth' with her play *Sex*

MUSIC HIT

15 Sept: 'Jelly Roll' Morton and his band the Red Hot Peppers cut their first record – their blend of ragtime with brass band style is a key development in jazz

NEW WORDS

gig *n*: a single booking for jazz musicians; the performance itself
gimmick *n*: something designed to attract extra attention, interest or publicity

The all-singing, all-dancing, glamorously costumed revue known as the Ziegfeld Follies has been performing to packed houses on Broadway for over 15 years. Florenz Ziegfeld's troupe launched the careers of Fanny Brice and Irving Berlin.

CRIPPLING STRIKE CALLED OFF

12 MAY, LONDON

The General Strike that has gripped Britain for nine days is over.
Railwaymen, transport workers, dockers, builders, printers, engineers, and gas and electricity workers all downed tools in support of an existing miners' dispute with mine owners over pay and working hours. Today the unions called off the strike, unwilling to prolong the direct conflict with the government. The miners' dispute remains unsettled.

The crisis arose after negotiations between the government, mine owners and the Trades Union Congress (TUC) broke down. On 1 May the miners, railwaymen and transport workers came out on strike, shortly followed by the gas, electricity and building workers. By 4 May more than a million workers had downed tools, bringing the country to a virtual standstill.

The government immediately declared a state of emergency. Its priority was to keep essential services going and to maintain law and order. Volunteers drove buses, trams and lorries, unloaded ships, delivered the mail and kept passenger trains running. Private lorries, escorted by armoured cars, carried food from the docks to

SECONDARY ACTION Workers blocked roads and tramways to bring public transport to a halt.

distribution depots. National newspapers virtually disappeared for the duration of the strike, but the government published a daily paper, the *British Gazette* – edited by the confrontational chancellor of the exchequer, Winston Churchill. In addition, news bulletins on the wireless and notices in shop windows were vital to keep the public informed.

The atmosphere started off as good, with friendly football matches between police and strikers, but the situation became increasingly violent. Buses driven by workers who ignored the strike were overturned, and in some areas police clashed with angry workers, clearing the streets with baton charges and keeping the peace with armoured cars.

Now that the General Strike is over most believe that it has achieved nothing. The miners are still on strike, determined to hold out no matter what hardship.

··· JOSEF GOEBBELS IS APPOINTED CHIEF OF THE NAZI PARTY'S BERLIN DISTRICT ···

Cobham travels around the world in 93 days

1 OCTOBER, LONDON

A hero's welcome greeted British pilot Alan Cobham as he landed his red and silver seaplane on the river Thames in front of the Houses of Parliament today at the end of a 43000-kilometre (26700-mile) round trip to Australia.

Cobham – a veteran of such trips – made the flight to work out a route and establish landing sites for future commercial air services to Australia by the British national airline Imperial Airways. In 1925 he had made a similar trip to Burma. Earlier this year he flew his plane, the second de Havilland DH 50 ever built, on a 25750-kilometre (16000-mile) route-proving round trip to Cape Town, South Africa. Cobham took off on 30 June in the same aircraft; it had been converted into a seaplane for the journey to Australia, which would be largely over water.

The Australian flight was marred by the death of his engineer Arthur Elliot, killed by a stray bullet from a Bedouin's gun as they flew over Iraq.

SPLASHDOWN Vehicles come to a standstill and crowds cheer as Cobham lands at Westminster.

New invention could bring movies to every home

PICTURES FROM AFAR Logie Baird peers into the spinning disc that 'scans' images for transmission.

27 JANUARY, LONDON

A Scottish electrical engineer, John Logie Baird, demonstrated a new machine that transmits moving pictures using radio technology.

In a darkened room in London's Soho, members of the Royal Institution peered at a dimly flickering oblong of light barely bigger than a visiting card. They took turns to sit in front of the 'televisor' while the others watched the image in another room, straining to convince themselves that what they were seeing was really a human face.

Baird was secretive about his system, refusing technical journalists an opportunity to see it, but it is based on an idea first suggested by the German Paul Nipkow in 1884. A spinning disc containing a series of lenses converts light from the image into electrical signals, which can be sent by wireless to a receiver, where they are converted back into an image on a fluorescent screen using a cathode-ray tube, a device invented in the 1890s.

The 'television' images measure just 5 centimetres (2 in) long by 3 centimetres (1½ in) wide, and are of poor quality. But Baird believes there is enormous potential for his invention and that every home could one day have its own receiving set – even if his belief in a mechanical television system is shared by very few other engineers.

··· ACTRESS JOAN CRAWFORD PIONEERS THE FASHION FOR BARE LEGS WITH EVENING WEAR AS HEMLINES RISE ···

Women no longer the weaker sex

6 AUGUST, DOVER

An American swimmer has landed a blow for women's sport by swimming the English Channel in a record-breaking time. At 14 hours and 31 minutes, the attempt beat by more than two hours the time established by Enrico Tiraboschi, which was the fastest effort since Captain Webb first swam the Channel back in 1875.

Gertrude Ederle, bronze medallist in the 400 metres freestyle at the 1924 Olympics, becomes the first woman to make a successful crossing and the first to do it from France to England.

The distance itself is not great – about 33 kilometres (20 miles) at the shortest crossing from Cap Gris Nez to Dover, the route take by Ederle. However, strong tides and swirling

currents make the actual swim a great deal longer. In addition, the swimmer must take on the icy cold and choppy water of the Channel and be ready to put up with the ever-present menace of stinging jellyfish. It all adds up to making the Channel swim an almost unbeatable test of strength and stamina. But the 18-year-old was prepared for her ordeal by a rigorous training programme, and was also protected from the elements by a thick layer of grease.

The *Daily Mail* can hardly have picked a worse time than this very morning to publish its opinion that 'even the most uncompromising champion of the rights and capacities of women must admit that in contests of physical skill, speed and endurance, they must remain forever the weaker sex'.

BON VOYAGE Covered in protective grease, Gertrude Ederle gets a supportive send-off in France for her cross-Channel swim.

Illustrious, peaceful era begins

25 DECEMBER, TOKYO
In a solemn ceremony within the royal compound, Prince Hirohito ascended Japan's chrysanthemum throne today. The new Emperor is a curious mixture of ancient and modern. With his spectacles and gentle demeanour he looks more like a science teacher than the latest in an ancient line.

But, like his predecessors, to the Japanese the young Emperor is divine. The royal family claims to be directly descended from Japan's native gods, and their bloodline goes back over 1000 years – longer than any other royal family in the world. Yet Hirohito is the first of his family to have

NEW DAWN Japan's Prince Hirohito, crowned Emperor today.

been to Europe and North America. He is also the first emperor to have a university degree, in marine biology.

Regent for the past five years since his father, Yoshihito, was declared insane, Hirohito has, as tradition dictates, chosen a title for his reign: *Showa*, or 'Illustrious Peace'.

Missing mystery queen found

14 DECEMBER, YORKSHIRE
Agatha Christie has been found safe and well at a Yorkshire spa, checked in under a false name. The best-selling authoress of murder mysteries disappeared on 5 December; her abandoned

car was found at the edge of a cliff. An intensive search of the area revealed no clues.

In a twist to rival her own plots, Mrs Christie is suffering from amnesia and remembers nothing about the past nine days.

STILL WATERS Police dragged lakes and pools in search of the missing woman.

WHEN LAUREL MET HARDY

Hollywood producer Hal Roach is tipping his protégés Stan Laurel and Oliver Hardy to become big stars as a double act. Roach signed up the two men separately, then saw their potential as a partnership. He has set them to work on the first 'Laurel and Hardy' short – *Putting Pants on Philip*.

Both men started out in vaudeville. Laurel, who comes from Lancashire, toured the USA in 1912 as Charlie Chaplin's understudy in the Fred Karno vaudeville show. After the tour he stayed in the USA, making his movie breakthrough in 1917. In one of his first films, *Lucky*

RISING STARS Timid Stan Laurel, bumptious Oliver Hardy and friend.

Dog, he played opposite Hardy, although they were not then a team. Hardy, who gave up a career as a lawyer because of his passion for the movies, hails from Harlem, Georgia. The two are developing a clowning double act, in which Laurel plays the helpless thin man, and Hardy his brash partner.

Birth of a princess

21 APRIL, LONDON
There is rejoicing in royal circles today with the announcement of the birth of Princess Elizabeth to the Duke and Duchess of York.

The baby was born at 17 Bruton Street, London, at 2.40 am, and was delivered by Caesarean section after the birth developed some complications. Queen Mary, the princess's grandmother, described the infant as 'a little darling with a lovely complexion'. She has been named Elizabeth Alexandra Mary – after her mother, rather than Queen Elizabeth, as it is unlikely that she will ever come to the throne.

··· SPANISH YOGHURT-MAKER ISAAC CARASSO MARKETS PREPACKED YOGHURT WITH ADDED FRUIT ···

1927

BORN
4 July: Gina Lollobrigida, Hollywood actress
13 Aug: Fidel Castro, Cuban Communist leader

DIED
14 June: Jerome K Jerome, British author
14 Sept: Isadora Duncan, US dancer

ASSASSINATED
10 July, Dublin: Kevin O'Higgins, Irish minister for justice and vice-president of the Irish Free State, by a faction of IRA

FLEW
15 Oct: French Capt Dieudonné Costes and Lt-Commander Le Brix, in *Nungesser et Coli*, from Senegal, W Africa, to Natal, Brazil, the first nonstop air crossing of South Atlantic; 18 hrs, 3360 km (2100 miles)

PUBLISHED
Virginia Woolf, *To the Lighthouse*
Martin Heidegger, *Being and Time*

FOUNDED
1 Jan, London: British Broadcasting Corporation; previously a company owned by wireless manufacturers, the BBC is made a public corporation
14 Mar, New York City: Pan-American Airways
26 Sept, New York City: Columbia Broadcasting System (CBS), new name and revamp for radio network United Independent Broadcasters
18 Nov, France: soccer World Cup, announced by Jules Rimet, head of International Football Association
Hollywood: the Academy of Motion Picture Arts and Sciences

Short hair and cloche hats continue to characterise the boyish fashion trends for women this year. The new look from Paris emphasises slim hips and flat chests – and style is defined by simple lines.

EXECUTED
9 June, Moscow: 20 alleged British spies
23 Aug, Massachusetts: Nicola Sacco and Bartolomeo Vanzetti, Italian political radicals convicted of murder
19 Dec, China: 600 people accused of being Communists, by Nationalists

UNVEILED
24 July, Belgium: Menin Gate war memorial at Ypres

FIRST NIGHTS
7 Apr, Paris: *Napoléon*, epic movie directed by Frenchman Abel Gance; shown simultaneously on three screens, it runs for 4 hrs 30 minutes
16 Apr, USA: *The King of Kings*, epic movie directed by Cecil B DeMille; it runs for 2 hours 35 minutes
22 Nov, New York City: *Funny Face*, musical with tunes by George Gershwin

27 Dec, New York City: *Showboat*, musical by Jerome Kern and Oscar Hammerstein II

OPENED
15 Jan, San Francisco: Dumbarton Bridge, first to carry cars over San Francisco Bay
29 Jan, London: Park Lane Hotel, first in Britain to offer a private bathroom for every bedroom

FLOODED
May, USA: Mississippi Valley, following heavy rains; hundreds drown and 675000 are homeless
1 Sept, Poland: parts of Galicia – 200 die, 15000 are made homeless
14 Sept, Japan: Kiu-Siu Island, hit by tidal wave; 3000 die

BANNED
18 Oct, Germany: dancing bears, from streets of Berlin

DISCOVERED
29 Oct, China: tomb of the 12th-century Mongol warrior leader Genghis Khan, by Russian archaeologist Peter Kozlov

SIGNED
20 May, Saudi Arabia: Treaty of Jeddah: Britain recognises independence of Saudi Arabia
14 June, Managua: US–Nicaragua treaty – US gains right to intervene in Nicaragua at times of unrest, in return for aid

FIRSTS
30 June: Ryder Cup golf contest; US team defeats British-Irish team
6 Oct: trading in foreign shares on New York Stock Exchange

27 Oct, New York City: news film with sound, the *Fox Movietone News*
13 Nov, London: automatic telephone exchange in Britain, at Holborn
13 Nov, New York City: tunnel under Hudson River

INVENTED
29 July, New York City: iron lung, by doctors Philip Drinker and Louis Shaw, at Bellevue Hospital

NEW WORDS
nappy *n*: a piece of soft towelling or other material wrapped around a baby to absorb its excrement
white-collar *adj*: belonging to the ranks of office workers

The opulent, clean lines of the Art Deco style, now at its height, are inspired by recent finds from ancient Egyptian and other non-Western art traditions. The interplay of geometric shapes, abstract patterns and brilliant colours is epitomised in architecture by the portal of London's Hoover Building, opened in 1932.

An epic flight from New York to Paris

LUCKY LINDY In flight, Lindbergh munched on home-made sandwiches.

21 MAY, PARIS
Cheering crowds mobbed US aviator Charles Lindbergh after he landed today at Le Bourget airfield following a gruelling 5800-kilometre (3600-mile) flight from New York.

The 25-year-old marched straight into the record books as the first person to fly solo and nonstop across the huge expanse of the Atlantic Ocean. During his flight, which lasted 33 hours and 30 minutes, Lindbergh triumphed over fog, ice – and a desperate urge to sleep. Because of intense preparations he had already been awake for 36 hours when he took off from Roosevelt Field, New York, in his Ryan aeroplane, the *Spirit of St Louis*. More than once during the flight he had

to stick his head into the freezing air outside the cockpit to keep himself awake.

The *Spirit of St Louis* was custom-built for the long-haul flight, with extra-wide wings, a powerful 237-horsepower engine and a vast fuel tank positioned in front of the cockpit, which meant that Lindbergh needed a periscope to see in front of him. When he took off early on 20 May he had 1215 kilos (2700 lb) of fuel on board. The Ryan lumbered into the air, only just missing a clump of trees at the runway's end.

Its pilot, a reserved young man from the midwestern USA, makes an unlikely hero. But flying is Lindbergh's passion. He bought his own Curtiss Jenny in 1922, and in two years he was a stunt pilot. Prior to this attempt Lindbergh was working as an airmail pilot on the St Louis–Chicago run.

He wins the $25000 prize offered for the first solo transatlantic flight – while his Ryan cost him just $6000.

CINEMA SPEAKS

'Wait a minute! ... You ain't heard nothin' yet!' said Al Jolson. Although a music accompaniment had always been part of the movies, these were the first words ever spoken on film.

The Jazz Singer, which opened in New York in October, is not a great picture. The story is corny and sentimental – the son of a Jewish cantor defies his father to become a Broadway star – and sound is mainly used for the songs, with only odd fragments of speech. But the words echoed around the world. Soon the silent movie will be a thing of the past.

AUDIBLE SUCCESS Al Jolson's famous words were ad-libbed.

··· THE FIRST TRANSATLANTIC TELEPHONE CALL COSTS $75 FOR THREE MINUTES – HALF THE COST OF A CAR ···

SULTAN OF SWAT Babe Ruth hits homer number 60 at Yankee Stadium.

Babe Ruth breaks home run record

How the Boston Red Sox have lived to regret trading Babe Ruth – admittedly for a record $125000 – to the New York Yankees seven years ago. This season he has hit 60 home runs, breaking his own record of 59 set in the 1921 season.

George Herman 'Babe' Ruth began his career as an outstanding pitcher and for Boston won twice as many games as he lost. But the Yankees bought him for his hitting, and the overweight, hard-drinking outfielder, who likes speakeasies more than training sessions, has handsomely repaid them. Year after year the 'Bambino' has consistently hit the Yankees to World Series victories.

1928

BORN
23 Apr: Shirley Temple, US actress
14 June: Ernesto 'Che' Guevara, Argentinian revolutionary
26 July: Stanley Kubrick, US film director
6 Aug: Andy Warhol, US artist

DIED
14 Jan: Thomas Hardy, British author
14 June: Emmeline Pankhurst, British suffragette
21 July: Ellen Terry, British actress

ENFRANCHISED
7 May: British women between 21 and 30, the 'flapper' vote

DISCOVERED
1 Mar: Vitamin F, by US scientist Dr Herbert Evans

INVENTED
The quartz crystal clock, by J W Horton and W A Morrison in the USA
Bubble gum, Fleer's Dubble Bubble, in the USA

FIRSTS
3 July, USA: television sets go on sale, at $75
14 Aug, New York: scheduled TV programmes shown by WRNY
1 Oct, USSR: Five-Year Plan announced by Stalin, to replace Lenin's New Economic Policy
20 Dec, UK: chip shop opened by Harry Ramsden, outside Bradford
Female judge, on the US Customs Court, Genevieve Cline
Royal Flying Doctor Service, in Queensland, Australia
Solo flight from England to Australia; Bert Hinkler flies London–Darwin in 15 days

Umberto Nobile's voyage across the North Pole in his airship Italia ended in disaster when the ship crashed; the crew spent 40 days on the ice before being rescued. Ironically, Roald Amundsen, the Norwegian explorer, was killed in a plane crash during a rescue attempt on the day that the lost crew was found.

RECORDS
19 Feb, Florida: land speed record of 332 km/h (206 mph) set by Malcolm Campbell at Daytona
26 Mar, New York City: record trading on US stock market, nearly five million shares sold in one day

SIGNED
27 Aug: Kellogg-Briand Pact to prevent war signed by 15 countries

CROWNED
1 Sept: King Zog of Albania, a newly declared kingdom

ELECTED
6 Oct: Chiang Kai-shek, president of China
7 Nov: Herbert Hoover, Republican President of the USA, winning a huge majority over Democrat Al Smith with his promise of 'a chicken in every pot and a car in every garage'

OPENED
28 July, Amsterdam: the eighth modern Olympic Games, with 46 countries participating

LAUNCHED
1 Aug: the Morris Minor, one of Morris Motors' most popular cars
22 Nov: the £1 and ten-shilling notes into circulation in Britain

BANNED
6 Apr: handshaking in Italy, pronounced unhygienic by Mussolini
July: *The Well of Loneliness* by Radclyffe Hall, deemed obscene for its open treatment of lesbianism

DEVASTATED
16 Sept: Florida, by a hurricane killing 2000 people

FLOODED
29 Dec, London: the Tate Gallery, when the river Thames overflows; priceless pictures stored in the basement are ruined

FOUNDED
Chicago: first US school for training models, L'Ecole de Mannequins
Atlanta, Georgia: the African-American daily newspaper *Atlanta World*

COMPLETED
15 Feb: the Oxford English Dictionary, after 70 years' work costing £300 000

PUBLISHED
Aldous Huxley, *Point Counter Point*
D H Lawrence, *Lady Chatterley's Lover* (printed privately in Florence)
Federico García Lorca, *Gipsy Ballads*
Evelyn Waugh, *Decline and Fall*
Virginia Woolf, *Orlando*

ABOLISHED
UK: the use of the lance as a weapon of war, by the British War Office

The first Ford Model A rolls off the production line, succeeding the famous Model T. The Model A can reach up to 114 km/h (71 mph), having twice the horsepower of the Model T. It also boasts a shatterproof windscreen and a raised gearstick for easier manipulation.

NEW WORDS
cocktail *n*: an appetiser of seafoods, mixed fruits, etc
media *n*: a collective noun that covers a variety of forms of communication, including print, radio and television
socialite *n*: a person who is or who seeks to be prominent in fashionable society

Bacteria's nemesis: a miraculous green mould

GERMBUSTER Fleming at his laboratory bench with cultures of the antibacterial mould *Penicillium*.

30 SEPTEMBER, LONDON

The Scottish biologist Professor Alexander Fleming has discovered an antibacterial agent that destroys many kinds of harmful bacteria. The unassuming mould, belonging to the genus *Penicillium notatum*, may turn out to be one of the most significant medical discoveries of the century.

A fortunate accident in Fleming's cluttered laboratory at St Mary's Hospital led to the discovery. After mistakenly leaving a dish of the *Staphylococcus* bacterial culture uncovered, he noticed that an interesting green fungus had formed on the surface, destroying the sections of bacteria with which it came into contact. With some amusement,

Fleming attributed the discovery to his untidiness, remarking that it could never have occurred in the pristine laboratories run by some of his colleagues.

As an army medic during the war, Fleming had to tackle the problem of rampant wound infections; often soldiers died of these infections rather than the underlying injuries. After the war Fleming returned to London and began his research into antibacterial substances. This year he was appointed professor of bacteriology.

The quest for an antibacterial drug is not new. In 1909 the German doctor Paul Ehrlich developed Salvarsan, which proved useful in combating the bacteria that caused syphilis. The problem has been to find a drug that destroys a wide range of harmful bacteria but is non-toxic to humans. Most of the drugs experimented with so far have had serious side-effects.

Fleming found that *Penicillium*, a relative of the mould that grows on bread, does not harm white blood cells, indicating that it may be safe for human use. The problem now is how to turn the fungus into a pharmaceutical drug.

··· BRITISH ACTRESS HERMIONE BADDELEY CAUSES SCANDAL BY WEARING TROUSERS AT HER WEDDING RECEPTION ···

Flyers now span the Pacific Ocean

9 JUNE, BRISBANE

Another great natural barrier has been conquered by aviators seeking a place in the history books. Australian ex-RAF pilots Charles 'Smithy' Kingsford Smith and Charles Ulm landed today after the first flight across the Pacific, the world's largest ocean. With American navigators James Warner and Harry Lyon, they left San Francisco on 31 May in their Fokker monoplane *Southern Cross* and touched

down in Hawaii and Fiji in the course of their 11770-kilometre (7300-mile) flight.

The first leg of their record-breaking flight, to Honolulu, took 27 hours. After refuelling there the Fokker was so heavy that they could not take off on the available runway and had to transfer to a beach. It took them a further 34 hours to reach Fiji. The worst part of the journey was just after Fiji when the Fokker's compass went wrong and they were

AUSTRALIAN DREAM The tri-motor *Southern Cross* is checked prior to take-off.

almost brought down by violent thunderstorms that raged around the aeroplane for four hours.

Ten days after the aeroplane left the United States the crew arrived in Brisbane to an ovation.

A surreal year

In the art world, attention continues to focus on the activities of the Surrealists. This controversial movement burst onto the scene four years ago, when André Breton issued his *Manifesto of Surrealism* – in it he called upon writers and painters to create art of the subconscious, in which dream and reality merged into 'an absolute reality, a super-reality'.

The Surrealists take their ideas from two main sources. They are inspired by the visual anarchy of Dadaism, a nihilistic art movement which reflects the horror and despair of war; and they are greatly influenced by Freud's theories about dreams and unconscious sexual drives. At the start Surrealism was chiefly a literary movement, but painting has now become its chief outlet, with two distinct approaches. Artists such as Max Ernst and Joan Miró attempt to tap into the subconscious by building up pictures from doodles and automatic drawings. Others, such as Dali and Magritte, create hallucinatory effects by juxtaposing strange objects, painted with dreamlike clarity.

This technique is not confined to painting. One of this year's notable achievements was the collaboration between Dali and the film-maker Luis Buñuel. Together they produced *Un Chien Andalou* (An Andalusian Dog), a bizarre 17-minute film.

IRREVERENCE Ernst's *Mary Spanking the Christ Child* (1926) challenges eyes and ideas.

HI-DE-HO Cab Calloway, the 'king of scat', helped to turn jazz into mainstream entertainment.

Popular music gets syncopated

Jazz came of age in the 1920s. It grew up in the brothels of New Orleans, where the 'jazzmen' played to entertain the customers, blending West African rhythms, European harmonies and gospel. The music was jaunty and fast-moving, a mix of ornate melodies played on high-pitched cornets or saxophones over a complex syncopated bassline, with a large dose of improvisation.

Jazz has spread like an epidemic across America to London and Paris. In New York the outrageously talented Louis Armstrong broadcasts regularly from the Savoy Ballroom, and stars with his 'Stompers' – featuring Earl Hines on piano – at the Sunset Café.

Meanwhile Duke Ellington rocks Harlem's Cotton Club with hits such as 'Creole Love Call'. 'Dixie' has evolved into an adventurous sophisticated sound, and its rhythms have been seized on by classical composers.

Jazz music has even featured in concert halls, with orchestras playing complex arrangements. No form of popular music has ever achieved such cultural dominance: this is the Jazz Age.

Americans lose face at Amsterdam Olympics

FLEET-FOOTED FINN Paavo Nurmi breaks the 10000 metres record, clocking in at 30 minutes 18.8 seconds.

12 AUGUST, AMSTERDAM
American track athletes, for many years supreme in international competition, have been brought down to earth with a bump at this year's Olympic Games in Amsterdam. Paavo Nurmi, hero of the Paris Games of 1924, and the crowd's favourite, stepped up to the 10000 metres distance and, despite suffering from injury and rheumatism, won the gold medal, finishing ahead of his compatriot Ville Ritola. Ritola had his revenge in the 5000 metres, pushing Nurmi into second place.

But what has really reddened American faces is the double victory of the Canadian sprinter Percy Williams in the 100 metres and 200 metres. No American finished in the medals in either race, and the once almost invincible team has returned home with only one athletics victory to its credit. The decline of the United States reflects the increasing international flavour of the Games, which this year drew competitors from 46 nations.

Americans have been partly consoled by the terrific performance of the romantic heart-throb Johnny Weissmuller in the pool. Immediately recognisable by his revolutionary high-in-the-water crawl stroke, Weissmuller added two gold medals – in the 4 x 200 metres freestyle relay and the 100 metres – to the three he won in 1924.

More notable than America's disappointing results has been the introduction of five athletics events for women, until now previously restricted to swimming races. Anxious to prove their worth, the women have suffered a setback. The 800 metres took such a distressing toll on the competitors that the event has been dropped from the next Games which will be held in Los Angeles in four years' time.

··· THE SMEAR TEST FOR UTERINE AND CERVICAL CANCER IS INVENTED BY A NEW YORK DOCTOR ···

Threepenny Opera earns high praise

1 SEPTEMBER, BERLIN
Bertolt Brecht's new play,
***The Threepenny Opera* – the fruit of his collaboration with composer Kurt Weill – opened last night** to an enthusiastic response from the audience, securing the German playwright's fame and literary reputation.

Loosely based on John Gay's 18th-century ballad opera *The Beggar's Opera*, but with the action placed in seedy Edwardian London, Brecht's version is a bitter satire on the corrupt bourgeois society of postwar Germany. Weill's musical score is a perfect complement to the play, boldly using the rhythms and motifs of jazz in a serious context.

The play's controversial characters and content have generated considerable media

MARXIST SUCCESS Bertolt Brecht, the 30-year-old poet and playwright.

interest and scandal – a phenomenon that has, if anything, added to its success – and the bourgeois circles that are satirised in the play are flocking to see it.

Brecht views his plays as social experiments, requiring detachment rather than passion from his audiences. But *The Threepenny Opera*, which was originally intended as a piece of avant-garde art, seems to be genuinely popular with the wider public.

1929

BORN

15 Jan: Martin Luther King, US civil rights leader
30 May: Audrey Hepburn, US actress
26 June: Anne Frank, German-born author of *The Diary of a Young Girl*
12 Nov: Grace Kelly, US actress and Princess of Monaco
12 Dec: John Osborne, British playwright

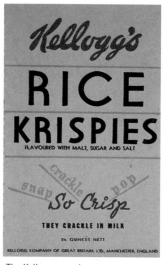

The Kellogg cereal company launches Rice Krispies, puffed rice that is said to 'snap, crackle and pop' in the breakfast bowl. The company, now more than 20 years old, is making a name for itself worldwide.

DIED

12 Feb: Lillie Langtry, British actress and courtesan
19 Aug: Sergei Diaghilev, Russian impresario

OPENED

8 Nov, New York City: Museum of Modern Art

Popeye the Sailor Man debuts in the 'Thimble Theatre' strip created by Elzie Segar. The strip has been running for ten years and depicts the adventures of Olive Oyl, her brother Castor Oyl and her boyfriend Ham Gravy. Popeye quickly becomes the principal and most popular character in the strip.

20 Nov, Paris: first exhibition of works by Salvador Dali

LAUNCHED

10 Jan: Tintin, created by Hergé (Georges Rémi) in a Belgian newspaper
7 July: Transcontinental Air Transport Co, the first US coast-to-coast passenger service, soon to become Trans World Airlines (TWA)
Oct: Bib-Label Lithiated Lemon-Lime Soda, soon to become 7-Up

FIRSTS

22 Apr: British municipal airport opens, at Chat Moss, Manchester
16 May: Academy Awards presented in Hollywood, by the Academy's president, Douglas Fairbanks
10 June: woman in British cabinet – Margaret Bondfield is minister of labour in Ramsay MacDonald's government
27 June: colour television pictures transmitted from New York to Washington
28–29 Nov: flight over the South Pole, by US naval commander Richard Byrd
Nudist colony, in New Jersey, USA

MASSACRED

Aug: 133 Jews, by Palestinians in Jerusalem, over use of the Wailing Wall

INVENTED

Car radio, by US engineer Paul Galvin
Synchromesh gearbox, installed in Cadillacs in the USA
Do-it-yourself hair colouring in ten shades (Nestlé Colorinse)
Front-wheel drive, in the 'coffin-nose' Cord L–29
Electric food waste disposal unit, by General Electric Company
Blattnerphone, an improved magnetic tape recorder by Louis Blattner, to help synchronise the soundtracks of his movies

JAILED

17 May: Al Capone and his bodyguard 'Slippery Frank' Cline, for one year, for carrying concealed deadly weapons

BANNED

14 Feb: dancer Josephine Baker from the Munich stage, for indecent behaviour
22 May: beauty contests in Italy, by Mussolini, who branded them immoral

SIGNED

11 Feb: Lateran Treaty, by Mussolini and the Pope, granting Vatican City State independence from Italy

CLASHED

22 Sept: Communists and Nazis on the streets of Berlin

Louise Brooks stars in Pandora's Box, *the silent film that makes a stir this year. Produced in Germany, the controversial film tells of a woman who kills her lover before becoming a prostitute. She is finally murdered in London by Jack the Ripper.*

EXILED

30 Jan, USSR: Leon Trotsky and 1600 followers, to Siberia for 'anti-Soviet' activities

SEIZED

4 July: 12 paintings of nudes by D H Lawrence from a London gallery by police, after complaints by the press and public

NEW WORD

lifestyle *n*: a set of attitudes, habits or possessions associated with a particular person or group; certain attitudes, etc, regarded as fashionable or desirable

SHARES PLUMMET ON 'BLACK THURSDAY'

WALL STREET CRASH Shocked crowds gather opposite the New York Stock Exchange as the market collapses.

24 OCTOBER, NEW YORK CITY
The financial boom of the last few years came to an abrupt end today when prices on the New York Stock Exchange in Wall Street fell dramatically, causing thousands of speculators to panic and sell their shares at virtually any price that was offered.

The financial crash was as sudden as it was devastating. In the years leading up to what has already been dubbed 'Black Thursday' there had been a period of wild speculation on the stock market, with investors rushing to make massive and quick profits. The market had seemed unstoppable and invincible – just weeks before the crash, on 3 September, a record high of eight million shares was sold. But panic hit as the bottom fell out of the market today, and share prices went into free fall.

Thousands of Americans have seen their life savings wiped out in a matter of hours, in the biggest catastrophe ever to hit the financial world. The disaster will affect economies all over the world and, it is feared, could trigger a serious depression worldwide.

··· 25 MAR: MUSSOLINI'S FASCIST PARTY CLAIMS 99 PER CENT OF THE VOTE IN ITALY'S GENERAL ELECTION ···

Mob takes on mob in bloody massacre on St Valentine's Day

14 FEBRUARY, CHICAGO
The war between Chicago's gangland bosses was stepped up a notch today as seven of 'Bugs' Moran's men were mercilessly shot to death.

The men were waiting to meet Moran at an illegal beerhall this morning when five men, three in police uniform, burst in. They lined the mobsters up against the wall and opened fire with sub-machine-guns.

The five supposed 'police' were in fact rival mobsters, probably from 'Scarface' Al Capone's gang. Moran is Capone's greatest rival and missed today's massacre only by minutes. Although Capone is currently in Florida, few doubt that he is behind the killings.

VIOLENT END Capone establishes his gangland supremacy when seven of Moran's men are gunned down.

Hundreds of mobsters have died in Chicago's gangland wars as Capone mounts a determined bid for control of gambling, protection rackets and illegal alcohol sales rumoured to be worth $100 million a year. Several key city officials, including the mayor, are said to be on Capone's payroll, and almost half of Chicago's police force is under investigation for alleged corruption.

1930

BORN
2 Mar: Stephen Sondheim, US composer
31 May: Clint Eastwood, US actor
5 Aug: Neil Armstrong, US astronaut
25 Aug: Sean Connery, British actor
10 Oct: Harold Pinter, British playwright

DIED
2 Mar: D H Lawrence, British author
8 Mar: William Howard Taft, US statesman
7 July: Sir Arthur Conan Doyle, British author

DISCOVERED
1 Jan: the site of the biblical city of Sodom, north of the Dead Sea
30 July, China: the million-year-old skull of a man, at Chou Kou Tien

LAUNCHED
Bugatti Royale, largest production car ever built, by Italian automobile manufacturer Ettore Bugatti

Otto Rohwedder's first attempt at sliced bread in 1928 proved unsuccessful – his device for holding the loaf together was a hatpin. But he has now developed a machine that wraps as well as slices bread, and the idea has taken off. A bakery in Battle Creek, Michigan, turned out the first loaf, and sliced bread was soon on sale around the world.

FIRSTS
3 Feb, India: 'untouchable' elected onto local council, in Bengal
25 Apr, Darwin: woman to fly solo to Australia; Amy Johnson left Britain on 5 April
Sept, New Jersey: electric passenger train
Airline stewardess: Ellen Church, employed by United Airlines after a second pilot spills coffee over a passenger

INVENTED
Analog computer, or differential analyser, by electrical engineer Vannevar Bush, at Massachusetts Institute of Technology, Boston
Electric kettle with automatic cut-out, by General Electric Company

KILLED
USSR: a daily average of 40 *kulaks* (wealthy peasants) by Stalin's forces, as part of the collectivisation programme

SUPPRESSED
300 films, by British Board of Film Censors, for depicting intoxicated women, clergy in 'equivocal situations', affluent criminals and marital infidelity

APPROVED
14 Mar: a proposed tunnel linking England and France, by the Channel Tunnel Committee
14 Aug: the cautious use of contraception, by the Church of England

BANNED
30 Dec: contraception for Catholics, by the papal encyclical of Pius XI

On February 18, 24-year-old amateur astronomer Clyde Tombaugh discovers Pluto, the smallest planet in the solar system. Tombaugh was working at the Lowell Observatory in Flagstaff, Arizona. This is an artist's impression of Pluto (pink) and its moon Charon (blue).

ARRESTED
10 Feb, Chicago: 158 people and 31 corporations, for bootlegging – held responsible for sales of 27 million litres (7 million US gal) of whiskey across the USA

RECORDS
6 Jan: Australian cricketer Don Bradman scores 452 not out in a single innings
Ocean dive to 1400 feet by American explorers Otis Barton and William Beebe, using the new bathysphere, a deep-sea observation instrument

TRIUMPHED
15 Sept, Germany: the Nazis poll 6.5 million votes in the general election, becoming the second largest party in the country
7 Dec, London: 13-year-old US violinist Yehudi Menuhin plays to an audience of more than 5000 in the Albert Hall

SHOWN
American Gothic, painting by Grant Woods, which caused a sensation when exhibited at the Art Institute of Chicago

SCREEN HITS
Animal Crackers, starring the Marx Brothers
The Blood of a Poet, directed by Jean Cocteau
Blackmail, directed by Alfred Hitchcock

AWARDED
4 May: Pulitzer Prize to US poet Robert Frost for *Collected Poems*
10 Dec: Nobel Prize for literature to US novelist Sinclair Lewis

On 2 November, Ras Tafari, regent of Ethiopia, is crowned Emperor and takes the name Haile Selassie ('Might of the Trinity'). His ascension follows the death of his cousin, the Empress Zauditu. Haile Selassie claims descent from the line of Solomon and the Queen of Sheba.

NEW WORDS
whodunnit *n*: a novel, play, etc, dealing with a crime, usually murder; from the question 'Who done it?'
odds and sods *pl n*: miscellaneous items or articles

Airship explodes on maiden voyage

5 OCTOBER, BEAUVAIS, FRANCE Flames raged in the night as the British airship R 101 – carrying thousands of cubic metres of hydrogen – exploded after crashing on its debut flight from Britain to India. British Secretary of State for Air Lord Thomson was among the 48 passengers and crew who died in the inferno. An eyewitness says it was 'as if the whole world had exploded'.

The R 101 was one of two airships built under the government's Imperial Airship Scheme to fly to distant British territories. Built by the privately owned Vickers company, the R 100 made a successful maiden flight two months ago. The R 101, built by the nationalised Royal Airship Works, was rushed into service before it was fully ready – partly because of competition with its sister ship.

The R 101 handled badly from the start; bad weather made things worse, forcing the ship down near Beauvais. It bumped along the ground, buffeted by gusts, and finally exploded into flames all along its 237-metre (777-ft) length.

SUMPTUOUS SELF-CONFIDENCE Chrysler's building is decorated with motifs influenced by car design.

Elaborate Chrysler Building is world's tallest

New York's most flamboyant skyscraper, the Chrysler Building, has been built for the car manufacturer Walter Chrysler by the architect William van Allen.

Under construction at the same time as the new Bank of Manhattan, the Chrysler Building was to be 280 metres (925 ft) high, just half a metre less than its rival. But thanks to the last minute addition of a stainless steel sunburst-patterned spire – built in secret – the skyscraper, at 317 metres (1046 ft), is the tallest in the world. This stunning Art Deco masterpiece is a monument to the business boom of the 1920s – now fast fading into memory.

UNGAINLY GIANT The R 101 at its mooring mast.

··· 'BLONDIE AND DAGWOOD', THE US COMIC STRIP, IS CREATED BY CHIC YOUNG ···

PEACEFUL DEFIANCE The slight figure of Mahatma Gandhi with his supporters on the long march for salt.

Gandhi marches for salt in India

12 MARCH, ASIALI, INDIA
Indian nationalist leader Mahatma
Gandhi has begun his march to the sea.
The march is part of the campaign of
non-violent 'civil disobedience' that he
hopes will end British rule in India.

Gandhi and a group of followers plan
to walk to the Gulf of Gambay from
central India. At the seashore they will
make salt; this breaks British law, which
protects a government monopoly on salt

manufacture. All salt in India is taxed, and
all the tax belongs to the British Crown.

Despite Gandhi's non-violent stance,
British troops have been put on the alert
across India. The bespectacled leader,
who dresses in a holy man's white *dhoti*,
has many followers, and the authorities
are expecting noisy demonstrations.

Gandhi is likely to be arrested, but
he said that he was prepared 'for the worst,
even death, in defiance of the salt tax'.

Uruguay wins football's first World Cup

30 JULY, MONTEVIDEO, URUGUAY
The host country, Uruguay, has won a
dramatic victory in the first
tournament for football's World Cup,
coming from 2–1 behind at half time to
defeat Argentina 4–2 at the final whistle.

MOMENTOUS OCCASION Jules Rimet, president of
FIFA, presents the trophy to the Uruguayans.

It was no surprise that the game,
fought out in front of 90 000 fans packed
into Montevideo's Centenario Stadium,
was an all-South American affair. Teams
from Great Britain, embroiled in a
dispute with FIFA over professionalism
versus amateurism and other matters,
were ineligible, and only four European
sides – from Belgium, France, Romania
and Yugoslavia – made the arduous
transatlantic journey to compete in the
tournament. By lifting the Jules Rimet
trophy – named after the French
president of FIFA – Uruguay's footballers have put the icing on the cake
for their country's celebrations of 100
years of national independence.

Freezing technique heralds new food age

6 JUNE, MASSACHUSETTS
A new product has gone on the market
today: frozen peas. Frozen meat has
been available for some time, but peas
are the first vegetable to be frozen
successfully. Consumers can now eat
food out of season, or transported from
the other side of the world – heralding
a revolution in our eating habits.

The idea of freezing food to
preserve it is nothing new, but the
problem has been to prevent the food
from becoming tasteless and soggy
when thawed. A few years ago the
American businessman and inventor
Clarence Birdseye pioneered a method
of freezing small packages of food
between two refrigerated metal plates, a
technique that worked more efficiently
– and preserved taste more effectively –
than anything hitherto devised.

Birdseye, a former fur-trader, was
inspired to experiment by his
observation of the food-preserving
techniques of the people of Labrador.
He founded his General Seafood
Company in 1924, selling out in 1928;
this year he became president of
Birdseye Frosted Foods, ushering in a
new era of convenience and choice.

BIRDSEYE VIEW Peas and other 'frosted' vegetables
are now available, thanks to Clarence Birdseye.

Dietrich triumphs in *The Blue Angel*

STAR QUALITY Marlene Dietrich's sizzling performance in *The Blue Angel* is a masterpiece of sensuality.

German movie actress Marlene Dietrich rocketed to stardom this year as a seductive cabaret singer in the talking picture *The Blue Angel*. It was Dietrich's first major film role, although she had already acted in 17 movies over a period of seven years. It was also her first collaboration with director Josef von Sternberg, who described *The Blue Angel* as 'a celluloid monument' to the actress.

Dietrich gives a provocative performance as the heartless dancehall singer Lola, who ruins the life of a respectable school professor hopelessly obsessed with her. The film has been an international success – for many, it is the definitive portrait of decadent city life in postwar Germany.

··· WORLDWIDE, 250 MILLION PEOPLE GO TO THE CINEMA EVERY WEEK ···

Bobby Jones wins golf's prestigious grand slam

27 AUGUST, PHILADELPHIA

Robert Tyre (Bobby) Jones, the finest amateur golfer in the world and the only one consistently to beat the professionals, has compiled one of the towering records in sport by pulling off the grand slam.

The young American sporting hero, unassuming and undemonstrative, but accompanied wherever he played by an adoring band of disconcertingly noisy admirers, has held on to his copybook form throughout the long season to win the Open and Amateur championships of both the United States and Great Britain. The British Amateur victory, of which he said 'There has been nothing in golf I wanted so much', had eluded him for nine years; the American Open he won in temperatures that soared over 38° C (100° F). His extraordinary triumph of technique and temperament has never before been achieved, and most experts in the game thought it was virtually impossible.

Jones, an engineering graduate from Georgia Tech and a practising lawyer, announced his retirement from competition almost immediately. Over his career the 28-year-old won five US Amateur championships, four US Opens, three British Opens and one British Amateur – all in the space of eight years.

In 1934, with Clifford Roberts, he will found the Augusta National Golf Club in Georgia, the site every year thereafter of the Masters' championship.

NATIONAL HERO Victorious Bobby Jones has no more golfing challenges left.

1931

BORN
8 Feb: James Dean, US actor
2 Mar: Mikhail Gorbachev, Soviet leader
11 Mar: Rupert Murdoch, Australian media tycoon

DIED
23 Jan: Anna Pavlova, Russian ballerina
23 Feb: Dame Nellie Melba, Australian soprano
18 Oct: Thomas Alva Edison, US inventor and businessman

CINEMA IDOLS
James Cagney in *The Public Enemy*
Clark Gable in *A Free Soul*

CONVICTED
25 Mar, Alabama: nine black Scottsboro boys, for raping two white girls on a train, provoking outcry in their defence; convictions later overturned
17 Oct: Al 'Scarface' Capone, for tax evasion, sentenced to 11 years in jail

INVADED
18 Sept: Manchuria, by the Japanese army

SCREEN HITS
Dracula, starring Bela Lugosi
Frankenstein, starring Boris Karloff, launching his career as a horror-film icon – the part was turned down by Bela Lugosi

BUILT
Christ the Redeemer, a monumental concrete statue on a hilltop in Rio de Janeiro, Brazil – it stands 38 m (125 ft) tall and the out-stretched arms span 28 m (92 ft)

PUNCHED
14 May, Rome: the conductor Arturo Toscanini, for refusing to play the Fascist anthem; his passport was later taken away

OPENED
14 July, Spain: Republican Cortes (parliament), after the abdication of the King
25 Oct, New York City: George Washington Bridge, the world's longest suspension bridge
13 Nov, New York City: the Whitney Museum of American Art
Sadler's Wells Theatre, recently rebuilt, in London

Alka Seltzer is launched using the advertising gimmick Speedy. The alkaline remedy, a cure for upset stomachs and hangovers, comes in tablet form which fizzes and dissolves when added to water.

MARRIED
7 Feb: aviator Amelia Earhart to New York publisher George Putnam, on the condition that she retains her full independence after marriage

British Prime Minister Ramsay MacDonald leads the first meeting of the new cabinet. To avert an economic crisis, MacDonald, who has led the Labour government since 1929, forms a controversial coalition with the Conservative opposition.

INVENTED
Electron microscope, by Max Knott and Ernst Ruska in Berlin
Electronic flash photography, by Harold Edgerton of Massachusetts Institute of Technology, Boston

PUBLISHED
Virginia Woolf, *The Waves*

BANNED
31 Dec, Moscow: the music of Sergei Rachmaninov, for being 'decadent', in the USSR

SHAKEN
7 June: Britain, by its most violent earthquake on record

ENTERTAINED
4 Nov, London: Mahatma Gandhi, wearing a loincloth and shawl, by George V and Queen Mary in formal attire, at the Round Table Conference

WRECKED
22 Dec, Rome: the Vatican Library, by a collapsing roof

INTRODUCED
10 Jan, UK: Mrs Wallis Simpson to the Prince of Wales, the start of a scandalous affair

LAUNCHED
6 Mar, USA: the comic strip *Little Orphan Annie* as a radio show by NBC, featuring Annie and her rich benefactor Oliver 'Daddy' Warbucks
USA: pick-up truck, by Chevrolet; the vehicle comes with a drop-back for easy loading and unloading

On 2 February, *Charlie Chaplin's new film* City Lights *premieres in London. One of the scenes, in which a blind flower-seller recognises Chaplin as a rich man, took 343 takes to get right, over a period of six months.*

NEW WORDS
black market *n*: the act of illegally buying and selling goods in violation of legal price controls; a place in which to do so
microwave *n*: an electromagnetic wave of extremely high frequency
pulp fiction *n*: a magazine or book containing trite or sensational material, usually printed on cheap, rough paper

Matterhorn's north face is scaled

SUPREME CHALLENGE The Matterhorn's distinctive peak towers above Zermatt in Switzerland.

4 AUGUST, SWITZERLAND
Two young German students, brothers Franz and Toni Schmid, have conquered the Matterhorn's north face – where all before them had failed.

Sixty-six years after the Matterhorn, which straddles the Swiss-Italian border, was first scaled from the easier southern approaches, the brothers, both still in their twenties, have reached the summit by the treacherous northern route.

They left the Tiefenmatten glacier at daybreak and, assisted by fine weather,

made rapid progress up the side of the 4478-metre (14 640-ft) mountain. At 8.30 pm they hauled themselves on to the 'shoulder' at its summit, thus meeting the last great challenge of Alpine mountaineering.

And for their bravery and skill the 1932 Olympic committee will award them an extraordinary gold medal. However, only a few weeks later Toni, aged 23, will tragically be killed in a fall while climbing the north-west face of the Wiesbachhorn.

Tobacco companies say smoking is good for you

Arguments have raged over the effects of smoking on health ever since Sir Walter Raleigh brought tobacco to Europe. In the past few years competition has intensified, yet people have become more health-conscious, so cigarette companies have begun to promote their brands' health benefits.

The more modest of them merely claim that their cigarettes are less damaging than rival brands, usually thanks to filters: 'You needn't cut down smoking if you smoke Cooltipt', or 'Du Maurier … the filter tips will keep you fit'. Others go further, suggesting that

ATTRACTIVE PROMISE Cigarette advertisements claim that smokers are both stylish and healthy.

their brands could help smokers to lose weight – a claim that many ex-smokers will admit has at least a grain of truth.

In the absence of any legislative control, some advertisements have gone over the top, touting cigarettes as an aid to digestion and relieving fatigue. One asks readers to try to unbutton and rebutton their waistcoats with one hand, from top to bottom; if you can't do it in 12 seconds you probably have bad nerves and should take up smoking. As far as the smoking public is concerned, the habit is free of risks to health.

Top cop: Dick Tracy is an instant hit

Dick Tracy, America's most famous detective, made his first appearance this year in the *Detroit Mirror*. The square-jawed sleuth, with his trademark snapbrim fedora, is the creation of cartoonist Chester Gould, who draws him every day, including Sundays.

Tracy began as an amateur detective, but he soon joined the police force, where he has a full range of crime-fighting tools at his disposal – including the famous two-way wrist radio. The combination of colourful villains and black-and-white morality is a winning formula that will ensure the success of the strip for many years and inspire a radio series and several films.

At last, American anthem is officially adopted

3 MARCH, WASHINGTON DC
More than 150 years after the US Declaration of Independence, the 'land of the free and the home of the brave' at last has a national anthem. Whether most people can sing the tune is another matter, for it certainly tests the limits of any ordinary vocal cords.

'The Star Spangled Banner' will already be familiar to many Americans. Since the 1890s the army has been using a John Philip Sousa arrangement of the tune whenever an anthem was called for.

The words, which describe the American Revolution, were penned by Francis Scott Key in 1814 and are suitably stirring and patriotic. The origin of the tune, however, is obscure. Certainly it was sung during the Revolution, and

STAR PATRIOT Francis Key, who wrote the words.

apparently it was a drinking song – a hymn to the joys of Venus, the goddess of love, and Bacchus, the god of wine.

··· 'WATCH TOWER BIBLE AND TRACT SOCIETY' CHANGES ITS NAME TO 'JEHOVAH'S WITNESSES' ···

CAMPBELL IS FASTEST MAN ON LAND

5 FEBRUARY, DAYTONA, USA
British driver Malcolm Campbell seized the world land speed record from his late rival and countryman Henry Segrave today, reaching 395 kilometres per hour (246 mph) in his custom-built car *Bluebird* at Daytona Beach, Florida.

In wet and misty conditions on Daytona's hard-packed sands, Campbell broke the record on his first run. The only scare came earlier, during practice, when some spectators appeared on the race course. However, there was nothing to compare with the near-disaster of an earlier record triumph in February 1927, when he was blinded for a few seconds at full speed after the wind whipped his goggles off – 'a most terrifiyng moment,' Campbell said afterwards.

Today's triumph is the fifth time that Campbell has set the land speed record since 1924. With Segrave, he has given Britain the edge in a keen rivalry with the United States. In 1928 the American driver Ray Keech grabbed the record

FLYING FINISH Malcolm Campbell flashes across the finishing line, setting the new land speed record.

after Campbell had held it for two months. Then on 29 March 1929 Segrave took it back for Britain, hiking it to 372 kilometres per hour (231 mph). But Campbell's good-natured rivalry

with Segrave is sadly over, as the latter died on 13 June last year in an accident during a world water speed record attempt on Lake Windermere in northern England.

Empire State Building dwarfs all others

1 MAY, NEW YORK CITY
The world's tallest building was opened today. Planned in a boom but built in a slump, the Empire State Building is one of the few encouraging developments of Depression-hit America.

Towering over the New York skyline, it rose at the dizzying speed of five-and-a-half storeys a week to a height of 380 metres (1250 ft), with 102 storeys. The building contains 60 000 tons of steel beams, and was riveted together by teams working high above the ground. Iroquois and Mohawk Indians, bearing out their reputation for having no fear of heights, proved particularly adept.

With no place to store materials, every girder was delivered from Pittsburgh to a precise schedule, numbered to show where it should go, and in position within three days of manufacture. On each successive floor a small-gauge railway was set up to carry materials to the right spot, and portable kitchens provided lunch so that workers did not waste time descending to ground level.

TRIUMPH OF CONSTRUCTION Al Smith, head of the construction firm, salutes a model of the Empire State.

··· GERMAN FILM *MÄDCHEN IN UNIFORM* (GIRLS IN UNIFORM) IS THE FIRST CINEMA PORTRAYAL OF LESBIAN LOVE ···

Rickenbacker's Electric Guitar

Popular music has been transformed by developments in instrument technology. Rickenbacker is the market pioneer with its 'Frying Pan' steel guitar – the 'Electro Spanish' is another favourite, much copied by other manufacturers.

Adapted for use with amplification, guitars can now create sounds resembling the human voice. Notes can be sustained for longer, and the electric guitar is fast becoming the favourite instrument for solo passages, which have been made popular by blues and jazz and performed by the likes of Charlie Christian.

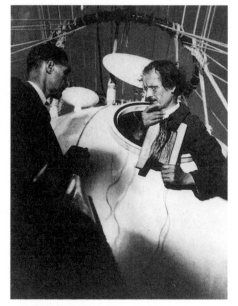

ELEMENTAL ASCENT Auguste Piccard's balloon flight was devised to study mysterious cosmic rays.

Piccard touches heaven

27 MAY, AUGSBURG, GERMANY
Swiss physicist Auguste Piccard and his assistant ascended in a balloon to an altitude of 15 780 metres (52 000 ft) – the first people to reach the stratosphere.

The men were carried in a pressurised gondola, with one side painted white to repel the Sun's rays and the other black to absorb them. Piccard planned to keep the temperature stable inside by using an electric motor to rotate away from the Sun or towards it. But the motor froze, temperatures rose and they were able to descend only when temperatures fell and the balloon's gas contracted.

1932

BORN
6 Feb: François Truffaut, French film director
27 Feb: Elizabeth Taylor, British-born actress
17 Aug: V S Naipaul, Indian author
29 Nov: Jacques Chirac, French statesman

DIED
6 Jan: André Maginot, French politician
14 Mar: George Eastman, founder of Kodak camera company

ABOLISHED
17 Apr: slavery in Ethiopia, by Emperor Haile Selassie

On **5 May,** *French president Paul Doumer is shot by a fanatical Russian anarchist, Pavel Gorgulov. Officials do their best to dissuade photographers as the injured president is carried away. The next day Doumer dies; his assassin is later guillotined.*

AWARDED
2 May: Pulitzer Prize to Pearl Buck for *The Good Earth*
10 Dec: Nobel Prize for literature to British writer John Galsworthy

OPENED
22 May, London: BBC Broadcasting House in Portland Place

The Mars bar is invented by American Forrest Mars in his laboratory in Slough, England, after experimenting on the Milky Way recipe given to him by his sweet-manufacturer father. Forrest Mars covered the Milky Way in caramel and chocolate to create the first ever chew bar – the Mars bar.

27 Dec, New York City: Radio City Music Hall, the world's largest theatre, in the Rockefeller Center

FIRSTS
27 Apr: regular airline service, between London and Cape Town
25 June, UK: Indian test match at Lord's cricket ground
25 Dec, UK: royal Christmas broadcast, by King George V

DECLARED
2 Jan: puppet state republic of Manchukuo in Manchuria, by the invading Japanese; ex-Emperor of China, Pu Yi, made president in March
18 July: new language regulations in Belgium; French becomes the official language of Walloon provinces and Flemish of Flanders

MUSIC HIT
Night and Day, by Cole Porter

DEFEATED
13 Mar: Adolf Hitler, by Field-Marshal Paul von Hindenburg, in German presidential elections, though Nazis go on to double their seats in the Reichstag in July

SPLIT
The atom, by John Cockcroft and Ernest Walton in Cambridge, demonstrating a new power source, nuclear energy

DISCOVERED
4 Apr: vitamin C, isolated by scientists C G King and W A Waugh at Pittsburgh, Pennsylvania
The neutron, by British physicist James Chadwick, at the Cavendish Laboratory, Cambridge

ELECTED
16 Feb: Eamon de Valera, president of the Irish Free State

INVENTED
Air conditioning, by Carrier Corp, USA

LIT UP
Piccadilly Circus, London, with flashing advertisements, 12 years after the first demonstration of neon lighting in Paris

REDUCED
June: German war reparations from $26 billion to $714 million, at the Lausanne Conference, Switzerland
15 July: President Hoover's salary, by a voluntary 20 per cent

CELEBRATED
Ireland: the 1550th anniversary of the arrival of Saint Patrick, the patron saint of Ireland

SCREEN HITS
Tarzan, The Ape Man, with Johnnie Weissmuller
Shanghai Express, directed by Josef von Sternberg, with Marlene Dietrich
Dr Jekyll and Mr Hyde, directed by Rouben Mamoulian

PUBLISHED
Ernest Hemingway, *Death in the Afternoon*
Aldous Huxley, *Brave New World*
Stella Gibbons, *Cold Comfort Farm*
Damon Runyon, *Guys and Dolls*
James Thurber, *The Secret Life of Walter Mitty*

NEW WORD
backlog *n*: an accumulation of uncompleted work
sweatsuit *n*: a set of garments made of soft, absorbent fabric, consisting of sweatpants and sweatshirt, often worn during athletic activity

Greta Garbo stars in yet another hit film, Grand Hotel, *in which she utters the memorable line: 'I vant to be alone'. The film consolidates her successful transition from silent to talking films. The Swedish actress arrived in America in 1925 and already has a string of films and an Oscar nomination behind her.*

WORLD PLUNGED INTO DEEP DEPRESSION

DEPRESSING SCENE North America is gripped by poverty and hunger, and many children are starving.

The depression has meant misery for the millions who have lost their jobs. By 1932 there were six million unemployed in Germany, three million in Britain, and more than 12 million in the USA. It is estimated that the income of more than a quarter of the American population comes from begging, charity handouts and limited public welfare. In many big cities, soup kitchens serving free food have been set up to feed the hungry.

Mass unemployment has led to homelessness; many people have been reduced to living in shanty towns made of tin and cardboard, dubbed 'Hoovervilles' after President Hoover. Farmers have been especially badly hit, since over-production led to an agricultural slump in the 1920s, and now a widespread drought has turned their land into a dust bowl.

The middle classes have also been affected, as small businesses and banks collapse. In the USA, investors have lost $74 billion on the stock exchange, 5000 banks have failed, and 86000 businesses have closed down. Around the world few governments have seemed able to cope with the crisis.

The worldwide depression, precipitated by the 1929 Wall Street Crash, reached an unprecedented peak this year.

The United States has been hit the hardest, but with many nations following its lead in imposing import tariffs to protect their own industries, prices and profits fell globally, as exports of raw material plummeted 70 per cent from their 1929 levels, ruining many countries.

··· FIRST PUBLICATION OF *FAMILY CIRCLE* MAGAZINE – DISTRIBUTED AT PIGGLY WIGGLY SUPERMARKETS IN USA ···

Roosevelt's New Deal sweeps him to power

8 NOVEMBER, WASHINGTON DC
In a resounding victory, the Democrat Franklin D Roosevelt has been elected as the new US President with one of the largest margins of victory ever seen in American politics. On a promise of a 'new deal for the American people', Roosevelt won the support of 42 states, while the defeated incumbent Herbert Hoover took only six.

The 50-year-old President-elect has been until now a successful and popular governor of New York State. Although paralysed from the waist down by polio for the past ten years and confined to a wheelchair, he fought an energetic campaign that took him all over the United States and brought him into contact with 'the forgotten man'.

The main issue in the election was how to revive the economy in the face of the current massive trade depression and soaring unemployment. Roosevelt has promised to take immediate action to solve the crisis and end the Great Depression when he takes office next year. The new President's ebullient personality, energy and enthusiasm have filled millions of Americans with renewed hope for the future.

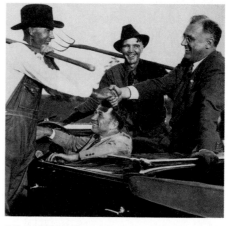

IT'S A DEAL Franklin D Roosevelt shakes hands with farmers while on a campaign tour in Georgia.

Flying hero's kidnapped son is found murdered

12 MAY, NEW JERSEY
The body of a baby boy found earlier this morning has been confirmed as that of Charles Lindbergh's son, who was kidnapped two months ago. The body was found less than 8 kilometres (5 miles) from his parents' home. A police spokesman said that it appeared that the child had been brutally murdered soon after the kidnapping.

On 2 March the 20-month-old toddler, Charles Junior, was snatched from his crib as his parents ate dinner. Kidnappers demanded $50000 from flying ace Lindbergh for the safe return of his son. The baby's distraught parents agreed to pay the ransom, but after the

money was delivered the kidnappers did not keep their part of the bargain.

After the infant was abducted, police moved swiftly to mount the biggest manhunt in history. More than 100000 officers as well as numerous volunteers searched the country for the missing boy. The kidnapper left plenty of clues: a set of muddy footprints in the bedroom, a home-made ladder against the wall, and the ransom note in broken English pinned to the windowsill.

Nevertheless, police are still no nearer to tracking down the criminal – who is now wanted for murder.

FATHER'S PLEA The nation is alerted.

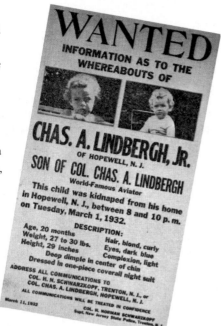

GIRDER BY GIRDER Sydney's soaring bridge cost £9 million and took eight years to build.

Massive bridge spans harbour

19 MARCH, SYDNEY
The world's longest single-arch bridge, spanning Sydney harbour in Australia, was opened today, carrying four railway lines, a road and a footway, and linking the northern suburbs with the city.

At 1140 metres (3770 ft) long, the bridge contains more steel than any other bridge ever built. Before it was

opened to traffic it was tested by leaving 81 railway locomotives standing on it for eight days. Designed and built by the British firm of Dorman, Long, Sydney's bridge is one of the heaviest steel fabrications ever constructed – weighing just under 53000 tons – and is held together by rivets 4 centimetres (1½ in) in diameter.

A new look for *The Times*

3 OCTOBER, LONDON
Readers of *The Times* got a shock this morning. Britain's longest-running newspaper, first published in 1785, has had a makeover, and the venerable 'Thunderer' has lost its Gothic look and become a fashionable young thing.

Typographic consultant Stanley Morison has designed an entirely new typeface, which he calls 'Times New Roman'. The face is clear, modern and streamlined, although Morison has retained the 'serif', the curly ornaments on the edges of letters.

New lighter promises instant flame

The Zippo, a stylish cigarette lighter made of stainless steel, was introduced this year. Designed by the American George Grant Blaisdel, it boasts a long 'chimney', to protect the flame from wind, and is intended to light at the first flick. The Zippo's combination of style and function ensures that it will become a genuine design classic.

Zany family delights audiences once more

Paramount Studios have released their fourth Marx Brothers film, which has been an instant box-office success.

An American university campus is the setting for *Horse Feathers*, the latest offering from the funniest comedy team around. The title is a euphemism for 'bunk' or 'baloney', and the film is a madcap parody of academic life. Football, sex and punning are on offer at Groucho's Huxley College, and the thin plot is more than compensated for by outstanding comic performances and wild, anarchic humour.

Sons of a poor tailor, the brothers were pushed into vaudeville by their ambitious mother. They developed their individual comic personalities on Broadway, where Harpo's silent lechery and capacious coat, Groucho's quick-fire punning and Chico's fake Italian accent became part of the brothers' much-loved repertoire.

LEAPS AND BOUNDS A record-breaking hurdles time bagged one of three medals for 'Babe' Didrikson.

Golden muddle at LA games

14 AUGUST, LOS ANGELES
An 18-year-old typist from Texas, Mildred 'Babe' Didrikson, has stolen the show at the second Olympic Games to be held in the United States – and but for the pig-headedness of the Olympic committee her tally of two gold medals and one silver would have been three golds.

The judges penalised her for her novel head-first-over-the-bar technique in the high jump and, although she set a new world-record height in the event, awarded her only second place. Another world record of 11.7 seconds in the 80 metres hurdles brought her gold in a photo-finish with her compatriot, Evelyn Hall. Didrikson also won the javelin competition, the event in which she burst on to the stage by setting a world record at the age of only 16.

Unlike the 1908 Olympiad at St Louis – to which few international athletes bothered to travel – this year's games have been an undoubted success. A new Olympic record has been set for every athletics event except the men's long jump – and Tommy Hampson of Great Britain recorded the fastest time ever in the 800 metres. In another odd decision the gold medal in the 400 metres hurdles was awarded to Robert Tisdall of Ireland, but the world-record time that he set was disallowed because he knocked over one hurdle.

The spread of gold medallists was truly international; perhaps the most surprising turn of events was the capture of five of the six swimming golds by the well-drilled team from Japan. The USA won most of the field events.

RIDING HIGH Harpo (driving), Groucho and Chico got their nicknames at a poker game back in 1918.

1933

BORN
16 Jan: Susan Sontag, US cultural critic and writer
18 Aug: Roman Polanski, Polish film director

DIED
5 Jan: Calvin Coolidge, former US President
22 Apr: Sir Henry Royce, co-founder of Rolls-Royce car manufacturers

PUBLISHED
George Orwell, *Down and Out in Paris and London*

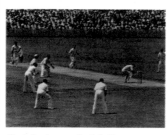

'Bodyline', one of cricket's greatest scandals, is the talk of the fourth Test at Brisbane. Bodyline is a dangerous bowling tactic used by the English team to prevent Australian batsmen from scoring. England wins the series but Australia bitterly contests the victory.

PROTESTED
20 July, London: 50 000 Jews, against Nazi persecution of German Jews

DECLARED
10 Jan, Spain: martial law by the premier, Manuel Azana, in the face of communist unrest
27 Oct, Palestine: state of emergency in coastal towns, after riots protesting at Jewish immigration

RECOLONISED
21 Dec: Newfoundland, which became a dominion in 1917, by Britain following government's financial collapse

SPLIT
25 Feb: Japan, from League of Nations
14 Oct: Germany, from League of Nations

ON SHOW
25 Sept, Italy: the Turin Shroud, which allegedly bears an imprint of Jesus Christ's face

FLED
From Germany: Arnold Schoenberg, composer; Otto Klemperer, conductor; Bertolt Brecht, dramatist, and Kurt Weill, composer; Fritz Lang, film director; Wassily Kandinsky and Paul Klee, artists; Thomas Mann, novelist

DICTATOR
23 Mar, Berlin: Adolf Hitler, who will rule by decree under the new Enabling Act

BOYCOTTED
1 Apr, Germany: Jewish businesses and shops, by government order

BANNED
19 Apr, UK: Soviet imports
14 July, Berlin: opposition political parties, by Nazi government
21 Aug, Berlin: aerial photography over Germany, by Hermann Goering, Nazi aviation minister
22 Aug, Dublin: fascist group the Army Comrades Association, nicknamed the 'Blueshirts'

US choreographer Busby Berkeley dominates Hollywood's musicals this year by directing the dance routines in three top films: Gold Diggers of 1933, 42nd Street *(above) and* Footlight Parade. *Berkeley's lavish and visually stunning dance numbers have transformed musical cinema.*

OPENED
20 Mar, Germany: first concentration camp, for Nazi Party's political opponents, at Dachau
3 July, London: Chiswick and Twickenham bridges over river Thames

FOUNDED
1 Apr, India: Indian Air Force
30 June: French national airline, Air France
New York City: *Newsweek* magazine, *Esquire* magazine

ANNOUNCED
26 July, Germany: sterilisation programme for Germans suffering from blindness, deafness, epilepsy and certain deformities
30 Sept, USA: $700 million aid programme for poor Americans, by President Franklin D Roosevelt
5 Oct, Birmingham: five-year, £95 million programme to clear British slums

EXECUTED
20 Mar, Florida: Giuseppe Zangara, who attempted to murder President-elect Roosevelt in February

COUP
12 Aug, Cuba: led by army, ousts President Gerardo Machado and installs Dr Carlos de Cespedes

CHAMPIONS
29 June, New York City: Italian Primo Carnera, world heavyweight boxing champion, knocks out Jack Sharkey

ELECTED
24 Jan, Ireland: Fianna Fáil government, with a majority of one seat

NEW WORD
the Mob *n*: a gang of criminals, especially the Mafia

On 22 July, *Wiley Post is greeted by a cheering crowd of 10 000 people at Floyd Bennett Airport, New York, after flying around the world in 8½ days. Post, who is blind in one eye, set the sensational round-the-world record in an aeroplane, the* Winnie Mae, *that he borrowed from his employer. Previous attempts had taken six months.*

Hitler becomes leader of Germany

30 JANUARY, BERLIN
Adolf Hitler, leader of Germany's National Socialist (Nazi) Party, has been sworn in by President Paul von Hindenburg as chancellor of the German Reich.

Known derisively as the 'Bohemian corporal', 44-year-old Hitler has never sat in the German Reichstag (parliament) nor held political office. The decision of the conservative Nationalist Party leadership to invite him to head a coalition government of Nazis and Nationalists is a calculated gamble that the office will tame the fiery orator, who has made no secret of his virulent anti-Semitism and contempt for democracy.

The chancellorship is also a measure of the extent of Hitler's success in catapulting the Nazi Party to its current position of strength.

Hitler's triumph was celebrated last night in scenes that are rapidly becoming familiar to Germans. A torch procession, led by disciplined files of young, brown-shirted Nazi stormtroopers, streamed for hours past the Chancellery. The marchers' arms were outstretched in the Nazi salute as they passed the new chancellor.

From the glowing, eager faces of the Nazi fanatics brandishing swastikas, and the shouts of 'Heil Hitler', it was evident that a new generation had entered into its political inheritance.

HARD HITTING In a 1932 election poster for the Reichstag presidency, Hitler is sold to the impoverished German masses as 'our last hope'.

··· 5 FEB, USA: PROHIBITION ENDS AND 1.5 MILLION BARRELS OF BEER ARE DRUNK THAT NIGHT ···

BURNING PYRE Nazi supporters destroy books and pamphlets considered subversive and anti-German.

THE NAZI PATH TO POWER

When Adolf Hitler first attended a meeting of Anton Drexler's fledgling German Workers' Party in a Munich beer-cellar in 1919, the party had only a handful of supporters. In little more than a year he imposed himself, by sheer force of personality, on the party and its leadership, adding the words 'National Socialist' to its title.

Hitler had a flair for organisation and propaganda – and for promoting a cult of leadership. From the outset he laid siege to the democratic institutions of the Weimar Republic, scourging the postwar government – the 'November criminals' – for accepting the crushing terms of the Treaty of Versailles. He also warned in his speeches of the sinister purposes of the Marxist, Jewish and capitalist enemies of Germany, both without and within.

His party made limited headway until the Great Depression that followed the worldwide financial crash of 1929 and left millions of Germans out of work. The desperate situation in which many found themselves provided an audience for Hitler's dramatic policies, and the elections of 1930 saw the Nazi Party suddenly emerge as the second-largest party in the German parliament. Two years later it pushed the Social Democrats into second place.

After Hitler was appointed chancellor he immediately set about acquiring absolute power. Further elections took place in March this year, with the Nazis winning 44 per cent of the vote – more than any other party. Hitler's government assumed dictatorial control on 21 March.

FDR's New Deal breathes life into US economy

TURNING TIDE Roosevelt promises a new era at his 1933 inaugural address.

31 DECEMBER, WASHINGTON DC
In his first year in office the Democratic President of the United States, Franklin D Roosevelt, has more than honoured his pledge of 'a new deal for the American people'.

Swept into power by popular frustration and anger at high unemployment, failing business and a depressed agriculture, the President moved swiftly to counteract the effects of the great Wall Street Crash of 1929. Confined to a wheelchair after a bout of polio in 1921, Roosevelt launched a series of Sunday night radio broadcasts, dubbed 'fireside chats', to reassure the nation and explain his policies to the people.

One of his first aims was to restore public confidence in the country's banking institutions by a series of measures. An Agricultural Adjustment Act, intended to bring parity between agriculture and business by raising the level of commodity prices and easing the credit and mortgage burden, was followed by a scheme to refinance private home mortgages. New life was breathed into the stock market, and stock prices rose after the gold standard was abandoned; this was followed by the devaluation of the dollar. However, the cornerstones of the New Deal have been to tackle unemployment through the provision of government-sponsored public works, and to ease the burden on industrial workers by reducing work hours and at the same time raising wages.

With fascism and communism on the march throughout Europe, the New Deal is seen as a bold initiative to save capitalism for the United States. Nevertheless, such unprecedented government intervention in the free market economy is already raising hackles, and President Roosevelt's policies may not have an entirely easy ride.

··· RUTH WAKEFIELD INVENTS CHOCOLATE CHIP COOKIES AT THE TOLL HOUSE INN, WHITMAN, MASSACHUSETTS ···

Elegance enters the factory production line

Two new products were introduced this year that epitomise the decisive shift taking place in the look of everyday objects. The new-style design is based on functional elegance.

At one end of the scale the new look consists of concealing the inner workings, as with the Goblin Teasmade, which combines an alarm clock with a teapot – and even pours the tea itself. It hides its kettle component behind a gleaming chrome façade – according to one commentator, reminiscent of 'a miniature Art Deco cinema'.

At the other extreme, functional elegance means that the workings are made integral to the design, as with the Anglepoise lamp designed by George Carwardine. This is a desk lamp with a

ADJUSTABLE COMPANION The Anglepoise desk lamp is marketed as a versatile workmate.

sprung and jointed arm – based on the mechanism of the human arm – which makes it almost infinitely adjustable.

The new design style is partly a reflection of new manufacturing technology. More significantly, it is a result of the rise of the middle classes;

EVERYDAY BEAUTY The shining Goblin Teasmade wins praise for its clean Art Deco lines.

with ever larger numbers of people able to afford beautiful things, the mass-produced item no longer has to be a poor relation of the handmade.

Scotland's monster of the deep is the star attraction

BIG BUSINESS Tourists flocked to Loch Ness to find souvenirs rather than the 'queer beastie' herself.

The people of Loch Ness, a long lake cutting through the heart of Scotland, have an unusual friend to thank for this year's boom in the local tourist industry. Ask anyone who makes a living in the area who is responsible for the sudden increase of visitors and the reply will be exactly the same: 'Nessie.'

Nessie is, of course, a monster who lives in the loch. She was first sighted on 14 April this year by Mr and Mrs John Mackay as they drove home one night along the new road that circles the shore. They saw 'an enormous animal' in the dark waters of the loch. The Mackays stopped and watched as the creature 'disported itself, rolling and plunging for fully a minute'.

Like the Loch Ness monster herself, the story might have sunk without trace, but the Mackay couple's alleged sighting made the local newspaper, the *Inverness Courier*, and has since been wired around the world.

The paper described Nessie thus: 'It has a long tapering neck, about 6 feet [2m] long, and a smallish head with a serpentine look about it, and a huge hump behind.' Altogether, Nessie is claimed to be more than 9 metres (30 ft) long from head to tail.

Since the appearance of the story in the international press, monster-watchers have flocked to the loch, determined to spot Nessie. One inn at Drumnadrochit is doing particularly brisk business. It happens to be owned by a Mr and Mrs John Mackay.

DANCERS AND SKYSCRAPERS

Musicals continued to dominate the scene this year, and leading the pack was the American choreographer and director Busby Berkeley with his kaleidoscopic set pieces, including *Gold Diggers of 1933*. This contained the spectacular 'Shadow Waltz' number, where hundreds of dancers swirled round with illuminated violins.

Equally lighthearted, though in a very different vein, was *King Kong*, set to become one of the cinema's best-loved fantasy films. Its spectacular climax, set on the roof of the Empire State Building, has an escaped giant ape, King Kong, shot down by a swarm of military aeroplanes as he clutches the beautiful Fay Wray, with whom he has fallen in love. The monster's epitaph: 'It wasn't the aeroplanes. It was beauty killed the beast.' The quality of the special effects by animator Willis O'Brien – who created the monster with a series of 45-cm (18-in) models – has amazed audiences.

1933 was also notable for a number of serious films. In *Queen Christina* Greta Garbo turned in a sphinx-like performance, while Charles Laughton won an Oscar for his part in *The Private Life of Henry VIII*. The most successful film of the year was *Cavalcade*, based on Noel Coward's play, which won Academy Awards for best picture and best director. The most controversial was *Ecstasy*, with Hedy Lamarr enjoying a nude dip, which fell foul of the censors.

HIGH DRAMA Perched above Manhattan, King Kong fends off fighters.

1934

BORN
9 Mar: Yuri Gagarin, Russian astronaut
20 Sept: Sophia Loren, Italian-born Hollywood actress
28 Sept: Brigitte Bardot (born Camille Javal), French actress

DIED
25 May: Gustav Holst, British composer
2 Aug: Paul von Hindenburg, president of Germany

Hollywood child star Shirley Temple is awarded a special Oscar for her string of hit performances over the past three years. Her dimples, ringlets and adorable personality have proved a winning formula, and she is fast becoming one of the biggest box-office successes in the world.

ASSASSINATED
22 Feb, Nicaragua: General Augusto Sandino, by members of the National Guard

Inventor John Logie Baird demonstrates the latest development in his patented colour television process; pictures are transmitted in 30 horizontal lines by electronic scanning. Baird is now developing three-dimensional images.

ARRESTED
28 Sept, New York City: Bruno Hauptmann, German immigrant to USA, for the murder in 1933 of US aviator Charles Lindbergh's baby

FREED
1 Aug, Louisiana: blues singer Leadbelly, from jail, after he wrote a song for the Louisiana governor begging for a pardon

IN POWER
19 May, Bulgaria: Fascists, following successful coup

DECLARED
8 Oct, Spain: national strike, and an attempt to make Catalonia in northern Spain independent
27 Dec, Teheran: that Persia will be renamed Iran, by government

OPENED
18 July, Liverpool: Mersey Tunnel, world's longest underwater tunnel, by King George V

KILLED
10 Jan, Germany: Marinus van der Lubbe, executed for allegedly burning down the Reichstag building
23 May, Louisiana: Bonnie Parker and Clyde Barrow, US criminals 'Bonnie and Clyde', in police trap
30 June, Germany: around 100 leading Nazis, enemies of Hitler, in 'Night of the Long Knives'
22 July, Chicago: US bank robber John Dillinger, 'Public Enemy No One', while on the run, by FBI

VOTED
2 June, Washington DC: $6 million aid package by Congress, for farmers suffering drought

APPROVED
19 Aug: Adolf Hitler's new position of *Führer* (Leader), by 89.9 per cent of voters in plebiscite

RECALLED
6 Aug: US marines, from Haiti, ending 19 years' occupation

CHAMPIONS
10 June: Italy, winners of first soccer World Cup to be held in Europe, beating Czechoslovakia 2–1
14 June, New York City: US boxer Max Baer, world heavyweight champion after he beats Primo Carnera

PUBLISHED
Agatha Christie, *Murder on the Orient Express*
Robert Graves, *I Claudius; Claudius the God*
Henry Miller, *Tropic of Cancer*

SCREEN HITS
The Scarlet Pimpernel, starring Leslie Howard, directed by Harold Young
The Man Who Knew Too Much, directed by Alfred Hitchcock
The Gay Divorcée, directed by Mark Sandrich, starring Fred Astaire and Ginger Rogers together for first time
Wise Little Hen, Disney cartoon introducing Donald Duck

FIRSTS
7 Dec: artificially made hormone, anderosterone, by US scientists
31 Dec: woman airline pilot in USA: Helen Richey, on Central Airlines' Washington DC–Detroit flight

BANNED
28 Mar, Austria: jokes about Chancellor Dollfuss's small size

NEW WORDS
call girl *n*: a female prostitute with whom an appointment can be made by telephone, or who is available to be called at a brothel
fix *n*: a dose of a narcotic drug to which one is addicted

BABY BOOM The Dionne quins were heralded as a wonder of human fertility.

Quins capture the public heart

29 MAY, ONTARIO
The residents of the sleepy hamlet of Corbeil in northern Ontario were stunned and overjoyed at the birth of female quintuplets in the town.

Born two months prematurely to Oliva and Elzire Dionne, the five baby girls weigh less than 1 kilo (2 lbs) each, but all are said to be doing well. The babies are the world's first known surviving quintuplets.

The girls, named Cécile, Yvonne, Annette, Emilie and Marie, are fast becoming celebrities, with messages flooding in from well-wishers around the world. Mr and Mrs Dionne already have two

daughters and three sons. The couple are said to be delighted – though perhaps a little daunted – at the arrival of five more children.

Representatives of Chicago World's Fair are reported to have offered a substantial sum to place the infants on exhibit; other sources say that there are moves to make them wards of the Ontario government. Dr Allan Dafoe, the physician responsible for the successful delivery of the babies, warned that in any event the quins need very special attention – perhaps more than the parents can give – and that it may be some time before they are allowed home.

··· AUSTRALIAN-BORN ACTRESS PAMELA TRAVERS PUBLISHES HER FIRST BOOK, *MARY POPPINS*, AT THE AGE OF 28 ···

Death for 'America's most wanted'

Three of America's most notorious criminals met bloody ends this year – the bank robber John Dillinger, named 'public enemy number one' by the FBI, and the murderous duo Bonnie Parker and Clyde Barrow, better known as 'Bonnie and Clyde'.

Dillinger and his gang terrorised the Midwest, and he was held responsible for ten or more killings in the course of his robberies. He was betrayed for the reward money offered on his head, and was shot by FBI agents when leaving a cinema in Chicago.

Bonnie and Clyde met in 1930 in Dallas, becoming small-time crooks who killed indiscriminately but whose exploits were glamorised in newspaper reports. They died in a police ambush near Shreveport, Louisiana; their car was riddled with more than 100 bullets.

Melt the cheese and create a world staple

This was the year in which a flash of culinary inspiration came to restaurant proprietor Carl Kaelen, when it occurred to him to place a slice of cheese

on to a hot meat patty and let it melt before serving. The 'cheeseburger' was an instant success at Kaelen's burger bar in Louisville, Kentucky, and took off around the country.

BIG CHEESE
A new culinary
delight from the USA.

Citroën Traction sets the standard

When the Citroën Traction Avant first rolled off the production line this year in France, it was recognised as one of the world's most revolutionary cars.

Sporty in appearance, it has a low-slung, streamlined look. Among other innovations the Traction has front-wheel drive and hydraulic brakes, and is an excellent road-holder. The design of the car, in which the chassis is an integral part of the structure, makes it longer-lasting and more solid. It is also one of the first cars to have undergone crash-tests before going on sale.

ROLLING OUT Citroën's new Traction Avant combines safety, speed and style.

America saved from Hollywood smut

**13 JUNE, LOS ANGELES
Cinema-goers worried about the excesses of Hollywood can breathe a sigh of relief today, as the film industry publishes its Production Code establishing moral guidelines for studios.** The industry's self-regulating body, the Motion Picture Producers and Distributors of America (MPPDA), has also authorised cinema owners to refuse to screen films that were produced prior to the code which they consider to be in contravention of it. The regulation will be known as the Hays Code after Will H Hays, head of the MPPDA. Any required changes to offending scenes, such as those containing nudity and profanity, will cost film-makers $25 000.

The news will be welcomed by concerned movie-goers across the nation – including the letter-writer to *Film Daily* who complained about 'smut in cartoons' in February 1933.

··· THE US PRISON BUREAU BUYS THE ISLAND OF ALCATRAZ IN SAN FRANCISCO BAY AS A SITE FOR A NEW PRISON ···

Radio days

Radio has transformed the lives of people throughout the world, becoming the principal form of home entertainment. Much pioneering work has been done in the United States, where two nationwide networks – NBC and CBS – were established by the start of this decade.

Many of the programmes are lighthearted in content, offering listeners a welcome – if temporary – release from the rigours and hardship of the Great Depression. Significantly, sales of wireless sets continue to soar while many theatres and dancehalls stand empty. Favourite American programmes feature comedians, such as Ed Wynn and

THAT'S ENTERTAINMENT A wireless in every home.

George Burns. Adventure tales such as *The Shadow* and *The Lone Ranger* are also becoming popular.

In Britain the structure of broadcasting is different. From the start the emphasis has been on public service radio, financed by a licence fee and typified by the King's Christmas message, broadcast throughout the Empire. 1934 saw the beginnings of commercial competition with the launch of Radio Luxembourg. The most popular listening is provided by *In Town Tonight* or by dance music from the likes of Ambrose and Harry Roy. For children there are the Ovaltineys and Uncle Mac.

The radio set itself is rapidly becoming an important and versatile item of furniture.

While traditionalists opt for large cabinets, often designed in a fake-antique format, modernists prefer jazzy Art Deco styles, invariably made out of the fashionable new material of Bakelite.

Wheeling and dealing game is great success

By late 1934, Parker Brothers, board-game manufacturers in the United States, were eyeing a new game in which players use pretend money for simulated property and financial dealings. A single game can go on for hours – even days – with losers ending up 'bankrupt' and the winner a 'millionaire'.

Initially, Parker Brothers rejected the suggestion from 'Monopoly' creator Charles Darrow that they should manufacture the game, claiming that it was too long and complex with no obvious finish. However, after Darrow sold 5000 sets to Wanamakers, a department store in Philadelphia, they decided to buy and market it, giving Darrow royalties on all sets sold.

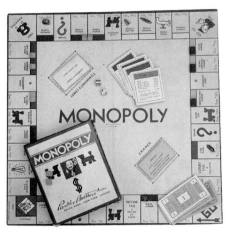

PASS GO Charles Darrow's original game used the street names of Atlantic City in New Jersey.

Within weeks of the game's official launch across the United States, the company was producing 20000 sets a week to meet the demand. Darrow himself is set to become the world's first millionaire game designer.

Catseyes are a reflective invention

This year saw the introduction of 'Catseyes' to British roads. Invented by engineer Percy Shaw, these glass studs are set along the edges of main roads to reflect the headlights of vehicles.

The inspiration for the invention came to Shaw when he was driving through thick fog and saw the glowing eyes of a cat reflected in his headlights in the road ahead. Having braked suddenly to avoid the animal, he realised that he had been driving perilously close to the edge of a cliff.

The first Catseyes, introduced in Bradford, Yorkshire, stopped working when they became dirty – so Shaw set them in rubber supports, which wipe them clean when they are run over.

··· THE WORLD'S FIRST LAUNDERETTE, A 'WASHETERIA', OPENS IN TEXAS WITH FOUR ELECTRIC WASHING MACHINES ···

Wimbledon shocked by women in shorts

8 JULY, WIMBLEDON
Decorum has once again taken a back seat at this year's tennis championships at the All England Club in Wimbledon. Last year Bunny Austin, the English Davis Cup player who lost in the final of the men's singles, discarded his long white trousers and appeared on Centre Court in shorts, and his defiant stand seems to have encouraged the ladies, who this year are everywhere to be seen in similar garb.

In fact, women were the first to brave the wrath of the All England Club management committee. In 1929 the Spanish star Lilli de Alvarez, who fought and lost three singles titles in a row from 1926 to 1928, introduced the wearing of culottes; and, more brazenly, Billie Tapscott of South Africa appeared without stockings.

The Wimbledon establishment, although keen to maintain standards

NEW LOOK Women win their fight with the establishment to play tennis in freer, more practical clothing.

of modesty, has had little choice but to accept the women players' demands for clothing that gives them greater freedom of movement.

However, the club is determined to maintain one tradition at least – the rule that all clothing must be white remains beyond challenge.

1935

BORN
8 Jan: Elvis Presley, US singer
1 June: Norman Foster, British architect
1 Dec: Woody Allen, US film director

DIED
19 May: T E Lawrence, aka 'Lawrence of Arabia', British adventurer and writer
3 July: André Citroën, French motor car manufacturer

QUIT
7 June: Ramsay MacDonald, British prime minister, for health reasons; Stanley Baldwin succeeds – National Coalition government continues

RETIRED
25 Feb: Jack Hobbs, from first-class cricket, after scoring more centuries than any other cricketer

OPENED
5 Jan, New York: Municipal Airport 2, forerunner of LaGuardia Airport

Two women give a demonstration of how to open cans and pour beer from them as Kreugers launch the first canned beer in New York. The company assures the beer-drinking public that thanks to a lining the beer never comes into contact with the metal. Customers are also told that empty cans should be thrown away.

On July 16, shortly after the world's first parking meters go into service in Oklahoma City, a local resident tries to work out how to use them. The meters are the brainchild of the editor of the local newspaper, who sits on the city's traffic committee.

TRIUMPHED
25 May, Michigan: 21-year-old student Jesse Owens, who sets three world records in one day: long jump, 220 yds, and 220 yds hurdles

BOMBED
27 Dec, Hawaii: the Mauna Loa volcano, by five US Army Air Corps pilots, trying to prevent its eruption from harming a nearby town

KILLED
16 Jan, Florida: Kate 'Ma' Barker, US leader of bank-robbing Barker gang, by FBI agents
23 Oct, New Jersey: gangster Arthur Flegenheimer, aka 'Dutch Schultz', by rival Charles 'Lucky' Luciano

LAUNCHED
Oct, London: Jaguar car, by Swallow Sidecar Company, costing £385

FOUNDED
June, USA: Alcoholics Anonymous

29 Oct, London: British Airways, by merger of Hillman, Spartan and United Airways
USA: 20th-Century Fox film company, by merger of Fox and Twentieth Century companies
USA: American Institute of Public Opinion, by George Gallup, to carry out market and political research

BANNED
28 Feb, Ireland: sale or import of contraceptives
31 Aug, USA: sale of arms to warring countries, under Neutrality Bill, signed by President Roosevelt

DENOUNCED
17 Apr, Geneva: Nazi military expansion, by council of League of Nations

CHAMPION
13 June, New York City: Jim Braddock, who defeats Max Baer to become world heavyweight boxing champion

RECORDS
3 Sept, Utah: Briton Malcolm Campbell sets new world land speed record of 482 km/h (301 mph) in his car *Bluebird*
Atlantic: French liner *Normandie* makes record 4 days 3 hrs crossing from Europe to New York
11 Nov, USA: Orvil Anderson and Andrew Stevens fly balloon to 21 800 m (74 000 ft) altitude

ELECTED
9 Mar, USSR: Nikita Khrushchev, chief of Moscow Communist Party
8 Oct, London: Clement Attlee, leader of British Labour Party

IN THE MONEY
17 May, London: 19-year-old actress Vivien Leigh signs a £50 000 film deal

DIVORCED
10 Jan, Los Angeles: Mary Pickford and Douglas Fairbanks

SCREEN HITS
Anna Karenina, starring Greta Garbo, directed by Clarence Brown
The Thirty-Nine Steps, starring Robert Donat, directed by Alfred Hitchcock

The first hearing aid designed to be worn by the user is launched. The new electric valve replaces devices such as the Klaxon horn, held up to the ear to magnify sound, and the Acousticon, a large, portable, battery-operated amplifier with a telephone-type receiver for the ear.

NEW WORDS
ecosystem *n*: an ecological term to describe a system involving the interactions between a community and its environment
mammogram *n*: an x-ray photograph of a breast, used for the detection of tumours

ITALY'S GRAB FOR ABYSSINIA PROVOKES SANCTIONS

FORWARD MARCH Mussolini's tanks have decimated Haile Selassie's forces, which rely on mules and horses.

11 OCTOBER, GENEVA
The League of Nations has voted to impose economic sanctions against Italy following the country's invasion of Abyssinia [present-day Ethiopia] on 3 October. Having massed on the Abyssinian border, last week Italian troops poured across the frontier, backed up by fighter planes which bombed strategic targets and border towns.
The independent African nation, lying between the Italian possessions of Somalia and Eritrea, is a tempting target for Mussolini's imperial schemes. The country has long been regarded as a natural target for colonial expansion. An earlier invasion attempt in 1896 ended with Italian forces defeated at Adowa – the town was one of the first targets for Mussolini's bombers this time around.

During the summer the world watched as 25 Italian infantry divisions – numbering around 650 000 men – and 2 million tons of supplies were shipped out to East Africa. Mussolini sounded out international opinion to ensure that there would be no interference from other European powers, but the attack has caused a range of reactions. As the Italian troops entered Abyssinia, the move was greeted with indifference at home and with outrage abroad. Abyssinia's Emperor, Haile Selassie, mobilised his army immediately and denounced the Italian invasion to the League of Nations.

The League is unwilling to take military action against an ally, but has put its faith in economic sanctions. These do not, however, include an oil embargo and will be hard to enforce. There is also a danger that sanctions will be counterproductive; the League's opposition could help Mussolini to rally Italian public opinion to his cause.

··· WORLD'S FIRST SCHOOL FOR AIRLINE STEWARDESSES IS FOUNDED IN LOS ANGELES BY TRANS-WORLD AIRLINES ···

Hitler steers Germany towards dictatorship

The Nazi grip on power in Germany is becoming ever tighter, and a slide towards war is beginning to appear unstoppable. Since taking power two years ago, Adolf Hitler has chosen an isolationist route, shown by Germany's withdrawal from the League of Nations, that is causing international concern. Germany's parliament, the Reichstag, has been rendered powerless, and trade unions and opposition parties have been abolished.

When President Hindenburg died in August, Hitler gained absolute control. He ordered that the Nazi swastika – a Hindu symbol of luck and prosperity – was to become the official national flag. It is often emblazoned on a white circle, supposedly representing purity and the Aryan ideal, set on a red background symbolising socialism. Huge banners with the swastika wave proudly over every Nazi event.

The greatest of these are the party rallies held at Nuremberg every September, and this year Hitler used them to announce new laws to further Nazi racial policies. These so-called Nuremberg laws enshrine the Nazi Party's anti-Semitism, and define the Jewish people as second-class citizens with drastically reduced civil rights.

PATRIOTIC PUPILS German children wave their new national flag, symbol of Nazism.

Long march to freedom is finally over

FINAL ADDRESS Speeches marked the arrival of Mao's followers in Shaanxi after a year on the run.

20 OCTOBER, CHINA

After a supreme feat of endurance the weary Communist forces of Mao Zedong have finally completed their Long March, reaching a safe haven in the north-western province of Shaanxi. This epic year-long trek involved them in a journey of 9600 kilometres (6000 miles) through swamps, gorges and mountain ranges, being continually harassed by Nationalist troops and provincial warlords. At the end of the ordeal, only about a third of Mao's original 100000-strong army survived.

This rearguard effort followed the rise to power of Nationalist leader Chiang Kai-shek, who became president of the Chinese Republic in 1928 and began a purge of Communist elements in the army. Resistance was led by Zhu De and Mao Zedong, who organised peasant uprisings in the south-eastern provinces of Hunan and Jiangxi. In 1933 Chiang surrounded the area to starve out the rebels. The plan seemed to be working, but Mao refused to surrender and broke through the blockade to try his 'impossible' escape.

The Long March has cemented Mao's position as leader of China's Communists, and he will now begin to establish a new Communist power base from which to oppose the Nationalists.

··· 22 MAR, BERLIN: FIRST HIGH-DEFINITION TELEVISION SERVICE IN THE WORLD IS LAUNCHED ···

From Russia with style

15 MAY, MOSCOW

Moscow's first underground railway line opened today, consisting of a network of 13 stations from Socolniky to Gorky Park. The line is 11.6 kilometres (7 miles) long, and can carry about 177000 passengers daily.

The system has opened four years after building work first began on the Russian capital's underground railway network, and 34 years after the first draft proposals for the Moscow metro were drawn up.

The metro is notable for its classically beautiful architecture and includes the first ever escalators to be installed in the Soviet Union. Certain sections resemble the foyers of luxury hotels rather than humble stations. Some

FIRST CLASS More than 150000 Russians travelled on the Moscow metro on its opening day.

of the country's most well-known architects were involved in the design, and more than 20 different types of marble were used to complete the grandiose effect. Each station has been designed differently, and the network is already a source of national pride.

Polymer 6.6 could be fabric of the future

As with many inventions, the discovery of nylon was a complete accident. Wallace Carothers and his team at the DuPont chemical company in the United States had been trying for years to produce an artificial material that resembled silk. Playing around with polyamide, a man-made substance, researchers found that it formed a long, strong fibre when melted and stretched. This material, first called 'polymer 6.6' because two of the chemicals used to make it had molecules of six linked carbon atoms, was later renamed 'nylon'. Possible uses include fishing lines, surgical thread and toothbrush bristles, and it even has potential as a light yet strong textile fibre – one day nylon stockings could be as common as silk ones.

Pick up a Penguin for a good read

The world of books was taken by storm this summer when Allen Lane, managing director of The Bodley Head, published a range of small, cheaply printed books with paper covers, to be sold for sixpence each – the same price as a packet of cigarettes. The idea is to make good reading affordable to the masses – titles in his paperbacked Penguin range cost a tenth of the price of the same books published in hardback.

Coming at a time when there is little inexpensive public entertainment, paperbacks proved an instant success. Lane aims to publish two colour-coded sets of ten books within a year of the launch and intends to concentrate on popular authors including Ernest Hemingway, Agatha Christie and Compton Mackenzie.

Each book is eagerly awaited by a public hungry for a good read. People in bookshops can already be heard simply asking for 'the latest Penguin'.

Hammer and sickle power

One day's extraordinary output by a young coal miner has led to the introduction of what has become known as the Stakhanovite movement in the Soviet Union. In August Alexei Stakhanov was reported to have cut 102 tons of anthracite in a six-hour shift at the Irmino coal mine in the Ukraine. That is more than 15 times the volume of the best Soviet mines and ten times better than crack German miners achieve. The Communist Party has made Stakhanov into a national hero and told Soviet workers to emulate him, thus demonstrating the economic and industrial superiority of the socialist system over the capitalist production methods of the West.

BIRD IN THE HAND The first Penguin paperback was André Maurois' biography of the Romantic poet Shelley.

TOP HAT TALES WIN HEARTS

Fred Astaire and Ginger Rogers danced their way into audiences' hearts in *Top Hat*, one of the most enchanting of their romantic musical comedies. The plot was flimsy, but what really mattered was the music by Irving Berlin and the duo's faultless dancing. Memorable songs included 'Cheek to Cheek' and 'Top Hat' itself, which Astaire sang as to the manner born. The Marx Brothers provided yet more laughs with their zany *A Night at the Opera*. In Britain, two of the best films starred Robert Donat, one of the greatest of all romantic leads. In *The Ghost Goes West*, directed by Frenchman René Clair, he played the double role of the owner of a Scottish castle and his ghostly 18th-century ancestor who is transported across the Atlantic when the castle is bought by an American millionaire. In Alfred Hitchcock's *The Thirty-Nine Steps*, a suspenseful spy drama, Donat played the dashing hero Richard Hannay.

DANCING SHOES Fred and Ginger in *Top Hat*.

1936

BORN

3 Mar: Ursula Andress, Swiss-born actress

18 Mar: F W de Klerk, South African politician

1 Aug: Yves Saint Laurent, French fashion designer

Billy Butlin opens his first holiday camp at Skegness, Lincolnshire. Such camps became a British institution after the first was set up at Caistor-on-Sea, Norfolk, in 1906. They have become popular as they provide a cheap option for blue-collar workers who now receive paid holidays.

DIED

27 Feb: Ivan Pavlov, Russian scientist

19 Aug: Federico García Lorca, Spanish writer

10 Dec: Luigi Pirandello, Italian playwright

BESTSELLER

Margaret Mitchell, *Gone With the Wind*

PROCLAIMED

28 Apr: Crown Prince Farouk as King of Egypt

DENOUNCED

8 Apr: Italian troops' use of mustard gas against Abyssinians, by British foreign secretary Anthony Eden

ELECTED

8 Feb, India: Jawaharlal Nehru, president of the Indian National Congress

RE-ELECTED

3 Nov: Franklin D Roosevelt, US President (Democrat); 523 electoral college votes give him biggest victory to date in history of US elections

FREED

3 Jan, Warsaw: 27000 prisoners, under general amnesty

LAUNCHED

14 July, UK: mass production of gas masks, with aim of producing one for every citizen

2 Nov, UK: regular BBC television service

USA: automatic food-vending machines

On 4 July, *the Douglas Commercial No 3 (DC–3), one of the most famous airliners in civil aviation history, made its inaugural flight as a passenger service. Run by American Airlines, the flight was from Chicago, Illinois, to Glendale, California. The DC–3 is a development of the earlier models the DC–1 and the DC–2.*

When Adolf Hitler summoned Ferdinand Porsche to a meeting in 1933 he asked for a blueprint for a 'people's car'. The result three years later is the Volkswagen – nicknamed the 'Beetle' because it looks like the insect.

BURNT DOWN

30 Nov, London: the Crystal Palace

TRIUMPHED

USA: Louis Meyer, winner of Indianapolis 500 motor race for record third time

3 July, London: British tennis star Fred Perry, winner of Wimbledon singles title for third year running

FOUGHT

Tel Aviv, Palestine: Arabs and Jews; nine die and 50 are injured

On 26 October, *the Jarrow March, a procession of 200 unemployed men from Jarrow, near Durham, passes by Bradford on its way to London. The marchers want to draw attention to their case; their mining and shipbuilding town has been devastated by the Great Depression.*

REBELLED

17 Feb, Paraguay: the army, against President Eusebio Ayala; results in creation of South America's first fascist regime

FIRSTS

4 Jan, USA: 'hit parade' listing; it is published in *Billboard* magazine

18 May, UK: women announcers on BBC, Jasmine Bligh and Elizabeth Cowell

FLEW

5 Mar: British Spitfire fighter, for first time

6 Sept: British aviator Beryl Markham, UK–Nova Scotia

OPENED

6 June, UK: Gatwick airport

NEW WORD

satellite *n*: a country under the domination of a foreign power

Spain's divisions blow up into civil war

31 JULY, MADRID

In the few short weeks since the left-wing Republican Party's victory in the elections, Spain has been plunged into a bitter civil war. Battle commenced when the Nationalist party leader General Francisco Franco landed at Cadiz with a party of Moroccan troops. 'Spain is saved,' he announced, demanding the resignation of the left-wing government. With General Mola advancing from the north, the rebel armies could meet in Madrid by Christmas.

Franco and his followers have powerful allies. In Germany, Adolf Hitler has pledged his support, and the Italian leader Benito Mussolini is said to have sent planes to help Franco.

The Allies appear to be doing nothing. The French have little stomach for war and will certainly remain neutral,

FIGHT FOR FREEDOM Republican supporters fire at Nationalist troops in Irun, in the Basque country.

but there has been a great deal of grass-roots sympathy for the Republican cause. Idealistic volunteers from all across Europe and the United States are already flocking to join the International Brigades to fight against fascism.

Anti-glare glasses

SHADY BUSINESS Military pilots are among the first to wear Edwin Land's specialised sunglasses.

The American physicist Edwin Land has developed a new type of sunglasses, based on a material that cuts the glare of reflected light by filtering out light waves that are aligned in the same plane. Land – a Harvard dropout – developed 'Polaroid' in 1932 by embedding special crystals in a thin plastic sheet. It could, he says, enable anglers to see through the reflective surface of the water to the fish below.

HITLER FLOUTS PEACE TERMS

7 MARCH, BERLIN

German troops have marched into the demilitarised zone of the Rhineland, violating treaties signed after the Great War. Adolf Hitler claimed he had been forced into the move because of the 'iron ring' France had put around Germany, occupying the industrial Rhineland district after Germany fell behind in reparation payments.

Military service has only been mandatory in Germany for a year, but the men who goose-stepped into Cologne looked as if they meant business. With their gleaming bayonets, polished boots and unmistakable curly helmets, Hitler's soldiers have stirred up unpleasant memories of the Great War.

Hitler worried the international community even more by asserting that he no longer considered himself bound by any treaties. He claimed that France's mutual assistance pact with the Soviet Union negates any agreements that Germany made after the last war.

THEY'RE BACK German troops march back into the Rhineland – and many welcome them.

Perhaps France can take some comfort from the fact that he told the Reichstag (parliament) that this move signalled 'the close of the struggle for German equality'. Observers of the German political scene, however, warn that the dictator's military ambitions are unlikely to stop at Cologne.

EDWARD RENOUNCES THRONE FOR LOVE

LOVE OVER DUTY Edward VIII, now Duke of Windsor, will go to live in France with the woman he loves.

11 DECEMBER, LONDON
In a moving and dignified radio broadcast to the nation, King Edward VIII announced his abdication today, saying that he had found it impossible to discharge his royal duties 'without the help and support of the woman I love'.

The prospect of a marriage between Edward VIII and a twice-divorced American socialite, Wallis Simpson, had been greeted with dismay by both Parliament and the Church, and had sparked a constitutional crisis. The King's role as Defender of the Faith means that he has to uphold the values of the Church of England, which disapproves of divorce. He is also the linchpin of the Empire, and many of the Dominions had indicated to the British government that they could not support such a marriage. Threatened with the breakup of the Empire, the King was compelled to choose between his lover and his throne.

Owing to the self-restraint of the British press it has only been during the past week that the British people have officially been informed of the affair – although rumours have been rife in the foreign newspapers.

Wallis Simpson and Edward met while he was still Prince of Wales and living the life of a playboy. As rumours of their affair snowballed, Edward came under pressure to make his choice. Popular opinion was very much behind the King, and the mood of the country as Edward – who was never crowned – sailed into exile was one of sadness and regret. His brother, the Duke of York, will succeed him as George VI.

··· TAMPAX INTRODUCES THE FIRST COTTON TAMPON WITH A STRING ATTACHED ···

Blackshirts and reds slug it out as Fascism comes to London

RUNNING BATTLE Marchers flee as police disperse Mosley's Fascists and their opponents.

19 OCTOBER, LONDON
London has been rocked by a week of violence, some of the worst the capital has ever seen. Fascists rampaged through the predominantly Jewish district of Whitechapel in the East End, clashing with residents and their supporters.

In a vicious anti-Semitic campaign, Oswald Mosley's 'blackshirts' have daubed Whitechapel walls with the letters 'PJ' (Perish Judah) and harassed the local Jewish population. On 5 October, Mosley and 7000 members of the British Union of Fascists paraded through the East End, to find themselves confronted by thousands of Communists and Jews who barred their way. In the fight that ensued – dubbed the 'Battle of Cable Street' – 80 people were injured, among them 15 policemen. A week later Mosley's men returned in the so-called 'Mile End pogrom', when they beat up Jews on the street and smashed the windows of businesses that they suspected were owned by Jews.

Mosley has cast himself in the role of the 'modern dictator' which he believes Britain needs, but his bully-boy tactics have lost him much support – including that of Lord Rothermere, owner of the *Daily Mail*, who had until this month's disturbances been an admirer. Parliament is also considering a public order act which will give the police the right to ban any marches that may cause a breach of the peace.

Jesse Owens sets Olympic gold standard

16 AUGUST, BERLIN
Hitler wanted the 1936 Olympic Games to be an 'Aryan' triumph, a showcase for the Nazis' racist doctrine of Nordic supremacy – but one man, the black American athlete Jesse Owens, has put paid to that idea.

Owens arrived in Berlin after a phenomenally successful year. On 25 May 1935 he had achieved what is perhaps the greatest individual feat in the history of sport by posting four world records – for the 100 yards, 220 yards, 220 yards hurdles, and long jump – in the space of a single afternoon. This year he has lived up to the high expectations pinned on him by winning four gold medals: for the 100 metres, 200 metres, 4 x 100 metres relay, and long jump. The man he beat into second place for the long jump was the very Aryan, blonde German champion Lutz Long – who made a point of publicly befriending him.

The German press had labelled the black members of the American team 'mercenaries' and 'auxiliaries', and Adolf Hitler, the German chancellor, left the Olympic stadium rather than acknowledge Owens's fourth victory, in the long jump. Hitler also refused to be photographed with him.

FRIENDLY FOES Lutz Long posing with Jesse Owens at the Berlin Olympics.

In the circumstances, it is only partial consolation for the Nazis that the German team has come top of the overall medals table, thanks in great part to their superbly trained rowing, equestrian and weight-lifting squads.

··· FIAT INTRODUCES THE TOPOLINO AS ITALY'S 'PEOPLE'S CAR' – RIVAL TO THE VOLKSWAGEN BEETLE ···

Boulder Dam busts all records

26 OCTOBER, ARIZONA
The Boulder Dam, the biggest in the world, which holds back the greatest man-made lake, started producing electricity today when the first generator went into action. The dam has taken five years to construct and is – perhaps surprisingly – the heaviest man-made structure to be built since the Great Pyramid of Giza in Egypt.

The dam is 190 metres (626 ft) high and 377 metres (1244 ft) long and curves like a tightly-strung bow between the rock abutments on either side of the Colorado River. The curve enables it to resist the force of the water of Lake Mead, a reservoir 185 kilometres (115 miles) long. It is made of enough concrete to build a road 5 metres (16 ft) wide and 20 centimetres (8 in) thick from San Francisco to New York. Its massive weight combines with its shape to keep it upright.

The project has taken eight years to come to fruition and required a special act to be passed by the US Congress. Built by the Federal Bureau of Reclamation, the dam is designed for flood control and the generation of electricity as well as the provision of domestic and industrial water supplies.

WATER WORKS The Boulder Dam (later renamed the Hoover Dam) is wedged tightly into Black Canyon on the Nevada–Arizona border.

1937

BORN

30 Jan: Vanessa Redgrave, British actress

9 July: David Hockney, British artist

8 Aug: Dustin Hoffman, US actor

21 Dec: Jane Fonda, US actress

Marcel Boulestin is the world's first television cook in Britain, appearing on the BBC's Cook's Night Out. *He is shown here filming his regular spot,* Dish of the Month. *The BBC is building up its entertainment output.*

DIED

23 May: John D Rockefeller, US industrialist

7 June: Jean Harlow, US actress

26 Sept: Bessie Smith, US blues singer

EXECUTED

1 Feb, Moscow: 13 enemies of Stalin, accused of being 'Trotskyites'

25 Feb, Abyssinia: Ras Desta Demtu, son-in-law of exiled leader Haile Selassie, by Italians

12 June, Moscow: eight Red Army generals, accused of planning a coup against Stalin

PUBLISHED

George Orwell, *The Road to Wigan Pier*

John Steinbeck, *Of Mice and Men*

J R R Tolkien, *The Hobbit*

FIRST NIGHTS

14 Apr, New York City: musical *Babes in Arms*

19 July, Berlin: exhibition of 'Degenerate Art' – official show, intended as mocking, of art condemned by Nazis

21 Dec, Los Angeles: *Snow White and the Seven Dwarfs*, first feature-length cartoon, directed by David Hand, produced by Walt Disney

EXILED

9 Jan, Mexico: Leon Trotsky, former leading Soviet Communist

FLOODED

22 Jan, USA: Ohio River – 16 killed and 150000 made homeless

OPENED

27 May, San Francisco: Golden Gate Bridge, 1280 m (4200 ft) long – world's longest suspension bridge

14 Oct, London: first London Motor Show

REOPENED

17 Oct, France: Rheims Cathedral, badly damaged in the Great War, after repair; a service of reconsecration is held

FASTEST

2 Sept, Switzerland: Briton Malcolm Campbell, who sets world water speed record of 208 km/h (129 mph), in his boat *Bluebird* on Lake Maggiore

19 Nov, USA: British driver George Eyston, who sets land speed record of 501 km/h (311 mph)

On 22 June, Joe Louis knocks out James Braddock in the eighth round to take the world heavyweight boxing championship in Chicago. Louis, who comes from Detroit, has spoken out in support of the black civil rights cause.

QUIT

16 May, Spain: Spanish premier Largo Caballero

28 May, London: Stanley Baldwin retires as British prime minister; Neville Chamberlain takes over

21 June, Paris: French premier Léon Blum after French senate denies him financial powers

11 Dec, Geneva: Italy, from the League of Nations

HARD WORKER

Humphrey Bogart, who stars in eight films in one year: *Black Legion, The Great O'Malley, Marked Woman, Kid Galahad, San Quentin, Dead End, Stand-In* and *Swing Your Lady*

PROMOTED

4 Oct, Washington DC: Judge Hugo Black, a former member of the racist Ku Klux Klan, to US Supreme Court

INVADED

7 July: China, by Japan

EASIER

23 July, UK: divorce under Matrimonial Causes Act, which adds new grounds of insanity and desertion to existing one of adultery

LAUNCHED

20 Apr, Birkenhead: *Ark Royal*, British aircraft carrier

29 Nov, London: new emergency number for calls to police – 999

FOUNDED

31 Aug, France: national railway company, the Société National de Chemins de Fer Français (SNCF)

NEW WORDS

blood bank *n*: a place where whole blood or blood plasma is stored until transfusion

wide boy *n*: unscrupulous and astute man, often a Londoner

On 12 May, the coronation of King George VI and Queen Elizabeth takes place at Westminster Abbey. The new King and Queen greet their subjects on the balcony of Buckingham Palace, with their young daughters, princesses Elizabeth and Margaret (adjusting her coronet). The whole ceremony is televised by the BBC.

Amelia Earhart vanishes on round-the-world flight

AVIATION HEROINE Amelia Earhart's tragic disappearance was never solved.

3 JULY, HONOLULU
Fears are growing for the safety of Amelia Earhart, the aviator whose epic flights have made her an American heroine. At 10.00 am yesterday she set off from New Guinea on the latest stage of her attempt to become the first person to fly around the world along the equator. Her destination was Howland Island, a tiny speck of land in the Pacific, just east of the International Dateline and more than 4000 kilometres (2500 miles) from her starting point in New Guinea. She and her navigator, Captain Frederick Noonan, made intermittent radio contact with American ships patrolling the ocean beneath. The aviators were last heard at 8.43 am today, and it was not possible to locate their position.

At 10.30 Captain Warner Thompson of the USS *Itasco*, anchored near Howland Island, radioed Honolulu to say that he thought the aeroplane – a specially adapted twin-engined Lockheed Electra – was probably down at sea and that he was about to begin a search. Other ships of the US Navy have been ordered to the area to augment the search.

Miss Earhart has set many aviation records. She was the first woman to fly solo across the Atlantic and the first person to fly nonstop from Mexico City to New York.

··· 'SPAM', TINNED PROCESSED PORK AND HAM, IS LAUNCHED BY THE HORMEL COMPANY ···

Giant airship becomes blazing inferno

6 MAY, LAKEHURST, NEW JERSEY
Stunned crowds watched in horror as the *Hindenburg*, the largest airship in the world, caught fire and turned into a blazing inferno. It took less than a minute for the imposing cigar-shaped vessel to be consumed by the flames.

The gruesome spectacle was caught on film by a news team which had come to report on the landing – the cameraman captured the faces of passengers clustering at the windows just seconds before the disaster. In all, 36 people were killed.

The *Hindenburg*, designed in Germany, came into service in 1936. It was the first commercial aircraft to make regular transatlantic crossings, completing the trip in around 55 hours. On its last journey it had travelled from Frankfurt. There will be an investigation into the disaster, but despite rumours of

UP IN FLAMES Amazingly, many survived by leaping out as the burning airship drifted to the ground.

sabotage it was probably the result of a freak accident in which hydrogen at the rear of the vessel was ignited by an electrical storm. Whatever the cause, the tragedy is bound to have implications for the future use of passenger airships.

1938

Italian designer Salvatore Ferragamo brings glamour to the shoe world when he patents the famous cork wedge heel. His designs are imitated around the world and start a trend for platform-soled peep-toe sandals in a range of crazy colours.

BORN
17 Mar: Rudolf Nureyev, Russian dancer
3 Oct: Eddie Cochran, US singer

DIED
1 Mar: Gabriele d'Annunzio, Italian soldier-poet
7 Aug: Constantin Stanislavsky, Russian theatre director
10 Nov: Mustafa Kemal (Atatürk), Turkish statesman

PUBLISHED
Daphne du Maurier, *Rebecca*
George Orwell, *Homage to Catalonia*
Graham Greene, *Brighton Rock*

KNOCKED OUT
22 June, New York City: German challenger Max Schmeling, in first round of world heavyweight boxing title, by champion Joe Louis

SCREEN HIT
Bringing Up Baby, starring Katharine Hepburn and Cary Grant

QUIT
20 Feb, London: Anthony Eden as British foreign secretary, in protest at direction of British foreign policy
8 Apr, Paris: Léon Blum from second term as French premier; replaced by Edouard Daladier

BANNED
Jan, USA: Mae West, from US radio stations after sketch on NBC radio that Federal Communications Commission found 'indecent'

EXILED
6 Jan, Vienna: Austrian psychoanalyst Sigmund Freud to London, to escape Nazi persecution
2 Dec, UK: 206 German Jewish schoolchildren

ELECTED
21 Apr, Ireland: Douglas Hyde, president

SET
25 June, Washington DC: minimum wage for workers – 25 cents per hour

EXECUTED
14 Mar, Moscow: 18 leading Communists after show trial, in Stalinist purge

LAUNCHED
3 Jan, London: BBC's first foreign-language radio service, in Arabic
27 Sept, UK: 80000-ton *Queen Elizabeth*, world's largest liner
USA: Teflon, fibreglass
UK: *The Beano,* children's comic

FIRSTS
31 May, UK: television game show, *Spelling Bee,* broadcast by BBC
29 July: person to swim the Baltic Sea, Danish woman Jenny Kammersgaad
31 Dec: pressurised airliner, Boeing Stratoliner, makes maiden flight

A living specimen of the coelacanth, a fish thought to have become extinct 75 million years ago, is found in the Comoro Islands. The specimen is taken to East London in South Africa for examination and is believed to be a close relative of the group of fish that gave rise to land-living vertebrates.

FASTEST
20 Aug, London: Briton Sydney Wooderson, who sets world record running half-mile in 1 min 49.2 secs
16 Sept, USA: British driver George Eyston, who sets new land speed record of 575 km/h (357 mph)

RECORDS
2 July, London: US tennis star Helen Wills Moody, 32, wins Wimbledon ladies' singles for eighth time
4 Aug, UK: Wolverhampton Wanderers soccer club sells its player Bryn Jones to Arsenal for £13000

FOUNDED
26 May, Washington DC: House Committee to Investigate Un-American Activities

On 3 July, *the British Mallard locomotive sets a world speed record for a steam-driven engine, reaching 202.8 km/h (126 mph) over a distance of 8 km (5 miles). The locomotive is run so hard that the engine is eventually damaged.*

FIRST HEARD
11 Nov, USA: *God Bless America,* song written by Irving Berlin, sung by Kate Smith on her radio show

NEW WORDS
Muzak *n, trademark:* recorded light music played in shops, factories, etc
nylon *n:* a class of strong, synthetic materials of which fibres can be spun to make women's stockings, brush bristles, etc
one-armed bandit *n:* fruit machine operated by pulling down a lever at one side

AUSTRIA FALLS UNDER HITLER'S SPELL

14 MARCH, AUSTRIA

Hitler made his triumphal entry into Vienna today, after yesterday's proclamation of the *Anschluss* – the political union of Germany and Austria – which was expressly forbidden in the Treaty of Versailles. The proclamation follows Germany's defiant show of power three days ago, when Nazi forces streamed across the Austrian border and seized control of the country. Hitler now rules with absolute power over an empire of 74 million people, as he ruthlessly pursues his plans for creating Germany's 'Third Reich' ('third empire'), which he claims will last for 1000 years.

Chancellor Kurt von Schuschnigg of Austria has been manipulated by Hitler over the past few months, forced to concede ever more rights to Germans in Austria and to appoint pro-Nazi officials. On 9 March he called for a referendum on the issue of Austria's independence, but before it could happen he was forced into resigning. He was succeeded by the Nazi sympathiser Arthur Seyss-Inquart who, on 11 March, invited German troops into the country.

Since the Austro-German treaty of 11 July 1936 the Nazis have been gradually gaining a foothold in Austria, Hitler's native land. Throughout 1937 their agents led a campaign of terror, planting bombs and staging rallies. Most of Austria's population is in favour of the annexation, as demonstrated by the ecstatic reception the dictator was given.

IMPERIAL AMBITION With the formal proclamation of the *Anschluss*, Hitler takes another step towards a 'Greater Germany' to dominate Europe.

··· NESTLE OF SWITZERLAND PRODUCES THE FIRST COMMERCIALLY SUCCESSFUL INSTANT COFFEE, NESCAFE ···

Munich Pact gives Hitler what he wants

29 SEPTEMBER, MUNICH

In an attempt to prevent another world war, leaders of the principal European powers have framed a treaty signing over part of Czechoslovakia to Hitler. The summit meeting was called after German threats to take control of the Sudetenland, a part of Czechoslovakia with a German-speaking minority. Britain, France, Italy and Germany attended the conference, with the Czech president conspicuous by his absence.

After signing the pact, Prime Minister Neville Chamberlain returned to Britain in triumph, claiming that he had secured 'peace in our time'. His view is not shared by Winston Churchill, who

warned: 'The belief that security can be obtained by throwing a small state to the wolves is a fatal delusion.'

The Munich Pact continues the policy of appeasement that Britain and France have adopted towards Hitler. As a result Germany has broken several key clauses of the Versailles Treaty, including the occupation of the demilitarised zone in the Rhineland and the annexation of Austria. In May German forces massed on the Czech border, and in June the SDP (Sudeten German Party) leader called for full autonomy for the region. With little apparent support coming from France or Britain, Eduard Beneš, the Czech premier, was forced to make

PIECE OF PAPER Back from Munich, Neville Chamberlain waves the agreement aloft.

a string of concessions – culminating in the loss of the Sudetenland at Munich. Even this may not satisfy Hitler for long.

GERMANY'S NIGHT OF BROKEN GLASS

A nation that has declared war on Jews

SHATTERED LIVES Many ordinary Germans are appalled by the orchestrated violence of *Kristallnacht*.

12 NOVEMBER, BERLIN In a meeting chaired by Marshal Goering, German ministers today passed a series of punitive anti-Jewish measures − their pretext being the eruptions of violence on the streets during the past week.

The seeds of the trouble were sown on 7 November when Herschel Grynszpan, a young Polish Jew angered by government persecution of his parents, walked into the German Embassy in Paris and shot an official, Ernst von Rath. The latter died two days later, and the Nazi propaganda minister Josef Goebbels used the incident to urge 'spontaneous' reprisals against German Jews.

On the night of 9 November a mob of Nazi activists carried out a series of violent attacks across Germany. Almost all the country's synagogues were burnt down, more than 7000 shops destroyed, and hundreds of Jews savagely beaten. Fire brigades were instructed to ignore damage to Jewish property. More than 90 Jews died; 30 000 were arrested and later sent to concentration camps. The pogrom has been nicknamed *Kristallnacht* ('night of broken glass') after the debris of shop windows that littered the streets.

Today's measures add further insult, as Jews are fined for the damage and, additionally, required to hand over any money reclaimed from insurance companies.

Germany's anti-Semitic policies date back to 1933 − a year that saw the introduction of a wave of measures aimed at excluding Jews from public office and key professions such as medicine, dentistry, law and teaching. The bulk of anti-Jewish legislation came in 1935, when the so-called Nuremberg Laws deprived German Jews of their citizenship. At the same time marriages between Jews and Gentiles were made illegal, even if they were conducted before the Nazi era.

This year the process accelerated, and the ban has been extended to include midwifery, police work and even acting as tour guides. There is also segregation, with Jews barred from many theatres, cinemas, restaurants, swimming pools and even park benches. Since 26 April, Jews have had to declare all their financial assets.

Measures such as these are intended to persuade Jews to emigrate − preferably without their posessions. Forced deportations are also becoming more common. The family of Herschel Grynszpan was among those affected by this policy; their deportation to Poland prompted him to commit the fatal act of violence that would spark off the brutal reprisals of *Kristallnacht*.

··· BAKED POTATOES WITH TOPPINGS ARE FIRST SERVED, AT LAWRENCE FRANKS'S RESTAURANT IN BEVERLY HILLS ···

Offices spurn new copying invention

An American, Chester Carlson, has invented a new copying process that could revolutionise office work.

Carlson made his major technical breakthrough in a makeshift lab above a bar in Astoria, where he works with Otto Komei, a young German physicist. Together they created the near-perfect duplicate of the notation '10-22-38 ASTORIA' (the date and location of the experiment) and were then able to make permanent copies of it on wax paper. Carlson patented his idea, known as 'xerography', to protect its originality.

The ability to copy documents quickly will be a major boon in busy offices. Unfortunately, no one will yet be able to benefit from Carlson's invention, as it has been turned down by more than 20 companies.

Now it's none for the road

The police department of Indianapolis, Indiana, this year became the first to use the 'drunkometer', which analyses the breath of anyone blowing into it. Until now, the only way to get hard evidence of the amount of alcohol a person had drunk was by a blood sample. The drunkometer is a far easier way to breath-test drivers suspected of being under the influence of alcohol – which is not illegal in Britain.

NO JOKE Orson Welles's broadcast shows he is a talent to be watched.

Panic in the streets as 'Martians' invade USA

1 NOVEMBER, USA

Chaos reigned for several hours in the United States yesterday evening as radio listeners took to the streets in terror, fleeing for their lives – from an alien invasion. Nationwide panic ensued when 23-year-old actor Orson Welles – already a Broadway sensation – broadcast a dramatisation of H G Wells's novel *The War of the Worlds*, a highly realistic account of a Martian invasion of Earth. Simulated 'news bulletins' interrupted a music show to give listeners updates of the devastation caused by an alien attack. 'On-the-spot reports' from breathless reporters tracked the invading Martians' progress from their landing site in New Jersey as they advanced towards New York City.

Millions of Americans, under the impression that this drama programme was an actual news report, succumbed to hysterical anxiety. Streets were filled with people fleeing the cities, switchboards were jammed and churches were packed. Many were genuinely convinced that the end was nigh – this reaction from a woman in Indianapolis was typical: 'It's the end of the world. You might as well go home to die. I just heard it over the radio.'

The broadcast, from Lincoln's Mercury Theater, was interrupted four times with the announcement 'This is purely a fictional play', but this seemed to do little to calm the audience. Orson Welles, who directed and starred in the broadcast, made a public apology on behalf of the Mercury Theater, stating: 'We can only suppose that the special nature of radio, which is often heard in fragments … has led to this misunderstanding.'

··· 1 JUNE, OKLAHOMA: SUPERMARKET TROLLEYS ARE INTRODUCED ···

Don Budge is first to win tennis grand slam

24 SEPTEMBER, FOREST HILLS, NEW YORK

Lanky Californian tennis star Don Budge has written his name in big letters in the history books by becoming the first player to win a 'grand slam' of the world's top tennis championships – in Britain, France, Australia and the USA. Budge, aged 23, powered to victory in the men's singles at the US Open today, beating Gene Mako by three sets to one, 6–3, 6–8, 6–2, 6–1.

Mako knows Budge's game better than anyone else because he is his usual partner in the men's doubles. He did well to hold the champion up at all – the set he won was the only one Budge dropped in the entire competition. Budge (born John Donald) also completed a memorable triple hat-trick: the singles, doubles and mixed doubles at

CHAMPION Budge's elegant play.

Wimbledon both last year and this, and at Forest Hills this year.

1939

BORN

29 Jan: Germaine Greer, Australian feminist writer

26 June: Francis Ford Coppola, US film director

18 Oct: Lee Harvey Oswald, alleged assassin of John F Kennedy

On 2 May, *Eugenio Pacelli is elected pope and takes the name Pius XII. His appointment follows the death of Pius XI, for whom Pacelli served as secretary of state. The new Pope's priority will be to maintain the independence of the Roman Catholic Church in Fascist Italy.*

DIED

28 Jan: W B Yeats, Irish poet and playwright

23 Sept: Sigmund Freud, founder of psychoanalysis

12 Dec: Douglas Fairbanks Sr, Hollywood actor and producer

PUBLISHED

John Steinbeck, *The Grapes of Wrath*
Henry Miller, *Tropic of Capricorn*
Raymond Chandler, *The Big Sleep*
Christopher Isherwood, *Goodbye to Berlin*

James Joyce, *Finnegan's Wake*
T S Eliot, *Old Possum's Book of Practical Cats*

LAST

Public guillotining in France, of triple murderer Eugen Wiedmann; takes place outside Versailles

VISITED

8 June: the USA by King George VI, the first visit by a reigning British monarch

SHOWN

'Grandma' Moses's paintings at the Museum of Modern Art, New York City; Anna Mary Robertson Moses's rural landscapes were discovered in a drugstore by an art collector; she was aged 78 when she took up painting

An increasing number of new passenger services are launched by airline companies as flying is recognised as a safe, fast and comfortable way to travel. Competition between airlines has lowered fares and made air travel more accessible. This promotion by Air France reflects flying's growing popularity.

INVADED

7 Apr: Albania, by Italy
1 Sept: Poland, by Germany
17 Sept: Poland, by the USSR
30 Nov: Finland, by the USSR

NEUTRALITY DECLARED

1 Sept: by Italy
3 Oct: by the USA

DEVASTATED

Jan, Chile: earthquake kills 30000 people

Dec, Turkey: earthquake kills 45000 people

MARRIED

Clark Gable and Carole Lombard, Hollywood stars

APPOINTED

3 Sept: Winston Churchill to British cabinet, after ten years out of office

EXPELLED

14 Dec: Soviet Union from the League of Nations

SNUBBED

Marian Anderson, renowned contralto, is refused permission to perform in Constitution Hall, Washington DC, because she is black

WARNING

2 Aug, USA: in a public letter to President Franklin Roosevelt signed by Albert Einstein, Edward Teller and Alexander Sacks, that German scientists might be developing an atomic bomb

On 20 December, *after being defeated in battle by the Royal Navy, the German battleship* Graf Spee *is scuttled by her own commander, Captain Langsdorff. Acting on direct orders from Hitler, Langsdorff blew up the ship and shot himself.*

ENDED

4 Nov: US embargo on arms sales to Britain and France

INVENTED

DDT (dichlorodiphenyltrichloroethane), chemical insecticide, by Swiss scientist Paul Müller

SET OUT

White Paper by British government, determining policy on Jewish settlement in Palestine

NEW WORDS

intercom *n*: system of communication by telephone or radio in vehicles or buildings

telegenic *adj*: having an appearance that looks pleasing on television

FRANCO CRUSHES SPANISH REPUBLICANS

1 APRIL, MADRID

The 32-month-old Spanish Civil War is over. Fascist General Francisco Franco controls all of Spain and has declared himself the country's new leader.

The end was slow in coming, as exhausted, hungry government troops slowly retreated before the firepower of the rebels. The consequences of a fascist victory will be grim for Republican soldiers. Already more people have died in reprisals and executions than in fighting – of the half-million dead, perhaps only a fifth died in battle.

Defeat had looked certain for the Republicans since last autumn when the International Brigade was sent home at the end of October. The Brigade's numbers had been decimated – 20 per cent killed and 15 per cent badly wounded. At their farewell in Madrid the communist orator Dolores Ibárruri, known as 'La Pasionaria', told them: 'You can go with pride … You are the heroic example of the solidarity and universality of democracy.'

However, with no one to aid them and the combined might of Italy and Germany lined up against them, the

EVER ONWARD General Franco checks his position as he makes steady progress on the Catalan front.

Republicans knew that the end was near. Franco's final offensive began last year on 23 December; in January he took the Republican stronghold of Barcelona; and by March he was marching on Madrid.

Refugees have been streaming across the borders to France and Portugal, and gathering on the beaches in the south hoping to escape to North Africa. They say that this is a defeat not merely for Spain but also for Europe.

··· FIRST REFRIGERATOR WITH FREEZER COMPARTMENT IS LAUNCHED BY GENERAL ELECTRIC COMPANY IN USA ···

Transatlantic flying-boat service starts with a splash

28 JUNE, NEW YORK CITY

The world shrank a little today as US airline Pan American launched the first scheduled passenger flights across the Atlantic. The Boeing 314 flying boat *Dixie Clipper* took off from the Hudson River bound for Marseilles carrying 22 passengers. Tickets are $375 single or $675 return.

Flying boats are not really boats but large seaplanes which take off from and land on water. The vast Boeing 314s, fitted like ocean liners with state rooms and plush dining areas, can carry more than 70 people. They have a range of 5600 kilometres (3500 miles) and a cruising speed of 275 kilometres per hour (170 mph). Pan Am also used 314s to begin the first scheduled transatlantic airmail flights on 20 May.

ALL ABOARD The first transatlantic passengers board the Pan Am seaplane.

Despair as Hitler marches into Czechoslovakia

WEEPING WELCOME Ethnically German Czech women greet the arrival of the Nazis with tears of joy.

15 MARCH, PRAGUE
German forces today marched into the Czech territories of Bohemia and Moravia, thus taking possession of most of Czechoslovakia. The third region of the country, Slovakia, declared itself independent yesterday. Czechoslovakia is in a state of chaos.

As Hitler's troops goose-stepped into the Czech capital, Prague, they were greeted by the boos and jeers of angry crowds. Many were weeping, while others defiantly sang the Czech national anthem. Such a reaction is in marked contrast to the joyous reception given to the Nazis by the citizens of the Sudetenland and of Austria – which were both annexed by Hitler last year in direct contravention of treaties.

These events are the culmination of a period of uncertainty and tension during which Hitler has used force or the threat of force to expand the boundaries of his country. This latest move, however, is the first time that he has seized territory that has a majority non-German-speaking population. Only a few months ago Hitler declared that he had no more territorial claims in Europe, while the British prime minister, Neville Chamberlain, said that the Munich Pact (by which the Sudetenland was ceded to Hitler) had secured 'peace for our time'. But the Pact did not halt Germany's ruthless expansion, which has now led Europe to the brink of war.

City children evacuated to safety in the country

4 SEPTEMBER, LONDON
In the past three days almost a million children have been moved from Britain's towns and cities to safer areas, in anticipation of the war with Germany. Some were accompanied by their mothers, but many went alone.

The evacuees assembled at pre-arranged points, often the local school, and then were taken to the appropriate main-line station. The mass exodus has been a triumph of government organisation, for not a single child has been reported missing or injured. At their destinations, local committees have worked wonders of improvisation trying to find accommodation for everyone, but there have been many scenes of desperately tired women and children trailing from door to door behind the billeting officer trying to find someone to take them in.

For many children, the journey that started as an adventure turned into a nightmare as excitement gave way to tedium and discomfort. Some children have reacted with amazement to their new surroundings, having lived all their lives in towns and knowing nothing of country ways – many had not seen farm animals before, and did not know that milk came from cows.

Householders who provide accommodation will be paid an allowance for each child. A difficult period of adjustment lies ahead, for no one knows when it will be safe for the children to return to their homes.

SAD EXODUS London children board the train for the provinces, not knowing when they will return.

··· ONLY 3 PER CENT OF US POPULATION (670 000 PEOPLE) EARN ENOUGH TO PAY INCOME TAX ···

Nazis and Soviets in devilish pact

24 AUGUST, MOSCOW
In the early hours of this morning the foreign ministers of Germany and the Soviet Union signed a treaty between their countries that has shocked Europe. For several years the Soviet Union has joined other nations in condemning Germany's aggressive policy towards its neighbours, but now, with Europe moving inexorably towards bloody conflict, Germany and the Soviet Union have agreed that in the event of war they will not take up arms against each other. The pact was signed in the Kremlin by Joachim von Ribbentrop for Germany and Vyacheslav Molotov for Russia, and comes into immediate effect.

With no fear of retaliation from the great power in the east, the way is now clear for Germany to extend its aggression into Poland. The chance of preventing a European war is looking ever more unlikely.

HITLER INVADES POLAND

RIDERS Nazi outriders herald the army's arrival in Polish towns.

1 SEPTEMBER, WARSAW
At dawn this morning Germany launched a massive invasion of Poland. An attack had been expected for some time, but the huge scale of the operation has taken the defenders by surprise.

Squadrons of German aeroplanes attacked airfields, seizing the initiative in the air, and hundreds of tanks and other armoured vehicles have crossed the border into Poland. The frontier is about 2800 kilometres (1750 miles) long, so it is impossible to guard all of it effectively. The Poles are resisting bravely, but the Germans outnumber them and, following years of building up powerful stocks of armaments, are far superior in equipment.

Five years ago Germany and Poland signed a non-aggression pact, but this has been swept aside. Hitler has shown that none of his neighbours is safe from his territorial ambitions. During the past 18 months he has successfully gambled that he could seize Austria and parts of Czechoslovakia without other nations intervening – but Poland has agreements of mutual aid with Britain and France, and these two countries are expected to declare war on Germany without delay.

KNIGHTS IN ARMOUR The Polish cavalry offer a courageous, if hopeless, challenge to Hitler's mechanised invasion.

··· IN BRITAIN 88 PER CENT OF WEALTH IS OWNED BY 10 PER CENT OF POPULATION ···

Britain declares war; Europe prepares for conflagration

3 SEPTEMBER, LONDON
Prime Minister Neville Chamberlain today announced that Britain had declared war on Germany because of the invasion of Poland two days ago. In a national radio broadcast he said: 'This morning, the British Ambassador in Berlin handed the German government a final note stating that, unless we heard from them by 11 o'clock that they were prepared at once to withdraw their troops from Poland, a state of war would exist between us. I have to tell you now that no such undertaking has been received, and that consequently this country is at war with Germany.'

Following a similar ultimatum to Germany, France has also declared war.

Russian designer's helicopter dream comes true

WHIRLYBIRD Immaculately dressed, Sikorsky ascends gingerly into the air in his new helicopter.

14 SEPTEMBER, CONNECTICUT
The Russian-born aeroplane designer
Igor Sikorsky fulfilled a personal dream
today when he made a successful
tethered flight of his VS-300 helicopter
prototype. The machine has a large
three-blade rotor on top, which moves
horizontally, and a small vertical rotor
at the back. Sikorsky piloted it on
several short hops while it was tethered
with ropes to sticks sunk in the ground
as a precaution.

Sikorsky has close on 30 years'
experience in designing giant
aeroplanes. He left Russia in 1917
because of the revolution and later set
up his own company in the United
States. He was responsible for building
some of the huge flying boats used by
Pan Am. However, right from the
beginning of his aviation career he has
been working on his true interest –
helicopter designs.

Helicopters are poised for a
breakthrough. The German Heinrich
Focke created the first really successful
helicopter, the FA 61, which first flew on
26 June 1936. This had twin rotors fitted
on arms extending from the sides of the
machine. Focke's design won him a
contract for a large machine from the
German military, and the first fruits of
that labour are reportedly almost ready.
Sikorsky's success is sure to attract the
interest of the US Army Air Force. The
helicopter has enormous potential as a
military aircraft.

··· THE FIRST CAR WITH AIR CONDITIONING IS PRODUCED BY NASH CAR MANUFACTURERS IN THE USA ···

HOLLYWOOD'S ULTIMATE WEEPIE WINS HEARTS – AND OSCARS

Representing the pinnacle of Hollywood glamour, *Gone with the
Wind* was a colossal success, establishing box-office records that
will take some beating. Clark Gable and Vivien Leigh were the
leading stars in this sweeping romantic tale set against the
background of the American Civil War. It was one of several
enduring classics of very different types to be premiered in a great
year for Hollywood. John Wayne leapt to stardom in the western
Stagecoach; Judy Garland captured hearts in *The Wizard of Oz*, a
wonderful children's fantasy that adults too find irresistible; Charles
Laughton gave an unforgettably moving performance as the
deformed bellringer Quasimodo in *The Hunchback of Notre Dame*, a
superbly atmospheric medieval drama; and Greta Garbo, the
screen's supreme tragic love goddess, surprised everyone when she
revealed a flair for comedy in the delightful *Ninotchka*.

LOVE AND WAR Vivien Leigh won an Oscar for her portrayal of Scarlett.

Riggs and Marble are tennis triple champions

PASSING SHOT Triple champion at first go: the young and talented Bobby Riggs.

8 JULY, WIMBLEDON
The American tennis player Bobby Riggs became the toast of Wimbledon today when he completed an amazing treble, winning the two major men's titles and the mixed doubles at the world's leading tennis tournament. His fellow American Alice Marble also won all three titles. This meant that, remarkably, only four names adorned the championship roll this year.

Riggs beat Elwood Cooke to win the men's singles title yesterday; today he partnered his defeated rival and added the men's doubles to his tally, followed by the mixed doubles in which he partnered Alice Marble. Miss Marble, who won the women's singles title

without yielding a set, is an experienced player. Her powerful serve-and-volley game is widely considered to make her the world's best woman player. Bobby Riggs, however, is only 21, and this is the first time that he has played at the Wimbledon championships. No one before has ever won all three titles at the first attempt.

Riggs started playing tennis at the age of 12, and by the time he was 15 he was entering and winning senior tournaments. Although he is slightly built compared with some of his more muscular rivals, he makes up for this in speed and skilful tactics. He has a wide range of shots and plays with flair, confidence and determination.

··· 11 APR: GLASGOW CITY OUTLAWS DARTS IN PUBS BECAUSE THEY ARE 'TOO DANGEROUS' ···

Superheroes fight it out

Superman, the mighty hero from the planet Krypton, made his debut in *Action Comics* in June 1938, but this year saw him gain a comic all to himself: *Superman*. The character was devised by writer Jerry Siegel and artist Joe Shuster. Their creation of a powerful, mysterious, strangely attired hero who rights wrongs and punishes the wicked has been highly influential, inspiring a number of other costumed superheroes.

One such is Batman, created by Bob Kane, who traced over Superman illustrations to see how his own hero would look in different costumes. Batman made his first appearance in May, and a *Batman* comic is planned for next year.

EXOTIC HEADGEAR Miss Miranda strikes a typically vivacious pose.

Fruity Latin temptress bowls on ahead

The American film actress Carmen Miranda has enlivened the fashion world this year by wearing eccentric head-dresses in the shape of piles of tropical fruit. The flamboyant Miranda was born in Portugal (her real name is Maria de Carmo Miranda de Cunha), but she has become known in Hollywood as the 'Brazilian Bombshell'.

She is not much of an actress, but she can sing and dance with gusto and has an exuberant sense of fun that makes her a hit with audiences. Her popularity is part of the current fashion for Latin-American dance music that is sweeping the United States.

1940

BORN
9 Oct: John Lennon, UK singer and member of the Beatles
14 Oct: Cliff Richard (born Harry Webb) UK pop singer and actor
23 Oct: Pelé, born Edson Arantes do Nascimento, Brazilian footballer

DIED
29 June: Paul Klee, Dutch artist
9 Nov: Neville Chamberlain, former British prime minister
21 Dec: F Scott Fitzgerald, US novelist

CANCELLED
The 12th Olympic Games in Tokyo, because of the war

The Japanese Zero goes into production, taking the fighter plane to a new level of agility and effectiveness. With an extra fuel tank, its weaponry includes machine-guns and cannons. Allied fighters are inferior in comparison.

APPOINTED
22 Feb: Tenzin Gyatso as the 14th Dalai Lama in Lhasa, at the age of five
10 May: Winston Churchill, British prime minister, following the resignation of Neville Chamberlain
11 July: Marshal Philippe Pétain, president of the French State (Vichy France)

20 July: the Duke of Windsor, formerly Edward VIII, governor of the Bahamas

INVADED
9 Apr: Denmark and Norway, by Germany
10 May: Belgium and the Netherlands, by Germany
14 May: France, by Germany
30 June: the Channel Islands, by Germany
28 Oct: Greece, by Italy

FLED
King Haakon of Norway, to Britain; he led the resistance of his country against German aggression
Queen Wilhelmina of the Netherlands to Britain, when her country was overrun by the German army; she headed the government in exile
General Charles de Gaulle, from France to Britain, as French defeat became evident; he then declared himself leader of the Free French

CREATED
July: the Home Guard in Britain, enrolling men who were too old or too young for conscription

SUNK
3 July: the French fleet, by the Royal Navy
11 Nov: the Italian fleet, by the Royal Navy

DISCOVERED
Rhesus factor in blood, by Austrian pathologist Dr Karl Landsteiner in the USA; discovery so named because it was found in the Rhesus monkey
Freeze drying process for food preservation in the USA

As Germany's aerial Blitz is stepped up, Londoners take shelter in Underground railway stations. At the sound of the air-raid sirens, thousands of people file down to spend the night below ground while the city is being bombed overhead.

ISSUED
English phrasebook to German troops, in preparation for the invasion of Britain

RE-ELECTED
5 Nov: President Franklin D Roosevelt, for a third term of office

FIRST
African-American woman to win an Oscar – Hattie McDaniel for her role in *Gone With the Wind*

DEVELOPED
The first penicillin for medical use, by Howard Florey and Ernst Chain, in Oxford, England
Colonel Sanders' recipe for Kentucky Fried Chicken in the USA
M & M sweets in the USA, first introduced by the US military as part of ration packs

DEMONSTRATED
First electron microscope, at RCA laboratories in Camden, New Jersey

DECLARED
The Serengeti, in Tanzania, as a national park, with wildlife protected

PUBLISHED
Ernest Hemingway, *For Whom the Bell Tolls*
Graham Greene, *The Power and the Glory*
Eugene O'Neill, *Long Day's Journey into Night*

ON SALE
Nylon stockings, nationwide in the USA for the first time, launched by Du Pont of Delaware

On 31 May, Oswald Mosley, the leader of the British Union of Fascists, is interned by the British government, along with 763 other members of his organisation.

NEW WORDS AND PHRASES
blitz *vb*: to attack suddenly with great violence
hunk *n*: a sexually attractive or conventionally handsome man
loo *n*: (informal) lavatory

UNSTOPPABLE FORCE A German soldier takes cover behind a panzer tank.

Low Countries running scared in the face of German blitzkrieg

11 MAY, LOW COUNTRIES
Belgium and the Netherlands have been attacked by a German 'blitzkrieg', or 'lightning war'. This tactic, which was used against Poland last year, relies on planning and speed. First, bombers hit the enemy's defences; then paratroops take key positions, and finally the land forces roll in.

Yesterday's assault on the Low Countries – including neutral Luxembourg – followed the pattern exactly Waves of Junkers, Heinkel and Dornier bombers smashed Dutch and Belgian airfields. Vast DFS gliders dropped paratroops who took control of important bridges at Dordrecht, Rotterdam and Moerdijk in the Netherlands and on the Albert Canal in Belgium. Stuka dive-bombers terrorised the enemy defenders. Ground troops came in panzer tanks with powerful 37 mm guns.

The greatest German success on a day of triumphs was the capture of the strategically crucial Belgian fort of Eben Emael near Liège – a concrete box manned by 1200 defenders. Gliders came in silently and landed on top of the fort, disgorging 78 crack German assault troops. They quickly disabled the guns, which were positioned to fire on attackers coming from below.

The Germans were aided by sympathisers, but the defenders had two crucial weaknesses: the Dutch army lacked armoured vehicles, and Belgium, determined to cling to its neutrality, did not integrate its army's actions with those of the Dutch.

Both armies will be trusting that the Allied forces will come to their aid. Against the onslaught of the German war machine, it can only be a matter of time before both countries' resistance crumbles.

Paris falls to the Germans

14 JUNE, PARIS
German invaders today marched into the French capital, Paris. They tied the Nazis' swastika flag to the Arc de Triomphe, pinning a notice to the door of the Chamber of Deputies that spells out the reality of the war so far: 'Germany conquers on all fronts.'

The German advance across northern Europe in the past month has been swift, decisive – and apparently unstoppable. After seizing Norway and Denmark in April, the Germans launched a devastating assault on the Netherlands and Belgium on 10 May. Successes there allowed them to roll on into France, simply bypassing the vaunted Maginot Line of fortifications, which had been built by the French to reinforce the German border but did not cover the Belgian frontier.

German troops surprised the French by attacking through the woods of the Ardennes plateau in Belgium rather than further west where the land was easier to cross. On 14 May panzer tanks and soldiers under Lieutenant-General Heinz Guderian made a breakthrough at Sedan on the Meuse River.

The Germans then stormed on to the Channel coast. Belgium's King Leopold, convinced that the Allies could not now win the war, commanded his army to surrender on 28 May. London ordered the British Expeditionary Force in northern France to ready itself for evacuation.

By 10 June the Nazis were 80 kilometres (50 miles) from Paris, and the French government decamped to Tours in the west. Gloom settled on the people of Paris. They knew their days of freedom were numbered, and many have now fled to the south.

STEALTHY KILLER A bomb falls away from a Junkers JU-87 Stuka dive-bomber.

Fleet of 'little boats' evacuates Allies from Dunkirk

BATTLE WEARY Captured Allied soldiers, who will sit out the rest of war in PoW camps, at Dunkirk.

4 JUNE, DUNKIRK

The last Allied troops were snatched from the clutches of the Germans at Dunkirk in northern France today, bringing a daring week-long evacuation to an end. Since 27 May, 338226 men – British, French and Belgian – have fled across the English Channel in a makeshift fleet comprising destroyers, pleasure steamers, coasters and small private boats.

The retreat of the British Expeditionary Force (BEF), sent to France last September, became the only option after the German advance through Belgium and France. An evacuation fleet began to assemble at Dover on 20 May. Yet despite the boldness of the plan, codenamed 'Operation Dynamo', many of the men recovering in England owe their freedom to Hitler. His decision on 24 May to halt the line of German tanks closing in on the BEF proved a costly mistake. It seems he believed the boast of Luftwaffe chief Hermann Goering that his bombers could finish off the BEF on their own.

··· 1 OCT: THE PENNSYLVANIA TURNPIKE, THE FIRST MODERN LONG-DISTANCE ROAD IN THE USA, OPENS ···

Bombs come with the night

30 DECEMBER, LONDON

Waves of Luftwaffe bombers droned over Britain last night, dropping 10000 incendiary bombs which unleashed a raging firestorm in the historic city of London. The Germans planned the raid to hit when the Thames was at low tide – so that it would be harder to pump water to the fires – and then bombed the water mains. Scores of buildings were damaged and many destroyed, including three hospitals, and eight churches designed by the 17th-century architect Sir Christopher Wren. But this morning St Paul's Cathedral loomed defiantly above the smoking rubble.

The people of Britain have endured almost four months of bombardment by Hermann Goering's Luftwaffe. Attacks on London began on 7 September, with around 450 people killed and 1600 injured in that first raid. As the onslaught continued, Londoners took to sleeping in Underground railway stations and many children were evacuated. The Midlands city of Coventry was flattened in a firebomb raid on 14 November,

NO SURRENDER St Paul's survived the Blitz, but it lost its high altar in October.

the Blitz's worst bombing to date. Liverpool, Bristol, Southampton, Glasgow and Manchester all suffered major raids that month. But the British people remain defiant. The firewatchers and firemen fight on.

Hitler calls off invasion after losing air battle

17 SEPTEMBER, LONDON

Adolf Hitler, convinced that the RAF remains strong enough to see off the Luftwaffe, today cancelled 'Operation Sea Lion', Germany's planned sea invasion of Britain. In two months of dogged fighting the RAF has repulsed the Luftwaffe's attempt to win control of the skies over Britain. On 15 September, RAF fighters won what is being hailed as their greatest victory of all. Two waves of attackers, intended to clear the sky of the British, were chased back to France. The Luftwaffe lost 61 aircraft to the RAF's 29.

Victory has been a close-run thing. Continued assaults on airfields brought the RAF to a state of crisis in early September, but on 7 September Luftwaffe chief Hermann Goering turned from the airfields to launch a 'blitz' on British cities, giving the RAF time to regroup.

Britain's secret weapon is its radio direction finding equipment (RDF). Pioneered by British scientist Robert Watson-Watt in the mid-1930s, RDF can plot the approach of bombers, giving British fighters time to scramble and intercept the bombers before they unload. Churchill has paid glowing tribute to the RAF's achievement. On 20 August he saluted the pilots: 'Never in the field of human conflict was so much owed by so many to so few.'

ABOVE LONDON The Blitz was designed to strike at ports and industrial bases.

BAILING OUT A sequence of camera-gun film frames showing the pilot of a stricken Ju 88 parachuting to safety after being shot down by a British fighter.

Churchill becomes Prime Minister

10 MAY, LONDON

After two days of high drama at Westminster, the veteran politician Winston Churchill has taken charge of the British war effort. Conservative Prime Minister Neville Chamberlain has resigned, and Churchill will head an all-party government.

German successes in Belgium and the Netherlands today were the final blow for Chamberlain, but his position was already weak. The humiliating failure of Britain's efforts to force the

CHURCHILL A vocal opponent of appeasement.

German invaders out of Norway last month sparked a House of Commons debate two days ago. Chamberlain won a vote of confidence, but 40 Conservative MPs voted against him. Most dramatically, Tory MP Leo Amery attacked Chamberlain with the words used by the 17th-century leader Oliver Cromwell to contemporary MPs: 'Depart, I say, and let us have done with you! In the name of God, go!'

Labour Party leader Clement Attlee told Chamberlain that his party would join a wartime coalition but only under a new prime minister. Chamberlain wanted to hand over to Foreign Secretary Lord Halifax, but Attlee demanded the redoubtable Churchill, who is robustly confident of victory.

MUSSOLINI ISSUES BATTLE CRY

10 JUNE, ROME
Generalissimo Benito Mussolini, Italy's Fascist dictator, declared war on Britain and France today. Hostilities will start at the stroke of midnight.

'Il Duce', as Mussolini is known in Italy, responded with his usual theatrical oratory to the cheering crowd that had gathered outside his official residence. 'We will conquer!' he said. 'People of Italy to arms! Show your tenacity, your courage, your worth.'

The Italian foreign minister, Galeazzo Ciano, told Allied ambassadors that Mussolini was simply carrying out the plans he had already laid with Hitler. The move certainly came as no surprise to the Allies, since Italy and Germany had already fought on the same side during the recent Spanish Civil War.

But Mussolini's declaration may have tipped the balance in favour of the Allies as the United States, which has tried to dissuade Italy from entering the

INSPECTION DAY Mussolini sought to regiment the masses and revive ancient Rome's military glory.

war, might now be stirred to action. President Roosevelt said in a speech in Virginia that Italy had 'scorned the rights of security of other nations' and pledged US aid to Britain and France.

And the *New York Times* will tomorrow publish a blistering attack on Mussolini. 'With the courage of a jackal at the heels of a bolder beast of prey, Mussolini has left his ambush,' the editorial says.

··· THE FIRST USE OF OVERDUBBING IN A FILM OCCURS IN *HIS GIRL FRIDAY*, DIRECTED BY HOWARD HAWKS ···

Trotsky assassinated with ice pick

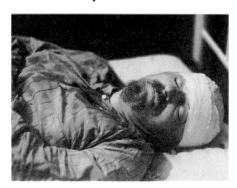

BOLSHEVIK HERO Trotsky was committed to the cause to the end. 'I am sure of the victory of the Fourth International,' he said on his deathbed.

21 AUGUST, MEXICO CITY
Leon Trotsky, one of the chief architects of the Russian Revolution, has died in hospital today from wounds suffered when he was attacked by a man with an ice pick at his home in Mexico City yesterday. He was 60 years old.

His murderer has been arrested and is believed to be a Spanish communist named Ramon Mercader. It seems that he had insinuated his way into the Trotsky household by posing as a supporter of the exiled Russian. While the two men were together in the study, Mercader plunged an ice pick into Trotsky's skull. There was a brief struggle, but the wounded man was no match for his assassin.

This was not the first attempt on Trotsky's life. Earlier this year, on 24 May, the villa was peppered with gunfire while he took shelter on the floor with his wife and grandson. Trotsky accused Stalin of being behind the May attack, and, although *Pravda* has described Mercader as a disillusioned Trotskyite, it is widely held that he was payrolled by Stalin.

'What's up, Doc?' demands rabbit

A new star was born this year – a cartoon rabbit. Bugs Bunny made his first screen appearance in *A Wild Hare*, looking up the barrel of a hunter's rifle and casually asking: 'Eh, what's up, Doc?'

Before Bugs, cartoon animals had been divided into the cute (such as Mickey Mouse) and the manic (Daffy Duck). Bugs's long, spindly body, laid-back personality and quick-fire, wisecracking dialogue are a new departure.

He takes his name from Warner Brothers animator Bugs Hardaway, but it was the innovative director Tex Avery who gave him his unique character – hip and snide – and his habit of chewing carrots. His voice is supplied by Mel Blanc.

French underground caves reveal the dawn of art

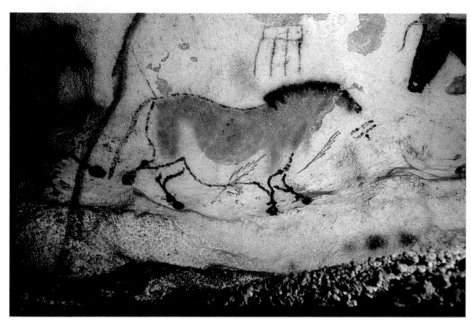

MAGICAL PAST The caves are adorned with mysterious symbols such as the jellyfish form above the horse.

1 NOVEMBER, FRANCE
An extraordinary archaeological discovery has been made by four boys lost in some caves in Lascaux, south-west France. After their dog fell into a hole, the boys climbed down to fetch him and found a cave covered with hundreds of lively images.

The cave consists of a main cavern and several steep galleries. The paintings and drawings are some 15 000 years old, dating back to the Stone Age – and as such are the earliest known works of art. Deer, bison, cattle and horses run across the walls with lifelike vigour. Some of the animals seem to be pierced by arrows, while others lie dying as if struck down in the hunt. Art historians have been excited by quality of the work. The execution of outline is confident, and anatomy is precisely rendered.

The purpose of these drawings, hidden as they are in inaccessible caves, is mysterious. It is certainly not decorative. The people who made them could only have seen their work by the light of flickering torches, and some of the drawings are scratched over others. The most likely explanation is a religious one. These early artists might well have been performing a kind of ritual. Were they chronicling or forecasting a successful hunt? Or were they impregnating the earth's womb with herds of magical animals?

One theory is that the precision with which the drawings are done points to the belief that these early Europeans were creating the animals as they drew them – or attempting to possess their life force. So the best artists would surely have been highly valued members of prehistoric society. Perhaps they were even venerated as shamans.

··· CBS MAKES THE WORLD'S FIRST TELEVISION BROADCAST IN COLOUR ···

ARABIAN NIGHTS AND MACHINE-GUN TALK

CROWNED HEADS Newspaper readers elected Bette Davis and Mickey Rooney 'King and Queen of the Movies' in a nationwide poll.

Undertones of war were evident in films such as Alfred Hitchcock's spy thriller *Foreign Correspondent*. But there were also opportunities to escape grim reality: Alexander Korda's magnificently colourful Arabian Nights fantasy *The Thief of Baghdad*, or Walt Disney's *Pinocchio* – a success to balance out the failure of his most ambitious film, *Fantasia*. Mickey Rooney and Judy Garland raised spirits in a rollicking high-school musical, *Strike Up the Band*. Audiences were dazzled by the machine-gun repartee of *His Girl Friday*, a fast-paced comedy starring Cary Grant and Rosalind Russell as warring newspaper hacks. The Rosalind Russell role had first been turned down by Jean Arthur and Ginger Rogers. Grant scored another hit with the elegant society comedy *The Philadelphia Story*, this time opposite Katharine Hepburn. Melodrama was well represented by *Rebecca*, with Joan Fontaine appealing as Laurence Olivier's second wife, overshadowed by the memory of the first, and *The Letter*, which found Malaysian rubber planter's wife Bette Davis facing blackmail. The latter was praised for its faithful interpretation of Somerset Maugham's play but censorship enforced an infuriatingly moral ending.

1941

BORN

Jan 9: Joan Baez, US folk singer
24 May: Bob Dylan (born Robert Zimmerman) US folk musician
8 Oct: Jesse Jackson, US politician and civil rights campaigner

Jane Wyman and Regis Toomey set a new world record for the longest kiss ever recorded in front of a motion picture camera. The kiss, filmed for the Warner Brothers' production You're in the Army Now, *lasted three minutes and five seconds.*

DIED

8 Jan: Lord Baden-Powell, founder of the Boy Scouts
8 Jan: Amy Johnson, pioneering British aviator
13 Jan: James Joyce, Irish novelist
28 Mar: Virginia Woolf, English novelist, by drowning herself
10 July: 'Jelly Roll' Morton, pianist and jazz band leader

WAR DECLARED

25 June: by Finland, on the USSR
27 June: by Hungary, on the USSR
5 Dec: by Britain, on Finland, Hungary and Romania
8 Dec: by the USA and Britain, on Japan
11 Dec: by Germany and Italy, on the USA

APPOINTED

26 July: General Douglas MacArthur, to command US forces in the Far East
16 Oct: General Hideki Tojo, leader of the 'War Party', prime minister of Japan

INVADED

6 Apr: Yugoslavia and Greece, by Germany
22 June: USSR, by Germany
25 Aug: Iran, by Britain and the USSR
10 Dec: Malaya, by Japan

SIGNED

13 Apr: a neutrality treaty between Japan and the USSR
13 July: a treaty of mutual aid between Britain and the USSR

SACKED

19 Dec: Field Marshal Walther von Brauchitsch, army commander-in-chief, after the German failure to capture Moscow – Hitler assumes personal command

LAUNCHED

USA: 'Big Boy', the biggest ever steam locomotive built by the Union Pacific railroad company

CALLED UP

9 Dec: single women in Britain between the ages of 20 and 30

REMOVED

1360 Soviet heavy industrial plants, eastwards, to prevent their capture by the advancing Germans

CAPTURED

25 Dec: Hong Kong, by Japanese forces

Spam, the tinned processed meat product, becomes a staple in the diets of millions of Allied soldiers. Nikita Khrushchev wrote in his memoirs: 'Without Spam, we shouldn't have been able to feed our army.'

FIRST NIGHTS

London: *Blithe Spirit*, by Noël Coward
Zurich: *Mother Courage and her Children*, by Bertolt Brecht

STANDARDISED

Manufactured clothing and furniture in Britain, with the introduction of wartime 'Utility' standards

FIRSTS

18 Aug, UK: National Fire Service set up in Britain
Aerosol insect sprays go on sale in the USA; invented by military scientists to protect troops from malaria
Wonder Woman cartoon appears in the USA

SUNK

27 May: German battleship *Bismarck*, claimed to be unsinkable, after being hunted down by the Royal Navy
14 Nov: British aircraft carrier *Ark Royal*, by an Italian submarine

ESTABLISHED

Fair Employment Practices Committee, to eradicate racist employment policies in the USA, by President Roosevelt

RETIRED

Greta Garbo, after poor reviews of her performance in the film comedy *Two-Faced Woman*

INVADED

Peru, by Ecuador, while the USA is tied up in the war in Europe

NEW WORDS

antibiotic *n:* substance that kills bacteria without injuring other forms of life
gremlin *n:* an imaginary imp jokingly said to be responsible for mechanical problems in the war
teenager *n:* person from 13 to 19 years of age

On 11 April, *the city of Coventry is once again the target of a heavy German air raid, only six months after it was razed to the ground by a massive German attack which involved around 500 aircraft and wiped out 60 000 buildings. Today's bombing was aimed at aircraft factories in and around Coventry.*

Hitler repelled from gates of Moscow

6 DECEMBER, RUSSIA
Russian forces under Marshal Zhukov today launched a huge counteroffensive against Hitler's troops, pushing them back from the perimeters of Moscow. Throughout Europe the news is raising hopes that this may prove to be the first genuine reversal for the German fighting machine.

The Eastern Front has been a major theatre of war since 22 June, when Hitler launched 'Operation Barbarossa', one of the most ambitious undertakings in military history. In a broad front, stretching from the Baltic to the Black Sea, German troops swarmed across the Russian border.

The attack was three-pronged: a northern unit marching towards Leningrad; a southern group, which advanced on Kiev; and an enormous central force – consisting of eight panzer divisions with 930 tanks – which pushed towards Moscow.

The Soviets were pitifully unprepared for the attack, having attached great value

ROLL ON Soviet T-34 tanks performed particularly well on the winter terrain.

to the nonaggression treaty with Germany, signed in 1939. At first the Germans made excellent headway. Smolensk and Kiev were

taken, Leningrad was besieged, and by mid-July the road to Moscow seemed open.

But the German army was halted while Hitler and the high command disagreed on the details of the main thrust of the attack. The march to Moscow only got under way on 30 September, when the weather began to change. As the autumn rains turned to ice and snow, the German advance slackened. Zhukov mustered his forces and waited on the Moscow Front until frostbite and disease took their toll on the enemy, before launching his own strike.

SMOKING BATTLEFIELD A German assault troop leader at the Eastern Front.

Hitler's top man baffles all with peace mission

11 MAY, SCOTLAND
Rudolf Hess, Hitler's deputy and confidant, secretly flew solo into Scotland last night, apparently seeking peace. His aeroplane crash-landed near Eaglesham, south of Glasgow, and he has been taken as a prisoner of war. Rumour has it he has been put in the Tower of London.

Hess, who is known to be directly responsible for Nazi Party organisation, is believed to have offered peace to Britain and recognition of her colonies in return for German domination of Europe.

There is no doubt that this astonishing offer is not authorised by the Reich; Hitler has moved fast to declare his former aide insane. The British government seems equally suspicious; Churchill said: 'This is one of those cases in which the imagination is baffled by the facts.'

The Hess affair had the unfortunate effect of deepening Stalin's mistrust of the Allied nations. Certain that Britain and Germany were plotting against the Soviet Union, Stalin ignored British and US intelligence reports of the impending German invasion.

Hess's sensational action was never satisfactorily explained – though there was speculation that the peace offer might have been a cover for an abortive attempt to contact Nazi collaborators in Britain.

Star of David clears way for persecution

6 SEPTEMBER, BERLIN
It was announced today that from 19 September it will be a crime for Jews in Germany to appear in public without a yellow Star of David sewn to their clothing. This order, published in the *Legal Gazette*, extends to all Jews 'who have completed their sixth year'. The order also says that Jews are not allowed to leave their areas of residence without getting permission from police.

This latest move was the most visible in a series of the anti-Semitic measures which started when Hitler first gained control of the German parliament in 1933. First he ordered a boycott of Jewish businesses, followed by the opening of a concentration camp for 'undesirables' at Dachau. In 1935, Jews were stripped of German citizenship and pension rights. It became illegal for Jews to use public transport, and to visit parks or libraries. Work in radio, theatre and the film industry was banned, and Jewish children were not allowed to attend public schools. Intermarriage between Jews and non-Jews was banned.

Rumours are starting to circulate that a 'final solution' to the 'Jewish problem' has been ordered. The murder of Jews is commonplace in occupied Russia, but new methods for systematic killing are believed to have been tested in the last few weeks at Auschwitz camp in Poland.

WARNING SIGN Posters declaring 'When you see this sign ...' reminded the public to avoid, or abuse, Jews.

··· RUSSIAN GALINA PUSHKOVA IS THE FIRST CAMERAWOMAN HIRED TO SHOOT A FULL-LENGTH FEATURE ···

Atlantic talks look forward to a time of peace

LIFELINE Roosevelt promised aid to Britain in the form of armaments from the 'great arsenal of democracy'.

11 AUGUST, NEWFOUNDLAND
The USA took a step nearer to joining the war today. Following meetings conducted in great secrecy, President Roosevelt and British Prime Minister Churchill issued a declaration of shared principles and aims. Foremost among these is 'the final destruction of Nazi tyranny' and a peace capable of delivering 'freedom from fear and want'.

The two men met aboard British and US warships moored in Placentia Bay, Newfoundland. The American public was told that the President had gone fishing, but Churchill's absence from Britain was a secret. The declaration, known as the Atlantic Charter, states that neither Britain nor the USA wants to gain land as a result of the conflict. Both countries recognise the 'right of all peoples to choose the form of government under which they will live', and look forward to disarmament: 'All the nations of the world, for realistic as well as spiritual reasons, must come to the abandonment of the use of force.' After the war there should be economic cooperation among nations.

Roosevelt has already shown his commitment to the British cause. The lend-lease agreement allows the USA to lend rather than sell armaments to Britain. It followed Churchill's announcement that Britain was facing bankruptcy and his plea: 'Give us the tools and we will finish the job.'

But Britain was hoping for more than the 'Europe first' strategy agreed in the event of US involvement in the war. 'Europe first' means merely defensive operations in the Pacific while attacks are mounted in Europe. Churchill was disappointed to find Roosevelt disinclined to commit to landings in North Africa or a Pacific offensive.

PEARL HARBOR BRINGS USA INTO WAR

GRAVEYARD OF BATTLESHIPS The rescue boat *West Virginia* searches for survivors after 353 Japanese fighter aircraft devastated the US base.

8 DECEMBER, PEARL HARBOR, HAWAII
As dawn broke over Hawaii yesterday morning, Japanese bombers attacked the US naval base at Pearl Harbor, on the island of Oahu. Early reports suggest that nearly 2500 members of the armed forces and civilians were killed.

News of the attack, which destroyed or severely damaged all eight of the battleships in the US Pacific Fleet, reached the east coast of the United States just as families, hardly able to believe what they heard, were sitting down to their Sunday roasts. On 27 November, Washington had sent a 'war warning' via Pearl Harbor of a possible imminent attack on the Philippines, Malaya or Thailand. No one had suspected that Pearl Harbor itself was in danger.

The disaster has shocked and embarrassed the White House, but President Roosevelt's reaction to what he has called 'a day that will live in infamy' has been swift. War has been declared on Japan. It is inevitable that the world's greatest democracy will soon be at war with Germany and Italy.

The attack on Pearl Harbor was timed to coincide with Japanese landings in Malaya and Thailand and aerial bombings of American bases on the Philippines, Guam, and Wake and Midway Islands. More than half of the British and American

aircraft in the Pacific have been destroyed. The Japanese Commander in Chief of the Combined Fleet, Admiral Isoruku Yamamoto, has for some time believed that the United States would be forced into the war. It is his hope that this pre-emptive strike will enable Japan to build an impregnable rim of air and naval bases around the central and south-western Pacific before the United States has recovered from the blow. In the USA's favour, it has been confirmed that the Pacific Fleet's three aircraft carriers all escaped the bombing, as they were at sea at the time.

Behind this new wave of aggression lies Japan's desperate search for oil and other strategic supplies. Throughout the autumn the American secretary of state, Cordell Hull, has repeatedly offered Japan financial credits and supplies in return for military withdrawal from China and Indochina. But Japanese Prime Minister Hideki Tojo rejected that offer. His own offer, to withdraw from Indochina in return for the 'unfreezing' of Japanese assets in the United States, would have left Japan with a clear run in China and cannot have been intended to receive American agreement. Indeed, both sides have known that the day of reckoning was at hand, though it has come sooner than Washington expected.

ROUGH GOING A couple of lieutenants take the new 4-cylinder, 2.2-litre GP for a gruelling test drive.

Versatile vehicle is GI Joe's best friend

The United States Army is very proud of this autumn's new recruit: a new go-anywhere, do-anything vehicle. The Willys 'General Purpose' vehicle, or GP, is a simple and robust four-wheel-drive vehicle which can act as a staff car, ambulance, reconnaissance car or load-carrier. Thanks to high ground clearance, the GP operates on almost any terrain. On the flat its maximum speed is 100 kilometres per hour (65 mph), and it is light enough to be carried in a glider and tough enough to be dropped by parachute.

The first GPs, soon known as Jeeps, were made in 1940 by the Bantam Car Company of Butler, Pennsylvania, but to step up production for the army both Willys and Ford submitted designs.

··· BIG BAND LEADER GLENN MILLER'S *CHATTANOOGA CHOO-CHOO* IS THE TUNE OF THE YEAR ···

Yankee Clipper sets home run record

16 JULY, CLEVELAND, OHIO
The hitting streak of Joe DiMaggio, the New York Yankees' star centre-fielder, has been halted by the Cleveland Indians after 56 games. For weeks America has been in the grip of a mounting excitement as the powerful, rangy slugger's ability to reach base safely with a hit continued game after game. Tonight, at Municipal Stadium, the odyssey ended, but DiMaggio had already gone way past the previous record of 41 games, set by George Sisler of the St Louis Cardinals in 1922.

Blessed with the smoothest of swings and a keen eye, DiMaggio rarely strikes out – unusual for a home-run hitter. Students of baseball are already hotly debating which is the greater achievement, this new record of the 'Yankee Clipper' or the 60 home runs hit by Babe Ruth in 1927.

HARD HITTER Joe DiMaggio hits another big one on 29 June, well into his record-breaking winning run.

HIGH PERCH At times, there were 70 men carving the heads with pneumatic hammers and chisels.

Great heads of government

6 MARCH, SOUTH DAKOTA
The man who grumbled that there was no monument in America 'as big as a snuff box' has died, his efforts to remedy the situation nearly complete. The spectacle of the vast heads of four American presidents carved into the towering granite cliff of Mount Rushmore was intended as a memorial for the nation, but it is also a tribute to its sculptor, Danish-born Gutzon Borglum.

Borglum started work in 1927, using dynamite to blast away the rock, and a system of pointers and plumb lines to transfer the shapes of smaller scale models to the 18-metre (60-ft) heads of Washington, Jefferson, Lincoln and Theodore Roosevelt. He created the pupils of the eyes by carving rings several feet across and deep enough to ensure they were always in shadow, with tiny pegs of rock left in the centre to reflect a spot of light. His son Lincoln will finish the memorial, due to be completed in November.

··· 1 JULY: THE WORLD'S FIRST COMMERCIAL RADIO STATION, WNBT, STARTS BROADCASTING IN NEW YORK ···

WELLES IS MASTER CRAFTSMAN

A blazing new talent burst onto the screen, although few people noticed. Orson Welles, already a star of stage and radio, directed and starred in *Citizen Kane*, a brooding, elaborate tale of a newspaper magnate corrupted by power. Critics were impressed by its brilliant photography and complex narrative structure, but it has not found favour with the public. A minor actor called Humphrey Bogart attracted notice as a dying gangster in *High Sierra* and a hard-nosed private eye in *The Maltese Falcon*. War-torn Britain produced anti-Nazi adventures such as *Pimpernel Smith*, *49th Parallel* and Humphrey Jennings's tender documentary *Listen to Britain*. Hollywood, too, geared up for war with *Sergeant York*: Gary Cooper won an Oscar playing a pacifist who conquered his scruples to become a World War I hero. But the power of film simply to entertain was celebrated in *Sullivan's Travels*, a satire about a Hollywood director who sets out to experience poverty for himself.

LOW DRAMA *Kane* used plenty of high- and low-angle shots for impact.

1942

BORN

17 Jan: Cassius Clay (later called Muhammad Ali), US boxer
31 Jan: Derek Jarman, British film-maker
25 Mar: Aretha Franklin, US singer
24 Apr: Barbra Streisand, US singer and actress
17 Nov: Martin Scorsese, Hollywood film director
27 Nov: Jimi Hendrix, US musician

Propaganda approaches an art form during World War II, and great use is made of posters. This drawing, which featured in Allied campaigns circulated in several countries, caricatures a German officer and reminds people: 'This is the Enemy.'

DIED

18 Apr: Gertrude Vanderbilt Whitney, US sculptor
29 May: John Barrymore, Hollywood actor

FIRST

2 Dec: controlled nuclear chain reaction, in a nuclear reactor built at the University of Chicago by Italian physicist Enrico Fermi

AWARDED

Feb, USA: the first gold disc, to Glenn Miller for selling a million copies of *Chattanooga Choo Choo*
Apr, UK: the George Cross to the island of Malta, for civilian heroism and courage during the German bombardment of the island

PUBLISHED

William Beveridge, *Social Security and Allied Services*, the blueprint for a welfare state in Britain
Albert Camus, *The Outsider*
Evelyn Waugh, *Put Out More Flags*

FOUNDED

July, UK: Oxford Committee for Famine Relief (later Oxfam)

INTERNED

Mar, USA: 110000 Japanese-Americans living near the Pacific coast, but not Germans or Italians

AGREED

Jan, Berlin: the 'Final Solution', by Nazi leaders meeting at Wannsee, to exterminate Europe's Jews, and to build special camps in Poland for the purpose

APPOINTED

1 Feb, Norway: Vidkun Quisling, pro-Nazi prime minister
23 Feb, UK: Air Marshal Sir Arthur 'Bomber' Harris, to head RAF Bomber Command
July, USSR: Georgi Zhukov, the 'general who never lost a battle', to command the Soviet southern armies

CAPTURED

15 Feb: Singapore and 70000 British and Commonwealth troops, by Japan

Plastics are being increasingly used by designers in the manufacture of household items. American Earl Tupper has used polyethylene to create lightweight containers with airtight lids, known as 'Tupperware'. This container is made to store cereal.

PROMISED

20 Mar: 'I shall return', by US General Douglas MacArthur, as the Philippines are overrun by the Japanese army

INTRODUCED

USA: the first national speed limit, set at 56 km/h (35 mph)

DEMONSTRATED

27 July, London: 60000 people in Trafalgar Square, demanding a second front in Europe to relieve German pressure on the Soviet Union

JAILED

9 Aug: leaders of the Indian National Congress – including Gandhi, Nehru and Azad – for launching the 'Quit India' civil disobedience campaign

ASSASSINATED

24 Dec: Admiral Jean François Darlan, former chief minister of Vichy France, now self-proclaimed pro-Allied French head of state; shot by outraged Frenchman

REJECTED

Errol Flynn, for military service, due to a heart defect, malaria and tuberculosis

CAPTURED

28 June, New York City: eight German spies on Long Island, after being landed by a U-boat

Kellogg's cereal company continues to prosper and launches a new product, sugar-coated corn flakes, called Frosted Flakes. Using Tony the Tiger as its advertising mascot, this marks the company's first venture away from its famously successful Corn Flakes brand.

NEW WORDS

freebie *n*: thing given free of charge
gung-ho *adj*: enthusiastic, eager
zap *vb*: to kill, destroy, deal a sudden blow to

Battle in the Atlantic

MAKING A SPLASH US sailors explode a depth charge in an attempt to deter a German U-boat.

JULY, LONDON

A grave error of judgement by Alfred Pound, the ailing First Sea Lord, led the PQ-17 convoy to disaster in Norwegian waters earlier this month. The convoy of 35 merchant ships, its escort including six destroyers, three minesweepers and two anti-aircraft carriers, set out from Iceland on 27 June. On 4 July, Pound – based in the Admiralty in London – ordered the convey to scatter, owing to fears that the German navy was intending to attack. He also recalled the convoy's escort.

German aircraft and U-boats immediately moved in to attack the undefended PQ-17. All but 11 of its ships went down, taking with them 430 tanks and 210 aircraft. More than 150 sailors are believed to have lost their lives.

Tragedy also struck another convoy, the PQ-13. On its return from the east it was driven off course by storms and lost six ships in an Allied minefield.

Since the beginning of the year the 'Battle of the Atlantic', as it has been dubbed by Winston Churchill, has been extended into northern waters. So far the Germans have gained the upper hand. In the early days of the war Admiral Doenitz attacked the convoys by sending out 'wolfpacks' of surface raiders at night, evading detection by the British underwater tracking device Asdic. This year Germany's development of long-range U-boats has carried the underwater attack to the coasts around the United States, and Allied convoy ships are being sunk at the rate of nearly 100 a month.

Cruel revenge in Czechoslovakia

10 JUNE, LIDICE

In a callous act of reprisal, German troops have razed the tiny Czech village of Lidice to the ground and butchered its male inhabitants. The brutal actions were carried out in retaliation for the death of Reinhard Heydrich, deputy chief of the Gestapo and 'protector' of Bohemia, one of the Czech regions annexed by Hitler in 1939. On 29 May two Czech patriots hurled a bomb at his car while he was driving towards Prague. The explosion shattered his spine, and he died from his wounds on 4 June.

Yesterday morning ten truckloads of German soldiers encircled the village and refused to allow anyone to leave. Starting at dawn today, they led away the men in batches of ten to a field behind a barn, where they gunned them down. More than 160 were killed. The 190 women of the village were rounded up and sent to the Ravensbrück concentration camp, where many of them were gassed. Almost 100 children were deported to be 'Germanised' at SS camps. After the massacre, the emptied village was utterly destroyed.

GRIM RETRIBUTION Nazis officers pose in front of the burning buildings of Lidice.

Japan's navy routed at Battle of Midway

EMBATTLED A stricken Japanese cruiser burns on the water after an American strike.

**7 JUNE, MIDWAY ISLAND, HAWAII
After four days of fierce fighting, the
revitalised US Pacific Fleet has inflicted
a crushing defeat on the Japanese navy
at Midway,** a small atoll at the northern
tip of the Hawaiian archipelago.

The victory, achieved with minimal
losses to the Americans, comes only a
month after the Battle of Coral Sea
thwarted Japan's attempt to clear the way
for an advance on New Guinea. The
Japanese navy has suffered some of its
most grievous losses – four carriers, two
heavy cruisers and nearly 300 aircraft.

After Coral Sea, the Japanese high
command decided to go all out in an
effort to regain the initiative in the
Pacific. Almost every capital ship in its
navy was deployed, under the overall
command of Isoroku Yamamoto, the
navy's commander-in-chief. The object
was not only to capture Midway, the site
of a large American air and naval base,
but also to lure the numerically inferior
forces of US Admiral Chester Nimitz
into battle.

The attack was launched on 4 June.
Helped by the cover of foul weather, a
four-carrier Japanese force advanced
and bombarded the US base without
battering it into submission. The
Japanese then turned away from the
base and sallied out to meet the
Americans in open water. That appears
to have been their fatal mistake. In the
afternoon American dive-bombers
exploded three carriers within minutes
and left them to blaze to their graves.
Torpedoes dispatched the fourth carrier
shortly afterwards.

This morning Japan was forced to
retreat from the battle, having sustained
its first decisive defeat of the war. Its
long-range striking capacity has been
effectively destroyed, and its ambition of
capturing New Caledonia, the Fiji
Islands and Samoa will now have to be
postponed. The American victory has
turned the naval balance in the Pacific
towards the Allies.

··· NEW YORK: PINBALL MACHINES ARE BANNED BECAUSE 'CHILDREN STEAL MONEY TO PLAY THEM' ···

New shirt fits to a 'T'

An icon of fashion came into being this
year when the US Navy came up with
specifications for the new 'T-type' shirt –
a knitted cotton vest with a round neck
and short sleeves set at right angles. This
design made for 'greater sweat
absorption under the arms'. Similar 'gob'
shirts (in American slang, a 'gob' is a
sailor) were available before the war, but
were thought of only as underwear.
Now the T-shirt has made the switch to
outerwear. Although created for the
armed forces, the T-shirt is already
proving popular in civvy street as a
casual, easy-to-wear top.

T TIME The US Coastguard was among the first to popularise T-shirts for everyday working clothes.

Bitter chill of defeat for Germans in Russia

24 DECEMBER, STALINGRAD

The German Sixth Army, trapped in Stalingrad in freezing temperatures for the past month, is staring defeat in the face. General Friedrich Paulus learned today that the Sixth Panzer Division is being withdrawn from the units that were sent to rescue him. It is now only a matter of time before he will have to order his forces to surrender.

This gloomy prospect could not have been foreseen at the start of the summer campaign. Hitler's chief target on the Eastern Front had been the Caucasus region in southern Russia, with its oilfields and its wealth of mineral resources. The initial objectives were met without encountering serious problems: Sebastopol fell on 9 July and Rostov-on-Don, the gateway to the Caucasus, was taken on 23 July. Six days later the Soviets' last rail link with the region was cut. Only Stalingrad, to the north-east of Rostov, still posed a threat. It is an important industrial centre and its situation, straddling the banks of the river Volga, gives it strategic value. There was also the possibility that, if the Russians counterattacked from this point and managed to break through the German cordon, the invading force in the Caucasus would be cut off from its supply lines. German military strategists decided that although it was

FIRING LINE Soviet troops take aim at the Germans from ruins in Stalingrad.

necessary to neutralise the city, perhaps with long-range artillery, it was not essential to take it.

However, Hitler did not appear to see it this way. Some observers believe that he became obsessed with the idea of taking Stalingrad. Acting on his instructions, General Paulus mounted a two-pronged assault on the city in late August. His attack was given initial impetus by a massive aerial bombardment, but in the city itself German forces met with stiff resistance. They tried to subdue the area street by street, but were hindered by snipers and could not make full use of their air power.

The Russian defence was spearheaded by Marshal Georgi Zhukov, who masterminded the counter-offensive outside the city. This consisted of a fierce attack on the German flanks, which were manned mainly by inferior Romanian and Italian troops who caved in quickly. By 23 November Paulus's troops, victims of the bitter cold as much as of the Red Army bombardment, had been encircled.

Since then the Sixth Army has been living on borrowed time. Despite promises that supplies would be airlifted to it, only meagre amounts have been received. Without fuel, ammunition and food, Paulus's position is hopeless.

TRIUMPHAL CRY A jubilant Soviet fighter celebrates the German army's defeat at Stalingrad on the river Volga.

The Desert Fox is stopped in his tracks

3 JULY, EL ALAMEIN, EGYPT

Field Marshal Erwin Rommel, the brilliant commander of the elite German Afrika Korps, has met with his first reversal, leaving the future of the North African campaign hanging in the balance. In Berlin there are mutterings that Hitler's favourite, the 'Desert Fox', has lost his invincible streak, while in Cairo and London hopes are rising that the fall of Egypt may yet be averted.

Rommel has had a meteoric rise up the military career ladder. He arrived in Libya in February 1941, when still a lieutenant-general, entrusted with the task of revitalising the African front. From the start his strategy was based on speed and surprise. His first

offensive brought the capture of Benghazi and Tobruk, and in 1942 he pressed on into Egypt, threatening to deprive the British of vital oil supplies and control of the strategically important Suez Canal. His rapid progress made this possible, but in the process he alienated many of his colleagues. They particularly resented the way that he was given resources that had been earmarked for other theatres of war, such as the assault on Malta.

Rommel's recent setback here is being attributed to his impatience. He attacked the British while his troops were exhausted after advancing 650 kilometres (400 miles) in just 36 days. Even so, his progress has been halted rather than defeated, and a greater conflict at El Alamein looms on the horizon.

BATTLE PLAN Montgomery had first gained military expertise in World War I.

British savvy wins the Battle of El Alamein

4 NOVEMBER, EL ALAMEIN, EGYPT

Before dawn today Field Marshal Erwin Rommel ordered his forces to retreat, as his Afrika Korps was reduced to just 30 tanks. The rout has shattered German ambitions in North Africa, and British and Commonwealth forces are now pursuing the enemy west towards Tunisia. It is estimated that the Allies have suffered some 25 000 casualties, with a further 30 000 taken prisoner.

The Allied attack was launched by British General Bernard Montgomery, or 'Monty' as his troops have nicknamed him, on the evening of 23 October. His move was made in the knowledge that the British position had strengthened in the past few months. He now had at his disposal 300 new Sherman tanks, sent across by US President Roosevelt, giving him a marked

numerical superiority in this field. In addition, the recent cracking of Germany's Enigma code by British scientists has meant that German messages can now be easily understood – a development that has enabled the Allies to pinpoint enemy positions exactly and target Rommel's supply ships.

Montgomery has also proved an imaginative commander in the field. He has used elaborate tricks to conceal his plans, such as deploying inflatable rubber vehicles to mislead aerial reconnaissance parties. Other tactical devices have included the novel method of employing infantry to open up a path for his tanks.

However the British general's *coup de grâce* was Operation Supercharge, a final push led by the New Zealand Division on 2 November. One day later the enemy line was broken, and victory was in sight.

OUTFOXED Rommel's first task in Africa was to bail out the Italians in Libya.

A gun named Dora smashes siege of Sebastopol

1 JULY, CRIMEA

A gun developed by a German armaments factory has been the Nazis' secret weapon in breaking the siege of Sebastopol. The weapon, designed in the 1930s by the Krupp company in order to smash the Maginot Line, dramatically bombarded 50 massive shells into the heart of the Russian fortress, ending a nine-month siege.

Dubbed *Schwere Gustav* ('Heavy Gustav') in honour of a member of the Krupp family, but now affectionately nicknamed 'Dora' by German troops, the gun fires 7-ton shells from its 80-centimetre (31-in) barrel. Mounted on rails, the siege gun is so massive that it has to be be taken apart in order to be moved and then reassembled at the desired firing position.

Although originally intended for Germany's attack on France, at that time Dora was neither ready nor needed, and it was not until 1942 that it was first test-fired in front of Adolf Hitler before being rushed to the Crimea.

BIG GUN Such a large weapon, capable of immense destruction, has never been used in warfare before.

··· THE FIRST KNOWN SELL-BY DATE IS USED ON A FOOD PRODUCT – A CARTON OF LYONS COFFEE IN BRITAIN ···

WEEPIES AND THE WAR

'Why ask for the moon when we have the stars?' Bette Davis asked Paul Henreid in *Now Voyager* - one of a spate of romantic weepies aimed squarely at women. Greer Garson's career was one of the main beneficiaries of the trend - she played an English rose who loses Ronald Colman (but finds him again) when he falls victim to amnesia in *Random Harvest*, and a similar role in *Mrs Miniver* playing a woman suffering in wartime Britain. According to Winston Churchill, the film was worth more to the war effort than a flotilla of destroyers. Humphrey Bogart also did his bit for the war effort in *Casablanca* with Ingrid Bergman; he played the cynical owner of 'Rick's Café' who helps his former lover and her resistance-leader husband to escape the Nazis. Bing Crosby gave audiences light relief in *Holiday Inn* and crooned 'White Christmas' for the boys fighting overseas.

WELL MET Bogart ponders Bergman's request for help which sparks off the movie's fatal chain of events.

1943

BORN

11 Feb: Mary Quant, British fashion designer
29 Mar: John Major, British prime minister
29 Sept: Lech Walesa, Polish trade union leader and statesman

DIED

28 Mar: Sergei Rachmaninov, Russian composer
4 July: Vladislav Sikorski, Polish soldier and politician
8 July: Jean Moulin, leader of the French resistance, under German torture

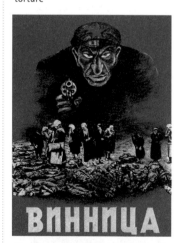

The Soviet secret police's practice of shooting anyone they thought likely to collaborate with the advancing German army was a gift to Nazi propagandists. This poster blames a demonised Jewish commissar for a massacre in the Ukraine in which 30 Russians were killed.

FIRST NIGHTS

31 Mar, New York City: *Oklahoma!,* stage musical by Rodgers and Hammerstein

14 Nov, New York City: Leonard Bernstein's debut as a conductor
2 Dec: *Carmen Jones,* stage musical by Oscar Hammerstein II

SCREEN HITS

For Whom the Bell Tolls, starring Gary Cooper and Ingrid Bergman
Lassie Come Home, the first Lassie film, starring the male dog Pal
Jane Eyre, starring Orson Welles, Joan Fontaine and Elizabeth Taylor
The Outlaw, starring Jane Russell, whose cleavage receives more publicity than the film itself

IN FASHION

USA: the zoot suit, a man's suit consisting of baggy trousers and long jacket with wide padded shoulders

PUBLISHED

Jean-Paul Sartre, *Being and Nothingness*
Hermann Hesse, *The Glass Bead Game*

BUILT

The Pentagon in Arlington, Virginia – the world's largest office building, to house American war administrators; it has 28 km (17 miles) of corridors

ESTABLISHED

Women's Airforce Service Pilots (WASPs), under director Jacqueline Cochran, to handle much of the USA's domestic flying

Rationing was imposed in Europe throughout the war and for many years afterwards. Items such as canned meat, coffee, sugar and clothing had to be purchased with stamps in ration books. As the war dragged on, many items were only to be found on the black market.

FOUNDED

Burma: the Indian National Army, by nationalist leader Subhas Chandra Bhose, to fight with the Japanese against the British
Washington DC: Congress of Racial Equality, to fight discrimination against African-Americans by non-violent direct action

SUNK

May: 41 German U-boats, ending the major threat to Allied shipping in the Atlantic

DEVASTATED

Bengal, by famine which kills over one million people

FIRST

Guided missiles used in action – the Luftwaffe sinks HMS *Egret*

DISCOVERED

12 Apr: the mass grave of 4500 Polish officers shot by the Soviet secret police at Katyn near Smolensk in 1940

ATTACKED

16 May, Germany: dams in the Ruhr, by the RAF using the 'bouncing' bombs designed by Barnes Wallis

MEETING

28 Nov, Teheran: the first between the 'Big Three' – Churchill, Roosevelt and Stalin

KILLED

29 Nov, Boston: 300 people by a fire at a nightclub; a further 150 people are injured

APPOINTED

24 Aug: Admiral Lord Louis Mountbatten, Allied supreme commander, South-East Asia
30 Nov: partisan leader Josip Broz ('Tito'), marshal of Yugoslavia, at a congress in the Bosnian town of Jajce

OPENED

USA: 'Big Inch' oil pipeline from Texas to eastern seaboard

ADMITTED

UK: women to membership of the Amalgamated Engineering Union

BEGUN

Muddy Waters's singing career, in Chicago, after being discovered on a plantation by folk singer Alan Lomax

NEW WORDS

chicken out *vb*: to withdraw through cowardice
soap opera *n*: a serialised drama, often dealing with domestic themes, broadcast on radio or television (so called because manufacturers of soap are typical sponsors)

Tide turns in the Pacific: USA takes Guadalcanal

9 FEBRUARY, SOLOMON ISLANDS

Japanese resistance has crumbled at Guadalcanal in the Solomon Islands – for the last six months a major strategic objective of the United States. The Japanese were building an airfield there intended to give them air supremacy in the region; now they are on the defensive in the Pacific.

The victory for Major General Vandegrift and his 19 000 men is the sweeter for having been accomplished against heavy odds.

The US troops were largely new recruits with no combat experience, least of all in the jungle, and the naval escort was untested in amphibious warfare. After seizing the enemy airfield last August they found themselves up against sapping

SPOILS OF WAR Troops display booty collected from fleeing Japanese soldiers.

heat, deadly stinging insects and a crack Japanese outfit. The carnage has been horrific, as night after night the 'Tokyo Express' brought in fresh supplies and men while warships bombarded the US dugouts. The decisive engagement took place on 13–14 November, when Japan suffered catastrophic losses – including two battleships, two cruisers and three destroyers – from which they never recovered.

For the last few weeks starving and disease-ridden Japanese soldiers have roamed the island, looting and scavenging, but the islanders have exacted a gruesome revenge: their traditional longhouses are now decorated with Japanese skulls. The Japanese have now, however, evacuated 13 000 men, leaving twice that number for dead.

Today there was an announcement from the US military headquarters: 'The Tokyo Express no longer has a terminal on Guadalcanal.'

··· CERVICAL CANCER IS THE BIGGEST KILLER OF WOMEN IN THE USA ···

Russians crush Germans

16 JULY, KURSK, RUSSIA

German forces are beginning their withdrawal from Kursk, following their defeat in the greatest tank battle of the war. Codenamed 'Operation Citadel', the massive German offensive was supposed to have demonstrated to the Allies that Hitler's army was not a spent force.

Nearly 3000 German tanks were committed to the attack, which was to begin at 3.30 am on 5 July. However, the day before, the Soviets received warning of the plan from a deserter, and as a result they were able to blunt the German assault by launching a pre-emptive strike at 1.10 am. Initially confused, the Germans regrouped and began their attack on time, though their progress on the first day was minimal.

Further minor gains were made over the next few days, but the key conflict was on 12 July, in the so-called 'slaughter of Prokhorovka'. Around this tiny village the German Tiger tanks were pitted against the Russian T-34s, fighting so ferociously that, as one officer put it, 'the earth was black and

ROLLING ALONG A soldier directs the Soviet Army's vast convoy of tanks.

scorched with tanks like burning torches'. Both sides sustained high losses, but the German advance had been halted. With this latest setback it is clear that the initiative on the Eastern Front is passing out of Hitler's hands.

Italian surrender comes as shock

8 SEPTEMBER, ROME

News of Italy's surrender was made official tonight in a broadcast by General Dwight Eisenhower, bringing an end to Italy's strained alliance with Germany. Marshal Pietro Badoglio, who became prime minister of Italy after the fall of Mussolini, made the announcement on Italian radio this evening.

The Allies invaded Sicily in July, and on 3 September, led by Field Marshal Bernard Montgomery, they crossed to the mainland and established beachheads along the coast. Since then they have advanced steadily up the Italian 'toe'. Yet Italy's unconditional surrender seems to have come as a shock to the Germans; just before Badoglio's broadcast Berlin radio praised Italian and German troops for their spirited defence of southern Italy. In fact, the ceremonial signing of the surrender took place secretly five days ago, on the day of the Allied invasion.

Italy's military position has become increasingly difficult in the two months since Mussolini, along with his Fascist war cabinet, was ousted from power on 25 July. Badoglio spent the following weeks disbanding the Fascist Party and arranging secret meetings with the Allies to negotiate the details of an armistice.

The main concerns of the Italian negotiators were to gain assurances of

LIBERATING ARMY American tanks rolling into Sicily face a population traumatised by German occupation.

maximum protection from the Allies for the Italian people and cities against the inevitable German reprisals. The German army will almost certainly try to wreak revenge upon its former allies, and Italy is clearly in a vulnerable position.

The Allies clearly hope that Italy will declare war on Germany. In his radio broadcast Eisenhower offered the Italians 'the assistance and support of the Allies' if they switch sides unconditionally and fight against the Nazis.

··· HITLER'S BOOK *MEIN KAMPF* (*MY STRUGGLE*) IS PUBLISHED IN THE USA ···

Nazis arrest pastor for treason

APRIL, BERLIN

The prominent Protestant theologian Dietrich Bonhoeffer was arrested this month, accused by the Nazis of conspiring to overthrow the German government. Bonhoeffer is one of the few members of the Church to have taken a consistently anti-Nazi line since Hitler first came to power. His

opposition to the Nazi regime and support for the Jews forced him into exile, but he returned to Germany at the start of the war and became actively involved in the resistance movement.

Last year he met the Anglican Bishop of Chichester, George Bell, and begged him to try to establish Allied support for the German opposition to

Hitler, but Bell's efforts since he returned to Britain have been in vain.

There has been little opposition to Hitler from either the Catholic or the Protestant Church. At best they have been sitting on the fence, although the Bishop of Württemberg's objection to Nazi treatment of the mentally ill slowed down the euthanasia programme.

STRATEGIC BOMBING FLATTENS GERMAN CITIES

MILITARY PRECISION US planes unleash hundreds of bombs over Germany.

HUMAN COST Bodies are laid out for identification in a gymnasium in Berlin.

31 JULY, HAMBURG

The heart of Hamburg has been wiped out by the intensive Allied bombing codenamed 'Operation Gomorrah'. More than 7000 tons of bombs have been dropped in the past five days – killing 40000 people, destroying 580 factories and knocking out three U-boats in the port area. On the night of 27–28 July, raging fire covered 5 square kilometres (2 sq miles) of the city and threw up a cloud of smoke 8 kilometres (5 miles) high. RAF Lancasters flew three mass night raids, while

US Eighth Army Air Force 'Flying Fortresses' made sure that Hamburg had no respite by mounting precision raids by day.

British and US forces have been aided by two new anti-radar devices, called Window and H$_2$S, enabling them to wreak unprecedented levels of destruction.

The Allies have directed their bombers against the German industrial area of the Ruhr since March. A celebrated triumph was the RAF's raid on the Mohne and Eder dams on 16 May with another new invention, the 'bouncing bomb'.

Warsaw Jews fight for their lives

16 MAY, WARSAW

At 8.15 tonight the Warsaw synagogue was blown up by SS General Jürgen Stroop, in a final symbolic act to support his claim that he has cleared the ghetto of its Jewish inhabitants.

In 1940 the ghetto was crowded with some 400000 Jews, brought from all over Poland by the Nazis. By February this year there were only 60000 left – the rest had died of starvation and disease. With a courage born of desperation, although weakened by lack of food, those remaining determined to die fighting. They put up some of the fiercest resistance the war has seen. It is not known how many German soldiers were killed before Himmler sent Stroop to sort out the crisis, but estimates run into hundreds.

BRAVE FIGHT Finally unearthed by the Nazis, Warsaw's last Jews are rounded up for the death camps.

On 24 April, the eve of the Jewish festival of Passover, Stroop gave the order for tanks to be sent in. He had told Himmler that he would be able to clear the ghetto within three days – in the event, the task has taken the Nazis three weeks.

Today Warsaw residents watched as Jews were herded onto trains bound for concentration camps. Around 4000 Jews were killed in the uprising, and 42000 went to their deaths in the camps. Only a few escaped, via the sewers, into the city's Christian sector.

Computer cracks the code for the Allies

DECEMBER, BLETCHLEY PARK, BUCKINGHAMSHIRE

Codebreakers at Britain's secret Code and Cypher School at Bletchley Park have a new and powerful ally: an electronic machine called Colossus. Built in 11 months by a team led by Post Office engineer Tommy Flowers, Colossus was put to the test by being asked to decode a German message which had already been solved using more primitive machines. The machine cracked it in just 30 minutes.

In amazement, the team ran the test again, with the same result. 'They just couldn't believe it,' said Flowers. 'They had never encountered that order of reliability and, of course, never that order of speed.'

Colossus is the first digital computer to use valves on a large scale – it contains 1500 of them. The idea that a machine might be able to break codes came from the work of mathematician Alan Turing – a staff member at Bletchley Park – who in the 1930s made pioneering studies of computation. When his Cambridge supervisor Max Newman arrived at Bletchley in late 1942, he put started to put Turing's ideas into practice.

MIGHTY MACHINE The 1500-valve Colossus is the world's first programmable computer.

The first machine was built at Dollis Hill, London, using a mixture of valves and relays. Called 'Heath Robinson' after the illustrator of bizarre machines, it worked, but too slowly. Colossus is a big advance, as it is the first machine to show that computers can do more than manipulate numbers, and it proves Turing's theory that they are logic machines with huge potential.

··· SWISS CHEMIST ALBERT HOFMANN ACCIDENTALLY DISCOVERS THE HALLUCINOGENIC PROPERTIES OF LSD ···

P-80 fighter plane could send the Messerschmitt into freefall

BLAST OFF The P-80 takes off in in Los Angeles.

31 DECEMBER, CALIFORNIA
The finishing touches are being put to a US jet fighter that is able to match Germany's Messerschmitt Me262. Lockheed's P-80 is ready to go, and will make its first flight in the next few days.

The Me262 made its first flight in July 1942. It was originally designed as a fighter aircraft, but the plans were changed when Hitler inspected it in November and decreed that it should go into production as a high-speed bomber. Its top speed is 160 kilometres per hour

(100 mph) faster than that of any Allied bomber – until now.

The P-80 is equipped with six guns and has a fuel tank at each wingtip that can be jettisoned if necessary. On paper the aircraft promises a performance which will be unrivalled by any other operational fighter. The plane will be capable of reaching speeds in excess of 880 kilometres per hour (550 mph). If initial tests go according to plan it will be ordered into production for the US Army Air Force as a front-line fighter.

Aqualung takes diving to new depths

French naval officer Jacques-Yves Cousteau and engineer Emile Gagnon this year successfully tested a device to allow divers to move freely underwater. The key to the success of the 'aqualung' is a valve designed by Gagnon that allows divers to use their own breathing to control the pressure of the air that reaches them. Air comes from a steel canister through a tube gripped in the teeth. Gagnon originally designed the valve to allow cars to run on gas.

The aqualung gives divers the freedom to move without the hindrance of heavy diving suits or pipes connecting them to the surface – the oxygen canister is strapped to the diver's back, leaving the hands free. The device is expected to have many applications in warfare, film-making and exploration.

Irish eyes are smiling after a cup of coffee

An entrepreneurial chef is lightening the load for passengers at Shannon Airport, Ireland, by serving them a new type of coffee that's sure to banish the travelling blues.

Joe Sheridan's 'Irish coffee' contains a generous tot of whiskey, with a dollop of fresh cream on top. Sheridan cooks for weary passengers who disembark from the transatlantic flying boat service run by Pan American Airways.

The last leg of the journey entails a short boat crossing from the seaplane to the shore, which tends to leave passengers cold and queasy as they enter the terminal building. An Irish coffee has proved just what's needed to warm them up, and Sheridan is now considering marketing his idea to restaurants and bars.

PHYSICAL ABANDON Jitterbugging offers young people a welcome release from the pressure of war.

Jitterbug whips up a frenzy

The latest dance craze that is sweeping across the United States is the jitterbug. This frenetic new dance started life as an altogether more sedate affair in the USA in the 1930s when it was known as the 'Lindy Hop'.

Now the dance has been completely revamped to match the new, faster jazz styles which have crossed over from the black American community to become popular throughout the world.

The USA's entry into the war has meant that the craze is spreading at lightning speed across the globe as American servicemen and -women posted in places as far afield as Britain and the Far East take the new dance with them.

The jitterbug has spawned a variety of variants, with names such as the Suzie-Q. All share the same structure: a basic two-step which is performed at a furious pace with jerky movements not previously known in dances.

The jitterbug also has a more fluid structure than has ever been seen before, allowing for bursts of wild, creative improvisation. It is all in stark contrast to the more conventional, formalised foxtrots and waltzes, which are suddenly beginning to look distinctly dated and old-fashioned. The new craze has the added benefit of keeping participants fit. Accomplished dancers have amazed onlookers by their energy and incredible gravity-defying feats.

··· 22 JAN, SOUTH DAKOTA: TEMPERATURE LEAPS FROM −20° C (−4° F) TO 12° C (54° F) IN 90 MINUTES ···

1944

BORN
9 Feb: Alice Walker, African-American author and social activist

DIED
23 Jan: Edvard Munch, Norwegian artist
13 Dec: Wassily Kandinsky, Russian artist

FIRSTS
30 Apr, London: 'prefab' (prefabricated home) on show
17 July, France: operational use of napalm, by US Air Force P–38 Lightnings during raid at Coutances

Rainbow Corner in London is one of the thriving social clubs where off-duty servicemen and -women gather to drink and dance. War has brought people closer together, and romance blossoms – especially between American GIs and British women.

ON STRIKE
8 Mar, Wales: 87000 miners, over attempts to introduce greater equality in mining wages across the country

DISCOVERED
10 Apr, USA: anti-malarial substance quinine, by Robert Woodward and William van Eggers
27 Aug, Poland: Nazi death camp at Majdanek

The first ballpoint pens go on sale in Buenos Aires. The ballpoint was invented by Laszlo Biro, a Hungarian journalist, who developed the idea after seeing the viscous, quick-drying ink used by printing machines.

New York City: preliminary findings on deoxyribonucleic acid (DNA) by German physicist Max Delbrück, who gives a series of groundbreaking lectures

RE-ELECTED
7 Nov, USA: Franklin D Roosevelt as US President, for fourth term

LAUNCHED
29 Jan, USA: USS *Missouri*, largest warship in the world
6 Apr, UK: PAYE (pay as you earn) for income tax
13 June: first German V1 rocket – or 'doodlebug' – fired at Britain
8 Sept: first German V2 rocket fired at Britain

PROMISED
22 June, Washington DC: education and housing for US war veterans, under GI Bill of Rights

DENOUNCED
28 Jan, London: Japanese treatment of US and British PoWs, by Anthony Eden, British foreign secretary

LIT UP
20 Nov, London: as blackout is lifted after five years

MASSACRED
10 June, France: inhabitants of village of Oradour-sur-Glane, near Limoges, in SS reprisal for killing of SS officer; 7 out of 700 survive

CANCELLED
Olympic Games due to be held in London, because of the war

ESCAPED
20 July, East Prussia: Hitler, from bomb attack; alleged leader of plot to kill him, Colonel Graf Klaus von Stauffenberg, is shot

COMMITTED SUICIDE
14 Oct, Germany: Field Marshal Erwin Rommel, after his knowledge of a plot against Hitler was revealed

LANDED
23 Feb, Cambridge: a German bomber with a full load of bombs, in a city garden, after the pilot bailed out
19 Mar, Germany: RAF Sergeant Nicholas Alkemade, safely in snowbank, after leaping from 5500 m (18000 ft) without a parachute; a fir tree saved him

NEW WORDS
angst *n*: acute but non-specific sense of anxiety or remorse
bebop *n*: type of jazz – derived from the 'nonsense' sounds of scat singing
fax *n*: abbreviation of 'facsimile': a telegraphy system that transmits documents via a telephone network

On 16 December, US jazz musician Glenn Miller mysteriously disappears on a flight from England to France and is never seen again. Miller's achievements were impressive – he was a band leader, trombonist and composer. He led the US Air Force Band, and his dance music was for many the soundtrack of the war.

Leap-frogging in the Pacific

The Allied victory at Guadalcanal last year brought the final assault on Japan a step nearer, but in the way lay hundreds of islands and atolls fitted out with airfields and fortifications, waiting to trap the Allied forces. Japan still held the Bismarck Archipelago, the Solomon Islands north of Guadalcanal and most of New Guinea.

To move through this Central Pacific maze General Douglas MacArthur, the US chief of staff, decided upon a strategy of 'leap-frogging' – bypassing Japanese strongholds such as Truk and Rabaul, but cutting them off with air and sea power, while establishing bases on less defended islands nearer to Japan. The strategy has paid rich dividends. By

INCHING FORWARD US marines advance after landing at Tarawa Atoll, in the Gilbert Islands.

midsummer 1944, American fleets had crashed through the Gilbert Islands, the Marshall Islands, New Guinea and the

Mariana Islands. With the autumn, MacArthur's forces came within bombing distance of the Philippines.

··· 22 JAN: ALLIED FORCES LAND AT ANZIO, SOUTH OF ROME ···

MacArthur's triumphant return to the Philippines

MISSION ACCOMPLISHED General MacArthur (left) wades to shore at Leyte.

25 OCTOBER, PHILIPPINES
Douglas MacArthur, the controversial American general, is back where, in his mind at least, he belongs – in the Philippines. MacArthur was given the joint command of

American and Filipino forces in the Far East in July 1941, but his troops were forced to leave when the Philippines fell to Japanese forces early in 1942. He vowed at the time that he would return, and he lived up to his promise on 20 August of this year. From Leyte Island he immediately broadcast a characteristically flamboyant message: 'People of the Philippines, I have returned!'

MacArthur has a strong emotional attachment to the Philippines, and has left no one in doubt that he considers the liberation of the islands not simply a highly strategic objective but also a sacred national obligation. The task at hand is a long slog from island to island, but already what must prove to be the clinching battle of the campaign has been won by the Americans. Even Japan's latest weapon – suicide pilots who deliberately crash their bomb-laden aircraft into enemy ships – was not enough to prevent an American victory in late October in the titanic Battle of Leyte Gulf. The two massive navies tested each other over an area as large as France, and at the end of the three days Japan's vaunted naval power lay in ruins. As the year ends – a year in which the tide in the Pacific has run ever more strongly in the Allies' favour – the United States is preparing for a final, and what must be a successful, drive to Manila. Meanwhile, speculation is rife that MacArthur is setting his sights on the White House.

GAINING A FOOTHOLD The Normandy landings, codenamed 'Operation Overlord', have opened the way to the liberation of France, at a cost of 10 000 casualties.

D-Day landings break German defences

6 JUNE, NORMANDY

A courageous and meticulously planned cross-Channel invasion of German-occupied northern France by British, American and Canadian forces has caught the German high command by surprise and re-opened the Western Front in Europe.

Fighting driving rain, blustery winds and high seas, a fleet of nearly 5000 warships and supporting craft with 176 000 men set out from England's southern coast shortly after midnight last night, heading for the beaches of Normandy. The Allied supreme commander, General Eisenhower, had given the go-ahead 18 hours earlier.

In preparation for the Normandy landings, Allied air forces have spent the past six weeks bombarding roads and bridges in northern France, leaving transportation links in chaos. Hitler's coastal defences were nevertheless formidable: underwater mines, pillboxes

and tank traps – and behind them 58 divisions of the German army. Two factors, however, stood in the Allies' favour. The weather was so bad last night that an invasion was discounted by the Germans, and they had in any case long expected landings to be made around Calais – the shortest route across the Channel – and had massed their defences there. Instead, the Allies chose a 100-kilometre (60-mile) strip of beach to the west of Le Havre for the landings.

By 3.00 am transports and landing craft were anchored off the Normandy coast. At 5.30 am warships began to shell the beaches. Artificial harbours, called 'Mulberries', were linked to the beaches by articulated steel roadways, and, before the shelling had stopped, the first assault troops were on their way.

The American infantry who landed on the 6-kilometre (4-mile) Omaha beach, where heavily overcast skies had ruled out air bombardment, met the

fiercest resistance. Many were trapped by underwater obstacles and drowned in the rising tide, and swathes of advancing troops were cut down by German fire from pillboxes and artillery strongholds while attempting to cross the 50 metres (165 ft) of shingle to the sea wall. But by 9.30 am, having scaled the bluffs beyond the beaches, the soldiers had opened a route inland. It is the first step on the long road to Paris.

LANDED Allied assault troops storm the beaches.

ALLIED FORCES LIBERATE PARIS

France's hero returns home

ALL OVER NOW Nazi prisoners are marched past the Arc de Triomphe today.

25 AUGUST, PARIS
Allied units swept into Paris today on what the American Major Frank Burk has called 'a physical wave of human emotion' – cheering crowds stretching out for 24 solid kilometres (15 miles). The fall of Paris after four years of Nazi occupation is an important milestone on the way to Berlin.

General Eisenhower, the Allied supreme commander, wishing to avoid costly street-fighting, had recommended skirting the historic city on the push to the German frontier. But last night he bowed to French opinion and, as Major General Dietrich von Cholitz continued to defy Hitler's orders to leave the city 'a field of ruins', news began to filter through that French troops had reached the Hôtel de Ville (town hall) in the city centre. Frenzied, ecstatic Parisians took to the streets in droves. At 2.30 pm troops closed in on the German headquarters in the Hôtel Meurice and forced Cholitz to surrender. A few skirmishes continued to break out, but by the end of the day more than 20000 German soldiers had been captured.

26 AUGUST, PARIS
General Charles de Gaulle, leader of the 'Free French' and head of the French Committee of National Liberation since 1943, ignored bullets from stray German snipers today as he led an Allied victory parade through Paris.

De Gaulle escaped to London after the fall of France in 1940 and did not see French soil again until the Normandy landings. He identifies himself as the saviour of France – President Roosevelt has referred to his 'Joan of Arc complex' – and his presence during the liberation of Paris ensures that the Communists will not take power. De Gaulle himself will head the first postwar French government.

··· GENERAL MACARTHUR AIRDROPS A MILLION CHRISTMAS CARDS OVER THE PHILIPPINES ···

Purge targets Nazi collaborators

The purge of French collaborators known as *l'épuration*, or 'purification', began in September this year, in an attempt to make a clean break after France's liberation and the abolition of the old administration. Amid great bitterness, thousands of people are accused of collaborating with the occupying Nazi forces. The head of the Vichy government, Marshal Pétain, and his prime minister, Pierre Laval, will stand trial; 'the way of collaboration' was Pétain's stated public policy.

Large numbers of public officials, bureaucrats and police are known to have cooperated with the Nazis.

The official punishment for those tried and found guilty is execution by firing squad, although women and children are to be spared. However, savage local reprisals are known to be taking place throughout France, especially in the Midi, where the resistance movement was the most active. Many collaborators are being rounded up and executed without trial.

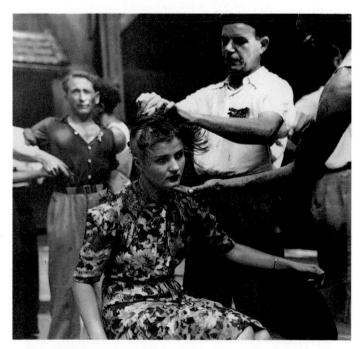

MARK OF SHAME A woman who fraternised with Nazi officers is cropped.

Allies forced to destroy historic monastery

MERCILESS DESTRUCTION A soldier walks through the ruins of Monte Cassino.

17 MAY, ITALY
The Allied forces gained an important military advantage today when British and Polish troops finally captured the ruins of Monte Cassino, taking 1500 German prisoners. Lying halfway between Rome and Naples, the town is geographically crucial, and it has been devastated by an Allied bombing campaign.

Back in January, fierce fighting centred on the historic Benedictine monastery on the Monte Cassino ridge – a building of particular strategic value as it blocked the road to Rome. Allied assaults from the ground failed to make any impact. Fighting conditions were atrocious, with mountain terrain made all the more treacherous by foggy weather. Attack from the air seemed the only option, and the monastery was flattened in a bombing raid on 16 February. Air raids on the town followed soon after. Today's conquest of Monte Cassino marks a big step forward in the Allied march towards Rome.

Rome is free again

4 JUNE, ROME
At long last Allied armies have entered Rome, liberating Italy's capital from the tyranny of the long Nazi occupation. Scenes of joy were widespread today as army jeeps rolled through the streets – Allied soldiers met with wildly enthusiastic, emotional crowds as they took possession of the 'eternal city'.

American General Mark Clark, one of the Allied army chiefs in charge of the Italian campaign, led the American 88th Division in its victorious procession into the capital. There was little resistance from the German soldiers remaining in the city. Their military leader, General Kesselring, had ordered a retreat northwards towards Florence, declaring Rome an 'open city' to avoid a bombardment and the destruction of its historic treasures and ancient buildings. Hitler had ordered his troops to blow up the famous Tiber bridges on retreat – fortunately his command was defied, and it seems that for the most part the city's ancient architecture has remained intact.

After months of hard fighting in southern Italy on the road to Rome, the capture of the capital has given the Allies an important psychological boost – it now seems inevitable that Hitler's military machine is doomed to destruction. President Roosevelt's response to the news has given voice to a universal feeling of optimism: 'The first Axis capital is in our hands. One up and two to go.' The Allied advance will continue northwards.

Grable is the pin-up queen

Peaches-and-cream Betty Grable is the Allied forces' favourite pin-up. She has topped the GI poll this year, beating the likes of Lana Turner and Rita Hayworth. Grable's long legs, which have become something of a legend, have been insured for $1 million by 20th Century Fox.

Grable began her career as a chorus girl at the age of 12. She made the transition to Hollywood, but was stuck with bit parts for ten years until she got her lucky break in 1940 when she landed the starring role in the top film musical *Down Argentine Way*. Grable's movie career has flourished ever since.

US SWEETHEART The pin-up craze is a new phenomenon in wartime.

Tormented figures express the horror of the current war

The self-taught and virtually unknown Irish-born painter Francis Bacon has exhibited a stunningly powerful picture that has made him him the most talked-about artist in Britain. The three panels that make up *Three Studies for Figures at the Base of a Crucifixion* may be intended for use at the base of a larger work depicting the Crucifixion, but these powerful images have the air of finished works in their own right.

Audiences have been shocked by the paintings' grotesque distortions and their intense sense of torment and suffering; some people find them merely unpleasant, but others believe that Bacon has expressed the predicament of the modern world with unrivalled force. The studies – depicting the Furies as inhuman figures – convey a sense of revulsion at the human condition, and Bacon has declared that death is

meaningless to him because humans are no more than meat.

Born in Dublin in 1909 to British parents, Bacon left the family home at the age of 16 when his father discovered him trying on his mother's underwear. He lived in Berlin and Paris before settling in London, where he worked for a time as an interior designer in 1928. It was not until 1930 that he began to paint seriously.

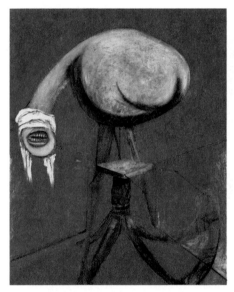

INNER DEMONS For many, Bacon's three figures haunting the scene of an execution represent the grotesque essence of man's inhumanity to man.

··· WALT DISNEY'S *THE THREE CABALLEROS* IS THE FIRST FILM TO COMBINE LIVE ACTION AND ANIMATION ···

GIRL LOVES HORSE Elizabeth Taylor gives National Velvet an affectionate hug.

FEMMES FATALES AND CHARMING GIRLS

The Hollywood *film noir* began in grim and deadly earnest this year: former song-and-dance man Dick Powell transformed his career playing a tough private eye in *Farewell My Lovely*; Gene Tierney was a murder victim and Dana Andrews the obsessive cop hunting her killer in *Laura*; insurance man Fred MacMurray was tempted into murder by Barbara Stanwyck in *Double Indemnity*. The *femme fatale* theme continued in *Arsenic and Old Lace*, a crazy comedy revolving around two sweet little old ladies with a nasty habit of poisoning people.

Laurence Olivier did his bit for the war effort as director and star of a brilliantly colourful, thrilling version of Shakespeare's *Henry V*. Carol Reed matched this achievement with *The Way Ahead*, a downbeat, realistic film about raw recruits being turned into hardened soldiers.

Elizabeth Taylor made a charming heroine in *National Velvet*, the story of two children who win a horse in a village raffle and train it to win the Grand National. Mickey Rooney and Angela Lansbury also starred. The film was shot in California, where Taylor was living as a war evacuee.

1945

DIED

26 Mar: David Lloyd George, British statesman
12 Apr: Franklin D Roosevelt, US President

DECLARED WAR

23 Feb: Turkey, on Germany
24 Feb: Egypt, on Germany and Japan
2 Mar: Finland, on Germany
27 Mar: Argentina, on Germany
8 Aug: Soviet Union, on Japan

RIOTED

30 Jan, Germany: Berliners, desperate for food

MARRIED

21 May, Ohio: Humphrey Bogart and Lauren Bacall
19 Sept, Hollywood: Shirley Temple and John Agar

On 26 July, *Clement Attlee is elected prime minister of Britain in a Labour landslide victory. The Labour Party won 393 seats, compared with the 199 won by the Conservative Party. Attlee has led the Labour Party since 1935, and today he becomes the first head of a Labour government with an independent majority.*

On 27 March, *Adolf Hitler decorates 20 young German soldiers who took part in battles against the Soviet army. Twelve-year-old Alfred Czech, the boy with whom Hitler is shaking hands, is being awarded the Iron Cross, second class.*

COMMITTED SUICIDE

23 May, Germany: Heinrich Himmler, head of SS

EXECUTED

15 Oct, France: Pierre Laval, former collaborationist leader
24 Oct, Norway: Vidkun Quisling, collaborationist leader

ON STRIKE

Oct, UK: dock workers demanding national minimum wage

PUBLISHED

Evelyn Waugh, *Brideshead Revisited*
George Orwell, *Animal Farm*
Jean-Paul Sartre, *The Age of Reason*
John Steinbeck, *Cannery Row*
Henry Miller, *The Air-Conditioned Nightmare*

REGISTERED

'Coke', as a trademark, by the Coca-Cola Company

FOUNDED

25–26 June, San Francisco: United Nations
20 Oct: Arab League
27 Dec, USA: International Monetary Fund (IMF); World Bank
Ebony magazine, by Chicago publisher John H Johnson
UK: Arts Council of Great Britain

PROCLAIMED

2 Sept: Democratic Republic of Vietnam
17 Nov: Republic of Indonesia
29 Nov: Federal People's Republic of Yugoslavia

FOUGHT

11 Oct, North China: Chinese Communists and Nationalists

ELECTED

Apr: Senator Albert Chandler (Kentucky), US baseball commissioner
16 June, Eire: Sean Kelly, president
13 Nov, France: Charles de Gaulle, president of French provisional government

CRASHED

28 July, New York City: B-25 bomber, into Empire State Building; 13 die and 26 are hurt

QUIT

21 Sept, Detroit: Henry Ford, as president of Ford Motor Company; his grandson Henry Ford II takes over

INVENTED

Microwave oven, by Percy LeBaron Spencer in Massachusetts; the idea came to him after a factory radar power tube melted the chocolate bar in his pocket

FIRSTS

16 July, New Mexico: detonation of an atom bomb, at the White Sands Missile Range; the flash was seen 288 km (180 miles) away
Car stickers, used in Kansas
Female executive producer in Hollywood; Virginia Van Upp was hired by Columbia Pictures to oversee 14 big-budget productions

OPENED

20 Nov, Nuremberg: war trials of leading Nazis

Swedish diplomat Raoul Wallenberg is arrested as a spy by the Soviet Army in Budapest. During the German occupation of Hungary he saved the lives of around 100 000 Hungarian Jews by placing them under Swedish protection.

NEW WORDS

additive *n*: a substance added to food to prevent deterioration; short for 'food additive'
genocide *n*: systematic extermination of a particular group of people
kamikaze *n*: a bomb-laden Japanese aircraft deliberately crashed on its target; the pilot who flies such an aircraft

NAZI CAMP SHOCKS WORLD

27 JANUARY, AUSCHWITZ, POLAND
Revelations by General Zhukov, whose
Red Army is driving relentlessly
through southern Poland towards
Berlin, have left the world in shock.
The Russians have liberated about
4000 prisoners from a large Nazi
extermination camp near the town of
Oswiecim (Auschwitz) – the first time
that the Allies have seen for themselves
the grim barbed-wire camps with their
lethal gas ovens.

Reports issued by the Polish
government since 1942 had alerted the
world to the scarcely believable
atrocities that the Nazis have committed
in Poland, but it is only now that the
full scale of Hitler's terrible vision is
becoming known. It is feared that
millions of people, most of them Jews,
were starved, worked as slave labour and
eventually murdered at Auschwitz. The
pits containing the corpses of the
victims of Nazi racism and the
emaciated, virtually fleshless bodies of
those who have been rescued are silent
testimony to the unspeakable horror
that has engulfed Europe in our time.

BARELY ALIVE The extermination camp at
Auschwitz-Birkenau, where 3 million died.

How race hatred turned to mass murder

MASS GRAVE Of the estimated 7 million people who went through the camps, only 500000 survived.

After his defeat at Stalingrad, Hitler
knew that, barring a miracle, Germany
could not win the war. He became
obsessed with his great objective: the
extermination of European Jewry.

From 1939 to 1941 official Nazi
policy was 'to assist the emigration of all
Jews from Germany', but already the
techniques of genocide were being
rehearsed in mental asylums, where,
under the 'euthanasia' programme, death
by gassing – referred to as 'disinfection'
– was practised. The rounding-up and
shooting of Jews in open countryside
had also begun in Poland, but by 1941
so many Jews had come under German
jurisdiction that killing them in this way
could not be done in secret or with
enough speed. In addition, the numbers
in the concentration camps were being
swollen by the daily arrivals in cattle-
trains of Jews exported from the Reich.

At the Wannsee Conference in
January 1942 the blueprint for the 'final
solution' was presented by Reinhard
Heydrich; special detachments of the SS
under Heinrich Himmler were detailed
to carry it out. The chief means selected
was gassing by Zyklon B, a form of
cyanide with which experiments had
already been conducted at Auschwitz.

Before Germany surrendered,
between five and six million Jewish
men, women and children had met a
cruel death, most of them in purpose-
built extermination camps such as
Auschwitz-Birkenau, Belsen, Treblinka
and Sobibor. Hundreds of thousands
were also murdered in their own villages
or starved to death in the ghettos. The
Jews were the principal focus of Nazi
hatred, but other groups such as
homosexuals, Jehovah's Witnesses and
gypsies were also slaughtered.

··· 31 DEC: EMPEROR HIROHITO MAKES RADIO BROADCAST REPUDIATING DIVINITY OF JAPANESE IMPERIAL LINE ···

Intense bombardment destroys Dresden

15 FEBRUARY, DRESDEN

Over the past two days British and American bombers have reduced Dresden, one of Germany's most beautiful cities, to a charred ruin. On the night of 13–14 February almost 800 RAF Lancasters, under the command of 'Bomber' Harris, dropped hundreds of tons of high explosive and incendiaries. The following day more than 300 American B-17 bombers added to the destruction. German air defences are now so weak that only six Lancasters were reported shot down.

Dresden was known to be a centre for refugees, and its population had almost doubled, to around a million. Up to 130 000 people died in the air raids, many killed by firestorms rather than by the bombs themselves. Firestorms are caused when a blaze sucks in oxygen from the surrounding air to feed itself; the air currents spread sparks and

SKELETAL REMAINS Dresden had been considered safe because of its unique architectural heritage.

burning debris, which cause other fires, until there is one vast conflagration.

The bombing raids formed part of a campaign to spread chaos and to undermine morale in Germany and prepare

the way for Allied troops, but Dresden had little strategic importance, and some senior military figures question the need to cause such ruthless devastation to the civilian population.

··· OF THE TOTAL 35 MILLION CASUALTIES OF THE WAR, MORE THAN 18 MILLION WERE FROM THE USSR ···

Germany's old men sent to war

DAD'S ARMY Old and young alike are being mobilised in a last-ditch attempt by Germany to win.

APRIL, BERLIN

As Soviet troops close on Berlin and Hitler's position becomes desperate, Germany is throwing boys and old men into the front line. Men and boys outside the normal 16–60 age range are

being called up. Thousands of members of the Hitler Youth, some as young as 12, are pitted against the might of the Red Army. Hitler expects the boys to be 'slim and slender, swift as greyhounds, tough as leather, and hard as Krupp steel'.

Death of the dictators

1 MAY, BERLIN

Two days after the death of Benito Mussolini in Italy, Adolf Hitler yesterday took his own life. With the two main enemy leaders dead, complete Allied victory in the war is now imminent.

For the past two years Mussolini had had power in name only, heading a puppet regime for the Nazis. As he tried to flee to Switzerland he was captured and shot by Italian partisans. His body was hung upside down in Milan with that of his mistress for public ridicule.

As Allied forces advanced on Berlin Hitler realised that his position was hopeless. He is thought to have killed himself with a cyanide capsule in the bunker from which he attempted to direct his nonexistent armies. His corpse is believed to have been burnt, along with that of his wife Eva Braun, who committed suicide with him.

Britain celebrates victory

8 MAY, LONDON

Ecstatic crowds danced in the streets today to mark the official end of the war in Europe. On 29 April German forces in Italy surrendered to Field Marshal Alexander, and on 4 May Field Marshal Montgomery accepted the surrender of German forces in the Netherlands, Denmark and north Germany. Berlin fell to the Russians almost a week ago. The formal end to the six-year conflict came yesterday at 2.41 am, when Germany signed its unconditional surrender.

Yesterday evening the BBC announced that the government had declared today a public holiday, to be known as Victory in Europe

IT'S ALL OVER Victory celebrations resound across the Allied world.

Day. The war against Japan in the Far East still continues, but nothing can dampen spirits in Britain or in the United States, which is also celebrating the victory today. The Soviet Union is to hold its celebrations tomorrow.

Prison camp atrocities revealed

Following the Allied successes in the Pacific, many Japanese prison camps have now been liberated, revealing a shameful catalogue of atrocities. The soldiers who surrendered during the dark days of 1942 were kept in cramped, disease-ridden conditions, or else were used as forced labour.

Some were sent to the mines in Manchuria, others made to build railways through malarial jungles. Most notorious of these was the Burma Railway, where thousands of British and Australian servicemen worked until they perished of disease or hunger.

Civilians fared little better. In the Philippines 3000 Americans were crammed into the former campus of St Thomas University; conditions in the occupied colonies of Hong Kong, Singapore and Java were even worse. Rape, torture and summary execution were common.

The extent of the brutality is said to result from the military training of the Japanese. Commanders of the camps reportedly paid less attention to the Geneva Convention than to the *Bushido* discipline – the ancient code of the Samurai. According to this ethic, surrender is worse than death and those who allow themselves to be taken prisoner are beneath contempt.

··· JAPANESE SCHOOLCHILDREN COLLECT 1 MILLION TONS OF ACORNS TO EASE FOOD SHORTAGES ···

Another island falls as US net widens over Pacific

23 FEBRUARY, IWO JIMA

American troops have gained an important foothold on the Pacific island of Iwo Jima, raising the US flag on Mount Suribachi. The campaign to take this tiny but strategically important site began four days ago with the landing of 9000 marines. They faced a garrison of 22 000 Japanese dug into secure positions. Despite heavy bombardment from naval shells the defenders pinned the marines down, inflicting 2000 casualties on the first day.

Initially progress was pitifully slow; the troops gained less than 400 metres (1320 ft)

SUCCESS SYMBOL The raising of the flag is captured on film for posterity.

a day. At sunrise today Lieutenant Harold Schirer and a 40-man combat team fought their way up to the summit of Mount Suribachi. Finally, at about 10.30 am, they

succeeded in planting a small American flag on the peak. Such was the symbolic value of this achievement that the same men staged the event again four hours later – this

time using a larger flag – so that Joe Rosenthal of the Associated Press could capture the moment on film.

The assault on Iwo Jima marks an important turning point in the war, bringing US forces within striking distance of the Japanese mainland. Until now the enemy aircraft stationed on the island have hampered US bombing raids, while radar installations have given Tokyo early warning of trouble. Once these are neutralised it is hoped that American forces can establish an air base on Iwo Jima, which will provide protection and shelter for its B-29 bombers.

HIROSHIMA OBLITERATED BY ATOM BOMB

6 AUGUST, HIROSHIMA

The Japanese city of Hiroshima has been completely destroyed by a single bomb – the most powerful weapon the world has ever known. Nicknamed 'Little Boy', the bomb weighed 4 tons but packed as much explosive power as 20 000 tons of TNT. An estimated 80 000 people have been killed. A pall of smoke hangs over the flattened city, and fires continue to rage around its edges.

At 8.15 on a clear morning, Little Boy was detonated 560 metres (1850 ft) above the city with a searing flash of bluish-white light – as bright as the Sun, according to one of the US Navy officers who witnessed it. The bomb was carried to its target by an American B-29 Superfortress, named *Enola Gay* after its pilot's mother. The plane took off from the western Pacific island of Tinian at 2.45 am, with a crew of 11 under the command of Colonel Paul Tibbets.

Thousands of people immediately below the blast were vaporised instantly as temperatures reached 9000° C (16 200° F). The shock wave, as powerful as an 800 kilometre-per-hour (500 mph)

NOTHING LEFT The flattened wastes of Hiroshima. Radiation effects continued to kill for years afterwards.

wind, levelled everything within a radius of 3 kilometres (2 miles), and a huge mushroom-shaped cloud of dust and debris rose 8 kilometres (5 miles) into the air. Below it tens of thousands of people died from radiation, blast and fire, and every building in the city centre was destroyed. Dazed and injured

survivors gathered by the wreckage of their homes, unable to believe or understand what had happened to their city.

The American team responsible for the bomb are celebrating – they calculate that it will bring the war with Japan to a swift end and save hundreds of thousands of American lives.

Deadly secret of the Manhattan Project

The bombs used on Hiroshima and Nagasaki are the culmination of a secret research programme codenamed the 'Manhattan Project'. After nuclear fission – the splitting of uranium atoms in a chain reaction – was discovered, a team of physicists was assembled by Dr Robert Oppenheimer at Los Alamos, New Mexico, in 1943, to try to harness the process to make a bomb.

The team worked flat out, and the first atom bomb was detonated on 16 July – too late for Europe, but in time to end the war in Japan.

Hirohito broadcasts ceasefire message

FINAL PEACE The Japanese delegation is received on the USS *Missouri* to sign the treaty.

15 AUGUST, TOKYO

In a radio broadcast Emperor Hirohito has informed his people that the war is over: Japan has ceased hostilities. Defeat

has been inevitable ever since the second atom bomb was dropped on Nagasaki on 9 August, but there were fierce disagreements among government ministers, and the Emperor had to take the unprecedented step of imposing his decision on the Japanese War Council.

During the night hardliners tried to break into the palace and destroy the tape of Hirohito's message, which he recorded yesterday. National pride has taken a severe dent, and wailing crowds have gathered at the imperial palace.

General MacArthur, the Allied supreme commander, will receive Japan's formal unconditional surrender today.

··· 5 DEC: FLIGHT 19, A GROUP OF NAVAL TRAINING CRAFT, VANISHES IN THE BERMUDA TRIANGLE ···

EUROPE CARVE-UP AGREED

11 FEBRUARY, YALTA, UKRAINE
After a week of intensive talks, the summit meeting at the Black Sea resort of Yalta has ended amid general agreement about the shape that a post-war Europe should take. Headed by Churchill, Roosevelt and Stalin, the conference has resolved that after Germany's surrender the country should be administered by four occupied zones, run by the Allies. Agreement has also been reached about the future of Poland. Its boundaries have been fixed

and there have been guarantees of free elections. In addition, a date has been fixed for another conference later in the year, which will deal with the creation of the United Nations.

Details of a secret agreement with Russia will not emerge until later. In return for declaring war against Japan once Hitler is defeated, Russia will be granted substantial territories which were lost in the Russo-Japanese War of 1905. The full text of the Yalta treaty will not be made public until 1947.

LASTING SUCCESS Celia Johnson and Trevor Howard have a *Brief Encounter*.

WOMEN'S YEAR

British audiences packed cinemas to see *Brief Encounter*, starring Celia Johnson and Trevor Howard. This accomplished film by director David Lean explored the heady passion of an illicit affair tempered by the dead hand of British inhibition and reserve, underscored with a searing Rachmaninov soundtrack.

Women took centre stage in Hollywood movies, playing a variety of self-assured independent careerists that would have been unheard of before the war. Joan Crawford made a stunning comeback in *Mildred Pierce*, her first major film for two years, playing an ambitious go-getter battling her way from rags to riches despite a no-good husband and a scheming daughter. Ingrid Bergman's Nordic cool was shown off to the full in her portrayal of the self-assured psychiatrist treating Gregory Peck's twisted subconscious in Hitchcock's *Spellbound*. Jane Wyman played a strong supporting role in Billy Wilder's Academy award-winning *The Lost Weekend*, although Ray Milland's uncompromising performance as an alcoholic writer who can only look at life through the bottom of an empty whiskey glass could never be eclipsed.

THE BIG THREE Churchill, Roosevelt and Stalin – and advisers who helped to negotiate the world's future.

Moscow squad's dynamic gesture

13 NOVEMBER, LONDON
A football team from the Soviet Union, Moscow Dynamo, startled 85 000 fans at Chelsea's Stamford Bridge stadium by trotting onto the pitch at the start of the match with a bouquet of flowers for each of their opponents. Dynamo is on a four-match tour of Great Britain to foster goodwill between the wartime allies, but the gesture was still tinged

with irony, since the team, the first from the Soviet Union to visit these shores, has always been considered as the footballing arm of the KGB.

The Moscow Dynamo 11 is actually a crack squad assembled from the whole of the country. Although down 3–0 to the Blues at half-time, they drew on their highly skilled short-passing game to finish level at 3–3.

··· THE US MINT BEGINS USING SALVAGED SHELL CASINGS TO MAKE COINS ···

1946

BORN

12 Mar: Liza Minnelli, US singer and actress

19 Aug: Bill Clinton, US President

DIED

21 Apr: John Maynard Keynes, British economist

14 June: John Logie Baird, British television pioneer

29 July: Gertrude Stein, US author

13 Aug: H G Wells, British author

25 Dec: W C Fields, US actor

ELECTED

2 Mar: Ho Chi Minh, president of North Vietnam

28 June: Enrico de Nicola, president of Italy

PUBLISHED

Bertrand Russell, *The History of Western Philosophy*

Eugene O'Neill, *The Iceman Cometh*

On 24 February, *Juan Perón is elected president of Argentina with an overwhelming majority. Perón led a revolt three years ago, and was subsequently made vice-president. But he was imprisoned earlier this year, until mass demonstrations, largely organised by his wife, Eva, secured his release.*

RIOTED

21 Feb, Cairo: Egyptians, over level of foreign influence in the country

3 May, Jerusalem: Arabs, over British plans to partition Palestine

13 June, Rome: Italian monarchists, angry at departure of King Umberto II following pro-republic referendum result

17–19 Aug, Calcutta: Muslims and Hindus, over British proposals for Indian independence

Following the reopening of shipping routes, and after a lengthy absence from the shops, London's first postwar bananas go on sale at Covent Garden Market. However, rationing of food items looks set to continue for a few years, and a shortage of wheat has even brought the unwelcome return of bread rationing.

BOMBED

22 July, Jerusalem: King David Hotel, British Palestine Army HQ, by Jewish terrorists; 91 killed

DECLARED WAR

19 Aug, China: Chinese Communists led by Mao Zedong, on Guomindang Nationalists led by Marshal Chiang Kai-shek

FOUNDED

6 Nov, UK: National Health Service

MARRIED

10 Jan: a GI bride and her groom, by transatlantic telephone link

FIRST NIGHTS

16 May, New York City: *Annie Get Your Gun,* musical by Irving Berlin

12 July, UK: *The Rape of Lucretia,* opera by Benjamin Britten, at Glyndebourne

COMMITTED SUICIDE

15 Oct: Hermann Goering, a leading Nazi who had been sentenced to death, with cyanide pill

PROCLAIMED

11 Jan: People's Republic of Albania

SQUATTED

8 Sept, London: empty homes in Kensington and Bloomsbury, by homeless families

LAUNCHED

24 Mar, London: BBC broadcasts in Russian

20 Sept, France: Cannes Film Festival

WOUND UP

18 Apr, Geneva: the League of Nations

OPENED

31 Mar, UK: London airport, at Heathrow

USSR: world's first nuclear reactor site

QUIT

20 Jan, France: Charles de Gaulle as French president, because of Communist opposition; Félix Gouin (Socialist) takes over

Procter & Gamble launch Tide, the first detergent specifically for clothes. The new soapless cleaning agent, developed during the war to clean military uniforms, can be used in the latest washing machines which help lighten the washday load.

NEW WORDS

data processing *n*: operations on data, especially those performed by a computer, in order to extract information, reorder files, etc

iron curtain *n*: political barrier between capitalist Western Europe and communist Eastern Europe

NAZI CHIEFS FACE VICTORS' JUSTICE

IN THE DOCK Nazi leaders, including Goering and Hess, listen carefully as the proceedings unfold.

31 AUGUST, NUREMBERG
The Nuremberg war trials are over, and
12 of Hitler's leading henchmen have
been sentenced to death as war
criminals. Seven were given prison
terms ranging from ten years to life, and
four, including Franz Papen, who was
vice-chancellor in the early days of the

Third Reich, and Hjalmar Schacht,
finance minister in the 1930s, were
acquitted.

In the 1930s Nuremberg's vast arena,
which was designed by the chief Nazi
architect and armaments minister Albert
Speer, was the setting for spectacular
mass rallies to celebrate the

achievements of Nazism. Now this
historic town has become the home of
an international court and, far from
being feted, Speer and his fellow Nazis
have faced the verdict of the victors.

A tribunal of judges drawn from the
major Allied countries has been hearing
evidence against them for the past ten
months. The legal basis for the trials has
been questioned, but doubts about the
court's authority have been have been
swept aside by the emotional torrent
demanding that the perpetrators of evil
should be made to answer for their
atrocities to humankind.

Twenty-three leading Nazis were
charged with crimes against peace and
humanity, and 18 of them appeared in
the dock. Details of the horrors of the
extermination camps appalled the court,
as did Hermann Goering's unrepentant
defence of the Nazi regime. Several of
the Nazi leaders – including Rudolf
Hess, staring into the distance with
glazed eyes, and Julius Streicher, sweating
profusely – looked overwhelmed by
their fate. Again and again the
defendants fell back upon the plea that
they had only carried out orders. It was
a defence that left the judges cold.

··· HUNGARY ISSUES THE ONE-HUNDRED-TRILLION PENGO NOTE, MARKING THE WORST INFLATION IN HISTORY ···

American dreams of the GI brides

From January to July, 'bride express'
trains have been steaming out of British
stations, gradually moving 50 000 'GI
brides' on their long journey from
Britain to the United States. The
women had fallen in love with US
soldiers, sailors and airmen stationed in
Britain during the war – known as GIs
after the words 'government issue'
stamped on their uniforms, equipment
and other many goods. Some married
before parting company after the war;
many others are looking forward to a
wedding in the USA.

The first convoy left on 22 January,
bound for a special camp at Tidworth
Garrison in Hampshire. From there the
brides travelled to Southampton and the
Queen Mary liner for the week-long
passage across the Atlantic.

The first shipment of British brides
arrived in New York on 10 February.
From there they were transferred all
over the USA to be reunited with their
sweethearts and start new lives. The
women took with them a total of 116
children. The youngest GI bride was just
16 years old.

US BOUND GI brides look forward to the future.

ENIAC is an intellectual heavyweight

**14 FEBRUARY,
PHILADELPHIA**
**A gigantic electronic 'brain'
was unveiled by scientists
at the University of
Pennsylvania today.** The
Electronic Numerical
Integrator and Calculator
(ENIAC) weighs 30 tons and
takes up 150 square metres
(1600 sq ft) of floor space.

ENIAC's inventors,
J Presper Eckert and John W
Mauchly, were originally
trying to develop a top-secret
calculating device that could
work out gun trajectories
and artillery strategies for the
US Army, but the machine
was not finished in time to
help the war effort.

The machine's 'thinking'
is done by 18000 electronic
valves, which are told what
to do ('programmed') by
scientists manually plugging
and unplugging leads. The
electronic brain's calculations
use a great deal of energy –
more than 100 kilowatts –

GIANT BRAIN Scientists work on ENIAC's thousands of valves.

and tend to make it overheat,
so it has its own air-
conditioner which struggles
to keep it cool.

ENIAC can perform up
to 5000 additions or
subtractions every second.

Although the machine is
only used to perform simple
arithmetic, Eckert and
Mauchly are confident that
the possibilities for future
generations of thinking
machines are almost limitless.

'Dr Death' is guilty

26 MAY, PARIS
**Dr Marcel Petiot went to
the guillotine today,** after a
jury had found him guilty
of murdering 27 people. The
evil doctor had plied a
gruesome trade in human
flesh during wartime Paris.

He lured wealthy Jews to
his home, at 21 rue Lesueur,
by promising that he could
help them to escape from
Nazi-occupied territory, but
instead he killed them,
dismembered their bodies
and disposed of their remains
in a furnace in his basement.
It was the stench from these
flames that first alerted the
police to the dark goings-on
in the cellar.

At his trial Petiot claimed
that all his victims victims
had been German soldiers,
but police found a hoard of
suitcases stuffed with
valuables from his
unfortunate Jewish clients.

KISSING TO BE CLEVER

The world went cinema-crazy this year, with annual box-office
receipts breaking all records. In Britain, 30 million people packed
out the cinemas, and in the USA audiences reached 90 million.

Burt Lancaster made an impressive screen debut in the stylish
film noir thriller *The Ladykillers*, teaming up with rising star Ava
Gardner for this explosive melodrama. Newlyweds Humphrey
Bogart and Lauren Bacall got together in Raymond Chandler's *The
Big Sleep*, Bogey playing world-weary Philip Marlowe to perfection.
Rita Hayworth blazed a trial of sensuality in *Gilda*, which some
saw as no more than a vehicle for her raw sex appeal; and
Hitchcock hit the headlines with *Notorious*, in which his camera
lingered on a passionate kiss between Cary Grant and Ingrid
Bergman for longer than had ever before been seen in film.

Away from the escapism, *The Best Years of Our Lives* was a fine
postwar readjustment movie from Hollywood. William Wyler's
story of three war veterans returning to the American Midwest

SEXUAL CHEMISTRY Lancaster smouldered with Gardner in *The Ladykillers*.

captured the mood of the year with its social realism, pathos and
comedy, along with an exceptional performance from Harold
Russell – a real-life war veteran who lost both arms in the conflict.

Mothers listen to Dr Spock

Child care has been revolutionised by a new book, *The Common Sense Book of Baby and Child Care*, by a New England doctor, Benjamin Spock.

Spock's book signals a new direction in child care, steering parents' approach away from the rigid regimes that many paediatricians and psychologists have previously advocated.

The philosophy in the book is unashamedly liberal, although some critics believe that this approach could encourage unruly behaviour and even create an entirely undisciplined generation.

However, Spock's book has found favour with parents. His simple advice on everything from bedwetting to whooping cough makes the book an indispensable item in many households. It will go on to sell 40 million copies, and will be translated into 38 languages.

'Indecent' swimwear is an explosive hit

11 JULY, PARIS
The world of fashion has been astonished by a new two-piece swimsuit, dubbed the 'bikini' by its creator.

There were gasps from the audience at designer Louis Réard's Paris show as model Micheline Bernardini appeared in a garment that is so brief compared with ordinary swimsuits that it is being called indecent.

Until now swimsuits have been conservative affairs covering up much of the body. Réard's design shows a generous portion of midriff. The costume is made of fabric printed with fragments of newspaper text, suggesting that the canny designer has an inkling of the acres of coverage his daring creation will pick up from the world's newspapers.

The bikini takes its name from the South Pacific atoll of Bikini, the scene of recent American atomic tests. The garment has had a similar explosive effect.

IN THE FLESH   Micheline Bernardini shows off the world's skimpiest swimsuit.

Stylish and practical Vespa scoots to success

ITALIAN JOB   Within ten years Piaggio's firm had sold over one million Vespas.

The motorcycle industry was revolutionised this year by the introduction of the Piaggio Vespa – the first scooter to achieve mass popularity. The machine was conceived by Enrico Piaggio as an easy way for workers to move around his family's vast engineering works at Pontedera, Italy.

The Vespa aims for neatness and convenience rather than power. The small two-stroke engine is entirely enclosed, the tiny wheels are easily removed when a tyre needs changing, and the flat footboard offers a comfortable riding position; importantly, it is also easy and cheap to manufacture.

Conventional motorcyclists have not been complimentary about the new machine, and its novel appearance has been seen by some as rather ugly. However, others regard the scooter as the embodiment of classic Italian design. Whatever the arguments, practicality is winning the day and the firm's order books are full. The Vespa is moving at full throttle.

1947

BORN

19 June: Salman Rushdie, Indian-born British novelist
9 July: O J Simpson, US footballer and alleged murderer

DIED

25 Jan: Al Capone, US gangster
7 Apr: Henry Ford, founder of Ford Motor Company

Subbuteo football game, invented by Peter Adolph, is launched in Britain. In these postwar rationing days many materials are still in short supply, and the game comes supplied with chalk to mark up a pitch on an old blanket. The football players, available in 24 colours, are made of cardboard.

8 May: Henry Gordon Selfridge, US founder of London department store
21 Aug: Ettore Bugatti, Italian car designer and manufacturer
4 Oct: Max Planck, German physicist

STARTED

15 Aug: UK's first atomic reactor, at Harwell, Oxfordshire

PROPOSED

5 June, USA: 'Marshall Plan' for US financial aid to help European economic recovery, by US Secretary of State George Marshall

BANNED

23 June, Washington DC: union 'closed shop' (under which all workers have to be union members)

LAUNCHED

17 Feb, Washington DC: 'Voice of America' broadcasts in Russian
24 Aug: Edinburgh Festival
27 Aug, UK: austerity cuts, including further food rations
20 Oct, Washington DC: investigation, by House Un-American Activities Committee, into allegations of communist bias in film industry

CEASED FIRE

3 Aug, Indonesia: Dutch troops and Indonesian nationalists, following United National Security Council resolution; first UN success

AGREED

29 Nov: plans to partition Palestine into Jewish and Arab states, by United Nations General Assembly

FIRSTS

5 Oct, USA: presidential address on television
14 Oct, USA: man to break sound barrier, Chuck Yeager in Bell X–1 rocket plane

ORDERED

21 Mar, Washington DC: FBI 'loyalty tests' for all US federal employees

CHAMPION

UK: cricketer Denis Compton of Middlesex, who scores 3816 runs and 18 centuries in one season, both records; he also plays professional football for Arsenal football club

QUIT

30 Dec, Bucharest: King Michael of Romania, pushed into abdicating by Communist government

SHIVERED

Jan–Feb, UK: Britons suffering 'big freeze'

EXPLODED

16–18 Apr: ships, factories and oil refineries in Texas City fire disaster; more than 700 killed

The first solid-body electric guitar is built by US musician Les Paul, who has spent years working on prototypes. Prior to this model, electric guitars have merely amplified the acoustic guitar sound. Guitar manufacturing company Gibson later picked up Paul's design, marketing the first model in May 1952.

On 20 November, *following a brief engagement, Princess Elizabeth marries Philip Mountbatten, Duke of Edinburgh, a cousin whom she met at her parents' coronation in 1937. They honeymoon at Broadlands, Hampshire.*

BOMBED

24 Apr, Palestine: police barracks at Sarona near Tel Aviv, by Stern Gang terrorists; four killed

THEATRE STAR

New York City: Marlon Brando, on Broadway in Tennessee Williams's *A Streetcar Named Desire*

SIGNED

10 Feb, Paris: postwar peace treaties, under which Italy gives up North African colonies and loses Dodecanese islands to Greece

RENOUNCED

3 Mar, Japan: war, under new constitution

NEW WORD

cold war *n*: state of antagonistic opposition between communist Eastern Europe and capitalist Western Europe with the USA**.**

The painful birth of Indian independence

PEACEMAKER Mahatma Gandhi, spiritual leader of the Indian people, with the Mountbattens.

15 AUGUST, INDIA
The subcontinent celebrated its hard-won freedom from the British Empire at the stroke of midnight last night. In New Delhi thousands of people crowded around the Council of State buildings. Jawaharlal Nehru, India's first prime minister, told his government: 'A moment comes, which comes but rarely in history, when we step out from the old to the new … when the soul of a nation, long suppressed, finds utterance.'

The Raj is gone, but the nation's partition into the Hindu-dominated state of India and the Muslim nations of East and West Pakistan is causing great suffering for ordinary people. Already there are reports of killings in Punjab, an area cut in half by the new border.

There has even been criticism of Lord Mountbatten, the last British viceroy, over this emotional issue. His detractors accuse him of responding to pressure for a separate Islamic state by Muhammad Jinnah's Muslim League with impetuous – even draconian – decisiveness. The timetable for the transfer of power was accelerated, as was the mapping out of the new borders by English jurist Sir Cyril Radcliffe.

Partition will lead to one of the greatest mass migrations ever seen in history, costing the lives of an estimated 500 000 people.

··· INDIA OUTLAWS DISCRIMINATION AGAINST 'UNTOUCHABLES' IN THE OLD CASTE SYSTEM ···

DESERT SCROLLS ILLUMINATE SCRIPTURES

The oldest known version of the Bible was discovered this year by a Bedouin shepherd in Jordan. Muhammad ad-Dibh was looking for a lost sheep when he threw some pebbles into a cave near the north-western shore of the Dead Sea. He heard the sound of something shattering and decided to investigate. Ad-Dibh found a cache of leather and papyrus manuscripts hidden inside clay jars.

The Dead Sea Scrolls, as they have been called, are a find of immense importance. They date from the 1st century AD, and are written in Aramaic, believed to be the language of Jesus, and Hebrew. They comprise fragments of every book of the Hebrew Bible except Esther, as well as poetry, calendars and biblical apocrypha.

Scholars have been fascinated to discover that the texts were hidden by an ascetic brotherhood called the Essenes. The scrolls shed new light on the relationship between Judaism and very early Christianity. It seems that the Essenes, who were strict Jews, may have been in competition with early Christians. One theory holds that the 'Righteous Teacher' in the texts is Jesus' brother James, while Jesus himself may be the one referred to as the 'Evil Priest'.

PRICELESS Some 400 scrolls have been recovered so far.

Are extraterrestrial craft stalking Earth?

The USA has been buzzing with reports of 'flying saucers' lighting up the night sky. Since the first report from a remote spot in Washington state by pilot Kenneth Arnold on 24 June, thousands of people have said they have seen brightly lit flying objects.

Arnold was out for a spin on a clear night when he saw nine discs shimmering against the background of the Cascade Mountains. An experienced pilot, he estimated that the objects were moving at 1600 kilometres per hour (1000 mph). Later he told a local journalist that the lights moved like a saucer skipping across water.

The US Air Force launched an investigation and declared that Arnold's flying saucers were not visitors from another planet, but simply products of his imagination. Many are accusing the authorities of a cover-up.

Dior puts glamour back into the wardrobe

STYLE GURU The House of Dior is sometimes picketed by those who find the 'New Look' indulgent – especially these evening gowns.

FEBRUARY, PARIS
The ration books are still in place, and wartime austerity continues to holds sway, but that has not marred the success of Christian Dior's first collection, which was launched in Paris this month. The 'New Look' collection, boasting glamorous, soft-structured clothes, has caused a sensation all over Europe.

The broad-shouldered dresses of the war years have given way to long, full skirts and a fetching 'figure-of-eight' look. The British government condemned the collection as 'irresponsibly frivolous', but copies of the clothes have sold out as fast as tailors could make them.

Christian Dior started life as an art gallery owner in Paris, promoting painters such as Salvador Dali and Jean Cocteau. After his business failed during the Great Depression of the 1930s he turned reluctantly to fashion.

··· US CHEMIST FRANK LIBBY DEVELOPS CARBON-DATING TECHNIQUE FOR ARCHAEOLOGICAL REMAINS ···

Photographs in an instant

SNAPPY IMAGES The Polaroid can print photographs in 60 seconds.

21 FEBRUARY, BOSTON
A camera that produces almost instant photographs has been invented by a man who never graduated from university. Edwin H Land, founder of the Polaroid company, launched his new Polaroid Land camera with a black-and-white self-portrait produced by the camera.

The idea for the Polaroid struck Land, a Harvard dropout, on a family picnic. After he had taken a picture of his young daughter, she asked to see it and was disappointed when told she would have to wait.

His new camera processes photos inside its body, using chemicals contained in a pod at the side of the film. As the film passes between rollers, the pod is crushed and the fluid develops the exposed image.

Jack the Dripper takes New York

Splashing and dripping paint on a canvas laid on the floor, Jackson Pollock has changed the course of art. He is the leading figure of a group of painters called 'Abstract Expressionists', whose aggressive work seems set to dominate American art in the postwar years. New York City is fast becoming the world capital of contemporary art.

Pollock's paintings are as explosively energetic as his method, called 'Action Painting', in which he splashes paint on the canvas as he hops around it. He believes the spontaneous action taps directly into his creativity.

Browse before you get there

The world's first 'duty free' shop for passengers travelling by air opened this year in Shannon, Ireland. Selling liquor, perfume and tobacco products, the store has taken advantage of its position at the international airport to offer products without the local excise duty being imposed. Shannon is an important hub on transatlantic flight routes, providing a refuelling stop for the long journey.

'Spruce Goose' lifts off

RISKY BUSINESS The 'Spruce Goose', which was in fact made of birch, gathers power for a brief flight.

4 NOVEMBER, LONG BEACH, USA
Millionaire playboy, movie mogul and aviator Howard Hughes took to the air today in the largest aeroplane ever built, little more than a year after he was almost killed while testing another of his company's prototype aircraft.

The Hercules HK-1, nicknamed the 'Spruce Goose', is a seaplane capable of carrying 700 people. It was airborne for less than a minute, and flew no more than 2 kilometres (1¼ miles).

Despite the flight's success, the future of the aeroplane is in doubt. The US government says that it no longer needs an airborne troop carrier, and furthermore, all Hughes's government contracts are under investigation by the FBI.

Nonstop fire power from Kalashnikov

20 FEBRUARY, IZHEVSK, USSR
An efficient new machine-gun has been invented by Mikhail Kalashnikov, a former sergeant in the Soviet army. Wounded in 1941, Kalashnikov heard many complaints in hospital that the cumbersome carbines issued by the Soviet infantry were no match for the rapid-firing German Schmiessers.

The automatic gun he has designed, called the AK-47, is almost unjammable. Its magazine uses intermediate power ammunition and holds 30 rounds, which can be fired either singly or automatically, at 600 rounds per minute.

Kalashnikov found it impossible to convince his military superiors that a mere sergeant with no qualifications could produce a weapon to match sophisticated German arms. The gun sat on the shelf throughout the war and was only formally introduced to the Soviet army this year.

Robinson dodges discrimination

15 APRIL, NEW YORK CITY
Jackie Robinson has broken through one of America's most entrenched racial barriers by taking the field today for the Brooklyn Dodgers, as the team opened the new baseball season at home to the Boston Braves. The 28-year-old is the first black American to play in the major leagues this century.

Robinson was signed two years ago by the Dodgers' general manager, Branch Rickey, and has spent the last two seasons with the Montreal Royals in the minor leagues. He will have to show great forbearance in his trail-blazing role, as it is likely he will be spiked, 'accidentally' hit by pitchers or taunted by some Dodgers fans.

Robinson is a player of great talent – as a fielder, hitter and base-stealer – and

TRAIL BLAZING Jackie Robinson, who went on to lead the Dodgers in the World Series, makes a home run.

his entry into major-league baseball is certain to pave the way for more players from the Negro leagues.

Later this year Robinson will go on to win the National League Rookie of the Year award.

1948

BORN
14 Nov: Prince Charles, heir to British throne
27 Dec: Gérard Depardieu, French actor

DIED
8 Jan: Kurt Schwitters, German artist
30 Jan: Orville Wright, US aeroplane pioneer
16 Aug: George Herman 'Babe' Ruth, US baseball legend

DENOUNCED
USSR: composers Dmitri Shostakovich and Sergei Prokoviev, for writing 'decadent' music, by Andrei Zhdanov, Soviet culture commissar

On **30 January**, *Mahatma Gandhi, aged 79, is assassinated by a Hindu extremist. Only a few days previously Gandhi, whose title Mahatma means 'Great Teacher', had completed a five-day fast to encourage peace. The assassination ended a lifetime's campaigning for the end of colonial oppression in South Africa and India.*

DISPLAYED
July, New Jersey: first transistor, by Bell Laboratories at Murray Hill

PUBLISHED
Graham Greene, *The Heart of the Matter*

COUP
25 Feb, Prague: by Czech communists

QUIT
7 June, Prague: Czech president Eduard Beneš, after refusing to ratify a new constitution for a 'People's Democracy'
30 July, Budapest: Hungarian president Zoltan Tildy, over the collectivisation of farms
14 Aug, London: Australian cricketer Don Bradman, who plays last Test innings
4 Sept, The Hague: Queen Wilhelmina, who abdicates; her daughter Juliana takes over

OPENED
29 July, London: Olympic Games, by King George VI

BANNED
12 Jan, Washington DC: use of race as a criterion in judging applications to law school
15 Mar, London: suspected or known communists or fascists in British civil service
30 July, Washington DC: racial segregation in US armed forces
20 Sept, Israel: Stern Gang terrorist group

FIRSTS
29 Jan, San Diego: flying car, Hall Flying Automobile, takes off
Sept, UK: British comprehensive schools established
3 Dec, Washington DC: female officer in US Army, Colonel Mary Agnes Hallaren
Cortisone injections, for arthritis, developed by US chemist Perry Julian

On **3 June**, *Daniel François Malan, head of the National Party, is elected prime minister of South Africa. Malan plans to institute* apartheid – *systematic racial segregation – as official government policy, and has been given a mandate to do so today.*

ELECTED
11 May, Italy: Luigi Einaudi, president
16 May, Israel: Chaim Weizmann, president

RE-ELECTED
29 Mar, China: Chiang Kai-shek, president, by Nanjing Assembly

TV DEBUT
USA: *Candid Camera*

EXECUTED
23 Dec, Tokyo: seven Japanese officials convicted of war crimes, including former premiers Hideki Tojo and Koki Hirota

LAUNCHED
3 Apr, Washington DC: Marshall Plan, $6 billion military and economic aid for Europe
18 June, West Germany: new currency, Deutschmark, to replace Reichsmark

INDEPENDENT
4 Jan: Burma, from Britain
4 Feb: Ceylon, with dominion status
16 Dec: Cambodia, from France

PROCLAIMED
9 Sept: Republic of North Korea

CHAMPION
25 June, New York City: Joe Louis, who knocks out 'Jersey Joe' Walcott in 11th round to retain heavyweight boxing champion crown

NEW WORD
cybernetics *n*: the scientific study of electronic and mechanical control systems; term introduced by mathematician Norbert Wiener

Alger Hiss, a highly placed official in the State Department, testifies before the House Committee on Un-American activities. He is accused by Whittaker Chambers, the editor of Time *magazine, of passing secret papers to the USSR. Congressman Richard Nixon plays a prominent role in the Committee's investigations.*

ALLIED AIRLIFT BRINGS RELIEF TO BESIEGED CITY

VITAL LIFELINE Children wave to a cargo aeroplane from the Allied forces, which are keeping up a tight schedule of an aeroplane landing and leaving every three minutes.

31 JULY, WEST BERLIN

Over the past month huge quantities of food, fuel and other supplies have been airlifted into West Berlin, a city faced with starvation. The operation, which began on 26 June, has been made necessary by the Soviet Union's act of severing water supplies and road and rail communications between West Berlin and the rest of Europe.

This is the first attack by the Soviets on the Western European powers since the end of the war, when Germany was divided into an eastern zone, controlled by Russia, and a western zone under a joint British, US and French administration. Berlin itself was partitioned into four sectors: the Soviet Union controls the east of the city, and the rest is divided into American, British and French districts.

Because Berlin lies deep within the territory controlled by the Soviet Union, access to the city from Western Europe has depended on the cooperation of the Soviets, and they have been angered by currency reforms in West Germany which have underlined the weakness of the economy in the Soviet zone. The isolation of West Berlin is an attempt to intimidate the Western powers into pulling out of the city, but the Allied nations have risen to the challenge. It is an enormous task to provide two million West Berliners with the provisions they need, and the operation will undoubtedly become more difficult as winter approaches. The Allies estimate that they need to take in 2500 tons of food a day. So far the airlift is running smoothly, and the Allied air forces are even flying industrial exports out of the city.

··· 2 NOV, MAINE: MARGARET CHASE SMITH, THE FIRST FEMALE US SENATOR, IS ELECTED ···

War without battlefields shapes a new world

The United States and the Soviet Union were allies against Germany during the war, but mutual mistrust also existed. Since the end of the war their rivalry for power and prestige has intensified, and the situation is developing into a new world order. The European powers are marginalised, and the new superpowers are locked into what has become known as the 'Cold War' waged between the communist and capitalist camps.

Europe has become the main theatre for these tensions, which Winston Churchill has likened to the descent of an 'iron curtain'. The division is further exacerbated by the Soviet Union's refusal to allow its satellites to accept the Marshall Plan, a programme for European economic recovery. The Communist states are permitted only to sign agreements among themselves.

Controversial birth of a new nation

Israel and Arab states explode into conflict

STAKING A CLAIM Jewish troops in Nazareth.

14 MAY, TEL AVIV
A long-cherished dream was realised today with the creation of Israel – the first Jewish state since biblical times.

The country has been carved out of Palestine, a region that since 1922 has been administered by Britain under the auspices of the League of Nations. Throughout this time Jewish leaders have been campaigning for a homeland for their people, focusing on Palestine, where many European Jews settled after fleeing the Holocaust.

Following United Nations recommendations that Palestine be divided into a Jewish state, a Palestinian state, and a small international zone including Jerusalem, Britain withdrew from the region, and the Jews immediately proclaimed their nationhood.

It seems, however, that there is trouble ahead. The Palestinians have already expressed outrage that Israel comprises over half the territory, including most of the valuable coastal area. The Israeli state, they say, is out of proportion to the relative number of Jews to Palestinians. Arab leaders will be very reluctant to recognise the recommendations.

No sooner was the new state of Israel created than it was under attack from the neighbouring Arab countries. The Palestinians claim that the British recognised their self-determination and are angry at their land being given to Jews. On 15 May, the day after Israel proclaimed its new status, the new country was invaded by Egypt, Iraq, Lebanon, Jordan and Syria. However, Israel was prepared for aggression, and, although it surrendered part of Jerusalem on 28 May, it held on elsewhere and made territorial gains in several places.

Fighting continued intermittently for the rest of the year, with a few temporary truces and Israel increasing its territory by about a third. The United Nations is acting as mediator in the hope that a lasting ceasefire may be achieved, though that seems unlikely considering the uncompromising line taken by both sides.

··· BRITISH CARMAKER DAIMLER INTRODUCES THE FIRST ELECTRIC WINDOWS IN CARS ···

Cars shape up for postwar market

The first major new car designs since 1939 lifted the gloom of postwar austerity this year, giving the prospective car buyer greater freedom of choice. The Morris Minor, a family saloon with eye-catching modern styling, was one of the stars of the London Motor Show in October. Designed by Alec Issigonis, it has a wider body than any other family car – allowing more room inside and giving better handling on corners. These qualities make up for the Minor's rather small 918 cc engine and its fairly low top speed of 100 kilometres per hour (60 mph). The first Morris Minor came off the production line on 8 October.

At the Amsterdam Motor Show the British firm Rover unveiled its Land Rover, a sturdy four-wheel-drive vehicle designed by Maurice Wilkes for rough off-road surfaces. Its powerful four-cylinder 1595 cc engine is the same as that used in Rover's P3 saloon. The Land Rover is Britain's answer to the Jeep, which was built in the United States by Willys and Ford as an all-purpose, all-terrain car for military use.

In Paris, Citroën launched its plucky 2CV, named after its two-horsepower engine, which was built in response to the massively successful German Volkswagen Beetle. Citroën's aim is to meet a practical need for cheap and reliable cars. The simply constructed 2CV is a perfect family car but is also aimed at the large rural French market – especially at farmers. Its self-levelling suspension system can cope with bumpy conditions so well that a basket of eggs carried in the car will remain intact.

FETCHING STYLE The Minor can hold all the family.

ROVING SUCCESS The term 'Land Rover' will become a byword for all four-by-four vehicles.

Whistlestop campaign works for President Truman

3 NOVEMBER, WASHINGTON DC

Against all the odds, Harry S Truman has been re-elected and will serve a second term of office as President of the United States. The surprise election victory is a comfortable one, with Truman winning a two-million majority of the popular vote over his Republican rival, Thomas E Dewey, governor of New York.

The Democrats have been voted back into both Houses of Congress, to the astonishment of pundits and pollsters alike, who had been consistently predicting a crushing defeat for the incumbent President and his party. Dewey conceded defeat at 11.00 am. For Truman, who succeeded Franklin Roosevelt on his death in 1945, the result is a personal as well as a political triumph. Always confident of success despite his low ratings in the polls, he has proved the sceptics wrong.

His energetic campaign evidently struck a chord with the majority of Americans. In what has become known as the 'whistlestop campaign', Truman travelled about 22000 kilometres (13400 miles) in just two months, making 275 speeches to win over the electorate.

LAST LAUGH A beaming Truman displays a premature headline which became one of the press's most famous blunders. The *Chicago Daily Tribune*, which held the popular view that Truman would lose, based its splash on early results from the East Coast, only to find that West Coast voters reversed the trend.

··· THE KINSEY REPORT REVEALS THAT 56 PER CENT OF US MEN HAVE BEEN UNFAITHFUL TO THEIR PARTNERS ···

Balsa raft braves challenge of the greatest ocean

LITTLE CONQUEROR The *Kon-Tiki*, bedecked with the flags of many nations.

This year the world has been held enthralled by the extraordinary journey of Norwegian adventurer Thor Heyerdahl, who with five companions crossed the Pacific by raft from South America to Polynesia. In doing so, he resoundingly proved the sceptics wrong, and added weight to his theory – dismissed by many of his fellow academics – that the Polynesian islands might have been populated centuries ago by South Americans travelling by boat.

Heyerdahl, a trained anthropologist, built his boat using only the techniques that would have been available to the Incas. The 14-metre (45-ft) raft was made without nails or wire; the bamboo and balsa-wood logs were tied together with rope. A small cabin on the deck housed a kerosene lamp, army rations, fishing equipment and a radio. Heyerdahl named the boat *Kon-Tiki*, after the Polynesians' god from the east.

On 28 April last year the *Kon-Tiki* set sail from the port of Callao in Peru. Critics predicted that the balsa wood would be waterlogged within a few days, but the *Kon-Tiki* stayed as buoyant as a cork across the open ocean, and 101 days and 6900 kilometres (4300 miles) later the crew landed on Raroiya, a palm-fringed island in the Tuamotu archipelago. Heyerdahl, who, with his crew, has braved sharks, dangerous reefs and bad weather, is vindicated and has hinted that he is planning a lecture tour of Europe and the United States. There is also talk of setting up a museum in tribute to the voyager.

Babe takes the fairway – and the titles

ALL-ROUNDER The unstoppable Zaharias brandishes trophy and cheque.

This year, Mildred 'Babe' Didrikson Zaharias added more lustre to her glittering sporting record by winning the US Women's Open golf championship. The victory was executed in fine style, being won by a margin of eight strokes, and Babe gave a matchless display of fairway shot-making.

A former All-American baseball and basketball player, Babe married the professional wrestler George Zaharias in 1938. The outstanding female Olympic athlete of the 1930s, she took up competitive golf in 1940 – and since then there has been no stopping her. Her first Open title comes after her series of stunning performances last year, when she won 17 tournaments in a row.

In 1950 the sports writers of America will unanimously vote for Babe Zaharias as the top sportswoman of the first half of the century.

USA is home to angels from hell

California was this year alerted to a new menace: 'Hell's Angels' – roving outlaw gangs of Harley-Davidson owners, who look for thrills and live outside the law. The fear of the biker gangs is probably greatly exaggerated, but it has some basis in reality. On 4 July last year 3000 of these motorcyclists converged on the town of Hollister, in northern California, where a riot ensued.

As postwar America slowly returns to normality, the leather-clad biker represents a new spirit of freedom and rebellion.

··· THE KENWOOD CHEF FOOD MIXER IS DESIGNED AND BUILT BY KENNETH WOOD IN WOKING, ENGLAND ···

Olympian triumphs

15 AUGUST, LONDON
Fanny Blankers-Koen has taken the athletics world by storm yet again.
Twelve years after her first appearance in the Olympics, the 30-year-old Dutch mother of two has swept away the opposition to win four of the nine gold medals available to women competitors at this summer's games. She came into the competition as the world record-holder in six events – sprinting, hurdling, the high jump and the long jump – and here she has won the 100 metres, the 200 metres and the 80 metres hurdles, and was one of the 4 x 100 metres relay winning team. Her neighbours in Amsterdam are to present her with a bicycle – so that she will not have to run so much.

The other headline-grabber at the Games has been the USA's Bob Mathias, who won the decathlon. The 17-year-old, who took up the event

FLYING HOUSEWIFE Blankers-Koen (right) takes the last hurdle before winning the 80 metres race.

only three months before qualifying for the American team, is the youngest man ever to win an Olympic gold medal – a triumph wildly celebrated in his home town of Tulare, California. When the news of his win broke, factory whistles and sirens blared for hours, and the roads were clogged with jubilant motorists.

Automatic jukeboxes bring music to every bar

MUSIC MAKER The 1100 jukebox is inspired by car design.

This is the year in which the flashiest jukebox ever seen came to town. The world's most fashionable bars and cafés are installing the latest sensation from America: the Wurlitzer 1100 jukebox. The brightly coloured music machines with their flashing multicoloured lights and polished chrome will – for a small fee – play your choice from a revolving record selection which can display up to eight singles at a time.

The Wurlitzer company was founded in North Tonawanda, New York, by Robert Hope-Jones, an immigrant from Liverpool. The company started out by making the organs that enlivened film screenings in the earliest nickelodeons. Hope-Jones was a perfectionist, and continually sought to improve his product by tinkering with its design. However, this infuriated his employees so much that one day they locked him out of his own factory. The inventor was so shocked that he committed suicide.

Hope-Jones's company has since gone on to prosper and is now the world's leading manufacturer of jukeboxes as well as the ever more elaborate cinema organs. The Wurlitzer 1100's design is widely credited to designer Paul Fuller; its success has resulted in Fuller being viewed as the genius of jukeboxes.

Long player is a threat to 78s

The Columbia Record Company ushered in a new era of sound this year in the United States with the launch of its 33⅓ records, sparking fears that the 78 revolutions per minute system may become obsolete. The new disc is played at 33⅓ rpm, and can hold up to 20 minutes of recordings – 78s had been criticised for only playing for a maximum of five minutes, and for their crackling sound quality. The new 'long-players' look similar to 78s but are made out of flexible plastic, making them light and shatterproof.

Peter Goldmark, launching the product for Columbia, said the new system was a winner, and predicted that every home would soon be dancing to music on a 33⅓ disc.

··· A JUDGE RULES THAT IT IS ILLEGAL FOR US HOMEOWNERS TO REFUSE TO SELL TO BLACK BUYERS ···

HOLLYWOOD ACCOLADES FOR OLIVIER

Five Oscars went to Laurence Olivier's film of *Hamlet,* which he produced, directed and starred in himself. It is an impressive version of Shakespeare's play, with brilliant camerawork by Desmond Dickinson and stirring music by William Walton as well as magnificent acting. Olivier himself won the Oscar for best actor for his interpretation of the title role.

Another outstanding European film was *Bicycle Thieves* by the Italian director Vittorio de Sica. It deals with the theme of unemployment, a topical subject for Italy, telling the poignant story of a man, long

out of work, who is robbed of a bicycle he needs for a new job. Using non-actors and filmed on location, it is one of the finest examples of the neo-realism currently favoured in Italian cinema. As de Sica said: 'My idea is to de-romanticize the cinema.'

In Hollywood, Humphrey Bogart was at his peak in *The Treasure of the Sierra Madre*, directed by John Huston, an enthralling adventure yarn, filmed partly in Mexico, about a trio of men consumed with lust for gold. The director's father, Walter Huston, won the Oscar for best supporting actor for his role as one of the drifters.

SIMPLE REALISM Father and son hunt for their bicycle in the moving film *Bicycle Thieves*.

1949

BORN

22 June: Meryl Streep, Hollywood actress
23 Sept: Bruce Springsteen, US musician

DIED

6 May: Maurice Maeterlinck, Belgian author
6 Sept: Richard Strauss, German composer

On **11 June**, *country singer Hank Williams debuts as a guest on the Grand Old Opry radio show in Nashville, Tennessee. He brings the house down and performs an unprecedented six encores.*

RIOTED

13–15 Jan, Durban: Indians and Africans over rumour that an Indian had killed an African; 105 killed

PROTESTED

23 Feb, Berlin: Jews, at portrayal of Jewish character Fagin by Alec Guinness in film *Oliver Twist*

BANNED

1 Apr, UK: Tudor IV airliners, following a series of accidents

JAILED

9 Feb, Los Angeles: actor Robert Mitchum, for smoking marijuana; his sentence is two months
14 Feb, Hungary: Catholic Church leader Cardinal Mindszenty, for life; he is accused of plotting against the Communist government

FOUNDED

4 Apr: NATO (North Atlantic Treaty Organisation)
18 Apr: Republic of Ireland
5 May: Council of Europe
23 May: Federal Republic of Germany (West Germany)
12 Oct: German Democratic Republic (East Germany)

MOVED

13 Dec: Israel's capital, from Tel Aviv to Jerusalem

The world's first training shoe is launched by the German sportswear manufacturer Addas (later Adidas). The three-strip shoe was designed by Adolf Dassler.

ATTACKED

20 Apr, China: British warship *Amethyst* on the Yangtze River by Chinese Communists; 17 crew killed

CEASED FIRE

24 Feb: Israel and Egypt
11 Mar: Israel and Jordan

TESTED

21 Sept, USSR: atom bomb

FIRST

2 Mar, Texas: nonstop round-the-world flight, by Captain James Gallagher in Boeing B–50A *Lucky Lady II*; 37 743 km (23 453 miles) in 94 hrs, refuelled four times in flight

PROCLAIMED

1 Feb: People's Republic of Hungary

ELECTED

13 Aug: Konrad Adenauer, chancellor of Federal Republic of Germany
16 Dec: Ahmed Sukarno, president of Indonesia

EXECUTED

15 Nov, India: Nathuram Godse, assassin of Mahatma Gandhi

TV DEBUT

USA: *The Lone Ranger*

TRIUMPHED

24 Aug, UK: Essex cricketer Trevor Bailey who bowls all ten Lancashire batsmen out in first innings

ENDED

12 May, Germany: Soviet blockade of Berlin
16 Oct: three-year Greek civil war; communist rebels defeated

EXPANDED

3 Nov, London: BBC, which buys Lime Grove film studios from Rank to make television programmes

Hollywood star Rita Hayworth causes a media sensation when she marries one of the richest men in the world, Ali Khan, heir to the Aga Khan, at Vallauris town hall in France. The town's whole population turns out.

OVERRULED

29 Nov: British House of Lords – against its wishes it has to accept the Parliament Bill, which limits its powers to delay legislation

FLEW

4 Sept, Bristol: Bristol Brabazon, world's largest airliner, weighing 130 tons, on its maiden flight

AWARDED

2 May, New York City: the Pulitzer Prize to playwright Arthur Miller, for *Death of a Salesman*

DECLARED

28 Dec, Ohio: flying saucers do not exist, by US Air Force, following investigation into reported sightings of UFOs

NEW WORD

baby boom *n*: temporary increase in the birth rate; period reflecting sharp postwar increase in US birth rate

CHINESE COMMUNISTS COME TO POWER

NEW REGIME Trucks rumble through the streets as Communist troops enter Shanghai.

1 OCTOBER, BEIJING
Mao Zedong today hailed the victory of the Chinese Communists in the long war against the Nationalist Party in a speech to hundreds of thousands of cheering supporters in Beijing's Tiananmen Square. 'Ours will no longer be a nation subject to insult and humiliation,' he said, in announcing the birth of the People's Republic of China.

'The Chinese people have stood up!' For the outgoing ruler Chiang Kai-shek and his defeated Nationalists the only refuge now will be the small island of Formosa.

China has become the world's largest Communist state, and the country's new government was at once given official recognition by the Soviet Union. Great Britain is expected to follow the Soviet example, but the United States, which has propped up the corrupt and increasingly inept government of Chiang Kai-shek for many years, will almost certainly continue to regard the Formosa regime as the legitimate government of China.

Mao now faces a multitude of problems. The remaining pockets of the country that are occupied by Nationalist troops have still to be pacified and, after years of military operations, the Communist Party itself must try to adapt to civilian rule and establish an administration capable of governing the vast territory of China and able to revive the Chinese economy.

··· 13 JULY: POPE PIUS XII EXCOMMUNICATES ALL COMMUNISTS FROM THE ROMAN CATHOLIC CHURCH ···

India's new constitution is for all

26 NOVEMBER, NEW DELHI
A new constitution has turned India into the world's largest democracy. The entire adult population – 173 million voters – will be entitled to vote in elections. The constitution will come into effect on 26 January of next year, turning the country from a Dominion of the British Crown to a fully fledged independent nation.

There had been fears that Jawarhalal Nehru's Congress Party might exclude groups such as the low-caste 'untouchables' from the democratic process, but the Indian prime minister rebuffed his critics by saying that the constitution's aim was to achieve justice, liberty, equality and fraternity for all

Indians. He outlined a vigorous programme of important social and economic reforms.

India has seen a tempestuous year since British rule ended and the country was partitioned. The war with its new neighbour Pakistan over control of the province of Kashmir shocked the country, while the assassination of Mahatma Gandhi on 30 January sent the whole subcontinent into mourning. Nehru has promised that the new federal system will leave the regions with a large measure of autonomy from New Delhi. But some have said that making Hindi the country's official language will cause resentment among Muslims and other minority linguistic groups.

ON PARADE Prime Minister Nehru salutes cheering crowds in the United States.

Britain leads the way as jet airliner takes to the skies

FLYING SUCCESS The world's first regular jetliner service (to Johannesburg) was inaugurated on 2 May 1952.

27 JULY, HERTFORDSHIRE
The world's first jet airliner, the De Havilland Comet, made its maiden flight at the Hatfield airfield under the control of test pilot Group Captain John Cunningham – a World War II fighter ace – who took it to a height of 2438 metres (8000 ft).

Powered by four Ghost turbojets each capable of a 2250-kilo (5000-lb) thrust, the Comet represents Britain's intention to become the world leader in aviation transport. The airliner is designed to fly at 800 kilometres per hour (500 mph) and 12000 metres (40000 ft) – twice as fast and twice as high as any existing airliner. The airliner carries its fuel inside tanks located in the wings, and is so smooth a design that it needs 'airbrakes' to slow it down for landing.

Developed in secrecy, the Comet was first designed as a mail plane because it was believed that jet engines would be capable of only a small range and a modest payload. During design, however, opinions changed, and the prototype was fitted with 36 seats.

Although there are doubts that jet engines will ever be economical enough for air transport over long distances, British Overseas Airways has ordered 16 of the aircraft, which are planned to come into service in 1952.

··· POSTWAR RATIONING OF SWEETS IS ENDED IN BRITAIN AND THEN RE-INTRODUCED A FEW MONTHS LATER ···

The rise of Mao

Mao Zedong, the head of the new Chinese government, has devoted his life to Communist revolution and in the process won a place in the hearts of the people as a national saviour.

Born in 1893 into a well-off peasant family in Hunan province, as a young man Mao studied the works of Karl Marx and in 1921 was instrumental in founding the Chinese Communist Party. He rose to prominence in 1934–5, when he masterminded the spectacular 'Long March' and established the Communists in the peasants' eyes both as the friend of the landless against the provincial warlords and as the patriotic foe of the Japanese occupiers of northern China. Mao now has the opportunity to elevate China into a major world power.

Small-town shooting frenzy: 13 massacred

9 SEPTEMBER, NEW JERSEY
A crazed war hero went berserk in small-town America today, butchering 13 people in a matter of minutes. To his neighbours 28-year-old Howard Unruh seemed a harmless oddball: a quiet, Bible-reading fellow, who had distinguished himself at the Battle of the Bulge. In reality, though, Unruh was a deeply disturbed young man.

At his home in Camden after the war he became a recluse. He kept a detailed notebook listing the imagined insults he had suffered. This simmering resentment broke loose earlier today, when Unruh strode out of his house, smartly dressed in a suit and bow-tie, and embarked on a killing spree. With two pistols he gunned down several people he had known since his childhood and a number of strangers. Shortly afterwards police arrested him at his home. Unrepentant, Unruh stated: 'I'd have killed a thousand if I'd had bullets enough.'

TRAGIC VICTIM Rose Cohen died along with her husband and mother in Unruh's shooting spree.

Ealing Studios' comedy success

This was a great year for the British film industry, with a string of hits released from the phenomenally successful Ealing Studios. Executive producer Michael Balcon and his team of talented writers created a trio of gentle comedies: *Kind Hearts and Coronets, Passport to Pimlico* and *Whisky Galore*. All are original, clever and witty creations, and seem to catch a mood of mild anarchy in postwar Britain. The films are quickly becoming modern comedy classics.

ORIGINAL STYLE Alec Guinness as Lady d'Ascoyne in *Kind Hearts and Coronets*.

Bleak vision of the future

8 JUNE, LONDON
George Orwell's new novel, *Nineteen Eighty-Four*, is a chilling prophecy about what may happen to Britain. But it is also intended as a fable about how millions of people live under totalitarian regimes in the present.

The author of *Animal Farm* – a satire on the Russian Revolution, in which the revolutionary leaders are portrayed as pigs – struggled to complete his latest novel in between long spells in hospital being treated for tuberculosis. The desperate state of his health means that *Nineteen Eighty-Four* may be his last work.

The novel describes a future world in which politicians, hiding behind the character of 'Big Brother', are all-powerful, controlling people's minds, distorting the truth and rewriting history.

Orwell denies that his book is an attack on the present British Labour Party, and describes himself as a socialist. His experiences as a policeman in Burma in the 1920s turned him into a champion of the poor and the oppressed. Nevertheless, he has had a dread of communism – the real target of *Nineteen Eighty-Four* – ever since he fought with the International Brigade during the Spanish Civil War. Instead of fighting fascists, he found himself in a life or death struggle with communist factions determined to stamp out opposition to their ideas.

··· PADDIPADS, WORLD'S FIRST DISPOSABLE NAPPIES, ARE MARKETED BY ROBINSON'S OF CHESTERFIELD, BRITAIN ···

FILM-MAKERS MOVE OFF THE SET AND ONTO THE STREETS

The city became the star this year as Stanley Donen abandoned the traditional Hollywood lot to film the innovative Gene Kelly musical *On the Town* in the streets of New York and Carol Reed captured the run-down, decadent atmosphere of Vienna so powerfully in *The Third Man* that the location almost upstaged the actors. Written by Graham Greene and starring Orson Welles as the suave, menacing racketeer Harry Lime, *The Third Man* is filled with the growing tension of Cold War Europe. Its air of eerie suspense is sharpened even further by the ghostly zither music that accompanies Lime as he wanders the streets, hunting for his victims.

The Third Man is one of many British films to enjoy critical success. Academy Awards went to Lawrence Olivier's *Hamlet* and Powell and Pressburger's *The Red Shoes* (both made last year). The Ealing Studios produced a rich crop of their trademark comedies, the most successful of them dealing, in different ways, with people trying to escape from austerity.

On the other side of the Atlantic, James Cagney gave a mesmerising performance as a gangster who gets what he deserves when an FBI agent penetrates his gang in *White Heat*. One critic called the movie 'the most gruesome aggregation of brutalities ever presented under the guise of entertainment'. *All the King's Men* was a political melodrama worthwhile for its vivid portrayal of an honest man corrupted by power.

ON LOCATION Orson Welles in the memorably stylish and atmospheric thriller *The Third Man*.

1950

BORN
2 Mar: Karen Carpenter, US singer
13 May: Stevie Wonder, US singer

DIED
6 Jan: George Orwell, British author
2 Nov: George Bernard Shaw, Irish author and playwright
11 Sept: Jan Smuts, South African politician and soldier

On 25 December, *Scottish nationalists steal the Stone of Scone from its traditional place under the Coronation Chair in Westminster Abbey, London. The stone, carried off from Scotland by King Edward I in 1296, is recovered four months later from Arbroath Abbey.*

PUBLISHED
Graham Greene, *The Third Man*
Betty Crocker, *Betty Crocker's Picture Cookbook*
L Ron Hubbard, *Dianetics: The Modern Science of Mental Health*

SURVIVED
1 Nov, USA: President Truman, assassination attempt by two Puerto Ricans

SEIZED
4 Apr, UK: at Liverpool docks, £80000 worth of smuggled nylon stockings destined for black market
30 Apr, UK: by Atomic Energy Commission, 30000 copies of *Scientific American* magazine reported to contain information on how to make an H-bomb

ELECTED
23 Feb, UK: Labour Party, in general election, with a majority of five
26 Mar, Yugoslavia: the People's Front Party led by Tito, with 93.2 per cent of vote in one-party election

ACCUSED
Feb 22, USA: 205 members of the State Department of being communists, by Senator Joe McCarthy

IMPRISONED
1 Mar, UK: British nuclear scientist Klaus Fuchs, for passing atomic secrets to the Russians

ISSUED
USA: 'Ten Most Wanted Criminals' list by the FBI – three are spotted by members of the public and arrested immediately

MARCHED
30 Apr, USA: five million Americans in anti-communist 'Loyalty Day' parades

ENDS
9 Sept, UK: soap rationing

FIRST
1 Oct, New York City: credit card, issued by Diners Club, giving credit at 27 restaurants
Kidney transplant, performed by Dr Richard Lawler at the Little Company of Mary Hospital, Chicago
Sex change operation, performed in Denmark by a medical team led by Dr Christian Hamburger; New Yorker George Jorgensen becomes Christine
UFO photograph, taken by farmers Mr and Mrs Paul Trent from McMinnville, Oregon

INVENTED
USA: passenger lift with automatic doors, installed by Otis at Atlantic Refining Building, Dallas; lift attendants are not impressed

URGED
4 Dec: USA, not to use nuclear weapons in the Korean War, by British Prime Minister Clement Attlee

12 Jan, New York City: no shaving, no bathing, as the city attempts to ease its water shortage

WARNED
11 Feb, USA: men, that there is no cure for baldness, by the New York Academy of Science
11 Feb, USA: atomic powers, not to produce H-bomb, by Albert Einstein

TELEVISED
USA: hearings before the Senate Crime Investigating Committee, featuring testimonies of gangsters

DISCOVERED
Living organisms at a depth of 10370 m (34000 ft), by Danish deep-sea exploration team in SS *Galathea* in the Pacific Ocean
Largest known crater in remote part of Quebec, Canada – 3341 m (11136 ft)

NEW WORDS
ergonomics *n*: the study of the relationship between workers and their environment
fallout *n*: the descent of radioactive material after a nuclear explosion
hassle *n*: a prolonged argument; a great deal of trouble

PEANUTS   By Schulz

Charles Schultz creates the first 'Peanuts' cartoon strip, launching a new type of cartoon-strip humour, which features wry, philosophical takes on life from a child's perspective. Back in 1937, 12-year-old Schultz had submitted a cartoon to Ripley's 'Believe it or Not' featuring a dog that ate razor blades. That dog eventually became Snoopy of 'Peanuts' fame.

MARINES MARCH INTO NORTH KOREA

TAKING A BREATHER US marines await orders in front of a flaming tobacco warehouse in Inchon.

1 OCTOBER, SEOUL
The war in Korea has taken a dramatic turn. United Nations and South Korean forces have crossed the thirty-eighth parallel, and President Truman has ordered General Douglas MacArthur, commander of the UN army, to advance into Communist North Korea and destroy the North Korean army.

Since June – when North Korean divisions invaded the south, captured the capital, Seoul, and all but eliminated the South Korean army as an effective fighting unit – the Communists have held the upper hand. In the last two weeks the momentum has shifted. On 15 September the US Tenth Corps launched an amphibious assault on the island of Wolmi-Do, which commands the approaches to Inchon, a port on the west coast not far from Seoul. The massive attack – in which 260 ships participated – took the North Koreans entirely by surprise, and the marines secured the island in just one-and-a-half hours. Naval and air bombardment of Inchon began almost immediately, and 11 hours later the port was stormed by the First Marine division and four South Korean marine battalions.

The next day the Eighth Army attacked, making a rendezvous with troops at the Inchon bridgehead and then advancing along the line westwards to Seoul. By 26 September the capital was surrounded, and all escape routes for the Communist insurgents were sealed off. Half of the invading North Korean troops found themselves trapped and facing either death or capture.

The question hanging over the war now is whether Communist China will enter the lists to help revive the North Korean cause.

··· 3 MAY, CHINA: THE COMMUNIST GOVERNMENT BANS POLYGAMY AND THE SALE OF WOMEN ···

Tibetans resist China

17 NOVEMBER, LHASA
The authorities in Tibet, the only country in the world to be ruled by priests, have invested the 15-year-old Dalai Lama with full powers of government. Usually the Dalai Lama is 18 before he assumes power: the decision signals to Beijing that Tibet will resist Chinese encroachments on its autonomy.

China has been building up its military occupation of eastern Tibet in its campaign to 'liberate the Tibetan people by force' and bring them into the fold. International protests have met with the reply that China will brook no foreign interference. Beijing aims to make the 13-year-old Panchen Lama its puppet ruler in Lhasa.

BITTER FREEDOM 'Freed' Tibetans parade with banners of Mao Zedong.

Peat bog reveals gruesome secret

The discovery of a 2000-year-old corpse in a peat bog in Denmark has stunned scientists around the world. The remarkably well-preserved body, found at the Tollund Mose bog near Jutland, was excavated by the leading archaeologist Professor P V Glob.

The corpse is that of a man killed with a leather rope, by either hanging or strangling – the rope is still stretched tightly around his neck. Some academics believe that the man could have been the victim of an ancient sacrificial ritual, perhaps to a fertility goddess.

Radio-carbon analysis has managed to date the organic remains to around 240–220 BC. Indeed, the body has been so effectively 'pickled' (due to low temperatures, low oxygen content and

the presence of considerable amounts of tannin in the bog) that scientists can establish that the dead man last ate between 12 and 24 hours before his untimely demise. He had consumed no meat for at least three days, surviving instead on a gruel of grain and seeds.

It is thought that the man was 30–40 years old when he died, and about 1.6 metres tall (5 ft 4 in). Naked except for a leather cap and belt, the man died curled in a foetal position, and his chin is rough with three days' growth of stubble. These details somehow add to the human pathos of this compellingly grisly archaeological find.

ETERNAL SLEEP The preserved corpse of 'Tollund Man' bears traces of an unnatural, violent end.

··· COCA-COLA'S SHARE OF THE US COLA MARKET IS 69 PER CENT; PEPSI-COLA'S IS 15 PER CENT ···

America's biggest holdup

18 JANUARY, BOSTON
Thieves yesterday pulled off one of the most daring and successful robberies of all time, netting a haul of almost $3 million in 15 minutes.

Their target was the North Terminal Garage in Boston, owned by Brinks Security Company. Every detail of the daring raid was planned to perfection. Before making their play the crooks acquired Brinks uniforms, along with keys to every door in the building. With these the 11 robbers let themselves in by a side staircase and walked up to the second floor. Then they crossed the hall and passed through the accounts department before reaching the high-security area.

SCENE OF THE CRIME Detectives and staff check over the empty bank vault.

Two barred doors separated them from the vault, but the thieves also had keys to these. Moments later they held up the five guards at the vault, who were astonished at being confronted by men in company uniform wearing halloween masks. Once inside the vault the robbers wasted no time in clearing out a fortune in cash, cheques and securities.

New trends for future holidays

1950 has been an exciting year for those prone to wanderlust. Two important developments in the tourism industry look set to transform our holidays.

Gérard Blitz, a Belgian, put a small notice in a French newspaper to advertise the first 'holiday village', where people can socialise in an idyllic seaside location in Majorca. Accommodation was cheap, with holiday-makers of the new 'Club Mediterranée' put up in army surplus tents.

Inexpensive air holidays are also fast becoming a reality, thanks to Vladimir Raitz. He used an inheritance of £2000 to charter a plane to Corsica, where he offered basic camping facilities. The total holiday 'package' cost only £35 10s per person.

Film's scandalous pair wed

19 NOVEMBER, ROME

Ingrid Bergman married the Italian director Roberto Rossellini yesterday, less than a month after her divorce from estranged husband Peter Lindstrom. The Swedish-born actress – star of such film classics as *Casablanca* – shocked her fans the world over when she left her husband and daughter to live with the controversial film director last year. Rossellini already has a reputation for challenging film conventions, combining neo-realism with melodrama and Hollywood narrative; the union with the beautiful actress has only added to his reputation.

Protest groups were formed to condemn the actress, and a US senator, Edwin Johnson, became involved in attacking the behaviour of the formerly popular film star. Bergman had stoked the fires of puritan outrage by refusing to apologise for her actions, saying: 'Americans do not understand that a mother might be blinded by passion to the point of sacrificing her daughter.' *Stromboli*, a volcano disaster movie set on an Italian island, and the first film the pair have made together, was released in the United States to unkind reviews.

IN LOVE Bergman and Rossellini take a break from the set of *Stromboli*.

··· 52 MILLION HOUSEHOLDS IN THE USA, 4.5 MILLION IN THE UK AND 3 MILLION IN WEST GERMANY OWN A CAR ···

HITS ON BOTH SIDES OF THE ATLANTIC

Hollywood's love–hate relationship with itself has never been better illustrated than in *Sunset Boulevard*, Billy Wilder's satire on the good old days of the movies. William Holden played a washed-up screenwriter, and Gloria Swanson was memorable as the forgotten silent-screen star Norma Desmond, still a legend in her own eyes. 'I am big,' she famously tells Holden. 'It's the pictures that got small.'

Holden appeared in far lighter vein opposite 'dumb broad' Judy Holliday later in the year in the hit comedy *Born Yesterday*, while Elizabeth Taylor played Spencer Tracy's daughter in the year's other comedy smash, *Father of The Bride*. James Stewart was upstaged by an invisible rabbit in the film version of the successful stage play *Harvey*, and Bette Davis swept all before her as a veteran Broadway star betrayed by the young actress she befriends and then tries to help in *All About Eve*, which went on to win the Academy Award for best picture.

FADED STAR Gloria Swanson gets ready for her close-up at the end of *Sunset Boulevard*.

In Paris, *Les Enfants Terribles* was released to great acclaim. Based on Jean Cocteau's novel, it concerns the intense relationship between a teenage sister and brother, with a powerful and tragic ending. Cocteau himself made a haunting film of his play *Orphée*, starring Jean Marais and featuring wonderful special effects.

Bobbysoxers swoon for Ol' Blue Eyes

Music lovers of a new type surfaced this year. They have followed Frank Sinatra since his days with the Tommy Dorsey Orchestra, they are young, female and excitable, and they're called bobbysoxers, after the knee-length stockings they wear.

They began by queuing round the block for Sinatra's dates at New York's Paramount Theater with the Dorsey Orchestra in 1942 and they have followed him ever since.

The 'skinny kid with big ears' from Hoboken, New Jersey, is the hottest act around. Sinatra sings with such intimacy that every girl in the audience thinks that he is singing directly to her. And whenever he starts to sing the teenagers start sighing in carefully choreographed unison. Some even manage to get so over-excited at 'the Voice' that they faint in the aisles. It has been suggested that some of this fainting is planted – but the bobbysoxers' admiration of their idol is real enough.

1951

BORN
4 Feb: Kevin Keegan, English footballer
23 May: Anatoly Karpov, Russian chess champion

DIED
6 Mar: Ivor Novello, British songwriter
29 Apr: Ludwig Wittgenstein, Austrian-born philosopher

WARNED
Smokers, that smoking is linked to cancer, by the *Reader's Digest*

POISONED
Aug 17: 300 people in south of France after eating rye bread made from ergot-infected grain – three die and 50 go insane

CLAIMED
13 Mar: by Israel, $1.5 billion in war reparations from Germany

Eva Perón greets a rally staged in Buenos Aires to demand that she run for the position of vice-president beside her husband, President Juan Perón, in Argentina's next election. Eva Perón's tremendous popularity has grown steadily since her husband's election in 1945. She campaigns on poverty, labour and women's issues.

FIRSTS
1 Jan, Chicago: cable television, introduced by the Zenith Radio Corporation; three films were shown and the subscription fee was $1 per film – scrambled signals were decoded via the telephone system
1 May, Johannesburg: major anti-apartheid demonstration; 18 killed
Space flight by living creatures when the USA sends four monkeys 140 km (85 miles) into the stratosphere
USA: power steering, in Chrysler Crown Imperial sedans and convertibles

IMPORTED
Australia: myxomatosis virus by sheep farmers to kill off rabbits, which are consuming enough grass to feed 40 million sheep

CONSUMED
UK: 53 000 horses for food, due to a beef shortage

Bluesman Muddy Waters has a hit with 'Rolling Stone' – a song title from which a band and a magazine will derive their names. Waters fuses traditional folk blues from his birthplace near the Mississippi delta with dance music from Chicago to produce his distinctive sound.

WORST
19 July: floods in US history hit Kansas and Missouri; 41 people are killed and 200 000 made homeless

AGREED
The Schuman Plan by France, West Germany, Italy, Belgium and Luxembourg, creating the European Coal and Steel Community and dismantling trade barriers

IMPORTED
USA: Lacoste tennis shirt from France; it quickly becomes a status symbol

CONTAMINATED
June 12, USA: hundreds of square kilometres of the Nevada Desert, after the government carries out above-ground nuclear tests

INVENTED
14 June, USA: first commercially available computer, the Univac 1, made by Remington Rand

CLASSIFIED
South Africans, forced to carry identity cards which categorise them as Black, Coloured or White

MET
21 Feb, East Berlin: the communist-sponsored World Peace Council

On 26 October, *Winston Churchill becomes prime minister of Britain for the second time, at the age of 77, having defeated Attlee's Labour government in the general election. Attlee had ousted Churchill from office six years ago.*

PUBLISHED
John Wyndham, *The Day of the Triffids*
James Jones, *From Here to Eternity*

NEW WORDS
hype *n*: intensive or exaggerated publicity or sales promotion
meter maid *n*: a female police or traffic-control officer
moonlight *vb*: to have an extra job on the side

USA DRAWS BACK FROM ATTACKING CHINA

OUT OF THE BLUE Hundreds of UN troops parachute into Korea.

12 APRIL, WASHINGTON DC

President Truman has asserted civilian control over the military by asking the United Nations to dismiss General Douglas MacArthur from his post as commander of the UN forces in Korea. The popular MacArthur, famous for his exploits in the Pacific during the last war, had made a series of public statements in conflict with official US policy in the Far East.

Ever since the UN forces drove the Communist North Korean armies out of South Korea last autumn, a debate has raged between the advocates of containment – consolidating UN positions on the thirty-eighth parallel and suing for a settlement – and the supporters of an aggressive policy, favoured by MacArthur, of conquering North Korea and ousting the Communist government. The White House agreed to the aggressive option, partly owing to MacArthur's belief that China would not enter the war.

However, last November Mao's volunteers launched a ferocious attack on the UN armies, winning back all the territory lost in North Korea and driving MacArthur and his men back into South Korea. Since then MacArthur, under criticism for wrongly assessing Chinese reactions and for deploying his troops ineptly, has been publicly blaming the White House for its policy of 'limited war'. On 24 March he threatened China with attack, and he continues to insist that 'there is no substitute for victory'. But the combatants in Korea have been locked in stalemate for some time, and President Truman, who wants to avoid open war with China or the Soviet Union, has decided the time is ripe for serious negotiations for a ceasefire to begin.

··· 19 APR, LONDON: THE FIRST MISS WORLD CONTEST, HELD AT THE LYCEUM THEATRE, IS WON BY MISS SWEDEN ···

The Abominable Snowman lives

The 'Abominable Snowman' is real – and the British mountaineer Eric Shipton has photographs to prove it.

Earlier this year Shipton returned from an expedition to the Himalayas with the first evidence that the legendary Abominable Snowman, or yeti, really exists: photographs of giant footprints in the snow. Shipton spotted the trail of footprints while climbing on the south-western slope of Menlung-Tse. He followed them for about 1500 metres (1 mile) before they petered out on a sheet of ice. Unlike previous climbers who have reported seeing similar prints, Shipton had the presence of mind to photograph them, showing them beside an ice pick and a boot to give an idea of scale. The prints are about as big as the boot – much bigger than a naked human foot – and there are five distinct splayed toes.

Stories of the yeti abound in the Himalayas. It is said to be a large, hairy, apelike creature which walks upright. The yeti lives a solitary existence; it appears to be shy and has certainly never posed a threat to human beings.

MYSTERIOUS MONSTER Enormous footprints in the snow may lead to the yeti's hiding place.

British diplomats suspected of spying for Russia

28 MAY, LONDON
Scotland Yard and MI5 launched a manhunt today for two suspected British double agents who slipped through their security net three days ago. Guy Burgess and Donald Duart Maclean were last seen on the evening of Friday 25 May, when they boarded a cross-channel steamer at Southampton and eventually caught the train for Paris. Then they dropped out of sight. Their ultimate destination is suspected to be the Soviet Union.

Burgess and Maclean both held influential positions with the Foreign Office, but they had been under suspicion as traitors for some time. Burgess was recalled from Washington this year for 'serious misconduct', and Maclean was due to be interrogated today. But, as it turns out, the authorities acted too slowly, and the disappearance of Burgess and Maclean is highly embarrassing for the British government.

Both men were undergraduates at Cambridge in the 1930s, and it is thought that this is when they were recruited by

TREACHEROUS LIVES Like a whole generation of young idealists, Maclean (left) and Burgess both became communists at Trinity College, Cambridge.

Russian spymasters. Their escape has aroused suspicions that they were tipped off by a 'third man' – probably someone high up in the British establishment, whose identification is now a matter of some importance.

··· A DROUGHT IN AUSTRALIA KILLS MILLIONS OF CATTLE AND LEADS TO THE RATIONING OF DAIRY PRODUCE ···

Britain gives itself a pat on the back

4 MAY, LONDON
Thousands gathered on a reclaimed bomb-site in south London to watch King George VI and Queen Elizabeth open the Festival of Britain – a celebration of the nation's culture.

According to the foreign secretary, Herbert Morrison, it's time for the British people to give themselves a 'pat on the back' for struggling through the years of austerity. Some critics say that austerity is still with us, and that Britain cannot afford such a lavish party.

About 13 hectares (27 acres) of land on the south bank of the Thames has been reclaimed, at a cost of more than £8 million, to stage the extravaganza. In an effort to recreate the excitement the Great Exhibition of 1851, a team of architects under Hugh Casson has erected imaginative modern buildings, including the Royal Festival Hall, a vast Dome of Discovery and a towering aluminium needle called the Skylon.

END OF AUSTERITY The Festival celebrates the nation's art, design, industry and architecture.

Catcher captures youth following

16 JULY, NEW YORK CITY
Christian organisations have denounced J D Salinger's first novel, *The Catcher in the Rye*, as a display of 'amateur swearing', but its many supporters claim that the book captures the authentic, angry voice of a new kind of 'anti-hero' – the modern American teenager.

The central character, Holden Caulfield, is a sensitive, troubled, rebellious adolescent, disgusted with the 'phony' world of adulthood. From the sanctuary of a psychiatric clinic he describes two-and-a-half humiliating days spent in New York City, his conflicts with teachers and parents, and his love for the young sister whom he considers the only 'pure' thing in his world. Holden is already being compared to his creator. Salinger is becoming increasingly reclusive and is rumoured to have had a nervous breakdown after returning from wartime Europe.

Sugar Ray loses title fight

11 JULY, LONDON

Against all the odds, Randy Turpin of Great Britain has wrested the world middleweight boxing title from the peerless American Sugar Ray Robinson.

The general opinion, that Turpin's only chance was to deliver one mighty knockout blow, was confounded, as the gritty 23-year-old outpointed Robinson over the full 15 rounds. Sugar Ray, the welterweight champion from 1946 to 1951, moved up a step to gain the middleweight crown from Jake La Motta in February. But last night at Earl's Court his silky movement around the ring could not save him from Turpin, who was decisive with his counter-punching and the stronger man in the clinches.

Britain has thus claimed the middleweight title for the first time since Bob Fitzsimmons won it in 1891. For most of the contest the arena was filled with the deafening roars of the 18 000 spectators, and, when Turpin was presented with a silver gilt globe that has become the symbol of British success in boxing, the crowd rose to its feet and sang 'For He's a Jolly Good Fellow'.

TIGER'S FURY Sugar Ray Robinson smashes a fist into Jake La Motta's head in the last round of their fight.

··· 58-YEAR-OLD US OIL BARON JOHN PAUL GETTY IS THE WORLD'S RICHEST MAN ···

HOLLYWOOD'S YEAR OF SPECTACLE AND ADVENTURE

PURE DESIRE 26-year-old Brando smoulders from the silver screen.

Japanese cinema was reintroduced to the West by Akira Kurosawa's *Rashomon*, a story set in 11th-century Japan and told from four different viewpoints. *Quo Vadis?*, the most expensive film since *Gone With the Wind*, was also made outside Hollywood, at the new Cinecittà studios in Rome. *Quo Vadis?* cost $7 million to complete, and stars Robert Taylor as a Roman legionary and Deborah Kerr as the Christian slave with whom he falls in love; Peter Ustinov is convincingly deranged as the Emperor Nero. The year's other epic adventure was John Huston's *The African Queen*, starring Humphrey Bogart and Katharine Hepburn.

However, for sheer spectacle, neither film could compete with the Vincente Minelli musical *An American in Paris*, starring Gene Kelly. The film is memorable for a long ballet scene choreographed by Kelly for himself and newcomer Leslie Caron.

On a more intimate scale, two Broadway plays made the difficult transition from the stage to the cinema screen. Arthur Miller's *Death of a Salesman* drew a virtuoso performance from Fredric March as the failed and fading salesman of the title, Willy Loman. The film of Tennessee Williams's *A Streetcar Named Desire* allowed Marlon Brando to recreate the sweaty, sexually charismatic role of Stanley Kowalski that first made him famous in the theatre. After only his second film, Brando is already being touted as the voice of a generation.

1952

BORN

11 Mar: Douglas Adams, British writer

2 Sept: Jimmy Connors, US tennis player

25 Sept: Christopher Reeve, US actor

DIED

6 May: Maria Montessori, Italian educationalist

26 July: Eva Perón, Argentinian political campaigner

ANNOUNCED

3 Oct: Britain has the atom bomb

REMOVED

27 June: the ban on immigration from Africa and Asia to the USA

WITHHELD

19 Sept, USA: Charlie Chaplin's entry visa, pending allegations of communist activities

TELEVISION HITS

UK: *Bill and Ben*

USA: *The Liberace Show, This is Your Life*

FIRST NIGHTS

London: *The Mousetrap* by Agatha Christie at the Ambassadors Theatre

London: *Norma,* opera with Maria Callas at Covent Garden

INVENTED

29 Dec, USA: the miniature hearing aid, by Sonotone Corporation

Pocket-sized transistor radio, by Sony of Japan

ESCAPED

31 Aug: 16000 people from East to West Berlin during the past month

On 4 November, *Dwight Eisenhower is elected President of the United States in a Republican landslide victory. Eisenhower, known affectionately as 'Ike', won the largest popular vote yet.*

WEPT

24 Sept: Richard Nixon, on television, after denying that he has embezzled Republican Party funds

KILLED

3 Feb, UK: 283 people, after gale force winds and high tides cause major floods on the east coast of Kent; thousands left homeless

8 Oct, UK: 112 passengers and 200 injured, when three trains collide at Harrow in Britain's worst train crash

Dec, UK: over 4000 people by smog in London, when industrial pollutants become trapped in atmosphere; a further 8000 deaths from respiratory disease are also linked to the smog

USA: 3300 by polio epidemic; thousands left disabled

PUBLISHED

Evelyn Waugh, *Men at Arms*

John Steinbeck, *East of Eden*

FIRSTS

2 May: passenger service by jet introduced by BOAC on the London–Johannesburg route, covering 10750 km (6720 miles) in under 24 hours

21 Sept: film made using CinemaScope technique, *The Robe*; the image is compressed on film and widened when projected on screen

31 Dec: year since the end of the Civil War that the USA has been free of lynching attacks

Car safety belts manufactured in the USA

Holiday Inn opened, on US Highway 70 in Memphis, by hotelier Kemmon Wilson

Tranquillising drug, Reserpine, developed by British biochemist Robert Robinson and Swiss pharmacologist Emil Schittler

Woman to swim the 21-mile channel between Catalina Island and Los Angeles, Florence Chadwick

DISCOVERED

Australia: a solid mountain of iron ore in the outback by prospector Lang Hancock, making him the country's richest individual

Ancient Greek ship off the coast of Marseilles by marine archaeologist Jacques Cousteau; it contains 3000 full wine urns

NEW WORDS

DIY *adj, n*: abbreviation for do-it-yourself, often applied to household maintenance

joint *n*: a cannabis cigarette

take the mickey out of *vb*: to tease someone

On 1 November, *the USA detonates the first hydrogen bomb (H-bomb) at Eniwetok Atoll in the Marshall Islands. The explosion creates a fireball 5 km (3 miles) wide, and it takes a full ten minutes for the huge mushroom cloud to develop. Physicist Edward Teller has been working on the H-bomb for ten years.*

Secret society targets white settlers

NO ESCAPE Kenyan soldiers round up fellow countrymen suspected of being Mau Mau fighters.

21 OCTOBER, NAIROBI
A state of emergency was declared in Kenya today by the government of the troubled British colony. The drastic move comes as a result of weeks of violence, during which a secret black organisation called the 'Mau Mau' has been attacking white farmers in an attempt to drive them from the country.

The Mau Mau's members belong to the Kikuyu tribe, Kenya's largest ethnic group. Resentment has been slowly building up against the white minority's ownership of Kenya's best farmland.

Guerrilla war has effectively broken out, with Mau Mau fighters killing more than 40 people in recent weeks. Fatalities include Senior Chief Waruhui, a well-known Kenyan, who was speared to death in a busy street. This murder happened in broad daylight, indicating a change of tactics by the Mau Mau, who had initially struck only under cover of night. Levels of violence have increased, and the Mau Mau are now armed with stolen firearms in addition to tribal weapons.

The white community in Kenya has responded by forming a European Home Guard to patrol vulnerable residential areas. Army support is on its way in the shape of British troops, who have been dispatched to Nairobi to help keep the peace. Meanwhile the colonial government is clamping down on disorder and beginning to round up suspected Mau Mau activists. In the longer term, social and economic conditions for the vast mass of Kenya's population must be improved. A programme of positive reform is under way, set to include the construction of badly needed hospitals and housing.

··· FIRST DIET SOFT DRINK IS LAUNCHED, 'NO-CAL GINGER ALE' DEVELOPED BY KIRSCH BEVERAGES OF NEW YORK ···

The King is dead – long live the Queen

6 FEBRUARY, BRITAIN
In the early hours of this morning King George VI passed away quietly in his sleep, after a blood clot stopped his heart. He died at home on his Sandringham estate after a long illness. Doctors had diagnosed cancer last year, and operated to remove his left lung on 23 September.

The King – always a heavy smoker – was not informed of the precise nature of his condition. The operation went well, although it affected his larynx so that, for the past few months, he has only been able to speak in a husky whisper. For the first time the traditional royal Christmas message had to be pre-recorded.

The end came comparatively quickly. Yesterday the King was out on the Sandringham estate, shooting rabbits and pigeons with his gamekeepers. Nothing seemed amiss when he went to bed at around 10.30 pm.

The King is succeeded by his eldest daughter, Princess Elizabeth, who is on holiday in Kenya at present with her husband, Prince Philip. The 25-year-old princess, now Queen, has been informed, and is hurrying back to Britain to be with her mother, Queen Elizabeth, and her sister Margaret.

THREE QUEENS Elizabeth II, Queen Mary and Queen Elizabeth the Queen Mother unite in mourning.

Designers recognise finger power

Two inventions brought a note of style to simple tasks at the flick of a finger. The flip-top cigarette pack – developed in 1939 – has now begun to replace the traditional soft pack. Rothmans has introduced hinged-lid packets for its king-size filters in South Africa, while, in Britain, Churchman's No 1 brand now comes in a flip-top packet.

Another ingenious invention is taking America's offices by storm. The Rolodex card index, designed by Arnold Neustadter, is revolutionising simple filing tasks. As well as being an essential desktop accessory, this compact, rotating, alphabetically divided index makes information easy to find.

FANNED OUT The Rolodex is an executive must.

Television is catching on, but slowly

WATCHING THE BOX A British family settles down to enjoy an evening of black-and-white entertainment.

The new medium of television came of age in the United States this year, with a broadcast on 24 September by Senator Richard Nixon in which he refuted charges of corruption. It was the first time that a politician had used television to broadcast this type of statement, and Nixon's use of the medium is widely credited with saving his career – he was elected vice-president in November.

Commercial television was launched in the USA in 1946 and had an almost immediate effect: cinema attendances fell for the first time in decades. By the end of this year more than 75 million Americans were regularly tuning in to one of four east-coast-based commercial television networks.

In Britain, the British Broadcasting Corporation's television service began in 1936 but was suspended during the war years. Now it is just starting to take off again, but at the moment British viewers have no choice of channel.

··· US COMPOSER JOHN CAGE'S LATEST WORK, 4' 33", IS 4 MINUTES, 33 SECONDS OF SILENCE ···

Husband-and-wife team grab double gold in athletics

4 AUGUST, HELSINKI
The Olympic stadium has been the scene of a heart-warming husband-and-wife double act. The Czech soldier Emil Zatopek and his wife Dana, who were born on the same day 29 years ago, have each collected gold at this summer's Games.

On the same afternoon that Emil overtook three runners down the final straight to break the tape first in the 5000 metres, Dana (having put her husband's gold medal in her bag 'for luck') collected the gold in the women's javelin competition. But the family contest was won decisively by Emil, who also took gold in the 10000 metres and the marathon, completing the latter event so far ahead of the favourite, Jim Peters of Great Britain, that he was already signing autographs by the time that Peters staggered across the finishing line.

No one before has won all three long-distance events and, like Dana, Emil set a new Olympic record in each of them.

GOOD DAY'S WORK After his triumphs Zatopek was promoted to lieutenant-colonel in the army.

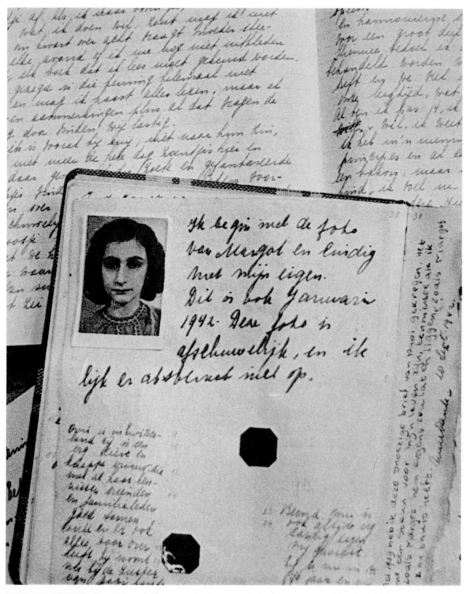

PERSONAL RECORD Anne Frank's diary survived to reveal the human cost of the Nazi Holocaust.

Diary of Anne Frank reveals moving tale

15 JUNE, AMSTERDAM
One family's ordeal during the Nazi occupation of the Netherlands has been brought to light with the publication of *The Diary of a Young Girl*, by Anne Frank. The poignant diary describes a childhood spent hiding from the Nazis in a secret bolthole.

In 1942, when Anne Frank was only 13 years old, she, her family and four other Jewish refugees shut themselves into a secret annexe off Otto Frank's office in Amsterdam. A few trusted friends brought them food, and they remained in their cramped hideout until an informer tipped off the Nazi authorities. In August 1944 the Gestapo raided the building, and the Franks were transported to Auschwitz concentration camp in Poland. Otto Frank survived, but Anne had been moved on to Bergen-Belsen, where she died just before the war ended, three months short of her sixteenth birthday.

Anne's diary was recovered after the war, and Otto Frank decided to honour his daughter's wish by publishing it. The diary gives a moving and honest account of a young girl forced to grow up in fear, isolated from the outside world.

··· THE FIRST COFFEE CREAMER, 'PREAM', IS INTRODUCED BY M AND R DIETETIC LABORATORIES OF OHIO, USA ···

HOLLYWOOD MUSICAL HITS NEW HEIGHTS

Representing one of the high points of the Hollywood musical, this year's lavish period piece *Singin' In The Rain* was, at $2.5 million, one of the most expensive films yet made by Hollywood, and has been one of its most successful. Gene Kelly and Debbie Reynolds were the leading stars in this intricate story set in the 1920s – the age of the flapper. It was also a memorable year for another Kelly, Grace Kelly this time, who had her first starring role as the fiancée of lawman Gary Cooper in the classic western *High Noon*. Neither of these films was chosen for the Academy Award pick of the year, however, although Cooper was handed the best actor statuette.

The award for best picture went to Cecil B De Mille for his circus melodrama *The Greatest Show on Earth*, which starred James Stewart as a clown and offered Charlton Heston his first lead role.

BROLLY TIME Gene Kelly is *Singin' In The Rain*.

1953

DIED
1 Jan: Hank Williams, US country and western star
9 Nov: Dylan Thomas, Welsh poet

DEVASTATED
Aug, UK: Britain's rabbit population, by the myxomatosis virus, after it spreads from continental Europe

PUBLISHED
William S Burroughs, *Junkie*
Raymond Chandler, *The Long Goodbye*
Ian Fleming, *Casino Royale* (the first 'James Bond' thriller)

FIRSTS
23 Mar, France: Baron Bich's low-cost disposable pen, the Bic ballpoint, on sale at 50 centimes
3 Apr, USA: television guide published
17 Apr, UK: woman at No 1 spot in UK chart, Lita Rosa with 'How Much is that Doggy in the Window?'
Cellulose-tipped cigarettes, introduced by L & M
Use of fibreglass to make the entire bodywork of a car, by US car manufacturer Chevrolet for its Corvette model
Woman to win the tennis Grand Slam, US player Maureen Connolly

FOUNDED
12 Nov, London: Samaritans helpline by Reverend Chad Varah, at St Stephen's Church, Walbrook

CRUSHED
17 June, East Berlin: general strike involving 200000 workers, which became an uprising against the Communist government; by Soviet troops, killing 16 people

FLOODED
31 Jan: coasts of Britain and the Netherlands, killing over 2000 people

CONSIDERED
30 Aug: a plan by Christians in West Germany to float Bibles by balloon behind the 'Iron Curtain'

DROWNED
31 Jan: 128 people, when Irish car ferry *Princess Victoria* sinks

BANNED
21 Aug: lobotomy in the USSR

INTRODUCED
Five-Year-Plan in China by Mao Zedong, in order to achieve more rapid industrialisation

SCREEN HITS
Gentlemen Prefer Blondes, starring Jane Russell and Marilyn Monroe
The Big Heat, starring Glenn Ford
Roman Holiday, starring Audrey Hepburn and Gregory Peck
Shane, starring Alan Ladd

From Here to Eternity *is the hit film of the year, winning eight Oscars. Based on the novel by James Jones, the film is a risqué account of US military life in the Pacific. The film includes one of the most passionate embraces on celluloid, between Deborah Kerr and Burt Lancaster.*

CREATED
USA: Department of Health, Education and Welfare, by the US government

INDEPENDENT
Cambodia from French rule, under Prince Norodom Sihanouk, after he dissolved parliament and declared martial law

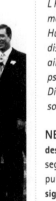

On 12 September, *John F Kennedy marries Jacqueline Lee Bouvier in Newport, Rhode Island. Kennedy is the senator for Massachusetts and Bouvier has, until recently, worked as a photographer for the* Washington Times-Herald.

INVENTED
USA: fish fingers by Gortons Fish Sticks, Worcester, Massachusetts

APPOINTED
5 Mar, USSR: Nikita Khrushchev, as First Secretary of the Communist Party

OPENING NIGHT
The Crucible by Arthur Miller at New York's Martin Beck Theater

L Ron Hubbard founds the Scientology movement in the United States. Hubbard, a former seaman, created a discipline called Dianetics, which aims to 'clear' neuroses by special psychotherapy. Scientology takes Dianetics further, offering a spiritual solution to personal problems.

NEW WORDS
desegregate *vb*: to eliminate racial segregation (as in schools or other public or common areas)
significant other *n*: a spouse, or a cohabiting partner to whom one is not necessarily married
think tank *n*: a research institute or body employed to solve problems

RUSSIA'S DICTATOR IS DEAD

7 MARCH, MOSCOW

Joseph Stalin's body lies in state at Trade Union House, Moscow, the scene of so many of the show trials during his reign of terror. The 73-year-old Russian leader died of a brain haemorrhage two days ago, on the evening of 5 March. His death was announced the following day on a black-bordered front page in the official newspaper *Pravda*, the publication he himself had founded and edited.

Now, ordinary Russians are coming to pay their last respects to their leader. A 10-kilometre (6-mile) queue waits to shuffle past the bier; inside, a military band plays Chopin's *Funeral March*. Outside the mood is less solemn. Bonfires light up the streets, and the sound of balalaikas can be heard.

Few can doubt Stalin's achievements. The son of a Georgian shoemaker, he became the leader of the USSR in 1929. Thanks to his shrewd diplomacy, Russia emerged from World War II as an international power.

However, Stalin's memory will always be tarnished by the increasing repressiveness and brutality of his regime, and the horrors of the purges that he carried out between 1934 and

REST IN PEACE Stalin's jovial image as 'Uncle Joe' belied a more sinister reality.

1938, when millions of Communist Party members, government officials and intellectuals were killed or exiled. The Supreme Soviet has yet to appoint a successor.

··· 1 DEC, USA: FIRST COPY OF *PLAYBOY* MAGAZINE FEATURES A CENTREFOLD OF MARILYN MONROE ···

British scientists define DNA, the key to life's secrets

LIFE FORCE Watson (left) and Crick show off their model of DNA.

25 APRIL, CAMBRIDGE
Two Cambridge scientists have won the race to explain the structure of the most important molecule in biology. In an article in the journal *Nature*, Francis Crick and James Watson have defined the structure of deoxyribonucleic acid (DNA) – the material of heredity.

Every form of life, from bacteria to human beings, is based on genetic information stored in DNA, but until now its structure has not been understood. The research of another British scientist, Rosalind Franklin, provided essential evidence which enabled Crick and Watson to complete their work. They propose that DNA takes the form of a double helix – two spirals wound around one another. The spirals consist of sugar-phosphate chains, held together by flat, ring-shaped molecules which the scientists call bases.

Crick and Watson suggest that whenever a cell divides, the two spirals unwind and separate, one half going to each new cell and creating a new matching half for itself – thus replicating the original double helix. The hereditary information, they suspect, is stored in the molecule in the form of a code spelt out by the bases – an alphabet of just four letters – whose order determines exactly what sort of protein each cell will make and what kind of living being will result.

The double helix is an inspired guess which fits all the facts known about DNA. Crick has no doubt that it is right. The day he and Watson worked out their thesis, he rushed into his local pub, The Eagle, and announced to the startled lunchtime regulars that he had discovered the secret of life.

Everest falls to brave climbers

29 MAY, NEPAL

The highest peak in the world has finally been conquered. At 11.30 am today the New Zealand mountaineer Edmund Hillary and his Sherpa guide, Tenzing Norgay, climbed on to the snow-covered summit of Mount Everest, 8853 metres (29078 ft) above sea level.

In clear, settled weather the pair spent 15 minutes on the summit, where they planted the Union Jack, the Nepalese national flag and the flag of the United Nations. They ate some mint cake and took photographs, and Tenzing left a Buddhist offering, before they began the long descent to base camp.

The conquest of the highest peak in the Himalayas was a triumph of planning and modern equipment. Many previous expeditions have been defeated by the thin atmosphere near the top of Everest. Hillary and Tenzing succeeded

PEAK PERFORMANCE Hillary and Tenzing relax after climbing the world's highest peak.

with the help of oxygen masks, and weatherproof clothing made from nylon. At −26° C (−15° F) it was bitterly cold on top of the mountain.

Expedition leader Colonel John Hunt studied previous expeditions and

weather records before picking the timing and route for the final attempt on the summit. The assault on Everest, planned with military precision, was based on the dictum that the mountain 'could not be rushed'.

··· A WOMAN IS IMPREGNATED WITH FROZEN SPERM AT THE UNIVERSITY OF IOWA ···

Pomp and circumstance mark the Coronation

HAPPY AND GLORIOUS Elements of the ceremony date from AD973.

2 JUNE, LONDON

Queen Elizabeth II was crowned today in London's Westminster Abbey. The 26-year-old is monarch of

more than 650 million subjects throughout Britain and the Commonwealth.

Despite a penetrating persistent drizzle, around

30000 people camped out on the London streets to have a good view of the procession from Buckingham Palace to Westminster Abbey.

The Queen's royal carriage, drawn by horses, was followed by dignitaries from the Commonwealth nations in a stately yet joyful procession. The ceremony was also broadcast live on television, although few people in Britain yet possess a set. The presence of the cameras represents a break with tradition, perhaps marking a foretaste of what many are already describing as a 'new Elizabethan Age'.

Certainly the Queen seemed reluctant to let the festivities come to an end. Together with her husband Prince Philip, she made no fewer than six appearances on the balcony at Buckingham Palace, the last of them after midnight, as crowds continued to celebrate.

The smoothness of the event reflects the thorough preparations made by the organisers. Among their many headaches was the hurried retrieval from the Royal Mews of vital carriages which had recently been sold to the film-maker Alexander Korda.

TRAITORS The Rosenbergs were convicted after Ethel's brother, David Greenglass, testified against them.

Atomic spy couple go to their deaths

19 JUNE, NEW YORK CITY
After one of the most controversial trials of the decade, Julius and Ethel Rosenberg went to the electric chair.

The couple, from Knickerbocker Village, New York, were convicted of treason on 30 March 1951 for passing secrets to the Soviets about the atom bomb. The couple's execution comes at the end of a series of failed appeals for clemency.

The Rosenbergs' treachery first came to light in 1950, after the arrest of Klaus Fuchs, a German physicist working in Britain. He revealed to officials details of an active Soviet spy ring in the United States. It was from these allegations that investigators became convinced that the Rosenbergs were working directly for Anatoli Yakovlev, the Soviet vice-consul in New York. Julius Rosenberg had been an electrical engineer who worked for the US Army Signal Corps.

All along, the case has aroused high passions. At their trial the couple were admonished by Judge Kaufman, who said: 'I believe your conduct has already caused the Communist aggression in Korea, resulting in more than 50 000 American casualties.'

However, some liberals believe that the death sentence was too harsh, and that it has only been carried out due to the anti-communist hysteria which has been whipped up in the United States recently by Senator Joseph McCarthy.

··· US PHYSIOLOGIST ANCEL KEYS SUGGESTS THERE IS A LINK BETWEEN HEART DISEASE AND A HIGH-FAT DIET ···

New knight rides to Derby victory

6 JUNE, EPSOM, ENGLAND
Sir Gordon Richards, who received his knighthood at Buckingham Palace six days ago, has at last won the Derby. The jockey – arguably the best rider in the British Isles – won the race on the 5–1 joint favourite, Pinza.

Richards became a stable-lad at the age of 15 and began his career as a jockey two years later, in 1921. He has ended the flat-racing season as champion jockey 26 times, but the Derby, perhaps the most prestigious of all flat races, had always eluded him. This year, on his twenty-eighth attempt, he realised his ambition, coming four lengths ahead of the Queen's colt Aureole.

Richards's warm manner and modest personality has endeared him to the British racing public, and there has

KNIGHT TIME Richards won a record 4870 races.

been a great deal of press coverage of his unorthodox riding style, which sees the jockey sitting in an unusually upright position in the saddle and using a long rein.

Serial killer hanged

15 JULY, LONDON
John Reginald Christie, one of the most notorious killers of modern times, was hanged at Pentonville Prison earlier today. Christie was convicted of murdering his wife, but he is believed to have killed at least five other women, some of whose remains were found buried beneath the floorboards or in the garden of his home.

Christie strangled his victims after using gas to render them unconscious, raped them, and kept pubic hairs in a tobacco tin as a memento of his deeds.

Christie's conviction has raised severe doubts about the case of his mentally retarded lodger, Timothy John Evans, who was executed in 1950 for murdering his wife and child at the same address.

1954

BORN
18 Feb: John Travolta, US actor
25 Aug: Elvis Costello, UK musician
5 Oct: Bob Geldof, Irish pop singer and international fundraiser
21 Dec: Chris Evert, US tennis player

DIED
10 Apr: Auguste Lumière, French cinema pioneer
3 Nov: Henri Matisse, French painter

FOUNDED
USA: the Moonies (Unification Church) by Korean Reverend Sun Myung Moon

URGED
25 June: stricter tests on British drunk-drivers, who at present are made to recite tongue-twisters and walk in a straight line
7 Nov: French factory bosses, to provide workers with drinking-water fountains as well as wine coolers

On 30 June, *Senator Joseph McCarthy's communist witch-hunts are finally discredited when he is censured by the US Senate. After years of destroying the lives of state officials and public figures, McCarthy went one step too far when he accused the army of harbouring spies. McCarthy is shown above right with his chief adviser, Roy Cohn.*

DESTROYED
27 Nov, Turkey: Istanbul's ancient bazaar in a fire – 2000 shops burnt down, causing £178 million damage

AGREED
23 Oct: German rearmament – West Germany is allowed 400 000 soldiers, a 75 000-strong air force and a 25 000-strong navy

LAUNCHED
21 Jan, USA: *Nautilus*, first nuclear submarine capable of remaining submerged for weeks at a time

GROUNDED
11 Jan: all BOAC Comet airliners, after a series of mysterious crashes leaves hundreds dead and experts baffled

ECLIPSED
30 June: the Sun throughout Britain

SIGNED
19 Oct: Anglo-Egyptian Treaty, recognising Suez Canal as Egyptian

RULED
19 Oct, USA: constitutional and non-discriminatory to have 'negro' against name on ballot paper, by Judge Stephen Chandler in Oklahoma City

BANNED
17 May, USA: racial segregation in public schools
UK: biker film *The Wild One*

DROWNED
9 Dec: 121 French, Irish and English fishermen in hurricanes around the British Isles

NEW WORDS
discotheque *n*: an occasion or place at which people dance to pop records
far out *adj*: bizarre or avant-garde, wonderful, hip and happening

On 22 July, *General Nhiek Tioulong, commander-in-chief of the Cambodian army, and General Ta Quang Buu, Vietnam's minister of defence, sign the Indochina armistice. France will evacuate North Vietnam and recognise the independence of Cambodia, Laos and Vietnam.*

The conversion of a nation of tea-drinkers begins when coffee culture takes off in Britain and coffee bars are opened across the country. Even old-fashioned restaurants such as the Parisien Grill in London use the new espresso machines.

PUBLISHED
Kingsley Amis, *Lucky Jim*
William Golding, *Lord of the Flies*
Dylan Thomas, *Under Milk Wood*

FIRST NIGHT
New York City: *Cat on a Hot Tin Roof* by Tennessee Williams

RALLIED
16 Apr, London: 180 000 people to hear US evangelist Billy Graham at Wembley stadium

FIRSTS
23 Mar, USA: polio vaccines are used on children in Pittsburgh
27 June, USSR: nuclear power station begins producing electricity in Obninsk
15 July, USA: flight by a Boeing 707 leaves from Seattle
19 July, USA: single by Elvis Presley, 'That's All Right Momma'
1 Dec, Boston: successful kidney transplant, from Richard Herrick to twin Ronald

Salk's vaccine holds out hope for polio prevention

26 APRIL, NEW YORK CITY

The biggest clinical trial in the history of medicine was launched by the National Foundation for Infant Paralysis (NFIP) today. The foundation plans to test a vaccine against polio – against the wishes of its discoverer, Jonas Edward Salk.

Salk, from the University of Pittsburgh, has been working on a polio vaccine for several years, using methods developed by John Enders at Harvard. The vaccine consists of the polio virus itself, treated to make it incapable of passing on the disease but able to confer immunity. Aware of the terrible risks – a similar vaccine tested in 1935 gave healthy children polio, killing six of them – Salk is cautious. The virologist has tested the vaccine on some children, including his own three sons, but is uncertain that it is yet safe enough for a mass trial. 'When you inoculate children with a polio vaccine,' he said, 'you don't sleep well for two or three months.'

The NFIP, founded by President Franklin Roosevelt who himself was paralysed by polio, disagrees. Its trial covers 44 states, and will involve vaccinating 1.8 million children at a cost of $7.5 million. It is a brave decision which, if successful,

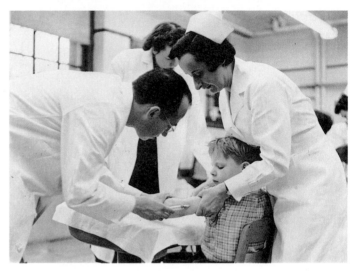

FUTURE HOPE Injections against polio will be soon be commonplace.

will assuage the fears of parents throughout the nation and could mark the beginning of the end for a disease that affects tens of thousands of children every year.

··· THERE ARE 94 MILLION TELEPHONES IN THE WORLD, OF WHICH 52 MILLION ARE IN THE USA ···

France abandons Indochina as battle of Dien Bien Phu ends in defeat

HASTY WITHDRAWAL French forces flee as Viet Minh rebels push forward.

8 MAY, DIEN BIEN PHU, INDOCHINA

European imperialism is on the retreat in Asia. France has been driven out of Indochina, surrendering Dien Bien Phu to the Communist forces of the Viet Minh after a two-month siege of the capital.

The decisive battle for control of Indochina began on 13 March, and from the beginning it was clear that all the advantages lay with the Viet Minh. General Giap had positioned 49 000 troops on high ground overlooking the French entrenchments, and an extraordinary amount of military hardware – howitzers, mortars, anti-aircraft guns and rocket launchers – had been laboriously hauled up the hillsides by gangs of peasants. Against that formidable array stood only 11 000 soldiers of the Indochina Union forces, woefully under-armed, in the valley below. By late April continual Communist bombardment had rendered the French position hopeless. The last week has seen the Viet Minh rebels wade through the mud and overrun the French trenches. Wave after wave of guerrilla assaults were marked by hand-to-hand fighting, and the airfield has been captured.

The French abandonment of Dien Bien Phu took place earlier today after the Communists had infiltrated the camp. The last message from the French compound came from General Castris to General Cogny: 'I am blowing up all our installations. The munitions depot is exploding already. *Adieu, mon général. Vive la France!*'

The withdrawal of France leaves the American government with the dilemma of whether to intervene militarily in Indochina to stop the Communist advance in the region.

BANNISTER BREAKS FOUR-MINUTE MILE

AGONY AND ECSTASY The fastest man in the world breasts the tape.

6 MAY, OXFORD
One of the most challenging barriers in sport has been crossed by a 25-year-old medical student from Oxford University. Roger Bannister has broken the record of four minutes for the mile, passing the line at three minutes 59.4 seconds, beating the previous best of four minutes 1.3 seconds set by Swedish runner Gunder Hägg in 1945.

The four-minute target had stood unbroken for so long that Bannister's great rival, the Australian John Landy, said recently that he was beginning to think it was impossible to overcome it. But Bannister's assault was many weeks in the planning, and when the wind dropped just before the start of the race on the cinder track at the university's Cowley athletics ground he sensed his moment had arrived. It was agreed that Bannister's running mates, Chris Brasher and Christopher Chataway, would lead for the first three laps and that Bannister would take over for the final lap. The plan worked perfectly. Bannister, who had no formal coach and was only able to train for an hour each day because of his studies, ran the last lap in 59 seconds and then collapsed into the arms of the Olympic 200 metres semi-finalist Nicolas Stacey.

The sporting hero fainted after he crossed the finish line and became temporarily colour blind. However, when he was spotted later drinking champagne in the early hours with a girl friend at a London club, Bannister told reporters that he felt 'like dancing until dawn, and I may yet do'.

··· USA: BELL TELECOMMUNICATIONS DEVISES THE FIRST PRACTICAL SOLAR BATTERY ···

Schoolgirl chums found guilty of murdering obstructive mother

30 AUGUST, NEW ZEALAND
A jury in Christchurch yesterday convicted the teenage killers whose cold-blooded crime has shocked New Zealand. Juliet Hulme and Pauline Parker, aged 15 and 16 respectively, were found guilty of bludgeoning Pauline's mother to death with a brick wrapped in a stocking.

The two girls had formed a bizarre and intense relationship at school, and, in a bid to break it up, Juliet's father decided to take his daughter with him for a lengthy visit to South Africa. Pauline was determined to join her there but feared that her mother might prevent this, so the two girls conspired to murder Mrs Parker.

In her diary Pauline, who was something of a loner, recorded: 'The happy event is to take place tomorrow. Next time I write, mother will be dead. How odd, yet how pleasing.'

In court this diary was cited as evidence. The prosecution used it to try to illustrate the premeditated nature of the crime, while counsel for the defence hoped it would show that both the girls were insane.

The authorities decided that the two young killers will serve their sentences in separate jails since, it is reckoned, this will add to their punishment. The girls smiled at each other across the dock as the judge read out their sentence of indefinite detention.

CRIME OF PASSION Juliet Hulme (left) and Pauline Parker could not let anyone stand between them.

Comedienne Lucille Ball finds global TV stardom

When Lucille Ball insisted that her situation comedy *I Love Lucy* be shot on film and not in the traditional, poorer quality, kinescope system it looked like extravagance. But now the top-rated American comedy series has become the first internationally syndicated television show and made its stars, Ball and her husband Desi Arnaz, world celebrities.

Lucille, a model and chorus girl from Celaron, New York, started off in Hollywood as a B-movie actress. Eventually her distinctive gravelly voice and sense of comic timing propelled her into television. Her new show, which was also the first situation comedy to be filmed in front of a live audience, was shot with three cameras to allow for better editing, and the sharp script and high production values have made it sought after by programme buyers around the world. The new ITV network in the UK, due to be launched on 22 September next year, has already signed up for the show.

HAVING A BALL Lucille dons a false nose in her *I Love Lucy* show 'LA at Last'.

··· A US TAXPAYER WITH AN INCOME OF $100 000 NOW PAYS $87 000 IN TAXES ···

End of an era: ration books are binned

3 JULY, LONDON
The British can finally eat as much beef as they like. As of today, rationing is over. In an un-British public demonstration of feeling, joyful crowds tore up the hated ration books in Trafalgar Square last night when the government announced the news. At Conservative Associations across the country, the books were burnt. The nation was fed up to the back teeth with 14 years of rationing.

Housewives needed to take a creative approach to cookery in order to feed their families on the dull rations that were available. Despite Home Office publications of recipes using powdered eggs, and valiant broadcasts by *Woman's Hour*, cheap substitutes for butter, cream, meat and eggs never set mouths watering. Dining out in London had never been so dreary.

Smithfield, the biggest meat market in Britain, opened its doors at midnight last night instead of the usual 6.00 am. A spokesman said they hadn't seen so much meat since 1939.

MUSICAL RELIEF FROM CITY CONFLICTS

PERFECT MATCH *Seven Brides for Seven Brothers* is the ultimate western musical.

Marlon Brando played the consummate anti-hero in *On The Waterfront*, Elia Kazan's Oscar-winning story of a washed-up ex-boxer battling union corruption. The film is thought to be inspired by the recent McCarthy investigations into un-American activities. It was left to Sam Spiegel to produce it after all the major Hollywood studios turned it down, no doubt shying away from its violent and controversial content.

Hollywood felt far more comfortable with tried and trusted formulas that had family appeal, such as MGM's *Seven Brides For Seven Brothers*, an all-singing,

all-dancing slice of apple-pie Americana that has seven Oregon farm boys looking for their respective Miss Rights.

Judy Garland gave a particularly moving performance as a young actress determined to reach the top in *A Star Is Born* – an intelligent musical melodrama studded with excellent songs by Ira Gershwin, Rodgers and Hart. Meanwhile, Alfred Hitchcock's *Rear Window* confirmed his status as the undisputed master of suspense. James Stewart and Grace Kelly starred in this tense study of voyeurism and murder, exploring the relationship between watched and watcher – which, by definition, includes the audience.

Also keeping viewers on the edge of their seats was *Bad Day at Black Rock*, directed for MGM by John Sturges. The star is Spencer Tracy, who plays a one-armed man arriving at a tiny country town. He receives a suspicious welcome from townspeople who are harbouring a secret. The story, which takes place over 24 hours, builds up a clock-watching tension that has led many to compare it to Fred Zinnemann's *High Noon*.

1955

DIED

18 Apr: Albert Einstein, German-born US scientist

12 Aug: Thomas Mann, German author

30 Sept: James Dean, US actor

QUIT

5 Apr, London: Winston Churchill, aged 80, as British prime minister because of poor health; Anthony Eden succeeds

19 Sept, Buenos Aires: Juan Perón, as president of Argentina, following coup; he flees to Paraguay

FASTEST

18 Sept, Soviet Union: runner Vladimir Kuts, who sets world 5000 m record of 14 mins 46.8 secs

On July 17, *the drawbridge is lowered on the entrance to Disneyland as Walt Disney opens his $17 million theme park at Anaheim, California. Most of the rides and attractions are based on the Disney cartoons, and visitors are delighted to see such characters as Mickey Mouse and Snow White come to life.*

EXECUTED

13 July, London: Ruth Ellis, for murdering her lover, David Blakely

TELEVISION DEBUTS

22 Sept, UK: ITV (Independent Television)

UK: *This Is Your Life* with Eamonn Andrews

USA: *Alfred Hitchcock Presents*

MUSIC RELEASES

8 Jan, USA: 'Milk Cow Blues Boogie', Elvis Presley's third single

2 Feb, UK: 'Majorca', Petula Clark's first record

23 July, USA: 'Maybelline', Chuck Berry's first single; reaches Top 10 pop chart

3 Dec, USA: 'The Great Pretender', by the Platters

FOR SALE

1 Aug, USA: IBM 700 line of computers

USA: Kentucky Fried Chicken, Kellogg's Special K

SIGNED

14 May, Poland: Warsaw Pact, by Soviet Union, Albania, Bulgaria, Czechoslovakia, East Germany, Hungary, Poland and Romania

DISCOVERED

UK: make-up of vitamin B12, by British chemist Dorothy Hodgkin

FIRSTS

Cyclist to win three consecutive Tours de France, Louison Bobet of France

European Cup competition in football; Scottish clubs participate, but not English ones

UK: experimental colour television broadcasts, by the BBC

PUBLISHED

Vladimir Nabokov, *Lolita*

Samuel Beckett, *Waiting for Godot*

J P Donleavy, *The Ginger Man*

C S Lewis, *The Magician's Nephew*

BLEW UP

1 Nov, Colorado: United Air Lines DC–6 in mid-air because of bomb in luggage, killing 44; John Gilbert Graham killed his mother, who was on board, for insurance money

PASSED

Clean Air Act in Britain, in response to the 1952 smog

Toy manufacturers are among the many celebrating the coming space age. This top-heavy wind-up robot is prone to falling over as it waddles around. Most robot toys of this period are manufactured in Japan.

The Seven Year Itch *launches Marilyn Monroe as a celluloid sex symbol. The comedy, directed by Billy Wilder, centres on an attraction between a married man (Tom Ewell) and his neighbour (Monroe). In this famous scene, Monroe cools down over a subway vent on a hot summer night.*

RIOTED

13 May, Florida: fans at Elvis Presley concert

20 Aug, North Africa: Algerians and Moroccans in coordinated anti-colonial demonstrations

BESTSELLER

Ian Fleming, *Moonraker*

NEW WORDS

beatnik *n:* a member of the Beat generation, which rejects social standards of the day; any person with long hair and shabby clothes

karate *n:* a style of martial art developed in Japan

jet set *n:* wealthy people of a fashionable social set who travel frequently by jetliner to parties and holiday resorts

VIOLENCE ERUPTS IN CYPRUS

SEARCHING FOR GUNS Under the state of emergency, British troops stationed in Cyprus were empowered to conduct random street searches in an attempt to crush the terrorist group EOKA – a public threat since 1954.

28 NOVEMBER, NICOSIA In response to the killing of five British soldiers on the British colony of Cyprus, Sir **John Harding, the governor of the island, has declared a state of emergency.** Since the spring the terrorist organisation EOKA has masterminded strikes, industrial sabotage and terrorist bombings in pursuit of its aim to unite Cyprus with Greece. The state of emergency entitles the governor to impose curfews, detain or exile terrorist suspects and seize property.

The violent campaign was instigated by the founder of EOKA, the Greek general George Grivas, and the people's hero, Archbishop Makarios, after the British authorities made it clear that they would grant neither independence nor union with Greece to the island, which also has a Turkish community estimated to comprise about 18 per cent of the population. Cyprus was annexed by Britain in 1914, when it declared war on Turkey. The last chance of peace disappeared about a year ago, when an appeal to the United Nations proved fruitless.

··· THE MILLIONTH VOLKSWAGEN BEETLE ROLLS OFF THE PRODUCTION LINE ···

The very modern romance of princess and the press

31 OCTOBER, LONDON After weeks of intense speculation, Princess Margaret announced today that she would not be marrying Group Captain Peter Townsend. The couple have been under virtual siege recently, with press reporters monitoring their every move and recording the precise amount of time that they spend together. Disappointing though the news is for romantics, the decision may at least bring some relief to Townsend and the princess. The former has admitted: 'We both feel mute and numbed at the centre of this maelstrom.'

The affair has focused international attention on the royal family and awakened uncomfortable memories of the 1936 abdication crisis of the then King Edward VIII and Mrs Simpson. Townsend was a distinguished fighter pilot, but he is also a divorcé with two children. Margaret, aged 25, could marry him at the cost of forfeiting her official income and her rights to succession but, like her uncle, she has suffered bitter recriminations from both the Church and parliament.

It had been hoped by the royal family that the affair would fizzle out during Townsend's recent two-year posting to Brussels but, in the end, the princess was forced to choose between duty and personal happiness.

DUTIFUL Margaret feels the pain of lost love.

The Comets rock the world around the clock

For a man who started out as a yodelling cowboy doing cover versions of Hank Williams songs, Bill Haley is a mean rock and roller. 'Rock Around the Clock' just scraped into the top 20 last year, but its appearance on the soundtrack of the film *The Blackboard Jungle* gave the number a welcome boost. A re-released version topped the charts in the UK and the USA this year, and the rocker followed that up with hits such as 'Shake, Rattle and Roll', and 'See You Later, Alligator'.

Bill Haley and his band, the Comets, are the ambassadors of a new type of music called rock and roll. Questioned about the success of the new music – a fusion of country music and the blues – Haley puts it down to the fact that young people can get involved with it, and that it's not too difficult for them to join in by singing along, clapping and dancing. However, some parents have expressed their concern about this new music trend and the wild dancing that goes with it.

CRAZY JIVE Haley and the Comets, renowned for an exuberant stage act, strike a rock-and-roll pose.

··· THE FIRST EDITION OF THE *GUINNESS BOOK OF RECORDS* IS PUBLISHED ···

Workwear becomes fashionable

HOT PANTS Blue jeans usher in an age of practical, hard-wearing fashions.

It used to be that jeans were strictly men's workwear, but this year the durable denim trousers have been hijacked by the young. Teenagers are also changing the shape in which these hardy perennials are made. The latest fashion is for figure-hugging blue jeans, and they are currently the number one bestseller for women in the USA, France, Britain and Canada.

'We ain't going to sit in the back no more'

8 DECEMBER, ALABAMA

Seven days ago a 43-year-old black woman made a decision that could have repercussions throughout the whole country. Mrs Rosa Parks boarded a public bus in Montgomery, Alabama, and sat near the front – in defiance of the segregation laws that insist that black people must sit at the back.

When Mrs Parks refused to give up her seat to a white passenger, the bus was stopped, the police were called, and she was arrested. After this events moved quickly. That evening a boycott of the city's buses was called by the black community.

The man appointed to lead the boycott is a young Baptist minister, Dr Martin Luther King, who recently received his PhD degree from the University of Boston. Dr King settled in the town last year as pastor of the Dexter Avenue Baptist Church and has quickly become a respected figure in the community. He is a powerful spokesman for equal rights for black citizens, and has gone on record as saying that he – like the late Mahatma Gandhi of India – is committed to achieving his goals by peaceful protest. Dr King believes that black Americans should no longer be content with 'anything less than freedom and justice'.

Black citizens make up about three-quarters of the bus commuters in the Montgomery area. Unless the council moves quickly, transport companies face a damaging campaign and a serious loss of revenue.

Catastrophe strikes Le Mans 24-hour race

11 JUNE, LE MANS, FRANCE
In the worst disaster in motor-racing history, 85 spectators and one driver lost their lives during the Le Mans 24-hour race. Two hours into the race, the Mercedes-Benz driven by Pierre Levegh collided at 240 kilometres per hour (150 mph) with an Austin Healey. Levegh spun several times in the air and dived over a bank into an enclosure that was densely packed with racing fans. Levegh died almost instantaneously as the wreckage burst into flames; the driver of the other car, Lance Macklin, was unhurt.

The race was allowed to continue, and spectators on the other side of the track had no inkling of the tragedy until, some hours later, an announcement was made over the public address system to a shocked crowd. Mercedes-Benz withdrew its cars from the competition, and the race was won by the British driver Mike Hawthorn and his partner Ivor Bueb, who stunned everyone by reaching a record-breaking average speed of 170 kilometres per hour (106 mph) in their Jaguar.

DISASTER AREA Race-track officials rush to pull out survivors.

··· RAVI SHANKAR, INDIAN SITAR-PLAYER AND COMPOSER, MAKES HIS DEBUT IN THE USA ···

DEAN'S REBEL BECOMES THE IDOL OF A GENERATION

Rebel Without A Cause, a story of teenage angst and rebellion, became James Dean's epitaph after he was killed in a driving accident in September at the age of 24. Youngsters used every trick in the book to see the film, which was released with an under-18 age restriction four weeks after his death. By the year's end, his cult status as a figure of disaffected youth was secure.

Robert Mitchum gave a performance of pure evil in Charles Laughton's *The Night of the Hunter*, a nail-biting thriller that deserved greater critical success, while famous villain James Cagney shone in a comic role in *Lady Killer*. Offering a few digs at the movie industry along the way, the film follows a small-time hood to Hollywood where he graduates to stardom. Its witty and fast-paced plot was well received, as was Cagney's stylish delivery. Ernest Borgnine won the best actor Oscar for his performance in *Marty*, a low-budget film about a Bronx butcher attracted to a plain-looking schoolteacher.

GENERATION GAP James Dean's on-screen defiance of his elders and betters made him a teen idol.

1956

BORN

31 Jan: John Lydon (aka Johnny Rotten), singer in the Sex Pistols punk group
6 June: Bjorn Borg, Swedish tennis player
18 Oct: Martina Navratilova, Czech-born US tennis player

DIED

31 Jan: A A Milne, British creator of Winnie-the-Pooh
11 Aug: Jackson Pollock, US artist
14 Aug: Bertolt Brecht, German writer

CONVICTED

22 Mar, Alabama: Martin Luther King, of organising boycotts of racially segregated bus services by black townspeople of Montgomery

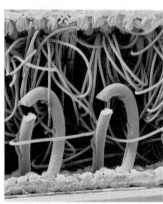

Swiss engineer Georges de Mertral perfects his fastening product, Velcro, after years of work. Inspired by the burdock seeds which cling to clothing and animals' coats, Velcro consists of two nylon strips. One is covered with thousands of tiny hooks and the other with loops to catch the hooks. The name 'Velcro' is a combination of the French velours (velvet) and crochet.

BANNED

13 Nov, Washington DC: racial segregation on buses, declared unconstitutional by US Supreme Court

ELECTED

23 June, Cairo: Colonel Gamal Abdel Nasser, president of Egypt

RE-ELECTED

6 Nov, Washington DC: Dwight Eisenhower, US President (Republican) for second term

RAISED

1 Mar, USA: minimum wage, from 75 cents to $1 per hour

MARCHED

30 Mar, UK: anti-nuclear protesters, from the Aldermaston research establishment to London

FLEW

4 July: the CIA's U–2 reconnaissance aeroplane, on first spying mission over Soviet Union

RIOTED

10 Mar, Cyprus: protesters at deportation of Archbishop Makarios, Greek Cypriot leader, by the British
29 June, Poland: workers, against Communist rule
Sept, UK: British teenagers at screenings of *Rock Around the Clock*

HIGHEST

6 Nov, Nebraska: US Navy Lieutenant Commander Morton Lewis and Malcolm Ross, who set new altitude record for manned balloon flight of 23 165 m (76 000 ft) in US Navy Stratolab

On 29 June, Hollywood actress Marilyn Monroe marries Pulitzer Prize-winning playwright Arthur Miller. It is her third marriage and his second. The union attracts unprecedented media attention.

EXPELLED

1 Mar, USA: Autherine Lucy, first black student at Alabama University, following riots by white students

FIRSTS

10 Mar, Sussex: aircraft to fly faster than 1600 km/h (1000 mph); Fairey FD–2, piloted by Peter Twiss, reaches a speed of 1820 km/h (1130 mph)
29 June, Los Angeles: athlete to clear 2.1 m (7 ft) in high jump, Charley Dumas
11 Oct, South Australia: British atom bomb, dropped over Maralinga by RAF

MARRIED

19 Apr, Monaco: actress Grace Kelly and Prince Rainier of Monaco

SEIZED

29 Oct–3 Nov: Gaza and Sinai, by Israel

PROCLAIMED

1 Jan, Khartoum: Republic of Sudan
23 Mar: Islamic Republic of Pakistan

OPENED

16 Jan, Italy: Winter Olympics, at Cortina d'Ampezzo
22 Nov, Melbourne: 16th modern Olympic Games

QUIT

27 Apr, USA: Rocky Marciano, undefeated world heavyweight boxing champion

On 25 September, the first transatlantic telephone system using an automatic exchange is opened. This service will substantially lower the costs of calls, making communication across the Atlantic more of an everyday activity.

INDEPENDENT

2 Mar: Morocco, from France
20 Mar: Tunisia, from France

NEW WORDS

flat top *n*: a style of haircut in which the hair is cut shortest on the top of the head
pop group *n*: a band of musicians which plays music of general appeal, especially to young people
wheeler dealer *n*: a shrewd operator, one who advances one's own interests

HUNGARIAN NATIONALISTS DEFY SOVIETS

26 OCTOBER, BUDAPEST

The long-simmering discontent in Hungary has at last boiled over into open defiance of the Soviet Union. For the last three days there has been fighting in the streets of the capital between ordinary people and the security police who, aided by the Soviet troops stationed in Budapest, are trying to restore order. Imre Nagy, the leader of the nationalist struggle for democracy, has assumed the prime ministership and today ordered Soviet troops to withdraw from Hungary. Reports suggest that much of Budapest is now controlled by the rebels and that the revolt is spreading beyond the capital.

The Hungarians' uprising against their Communist rulers began in March, following Khrushchev's denunciation of Stalin. The nationalist movement has been bolstered by the support of students and intellectuals. Prominent victims of Stalin's tyranny were honoured by public reburials, and statues of Stalin were toppled in towns throughout the country.

Violent discontent erupted after the meeting of the Writers' Union, a Communist-affiliated group, on 19 October. Sixteen resolutions were passed, calling for multi-party elections, the release of political prisoners, the liberalisation of the economy and the dismissal of Stalinists from official posts. Four days later hundreds of thousands of demonstrators burst on to the streets shouting anti-Soviet slogans and demanding the departure of Soviet troops. Public support for Nagy and for reform is widespread, but it is hard to believe that the Soviet Union will not send in its army to restore its authority.

PROVOCATIVE ACTION Protesters tear down a statue of Stalin in Budapest.

··· THE FIRST EUROVISION SONG CONTEST IS HELD IN LUGANO AND WON BY THE SWISS ENTRANT, LYSS ALYSSIA ···

Khrushchev orders in the tanks to crush democracy movement

IRON FIST Soviet tanks wreaked havoc in Budapest, destroying buildings and boulevards.

5 NOVEMBER, BUDAPEST

A massive show of force by Moscow has crushed the rebellion in Hungary and ended a spirited attempt to shake off dependence on the Soviet Union and form a democratic society. Three days of artillery fire from tanks, fighter aircraft and infantry have imposed a deathly silence on the capital. The last words heard from the rebels' radio station, early this morning, were a plaintive 'Help, help, help …'

The whereabouts of the ousted prime minister, Imre Nagy, are not known; he is to be replaced by the secretary-general of the Hungarian Communist Party, Janos Kadar.

Soviet tanks and troops crossed the Hungarian border on 1 November, and by the next morning they were at the gates of Budapest. Nagy appealed to the West to recognise Hungary's neutrality, but the United Nations did nothing beyond calling for a Soviet withdrawal. Molotov cocktails and grenades have been impotent against the might of the Red Army, which has moved through the capital butchering its citizens. It is believed that 25 000 people have been killed and 150 000 injured. A further 200 000 have fled the country.

Suez invaded by Britain and France

6 NOVEMBER, CAIRO
Six days after British and French forces began to bombard Egyptian airfields and radio stations, the troops have captured Port Said and are advancing southwards along the Suez Canal. The invasion of Egypt is in response to President Nasser's nationalisation of the canal, in which an Anglo-French company held the controlling shares.

Relations between Nasser's government and the West have soured since last year when he closed an arms deal with the Soviet Union and gave official recognition to Communist China. In retaliation the United States withdrew its offer to help finance the massive Aswan Dam scheme. On 26 July this year Nasser announced his nationalisation plans to a vast outdoor rally in Alexandria. The canal, he proclaimed, was 'our canal', and the

CASUALTIES After the battle, ships sunk by the Egyptians lie in the canal entrance at Port Said.

Aswan Dam would be built with the revenues from Suez. He also said the imperialists could 'choke on their rage'.

France, Britain and Israel have committed themselves to military action, but unless they are backed by the United States – an increasingly doubtful proposition – they may have to make a humiliating retreat.

Lady sings blues and tells all

IN THE LIMELIGHT Holliday, whose real name was Eleanora Fagan, wows a club with her stylish performance.

AUGUST, NEW YORK CITY
Billie Holliday's autobiography *Lady Sings the Blues* hit the book shops this month. It is a sensational self-portrait of the jazz singer whose life has been rocked by controversy and scandal. Holliday's first recording was with the Benny Goodman Band in 1933. Since then, her unique voice has assured her a string of hits, including the songs 'Lover Man' and 'God Bless the Child', but her professional success has been dogged by her tragic personal life.

The book chronicles the singer's battle with drink and drugs, and her time in prison after being convicted for drug possession. However, some critics question just how accurate the singer's memories really are, and co-author Bill Dufty has been accused of filling in the blanks when Holliday can't or won't remember her past.

Khrushchev denounces Stalin as despot

10 MARCH, MOSCOW
Nikita Khrushchev, the Soviet premier, has denounced Stalin and his 'cult of personality' at the Twentieth Congress of the Communist Party. In a long, emotional speech which has stunned the world, Khrushchev branded the late dictator a paranoid despot and a mass murderer. He further accused him of incompetence for ignoring warnings of Hitler's imminent invasion in 1941, of mishandling the war and of provoking a rift with President Tito of Yugoslavia.

Sources close to the Party made it clear that Khrushchev was in tune with the prevailing anti-Stalinist mood of the meeting. The Party, it seems, is eager for a return to a more collective leadership in the style of Lenin, and for a thaw in East–West relations.

Laker bowls into the record book

27 JULY, MANCHESTER
With one match left, England has taken a 2–1 lead in the Ashes series against Australia thanks to stupendous bowling at Old Trafford by Jim Laker. The Surrey off-spinner, who claimed ten wickets in an innings for his county against the Australians in May, has surpassed even that performance, ending the match with figures of 19 wickets for 90 runs – all the wickets being taken from the Stretford end.

Yorkshire-born Laker possesses a textbook high-arm action; his beautiful control of flight and spin have earned him an enduring place in cricket history as the only bowler ever to take ten Test wickets in an innings and the only one to take 19 wickets in a first-class match.

US HITS OF THE YEAR

1	HOUND DOG/DON'T BE CRUEL	*Elvis Presley*
2	SINGING THE BLUES	*Guy Mitchell*
3	HEARTBREAK HOTEL	*Elvis Presley*
4	THE WAYWARD WIND	*Gogi Grant*
5	LOVE ME TENDER	*Elvis Presley*

EPIC TALES, BIG PRODUCTIONS

EXOTIC COUPLE The King of Siam and the prim governess.

Cinemas were filled with long and lavish adaptations of classic stories this year. Michael Anderson's Jules Verne adaptation *Around the World in 80 Days*, starring David Niven and Shirley MacLaine, and Cecil B de Mille's biblical epic *The Ten* Commandments dominated the box office. Solemn, respectful versions of *Moby Dick*, directed by John Huston and starring Orson Welles, and *War and Peace*, starring Audrey Hepburn and Henry Fonda, found less favour.

In *The Searchers* John Wayne shook off his heroic image to play a ruthless cowboy searching for his niece and the Native American who kidnapped her. Audiences were charmed by Marilyn Monroe, showing that she could act in *Bus Stop*, and by the partnership of Deborah Kerr – though her songs were overdubbed – and Yul Brynner in Rodgers and Hammerstein's musical *The King and I*.

Elvis storms the charts

RISING STAR On stage, Presley's raw energy whips audiences into a fever.

The world of popular music was changed forever in April this year when a moody, dramatic recording of 'Heartbreak Hotel' by Elvis Presley stormed the charts on both sides of the Atlantic. The 21-year-old former truck-driver went on to conquer the hearts of teenage America with such hits as 'Blue Suede Shoes' and 'Don't Be Cruel'.

Nobody has ever heard or seen anything like him, with his indelible half-sneer and swivelling hips – leading to his nickname 'Elvis the Pelvis'. Some are horrified by his blatantly sexual appeal – one Cincinnati car-dealer offered to smash 50 Presley records for every car sold, and did a roaring trade. But Presley's stage performance is a hit with teenagers – especially teenage girls. One female fan was quoted in a national newspaper as saying: 'He's just one big hunk of forbidden fruit.'

Elvis's first appearance on the *Ed Sullivan Show* garnered a record television audience: more than 50 million people tuned in to watch him – about 82 per cent of the total American television audience.

1957

DIED

14 Jan: Humphrey Bogart, US actor
2 May: Joseph McCarthy, US senator, leader of anti-communist witch-hunts
24 Oct: Christian Dior, French *haute couture* fashion designer
17 Dec: Dorothy L Sayers, British novelist and playwright

RELOCATED

New York: US baseball teams the New York Giants and the Brooklyn Dodgers to California; the Giants go to San Francisco, and the Dodgers to Los Angeles

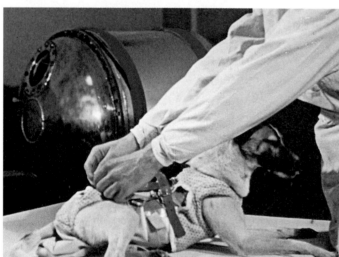

On 3 November, *the USSR launches its second space satellite,* Sputnik II, *carrying the first animal in space, a female dog called Laika. The aim is to study the effects of space travel on an animal in preparation for sending humans.*

FOUNDED

25 Mar: EEC, the European Economic Community, or 'Common Market', under Treaty of Rome; signed by France, West Germany, Italy, Belgium, the Netherlands and Luxembourg
29 July: International Atomic Energy Agency (IAEA)

PRIZEWINNER

6 May, New York City: John F Kennedy, Massachusetts senator, who is awarded Pulitzer Prize for *Profiles in Courage*

PUBLISHED

Muriel Spark, *The Comforters*
Patrick White, *Voss*
Samuel Beckett, *Endgame*
Boris Pasternak, *Dr Zhivago*

PROCLAIMED

25 Apr, Jordan: martial law, by King Hussein, following failed coup

WON AT HOME

20 July: Stirling Moss, winner of British Grand Prix in British Vanwall car; first victory for British driver-car combination since 1923

BESTSELLER

Dr Seuss, *The Cat in the Hat*

Dwight Eisenhower, sworn in as US President for a second term of office, announces the 'Eisenhower Doctrine' which increases the role of the United States in politics in the Middle East. The USA is concerned about the growing influence of the Soviet Union in Arab countries.

CONVICTED

31 May, Washington DC: playwright Arthur Miller, of contempt of Congress, when he refuses to name allegedly communist writers to the House Un-American Activities Committee

INDEPENDENT

30 Aug: Malaya, of Britain

QUIT

9 Jan, London: Anthony Eden, as British prime minister

APPOINTED

10 Jan, London: Harold MacMillan as British prime minister

FIRSTS

16 Apr: parking meters in London
6 July, London: black tennis player to win at Wimbledon; Althea Gibson wins the ladies' singles title

1 Aug, New Mexico: solar-heated commercial building, the Solar Building, in Albuquerque
18 Dec, USA: US atomic power plant, in Shippingport, Pennsylvania

LINKED

26 June, UK: smoking and lung cancer, in Medical Research Council report; the connection is 'one of direct cause and effect'

The world's first giant dish radio telescope is commissioned. The Mark 1A telescope, set up at Jodrell Bank, near Manchester, England, measures 76 m (250 ft) in diameter. The dish reflects and focuses astronomical radio waves.

PROPOSED

4 Sept, UK: legalisation of gay sex between consenting men aged over 21, in Home Office committee report

LONGEST

23 Jan, Barbados: test innings, by Pakistani cricketer Hanif Mohammed; he is in for 16 hours 10 minutes and scores 337

NEW PHRASE

see you later, alligator: way of saying goodbye taken from Bill Haley song title; reply is 'in a while, crocodile'

SPUTNIK BLASTS INTO SPACE

4 OCTOBER, KAPUSTIN YAR, KAZAKHSTAN

On the fiftieth anniversary of the Russian Revolution the Soviets have launched a satellite into orbit around the Earth – beating the United States in the 'space race'. Sputnik, a 56-centimetre (22-in) sphere, was fired into space using rockets based on the Nazis' wartime V2 weapons, which were developed to carry H-bombs enormous distances around the world.

The project's chief designer, Sergei Korolyev, is a survivor of the Kolyma Gulag. He was still under life sentence for treason at the end of the war when Stalin made him responsible for rounding up German rocket engineers in the Soviet zone to exploit their expertise.

But Korolyev wanted to build spacecraft, not weapons. His dream came true when Khrushchev needed a propaganda coup to bolster his image at home and convince the USA that the

SPACED OUT Sputnik's short development time meant that it contains little scientific equipment.

USSR had developed intercontinental missiles. Korolyev was given six weeks to design Sputnik. The tiny satellite

contains a battery-powered radio, which transmitted a message of triumph as it passed over Asia, Europe and the USA.

··· A NEW LOWEST-EVER TEMPERATURE IS RECORDED BY SCIENTISTS AT THE SOUTH POLE: –73.5° C (–100.4° F) ···

Troops signal death knell for segregation in Arkansas

ARMED GUARD The 'Arkansas Nine' are escorted into school at Little Rock.

25 SEPTEMBER, LITTLE ROCK
The President of the United States, Dwight Eisenhower, has sent troops to Little Rock, Arkansas, to enforce the racial desegregation of schools in the southern states.

Three years ago the US Supreme Court ruled that segregation in education was unconstitutional and must be ended 'with all deliberate speed'. But the President remained silent on the issue, even though no progress was made and 'White Citizens Councils' whipped up opposition to the court order throughout the Deep South. Backed by senators and congressmen, they mounted a campaign against the change.

This year a federal court ordered desegregation to start at the beginning of the new school year. The governor of Arkansas, Orville Faubus, called out the state militia to prevent black children from entering schools, but when another court order insisted that he withdraw the troops, Faubus backed down. Events came to a head at the Central High School, where mobs of white parents gathered to try to keep black pupils out.

Yesterday they could do nothing as 1000 federal paratroopers escorted six black girls and three boys into the school. These events have given a boost to the civil rights movement led by Dr Martin Luther King.

Teddy Boys cause a teenage rampage

Rock and roll has ripped up more than the songbook, it has changed attitudes, hairstyles and the way teenagers dress.

Leading the charge in Britain are the Teddy Boys, the first real youth tribe. Named because of the Edwardian-style clothes they wear, these rock-and-roll lovers distance themselves from the music of their parents and the people they call 'straights', who do not like the new music coming from the USA.

The Teddy Boys' frock coats, crepe-soled shoes and ruffled shirts were in evidence at Bill Haley's first British tour of 1957. But some Teds ripped out seats at the concerts and were branded thugs.

In Britain singers like Tommy Steele are taking their lead from US music and are becoming increasingly popular.

TED TRENDY For the first time young people have enough disposable income to allow them to buy the clothes and records required for being a 'Ted'.

Kerouac's beatniks take to the road

On the Road, a novel by 35-year-old author Jack Kerouac, has shocked Middle America with its graphic portrayal of sex and drugs. The story of two men journeying across the United States, running away from the monotony of American suburbia, has gained massive media attention.

Critics have said the novel's 'heroes' epitomise what is being called the 'beat generation', a whole section of American youth that is not prepared to conform – a subculture that likes to get high, listen to jazz and have pre-marital sex.

Kerouac has touched a nerve; along with fellow 'beatniks' Allen Ginsberg and William Burroughs, he has given a voice to young people who have until now been despised or ignored.

··· TROUSERS WITH PERMANENT CREASES ARE INVENTED BY AN AUSTRALIAN GOVERNMENT RESEARCH BODY ···

COOL DUDE Miles Davis's meteoric career rise occurred soon after he beat his heroin addiction in 1954.

Davis is Mr Cool

Jazz will never be the same again, thanks to Miles Davis and the pioneering sound he has created known as 'cool'.

In the last six months the 31-year-old trumpeter from Illinois has released albums that have astounded the jazz world with their originality and finesse. This is jazz unlike anything that has been heard before – music that seems to have little in common with the frantic pace of bebop played by the likes of Dizzy Gillespie and Charlie Parker. Instead audiences are treated to a velvety-smooth, laid-back sound, full of unhurried solos and urbane rhythms.

Davis has released two albums this year, both breathtakingly original. First came *The Birth of Cool*, recorded in 1948 but released now as the style crosses over to the mainstream. Davis followed up this triumph with *Miles Ahead* – an orchestral collaboration with composer Gil Evans that is set to become an all-time classic.

Ghana wins independence

6 MARCH, ACCRA
The British Union Jack no longer flutters over the parliament buildings in Accra, the capital of the new independent nation of Ghana in West Africa. At midnight yesterday a crowd of joyful Ghanaians cheered as the symbol of British imperial authority was lowered for the last time. The new country amalgamates two former British colonies – the Gold Coast, a British Protectorate since 1874, and British Togoland. The new nation will remain within the Commonwealth.

In the 18th and 19th centuries the country was a centre for the gold and slave trades, with European traders forcibly transporting thousands of people to the 'new' countries of the Americas.

Ghana has won its independence with very little bloodshed, and it is being hailed as a model for the smooth divestment of colonial power. Today's victory was the culmination of a process that began in 1946 when a new constitution guaranteed blacks a majority in the country's parliament.

It is a great triumph for Ghana's leader Kwame Nkrumah, imprisoned from 1950 to 51 for his part in fomenting illegal strikes. Nkrumah has been prime minister since 1952 and now becomes the head of the first sub-Saharan colony (with the exception of South Africa) to liberate itself from European rule.

Morocco, Tunisia and Sudan gained independence from their rulers last year.

Fangio drives into a record

31 AUGUST, ITALY
The champagne was flowing at Monza today as Formula One driver Juan Fangio carried off his fifth world championship, a feat that has never been accomplished in the history of the sport.

Fangio's great physical strength and stamina have enabled him to cheat Father Time and at 46 years and two months become the oldest man ever to become Formula One champion.

Racing pundits believe that the Argentinian will end on a high and make this his last full year of racing. His second place in a 250F Maserati at the last race of the year in Italy, and the four wins he achieved earlier in the season, earned him the title as well as a place in the record books.

Fangio's is a true rags-to-riches story. Born in 1911 of Italian immigrant parents in Buenos Aires, he worked in a garage from the age of 11 in order to save up enough money to buy his first ever car – a Model T Ford.

US HITS OF THE YEAR

1	JAILHOUSE ROCK	*Elvis Presley*
2	TEDDY BEAR	*Elvis Presley*
3	ALL SHOOK UP	*Elvis Presley*
4	LOVE LETTERS IN THE SAND	*Pat Boone*
5	YOUNG LOVE	*Tab Hunter*

··· *THE MOUSETRAP* BY AGATHA CHRISTIE BECOMES BRITAIN'S LONGEST-RUNNING PLAY WITH 1998 PERFORMANCES ···

All hail the 'inventor' of rock and roll

Alan Freed, a DJ with a taste for whiskey, gave the world the term 'rock and roll'. Back in 1952, Freed launched his show *Moondog's Rock 'n' Roll Party* on the WJW station in Cleveland, Ohio, and since coining the phrase he has shown that he has his finger on the pulse.

His liquor-fuelled rants do not win him any fans in authority but are popular with teenagers, and films like *Rock Around the Clock* have cemented his place at the forefront of the movement. Now his radio programme is the first rock show to be syndicated throughout the United States, as well as in Europe on Radio Luxembourg.

FRENCH UNDRESSING AS BB BARES ALL

BABE Bardot was 18 when she married Vadim.

Lying naked in the Mediterranean sun, Brigitte Bardot caused a sensation around the world in the opening scene of her husband Roger Vadim's *And God Created Woman*. Anglo-Saxon audiences were not used to seeing nudity in mainstream cinema, and even in France the censor felt it necessary to impose cuts. In Hollywood, Henry Fonda gave a powerful performance in *Twelve Angry Men*, a claustrophobic drama of a jury's verdict on a teenager accused of murder. The science fiction genre managed to shake off some of its B-movie reputation with Jack Arnold's *The Incredible Shrinking Man*. The film left audiences enthralled with its convincing special effects and a polished performance from lead actor Grant Williams.

1958

BORN

7 June: Prince Rogers Nelson (aka Prince, The Artist Formerly Known As Prince), US pop musician
16 Aug: Madonna Louise Ciccone, (aka Madonna), US pop musician
29 Aug: Michael Jackson, US pop musician

DIED

14 Mar: Christabel Harriette Pankhurst, British suffragette
2 Oct: Marie Stopes, British pioneer of birth-control education

KILLED

17 June, Hungary: Imre Nagy, prime minister in 1956 uprising, hanged
3 Aug, West Germany: British racing driver Peter Collins, in crash during German Grand Prix

LAUNCHED

4 Aug, USA: Hot 100 singles chart in *Billboard* magazine
USA: American Express credit card

On 25 October, Italian Cardinal Angelo Roncalli, aged 81, is elected Pope. He takes the name John XXIII. His appointment follows the death of Pius XII on 9 October. John XXIII has served as an apostolic delegate in several European countries and as papal nuncio (ambassador) to France after World War II.

The Boeing 707 passenger jet enters transatlantic service with Pan Am. Since the aircraft made its first flight four years ago it has gained a reputation for safety, comfort and speed. Pan Am is now planning a round-the-world jet service.

FOUNDED

1 Feb, Middle East: United Arab Republic, comprising Egypt and Syria
14 Feb, Middle East: Arab Federation, comprising Iraq and Jordan
17 Feb, UK: Campaign for Nuclear Disarmament (CND)
May, New York City: news service UPI (United Press International)
29 July, Washington DC: NASA (National Aeronautics and Space Administration)

DISCOVERED

UK: that thalidomide, a drug prescribed to expectant mothers for morning sickness during pregnancy, may cause birth defects

DISPATCHED

15 July, Washington DC: 5000 US marines to support President Chamoun's government in Lebanon
17 July, UK: 2000 British troops to support King Hussein of Jordan's regime

COUPS

14 July, Baghdad: against King Feisal of Iraq, by army soldiers; succeeds

31 July, Haiti: against President François 'Papa Doc' Duvalier, by army on behalf of exiled leaders Louis Dejoie and Paul Magloire; crushed
26 Sept, Rangoon: against Premier U Nu, led by General Ne Win; succeeds

FIRSTS

1 Feb: US satellite in space, *Explorer*
4 Oct, London: scheduled transatlantic jet service, by BOAC Comet 4
21 Oct, London: women peers in House of Lords
5 Dec, UK: British motorway – 8 km (5 miles) of bypass at Preston, Lancashire

After years of design and development, the Lego brick is finally launched by Danish toymakers Ole and Godtfred Kirk Christiansen. Lego (which comes from the Danish leg godt, meaning 'play well') comprises a range of plastic blocks and accessories which can be built into houses, vehicles and people.

BANNED

9 Feb, London: *Endgame*, play by Samuel Beckett, because of alleged blasphemy

KIDNAPPED

23 Feb, Cuba: leading racing driver Juan Fangio by Cuban rebels; he is released the next day

OUSTED

27 Mar, Moscow: Soviet Premier Marshal Bulganin, by Nikita Khruschchev

RIOTED

28 Jan, Cyprus: Turkish community, in anti-British demonstrations
3 May, Boston: audience at rock 'n' roll show *The Big Beat*, produced by US disc jockey Alan Freed
9 Sept, London: blacks and whites in race conflict, Notting Hill; follows earlier race riots on 30–31 Aug

QUIT

2 Mar, Athens: Greek premier Constantine Karamanlis
22 Sept, Washington DC: Sherman Adams, President Eisenhower's chief of staff, accused of accepting gifts in return for favours

CHAMPIONS

25 Mar, Chicago: Sugar Ray Robinson, aged 37, wins world middleweight boxing championship for fifth time by beating Carmen Basilio
29 June, Sweden: Brazil, winners of soccer World Cup 5–2 against Sweden; 17-year-old Pele plays
1 Sept, London: Surrey, winners of county cricket championship for seventh year running
19 Oct, Morocco: British racing driver Mike Hawthorn, winner of world championship, in a Ferrari

NEW WORDS

counterculture *n*: the lifestyle of people who reject dominant or conventional social values
high fidelity, or hi-fi, equipment *n*: radio or record players capable of reproducing new stereo recordings

TRAGIC END FOR BUSBY'S GIFTED BABES

7 FEBRUARY, MUNICH

Eight players of the Manchester United team who were carrying hopes for an English victory in the European Cup were killed last night in an air crash on their way home from Yugoslavia. All but one of the players killed were under 25. Also killed were eight journalists (among them the former England goalkeeper Frank Swift) and five substitute members of the squad. The team's manager, Matt Busby, is still in a critical condition in a Munich hospital, receiving blood transfusions and, although conscious, unable to speak.

This spells a tragic end for 'Busby's Babes' – the most promising United squad for years. Spirits were high on the aeroplane last night as the players were celebrating their victory over Belgrade Red Star, which advanced United to the semi-finals. The crash also revived memories of a previous disaster in 1949, when 18 players of Torino FC were killed in an air crash in Italy.

The accident happened when the airliner on which the team were travelling was taking off from Munich

DREAM TEAM Matt Busby discusses tactics before the Red Star game, fated to be the team's last match.

airport, where it had stopped to refuel. Suddenly, a blinding snowstorm blew up and the aeroplane caught fire after hitting buildings on the edge of the airport, seconds after take-off.

Lost to English football are the England fullback and Manchester United captain Roger Byrne and the

immensely talented young halfback Duncan Edwards. Two other England internationals – the promising forwards Tommy Taylor and David Pegg – and the Irish international forward Bill Whelan were also killed. Bobby Charlton escaped with minor injuries to the head.

··· 30 JAN, FRANCE: YVES SAINT LAURENT HOLDS HIS FIRST FASHION SHOW IN PARIS ···

No small wonder that it was invented – twice over

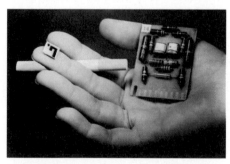

LITTLE WONDER The fingertip-sized integrated circuit (left) performs an identical function to a much larger conventional circuit (right).

This year two engineers, with 1000 miles between them, invented the first working integrated circuit. The circuit, which will

revolutionise the manufacture of electronic products, has been credited to both Jack Kilby, an engineer working for Texas Instruments in Dallas, and Robert Noyce, of Fairchild Semiconductors in Santa Clara, California.

Kilby had only recently started working at Texas Instruments and had not been there long enough to qualify for a holiday. While his colleagues were away, and he was alone in the laboratory, he had a brilliant idea: to eliminate the complexity of wires and soldering by combining transistors, resistors and capacitors in a single block of the semiconducting element germanium.

Noyce had had the same idea but approached it from a different angle. He realised that the circuits could be built much flatter, by stacking the semi-conductor layers inside rather than on top of one another.

Both firms announced their circuits at the same time, and a battle over the patent is expected. However, Kilby and Noyce consider themselves co-inventors, and so does the scientific community.

Although neither realised it, their idea was not new. A British engineer, G W Dummer of the Royal Radar Establishment in Malvern, had suggested it in 1952, but could not make it work.

Algerian crisis brings de Gaulle back to politics

2 JUNE, PARIS

General Charles de Gaulle, hero of the French Liberation forces of World War II, has been granted emergency powers to deal with the crisis in Algeria. De Gaulle took over as prime minister of France yesterday, and expectations of the new premier are high. He is widely considered to be France's only hope of stability as the country teeters on the brink of civil war.

Algeria, a French colony, has been in the throes of guerrilla warfare since 1954 in an effort to gain independence. The current crisis came to a head on 13 May, when a French army revolt in Algiers sparked a dispute which led to the fall of the French government. In the face of a threatened coup by settlers in Algeria, who opposed any concessions to Algerian nationalists, politicians called upon de Gaulle to come out of his 12 years in retirement.

The respected and formidable wartime leader accepted President René Coty's offer of the premiership, but only on his own terms. The French National Assembly has now granted de Gaulle sweeping new powers to address the current problems, together with a mandate to reshape French politics by rewriting the constitution. This may well spell the end for France's 'Fourth Republic' which began in 1946.

REINS OF POWER De Gaulle's assumption of the premiership ushered in the Fifth Republic.

··· THE SKATEBOARD IS INVENTED BY BILL AND MARK RICHARDS OF VAL SURF SHOP IN CALIFORNIA ···

CRAZY WHIRL Singer Georgia Gibbs records 'The Hula Hoop Song', which is a US hit.

Hula mania makes the world go round

Hips were set wiggling this year by the arrival of the hula hoop. Like so many fads – including the famous frisbee – the hula hoop hails from California.

The brainchild of Arthur Melin and Richard Knerr, who got the idea from Australian children's bamboo hoops, it is made out of Grex, a form of polyethylene. Competition to sell hoops was hot. Within weeks, rival manufacturers were selling their own versions; 25 million hoops were sold around the world before the craze died, as suddenly as it had sprung up, in the summer.

Elvis swops blue suede shoes for army boots

24 MARCH, MEMPHIS

The king of rock and roll has been drafted. Elvis Presley, whose provocative style inflamed teenagers and outraged parents, has shown that he's a loyal American citizen by joining the army. The celebrated quiff has been replaced by an uncompromising crew cut – photographs of the haircut have been reproduced in newspapers around the world – and for the next two years he will simply be US Private 53310761 Presley E A.

Presley's two-year military service will be spent mostly in Germany. His presence in the film industry will be maintained during his absence by the release of a series of films and extensive merchandising. Hits such as 'A Fool Such As I', 'Hard Headed Woman', 'I Got Stung' and 'A Big Hunk O' Love' maintain his high profile in the pop charts. And it is during his sojourn in Germany that Presley meets a 14-year-old girl, Priscilla Beaulieu, whom he will marry in 1967.

The future is glass

SHEER STYLE The innovative Seagram Building was copied around the world.

One of the landmarks of modern architecture was completed this year. Depending on your point of view, the Seagram Building in New York is either an elegant exercise in pure form or a soulless monolith. It was begun in 1954 and designed by the German-born architect Mies van der Rohe, who has lived in Chicago since 1937. The building towers 157 metres (516 ft) above Park Avenue, a sheer wall of glass and marble relieved only by bronze mullions. A low pavilion to the rear houses the Four Seasons restaurant.

Among the innovative features that have been praised by architects are the pillars that lift the whole structure a storey above ground level, the public plaza in front of the building, and the striking floor-to-ceiling windows of tinted glass. The combination of these elements produces a sense of lightness and bold modernity.

Jerry flees a hornet's nest

MAY, LONDON
Jerry Lee Lewis, Presley's rival for the title of 'King of Rock', has cancelled his British tour after only three concerts. Lewis recently topped the charts with 'Great Balls of Fire'. This setback to his career came after it was revealed this month that his wife, Myra, is also his 13-year-old second cousin. The scandal followed Lewis home, where his popularity began to wane.

By contrast, the clean-cut, bespectacled Buddy Holly saw his star continuing to rise. He had chart hits on both sides of the Atlantic, on his own and with his band, the Crickets. And another clean-living star has begun his career – Cliff Richard had his first hit in September with 'Move It'.

TUNESMITH Buddy Holly soared to fame with this year's tour of the UK.

NASA plans to send men into orbit

7 OCTOBER, USA
Project Mercury, a plan 'to send a man into orbit', has been announced today by the National Aeronautics and Space Administration (NASA), the body that was created earlier this year.

Preparations are already under way. NASA has begun to develop space suits that will insulate the first men in space, and to investigate the effects of zero gravity on the human body. Zero gravity is simulated by allowing jet aeroplanes to fall freely through the sky. The pressure caused by the high acceleration of a rocket when taking off and landing will be simulated in centrifuges – giant high-speed carousels – and rocket sleds which can exert as much as 80 times the normal force of gravity.

US HITS OF THE YEAR

1	IT'S ALL IN THE GAME	*Tommy Edwards*
2	THE PURPLE PEOPLE EATER	*Sheb Wooley*
3	AT THE HOP	*Danny & The Juniors*
4	NEL BLU DIPINTO DI BLU (VOLARE)	*Domenico Modugno*
5	TEQUILA	*Champs*

··· THE BLACK BOX FLIGHT RECORDER IS DEVELOPED IN AUSTRALIA BY DAVID WARREN ···

1959

BORN
16 Feb: John McEnroe, nicknamed 'Superbrat', US tennis player

DIED
7 Feb: Daniel François Malan, former South African prime minister and architect of apartheid
3 Mar: Lou Costello, US comedian
17 July: Billie Holliday, US singer
14 Oct: Errol Flynn, British actor

SWORN IN
25 June, Dublin: Eamon de Valera as president of the Irish Republic

FOUNDED
20 Aug, South Africa: anti-apartheid Progressive Party

The Morris Mini-Minor, one of Britain's first 'baby' cars, goes on sale. It has an 848 cc engine, and can reach a speed of 112 km/h (70 mph). The car's designer, Alec Issigonis (above, with his creation), also designed the other baby car of the year, the Austin Seven.

MARRIED
18 June, Paris: Jacques Charrier and Brigitte Bardot

BANNED
21 July, Washington DC: British writer D H Lawrence's novel *Lady Chatterley's Lover*, from US mail

On 19 April, Tibet's spiritual leader, the Dalai Lama, arrives in India seeking political asylum. He fled Tibet last month, following the intervention in the country by Chinese military. The Chinese were planning to arrest him.

SIGNED
20 Nov, Stockholm: European Free Trade Association (EFTA) agreement by Britain, Austria, Denmark, Norway, Portugal, Sweden and Switzerland, creating rival trade group to EEC

PUBLISHED
Saul Bellow, *Henderson the Rain King*
William Burroughs, *The Naked Lunch*
Laurie Lee, *Cider With Rosie*
Tennessee Williams, *Sweet Bird of Youth*

DUG
3 Apr, English Channel: test bores for a Channel tunnel
30 May, France: first excavations for road tunnel under Mont Blanc

CONDEMNED
10 Nov: South African apartheid, by United Nations General Assembly

DECLARED
27 Feb, Rhodesia: state of emergency, by British authorities

OPENED
26 June, Quebec: St Lawrence Seaway, linking the Great Lakes and the Atlantic Ocean

KILLED
22 Jan, Surrey: British racing driver and reigning world champion Mike Hawthorn, in non-racing motor accident
3 Feb, Iowa: US singer Buddy Holly, in aeroplane crash, with another rising star, Ritchie Valens

The Barbie Teenage Fashion Model is launched in the USA by Mattel. Barbie started her life some years earlier as Lilli, named after a risqué German newspaper character. The doll, which stands about 30 cm (12 in) tall, costs $3.

FIRSTS
22 Feb, Florida: Daytona 500, US stock car race, 800 km (500 miles) on speedway circuit; won by Lee Petty in an Oldsmobile at average speed of 218 km/h (135 mph)
Helicopter crossing over the English Channel

SCREEN HITS
North by Northwest, directed by Alfred Hitchcock
Some Like It Hot, directed by Billy Wilder

JOINED THE USA
3 Jan: Alaska, 49th state
20 May, USA: 5000 Japanese-Americans who had had their US citizenship revoked during World War II
21 Aug: Hawaii, 50th state

OPENED
23 Feb, Strasbourg: European Court of Human Rights

NEW WORD
psychedelic *adj*: relating to new or altered perceptions, as through the use of hallucinatory drugs

CASTRO LEADS CUBAN REVOLUTION

2 JANUARY, HAVANA
A ragged army of rebel guerrillas led by Fidel Castro has taken power in Cuba, ousting the government of the dictator General Fulgencio Batista.

Castro proclaimed the Cuban revolution from his headquarters in Santiago de Cuba, while his troops, led by Camilo Cienfuegos and Argentinian revolutionary Che Guevara, took over the barracks and the presidential palace. Their arrival was greeted by enthusiastic crowds. Batista and his immediate supporters fled by air to the Dominican Republic early yesterday morning.

Castro's triumph follows a two-year guerrilla war fought from the hills of the Sierra Maestre against a corrupt and unpopular regime. The charismatic 32-year-old leader first took arms against Batista in 1953 in a raid on the Moncada barracks in Santiago, which failed. When defending himself at his trial, Castro declared: 'History will absolve me.' This was to become a rallying cry for his supporters.

Freed two years later in an amnesty, Castro went abroad. He returned in 1956 aboard the *Granma* – a tiny, barely seaworthy vessel – as head of an invasion force. When his 82 men were caught in an

VIVA LA REVOLUCION Castro rallies support on the march to Havana.

ambush, nearly all of them were killed or captured. A small handful escaped to the hills, from where they rallied support, dodged capture and gained strength, until by December 1958 they were ready to march on the capital.

··· SINCE 1945 MORE THAN TWO MILLION EAST GERMANS HAVE CROSSED OVER TO WEST GERMANY ···

Little bubbles burst onto the motoring scene

Easy to park, easy to drive and so lightweight you could almost pick it up, the 'bubble car' has become the vehicle of the young urban cognoscenti.

As well as the ubiquitous Heinkel Trojan, which has become the defining shape of this tiny transporter, two other bubbles are roaming the streets of London.

The Messerchmitt KR200 is little more than a scooter with a chassis. It is 250 centimetres (99 in) long, but its 191 cc engine reaches a hair-raising 96 kilometres per hour (60 mph).

BABY CAR The tiny BMW Isetta has room for two adults and a child.

More stylish, with a roll-top and swing-up front door, is the BMW Isetta. Made in in Brighton, it has a 245 cc engine and three wheels, and is surprisingly stable – but getting out of the vehicle gracefully remains a problem.

Some light shed on the dark side of the Moon

18 OCTOBER, MOSCOW
The world has received its first glimpse of the hidden, 'dark' side of the Moon, in pictures transmitted by the Soviet spacecraft *Luna III*.

The images were taken seven days ago when the unmanned craft looped around the Moon on its way back to the Earth, but could not be transmitted earlier as *Luna III* was too far away.

The Russian authorities have hurried to exploit the pictures' propaganda value by naming lunar features after Soviet landmarks and heroes.

Kitchen sinks fuel drama as superpower leaders meet

HEATED DEBATE Khrushchev and Nixon argue before a fascinated crowd of Western journalists.

29 JULY, MOSCOW
In a refreshing departure from the Cold War climate of suspicion, ordinary Russians have been given details of a heated discussion between their leader and the American Vice-President. The exchange between Khrushchev and Nixon – which is already being dubbed the 'Kitchen Debate' – took place at the American National Exhibition in Sokolniki Park, Moscow.

This glittering show, housed under a giant dome, has captured the imagination of Muscovites. Young girls hand out free Pepsi-Colas, and visitors marvel at the colourful slides of American life showing rows of shiny cars, and at the mock-up of a typical ranch house.

The atmosphere between Nixon and Khrushchev was strained at the beginning of the visit, and by the time the men arrived at the ranch-house kitchen – which, Khrushchev sniped, was way beyond the pockets of ordinary Americans – the argument was in full flow. An animated discussion ensued as to whether capitalism or communism was the better system.

Commentators have been amazed at the openness and passion of the debate, which for once took place outside the realms of diplomatic protocol.

··· FIRST 'SMELLIE' FILM, *BEHIND THE GREAT WALL* – 72 SMELLS ARE PROVIDED, INCLUDING INCENSE AND ORANGES ···

Space flight is monkey business

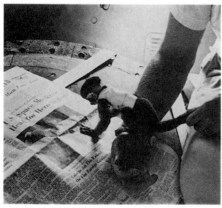

SHOT TO FAME Baker reads news of his mission.

29 MAY, FLORIDA
Two monkeys called Able and Baker were recovered unharmed from the Atlantic Ocean after being fired 480 kilometres (300 miles) into space. They are the first living creatures that the USA has sent safely to such an altitude.

Able and Baker both wore space suits, and were strapped into couches specially moulded to their body shapes to make them more comfortable during the acceleration take-off.

Throughout the 15-minute flight each monkey's heartbeat, breathing rate, body temperature and muscular tension were carefully monitored from mission control at Cape Canaveral, and the director of the Medical Research and Development Command of the US Army declared that both Able and Baker were in 'perfect condition'.

Able had a morse-code key attached to her spacesuit and had been trained to tap it when she saw a red light, so that scientists could monitor how zero-gravity affected her reactions. No signals were received, but a fault, rather than Able's disorientation, was blamed.

Makarios elected Cypriot president

13 DECEMBER, NICOSIA, CYPRUS
Archbishop Makarios has been elected the president of Cyprus, which from July next year will be independent of British rule. Makarios was exiled from the island by the British in 1956 for his part in the *enosis* movement which agitated for union with Greece. He returned at the beginning of March this year to a tumultuous reception.

In the run-up to the election the streets of Cyprus were strewn with myrtle when Makarios made a preaching tour. He received 67 per cent of the vote, beating his Turkish-Cypriot opponent by two votes to one. The world is now waiting to see whether the new president returns to the cause of union with Greece.

Remarkable museum becomes 'arrogant' architect's epitaph in stone

BETTER BY DESIGN The Guggenheim Museum took three years to construct.

21 OCTOBER, NEW YORK CITY
The Guggenheim Museum of Modern Art in New York, designed by Frank Lloyd Wright in the months leading up to his death, opened today. The architect died six months before the completion of what is being hailed as his *pièce de résistance*.

The public is now able to see the magnificent Guggenheim family collection of 20th-century masterpieces by Paul Klee, Marc Chagall, Wassily Kandinsky, Piet Mondrian and others, but the work of these masters is almost overshadowed by the building in which they will be housed.

The main part of the museum is a multi-storey cone. Visitors start at the top and walk down a large spiral ramp that curves around a central well. Paintings hang away from the wall on metal bars, so they appear to float in the air. Critics have questioned whether the sense of motion induced by the ramp and cone is ideal for the contemplation of paintings.

The building has been seen by some as arrogant, sitting in all its unique modernity among the sedate apartment blocks of the Upper East Side. But the same charge was levelled at Wright. He believed himself 'the greatest living architect' and preferred 'honest arrogance' to 'hypocritical humility'. The Guggenheim is a perfect monument to an irascible genius.

Hovercraft glides across Channel

25 JULY, DOVER
On the fiftieth anniversary of Louis Blériot's first flight across the English Channel, a craft that can float on air above the water has made the same journey. Designed by engineer Christopher Cockerell and built by Saunders-Roe on the Isle of Wight, the SR-N1 is the first practical hovercraft. It weighs 4 tons and is able to carry a crew of three at a speed of 25 knots over calm water.

Cockerell worked for the Marconi company for 15 years before setting up as a boat-builder in the Norfolk Broads. Trying to think of ways of making his boats go faster, he dreamt up the idea of floating them on a cushion of air. Experiments with a coffee tin, kitchen scales and vacuum-cleaner tubes convinced him it would work. The SR-N1, built in secret with a grant from the Ministry of Supply, proved it.

FLOATING ON AIR Cockerell's prototype will be developed for commercial use.

US HITS OF THE YEAR

1	MACK THE KNIFE	*Bobby Darin*
2	THE BATTLE OF NEW ORLEANS	*Johnny Horton*
3	VENUS	*Frankie Avalon*
4	LONELY BOY	*Paul Anka*
5	THE THREE BELLS	*Browns*

Copying just got easier

16 SEPTEMBER, USA
The first copier able to reproduce documents at the press of a button has been launched by Haloid. The 'Xerox 914' makes copies on standard 9 x 14 in (23 x 35.5 cm) paper. It represents the life's work of inventor Chester Carlson, whose patent was filed in 1937. Previously he had offered the idea to over 20 companies, who all rejected it.

1960

DIED

4 Jan: Albert Camus, French author
18 Apr: Eddie Cochran, US rock-and-roll star
30 May: Boris Pasternak, Soviet author
27 Sept: Sylvia Pankhurst, British suffragette
5 Nov: Mack Sennett, US film director
16 Nov: Clark Gable, US actor

KILLED

25 Apr, Mississippi: ten black Americans in race riot

DECLARED

30 Mar, South Africa: state of emergency

ENDED

11 June, Italy: marriage of Roberto Rossellini and Ingrid Bergman, in annulment
2 Dec, UK: marriage of Laurence Olivier and Vivien Leigh, in divorce
31 Dec, UK: national service for British men; last call-up cards issued

INDEPENDENT

27 Apr, Africa: French Togo, as Republic of Togo
30 June, Africa: Belgian Congo, as Congo Republic
12 July, Africa: Congo, Chad and the Central African Republic, of France
16 Aug: Cyprus, of Britain, with Archbishop Makarios as president
1 Oct, Africa: Nigeria, of Britain

TRIUMPHED

18 May, Glasgow: Spanish football side Real Madrid, which wins the European Cup for the fifth time, beating Eintracht Frankfurt 7–3

The US Mercury Seven astronaut team, chosen last year, begins its training for Project Mercury, NASA's first manned space flight. The astronauts are (front row, left to right) Walter Schirra, Donald Slayton, John Glenn, Scott Carpenter and (back row, left to right) Alan Shepard, Virgil Grissom and Gordon Cooper.

WRECKED

1 Mar, Morocco: Agadir, by tidal wave, earthquake and fire – 1000 killed and 40 000 made homeless
25 Apr, Iran: town of Lar, by earthquake – around 1500 killed

PUBLISHED

Harper Lee, *To Kill a Mockingbird*
John Updike, *Rabbit, Run*

QUIT

27 Apr, South Korea: Syngman Rhee, as president, following unrest in the wake of his election

FASTEST

21 June, New York: British sailor Francis Chichester, who arrives after record 40-day yacht crossing of Atlantic Ocean from Plymouth

ELECTED

24 Oct, UK: Bertrand Russell, to head Campaign for Nuclear Disarmament
9 Nov, USA: John F Kennedy (Democrat), as President

BANNED

27 Feb, Connecticut: *Playboy* magazine, from newsstands
25 Mar, South Africa: black political organisations

FIRSTS

20 June: heavyweight boxer to regain world championship, Floyd Patterson
26 Sept, USA: nationally televised presidential debate between candidates
14 Dec: cricket Test Match to end in a draw, West Indies versus Australia

FOUNDED

UK: Royal Shakespeare Company

BEHAVED BADLY

29 Sept, New York City: Soviet leader Nikita Khrushchev, who heckles during British Prime Minister Harold Macmillan's speech to United Nations General Assembly
12 Oct, New York City: Khrushchev again, who bangs his shoe on his desk during speech by Philippine delegate Lorenzo Sumulong

NEW WORDS

catsuit *n*: tight all-over piece of women's clothing
dropout *n*: person who abandons conventional society
mouse *n*: hand-operated mobile device attached to computer
sit-in *n*: peaceful occupation or obstruction of an area as a protest

SOUTH AFRICAN POLICE SHOOT 69 DEAD

AFTER THE VIOLENCE South African police examine victims' bodies following the Sharpeville shootings.

22 MARCH, SHARPEVILLE, SOUTH AFRICA

In a violent display of white power in South Africa, police yesterday opened fire on unarmed black protesters, killing 69 and wounding another 200.

Similar episodes have taken place in the past decade, but none so bloody as this.

Demonstrators, numbering about 20000, were attending a protest rally at the black township of Sharpeville, near Vereeniging in the Transvaal. They are outraged that the police continued to train their automatic weapons on the crowd even when it was fleeing from the scene. Robert Sobukwe, the leading activist in the South African black consciousness movement and the organiser of the rally, was arrested.

The demonstrators were protesting against the Pass Laws enacted by the National Party government three years ago. Any black male observed in a 'white area' is required to show a pass entitling him to be there. Each week thousands of blacks are stopped by the police and arrested if they are found not to have their passes with them.

Yesterday's outrage has been severely condemned by world leaders, and several international bodies have already indicated their intention to require South Africa to leave. The country's continued membership of the Commonwealth is now in jeopardy, and it is becoming more isolated in the international community.

··· 5 APR, LOS ANGELES: THE FILM *BEN HUR* IS AWARDED A RECORD TEN OSCARS ···

American pilot condemned as spy

19 AUGUST, MOSCOW

Cold War tensions were heightened today when pilot Gary Powers was found guilty of being an American spy. The trial lasted only three days, largely because of the cooperation of the defendant, and has proved an immense propaganda coup for the Soviet Union.

The first chapter in this tale of political intrigue took place on 1 May, when Powers, a 30-year-old civilian, was shot down while carrying out an aerial reconnaissance mission over Soviet territory. He was flying at 20600 metres (68000 ft) in a Lockheed U-2, taking photographs of Russian installations on a route between Afghanistan and Norway. While passing close to the industrial city of Sverdlovsk, however, his plane was brought down by a ground-to-air missile.

The Soviets did not acknowledge the capture of the airman until 7 May, when Khrushchev demanded an apology from President Eisenhower. The revelation was timed to cause maximum embarrassment, coinciding with the date when the two leaders were due to attend a summit meeting in Paris.

At first the USA issued denials, but the remnants of detailed maps, sophisticated camera equipment and surviving photographs disproved any arguments that the pilot had simply lost his way. Similarly, at his Moscow trial, Powers had little option other than to admit his guilt. He was sentenced to ten years' imprisonment. The Paris summit talks had fizzled out on 17 May.

FLYING SPY American pilot Gary Powers holds a model of the Lockheed U-2 reconnaissance plane.

LATECOMERS REFUSED ENTRY TO HITCHCOCK'S NEW THRILLER

CHILLER Anthony Perkins goes *Psycho* as motel keeper Norman Bates.

The most talked-about Hollywood film of the year was *Psycho*, partly because of skilful publicity. To emphasise the tension of the plot, cinemas that showed the film had to agree not to admit any customer once it had started. A masterly combination of mystery, horror and black comedy, it is one of Alfred Hitchcock's finest creations. The murder scene in the shower and the shocking unmasking of the killer have become part of movie legend.

In European cinema the most hotly discussed film – for very different reasons – was *La Dolce Vita* (*The Sweet Life*), directed by Federico Fellini. It follows a week in the life of a gossip columnist, played by heart-throb Marcello Mastroianni, and exposes the emptiness of the lives led by the rich and famous – many members of Rome's high society appeared in the film. The Vatican attacked it as 'decadent', but Italian audiences loved it, and a dubbed version has been successful in Britain and the USA.

Vessel explores ocean depths

24 JUNE, PACIFIC OCEAN
The deepest dive in history took place yesterday as the Swiss-built US Navy bathyscaphe *Trieste,* manned by its inventor's son Dr Jacques Piccard and USN Lieutenant Don Walsh, plunged 10 900 metres (35 800 ft) into the Mariana Trench in the Pacific Ocean.

The *Trieste* was built in 1953, and extensively revamped when it was acquired by the US Navy two years ago. The vessel works on the simple principle of gaining or losing ballast in order to sink or float. In order to sink, it gradually takes water into its ballast tanks. Two large chambers are filled with gasoline, which compresses as it descends. To rise, it releases iron shot that has been held in place by electromagnets; as it does so, the gasoline decompresses, allowing the vessel to float again. This means the bathyscaphe can go up and down, but cannot manoeuvre sideways. Once on the seabed, therefore, the *Trieste* was unable to explore its new terrain.

The cult of Citroën's revolutionary DS

BASKING SHARK Introduced in 1955, the DS is a technologically-advanced, futuristic-looking classic.

No car can have a more distinctive shape than the Citroën DS, known as the 'Shark'. Its low-slung aerodynamic shell, vast expanse of bonnet and sleek futuristic styling conjure up images of the dark streets of 1950s Paris and the mysterious figures of Maigret's underground. In fact the DS spans every level of French society – it is the official French presidential car and was a favourite of Charles de Gaulle, once saving him from a gun attack thanks to its remarkable ability to drive on two flat tyres.

Well ahead of its time, the DS features self-levelling 'hydropneumatic' suspension which gives its passengers one of the smoothest rides around. Also supplied as standard are power-assisted steering and power-operated brakes, gearbox and clutch. You can even change a tyre without using a jack.

··· THE AVERAGE BRITON'S STANDARD OF LIVING IS ONE-THIRD AS HIGH AS THE AVERAGE AMERICAN'S ···

Polio victim sprints to triple Olympic glory

12 SEPTEMBER, ROME
The Olympic Games have ended with the Soviet Union delighted by its athletes' stunning eclipse of a powerful team from the United States. The Soviets won 43 gold medals against the Americans' 34 golds and a total of 103 medals against the American tally of 71 – a repeat of the Soviet achievement four years ago. But the Games are really about individual effort, and two stories have captured this year's headlines.

The undoubted star has been the American sprinter Wilma Rudolph, the 20-year-old mother from rural Tennessee, who was the twentieth of her father's 22 children, born prematurely

and stricken in infancy with polio, double pneumonia and scarlet fever. Until the age of six she wore a leg-brace, and she did not throw away her orthopaedic shoes until she was 11. Since then sheer grit and determination have lifted her to the pinnacle of world sport. This year she has emulated the achievement of her team-mate Betty Cuthbert at the 1956 Games, by winning gold medals in the 100 metres, 200 metres and 4 x 100 metres relay.

In a tragic accident on the cycle track, Knut Jensen of Denmark collapsed from sunstroke in sweltering heat during the team time trial and died after fracturing his skull. He is the first

GOLDEN BOY Clay proudly accepts his medal.

competitor to die in an Olympic event since the 1912 marathon.

The light-heavyweight boxing gold medal went to a young, nimble-footed American named Cassius Clay.

··· US SUBMARINE *TRITON* MAKES THE FIRST ROUND-THE-WORLD UNDERSEA VOYAGE, LASTING 84 DAYS ···

Laser beam makes debut

The first device able to amplify visible light and produce a powerful beam has been developed by Theodore Maiman of Hughes Research Laboratories. Known as a 'laser', it is based on an idea that came to US physicist Charles Townes while waiting for a restaurant to open for breakfast.

The idea behind Townes's 'maser' – microwave amplification by the stimulated emission of radiation – led to Maiman's laser. Maiman uses a rod of ruby, bouncing the light to and fro and amplifying it by pumping in energy which stimulates the ruby molecules to release radiation. When the beam is powerful enough it bursts through the silvered end of the rod, an intense beam of visible light.

British workers walk on air

APRIL, WOLLASTON, NORTHAMPTONSHIRE
A brand new style of workboot has been launched in the UK by R Griggs and Company, a small family-run shoe manufacturer based in rural England. The chunky eight-eyelet utility boots are called

'Dr Martens' after their German inventor, Dr Klaus Maertens. Already highly successful across Europe, the 'comfort' shoes were first made in the 1940s.

Dr Maertens had injured his leg in a skiing accident and needed a suitable walking shoe. Together with an engineer friend, Dr Herbert Funct, Dr Maertens created the prototype for the boot; it features a soft, pliable sole, which is heat-sealed onto the leather upper for an 'air-cushioned' effect.

US TV HITS	
1	*Gunsmoke*
2	*Wagon Train*
3	*Have Gun, Will Travel*
4	*The Danny Thomas Show*
5	*The Red Skelton Show*

US HITS OF THE YEAR		
1	THEME FROM 'A SUMMER PLACE'	*Percy Faith*
2	ARE YOU LONESOME TONIGHT?	*Elvis Presley*
3	IT'S NOW OR NEVER	*Elvis Presley*
4	CATHY'S CLOWN	*Everly Brothers*
5	STUCK ON YOU	*Elvis Presley*

1961

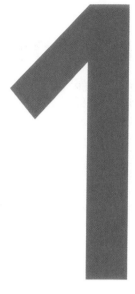

BORN

3 Mar: Eddie Murphy, US actor
14 June: George O' Dowd (aka Boy George), British pop singer
1 July: Diana Spencer, later Princess of Wales

DIED

6 June: Carl Jung, Swiss analytical psychologist
6 Mar: George Formby, British comedian
13 May: Gary Cooper, US actor

CURTAILED

USSR: Soviet authorities ban religious worship, then close all synagogues

SIGNED

The Supremes by Motown records

On 28 October, Russian and US tanks face each other in a standoff at the border of East and West Berlin on Friedrichstrasse. Tension has been high since the East German police partitioned the city with barbed wire on 13 August and began building a concrete wall to divide the communist east from the capitalist west.

PUBLISHED

Joseph Heller, *Catch-22*
V S Naipaul, *A House for Mr Biswas*
Muriel Spark, *The Prime of Miss Jean Brodie*

LAST

7 Oct: steam train on the London Underground, on the Central Line

IBM launches the 'golf ball' typewriter, so called because its innovative typing head is the size and shape of a golf ball. The new model, designed by Eliot Noyes, uses a carbon ribbon for sharp printing and comes with a selection of typefaces. Light and easy to use, the 'golf ball' looks set to revolutionise office work.

JAILED

3 May, London: former British diplomat George Blake, for 42 years; he pleads guilty to spying for KGB

FIRSTS

1 Feb: ICBM (Intercontinental Ballistic Missile), the *Minuteman*, is launched from the Nevada Desert
27 Dec: plane hijacked, diverted to Cuba by Marxist guerrillas
UK: government job for Margaret Thatcher, as joint parliamentary secretary at the Ministry of Pensions

UK: issue of the satirical magazine *Private Eye*
USA: musician to use computer for composing – US mathematician Milton Babbit applies theories of Austrian Arnold Schoenberg to create serial electronic composition

FOUNDED

Mar 1, USA: the Peace Corp
Oct 15, UK: Amnesty International, non-political organisation to help prisoners of conscience
UK: the World Wildlife Fund (later World Wide Fund for Nature), dedicated to saving wildlife
USA: Weight Watchers, by 97-kg (214-lb) Jean Nidetch, who decided to meet up regularly with overweight friends for mutual support

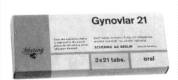

The oral contraceptive is launched, after being approved by the US Food and Drug Administration last year. The birth control pill, an oestrogen-progesterone hormone compound, blocks conception. It is taken by women for 21 days of the month.

ABOLISHED

UK: footballers' maximum weekly wage of £20; Fulham's Johnny Haynes becomes the top earner, with £100 a week

INTRODUCED

USA: Sprite soft drink by Coca-Cola, to challenge Pepsi's 7-Up
USA: in-flight movies, by TWA on the New York to Los Angeles route – first film shown is *By Love Possessed*

INAUGURAL SPEECH

USA: President Kennedy – 'Ask not what your country can do for you, ask what you can do for your country'

BOUGHT

New York City: Rembrandt's *Aristotle Contemplating the Bust of Homer*, by the Metropolitan Museum for $230000, highest price ever paid for a work of art at an auction

Last year's hit tune, 'Let's Twist Again', by 20-year-old Chubby Checker (right) is the theme tune for this year's dance craze, the Twist. The dance – performed by rhythmically bending the knees while pivoting the body on the balls of the feet – can be performed with or without a partner.

NEW WORDS

quirk *n*: a bizarre, unpredictable or odd trait or characteristic
serial killer *n*: a multiple murderer who kills a series of victims (usually in a similar fashion) over an extended period

Russia beats USA in the space race

HIGH ACHIEVER Yuri Gagarin in the cabin of *Vostok I*, the spacecraft in which he orbited the Earth.

5 MAY, CAPE CANAVERAL, FLORIDA
Lieutenant-Commander Alan Shepard of the US Navy became the first American – and only the second man – in space. The launch of Shepard's capsule was delayed by four hours while engineers wrestled with technical problems. Unfortunately the designers had provided no way for the astronaut to relieve himself, and at one point the hot, cramped and frustrated Shepard – who was lying on his back with his feet in the air and desperate to go to the lavatory – threatened to get out and fix the rocket himself.

Although the launch was delayed, the flight itself was perfect; *Freedom 7* took 15 minutes to complete a 190-kilometre (120-mile) high arc and parachute into the sea 500 kilometres (300 miles) away.

Yuri Gagarin, the 27-year-old Soviet cosmonaut who beat Shepard into space by several weeks, was not impressed. 'We sent some dogs up and down, just like Alan Shepard,' he said. Gagarin's flight, on 12 April, was in fact a much greater achievement. His spacecraft, *Vostok I*, made a complete circuit of the Earth. The flight lasted 108 minutes, reaching a height of 315 kilometres (195 miles).

Unlike Shepard, Gagarin had to eject from his capsule at a height of 6000 metres (20 000 ft), because the Soviets were not prepared to risk parachuting a 4.7-ton capsule onto solid land. The charred remains of *Vostok I* crashed to Earth on the Russian steppes, and Gagarin parachuted safely into a cow pasture. He was welcomed as a hero in the Soviet Union and was hailed by Khrushchev as a 'new Columbus'.

··· 20-YEAR-OLD BOB DYLAN PLAYS HIS FIRST GIG IN GERDE'S FOLK CITY, GREENWICH VILLAGE, NEW YORK ···

KENNEDY IS SHAMED BY BAY OF PIGS FIASCO

20 APRIL, HAVANA
Three days after their CIA-backed attempted coup, all the members of the ill-prepared armed force that invaded Cuba have been either killed or captured. About 1500 Cuban exiles hostile to the prime minister, Fidel Castro, had landed at Cochinos Bay (Bay of Pigs) on the southern coast, expecting to generate popular support on the island. However, government troops, who seem to have had advance warning of the invasion plan, had no difficulty in quashing the rebellion almost before it had begun.

This incident – backed by President Kennedy – has worsened the already sour relations between Cuba and the United States. Since Castro came to power in 1959 the USA has been aggrieved at losing much of its influence and many of its financial interests in Cuba. Castro has nationalised industries that were formerly American-controlled, and last year he strengthened contacts with the Soviet Union.

CASTRO'S ARMY Cuban troops pose beside one of the invaders' boats.

Jerusalem court sentences Eichmann to death

EXTERMINATOR Leading Nazi Eichmann gives evidence in court from a bullet-proof booth.

15 DECEMBER, JERUSALEM

Four days after being found guilty of crimes against humanity, the former Nazi leader Adolf Eichmann was today sentenced to death. His trial at Jerusalem District Court has been long and involved; it began in April, since when more than 100 witnesses have given evidence and well over 1000 documents have been examined.

Eichmann was the chief of operations in the Nazi plan to exterminate the whole of European Jewry. At the end of the war he managed to escape to Argentina, but Israeli agents tracked him down and brought him back last year to face trial.

His lawyers contended that he had been illegally abducted, and that the state of Israel did not exist at the time of his alleged crimes. After these objections had been dismissed, Eichmann did not deny that the crimes had taken place, but maintained that he was just a small cog in a vast machine. He is expected to appeal against his sentence.

··· THE MAXIMUM WAGE OF £20 A WEEK FOR ENGLISH FOOTBALL LEAGUE PLAYERS IS ABOLISHED ···

Ban-the-bomb demonstrators clash with police

3 APRIL, LONDON

This year's Aldermaston March, organised by the Campaign for Nuclear Disarmament, has been the largest yet. The annual march begins from the Atomic Weapons Research Establishment at Aldermaston in Berkshire and ends at Trafalgar Square in London, where the crowds are addressed by distinguished speakers. Today they included playwright John Osborne, actress Vanessa Redgrave and Bertrand Russell, the philosopher and ardent champion of pacifism. Russell addressed the 15 000-strong crowd, saying he regretted that he was too old at 88 to take part in the march itself.

The tradition of an Easter march, together with protests at Aldermaston, started in 1956. Comparatively few of the campaigners cover the whole route of 80 kilometres (50 miles); those who did so this year started out from Aldermaston three days ago.

As 3000 police struggled to arrest demonstrators staging 'sit-down' protests, violent clashes erupted and nearly 850 people were arrested.

Jaguar launches instant classic

MOTORING CHIC Jaguar's super-sleek E-Type sports coupé is the last word in exclusive style for drivers.

The year saw the launch of two classic cars – one at each end of the motoring spectrum. Taking the country roads at a speed of 220 kilometres per hour (140 mph), and making the heart race as its low-slung chassis flew along the road, the E-Type Jaguar leapt on to the motoring scene with immaculate styling and an almost unbeatable exclusivity. Already the favourite plaything of the super-rich, the E-Type Jag is becoming synonymous with leisure, high living and a lifestyle that has passed the ordinary person by.

For those with a more realistic budget (and lower speed expectations) Renault launched the Renault 4, a boxy little estate car which has quickly become a family favourite. With a capacity of 747 cc, the Renault 4's engine is less than a fifth the size of the E-Type's 3.8-litre powerhouse, but at least you have enough room for the kids and shopping in the back.

FAIRY TALES AND GRITTY REALISM

STYLISH *Breakfast* time for Hepburn and Peppard.

A star from Hollywood's golden age, James Cagney, bowed out with the fast and furious Cold War comedy *One, Two, Three*. Romance in New York made for two popular hits: romantic comedy *Breakfast at Tiffany's*, based on Truman Capote's novella, starred Audrey Hepburn as the enchanting 'party girl' Holly Golightly who captivates struggling novelist George Peppard; and *West Side Story*, an updated, musical version of *Romeo and Juliet* set among rival teenage gangs. Elizabeth Taylor plays a call girl in *Butterfield 8*, and Marlon Brando directs himself in *One-Eyed Jacks*. British cinema enjoyed a taste of gritty realism with Shelagh Delaney's tale of teenage pregnancy, *A Taste of Honey*, and *Victim*, starring Dirk Bogarde, one of the first films that deals openly with homosexuality.

Russian dancer leaps to freedom

16 JUNE, PARIS
Holidaymakers and business travellers at Le Bourget airport witnessed a dramatic spectacle today when a leading member of the Kirov Ballet defected to the West.

The 23-year-old Rudolf Nureyev, regarded by many as the most charismatic and talented male dancer of his generation, was among the 120-strong party that trooped into the waiting-room, ready to board a plane to London. Then, as two burly minders looked on, Nureyev made a bolt for the exit, running headlong into a crowd of travellers.

At first he held on to a pillar, screaming: 'I won't go back!' As the Russian ballet corps guards moved in on him, the dancer ran into the bar, where he threw himself into the arms of two bemused French policemen. It is thought that he will be granted political asylum.

··· 70 000 REFUGEES LEAVE COMMUNIST CHINA FOR HONG KONG ···

Cambridge student revue takes West End by storm

At first glance Alan Bennett, Peter Cook, Dudley Moore and Jonathan Miller might appear to be typical well-mannered Cambridge graduates. Those lucky enough to be in the audience for one of their Footlights revues at university or at last year's Edinburgh fringe festival will know otherwise. The mixture of sketches, political satire and songs scripted by the diminutive Moore has proved wildly successful. One critic dismissed the quartet by saying that 'they don't know the meaning of good taste'. The foursome concluded that that was probably the basis of their success.

Their student revue has now made a triumphant

CAUSTIC COMICS The four Cambridge students of the hit *Beyond the Fringe*.

debut in London's West End, and the four have become considerable comic stars. Miller, a doctor by training, has expressed a desire to turn his hand to theatre directing, but there seems little point in any of the four making alternative arrangements for their careers while the revue continues to play to packed houses in the West End.

US TV HITS	
1	*Gunsmoke*
2	*Wagon Train*
3	*Have Gun, Will Travel*
4	*The Andy Griffith Show*
5	*The Real McCoys*

US HITS OF THE YEAR		
1	TOSSIN' AND TURNIN'	*Bobby Lewis*
2	BIG BAD JOHN	*Jimmy Dean*
3	RUNAWAY	*Del Shannon*
4	WONDERLAND BY NIGHT	*Bert Kaempfert*
5	PONY TIME	*Chubby Checker*

1962

On 10 July, *Telstar 1, the first commercially developed satellite, is launched into orbit. Built by the American Telephone and Telegraph Company, the satellite receives messages from the ground – including complex data such as television pictures – and can re-transmit them immediately,*

BORN

17 Jan: Jim Carrey, US actor
3 July: Tom Cruise, US actor
19 Nov: Jodie Foster, US actress

DIED

6 July: William Faulkner, US novelist
28 Nov: Eleanor Roosevelt, US stateswoman

FIRSTS

29 Jan, USA: positive discrimination bill – firms with large government contracts must have 15 per cent black workforce
20 July, UK: hovercraft to carry passengers, across the Dee estuary, between Rhyl and Wallasey
1 Oct, USA: black student to attend lectures at Mississippi University; James Meredith has to be accompanied by US marshals and federal troops to protect him from race-hate mob

British record to top the US charts, *Telstar* by the Tornados
Tokyo: city to have a population of over ten million

BANNED

3 Feb, USA: all trade with Cuba, by President Kennedy – cigar smokers are badly hit

INVENTED

USA: cans that can be opened with tabs, by the Iron City Beer Company of Pittsburgh

KILLED

21 May: Adolf Eichmann, executed for war crimes
20 Aug: 18-year-old Peter Fechter, shot by East German border guards as he tries to escape to the West

PUBLISHED

Anthony Burgess, *A Clockwork Orange*
Ken Kesey, *One Flew Over the Cuckoo's Nest*
Alexander Solzhenitsyn, *One Day in the Life of Ivan Denisovich*

Two young American citizens play in a nuclear bomb shelter, built in the basement of their house. Families around the world are starting to consider the need for such protection as fears of an atomic war escalate, fuelled by the belligerent stance of both the American and the Soviet leadership.

FINAL

27 May: trip on the Orient Express train

ON STRIKE

8 Dec, New York state: New York's nine daily newspapers; strike continues for the next four months

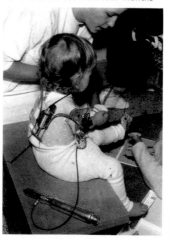

A victim of thalidomide is taught to use an artificial limb. More than 3000 babies have been born with malformed limbs and defects of the eyes and intestinal tract as a result of the prescription of the drug as a sedative to pregnant women in Britain and Germany.

CHARGED

25 June, Italy: Carlo Ponti and Sophia Loren, with bigamy

NEW WORDS

computer chip *n*: a tiny wafer of semiconductor material, such as silicon, which forms an electrical circuit in a computer
cryonics *n*: the practice of freezing a corpse in the hope of restoring it to life in the future

KHRUSHCHEV CLIMBS DOWN OVER CUBAN MISSILES

28 OCTOBER, VIENNA
After a week of excruciating tension, when nuclear war has at times seemed imminent, the conflict between the United States and the Soviet Union over Cuba was resolved peacefully today. The Russians have agreed to remove the missiles supplied to Cuba over the past few months, provided that the USA agrees not to invade the island.

Aerial reconnaissance had confirmed that these missiles were already being installed in Cuba – and every city in the USA would have been within their range. President Kennedy took a gamble in placing a naval blockade around Cuba a week ago, refusing to let Soviet ships through with their deadly cargo, but he has won the war of nerves with the Soviet leader Nikita Khrushchev.

Kennedy's firmness in a situation of enormous difficulty has enhanced his status at home and abroad, while Khrushchev's authority has been greatly undermined. However, some political observers deplore Kennedy's tactics. They think that the USA has no more right to determine whether Cuba possesses nuclear missiles than the Soviet Union has to determine the defence policies of its own neighbours. To them, Khrushchev is the true statesman for having the sense to back down rather than risk all-out war.

SEEN FROM ABOVE Soviet planes and missiles are visible on a Cuban airfield.

··· DECCA RECORDS TURNS DOWN THE BEATLES AND SIGNS BRIAN POOLE AND THE TREMELOES INSTEAD ···

Lucky escape for US astronaut

AMERICAN IN SPACE Pictures of Glenn were taken by an automatic camera inside the capsule.

20 FEBRUARY, CAPE CANAVERAL, FLORIDA
Colonel John Glenn of the US Marines survived a fiery drop into the Atlantic Ocean after becoming the first American to orbit the Earth. More than 100 million Americans watched on television as flaming chunks flew from Glenn's capsule, the *Friendship 7*, during its descent.

Problems started with the flight towards the end of the first orbit, when the capsule began veering and tumbling, and Glenn had to take it off autopilot and fly it manually for the remaining two circuits. Things grew worse still when it became evident that the capsule's heat shield was loose. If it came away, Glenn would burn up on re-entry, so the decision was taken not to jettison the braking rockets on the front of the capsule – the normal practice – in the hope that they would help to hold the heat shield on. It was a gamble, but it worked; Glenn's only injury was a cut on the knuckles, received when he opened the capsule's hatch.

Marilyn Monroe is found dead at 36

8 AUGUST, HOLLYWOOD
Film star Marilyn Monroe was found dead in her bed early this morning. The glamorous sex symbol died from an overdose of sleeping tablets, and was discovered lying face down and naked, clutching a telephone receiver. It seems likely that the verdict on the death will be suicide, although a certain degree of mystery surrounds the case.

Monroe is rumoured to have had close relations with the Kennedys, both the President and his brother Robert – perhaps this made her a threat to national security. It is also said that she had links with the Mafia – these could have been dangerous connections. The world awaits a full inquiry into the mysterious, untimely death of the ultimate screen idol.

Independence for Algeria

1 JULY, ALGIERS
Algerians have voted in huge numbers to free themselves from French rule and add their country to the list of African nations that in the past few years have thrown off the imperial yoke.

In a plebiscite negotiated in March by the Nationalist leader, Ahmed Ben Bella, with the French president, Georges Pompidou, 91 per cent of the voters have opted for independence.

The result brings to an end one of the bloodiest liberation wars in history, fought between the FLN (Front de Libération Nationale) and the OAS

(Organisation de l'Armée Sécrète), a union of 'pieds-noirs' – Algerians of French descent – and dissident soldiers of the French army. Just three weeks ago the OAS set fire to the Saharan oil wells, the basis of the national economy.

The fighting raged for eight years and cost a million lives – nearly one in ten of the Algerian population. A further two million people have been displaced from their homes.

Although the links between France and Algeria will be reduced, it is anticipated that trade will continue to flourish.

MIXED BLESSING? Algerians contemplate a future independent of France.

--- 28 JAN, USA: THE TWIST DANCE IS BANNED BY SOME CATHOLIC CHURCHES AS IMMORAL ---

New York hails Pop artist Warhol

EVERYDAY BEAUTY Andy Warhol's brightly coloured screen print of a Campbell's soup tin.

A new star burst on to the New York art scene this year. Following his hugely successful one-man show at the Stable Gallery, 34-year-old Andy Warhol has been hailed as the most brilliant talent in Pop art, the movement that is currently the hottest thing in the art world. Pop artists revel in the kind of images we see around us all the time, in TV and magazine advertisements and on packaging, but they make them bigger, bolder and brighter.

Warhol's favourite image of this kind is a tin of Campbell's tomato soup, which he has painted again and again. He says that he has a tin of this soup for his lunch every day.

Warhol comes from Pittsburgh, Pennsylvania, and moved to New York in 1949. Before taking up painting he worked as a commercial artist and won awards for his shoe advertisements. Pop art, Warhol claims, reflects the banality of modern American culture.

Catholic Church enters modern world

11 OCTOBER, VATICAN CITY
The largest gathering at any Council in the Catholic Church's history took place in Rome today, at the opening Mass of the Second Vatican Council. Plans for the Council were first announced three years ago by Pope John XXIII, shortly after his election.

Pope John has far-reaching ambitions for the Church, aiming to bring it up to date, particularly in the fields of science, economics, politics and morality. One of the Council's first recommendations will be that people should be allowed to celebrate Mass in their native languages.

Pope John is an energetic man despite his 81 years and failing health. His warmth, simplicity and charm, combined with his profound spiritual vision, have won him respect from Catholics and non-Catholics alike.

Beatles shoot to success

Since they were turned down by Decca Records in February, the Beatles have made a triumphant recording debut. The Liverpool quartet replaced drummer Pete Best with Ringo Starr to help secure a first record deal with Parlophone. Their first single, 'Love Me Do', broke into the UK Top 20 on 15 December. A second single, 'Please Please Me', shot to number two in the charts, and then a first national television appearance helped propel the band to still greater heights. Their appearance on *Thank Your Lucky Stars* attracted six million viewers and helped 'From Me to You' give the 'mop tops' their first number one record.

John, Paul, George and Ringo have created a whole new trend of haircuts, neat suits and an explosion of music from Merseyside.

FAB FOUR The neatly dressed Beatles wow Birkenhead's Majestic Theatre.

SEAN CONNERY LANDS ROLE OF JAMES BOND

LICENCE TO KILL Scottish actor Sean Connery brings wit as well as brawn to the role of 007.

A readers' poll in Britain's *Daily Express* newspaper chose the ex-body builder and model Sean Connery to bring Ian Fleming's super-spy James Bond to life in the international blockbuster film of Ian Fleming's *Dr No*.

Another dashing British hero was created by Peter O'Toole in David Lean's *Lawrence of Arabia*, an epic biography of the man who united the Arabs against the Turks in World War I. The film won seven Oscars, including best picture and best director for Lean.

The influence of the French New Wave reached Britain with Tony Richardson's atmospheric *The Loneliness of the Long Distance Runner*, starring Tom Courtenay as a Borstal boy who deliberately loses a race as an act of revenge against the school authorities. Among the more suggestive films of the year were *Lolita* – Stanley Kubrick's sly comedy about under-age sex, starring James Mason and Peter Sellers – and *Knife in the Water*, the debut by young Polish director Roman Polanski.

Brazil wins the World Cup

17 JUNE, SANTIAGO
Three misjudgments by the Czech goalkeeper, Schroiff, today helped Brazil to its second consecutive victory in the World Cup.

In the preliminary rounds the Czechs had held Brazil to a scoreless draw. Today, before 68 000 fans at the Estadio Nacional in Santiago, they were simply outclassed, and succumbed 3-1 after scoring the opening goal in the sixteenth minute. Brazil's goals were scored by Amarildo, Zito and Vavá.

Brazil played most of the tournament without its brilliant young forward, Pelé, at only 17 one of the stars of the 1958 tournament, who tore a leg muscle in the second match. Even without him Brazil glided past all opposition, beating England 3–1 in the quarter-finals and Chile 4–2 in the semi-finals.

US TV HITS	
1	*Wagon Train*
2	*Bonanza*
3	*Gunsmoke*
4	*Hazel*
5	*Perry Mason*

US HITS OF THE YEAR		
1	I CAN'T STOP LOVING YOU	*Ray Charles*
2	BIG GIRLS DON'T CRY	*Four Seasons*
3	SHERRY	*Four Seasons*
4	ROSES ARE RED (MY LOVE)	*Bobby Vinton*
5	PEPPERMINT TWIST (PT 1)	*Joey Dee & The Starliters*

··· USA: SILICONE BREAST IMPLANTS ARE INVENTED BY THE DOW CORPORATION OF MICHIGAN ···

1963

BORN
27 Mar: Quentin Tarantino, US film director
25 June: George Michael, British pop musician
9 Aug: Whitney Houston, US singer

DIED
31 Aug: Georges Braque, French artist
11 Oct: Edith Piaf, French singer

CLOSED
21 Mar, USA: Alcatraz prison; the last 27 prisoners are transferred

On **16 June,** *Soviet cosmonaut Valentina Tereshkova becomes the first woman in space when she pilots the Vostok 6 spacecraft. The flight lasts three days, and the spacecraft orbits the Earth 48 times.*

DISMISSED
USA: Timothy Leary from his lectureship in psychology at Harvard University, after carrying out experiments with psychedelic drugs

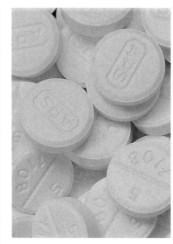

Valium (diazepam), a tranquillising drug, is launched in the USA by Roche Laboratories. Available on prescription, it helps to relieve tension and anxiety, and also has muscle-relaxant properties. However, some observers express fears that the drug may cause dependency.

INTRODUCED
18 Nov, USA: the push-button telephone – it quickly becomes the norm

INVENTED
New Zealand: prenatal blood transfusion
UK: 'hover' lawnmower, by Flymo
USA: holograms, using laser beams, by scientists at the University of Michigan

BANNED
1 Mar, USA: Bob Dylan, from singing his anti-segregationist 'Talking John Birch Society Blues' on the *Ed Sullivan Show*
17 June, USA: reading the Bible and saying prayers in schools

ARRESTED
Iran: Muslim leader Ayatollah Khomeini, for protesting against the Shah's plans to give votes to women

SET UP
30 Aug: a 'hotline' between the Kremlin in Moscow and the White House in Washington DC, to improve communication

WITHDRAWN
1 Jan, UK: the BBC ban on mentioning sex, religion, politics and royalty on comedy shows

FIRSTS
UK: kidney transplant, at Leeds General Hospital
USA: television instant replay; it is shown during an annual football game between the Army and the Navy – confused fans bombard the station with calls
USA: professional football Hall of Fame
USA: anti-smoking campaign; it is launched by the American Heart Association

PUBLISHED
Rachel Carson, *The Silent Spring*
Sylvia Plath, *The Bell Jar*
John Le Carré, *The Spy who came in from the Cold*
Mary McCarthy, *The Group*

FOUNDED
May, Ethiopia: the Organisation for African Unity (OAU), in Addis Ababa; its aim is to maintain solidarity between African leaders and to free the continent of oppression
USA: *New York Review of Books*
USA: Institute for Policy Studies

The latest nightclubs – or discotheques – now offer young people much more than a silvered ball above the dancefloor. Teenagers looking for a night out expect to find flashing lights, big dancefloors and amplified pop music.

KILLED
Caribbean: 6000 people, by Hurricane Flora

NEW WORDS
kinky *adj:* given to deviant, unusual or abnormal sexual practices
nitty-gritty *n:* the basic facts of a matter, the core issue
one-night stand *n:* a sexual encounter lasting only one evening or night

CIVIL RIGHTS LEADER PREACHES RACIAL HARMONY

29 AUGUST, WASHINGTON DC
Almost half a million people yesterday hung spellbound on the words of one man as Dr Martin Luther King made a speech that will surely be ranked among the world's classics of oratory.

In ringing phrases that echoed the rhythms and cadences of the Bible he loves, Dr King spoke of a time when there would be an end to racial injustice and all peoples would be able to live together in harmony. 'I have a dream,' he declared, 'that the sons of former slaves and the sons of former slave owners would sit together at the table of brotherhood.'

Dr King, a Baptist minister and champion of civil rights, has long been renowned as one of the most eloquent public speakers in the country, but even he has never before stirred the hearts and minds of such a huge gathering. His vast audience was gathered near the memorial to President Lincoln. Among the crowds there were many famous faces to be seen, including those of the singers Joan Baez and Bob Dylan.

The gathering was the culmination of a peaceful march on Washington

INSPIRATIONAL Dr Martin Luther King greets 500 000 marchers at the Lincoln Memorial, Washington DC.

organised by Dr King. He has been a focus for civil rights activities since 1955 when, at the age of 26, he became the leader of a group of people who refused to accept the racial segregation of public buses in Montgomery, Alabama. After they achieved their aim of desegregation

the following year, Dr King built up a national reputation as a lecturer on racial matters.

He has consistently advocated non-violent means of protest, such as sit-ins and protest marches, and he has been imprisoned several times for his beliefs.

··· FIRST NUDE SCREEN TESTS HELD FOR A FILM, *FOUR FOR TEXAS*; URSULA ANDRESS IS PICKED FOR A MAIN ROLE ···

Profumo Affair claims yet another victim as Stephen Ward dies

SERIOUS AFFAIR Christine Keeler leaves the Old Bailey after the trial.

3 AUGUST, LONDON
Dr Stephen Ward, the society osteopath involved in the Profumo scandal, died today in St Stephen's Hospital, Fulham. He had been in a coma since taking an overdose of barbiturates three days ago.

As Dr Ward's life slipped away, the jury at his Old Bailey trial delivered its verdict, finding him guilty of living off the immoral earnings of Christine Keeler and Mandy Rice-Davies.

Miss Keeler, who insisted she was not a prostitute, had had an affair with the former secretary for war, John Profumo, who resigned in June after initially denying the affair. It had made him a security risk, as Miss Keeler was also involved with Eugene Ivanov, an official at the Soviet Embassy.

The Profumo Affair has seriously tarnished the image of both the Conservative government and Prime Minister Harold Macmillan.

PRESIDENT KENNEDY KILLED

22 NOVEMBER, DALLAS
The world has been stunned by the murder of John F Kennedy, the charismatic young President of the United States. He was shot in the head by a hidden assassin as he drove through the centre of the city in an open limousine, watched by cheering, flag-waving crowds.

Dallas was the latest stop on a national tour as part of his campaign for re-election in 1964. Jacqueline Kennedy, who was seated beside her husband in the car, was spattered with his blood. She cradled him in her arms as the motorcade rushed to Parkland Memorial Hospital, about 5 kilometres (3 miles) away. Surgeons worked frantically to save the

President, but he never regained consciousness and was pronounced dead at approximately 1.00 pm local time, half an hour after the bullets struck. A Catholic priest read the last rites shortly before he died.

A 24-year-old man, identified as Lee Harvey Oswald, was arrested in connection with the killing of a Dallas police officer, Patrolman J D Tippit, soon after President Kennedy's murder. Questioned about the assassination of the President, the suspect has denied any involvement in either this or the killing of Patrolman Tippit.

Oswald, a former US Marine, settled in the Soviet Union in 1959 and is

BEFORE THE BULLET President and Mrs Kennedy prepare for the motorcade.

believed to have applied for Soviet citizenship. Last year he returned to America with his Russian wife and their baby girl. A week ago he began working at the Texas School Book Depository,

which overlooks Dealey Plaza where the President was shot. Police officers have found a rifle and three spent cartridges near a window on the sixth floor of the Book Depository building.

··· USA: SINGER STEVIE WONDER RELEASES HIS FIRST ALBUM, *LITTLE STEVIE WONDER, THE 12-YEAR-OLD GENIUS* ···

Lyndon Johnson sworn in on presidential jet

UNEXPECTED PROMOTION The shock of Kennedy's death still weighs heavily as Lyndon B Johnson takes the presidential oath. Beside him is Mrs Kennedy.

22 NOVEMBER, WASHINGTON DC
At 2.38 pm today Lyndon B Johnson was sworn in as the thirty-sixth President of the United States in succession to the assassinated John F Kennedy. Johnson, a former Texan schoolteacher, was a US senator from 1949 to 1960 and served as vice-president under Kennedy since 1961.

The ceremony was performed on board the presidential plane, *Air Force One*, shortly before it left Dallas for Washington, two hours after the assassination. As he took the solemn oath,

Johnson was flanked by his wife, Lady Byrd Johnson, and Jacqueline Kennedy, whose husband's body was carried back to Washington on the plane. Mrs Kennedy appeared to be in a state of deep shock, and her pink suit still bore the splashes of her husband's blood.

When the plane landed at Andrews Air Force Base, President Johnson, clearly shaken, said: 'I will do my best, that is all I can do. I ask for your help, and God's.'

President Johnson will serve the remainder of Kennedy's term of office, until January 1965.

Oswald shot in front of world's press

LAWLESS RETRIBUTION Ruby shoots Oswald at Dallas police headquarters.

24 NOVEMBER, DALLAS

In what must be the most public murder ever committed, Lee Harvey Oswald was shot dead today in front of the world's press. Oswald, accused of assassinating President Kennedy two days ago, was being moved from Dallas police headquarters to a more secure jail when the gunman struck.

At 11.20 am Oswald, handcuffed and flanked by detectives, was brought to a waiting car in a basement garage, where about 70 police officers and reporters were packed into the small area. As Oswald passed, a figure suddenly stepped out from the crowd and, before anyone could react and stop him, fired a single shot point blank into Oswald's stomach. Oswald was taken to Dallas's Parkland Memorial Hospital, where he died almost exactly 48 hours after Kennedy had died in the same hospital.

Oswald's killer, who was quickly overpowered at the scene of the murder, has been identified as Jack Ruby, a 52-year-old nightclub owner with a criminal record. He claims that he killed Oswald out of admiration for Kennedy and compassion for his widow and children.

Many local people have hailed him as a hero, a dispenser of frontier justice, but Dallas police have been severely criticised for allowing a known criminal to gain access to their headquarters at such a sensitive time.

··· 17 MAR, SWITZERLAND: A TYPHOID EPIDEMIC BREAKS OUT IN ZERMATT ···

Conspiracy theorists claim Oswald could not have acted alone

More has been written about President Kennedy's murder than about any other single crime in history. A week after the event, President Johnson announced the setting up of a commission to discover, as far as possible, the truth about the killing. The commission was chaired by Earl Warren, head of the Supreme Court; members included Gerald Ford, who later became President himself.

In September 1964 the Warren Commission published its findings in great detail, concluding that Lee Harvey Oswald had acted entirely alone in killing Kennedy, and that Jack Ruby had acted alone in killing Oswald; neither of them 'was part of any conspiracy, domestic or foreign, to assassinate President Kennedy'. Many people, however, refused to believe that Oswald

was a lone fanatic and have proposed that Kennedy was the victim of a well-orchestrated contract killing. The so-called 'conspiracy theorists' have four main suggestions.

The first is that the Mafia ordered Kennedy's assassination because of his crackdown on organised crime. Another is that the CIA was behind it because he was too 'soft' on communism or because he had refused to defend South Vietnam openly against communism. A third suggestion is that the KGB wanted revenge on Kennedy for the humiliation of the Cuban Missile Crisis. Lastly, some argue that a Cuban force (pro- or anti-Castro) wanted Kennedy dead either because of the Bay of Pigs fiasco or because he failed to authorise a second Bay of Pigs invasion.

FAMILY IN MOURNING Jacqueline Kennedy with her children, Caroline and John, at the funeral.

Railway robbers snatch millions

8 AUGUST, ENGLAND
An armed gang hijacked a train this morning and escaped with more than £2.5 million in a daring raid that has been dubbed the 'Great Train Robbery'. The Scotland to London Post Office Express was ambushed near Cheddington, Buckinghamshire, by at least 15 masked men.

The gang stopped the train at 3.10 am by using a glove to cover the green 'go' sign at the side of the track, and four torch batteries to turn on the red 'stop' signal. When the train's co-engineer tried to telephone from a set

at the side of the track he was ambushed. It took the robbers only 20 minutes to break into the carriages, overpower the staff inside and unload 120 mail bags into a waiting lorry. They had half an hour's head start before train driver Jack Mills – who was viciously beaten about the head – and his fireman David Whitby were able to raise the alarm.

Police believe that the robbers had inside information. They knew that the Post Office Express was carrying a fortune in old banknotes, on their way to be incinerated, and that the security carriages that would normally

CRIME SCENE A van was ready for the booty.

accompany the train were undergoing repairs. A full-scale inquiry into the security of the train has been ordered.

··· AN EQUAL PAY LAW FOR MEN AND WOMEN IS PASSED IN THE UNITED STATES ···

Exploding the myths of femininity

Betty Friedan's *The Feminine Mystique* appeared this year and became a founding text of second-wave feminism. Friedan's study explored the gap between traditional social roles for women in the United States and the new freedoms brought about by women's liberation.

Friedan completed a BA in Psychology, undertook graduate work and started a career before giving it all up to become a wife and mother. Her subsequent frustrations led her to undertake this project to find out how women in general were coping with recent changes to their social status. The book has helped to explode myths about femininity, and highlights the role of social conditioning in shaping women's lives.

Tension rises in South Vietnam

10 JUNE, SAIGON
A Buddhist monk burnt himself to death today in one of the most horrifying protests so far against the government of South Vietnam. The US-backed regime headed by President Ngo Dinh Diem is predominantly Catholic, whereas most of the Vietnamese population is Buddhist. Buddhists claim that they suffer unfair treatment under the present government.

Last month, troops opened fire on a peaceful demonstration protesting against the repression of Buddhism in Vietnam. When the smoke cleared, nine people were dead.

The sectarian divide in Vietnam is just one more ingredient in an already explosive cocktail. Diem is deeply unpopular. His regime is openly corrupt, and the president himself is widely

FLAMES OF PROTEST The Buddhist martyr makes the ultimate sacrifice.

seen as a ruthless tyrant with no regard for the well-being of most of the population. His government is believed to be marking time in power, content to enjoy the support of the United States.

The US government has not officially condemned the nominally democratic

regime's treatment of Buddhists, but the White House has threatened to do so unless positive steps are taken to redress the situation. The United States pumps money into South Vietnam as a counterbalance to the threat from the Communist regime in the North.

Bob Dylan and the many faces of rock

POPULAR PROTEST Bob Dylan's second album, *The Freewheelin' Bob Dylan*, struck a chord, selling 250 000 copies.

In a year dominated by the Beatles, their manager Brian Epstein added Billy J Kramer and the Dakotas to his stable of artists, which already included Gerry and the Pacemakers, and Cilla Black. In the USA, Bob Dylan walked out of his television debut on the *Ed Sullivan Show* when he was told he could not perform his controversial 'Talking John Birch Society Blues'. Dylan's album *The Freewheelin' Bob Dylan* was a triumph, and 'Blowin' In The Wind' and 'Don't Think Twice, It's All Right' became chart hits as well as protest anthems.

Meanwhile in leafy Richmond, south-west London, two young pop promoters, Andrew Oldham and Eric Easton, signed up an unknown band called the Rolling Stones. 'I knew what I was looking at,' Oldham is reported to have stated. 'It was sex.'

CLEOPATRA DIES AT THE MOVIES

The year's big release was *Cleopatra*, directed by Joseph Mankiewicz, which at $30 million is the most expensive film ever made. Starring Richard Burton and Elizabeth Taylor, the movie was a critical flop and Taylor herself called it 'the most bizarre piece of entertainment ever to be perpetrated'. Successful releases included Hitchcock's thriller *The Birds*, while *Tom Jones*, starring Albert Finney and Susannah York, picked up Oscars for best film and best director. *From Russia With Love* was Sean Connery's second outing as British secret agent James Bond. In the USA, Paul Newman starred in *Hud* with Patricia Neal and Melvyn Douglas, and Fellini's *8½* won the Oscar for best foreign film. Other notable movies were *The Leopard*, Visconti's tale of family life in Garibaldi's Italy, and *This Sporting Life*.

US HITS OF THE YEAR		US TV HITS	
1 SUGAR SHACK	*Jimmy Gilmer & The Fireballs*	1 *The Beverly Hillbillies*	
2 DOMINIQUE	*Singing Nun (Soeur Sourire)*	2 *Candid Camera*	
3 HE'S SO FINE	*Chiffons*	3 *The Red Skelton Show*	
4 HEY PAULA	*Paul & Paula*	4 *Bonanza*	
5 MY BOYFRIEND'S BACK	*Angels*	5 *The Lucy Show*	

FEATHERED FOES *The Birds* turn against humans.

1964

BORN

7 Jan: Nicolas Cage, US actor
27 Jan: Bridget Fonda, US actress

DIED

28 May: Jawaharlal Nehru, prime minister of India since independence
12 Aug: Ian Fleming, creator of James Bond
28 Sept: silent Marx Brother, Harpo
15 Oct: Cole Porter, jazz musician

CANCELLED

4 May: this year's Pulitzer Prizes, when the committee announces that no fiction, drama or music has been good enough

On 16 October, Britain elects a Labour Government for the first time for 13 years. Harold Wilson's party scrapes to victory with an majority of four. Its first challenge will be to deal with the economy; steel production, water and building land are scheduled to come under public control.

KILLED

Peru: 300 at worst-ever football disaster, when a stampede is caused after fans, unhappy at a disallowed goal, invade the pitch and are fired on by police with tear gas and revolvers

UK: John White, Tottenham Hotspur international forward, by a bolt of lightning while sheltering under a tree on Enfield golf course
USA: 110 people, in serious earthquake (8.4 on the Richter scale) in Alaska

MARRIED

19 Feb, UK: Peter Sellers and Britt Ekland, in London
15 Mar, Canada: Richard Burton and Elizabeth Taylor, in Montreal

RECORD

Finnish dockworker Toimi Solvo stays awake for 16 days and 10 hours, by snow massages and constant coffee-drinking

INTRODUCED

Switzerland: long-life milk, by Verbands Mölkerei
USA: Carlton low-tar cigarettes, by American Tobacco Company

CLASHED

15 May, UK: Mods and Rockers, at seaside resorts, causing panic and outrage; a judge describes the rioters as 'little sawdust Caesars'

FIRSTS

1 Jan, UK: *Top of the Pops* broadcast by the BBC
13 Apr, Hollywood: black actor to win an Oscar – Sydney Poitier for *Lilies of the Field*
23 June, South Africa: snow in Johannesburg since records began
31 July, USA: close-up pictures of the Moon's surface sent back by US satellite *Ranger 7*
15 Sept, UK: edition of the *Sun* newspaper

A soldier doll for boys, called GI Joe in the United States and Action Man in Europe, is launched by Hasbro. Both versions are an instant hit and are soon relaunched with new combat accessories and outfits.

ESCAPED

5 Oct, East Berlin: 57 people to the West, through a 98-m (320-ft) tunnel under the Berlin Wall

ANNOUNCED

27 Sept, USA: the findings of the Warren Commission into JFK's assassination – it says Lee Harvey Oswald acted alone
21 Dec, UK: the abolition of the death penalty in Britain, except for treason and setting fire to a naval dockyard
UK: Roman Catholics are forbidden to use the new contraceptive pill

BEATLEMANIA

11 Apr, USA: the Beatles occupy the whole of the *Billboard* Top Five

SHOCKED

30 Apr, USA: animal lovers, as President Johnson lifts up his beagles 'Him' and 'Her' by the ears at a press conference on the White House lawn

ON STRIKE

3 Apr, Belgium: 12 000 doctors against nationalisation; lasts 16 days, and kills dozens

OPENED

4 Sept, Scotland: suspension bridge over the river Forth
USA: the Verrazano Narrows Bridge at the entry to New York Harbour

NEW WORDS

biodegradable *adj*: capable of being decomposed by bacteria
hands-on *adj*: having practical experience of equipment

Clint Eastwood shoots to international stardom in A Fistful of Dollars *as the mysterious stranger who cleans up a Mexican border town. The film, directed by Sergio Leone, launches a craze for 'spaghetti westerns' and reinvents the cowboy genre as mean, moody and supercool.*

Independent Kenya elects its first president

INDEPENDENCE DAY Jomo Kenyatta (second from right) celebrates with other African leaders.

12 DECEMBER, NAIROBI
Today Kenya has become an independent nation within the Commonwealth, and Jomo Kenyatta, chief of the dominant Kikuyu tribe, has been installed as the first president.

As long ago as 1928 Kenyatta, whose first name means 'Burning Spear', helped to found the Central Organisation of the Indigenous People of Kenya, a body dedicated to driving the white European settlers from ancient tribal lands.

When the Mau Mau rebellion against British rule began in 1952 the imperial authorities fought vigorously to repress the movement; Mau Mau terrorism was crushed by 1956. Three years later, indignation at the deaths of 11 Mau Mau prisoners at the Hola prison camp impelled the British government to speed up its withdrawal from Kenya. Kenyatta himself, imprisoned since 1952, was released in 1959; the state of emergency imposed during the Mau Mau years was lifted the following year, and Kenya was granted self-governing status in 1963.

Mainly under colonial rule ten years ago, Africa is now almost entirely independent, except for the British and Portuguese colonies to the north of South Africa. South Africa, though independent, is still ruled by the white minority.

··· THE HEAD OF THE LITTLE MERMAID STATUE IN COPENHAGEN IS SAWN OFF AND STOLEN ···

BLACK NATIONALIST LEADER JAILED FOR LIFE

11 JUNE, PRETORIA
Nelson Mandela and eight other leaders of the black struggle against apartheid in South Africa have been convicted of conspiring to overthrow the government and sentenced to life imprisonment. They are to be transferred to the notorious maximum security prison on Robben Island, off Cape Town.

Before becoming an executive officer of the African National Congress in 1944, Transkei-born Mandela was a successful Johannesburg lawyer. He was known as 'the Black Pimpernel' for his ability to evade arrest during the 1950s, but he has been in police custody since August 1962. His colleagues were arrested last July after a raid on a farm near Pretoria, headquarters of the 'Spear of the Nation' military arm of the ANC.

The trial lasted for eight months. At the end Mandela addressed the court, giving a very lengthy and calmly delivered defence of the ANC. He finished by saying that the nationalist campaign was 'a struggle for the right to live'. It was, the 48-year-old liberation leader said, 'an ideal for which I am prepared to die'.

South Africa's blacks are excluded from political participation and denied basic civic rights; Mandela's imprisonment deprives them of their most powerful voice. The almost total segregation of whites and blacks is firmly established in the republic, and overt opposition to the ruling Nationalist Party – except from the few white opponents of the regime – has now been effectively stilled.

PEOPLE'S VOICE The ANC's leader, spokesman for South Africa's black population, is now in prison.

Coltrane comes out of the shadows and into the spotlight

Tenor saxophonist John Coltrane, a disciple of Miles Davis, has become one of the leading jazz players of the 1960s. In the 1950s, as part of the Miles Davis quintet, he appeared on the album *Kind Of Blue* and developed a high-velocity, frantic solo style which contrasted with Davis's easy-going West Coast 'modal' jazz.

In 1960 Coltrane switched style, falling in line with Davis's freer approach and experimenting with harmonies and structure. His 1960 composition 'My Favorite Things' gave soloists an unprecedented freedom to improvise for as long as they wanted, and this year's album *A Love Supreme*, marked by Coltrane's ever-increasing

AVANT GARDE Saxophonist John Coltrane leads his quartet in a recent concert in Amsterdam.

harmonic complexity, has earned him his place as a leader of the avant garde.

Some people find his style too extreme when compared with the more mainstream approach of artists such as

Stan Getz and Herbie Mann, but the influential *Down Beat* magazine considers him one of the best around – and *A Love Supreme* one of the best albums of the year.

··· INDIAN CINEMA-GOERS SEE WOMEN IN BATHING COSTUMES FOR THE FIRST TIME, BUT KISSING IS STILL TABOO ···

Soviet technology tames the mighty Nile

HIGH-POWERED Construction of the Aswan High Dam is scheduled to take four years.

14 MAY, ASWAN, EGYPT
The waters of the mighty Nile were diverted today, using all the powers of 20th-century technology. The next stage

of the billion-dollar Aswan Dam project is under way – a symbol of the Soviet-Egyptian 'honeymoon'.

The creation of the High Dam, conceived by the Egyptian president Gamal Abdel Nasser, involves flooding some of the greatest monuments in the world and putting most of Nubia under water. The dam will create a lake nearly 480 kilometres (300 miles) long and provide power for the whole country.

Egyptologists are already up in arms about the ancient remains along the Nile south of Aswan that will be drowned. An international team will move sites such as the temple of Abu Simbel and reassemble them along the lake. Some 800 ancient Coptic churches will be submerged.

A massive project to move the Nubian population to Middle Egypt is already under way. Villages are being planned for them, and land will be reclaimed from the desert.

Cassius Clay becomes world champion

25 FEBRUARY, MIAMI
Cassius Clay, the outspoken 21-year-old American boxer who four years ago won the light-middleweight gold medal at the Olympic Games, has become the world heavyweight champion.

Delighting the crowd with his speed of footwork and lithe athleticism, he knocked out Sonny Liston, the odds-on favourite to win and so retain his title. Suffering from eye cuts and an injured left shoulder, Liston was unable to come out for the seventh round.

Clay, a handsome heart-throb who drives a pink Cadillac, fulfilled the promise that he made at the weigh-in to 'float like a butterfly and sting like a bee'. He has now fought 20 professional contests without defeat and looks set to become one of the greatest boxers in the history of the sport.

MARY POPPINS BAGS THE PRIZES

The big hit of the year was the Disney musical *Mary Poppins*, which brought Julie Andrews to the screen and bagged her an Oscar for best actress. The movie shot up the box office charts and made songs such as 'Chim Chim Cheree' part of the national psyche on both sides of the Atlantic. Eight Oscars, including those for best film, best actor and best director, went to the Warner Brothers' musical *My Fair Lady*. The movie starred Rex Harrison with Audrey Hepburn as Eliza Doolittle – a role which had been created on stage by Julie Andrews. Hepburn's singing voice never matched up to Andrews' standard, and her songs on *My Fair Lady* were dubbed by Marni Nixon.

Other hits included *Zorba The Greek*, starring Anthony Quinn and Alan Bates, and the British-made comedy *Dr Strangelove; or, How I Learned to Stop Worrying and Love the Bomb*, Stanley Kubrick's black comedy starring Peter Sellers. Meanwhile, the third Bond movie *Goldfinger* made Sean Connery the top box–office star of the year. Other releases included *Night of the Iguana*, *The Umbrellas of Cherbourg* and the Beatles' first movie, *A Hard Day's Night*.

MAGIC JOURNEY Dick van Dyke and Julie Andrews take a ride in *Mary Poppins*.

The style leaders unite

FASHION QUEEN Mary Quant has her hair remodelled by the king of the bob, Vidal Sassoon.

Mary Quant, the miniskirt's great pioneer and advocate, now sports an uncompromising new haircut, courtesy of celebrity hairdresser Vidal Sassoon, which perfectly complements her clothes.

For the under-25s the Quant look is *de rigueur* – sharp little A-line dresses well above the knee and low shoes. Mary Quant's designs have liberated women of the 1960s from the constrictions of their mothers' styles. The look has no waist, no heels, no gloves, no hat and no stockings – a shame for the girl with an hourglass figure and fat legs.

New typewriter makes mistakes disappear

29 JUNE, NEW YORK CITY
The world's leading computer company has spared a thought for the typist, sentenced to a routine of relentless accuracy – any mistake, and a letter has to be entirely retyped. But not with IBM's new typewriter, in which the keystrokes are recorded on a magnetic tape as each line is typed, and displayed electronically within a window on the the machine before it is printed.

The typist can go back and make corrections to the line as many time as he or she wishes, then print it once it is error-free. Now the typist can produce flawless letters every time.

US HITS OF THE YEAR		
1	I WANT TO HOLD YOUR HAND	*Beatles*
2	CAN'T BUY ME LOVE	*Beatles*
3	THERE I'VE SAID IT AGAIN	*Bobby Vinton*
4	BABY LOVE	*Supremes*
5	OH PRETTY WOMAN	*Roy Orbison*

US TV HITS	
1	*The Beverly Hillbillies*
2	*Bonanza*
3	*The Dick Van Dyke Show*
4	*Petticoat Junction*
5	*The Andy Griffith Show*

1965

BORN

31 May: Brooke Shields, US actress

DIED

4 Jan: T S Eliot, US-born British writer and poet
24 Jan: Winston Churchill, British statesman
15 Feb: Nat 'King' Cole, US jazz musician
23 Feb: Stan Laurel, British-born film actor

MARRIED

8 Feb: Ringo Starr and Maureen Cox
15 Apr: French rock musicians Johnny Halliday and Sylvie Vartan

OPENED

14 July: the Mont Blanc tunnel, linking France and Italy

BANNED

UK: all cigarette advertising from commercial television

British pop singer Dusty Springfield sweeps into the USA on the back of her hit 'I Just Don't Know What To Do With Myself'. Many consider her the best female singer Britain ever produced; her first solo single 'I Only Want To Be WIth You' was an immediate hit in September 1963.

Roy Rogers, the all-American, all-singing movie cowboy, says goodbye to his faithful steed Trigger, who dies after 20 years as an animal star. When Rogers was at the height of his fame as Hollywood's highest-grossing 'western' actor, Trigger received as many as 200 fan letters each month.

INVENTED

UK: the McLaren buggy, a lightweight collapsible pushchair
UK: the Dolby sound recording system, by Ray Dolby and staff

ON STRIKE

26 Apr, Denmark: Danish brewers Tuborg and Carlsberg, creating a national beer shortage – thirsty Danes cross by ferry to Sweden for supplies

FINED

UK: the Rolling Stones, £5 for urinating against the wall of a petrol station

SAVED

Egypt: Abu Simbel temple, from destruction by the Aswan Dam project; UNESCO dismantles the temple and moves it 60 m (200 ft) to safety

FIRSTS

8 Mar: deployment of US troops in Vietnam
18 Mar: space walk; Soviet astronaut Alexei Leonov leaves his spacecraft *Voskhod 2*, 177 km (110 miles) above Earth, for ten minutes
1 May, UK: FA Cup win for Liverpool's football team, beating Leeds 2–1 in extra time
10 June, UK: airliner to make an automatic landing; a BEA de Havilland Trident, at Heathrow
28 June, Canada: multiplex cinema; it opens in Burnaby, British Columbia
1 Nov, Japan: high-speed train service; the Tokyo–Osaka 'bullet' train averages a speed of 162 km/h (101 mph)

On 21 February, Malcolm X (Malcolm Little), US black nationalist leader, is assassinated while attending a Muslim rally in Harlem, New York City. He made political enemies last year when he founded the Organisation of Afro-American Unity.

PUBLISHED

Kurt Vonnegut, *God bless you, Mr Rosewater*
Timothy Leary, *The Psychedelic Reader*

BIGGEST

15 Aug, New York City: attendance at a rock concert – 56 000 fans come to see the Beatles perform at Shea Stadium
9 Nov: power failure in history; it causes blackout all down the eastern coast of Canada and the United States for more than nine hours, leading to a surge in the national birthrates nine months later

On 3 June, US astronaut Edward White steps out of the space capsule Gemini 4 and dangles in space for 20 minutes, tethered only by a safety line. His co-pilot James McDivitt remains inside the capsule, which has undertaken the longest US space flight yet – four days.

FOUNDED

29 Nov, UK: the National Viewers' and Listeners' Association, by anti-filth campaigner Mary Whitehouse
USA: Hare Krishna movement, by a 59-year-old ex-accountant, A C Bhaktivedanta

NEW WORDS

flower power *n*: youth movement preaching the power of love; linked to experimentation with illegal drugs
rubber johnny *n*: condom

US FORCES UNLEASHED IN VIETNAM

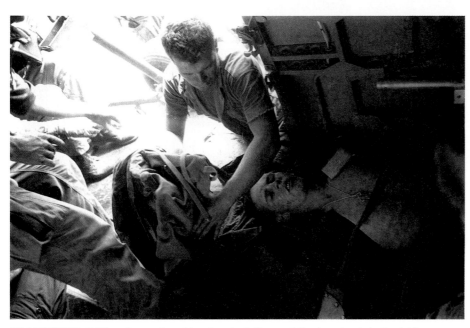

WAR WOUNDED A US marine receives aid on board a helicopter following a battle in South Vietnam.

13 FEBRUARY, WASHINGTON DC
President Lyndon B Johnson has ordered the US Air Force and Navy to start bombing military targets in the People's Republic of North Vietnam. Operation Rolling Thunder promises to be the first step in increasing American military involvement in the region.

Until today the American military have played an 'advisory' role to the South Vietnamese army, allegedly taking no part in the fighting. But 23 000 American troops are in Vietnam already, and are starting to suffer casualties.

The USA became involved in this war on the far side of the globe back in 1956 when civil war broke out between the Viet Cong rebels, backed by communist North Vietnam, and the South Vietnamese army. The USA supplied arms and advice to the South Vietnamese. In 1961 President Kennedy authorised American advisers to fight with the Vietnamese they were training.

Last August, after North Vietnamese attacks on US destroyers in the Gulf of Tonkin, Congress gave President Johnson the authority to take 'all necessary measure … to prevent further aggression'. The resolution gives the President full power to send in as many troops as he likes without declaring war.

Meanwhile, at home, anti-war protests have been escalating as Americans see their country dragged into a semi-covert war on the other side of the world.

··· 1 FEB, USA: HEALTH WARNINGS ON CIGARETTE PACKETS ARE NOW REQUIRED BY LAW ···

LA rocked by race riots

15 AUGUST, WATTS, LOS ANGELES
The past week has seen the worst race riots in the United States since the war. The centre of this outbreak of violence is Watts, a black suburb of Los Angeles, California. The trouble started on 9 August when LA police arrested a black man for drunk-driving; local youths who witnessed the arrest attacked the police officers, who then responded with force. The result was a full-scale riot in the Watts district, with many buildings quickly engulfed in flames.

Twenty thousand National Guardsmen spent yesterday inspecting the damage to the area, which is estimated at over $175 million. The human cost of the riots has been high – the 28 fatalities include children, and the 676 casualties include 70 police officers, 25 firefighters and four members of the National Guard. Tension continues in the district despite a lull in the fighting. It is clear that many young blacks have rejected the peaceful message of Martin Luther King, the black civil rights leader, in favour of the more aggressive Black Power movement.

NO SMOKE WITHOUT FIRE Deep racial tension lies behind the Watts riots.

Chilling 'Moors Murderers' are brought to justice

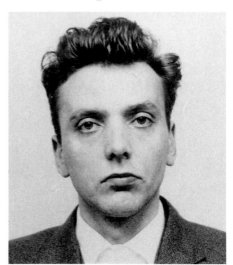

UNREPENTANT Ian Brady was silent in court.

ACCOMPLICE Hindley was under Brady's spell.

28 OCTOBER, HYDE, CHESHIRE
Angry scenes were witnessed today
outside the courthouse where a man
and woman were charged with the
cruel murder of ten-year-old Lesley
Ann Downey. Feelings of public outrage
were running so high that police used
decoy cars to divert the crowd of 200
demonstrators as the accused were
brought to the court hearing.

Ian Brady, aged 27, a stock-clerk, and
his girlfriend Myra Hindley, aged 23, a
typist, were arrested following the
discovery two weeks ago of the
schoolgirl's body, buried on the bleak
Saddleworth Moor near Manchester. A
full-scale police search has been
launched on the moors, suggesting that
further unsolved murders are involved in
the case. RAF photo-reconnaissance
bombers have been called in to help
with the search. Meanwhile, public
attention is fixed on Brady and Hindley,
at the centre of what is quickly
becoming one of the most notorious
murder cases of the century.

Cosmopolitan – the bible for sixties girls – is relaunched

American publishing has tuned into the
'swinging sixties' with the relaunch of
Cosmopolitan, the women's magazine
that gives its readers a clear message:
'Have fun, be single and have sex.' Until
now women's magazines have been
stuffy, predictable publications full of
recipes and knitting patterns, aimed at
housewives and homemakers.

Helen Gurley Brown, editor of
Cosmopolitan, has taken the controversial
ideas that she first developed in her
bestselling book of 1962, *Sex and the
Single Girl,* and put them into a glossy
magazine format with mass-market
appeal. The 'Cosmo girl' is a new role
model for women – independent,
ambitious and carefree, with neither the
time nor the inclination to think about
marriage or motherhood.

State funeral for wartime leader

30 JANUARY, OXFORDSHIRE
Sir Winston Churchill was laid to rest
today in a small churchyard near his
family's seat at Blenheim Palace. When
he died four days ago the nation was
plunged into mourning, and the world
paid homage to one of the 20th
century's greatest statesmen.

In 1940, when Europe had been
overrun by the Germans and it seemed
as if Britain might at any moment be
invaded, Churchill rallied the nation –
with his eloquent speeches as prime
minister as much as his bold leadership.
With a cigar clamped in his mouth he
toured bomb-torn areas, where his
presence put heart into a war-wrecked
people. It came as a bitter personal blow
to him when he lost the general
election to Labour in 1945.

But the British people showed their
appreciation of Churchill at his funeral.
Hundreds of thousands filed in a sober
procession past his coffin as his body lay
in state at Westminster Abbey.
Representatives of 110 nations attended
the state funeral service at St Paul's
Cathedral in London.

SLOW MARCH Churchill's funeral cortege keeps a
stately pace as it passes St Paul's Cathedral.

··· 12 IN 100 AMERICANS ARE BLACK, BUT 23 IN 100 US SOLDIERS IN VIETNAM ARE BLACK ···

RHODESIA DECLARES INDEPENDENCE

NEW ERA BEGINS Premier Ian Smith signs the document establishing Rhodesian independence.

11 NOVEMBER, RHODESIA
Britain's new Labour government is facing its first overseas crisis. In a radio broadcast to the people of Rhodesia the prime minister of the British colony, Ian Smith, has unilaterally declared independence from Great Britain.

Smith heads an all-white parliament in a country whose population is 90 per cent black. For some time British colonial officials have been trying to guide Rhodesia towards a more democratic path.

In his broadcast today Smith spoke of the 'separate and equal' status to which the people of Rhodesia are 'entitled'. Negotiations are likely to be difficult, but Britain will be reluctant to answer Commonwealth appeals for armed intervention.

··· USA: THE FIRST 'TEACH-IN' AGAINST THE VIETNAM WAR IS HELD AT THE UNIVERSITY OF MICHIGAN ···

Breedlove regains speed record

15 NOVEMBER, UTAH
The American driver Craig Breedlove, who set a new world land-speed record two weeks ago only to see it surpassed by Art Arfons a few days later, has reclaimed the record – reaching a speed nearly 80 kilometres per hour (50 mph) faster than his previous achievement.

Overcoming technical difficulties on earlier runs, he drove *Spirit of America – Sonic I*, with its narrow waist, pointed nosecone and high tail fin, to 961 km/h (600 mph) on the Bonneville Salt Flats in Utah. Arfons' briefly held record was 922 km/h (576 mph). Just ten days ago Breedlove's wife set the record for a woman driver of 494 km/h (308 mph).

The four-wheeled *Spirit of America* has several novel features. It is powered by a jet aircraft engine, the steering is by handlebars, and it is brought to a halt by disc brakes and a parachute.

JET POWER Despite its ambitious name, *Spirit of America - Sonic I* never reached the speed of sound.

Consumer champion Nader discredits General Motors

According to a book that is sending tremors through the auto industry, American automobiles are unsafe and responsible for killing and injuring thousands of people every year. *Unsafe at Speed*, by lawyer Ralph Nader, focuses particular attention on General Motors' Corvair model but claims that all manufacturers have been careless of their customers' safety.

Alarmed by the popularity of the book, which has quickly become a bestseller, General Motors employed private detectives to spy on 31-year-old Nader in an attempt to discredit him. This was a fatal error: a successful lawsuit for invasion of privacy cemented Nader's reputation as a consumer champion and gave him the money to set up a non-profit organisation in Washington to further his causes.

19**65**

Post Office Tower opens in London

7 OCTOBER, LONDON
London's tallest building has been opened, close to Tottenham Court Road in the West End. The 188-metre (620-ft) Post Office Tower was designed to relay microwave signals, which travel in straight lines, and this meant that it must be in direct line of sight with other towers in the Post Office network. Technically this dictated a pencil-slim tower rising well above surrounding buildings.

At the top is a public viewing gallery and a revolving restaurant with some of London's finest views, reached by Europe's fastest lifts. Anthony Wedgwood Benn, Postmaster-General, has called the tower the Big Ben of the 20th century.

··· GENERAL CHARLES DE GAULLE IS RE-ELECTED PRESIDENT OF FRANCE ···

Young consumers fuel boom

Britain's young people have burst out of the dreary postwar years of rationing and restriction into a new era of energy and freedom – thanks partly to their new-found spending power.

And Londoners who want to join in with the city's swing know how to do it. It's never been cheaper to be chic, or better yet 'trendy'. As any dollybird knows, Biba is the place to get kitted out, while if you have a new pad to furnish Habitat is just right.

Biba is not merely a boutique but also a fashion grotto. Sepulchrally dark, its interior is strewn with jewel-coloured feather boas, shiny beads, glittering Lurex dresses and velvet hats. Clothes are displayed in little clumps on bentwood hatstands. And of course the clothes are cheap. For £15 a girl can buy an entire outfit from hat to shoes, whereas at Mary Quant she'd get only a dress for the same price.

Meanwhile, a young man named Terence Conran has opened Habitat, a furniture shop that stocks simple Swedish-style furniture, beanbags and French cookware – all at affordable prices. His modest aim is to revolutionise the way the British live.

STREET STYLE The cheaply available miniskirt became a uniform for the young in London.

MODERN MASTERPIECE Finishing touches are made to the Post Office Tower, thrusting symbol of a new British confidence.

US HITS OF THE YEAR	
1 (I CAN'T GET NO) SATISFACTION	*Rolling Stones*
2 YESTERDAY	*Beatles*
3 TURN! TURN! TURN!	*Byrds*
4 MRS BROWN YOU'VE GOT A LOVELY DAUGHTER	*Herman's Hermits*
5 I GOT YOU BABE	*Sonny & Cher*

US TV HITS
1 *Bonanza*
2 *Bewitched*
3 *Gomer Pyle, U S M C*
4 *The Andy Griffith Show*
5 *The Fugitive*

Beatles fans besiege Palace

PROTECTING THE BEATLES Police attempt to restrain fans desperate for a glimpse of their idols.

25 OCTOBER, LONDON

Official honours have capped a year of triumphs for the Beatles. Today the 'Fab Four' made their way to Buckingham Palace to receive their MBEs from the Queen. The Beatles have won fans on both sides of the Atlantic, notching up a string of number one singles and albums.

After the group played at a Royal Command performance in London there were more than a million advance sales of the next single, 'I Want to Hold Your Hand'. Earlier this year they conquered America. Landing in New York in February they received the sort of rapturous welcome they are used to in Britain. Two appearances on the top-rated *Ed Sullivan Show* followed in April and helped boost their popularity all over the country. In August their second film, *Help!*, opened in US cinemas.

At one stage the Beatles had five top-selling singles in the *Billboard* Hot 200. The single 'Can't Buy Me Love' became the first record to reach number one simultaneously in the USA and the UK.

The new aristocracy

Fashion photographer David Bailey and his wife, French actress Catherine Deneuve, are reputed to be London's coolest couple. Bailey, son of an East End tailor, has had a sensational rise to the top, and when he married Deneuve earlier this year his transformation into the sultan of London hip was complete.

Society magazines such as *Tatler* and *Harpers & Queen*, which used to fill their social columns with the antics of the upper classes, now cannot get enough of Bailey, Deneuve and the rest of the 'Swinging London' set. Other members of the 'club' include actor Terence Stamp, designers Mary Quant and Ossie Clarke, singer Adam Faith and celebrity hairdresser Vidal Sassoon.

HIPSTERS Bailey and Deneuve take the air in Rome shortly after their August wedding.

THE SOUND OF SINGING NUNS SWEEPS ACADEMY AWARDS

LOVE-LORN Omar Sharif took the title role in *Doctor Zhivago*.

Julie Andrews built on her success in last year's *Mary Poppins* with the phenomenally successful *The Sound of Music*. One of the biggest box-office grossers ever, the sugar-sweet story of a singing nun and over-innocent children swept the board at the Oscars and had audiences singing along to 'My Favourite Things' and 'The Hills Are Alive ...' across the globe. This was also the year when English actress Julie Christie came to the fore. She won an Oscar for best actress in John Schlesinger's *Darling* – a tale of decadent high-flyers in the swinging 1960s – and starred opposite Omar Sharif in David Lean's epic *Doctor Zhivago*. Both films were huge successes. The Bond juggernaut rolled on with *Thunderball*; Michael Caine starred in *The Ipcress File*, Richard Burton triumphed in *The Spy Who Came in from the Cold* and Steve McQueen held audiences spellbound in *The Cincinnati Kid*, a study of the poker-playing underworld in 1930s New Orleans.

1966

DIED
1 Feb: Buster Keaton, US actor and film director
28 Sept: André Breton, French poet, author of the *Surrealist Manifesto*
18 Oct: Elizabeth Arden, French cosmetician
15 Dec: Walt Disney, US cartoon producer

INDEPENDENT
26 May: Guyana, of Britain
4 Oct: Lesotho, of Britain
30 Nov: Barbados, of Britain

Raquel Welch stars in One Million Years BC, *a tale of war between rival tribes in the Stone Age. The film is a remake of the 1940 film* One Million BC, *itself a remake of D W Griffith's* Man's Genesis. *Welch is being hailed as the new cinema sex symbol of the decade.*

MARRIED
21 Jan, UK: Beatle George Harrison and actress Patti Boyd
14 July, USA: Günther Sachs and actress Brigitte Bardot
19 July, Las Vegas: singer Frank Sinatra and actress Mia Farrow

ELECTED
19 Jan, India: Indira Gandhi, as prime minister

RE-ELECTED
2 June, Ireland: Eamon de Valera, aged 83, as president for second term

QUIT
30 June: NATO, by France

KILLED
6 Sept, South Africa: Prime Minister Hendrik Verwoerd, stabbed in the House of Assembly by Demetrio Tsafendas, a messenger

FOUNDED
8 Feb, UK: Laker Airways, airline specialising in cheap holiday flights, by British entrepreneur Freddie Laker

BANNED
6 June, Belfast: Ulster Volunteer Force
June, New York City: the Rolling Stones, from 14 hotels

LAUNCHED
30 Apr, UK: hovercraft service across the English Channel, from Ramsgate to Calais
15 Oct, London: *International Times*, underground newspaper

JAILED
14 Feb, USSR: writers Yuri Daniel and Andrei Sinyavski, sent to labour camp for having their banned novels published abroad
20 July, Ireland: Reverend Ian Paisley, convicted of breaching the peace at a church meeting

As Twiggy, 17-year-old Londoner Lesley Hornby becomes the most famous model in the world. She has turned ideals of female beauty upside down and made skinny androgyny fashionable. Her bobbed hair, big eyes and waifish awkwardness constitute a kind of 'anti-glamorous' glamour.

COUPS
24 Feb, Ghana: against President Nkrumah, led by military
1 Aug, Nigeria: Yakubu Gowon takes control

FIRSTS
17 Mar: space docking, of *Gemini 8* spacecraft with part of its Agena launcher, by US astronauts Neil Armstrong and David Scott
15 Sept: British nuclear submarine, HMS *Resolution*

CHAMPIONS
21 May, London: Cassius Clay, who beats British challenger Henry Cooper to keep world heavyweight championship
30 May, Indianapolis: British racing driver Graham Hill, who wins Indy 500 race at first attempt; average 230 km/h (144 mph) in Lotus-Ford

FOUND
7 Apr, Atlantic Ocean: US hydrogen bomb that fell into water after mid-air crash of B-52 bomber with airborne fuel tanker on 17 Jan

RIOTED
July, USA: inhabitants of Chicago, Brooklyn and Cleveland, in racial clashes
11 Sept, Georgia: black Americans in Atlanta
12 Sept, Mississippi: white Americans who attack black schoolchildren at racially integrated schools in Grenada

NEW WORDS
acid *n*: (slang) LSD
bootleg *n*: an illegally made musical recording

The clearing-up operation begins in Florence, Italy, after severe floods wreak havoc in the city. Rain and high winds fill the river Arno to bursting point until it overflows its banks. Many of Florence's art treasures, including paintings, books and sculptures, are damaged or lost in the swirling waters.

Mao's supporters unleash Cultural Revolution

15 AUGUST, BEIJING
Hundreds of thousands of students have begun a purge of intellectuals in Communist China as the 'great proletarian Cultural Revolution', announced by the Chinese leader Mao Zedong on 8 August, got under way.

The newly formed Red Guards – an unofficial movement composed mostly of teenagers – are sweeping through the country carrying portraits of Mao and copies of his 'little red book', which contains quotations from the Chinese leader's works. Their aim is to restore 'revolutionary zeal', and their targets include Communist Party officials as well as teachers, philosophers and artists whom they accuse of 'revisionism' – straying from the orthodox dogma of the Party set out by Mao himself. People are urged to denounce anyone suspected of not being a genuine Communist, including friends, neighbours and even family members.

Using bullying tactics and sheer force of numbers, the Red Guards have ransacked homes, closed down schools and made those found 'guilty' wear dunces' caps as they are paraded through the streets. Many locals are fighting back, but the Red Guards have the support of senior Communist Party figures. However, even high-up members of the Party have come under

MASS MOVEMENT The 'acceptable' activity of chanting Mao's thoughts.

attack. Tien Han, who composed Communist China's national anthem, has been publicly disgraced, and Kuo Mo-jo, a close friend of Chairman Mao's, was forced to confess that the many volumes of poetry, fiction and history he had penned did not apply to Mao's teachings, were worthless and should be burnt.

··· 29 JUNE, UK: THE FIRST BRITISH CREDIT CARD, THE BARCLAYCARD, IS INTRODUCED ···

CHILDREN KILLED AS SCHOOL IS ENGULFED

FADING HOPES Desperate parents and helpers dig through the slurry in the search for surviving children.

21 OCTOBER, ABERFAN, WALES
A total of 116 children and 28 adults died today when a rain-soaked colliery tip slid down into the Welsh mining village of Aberfan, burying the local school, a row of cottages and a farm.

Thousands of tons of slurry slid down the hillside just as the children were starting their morning classes, and the school was engulfed in seconds. The waterlogged tip, part of the Merthyr Vale coalfield, had towered over the village for more than 50 years.

As rescuers fought to save the children, one ten-year-old survivor described what happened: 'We heard a noise and saw all this stuff flying about ... Children were shouting and screaming. We couldn't see anything.' Others described hearing a rumbling noise 'like thunder' from as far as 5 kilometres (3 miles) away. Among the dead was the deputy headmaster, who was found buried with the bodies of five children in his arms. Hundreds of people are working into the night looking for survivors.

One theory is that an underground spring destabilised the tip and started the landslide. Prime Minister Harold Wilson said: 'I don't think any of us can find words to describe this tragedy.'

At last – the 'home of football' beats the world

SWEET VICTORY Captain Bobby Moore expresses his joy at winning the Cup.

30 JULY, LONDON
Jubilant crowds swarmed over London's West End tonight, endlessly chanting 'England! England!' to celebrate their team's winning of football's World Cup. The land that proudly calls itself the home of football has won the trophy for the first time, beating the 1954 winners, West Germany, 4–2 after extra time.

England, managed by Alf Ramsey and captained by the West Ham midfielder Bobby Moore, gained its place in the final by defeating Portugal 2–1 in a tense semi-final. At Wembley stadium today the home supporters were emotionally drained by a match in which England's fortunes fluctuated as much as the weather, which veered between sunshine and slanting rain. Germany scored first, in the thirteenth minute, but with seconds left in the match England was leading 2–1, thanks to goals by the West Ham forward players Martin Peters and Geoff Hurst. Then West German spirits were almost miraculously revived by a scrambled goal from Weber.

So, the cup snatched from it at the last moment, England had to pick itself up quickly, and with great resolve and resilience it did exactly that. Hurst's two goals in extra time brought the match to a story-book conclusion. Both goals were surrounded by drama. The first was hotly disputed by the Germans, who argued in vain that the ball, which struck the underside of the crossbar, had not crossed the line. The second, a rasping shot on the end of a beautifully weighted pass from Moore, was scored as sections of the crowd, believing that the final whistle had been blown, surged on to the pitch.

Hurst, somewhat unexpectedly selected to play instead of the prolific striker Jimmy Greaves, had collected the first hat-trick in a World Cup final. And for the sixth time in the last eight finals, the team that scored first ended up the losers.

Wembley was a sea of Union Jacks as the England players hauled themselves up the famous stairs to the royal box, where they received the trophy and their medals from the Queen.

··· THE KRAY TWINS SHOOT GEORGE CORNELL IN THE BLIND BEGGAR PUB, BETHNAL GREEN, LONDON ···

Lone yachtsman makes round-the-world bid

12 DECEMBER, SYDNEY
The English yachtsman Francis Chichester arrived in Sydney today, completing the first leg of his epic journey around the world. The 64-year-old mariner aims to become the first person to make a solo circumnavigation.

Chichester began his 47 400-kilometre (29 600-mile) journey 107 days ago. He set sail in his small boat – a 16-metre (53-ft) ketch called *Gipsy Moth IV* – from Plymouth on 27 August and sailed eastwards around Africa and the Cape of Good Hope. Today's landfall in Sydney marks the half-way point in his trip. He will spend a month or so preparing for the return journey – this time across the Pacific Ocean.

In 1960 Chichester won the first solo race across the Atlantic in *Gipsy Moth III*, yet the intrepid mariner only took up ocean sailing at the age of 52, having previously made a name for himself as an aeroplane pilot. His *Gipsy Moth* boats are named after the type of plane in which he made a solo flight to Australia in 1929.

LONELY ORDEAL *Gypsy Moth IV* ploughs through heavy seas as Chichester heads for Australia.

Television space series takes off

ENTERPRISING CREW Captain Kirk and his team – roving the universe.

9 SEPTEMBER, USA
It nearly didn't happen, but last night NBC premiered its most ambitious prime-time series for years: the space exploration drama *Star Trek*.

Star Trek enjoyed the unheard-of luxury of two separate pilot episodes. NBC was unhappy with the first, which it thought was 'too cerebral'. The network opted not to cancel the show, but instead advanced the money for a second pilot, this time without the services of the original star, Jeffrey Hunter. In his place, as Captain James T Kirk of the starship *Enterprise,* is William Shatner.

The series creator is Gene Roddenberry, the lead writer on the western *Have Gun Will Travel*, and a former script writer on *Dr Kildare*. Roddenberry has said the show is a sort of 'space western', and revolves around a racially diverse crew trying to stand up for good.

The most intriguing character, Mr Spock, played by Leonard Nimoy, was fortunate to survive into the series proper. NBC thought the character too dark, but Roddenberry fought successfully for his inclusion.

Beatles are 'more popular than Jesus'

A remark made by Beatles guitarist John Lennon to a British journalist earlier this year has sparked controversy in parts of the United States. Lennon's claim that 'We're more popular than Jesus Christ right now' had little effect in Britain, but when the interview was reprinted in a teen magazine in the United States it provoked unheard-of scenes across the American South.

An unholy alliance of the Christian Coalition and the Ku Klux Klan has condemned the band in an effort to protect American children from its worst excesses. All over the Deep South the Beatles have seen their records and pictures smashed and burnt, while hooded KKK members have picketed record shops that dare to stock anything by the band. They are demanding an apology from Lennon.

	US HITS OF THE YEAR	
1	I'M A BELIEVER	Monkees
2	THE BALLAD OF THE GREEN BERETS	S.Sgt Barry Sadler
3	WINCHESTER CATHEDRAL	New Vaudeville Band
4	(YOU'RE MY) SOUL AND INSPIRATION	Righteous Brothers
5	MONDAY MONDAY	Mamas & The Papas

	US TV HITS
1	Bonanza
2	Gomer Pyle, U S M C
3	The Lucy Show
4	The Red Skelton Hour
5	Batman

BRITAIN TRIUMPHS AT OSCARS

Paul Scofield, Wendy Hiller and Susannah York starred in Fred Zinnemann's *A Man for All Seasons*, an immaculate adaptation of Robert Bolt's stage play set in the court of Henry VIII. As well as picking up the Oscar for best film, Zinnemann won best director, Scofield best actor and Bolt best adapted screenplay.

Michael Caine had an immense box office success with *Alfie*, the story of a Cockney Don Juan, for which he received an Oscar nomination. Meanwhile, Elizabeth Taylor collected an Oscar for her performance in *Who's Afraid of Virginia Woolf?* in which she and Richard Burton starred as a couple constantly at each other's throats.

The year's other big news was the sale of *The Bridge on the River Kwai* to the ABC television network for a record $2 million. This could be the start of a major new source of film funding.

KNOCKOUT Michael Caine, star of *Alfie*, is a real hit with cinema audiences.

1967

DIED

7 June: Dorothy Parker, US author
10 June: Spencer Tracy, US actor
8 July: Vivien Leigh, British actor
3 Aug: Siegfried Sassoon, British poet
10 Dec: Otis Redding, US singer

FOUNDED

11 Jan, UK: Society for the Protection of Unborn Children
7 Feb, UK: National Front, fascist organisation

LEGALISED

27 July, UK: sexual intercourse between consenting men aged over 21

DEFECTED

9 Mar, India: Svetlana Alliluyeva, Stalin's daughter, to the West

On 1 May, *Elvis Presley and Priscilla Beaulieu are married in Las Vegas. The couple met in Germany in 1959 when Presley was stationed there with the US Army and Beaulieu, daughter of an air force officer, was attending high school in Frankfurt. The wedding caused scenes of hysteria across the USA among Presley's teenage fans.*

DISCOVERED

Greenhouse effect, the raising of climatic temperatures worldwide because of a concentration of carbon dioxide in the Earth's atmosphere

ARRESTED

16 Oct, California: singer Joan Baez, at anti-Vietnam War demonstration
21 Oct, Virginia: writer Norman Mailer, during anti-Vietnam War protests at Pentagon

SWORN IN

2 Jan, USA: Ronald Reagan, as governor of California
19 Dec, Australia: John McEwen, as acting prime minister, following death of Prime Minister Harold Holt

FIRSTS

25 May: British soccer team to win European Cup – Glasgow Celtic beats Inter Milan 2–1
8 Nov, UK: BBC local radio station, Radio Leicester
DNA successfully synthesised in a test tube by biologists in USA
Third Division football club to win Wembley final – Queen's Park Rangers beats holders West Bromwich Albion 3–2 to win League Cup

COMPLETED

28 May, Plymouth: solo round-world trip, by British yachtsman Francis Chichester, 46 500 km (28 500 miles)

FIRST NIGHTS

11 Apr, London: *Rosencrantz and Guildenstern are Dead,* play by Tom Stoppard
29 Oct, New York City: *Hair,* musical
21 Dec, UK: *Half a Sixpence,* musical starring Tommy Steele

On 27 January, *three US astronauts are killed when their spacecraft, Apollo 1, catches fire during a flight simulation at Cape Canaveral. Virgil Grissom, Edward White and Roger Chaffee were practising for a 14-day orbit scheduled for next month. The fire was caused by an electrical fault.*

VOTED

10 Sept: people of Gibraltar, to stay a British Crown Colony

OPENED

1 Mar, London: Queen Elizabeth Hall
2 Aug, London: Dartford Tunnel, beneath the river Thames

KILLED

4 Jan: British racing driver Donald Campbell, when his speedboat crashes as he attempts to beat the world water-speed record
24 Apr: Soviet cosmonaut Vladimir Komarov, when his *Soyuz* spacecraft crashes as he tries to return to Earth from orbit
23 July: by heat – Tommy Simpson, British racing cyclist, during Tour de France race

DECLARED OBSCENE

23 Nov, London: novel *Last Exit to Brooklyn* by Hubert Selby Jr, in court decision during trial of its publishers, Calder and Boyars

UNVEILED

11 Dec, France: Concorde prototype

FASTEST

3 Oct, California: X-15A-2 rocket-powered research aircraft; piloted by USAF Major Pete Knight, it hits 7254 km/h (4534 mph)

BOMBED

5 June: Egyptian airfields, by Israeli aircraft

ELECTED

5 Feb, Nicaragua: Anastasio Somoza, president
3 Sept, South Vietnam: General Nguyen Van Thieu, president

NEW WORDS

bell bottoms *n*: trousers with very wide flare from the knee
body bag *n*: bag used for removing corpses from battle

The Japanese watch firm Seiko launches the first quartz wristwatch, bringing precision timekeeping to everyday life. Quartz timekeeping was the invention of US clockmaker Warren Alvin Marrison, who discovered that quartz crystals vibrate at a fixed frequency that can be used to measure time accurately.

Decisive victory for Israel in Six Day War

WAR CONVOY Israeli troops on their way to the front pass a truck full of Egyptian prisoners of war.

10 JUNE, TEL AVIV

Six days after launching a surprise air attack on its Arab neighbours, Israel has accepted the United Nations' call for a ceasefire and halted its attack.

The Israelis' initiative has been a stunning success – won on virtually all fronts. This is the third war since the Jewish state was formed in 1948, and the third time Israel has come out on top.

The motivation for the Israeli assault was that Egypt and its Arab allies were about to invade Israeli territory. When Palestine was partitioned between the Jews and the Arabs after World War II to create a Jewish homeland, many Palestinians fled over the borders into neighbouring Arab states. Some of these people formed guerrilla groups whose sole aim was the destruction of Israel.

Israel's strike has thwarted the Arabs. On the first day of the war Israel wiped out the entire air capability of the Arab enemies – Syria, Jordan, Iraq and Egypt – whose armies were tightening their grip around Israel, and forced them to surrender large tracts of land. On 7 June Israel occupied East Jerusalem and the West Bank of the river Jordan – an area that is Jordan's economic heartland, and that also contains sites holy to both Judaism and Islam. After advancing as far as the Suez Canal, Israel gained control of the Sinai peninsula, the Golan Heights and the Gaza Strip. Its decisive victory is partly due to the element of surprise and to Arab disorganisation, but it owes much to the discipline of the Israeli army.

Hundreds of thousands of Arabs, mostly Palestinians, have been uprooted, and many have been taken prisoner by the Israelis. Palestinian refugees are streaming into Jordan and Syria.

The United Nations will almost certainly call upon Israel to retreat to its pre-war borders, but history suggests that the UN will not have the means to enforce its resolutions against a country which is the United States' chief ally in the Middle East.

··· ALBANIA DECLARES ITSELF TO BE THE WORLD'S FIRST OFFICIALLY ATHEIST STATE ···

Che Guevara, rebel with a cause, is shot dead

31 OCTOBER, BOLIVIA

Only weeks after his death was reported in Bolivia, the Latin American revolutionary Ernesto 'Che' Guevara has become a cult hero to the world's youth. Posters of the bearded figure are appearing on students' bedroom walls, poems are being written in his honour, and T-shirts emblazoned with the slogan 'Che lives' have become fashionable.

According to official Bolivian sources, Guevara was shot dead by government troops on 9 October. A

martyr's death has underlined the qualities that made Che appeal to so many. He was an intellectual as well as a man of action, a qualified doctor as well as a guerrilla fighter – and even those who did not agree with his ideology expressed admiration for his integrity.

Che had helped Fidel Castro in the Cuban revolution and served Cuba as a diplomat. After disappearing two years ago he arrived secretly in Bolivia, hoping to rouse the country's poor against the dictatorship of President Barrientes.

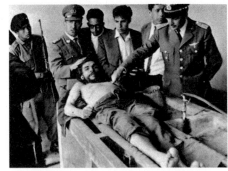

MARTYRED REVOLUTIONARY At a press conference, Bolivian generals show little respect for the corpse of guerrilla leader Che Guevara.

Disaster as tanker sinks

31 MARCH, CORNWALL
The last remains of the stricken oil tanker *Torrey Canyon* sank out of sight yesterday as RAF aeroplanes continued their bombing of the area to try to burn up any remaining oil. Several small fires have been started, but they are believed to have had very little effect.

The Liberian-registered tanker ran aground on the Seven Stones Reef, near the Scilly Isles, on 18 March, en route from Kuwait to Milford Haven in Wales. Despite concerted attempts at salvage operations, the ship broke up in heavy seas. She was fully loaded with more than 100000 tons of crude oil, and the spillage has spelt disaster for both marine life and seabirds in the area.

About 160 kilometres (100 miles) of the English shoreline have been affected, and oil is now also beginning to reach the French coast.

The Intergovernmental Maritime Consultative Organisation is meeting in emergency session. It is urgently aiming to secure international agreements to prevent another disaster of this type. Faulty navigation was the cause of the wreck.

WATERY GRAVE *Torrey Canyon's* oil spill was the worst ever in British waters.

··· THE WORLD'S FIRST MACROBIOTIC RESTAURANT OPENS IN CAMDEN, LONDON ···

Greek tragedy as Colonels seize power

21 APRIL, ATHENS
In the early hours of this morning the Greek army seized power in a bloodless coup which caught the country by surprise. This is the first successful coup in Western Europe since the end of World War II, and it has brought to an end a series of political crises in Greece which began just over two years ago, when Georgios Papandreou resigned the premiership.

The prime minister of Greece, Panagolis Kanellopoulos, has been put under arrest, along with other leading politicians. Hundreds of communists and left-wingers have been rounded up across the country for deportation.

The new military government is headed by a civilian, Konstantinos Kollias, who was sworn in this afternoon. Freedom of assembly and of the press have been abolished, but so far there has been little sign of popular resistance.

Barnard performs first ever heart transplant

4 DECEMBER, CAPE TOWN
Medical science took a huge step into the unknown yesterday when a human heart was transplanted from one person to another for the first time. The operation was performed by a team of surgeons, led by Dr Christiaan Barnard, at Groote Schuur Hospital.

Dr Barnard introduced open-heart surgery to South Africa and is one of the world's leading specialists. Yesterday he and his team took the heart from a man who had died in an accident and transplanted it to their patient, Mr Louis Washkansky, a grocer.

Mr Washkansky had been extremely ill with heart disease, and this operation was considered the only chance of saving his life. In the past, surgeons have transplanted other body organs, such as the lung and the kidney, with varying degrees of success. However, even after a successful transplant operation the team faces the possibility that the patient's body may reject the new organ.

HEART MAN Barnard was supported by a team of 30 assistants during the operation.

Barnard's transplant operation has ignited a debate about the ethics of the procedure, with some religious leaders saying that to interfere with the heart is tantamount to playing God.

Race riots shock Detroit

RUN RIOT High levels of racial prejudice within the US police forces intensified the rioting in Detroit.

30 JULY, DETROIT
After four days of the worst riots in US history, order has been restored to the streets of Detroit by federal troops. The city is now preparing to count the cost. About 40 people are dead and there have been more than 3000 arrests, many for looting. The cost of the damage will run to hundreds of millions of dollars.

The trouble started when police raided a nightclub popular with the Black Power movement and arrested more than 70 customers. Soon windows were smashed and fires started, and the destruction and violence escalated out of control. The events come at the end of a month that has seen racial tension sweeping across the country.

Thousands protest against Vietnam War

21 OCTOBER, WASHINGTON DC
The capital saw the biggest anti-government demonstration in the history of the United States today. Thousands of people converged on Washington in a massive rally protesting against continued US involvement in the Vietnam War.

This year will be remembered as the one in which Americans mobilised for peace. It was not only radical students who came to Washington – people from every walk of life have felt compelled to show the White House their anger. In a confrontation between the crowd and military police with batons and tear gas grenades, more than a dozen demonstrators were hurt and hundreds arrested.

More than half a million American soldiers have been sent to fight in Vietnam; tens of thousands have been killed since 1961, and government expenditure of public money on the war runs into billions of dollars. Public opinion polls show that support for President Lyndon Johnson's foreign policy is rapidly waning.

··· MUHAMMAD ALI IS STRIPPED OF HIS HEAVYWEIGHT BOXING CROWN AFTER REFUSING TO BE DRAFTED TO VIETNAM ···

First Super Bowl touches down

15 JANUARY, LOS ANGELES
Veteran quarterback Bart Starr has led the Green Bay Packers to a decisive victory in the first ever staging of the American Football Super Bowl.

Before a crowd of 63 000 at the Coliseum, and a national television audience of more than 45 million, the Packers, National Football League (NFL) champions, built a half-time lead of 14–10 against the Kansas City Chiefs, American Football League (AFL) champions. In the second half, after two superb passes by Starr to Max McGee, they ran away to a 35–10 victory.

The Super Bowl represents the end of a bitter feud in American football which has been played out in the courts and in the press. Until recently, the older NFL had virtually denied the existence of the new upstarts at the AFL.

However, the money behind the AFL from powerful business interests meant that it was only a matter of time before both league champions met on the field. Every player on the winning team will receive a bonus of $15 000, the most ever paid to a team player in any sport for a single game; Chiefs players will have to make do with $7500 each.

BOWL STARS In the closing minutes of the game the Green Bay Packers' Bart Starr hands the ball over to Elijah Pitts.

THOUSANDS TURN ON FOR SUMMER OF LOVE

FLOWER POWER Long hair, bell-bottomed trousers and colourful shirts became the hippy uniform.

If you're young, free and looking for an alternative way of living, San Francisco is the place to be. It all began in June with the Monterey Pop Festival, when 50 000 kids descended on the city for an outdoor concert featuring the Beatles, the Grateful Dead and Jimi Hendrix.

They never left. More young people arrived, until the Haight–Ashbury district was declared 'Hippie Haven' by the press. This summer Haight–Ashbury became so crowded with visitors that the city's infrastructure started to buckle. The hippies organised themselves, cleaned the streets, gave out free food and set up a special phone line for runaways.

San Francisco has become the centre of a US phenomenon with worldwide reverberations that has been dubbed the 'Summer of Love'. What this means is a matter of opinion, though a hippy philosophy of love and peace, the taking of drugs such as LSD and marijuana to find the 'inner self', and opposition to US involvement in the war in Vietnam all seem to be part of it. Some pundits see it as a middle-class rebellion against the Protestant work ethic.

The hippies are mostly young, white and middle class. According to one study 60 per cent are aged between 19 and 25; 68 per cent have had a college education. These intelligent young people are heeding drugs guru Timothy Leary's advice to 'turn on, tune in and drop out'. For many hippies, rebellion has its limits. They have to go back to school in September, and for them the Summer of Love has been only a brief flirtation with the politics of non-conformity.

··· 9 NOV: THE FIRST ISSUE OF *ROLLING STONE* MAGAZINE GOES ON SALE IN THE UNITED STATES ···

LSD offers a peek into Pandora's box

Not since Coleridge wrote the fantasy poem 'Kubla Khan' after taking opium has a drug had such a big impact on the way artists see the world. The drug in question is LSD (short for 'lysergic acid diethylamide'), a powerful synthetic hallucinogen which takes the subject on a 'trip' that can last seven hours. LSD, or 'acid', appears to make new connections in the mind, or to open 'the doors of perception', as Aldous Huxley, the late exponent of psychedelic drugs, put it.

In Britain and the United States musicians have been openly experimenting with narcotics. When Mick Jagger, lead singer of the Rolling Stones, was arrested for possession of drugs, he freely admitted taking them.

Pop music has been transformed. The Beatles latest LP is a 'concept' album, *Sergeant Pepper's Lonely Hearts Club Band*, the bizarre imagery and soundscape of which are a complete departure from their former style of music. The album's cover, designed by Peter Blake, is rich in

TAKING A TRIP The Beatles, once clean-cut Liverpool lads, have now produced a psychedelic masterpiece.

obscure symbolism. The LP may be influenced by drugs, but John Lennon has dismissed as coincidence the fact that one of the song titles, 'Lucy in the Sky with Diamonds', forms the initials LSD.

Other groups were quick to jump on the psychedelic bandwagon. The Rolling Stones' riposte was the single 'We Love You' and album *Their Satanic Majesties Request*, with tracks like 'She's a Rainbow'. Meanwhile *Piper at the Gates of Dawn*, by newcomers Pink Floyd, is being hailed as a modern-day classic. The album is full of surreal images, spooky lyrics and strange sounds which seem to be positively drenched in acid.

Aretha Franklin hits the top notes

Aretha Franklin has become the hottest property in pop, notching up four Top Ten hits, three of them million-sellers, in the United States this year. Talent runs in her family: her father, the Reverend C L Jackson, a gospel singer who commands $4000 a performance, is known as 'the Million Dollar Voice'.

Franklin released her first album, a collection of gospel songs, at the age of 14. She hit the big time when she signed to the Atlantic record label – her producer Jerry Wexler capturing the power of her four-octave voice. In March 'I Never Loved A Man' was her first big hit, followed by 'Respect', 'Baby I Love You' and '(You Make Me Feel Like a) Natural Woman'. With her blend of gospel, soul, R & B and pop, Franklin looks unstoppable.

QUEEN OF SOUL Aretha's 'Respect' became an anthem for the black and feminist movements.

Historic *Forsyte Saga* enthrals Britain

Six million viewers tuned into Britain's new third channel, BBC2, for *The Forsyte Saga*. The BBC's first costume drama was so popular that sports events and church services were rescheduled so that no one needed to miss the Sunday-evening instalments. Based on the novels of John Galsworthy, the series starred veteran actor Kenneth More as the merchant Jolyon 'Jo' Forsyte.

The series, spanning 26 episodes, followed the trials and tribulations of the Forsytes, a London merchant family living at the turn of the century. Each episode left audiences on the edge of their seats with a cliffhanger ending. The television rights to the drama have been bought all over the world.

··· 14 APR: THE BEE GEES' FIRST SINGLE, *NEW YORK MINING DISASTER 1941*, IS RELEASED ···

MRS ROBINSON GIVES DUSTIN HOFFMAN LESSONS IN LOVE

LEG MAN Hoffman graduates with honours.

Simon and Garfunkel coo-coo-ca-chooed their way to chart success on the soundtrack to *The Graduate* – Dustin Hoffman was the bored young man seduced by an older woman, his parents' friend, in the hippest film of the year. More bored young people were out for kicks in *Bonnie and Clyde*, with Faye Dunaway and Warren Beatty making bank-robbing look like a glamorous diversion. In *Guess Who's Coming to Dinner?* Spencer Tracy and Katharine Hepburn were anxious white parents coming to terms with having Sidney Poitier for a son-in-law. Race was tackled more daringly in the thriller *In the Heat of the Night* – Poitier again, this time as a black detective coming up against a gang of southern rednecks. Roger Vadim's film *Barbarella*, starring Jane Fonda, looked set for cult status. Based on a science fiction comic strip, its combination of high camp and soft porn meant that the censor insisted that some its more risqué scenes ended up on the cutting-room floor.

US HITS OF THE YEAR

1	TO SIR WITH LOVE	Lulu
2	DAYDREAM BELIEVER	Monkees
3	WINDY	Association
4	ODE TO BILLIE JOE	Bobbie Gentry
5	GROOVIN'	Young Rascals

US TV HITS

1	Bonanza
2	The Red Skelton Hour
3	The Andy Griffith Show
4	The Lucy Show
5	The Jackie Gleason Show

1968

Kodak's easy-to-use, lightweight Instamatic camera hits the shops. The cheap, compact Instamatic has a special drop-in film cartridge, a fixed-focus lens and only two exposure settings – sunny and cloudy. Taking snapshots couldn't be easier.

DIED

27 Mar: Yuri Gagarin, Soviet cosmonaut, first man in space
28 Nov: Enid Blyton, British children's author
20 Dec: John Steinbeck, US author

BIGGEST

30 June, Georgia, USA: Lockheed C-5 Galaxy troop transport, the world's biggest aircraft; 75.3 m (247 ft) long with wingspan of 67.6 m (222 ft)

FIRSTS

23 Apr, UK: British decimal coins
30 Sept, Washington: flight of a Boeing 747 jumbo jet
2 Oct, Birmingham: British sextuplets, born to Mrs Sheila Ann Thorns
31 Dec, Moscow: supersonic airliner to fly, Tupolev Tu-144
Wimbledon tennis championships open to professionals

CANCELLED

17 Sept: MCC cricket tour of South Africa, by South African Prime Minister John Vorster because of inclusion of Cape Coloured Basil d'Oliveira in the party

ATTACKED

21 Apr, UK: British immigration policy, by Conservative MP Enoch Powell: 'As I look ahead ... I see the river ... foaming with much blood'

The world's largest passenger ship, Cunard's Queen Elizabeth II, *receives some final touches in preparation for her maiden voyage next year. Cunard kept the name of the liner a secret until the moment of her launch last year. The ship's design will allow her to pass through the Suez and Panama canals.*

SEIZED

26 Apr, London: stash of drug LSD worth £1.5 million

CHAMPIONS

29 May, UK: Manchester United, which wins European Cup by beating Benfica 4–1 in the final at Wembley

SIGNED

1 July: Nuclear Non-Proliferation Treaty, by 36 nations

SHOT

3 June, New York City: Andy Warhol, artist, by Valerie Solanas, head of SCUM (Society for Cutting Up Men); he survives

PUBLISHED

Arthur Hailey, *Airport*
Philip K Dick, *Do Androids Dream of Electric Sheep?*
Tom Wolfe, *The Electric Kool-Aid Acid Test*

On 27 December, Apollo 8 *returns from Moon orbit with pictures of the Earth rising – stunning images of a fragile and beautiful blue planet surrounded by blackness. The US space programme is now preparing for a human landing on the Moon.*

ELECTED

5 Nov, Washington DC: Richard M Nixon, as President

INDEPENDENT

31 Jan: Mauritius, of Britain
6 Sept: Swaziland, of Britain

NEW WORDS

dayglo *adj*: denoting very bright colours that glow in daylight; originally a brand name
overkill *n*: excess; amount by which what is necessary is exceeded

Russia crushes Dubček's 'Prague Spring'

21 AUGUST, PRAGUE

The 'Prague Spring' is over. Meeting little serious resistance, Soviet tanks last night rolled into the Czech capital, bringing to an end the brief period of freedom engineered by the reformer Alexander Dubček.

After his election last January as first secretary of the Communist Party in Czechoslovakia, Dubček announced economic and political reforms which he promised would bring about the 'widest possible democratisation'. The reforms gave greater independence to individuals, trade unions and other institutions; even non-Communists could play a part in government. Press censorship was lifted, unfair trials ended and political prisoners pardoned. In what became known as the 'Prague Spring', Czech citizens had freedoms approaching those of the West.

Dubček promised the Soviet Union that Czechoslovakia would remain part

END OF AN ERA Moscow sent troops and tanks to Czechoslovakia to quash the new liberalism.

of the Warsaw Pact. However, he underestimated the threat that his reforms posed to the Moscow regime, whose troops, backed up by soldiers from satellite East Germany, Poland, Bulgaria and Hungary, have now taken back control of the capital. Dubček has been arrested and taken to Moscow, where he will be made to concede the reversal of almost every reform he brought about.

··· ROY JACUZZI OF WALNUT CREEK, CALIFORNIA, INVENTS THE WHIRLPOOL BATH ···

France's student rebellion turns into national strike

FACE TO FACE Riot police and protesters converge on the streets of Paris.

1 MAY, PARIS

Almost half of France's workforce is on strike today, as up to ten million workers join in the student protests that have rocked the country in the past few weeks. The workers are protesting about pay and conditions, censorship and discrimination; but the general strike is as much a show of solidarity with the students whose demands have plunged the country into chaos. In one incident a group of car workers locked their management in a room and 'tortured' them by playing them the socialist anthem, the 'Internationale', over and over again.

Student unrest caused the Nanterre and Sorbonne campuses of Paris University to be closed and classes to be suspended. Riots broke out as thousands of students took to the streets to protest against government expenditure, calling for more spending on education and social reform and less on maintaining France's armed forces. In an attempt to break up the crowd, police launched a brutal attack with batons and tear gas. The students threw bricks, stones and Molotov cocktails in response. Barricades were erected and cars burnt; so far, more than 1000 people have been injured in street fighting, which continues in parts of Paris.

President Charles de Gaulle has rebutted demands for his resignation and has intimated his willingness to use strong measures to suppress the revolt.

ASSASSINATIONS SHOCK AMERICA

MOURNING PARADE Martin Luther King's coffin is drawn through the streets.

For many Americans this year will be remembered most for the shameful assassination of two of its most prominent citizens.

The first tragedy struck on 4 April, when the civil rights leader Dr Martin Luther King was shot by a sniper in Memphis while standing on a motel balcony. King had come to the city to muster support for striking refuse collectors, although he knew that his life was in danger. The night before his murder, he told an audience: 'I've seen the Promised Land. I may not get there with you, but I want you to know that we as a people will get to the Promised Land.'

The gunman, James Earl Ray, escaped but was arrested two months later at London airport, three days after a new tragedy shook America.

On 5 June, shortly after completing a victory address to his campaign supporters, Senator Robert Kennedy was shot down in a Los Angeles hotel. In a room packed with onlookers, Sirhan Bishara Sirhan, a young Palestinian-American, emptied a full round of bullets into the senator. He later claimed that he was protesting on behalf of the Palestinian people against US patronage of Israel but, as in Dr King's case, there is a host of conspiracy theories.

··· THERE ARE 500 000 US SOLDIERS IN VIETNAM AT A COST OF $30 BILLION PER YEAR – 300 DIE EACH WEEK ···

Tet offensive reveals Viet Cong's might

31 JANUARY, SAIGON
As Vietnam began yesterday to mark the start of Tet, the Vietnamese New Year, the Viet Cong launched a fierce and unexpected attack on some 30 cities and US bases and hundreds of villages, overrunning the city of Hue and gaining control of the US Embassy in Saigon for several hours. Attempts to capture President Thieu's palace and the local radio headquarters failed, but street

fighting in the southern capital inflicted heavy casualties on both sides.

The Tet offensive shows both strong support for the Viet Cong and that the American 'pacification programme' is faltering. President Johnson faces severe criticism at home as US opinion begins to turn against the war in South-East Asia.

RUNNING FOR COVER Citizens of the South Vietnamese capital flee the fighting in the streets.

US HITS OF THE YEAR

1	HEY JUDE	Beatles
2	I HEARD IT THROUGH THE GRAPEVINE	Marvin Gaye
3	LOVE IS BLUE	Paul Mauriat
4	HONEY	Bobby Goldsboro
5	PEOPLE GOT TO BE FREE	Rascals

US TV HITS

1	The Andy Griffith Show
2	The Lucy Show
3	Gomer Pyle, U S M C
4	Gunsmoke
5	Family Affair

American Fosbury is no flop

27 OCTOBER, MEXICO CITY
The United States has dominated the Mexico Olympics, winning 45 gold medals against the 29 garnered by the Soviet Union, but team officials have been embarrassed by overt reminders of the racial discord back home. During the medals ceremony for the men's 200 metres, the black American sprinters who won gold and bronze, Tommie Smith and John Carlos, raised clenched fists in the Black Power salute as the national anthem was played.

For more conventional reasons another black American stole the show at this year's games. The long-jumper Bob Beamon, taking advantage of the thin air at Mexico City's high altitude, made a gigantic leap into the record books. On his first jump in the medal competition he met the take-off board perfectly and sailed through the air for 8.9 metres (29 ft) – the first jump in history over 8.5 metres (28 ft).

Another first was recorded in the high jump, which Dick Fosbury won for the United States with his unusual 'Fosbury flop', leaping head first with his back just skimming the bar.

NEW TWIST Using a technique now certain to be widely adopted, Dick Fosbury tackles the high jump at the Mexico Olympics in his own distinctive way.

··· SCIENTISTS DEVISE THE EPIDURAL ANAESTHETIC IN ORDER TO EASE THE PAIN OF CHILDBIRTH ···

Hendrix shakes up the world of pop

This has been the year for Jimi Hendrix – perhaps the greatest guitarist rock has ever seen. He arrived in London last year and was an instant hit, forming the Jimi Hendrix Experience (with Noel Redding and Mitch Mitchell) and wowing fans with songs such as 'Hey Joe' and the classic 'Purple Haze'. But 1968 has seen him triumph, with the albums *Axis: Bold As Love* and the sensational *Electric Ladyland* soaring up the charts, making this year his most commercially successful so far.

Hendrix is a revolutionary and influential showman with an intensely sexual and theatrical style. He has taken the electric guitar to new heights of innovative expression, playing it with his teeth or behind his back, and even burning his instrument after a set. Rock greats such as Eric Clapton, Jeff Beck and Jimmy Page hold him in awe, and he has even been compared to Charlie Parker for his original musical interpretations.

SCI-FI FANTASIES WITH A MORAL MESSAGE

OBSCURE VISION *2001: A Space Odyssey* deals with age-old questions about the human condition.

Reality was out of fashion this year. Instead, audiences flocked to see science fiction and the supernatural. Stanley Kubrick's *2001: A Space Odyssey* was the most ambitious (and confusing) science-fiction film yet made, with a plot that began with humankind ascending from the apes and ended in outer space.

Evolution took a different direction in *Planet of the Apes*, a film with an ironic twist, where a post-holocaust society is ruled by apes. Roman Polanski shocked some people – probably not for the last time – with the chilling *Rosemary's Baby*, in which Mia Farrow was sensational as the young wife impregnated by the devil.

1969

DIED

28 Mar: Dwight Eisenhower, US President 1953-61

2 July: Brian Jones, member of the Rolling Stones rock group

21 Oct: Jack Kerouac, US Beat generation author

FIRSTS

8 July: US units withdrawn from Vietnam

14 Oct, UK: 50 pence coins

13 Feb, UK: test-tube fertilisation of human eggs

PUBLISHED

John Fowles, *The French Lieutenant's Woman*

Laurie Lee, *As I Walked Out One Midsummer Morning*

JAILED

10 Mar, Tennessee: assassin James Earl Ray, for 99 years, after pleading guilty to murder of Martin Luther King Jr

The children's animated series Magic Roundabout, *with its surreal, 'trippy' storylines, attracts a cult adult following. Some viewers see the roundabout as a metaphor for an acid trip, and the dialogue from Florence, Dylan, Dougal, Ermintrude and Mr Rusty as containing subtle references to hippy drug culture.*

COMMITTED SUICIDE

19 Jan, Prague: Czech student Jan Palach, who sets fire to himself in protest at Russian occupation of Czechoslovakia

25 Feb, Prague: Jan Zajic, in second burning protest against Russians

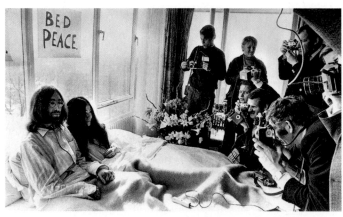

On 27 March, *newly married Beatle John Lennon and his wife, Japanese artist and writer Yoko Ono, hold a press conference to explain their seven-day 'bed-in' protest at war and violence in the world. The couple's unusual honeymoon takes place in the presidential suite at the Hilton Hotel in Amsterdam.*

SENT IN

19 Mar: British troops, to Caribbean island of Anguilla, to depose self-appointed president, Ronald Webster; there is no resistance

15 Aug: British troops, to Northern Ireland, following Protestant–Catholic rioting

PLAYED FOR FREE

30 Jan, London: the Beatles, who – unannounced – perform live on roof of Apple Records offices while filming *Let It Be*

5 July, London: the Rolling Stones, in Hyde Park

ARRESTED

1 Mar, Miami: Jim Morrison of the Doors; he is alleged to have exposed himself during a concert

QUIT

14 Jan, UK: Matt Busby, as manager of highly successful Manchester United soccer team

28 Apr, France: Charles de Gaulle, as president

29 Apr, Northern Ireland: Terence O'Neill, as prime minister

24 June, Rhodesia: Humphrey Gibbs, as governor

ELECTED

1 May, Northern Ireland: James Chichester-Clark, prime minister

15 June, France: Georges Pompidou, president

21 Oct, Germany: Willy Brandt, chancellor

SELECTED

3 Feb, Cairo: Yasser Arafat, as new leader of Palestine Liberation Organisation

SLICKED

28 Jan–9 Feb, California: beaches and birds around Santa Barbara, after underwater oil leak from platform

COUP

1 Sept, Tripoli: led by Colonel Muammar Gadaffi against King Idris

On 17 March, *Golda Meir is sworn in as prime minister of Israel at the age of 71. She has been an active political campaigner throughout her career and has served in the Israeli foreign ministry since 1948.*

ADMITTED GUILT

25 July, Massachusetts: Senator Edward Kennedy, to leaving scene of accident after death of Mary Jo Kopechne in car accident on 18 July at Chappaquiddick

CELEBRATED

20 Nov, Rio de Janeiro: soccer star Pele, who scores his 1000th goal

NEW WORDS

ego trip *n*: self-centred or self-obsessed action

road movie *n*: film in which action follows characters travelling by car or motorbike

APOLLO MEN WALK ON MOON

HISTORIC STEP Neil Armstrong lowers himself from the *Eagle* landing capsule onto the Moon.

20 JULY, HOUSTON, TEXAS

The largest audience for any single event in human history gathered before television screens across the world to watch Neil Armstrong become the first man on the Moon. As he hopped gingerly backwards from the ladder of the *Eagle* lunar capsule, Armstrong announced across nearly half a million kilometres: 'That's one small step for man … one giant leap for mankind.'

Apollo 11 blasted off from Cape Kennedy on 16 July. When the mission reached the Moon, Armstrong and 'Buzz' Aldrin descended to the surface in the *Eagle* capsule. They explored the Sea of Tranquillity, collected rocks, set up measuring equipment, talked by phone to President Nixon and raised the American flag – although the USA is making no claim to the Moon. The third crew member, Mike Collins, orbited overhead in the *Columbia* command module, waiting for the *Eagle* to return so that *Columbia* could begin its 60-hour trip back to Earth.

Their return will be the vindication of the Apollo project which was first announced by President Kennedy in 1961, at a time when the Russians – with the first space satellite, and the first man to orbit the Earth – seemed far ahead in the space race. Apollo (named after the Greek Sun god) was Kennedy's attempt to regain national pride. But the first Apollo mission never left Earth. On 27 January 1967, during an apparently routine check, a vicious electrical fire broke out in the capsule. When the technicians reached it, the entry hatch was red hot. By the time they got it open 14 seconds later, the three astronauts – Ed White, Gus Grissom and Roger Chaffee – were dead.

The whole world was stunned, but, despite this tragedy, by October an unmanned spacecraft, *Surveyor,* was taking photos of the lunar surface to prepare for a possible landing. A year later, *Apollo 7* lifted three astronauts into space for 11 days. *Apollo 8* successfully orbited the Moon on Christmas Eve last year, and the LEM (Lunar Excursion Module) that would actually touch down on the Moon was tested, but not landed, by Apollo missions 9 and 10.

Nevertheless, the triumphal flight of Neil Armstrong and his *Apollo 11* crew came within seconds of disaster this morning. When the *Eagle* landing module was 3 kilometres (2 miles) above the surface, the computers overloaded and Armstrong had to pilot the landing manually, talked down by a young engineer at flight control in Houston. He made it with only 20 seconds of fuel to spare, and after an agonising silence announced to the world: 'The *Eagle* has landed.'

MAN WAS HERE The astronauts took a photo of the first human footprint on the Moon's surface.

HUNGER IS THE KILLER IN NIGERIA'S BITTER WAR

TOO WEAK TO MOVE A starving child is left behind as relief supplies arrive.

1 DECEMBER, LAGOS
Biafra's attempt to secede from Nigeria and win status as an independent nation is taking a huge toll on its people, most of them members of the Ibo tribe.
The civil war that began in 1967 has continued far longer than the embattled Nigerian government expected, and earlier this year the air and sea blockade of arms and food to the Ibo was stepped up.

Biafra, formerly the eastern region of Nigeria, is the traditional home of the Ibo people. As many as a million Ibo fled there from northern Nigeria in 1966 after racial massacres in the north in which up to 30 000 of them were killed by members of rival Hausa tribes.

In May 1967, the head of the eastern region, Odumegwu Ojukwu, declared it independent, and fighting broke out.

Nigeria's government banned humanitarian aid to the Ibo in April this year and, although the ban on medical supplies was lifted in July, Biafrans are still being denied food from outside agencies. More than 300 000 people are now starving in refugee camps.

Last year the Red Cross estimated that 6000 people were dying each day, and the figure is currently rising. Already there have been 1.5 million deaths from hunger, and there seems to be little prospect of the Biafrans sustaining their drive for independence much longer.

··· IN FASHION, THE ANKLE-LENGTH 'MAXI' DRESS TAKES OVER FROM THE MINI SKIRT ···

Army sent to police Northern Ireland

15 AUGUST, BELFAST
Continuing sectarian violence in Northern Ireland has finally forced the hand of the Labour government in London, which today dispatched army troops to the turbulent province in an effort to restore order. Serious riots between Roman Catholics and Protestants broke out at various trouble-spots in mid-July, and three days ago unbridled warfare spilt on to the streets of Londonderry during the Orange Lodge's Apprentice Boys' Parade.

It was soon evident that the policemen of the Royal Ulster Constabulary lacked the resources to control events. Officers of the RUC – viewed by Catholics as a Protestant force – were not even able to enter the 'no-go' area of the Bogside, which is known to Catholics as 'Free Derry'.

UNEASY STANDOFF A British soldier stands guard opposite suspicious locals on a Belfast street.

Eight Catholics and two Protestants have died in the violence since the beginning of July. The British Army will prevent passions from erupting into full civil war, but it remains to be seen whether Westminster's hopes that the army's presence in Northern Ireland will be short-lived are fulfilled.

New York gays fight back at Stonewall

29 JUNE, NEW YORK CITY
Drag queens, gay men and lesbians have been rioting in New York's Greenwich Village following police raids on the Stonewall Inn, a gay bar, on the night of 27 June. Police harassment of homosexuals is common, but this raid met with anger never seen before – police were pelted with bottles and stones. The following night saw more violence, but as well as drama there was high camp – drag queens chanted: 'We are the Stonewall Girls.'

The riots have energised the gay and lesbian community. Militant groups such as the Gay Liberation Front have sprung up in both the United States and Europe, demanding an end to intolerance and police intimidation.

Aircraft get bigger and faster

SHAPE OF THE FUTURE? The sharp-nosed Concorde during its first flight.

2 MARCH, FRANCE
Less than a month after
Boeing's massive 747
aeroplane made its first
flight in Seattle, the Anglo-
French Concorde took off
for the first time at
Toulouse. They represent
diametrically opposed views
of the future of air travel: one
a huge people-carrier, with a
long range but no more
speed than the previous
generation of jets, the other a
futuristic supersonic airliner
with a shorter range and
scarcely 100 seats.

Concorde is the product
of collaboration between
Britain and France, a needle-
nosed marvel of 1960s
technology capable of
cruising at nearly twice the
speed of sound. Aérospatiale
and the British Aircraft

Corporation built it with
government money, and
believe they can sell 400 of
the aircraft around the world.
It is designed to make the
journey between London
and New York in 3 hours 20
minutes, and in the past
aircraft offering greater
speeds have always attracted
new customers. But
Concorde is complex and
will need intensive testing
before it can come into
service. As it took off on its
maiden flight, observers were
impressed by the crackling
roar of its engines, but
environmentalists warned
that the noise was intolerable
and that the 'sonic boom'
released as Concorde breaks
the sound barrier would
damage buildings. Only one
other supersonic transport,

the Russian Tupolev-144, has
been built; it first flew on 31
December last year.

The Boeing 747 is a huge
gamble by its makers, who
invested far more than the
total value of their company
to launch it, with only an
advance order from Pan
American for 25 aircraft to
encourage them. They are
betting on a huge expansion
in the market for air travel,
because the 747 is able to
carry up to 500 passengers
using conventional
technology. With its huge
bulbous nose and engines
slung below the wing like its
predecessor the 707, the 747
is no beauty. Rival 'jumbo
jets' are being built by
Lockheed and McDonnell
Douglas, but Boeing are sure
that they can sell enough
747s to make a profit.

ROOM TO RELAX The 747's wide
body means greater comfort.

British team reaches frozen goal in Arctic

31 MAY, SPITSBERGEN
The four members of the
British Trans-Arctic
Expedition, led by 34-year-
old Wally Herbert, have
become the first men to
cross the frozen surface of
the Arctic Ocean. Using sleds
drawn by 35 huskies, they
took 464 days to travel the
5760 kilometres (3600 miles)
from Point Barrow, Alaska, to
Seven Islands, just north of
Spitsbergen.

Fresh supplies were
dropped at regular intervals
by the Canadian Air Force. At
the beginning and end of the
journey, the expedition was
hampered by the need to
cross ridges or 'waves' of ice
as much as 10 metres (30 ft)
high, which had been
squeezed up by the move-
ments of ocean currents far
underfoot. Other hazards
included the ice's splitting
underneath the expedition's
winter hut in February, and
several encounters with polar
bears. On one occasion a
bear even ran off with the
dogs' rations.

It was only after the
explorers reached the North
Pole in early April (the first
Britons to do so) that they
started to make swifter
progress. They covered up to
20 kilometres (12 miles) a
day over smoother, newly
frozen ice floes. Herbert and
his men are the first North
polar explorers to have used
dog-drawn sleds since 1909,
when Robert Peary was the
first man to reach the Pole.

US HITS OF THE YEAR		
1	AQUARIUS/LET THE SUNSHINE IN	Fifth Dimension
2	IN THE YEAR 2525	Zager & Evans
3	GET BACK	Beatles
4	SUGAR SUGAR	Archies
5	HONKY TONK WOMEN	Rolling Stones

US TV HITS	
1	Rowan & Martin's Laugh-In
2	Gomer Pyle, U S M C
3	Bonanza
4	Mayberry R F D
5	Family Affair

DESPITE DOWNPOUR, PEACE REIGNS AT WOODSTOCK

DOING HER OWN THING One Woodstock devotee seems to feel or hear more than the fans around her.

20 AUGUST, NEW YORK STATE
In a sea of mud not far from the artists' colony of Woodstock, 400 000 young people have joined together in a weekend festival of love and music that has awed their elders. Torrential rain, mudbaths and a lack of facilities failed to dispel the good vibrations.

Billed as an 'Aquarian Exposition' by its four young promoters, the festival featured music by more than 32 rock and folk groups including Janis Joplin, Jimi Hendrix, Joan Baez, Arlo Guthrie, the Who, Jefferson Airplane, and Crosby, Stills and Nash.

The organisers expected about 50 000 people a day; in the event, about six times as many turned up. Traffic around the 225-hectare (600-acre) site ground to a halt, and toilets soon gave out. The rain started on Friday night, knocking down tents and makeshift shelters, drenching food and clothing. But despite the ankle-deep mud and a sleepless night, the peaceful atmosphere at the festival continued.

Local residents noticed marijuana being smoked openly and young people skinny-dipping in nearby ponds; some questioned the absence of arrests. But the local sheriff said: 'This is the nicest bunch of kids I've ever dealt with.' On Sunday evening a 19-hour marathon of music began, and the rain started again.

Cult is linked to Hollywood murders

KILLING INFLUENCE Manson's followers saw him as a kind of prophet; his hold over them was huge.

12 OCTOBER, CALIFORNIA
Police have arrested cult leader Charles Manson and 23 of his followers, known as the 'family', in a raid on the Barker Ranch in Death Valley. The group has been under suspicion for a range of crimes, from car theft, drug dealing and arson to the possession of illegal firearms, but there are now hints that it may be connected with something far more sinister – a series of chilling murders in Los Angeles.

The first of these atrocities took place in Beverly Hills on 8 August. Assailants broke into the exclusive Beverly Hills home of Sharon Tate, actress and wife of movie director Roman Polanski, and butchered her along with three of her guests and a passer-by. The killers scrawled the word 'pig' on a wall, using Tate's blood. The murder aroused particular repugnance as Tate was eight months pregnant at the time. Manson is also being linked with the murder of the wealthy supermarket tycoon Leno LaBianca and his wife Rosemary, which took place two days after the Tate killings. None of the cult members knew any of the victims.

Nixon takes office, facing a tough future

20 JANUARY, WASHINGTON DC
Richard Milhous Nixon was sworn in today as thirty-seventh President of the United States, following his narrow election victory over Democrat Hubert Humphrey last November. It was the second stab at the presidency for the 55-year-old Californian, who lost the 1960 race to John F Kennedy. But Nixon is no stranger to the White House – he was vice-president twice in the 1950s under 'Ike' Eisenhower.

Nixon, whose political career has not been without controversy, will have little time to rest on his laurels. He is under intense pressure to deliver on his election pledges, especially his promise to end US involvement in the Vietnam War. Anti-war protesters today made clear the strength of feeling on the issue among many Americans.

Television finds fresh appeal

This year saw the launch of two very different but equally innovative television series – one on either side of the Atlantic. In Britain the eccentric yet radical comedy series *Monty Python's Flying Circus* was first broadcast by the BBC on 5 October. The humour is typically 'British', paying particular attention to the ridiculous and the anarchic. The show is made up of a series of sketches which are loosely tied together with a running joke, often carrying on into and beyond the credits. The sketches are written and performed by a group of talented young actors.

Targeted at a different audience – pre-school children – a new educational series called *Sesame Street* was premiered in the United States on 10 November. The hour-long programme has a fast-paced delivery and uses a variety of teaching techniques – some borrowed from advertising. Repetition helps teach numbers and letters, and there are frequent songs and funny sketches, often involving 'Muppet' characters.

FIVE INTO ONE 'Whicker Island' is one of the Python's best-loved sketches.

Developed by Joan Ganz Cooney, executive director of the newly formed Children's Television Workshop, *Sesame Street* sets a new standard for children's television.

··· 1–6 NOV, COPENHAGEN: A SIX-DAY 'SEX FAIR' OF PORNOGRAPHY IS HELD ···

YEAR OF THE LAWBREAKER

Outlaws were everywhere: the big box-office hit was *Butch Cassidy and the Sundance Kid*, with Paul Newman and Robert Redford as easy-going bank-robbers. A more realistic Wild West was on show in *The Wild Bunch*, which broke new ground in cinema violence. Peter Fonda and Dennis Hopper drove across America with a consignment of LSD in *Easy Rider*. *Midnight Cowboy* was about a seedier kind of outlaw, with Jon Voight trying to make it as a gigolo in New York City. None of these was as unsettling as the horrors of English public schools evoked in Lindsay Anderson's *If....* For light relief, Barbra Streisand belted out the songs in *Hello Dolly!* – last of the big musicals.

MODERN OUTLAWS Easy riders on the road to the heart of the USA.

Czechs gain sporting revenge

PRIDE AT STAKE Political foes play hard when Soviet (l) meets Czech.

28 MARCH, STOCKHOLM The Czechoslovakian ice hockey team has failed in its bid to win the world championship, but no one in Prague seems to care. The only important games to the country's fanatical hockey supporters were the two group matches against the Soviet Union, held in almost universal contempt since the crushing of the 'Prague Spring' eight months ago. The Czechs won the two matches 2–0 and 4–3, and after the second victory deliriously happy men and women of all ages swarmed into Prague's central square where, beneath the statue of St Wenceslas, they chanted anti-Soviet slogans.

Czechoslovakia's two defeats against Sweden condemned them to the bronze medal position in the championship. The Soviet Union won the gold, finshing top of the table, one place above Sweden, after beating Canada in their last match. The result is uncannily like that at last year's Winter Olympics, when losing to Sweden in the last game, coupled with a Soviet defeat of Canada, cost the Czechs the gold medal.

1970

DIED
25 Feb: Mark Rothko, US artist
7 June: E M Forster, British author
18 Sept: Jimi Hendrix, US rock musician
9 Nov: Charles de Gaulle, French statesman

ELECTED
19 June, UK: Conservative Party; Edward Heath is new prime minister
5 Oct, Chile: Salvador Allende Gossens, president

On 3 July, *Australian tennis player Margaret Court (above) beats American Billie Jean King in the longest women's singles final in the history of the Wimbledon tournament. In a tense and thrilling match, Court wins 14–12, 11–9.*

QUIT
20 Dec, Warsaw: Vladislav Gomulka, Polish Communist Party leader, following rioting; Edward Gierek succeeds him

KILLED
22 May, Israel: eight children, in rocket attack on school bus by Popular Front for the Liberation of Palestine (PFLP)
5 Sept, Italy: Austrian racing driver Jochen Rindt, in crash while qualifying for Italian Grand Prix

LOST
23 Jan, London: passengers' luggage at Heathrow airport, when first Boeing 747 jumbo jet lands; airport staff are not used to processing so many passengers at once

BANNED
2 Jan, UK: Manchester United soccer star George Best, for one month, by Football Association because of 'disreputable behaviour'

COMPLETED
21 July, Egypt: Aswan Dam

SURRENDERED
12 Jan, Nigeria: separatists in Biafra, to Nigerian government

BESTSELLER
7 Mar, UK: the New English Bible, which sells one million copies in its first week of its publication

On 21 June, *Brazil wins the World Cup soccer tournament for the third time, beating Italy 4–1 in the final in the Azteca Stadium, Mexico City. The tournament, played in extremely hot weather and at a high altitude, is the first to be televised live and in colour around the world.*

CHAMPION
16 Feb, New York City: Joe Frazier, who wins world heavyweight boxing championship when he knocks out Jimmy Ellis

COUP
8 June, Argentina: against President Juan Carlos Ongania
13 Nov, Syria: led by defence minister, General Hafez el-Assad

ACCUSED
26 May, Colombia: England soccer captain Bobby Moore, of stealing jewellery; he is cleared on 20 Aug

REDUCED
1 Jan, UK: voting age, from 21 to 18

CELEBRATING
19 Aug, UK: British ITV soap opera *Coronation Street*, which screens its 1000th episode

On 4 October, *rock-blues singer Janis Joplin is found dead of a heroin overdose at the age of 27. Joplin, who often swigged from a bottle of Southern Comfort when she sang on stage, was one of the first successful white blues singers – but was also known for drug and alcohol abuse.*

FIRSTS
2 Aug, Northern Ireland: use of rubber bullets, by British troops in Belfast
27 Nov, London: demonstration by Gay Liberation Front

INDEPENDENT
10 Oct: Fiji, of Britain

COLLAPSED
15 Oct, Melbourne: Australia's biggest bridge, the West Gate Bridge, killing 33 people

NEW WORDS
black hole *n*: in space, exhausted and collapsed star that sucks in light and matter
jet lag *n*: tiredness and general malaise resulting from switching time zones during long-haul flights

Apollo 13 crew survive space explosion

HOME AGAIN Visibly relieved, the *Apollo 13* astronauts float next to their capsule, waiting to be picked up.

16 APRIL, HOUSTON, TEXAS
The astronauts of *Apollo 13* – the US
Moon rocket that was so nearly lost in
space – splashed down in the South
Pacific today within sight of a flotilla of
rescue ships and helicopters.

The first sign of trouble with the mission came three days ago, when Jack Swigert, Fred Haise and mission commander Jim Lovell were already 330 000 kilometres (206 000 miles) from Earth. An explosion in one of the main oxygen tanks left the command module without power or air. Fortunately the lunar landing module *Aquarius* had its own power and oxygen supplies, and in desperation the men decided to use it as an extraterrestrial lifeboat.

Swigert was a last-minute substitute for Ken Mattingley, who had come down with measles. But this turned out to be a stroke of luck: Swigert had written *Apollo 13*'s emergency manual.

If the crew could not control the command module, *Apollo 13*'s trajectory would take it round the Moon, shooting off into deep space. But they used *Aquarius*'s small landing engines to drag the command module into a new orbit that would catapult them back to Earth.

Sixty-three hours later, exhausted and irritable, the men crawled back into the command module, jettisoned *Aquarius* and made a perfect re-entry into the Earth's atmosphere.

··· THE WORLD TRADE CENTER IN NEW YORK CITY BECOMES THE WORLD'S TALLEST BUILDING AT 411 M (1350 FT) ···

Balls now in women's court

Are women being castrated by society? That is the what the Australian academic Germaine Greer argues in her book *The Female Eunuch*.

The book has caused a storm – partly because its author writes candidly about sex. She says that we need changes in social structure, in relations between men and women and in the way women perceive themselves.

Women have been rebelling against negative stereotypes for many years. In Greer they have found a spokeswoman who is both opinionated and articulate.

National Guard opens fire on student protesters

5 MAY, KENT, OHIO
Four students at Kent State
University were shot dead
yesterday by National
Guardsmen. Students had been protesting at the US invasion of Cambodia when the troops opened fire into the unarmed crowd. Ten other students were wounded. According to student leaders, the four who were killed were bystanders.

The demonstration had turned violent after students started throwing firebombs and bottles at police officers. This was then followed by three days of rioting. Ohio state governor James Rhodes ordered the National Guard

SHOOT TO KILL Students show their horror in the aftermath of the shootings.

on to the university campus, and declared: 'We are going to eradicate the problem.'

Today students at Kent are in mourning for their fallen classmates. Shock has been felt around the United States as people question how such a demonstration could end in a bloodbath.

Palestine terror group blows up three planes

12 SEPTEMBER, JORDAN
The Popular Front for the Liberation of Palestine (PFLP) is being held responsible for the blowing-up of three hijacked passenger aircraft in the Jordanian desert today.

In a synchronised operation, members of the organisation seized control of three Boeing 707s bound for New York and rerouted them to a military airstrip at Dawson's Field, near Zerqa. Some 600 passengers and crew were evacuated before the aeroplanes were blown up; most of them have been released, but the Palestinians are still

holding a further 56 hostages in a secret hiding-place.

This latest manoeuvre has been the culmination of a fortnight of mounting terror. On 6 September, Leila Khaled and a male accomplice failed to hijack an El Al Boeing 707. In a struggle inside the plane, Khaled was pinned down by passengers while her partner was shot by his own gun in a fight with one of the plane's stewards.

The PFLP is now demanding that Khaled be released from police custody in London before it surrenders any of its British hostages.

BLOWN AWAY Destroying the hijacked aeroplanes was a spectacularly pointless gesture of defiance.

End of Beatles' long and winding road

9 APRIL, LONDON
Paul McCartney is leaving the Beatles and launching a legal action to bring an end to the greatest pop group in the world. His High Court writ to dissolve 'the business carried on … as the Beatles & Co' coincides with his announcement of his new LP, called *McCartney*, made with his wife, Linda.

Asked if the pair would become 'the next John and Yoko', Paul replied: 'No, we'll be the first Paul and Linda.' He said that the break was due partly to business and musical differences, but mostly because he was having a better time with his family than with the group.

Insiders blame the growing tension between McCartney and his songwriting partner John Lennon. Officially the pair have collaborated on all the Beatles' songs, but they have been more or less writing separately since the *Revolver* album came out in 1966. McCartney said that he enjoys working solo, and that although he still loves John he cannot foresee any future for the Lennon–McCartney partnership.

··· 19 NOV, EAST PAKISTAN: 150000 PEOPLE ARE KILLED BY A TYPHOON AND TIDAL WAVE ···

Oh! Calcutta brings nudity to the London stage

27 JULY, LONDON
After months of controversy, press hysteria and the threat of prosecution, Kenneth Tynan's erotic revue *Oh! Calcutta* opened in London tonight. The only theatre that would take the show, which features blasphemy and full frontal nudity, was the Roundhouse, a converted engine shed in Camden.

Tynan, a celebrated theatre critic and literary manager of Britain's National Theatre, first devised a show

which would 'use artistic means to achieve erotic stimulation' in 1966. He solicited sketches and sexual fantasies from famous authors and playwrights, including Samuel Beckett, Tennessee Williams and David Mercer, although most never made it into the final revue.

When *Oh! Calcutta* first opened on Broadway in June last year, the *New York Times* described it as 'the kind of show to give pornography a dirty name'.

STRIP TEASE In this show, the cast never stays dressed for very long.

Jacklin tees off to US success

**21 JUNE, MINNESOTA
US golfers have had to play
second fiddle to an overseas
player for only the second
time in the long history of
the US Open championship.**

Tony Jacklin, the boyish
star from Potter's Bar, north
of London, has become the
first British player ever to
capture the title. He has done
so with great aplomb –
finishing seven strokes ahead
of the field at the Hazeltine
National Golf Club at
Chaska, Minnesota.

In cold, blustery winds,
which are familiar to British
golfers, Jacklin took the lead
with an opening round of 71
and never lost it.

The reason for Jacklin's
control of the match was a

HERO'S RETURN Jacklin shares his triumph with his wife and baby son.

masterful short game and
confident, steely putting. He
took only 113 putts for the
whole of the four days and
finished each round under
par, a feat which has only
been achieved once before.

Having won the British
Open last year, Jacklin now
joins all-time greats such
as Bobby Jones and Gene
Sarazen in the rare distinction
of holding both US and
British titles at the same time.

Floppy disk is a computer revolution

US business giant IBM has
introduced a computer that
can store data on so-called
'floppy disks'. Its new 3740
model records and stores
information on the flat,
flexible disks which are light
and easy to transport.

The invention dates to
1950, when Dr Yoshuiro
Nakamats of Imperial
University, Tokyo, patented
his concept of a magnetic
disk for recording data. A
prolific inventor, with more
than 2000 patents to his
name, Nakamats licensed the
technology to IBM.

Floppy disks are still not
able to store very much
information, but they are
better, faster and less bulky
than the magnetic tapes and
punched cards that have
been used by computers for
storing programmes or saving
back-up files. These systems
were cumbersome, and even
the super-fast tape readers
are not as quick as the new
floppy disks.

IBM believes that its
20-centimetre (8-in) wide
disks represent a definite leap
forwards in the world of
computer technology.

ALL'S FAIR IN LOVE AND WAR

SO IN LOVE O'Neal and McGraw.

'Love means never having to
say you're sorry' – according to
Love Story. The producers of
this film certainly didn't have
anything to feel sorry about
with this massive hit, which
showed that there was still a
market for raw slush; Ryan
O'Neal and Ali McGraw were
the tragic young lovers. There
was still plenty of disillusion
around: in *Five Easy Pieces*,

middle-class drifter Jack
Nicholson left a succession of
girlfriends in the lurch.

Public disillusion with the
Vietnam War was reflected in
a crop of war movies. Among
the best were *M*A*S*H* (set in
the Korean War) and *Catch-22*
(World War II) based on the
classic Joseph Heller novel.
Meanwhile *Airport* inaugurated
a wave of disaster movies.

US HITS OF THE YEAR		US TV HITS	
1 BRIDGE OVER TROUBLED WATER	Simon & Garfunkel	1 Rowan & Martin's Laugh-In	
2 I'LL BE THERE	Jackson Five	2 Gunsmoke	
3 RAINDROPS KEEP FALLIN' ON MY HEAD	B J Thomas	3 Bonanza	
4 (THEY LONG TO BE) CLOSE TO YOU	Carpenters	4 Mayberry R F D	
5 MY SWEET LORD/ISN'T IT A PITY	George Harrison	5 Family Affair	

HIGH TECH Operators of the IBM
3740 enjoy their 'paperless' office.

1971

DIED

10 Jan: Gabrielle 'Coco' Chanel, French couturier
16 Apr: Igor Stravinsky, Russian composer
3 June: Jim Morrison, US rock musician
11 Sept: Nikita Khrushchev, Soviet politician

SENT HOME

24 Sept, UK: 90 Soviet diplomats, accused of spying

PLAYED FOR FREE

1 Aug, New York City: rock musicians, in Concert for Bangladesh organised by ex-Beatle George Harrison; on stage are Ravi Shankar, Eric Clapton and Ringo Starr

On 31 December, *Austrian diplomat Kurt Waldheim takes office as secretary-general of the United Nations, replacing U Thant. After serving as a Nazi officer in World War II, Waldheim rose through the ranks of the Austrian foreign ministry to become permanent representative at the United Nations in 1960.*

The Ferrari Daytona sports car goes on sale, launching a new type of 'supercar' and bringing the qualities of a racing car to everyday driving. The aerodynamic design helps the Daytona to reach a top speed of 275 km/h (170 mph). Italian car designer Enzo Ferrari founded his company in 1929.

COVERED UP

26 July, French Riviera: topless women sunbathers, on orders of French riot police

CEASED FIRE

17 Dec: India and Pakistan, after two-week war that ended in defeat for Pakistan

DISQUALIFIED

15 Aug, UK: British showjumper Harvey Smith, as winner of British Showjumping Derby, when he makes a two-fingered 'V for Victory' gesture that is misinterpreted

MARRIED

12 May, France: Mick Jagger and Bianca Perez Morena de Macias

MADE EASIER

1 Jan, UK: divorce, under new laws – 'irretrievable breakdown of marriage' becomes legal grounds

FOUNDED

Canada: Greenpeace, environmental campaign group, by Canadian opponents of US nuclear testing

FIRST

31 July: ride in a vehicle on the Moon's surface – US astronauts David Scott and James Irwin go for a drive in a 'Moon rover'

KILLED

2 Jan, Glasgow: 66 football fans, in crush when barriers collapse at Ibrox Park football ground during Rangers vs Celtic match
9 Dec, Dhaka: 300 children, when an orphanage is hit by Indian bombs during Indian–Pakistani war

FIRST NIGHT

12 Oct, New York City: *Jesus Christ Superstar*, rock musical, with lyrics by Tim Rice and music by Andrew Lloyd Webber

SENTENCED

3 Mar, Johannesburg: Winnie Mandela, to one year in prison, for receiving guests at home contrary to government order
29 Mar, US: Charles Manson and three accomplices, to death, for murder of Sharon Tate and others

The invention of the microprocessor by Intel in the United States promises drastic reductions in the size of computers. Built into a tiny chip of silicon, the microprocessor (shown above, magnified) is a single integrated circuit that can perform basic computing functions.

PROCLAIMED

26 Mar, East Pakistan: independent state of Bangladesh, by Sheikh Mujibur Rahman; civil war breaks out

LAUNCHED

UK: the Open University

NEW WORDS

artificial intelligence *n*: human powers of reason in a machine
no-go area *n*: place that it is forbidden or too dangerous to enter
oil spill *n*: unintentional release of crude oil, generally into the sea from a ship or drilling platform

Bangladesh wins independence from Pakistan

16 DECEMBER, DHAKA
Pakistan's army has been routed by Indian forces after two weeks of fighting in the newly declared nation of Bangladesh. The Indian government gave official recognition to the new state, the former province of East Pakistan, separated from West Pakistan by 1600 kilometres (1000 miles) of Indian territory.

Last January the separatist People's League won an overwhelming majority in East Pakistan in the national elections. However, Pakistan's President Yahya Khan suspended the national legislature and sent the army into the eastern province. Civil war erupted on 26 March after a clandestine radio broadcast declared the independence of Bangladesh. An estimated one million Bengalis were killed, and by the beginning of this month up to 12 million refugees had poured over the border into India. On 3 December the Indian prime minister, Indira Gandhi, ordered the army to defend Bangladesh. This is the third time since partition that Pakistan – despite US support – has been defeated by India.

FIRE POWER A Bangladeshi commander demonstrates mines and grenades.

··· US TENNIS PLAYER BILLIE JEAN KING BECOMES THE FIRST FEMALE ATHLETE TO EARN $100 000 A YEAR ···

The bridge that crossed the Atlantic Ocean

7 OCTOBER, ARIZONA
London Bridge has been dismantled stone by stone and reassembled in a desert town in the United States. The bridge, remembered in the rhyme 'London Bridge is falling down', certainly puts the new resort of Lake Havasu City on the map. Oil tycoon Robert P McCulloch, who has invested $10 million in the new town, announced today that the Lord Mayor of London would formally open the bridge next week. However, some people are disappointed that it is not Tower Bridge, which stays in London as one of the city's prime tourist attractions.

WATER FEATURE London Bridge, built in 1831, now spans a man-made inlet of the Colorado River.

Christmas bombing in Belfast claims 15 lives

15 DECEMBER, BELFAST
There is little peace and goodwill for the battered people of Belfast this Christmas. The current spate of bombings – carried out by both Republican and Loyalist paramilitaries – culminated today in a ruthless strike by Loyalists at McGurk's Bar in central Belfast, in which 15 people were killed. Rescue operations were hampered as the army came under fire and rival crowds fought in the streets.

The past year has been the most violent since the recent 'troubles' began in 1968. The crisis intensified in August when the Ulster authorities introduced the new policy of 'internment' – which allows the police to detain suspects without trial for up to two weeks. On the day that the announcement was made, a total of 300 people were arrested – and riots broke out in the Republican areas of Belfast, Newry and Londonderry.

Hot pants, long legs

Long legs and a pert behind are this season's essential style accessories, as otherwise the latest fashion must – hot pants – looks less than fetching.

After the flop of the calf-length midi skirt – dubbed 'instant age' by the press – manufacturers realised that it was not going to be easy to entice women away from the leggy look. So they came up with hot pants – tiny shorts that just cover the behind. Women enjoy wearing them, men love them, and they even have the royal seal of approval – they have been allowed into the royal enclosure at this year's Ascot races, as long as the 'general effect' is pleasing.

This year's other success story is the return of the wedge shoe – a feature of the 'tarty' 1940s look. Now it has become popularly known as the platform shoe. Another trendy item of footwear is the knee-length 'kinky' boot with long laces. Either way, teamed with a pair of tiny, shiny shorts, the effect is of very long legs indeed.

The death of the midi was an expensive lesson for the clothing industry, proving that women will not accept a new look simply because it is supposed to be trendy. Instead of dictating style, the fashion houses now have to anticipate the market and look at what people are wearing on the streets.

BARE NECESSITY Hot pants became a common sight in the streets and discos.

··· NONTUPLETS, FIVE BOYS AND FOUR GIRLS, ARE BORN TO GERALDINE BRODERICK IN AUSTRALIA – SIX SURVIVE ···

Britain conforms to decimal currency

CASHING IN Lord Fiske, head of the Decimal Currency Board, goes shopping.

15 FEBRUARY, LONDON
Despite warnings that elderly people will never understand it, and that shops will use it to increase prices, **Britain has adopted decimal currency.** Out goes an ancient coinage based on pounds, shillings and pence, which included such well-loved oddities as the half-crown (two shillings and sixpence) but no crown. The pound has survived, but, no longer divided into 20 shillings, it is now made up of 100 'new pence'. The new penny is worth more than twice as much as the old one, while the new ten pence coin is the same as the old florin (two shillings).

Long planning went into the changeover, but there has been little public enthusiasm. Many market traders and shopkeepers swear they will never change to the decimal system, which was adopted in France in 1799. In fact, the new money will make most calculations easier.

Parachute skyjacker disappears

25 NOVEMBER, WASHINGTON STATE
The hunt is on for a daredevil skyjacker who last night parachuted from a Boeing 727 with $200000. During the flight the skyjacker slipped a stewardess a note claiming that his briefcase contained a bomb. He asked for $200000 – and a parachute. The aeroplane stopped at Seattle to swop passengers for the money, and when it was back in the sky the man – who called himself Dan B Cooper – leapt into the freezing night.

Led Zeppelin pave the way to heaven – or hell

The year opened with Andy Williams deposed from the top of the album chart by George Harrison's debut *All Things Must Pass*. With the Beatles still at each other's throats, Paul McCartney's new band, Wings, released their first album *Wildlife* in November. This was also the year that Led Zeppelin released their fourth LP, containing the rambling epic track 'Stairway To Heaven'. The song quickly became an all-time favourite and added to the band's decadent allure. Many Christians condemned its pagan lyrics as pure evil, and believed that satanic incantations could be heard if the album was played backwards.

Another highlight of the year was the release of Marvin Gaye's mould-breaking LP *What's Going On*. It was a concept album – the first to be produced by a black soul artist – and gave Gaye two top-ten hits almost immediately – 'Mercy Mercy Me (The Ecology)' and 'Inner City Blues (Make Me Wanna Holler)'.

IN CONCERT Led Zeppelin's Robert Plant and Jimmy Page.

Video moves into the home

20 MAY, LONDON
The first video cassette recorder (VCR) designed for the home market hit the shops today. The Philips N1500 costs £388.62, and plays a 1-centimetre (½-in) tape with a maximum duration of one hour. Recording anything longer will mean changing the tape.

Sony has already launched a similar machine, the U-matic, but that is aimed at professional or studio users. Philips, which unveiled its machine at a press conference at London's Savoy Hotel, claims that its VCR is 'the start of a revolution in home entertainment'.

Video recording using magnetic tape has been in use in television studios in the United States since the mid-1950s and in Britain since 1958. The BBC's first device used 1-cm (½-in) tape running at 500 cm (200 in) per second.

US HITS OF THE YEAR

1	JOY TO THE WORLD	*Three Dog Night*
2	MAGGIE MAY/REASON TO BELIEVE	*Rod Stewart*
3	IT'S TOO LATE/FEEL THE EARTH MOVE	*Carole King*
4	ONE BAD APPLE	*Osmonds*
5	HOW CAN YOU MEND A BROKEN HEART	*Bee Gees*

US TV HITS

1	*Marcus Welby, M D*
2	*The Flip Wilson Show*
3	*Here's Lucy*
4	*Ironside*
5	*Gunsmoke*

DISTURBING VISIONS OF THE PRESENT AND THE FUTURE

For the first time in cinema history audiences saw a kiss between two men, in John Schlesinger's tense *Sunday, Bloody Sunday*. A sensitive study of the British middle classes in love, the film starred Glenda Jackson, Peter Finch and Murray Head. Clint Eastwood made his directing debut in *Play Misty for Me*, a gripping tale of a disc jockey who is stalked by a female fan. He played the lead in the movie and also starred in the box-office smash *Dirty Harry*, playing a tough San Francisco cop who is not afraid to step outside the

bounds of the law. Gene Hackman gave a polished performance as Popeye Doyle in *The French Connection*, a stylish, violent thriller with one of cinema's classic car chases. Stanley Kubrick's *A Clockwork Orange* caused a stir with its portrayal of brutal torture set to sublime classical music. Prophesying a harsh urban society in which gangs of delinquent youths amuse themselves by committing rape and murder, the futuristic film was banned in Britain and many other countries – despite protests that it was in fact a moral fable.

JOLLY SADIST Malcolm McDowell gave a powerful performance in *A Clockwork Orange*.

1972

BORN
6 Mar: Shaquille O'Neil, US basketball player
21 Sept: Liam Gallagher, British rock musician

DIED
2 May: J Edgar Hoover, head of FBI since 1924
28 May: Duke of Windsor, ex-King of England

DECLARED
22 Jan, USA: a woman's right to choose abortion
9 Feb, UK: state of emergency by government to deal with power shortage caused by miners' strike

ABOLISHED
Vatican: obligatory tonsure for new priests and monks, by Pope Paul VI

Bob Marley, Jamaican reggae musician, lead singer of the Wailers, is the first reggae star to break into the mainstream. This year he is signed to the Island record label; next year's album Catch a Fire *is a big hit. Marley's lyrics express his trenchant views on black history and his Rastafarian religious beliefs.*

The US Environmental Protection Agency bans the insecticide DDT (above, being sprayed on a beach in 1945) after it is proven to be toxic. For years, in the face of increasing evidence to the contrary, the government has maintained that the pesticide is safe, but its widespread use in farming has damaged wildlife, and poisonous chemical residues have ended up in the human food chain.

ELECTED
13 Mar, India: the Congress Party, led by Indira Gandhi
7 Nov, USA: Richard Nixon, as President for a second term

FIRSTS
London: CT scanner – provides cross-sectional X-rays of human brain
Munich: US team not to win Olympic gold medal for basketball – it loses 51–50 to Russia
USA: Nike running shoes

LAST
11 Aug: US ground troops leave Vietnam

OPENED
Apr: the Berlin Wall for eight days, so that West Berliners can visit relatives over Easter

RECORD
7–19 Dec: *Apollo 17* astronauts spend 75 hours on the Moon

ENDED
27 Jan: World War II, for Shoichi Yokoi of Japan, who gives himself up on Guam Island in the Pacific, where he has hidden for 27 years

PUBLISHED
Richard Adams, *Watership Down*
Frederick Forsyth, *The Odessa File*
James Herriot, *All Creatures Great and Small*

DESTROYED
29 Jan: *Queen Elizabeth*, 83 600-ton liner once the pride of the British fleet, by fire in Hong Kong harbour
23 Dec, Nicaragua: Managua, capital city, by earthquake; kills 6000 people

KILLED
30 May, Israel: 25 people at Tel Aviv airport, by Japanese 'Red Brigade' terrorists armed with machine-guns and grenades
8 June, Rhodesia: 400 miners, in a pit explosion

DAMAGED
21 May, Rome: Michelangelo's *Pietà*, with a hammer, by deranged Australian Laszlo Tuth

BANNED
28 Sept, Munich Olympics: black US athletes Vincent Matthews and Wayne Collet, who are sent home for yawning during the national anthem
17 Oct, South Korea: long hair, by President Park Chung; 20000 youths queue to have their hair cut

On 22 January, the Treaty of Rome is signed, taking Britain, Denmark, Norway and Ireland into the Common Market. British MPs voted in favour last October (above). When Britain last applied, in 1966, French leader Charles de Gaulle vetoed the entry; since his retirement in 1969 there has been a new mood of expansion.

EXHIBITED
London: treasures of Tutankhamun's tomb, at the British Museum

NEW WORDS
acid rain *n*: rain containing acidic pollutants, mainly sulphur dioxide and nitrogen oxide
veggieburger *n*: vegetarian variant of hamburger

FIREBOMBS RAIN TERROR ON VIETNAM

HAUNTING IMAGE Children flee after their village of Trang Bang was mistakenly bombed by the Americans.

This spring the world was shocked by a picture of a young Vietnamese girl who had been hit by napalm (an incendiary liquid or gel) and was running naked in terror along a road away from the fighting near An Loc – an image that encapsulated the cruelty of the Vietnam War.

The use of napalm in incendiary bombs and flamethrowers is not new, and the impression given by the media that its use in Vietnam has led to thousands of villagers being burnt to death is false; nevertheless, it is hard to square the use of napalm with the clause of the Hague Convention that prohibits methods of warfare that cause 'unnecessary suffering'.

One of the worst incidents took place at Dak Song, north of Saigon, in December 1967, when Viet Cong guerrillas attacked the hamlet with flamethrowers, killing 252 villagers and leaving hundreds with severe burns. The number of people to have been killed by napalm is almost impossible to estimate: napalm burns are so deep that many victims die before getting medical attention. Those who survive live in constant torture.

This year the United Nations passed a resolution condemning the use of all incendiary weapons, but a ban has still to enter international law.

··· SALLY PRIESAND IS THE FIRST FEMALE RABBI, AT ISAAC M WISE TEMPLE, CINCINNATI, OHIO ···

Amin expels Uganda's Asians

6 AUGUST, KAMPALA
General Idi Amin today announced plans to expel Uganda's 50 000 British-passport-holding Asians from the country over the next three months. They will be sent to Britain. Although Asians form the most well-off section of Ugandan society, Amin accuses them of 'sabotaging the economy'.

Idi Amin seized power from President Obote in January last year. Partly because of his rejection of Obote's socialist policies, and partly because he had served in the British Army, Britain and the USA gave him a warm reception. However, Amin began a series of brutal 'reforms', suspending democratic rights and giving himself and the military almost unlimited powers. The Political Activities Decree ended all constitutional rights; another decree gave the army power to shoot on sight.

Amin's increasingly repressive regime has meant that international opinion is turning against him. But his power can hardly be contained, and thousands of people are already known to have been murdered by his soldiers.

INTO EXILE Uganda's Asian population had been settled in East Africa for more than 100 years.

British troops kill 13 on Derry's bloodiest Sunday

30 JANUARY, LONDONDERRY
British troops, sent to Northern Ireland more than two years ago to keep the peace, opened fire on civil rights marchers in Londonderry's Bogside area today, killing 13 of the Roman Catholic demonstrators and wounding another 17. A dispute has begun as to whether the paratroopers committed wanton murder or only acted after being fired upon themselves.

No matter how that question is resolved by later inquiries, 'Bloody Sunday' is certain to inflame the Irish Republican Army and encourage it to step up its campaign for a united, independent Ireland. Nationalist opinion in the province has become hostile towards the British government for the introduction, apparently at the behest of Protestant loyalists, of its internment policy, under which terrorist suspects can be detained without trial for an indefinite period. By the end of last year 1576 arrests had been made under the

MEAN STREETS Derry residents erected barricades as fighting broke out out after the killings.

new powers, and most of the 600 or so suspects now held in detention centres are Catholics.

The Derry killings, signalling the increasing difficulty of maintaining

order, have raised expectations that the British government in London will suspend Northern Ireland's legislative assembly at Stormont and impose direct rule from Whitehall on the province.

··· THE VOLKSWAGEN BEETLE BECOMES THE BIGGEST-SELLING CAR EVER, OUTSTRIPPING THE FORD MODEL T ···

Nixon and Mao shake hands

HISTORIC TALKS Nixon, seen here on the Great Wall, exhorted China to join the USA in the 'long march' to world peace.

28 FEBRUARY, BEIJING
President Nixon today ended the first ever official visit to China by a US leader. The historic trip is being hailed as a diplomatic triumph for Nixon and

a landmark in relations between the West and Asia's Communist giant.

Chinese premier Zhou Enlai welcomed President Nixon with full honours in Beijing on 21 February, but perhaps the most symbolic moment of the visit came when the head of the world's greatest capitalist state shook hands with Mao Zedong, the 79-year old founder of the People's Republic.

Before the President flew home, Nixon and Zhou summed up the 'serious and frank talks' held amid all the banquets and sightseeing. They agree to differ over the breakaway island of Taiwan and have pledged to boost cultural and scientific contacts. For the time being, though, full US recognition of Red China remains on hold.

Watergate is bugged

17 JUNE, WASHINGTON DC
The Democratic Party has demanded an explanation for a thwarted break-in earlier today at its offices in the city's Watergate complex. Five burglars were caught red-handed in the act of planting bugging devices in the headquarters of the Democratic National Committee, which runs the presidential election campaign of Democrat contender Hubert Humphrey.

Those arrested include James McCord, an ex-CIA man currently working for the Committee to Re-elect the President (CREEP), a secretive organisation set up by the Republican Party to help President Nixon win this year's election. Senior Republicans deny any connection with the burglary.

TERROR STRIKES MUNICH OLYMPICS

6 SEPTEMBER, MUNICH
The Olympic Games were suspended yesterday after Palestinian terrorists stormed the Israeli quarters in the athletes' village. Although the village was heavily guarded by plain-clothes policemen, eight Palestinians from the Black September group scaled a high wire-mesh security fence at 4.30 am.

The hooded terrorists entered the Israeli compound by an unlocked door and opened fire with sub-machine-guns, killing a weightlifter and a wrestling coach before taking captive nine team members. Holding the hostages at gunpoint they announced terms for their release: the freeing of 200 Palestinian political prisoners in Israel and safe passage out of Germany.

MASK OF TERROR Heavily disguised, the terrorists appeared on the balcony to threaten or negotiate.

When the Israeli government refused to negotiate, Willy Brandt, the German chancellor, stepped in. He promised the terrorists safe passage to Cairo in return for surrendering the hostages. The Palestinians, with their hostages, were taken to a military airfield outside Munich. Just before midnight, as they were about to board the plane, German police opened fire. Tragically, in the ensuing gun battle all the hostages, four terrorists and one policemen were killed.

The Israelis have withdrawn from the Games, which will resume today. A memorial service will be held in the main stadium.

··· *MR MEN* AND *LITTLE MISS* CHILDREN'S BOOKS ARE PUBLISHED ···

Spitz swims to glory, Korbut captivates the crowds

SMILE OF SUCCESS Olga Korbut beams as she waves one of her three gold medals.

11 SEPTEMBER, MUNICH
Almost a week after the blackest hour in Olympic history, the Munich Games have closed in sombre mood, but also with the memories of superb individual performances. The star of the Games has been the 22-year-old American swimmer Mark Spitz. His father told him from an early age that 'swimming isn't everything, winning is' – and Spitz has done his father proud by winning seven gold medals. No one before, in any branch of the Games, had won more than five golds at one Olympiad.

But even Spitz has been eclipsed in public adoration by the pixie-like Soviet gymnast Olga Korbut. Despite finishing in only seventh place in the all-round individual competition, the diminutive blonde Belarussian – a born performer – caught the public's attention by her spectacular routine on the uneven parallel bars during the team competition and by her sunny personality. And although a fall from the bars cost her the top position in the individual event, she captured the gold on the beam and in the floor exercise.

US HITS OF THE YEAR

1	THE FIRST TIME EVER I SAW YOUR FACE	*Roberta Flack*
2	ALONE AGAIN (NATURALLY)	*Gilbert O'Sullivan*
3	AMERICAN PIE (PTS 1 & 2)	*Don McLean*
4	WITHOUT YOU	*Nilsson*
5	I CAN SEE CLEARLY NOW	*Johnny Nash*

US TV HITS

1	*All in the Family*
2	*The Flip Wilson Show*
3	*Marcus Welby, M D*
4	*Gunsmoke*
5	*ABC Movie of the Week*

Teenybop idols are a screaming success

FAMOUS FIVE Young Michael Jackson with his musical brothers.

Pop music is no longer the preserve of rebellious teenagers. Now their younger sisters and brothers are getting in on the act: teeny-bop is here. Teenyboppers are teenage wannabes – 11- or 12-year-olds, usually girls, whose outlet is their fanatical devotion to their pop music heroes.

Teenybop icons serve up the latest in bubblegum pop.

There are several candidates for most popular idol. Some worship David Cassidy, star of television's popular *Partridge Family*; others adore the Osmonds, a clean-cut Mormon family ensemble who give out a wholesome glow with a touch of schmaltz; a third camp loves another family outfit – the Jackson Five, led by child prodigy Michael.

There were scenes bordering on hysteria recently as David Cassidy arrived in London – one girl was taken to hospital after fainting with excitement having waited three hours to catch a glimpse of her idol.

Record companies are encouraging the trend: this represents a new captive audience, prepared to spend its pocket money on a whole range of records and merchandise – everything from scarves and badges to dolls and bed linen – and as long as the bands continue to demonstrate a wholesome image, their parents surely cannot complain.

FAMILY Many thought the Osmonds, from Salt Lake City, too good to be true.

··· USA: CHARLIE CHAPLIN'S *LIMELIGHT*, BANNED FOR 20 YEARS FOR ALLEGED COMMUNIST LEANINGS, IS RE-RELEASED ···

Fischer sweeps to world chess victory

1 SEPTEMBER, REYKJAVIK
For years Bobby Fischer bragged that he was world chess champion in all but name; today the brooding, prickly 29-year-old American officially claimed the title by completing a 12½–8½ rout of the reigning champion from the Soviet Union, Boris Spassky.

At 14 Fischer was the youngest-ever US champion and at 15 the youngest-ever international grand master. The long contest between him and Spassky began on 11 July, after fears that it would never get off the ground because of Fischer's objection to the size of the prize money – a shared $125 000. Fischer made a poor start, dropping the opening game and defaulting the second. But from then on brilliant play

GRAND MASTER Fischer is the first native-born American to win the world chess championship.

swept him to the victory for which he always seemed destined. At one point security men from Spassky's team even took apart Fischer's chair to see if there were devices implanted in it for receiving information.

Easy calculations, instant photographs

This year saw the invention of a pocket calculator that can add, subtract, multiply and divide, using the newly developed microchip. The calculator was designed by a team at Texas Instruments; already Hewlett-Packard are planning a more sophisticated device, designed for scientific and financial calculations.

Polaroid, the pioneer of instant photography, brought out the SX-70 camera, which produces instant colour photographs from a single-sheet film. This film incorporates all the negative and positive layers needed for colour pictures. The user clicks the shutter, the photograph is ejected, and the image develops before one's very eyes.

Sensational hoax exposed

JUST KIDDING Irving faces the press. His book repeats many of the rumours about Hughes's harems of movie starlets, his codeine addiction, his obsession with cleanliness and other eccentricities.

13 MARCH, NEW YORK CITY
Author Clifford Irving has admitted that *The Memoirs of Howard Hughes*, which he claimed was a transcript of secret interviews with the millionaire recluse, is nothing but a hoax.

Hughes, a wealthy industrialist, became famous in the 1930s and '40s as a film producer and aviator; but since 1966 he has lived in a series of sealed hotel rooms, surrounded only by his Mormon aides, who control all communications between him and the rest of the world. Irving, who received £750000 for the book, was relying on the millionaire's fear of appearing in public to keep him from denouncing the book – but in a telephone interview on 7 January, Hughes broke his silence to tell reporters: 'I don't know him [Irving]. I never saw him.'

Survivors ate dead

29 DECEMBER, MONTEVIDEO
The survivors of the Uruguayan plane that crashed in the Andes ten weeks ago have publicly admitted that they cannibalised the bodies of their fellow passengers in order to stay alive.

The plane, en route from Montevideo to Santiago, Chile, came down on 13 October; of the 45 on board, 29 died in the crash or in an avalanche two weeks later. The 16 survivors – eight of them members of a rugby team – subsisted on chocolate and crackers. The food ran out after three weeks and, as the men became increasingly desperate, the unthinkable became the inevitable.

Church spokesmen have indicated that the act was justifiable under the circumstances. Out of respect for the families, the Chilean authorities buried the grim evidence on the mountain.

··· 15 NOV: BRITISH GOVERNMENT INTRODUCES KIDNEY DONOR CARD SCHEME ···

Ms. – a magazine for today's real women

What does a woman call herself in these liberated days? If she's a Miss, she's just some man's daughter; if she's Mrs, she's another man's wife. There is one way to get around the problem and that's to call herself 'Ms', a female equivalent of Mr.

The liberated Ms now has a magazine to call her own. The feminist monthly *Ms.* was launched in June and is available for $1 by mail. Headed by journalists Gloria Steinem and Letty Cottin Pogrebin, it has an impressive list of contributors. The first couple of issues included stories by black activist Angela Davis and feminist writer Kate Millett, a feature about Marilyn Monroe and one about vaginal self-examination.

The magazine, like any other, carries advertisements. But *Ms.* has a firm policy not to carry any that could be sexist – the operator in the telephone company advertisement has sideburns.

GODFATHER TANGOS TO SUCCESS

FAMILY MAN Brando played Mafia boss Don Corleone with powerful suppressed emotion.

Controversy surrounded *Last Tango in Paris*: Bernardo Bertolucci's film about a bizarre sexual relationship between an ageing widower and a young woman was variously banned or cut, but it gave people new ideas about what to do with butter, and Marlon Brando one of his best roles. However, it was for his role in *The Godfather* – Francis Ford Coppola's sprawling, operatic story of the Mafia as family business – that Brando received an Oscar nomination.

Two important political pictures were released this year. *The Candidate* starred Robert Redford as the would-be senator who keeps selling principles for votes, and ends up standing for nothing at all; and *Cabaret*, a musical set in Berlin against the background of the rise of the Nazis, was a chilling warning against political apathy – although two of the main reasons for seeing it were outsize performances by Liza Minnelli and Joel Gray, and some fabulous dance numbers choreographed by Bob Fosse.

1973

BORN

12 Feb: Monica Seles, Yugoslav-born US tennis player
16 May: Tori Spelling, US actress
21 June: Juliette Lewis, US film actress
28 Sept: Gwyneth Paltrow, US film actress

DIED

22 Jan: Lyndon B Johnson, former US President
8 Apr: Pablo Picasso, Spanish artist
2 Sept: J R R Tolkien, British author

POISONED

Spain: 50000 storks, herons, coots, ducks and other wild birds at the Donana National Park, by pesticides

Mastermind, launched by Invicta of Leicester, England, two years ago, has become one of the biggest-selling games of all time. The game of logic was invented by Israeli postmaster Mordechai Meirovitz. It requires two players, one of whom tries to deduce which combination of coloured pegs the other has chosen.

On 14 November, *Princess Anne and Captain Mark Phillips are married at Westminster Abbey, London. The wedding, policed by 4000 officers, is followed by a 1500-guest reception and a honeymoon in the Caribbean. The first royal wedding to be televised, it is watched by 550 million people across the world.*

LAUNCHED

10 Oct: LBC, first commercial radio station in Britain

INTRODUCED

1 Apr: Value Added Tax (VAT), to Britain
Japan: first colour photocopier, made by Canon

AGREED

26 Nov: a ransom of $1 million to be paid by the oil-rich Getty family for kidnapped son Paul, after receiving his ear in the post

REFUSED

28 May: an Oscar, by Marlon Brando, in protest at Hollywood's exploitation of Native Americans

AWARDED

7 May: Pulitzer Prize, to journalists Carl Bernstein and Bob Woodward for exposing Watergate scandal

ANNOUNCED

27 Jan: end of US involvement in Vietnam, by Richard Nixon
3 July: separation of Richard Burton and Elizabeth Taylor, after nine years of marriage
Australia: Aborigines to get the vote

INVENTED

California: the mountain bike, by members of the Marin County Canyon cycling club, for riding the slopes of the local canyons

FIRSTS

1 June, UK: black newscaster in Britain – Trevor McDonald for ITN
23 June, UK: graduates of the Open University receive their degrees

BANNED

The Netherlands: driving on Sundays, to preserve petrol supplies; other countries impose an 80 km/h (50 mph) speed limit

OLDEST

Cyprus: vessel (c200 BC) – raised off the coast, with a cargo of amphorae and kitchen utensils

CRASHED

21 June: Soviet supersonic airliner Tupolev Tu-144, on a demonstration flight at the Paris air show

EXPLODED

South Pacific: several nuclear devices over Mururoa Atoll, by France; worldwide condemnation follows

PUBLISHED

Thomas Pynchon, *Gravity's Rainbow*

On 19 July, *Bruce Lee, Chinese-American martial arts expert and movie star, dies suddenly at the age of 32. Lee had a cult following in the late 1960s, but only received international acclaim with* Fists of Fury *in 1971. His latest films,* Enter the Dragon *and* Return of the Dragon, *broke all box office records.*

FIRST NIGHT

London: *Joseph and the Technicolour Dreamcoat,* at the Albery Theatre

NEW WORD

child abuse *n*: physical, sexual or emotional maltreatment of a child by its parents or other adults responsible for its welfare

Israel loses battle – but wins the war

DEATH FROM THE SKY Israeli infantry soldiers gaze up as an Arab Skyhawk jet swoops in to attack.

24 OCTOBER, TEL AVIV
Israel is celebrating victory in the
fourth and fiercest Arab–Israeli war,
which ended today when the two sides
agreed to a United Nations ceasefire.

Israeli families were worshipping in synagogues on 6 October, the Day of Atonement, or Yom Kippur, when Egyptian and Syrian forces, reinforced by Palestinian units, invaded the Sinai peninsula and the Golan Heights, catching the whole nation by surprise. Radio stations broke their traditional silence on the holiest day in the Jewish calendar to broadcast news of the latest developments. Israel branded Egypt and Syria as aggressors, but Arab leaders were quick to claim that they had merely been responding to the shooting down of 13 Syrian jet fighters by Israel in September.

When the war began Yasser Arafat, the Palestine liberation leader, rejoiced. 'This isn't a spark,' he is reported to have said. 'It's a fire!' Certainly the courage and discipline of the Arab soldiers have raised Arab confidence. The capital of Syria, Damascus, was heroically defended with assistance from Jordan and military aid from the Soviet Union. And the massive tank battle on the Suez front – from which Egypt emerged with its positions on the east side of the canal intact – marked the first ever victory of Arab forces over an Israeli army.

But in the end it is Israel that has emerged once again the victor. Early estimates of loss of life are that around 2500 Israeli soldiers were killed, against 7000 from Syria and 15000 from Egypt. Pre-war boundaries have been confirmed, leaving Israel in control of all the lands it annexed in the Six Day War in 1967.

··· THE LONGEST SOLAR ECLIPSE IN HISTORY IS VISIBLE FROM THE SOUTHERN SAHARA DESERT ···

USA pulls out of Vietnam

FLYING OUT Crowds gather as released American PoWs leave Vietnam.

27 JANUARY, SAIGON
President Nixon has finally
been persuaded to pull
American troops out of
South-East Asia, bowing to domestic opposition to US involvement in the war in Vietnam. Today in Paris, after several false starts, a ceasefire was signed, although the terms that the US secretary of state, Henry Kissinger, have been able to wring from the Viet Cong are hardly satisfactory to South Vietnam. The accord implicitly legitimises the presence of Viet Cong troops in the South, and many observers believe that the United States has forsaken its ally.

Nixon said on television four days ago that the USA would continue to regard the government in Saigon as the sole legitimate government of South Vietnam, and he pledged support for the South should Hanoi violate the peace agreement. At the same time the Pentagon said that the last US troops would be out of Vietnam by the end of March.

Space laboratory blasts off

14 MAY, HOUSTON, TEXAS
The United States' $2.5 billion orbiting space station *Skylab* was launched today – but misfortune struck immediately. A protective heat shield tore away, carrying with it one of the main solar panels that was to power *Skylab*, and pinning the other to the vehicle's side. *Skylab*'s only source of power is now a windmill-shaped array of four smaller panels, intended only to power the telescope. Without the heat shield the temperature inside is hotter than anywhere on Earth, making the station uninhabitable.

Plans are already under way to send an outer-space repair crew to cut the remaining solar wing free. They will also take one of the strangest objects ever to go into space: a giant aluminised plastic parasol, which they will push through a hatch in Skylab's hull and then unfurl to protect the station from the Sun.

SPACE STATION *Skylab* is built from the cannibalised shell of an unused Saturn lunar rocket.

Two-thirds of *Skylab*'s 340-cubic-metre (10000-cu-ft) space is filled with a workshop, sleeping area, kitchen and bathroom, all designed for zero gravity; for example, water must be drawn down the sinks by suction pumps, otherwise it floats around the interior. The other third is an experiment chamber which will be used for metallurgical tests and to see how mice, minnows, fruit flies and other animals – including astronauts – cope with long periods in outer space.

··· THERE ARE ONLY 950 WINDMILLS LEFT IN THE NETHERLANDS ···

Nixon swears innocence in Watergate scandal

TRUTH-SEEKERS Woodward (left) and Bernstein uncovered the story.

17 NOVEMBER, FLORIDA
Richard Nixon chose Disney World as the place from which to tell America today that its President is 'not a crook'. Nixon denied his involvement in the 'Watergate affair' that has gripped the USA since last summer. The true extent of the scandal came to light after dogged investigations by *Washington Post* reporters Bob Woodward and Carl Bernstein.

Last year they revealed that there had been an attempt by senior Republicans to cover up the break-in at the Democratic headquarters, and that those involved included four top Nixon aides – attorney-general Richard Kleindienst, chief of staff Bob Haldeman, chief domestic affairs adviser John Ehrlichman and legal adviser John Dean.

All four resigned before a Senate committee began investigating the Watergate affair on 17 May. Nixon insisted he had known nothing about the burglary or the cover-up, but in June Dean told the committee that Ehrlichman and Haldeman had ordered the burglary and, sensationally, that Nixon was involved in the cover-up all along.

In July the Watergate hearings learnt that Nixon had tape-recorded all his conversations in the Oval Office, and asked him to hand over the tapes. After an initial refusal, he reluctantly gave way last month. This delay is widely seen as a blunder. If he is innocent, people wonder, surely the tapes would have proved it?

Greek Colonels stage another coup

25 NOVEMBER, ATHENS
The president of Greece, Colonel Georgios Papadopoulos, has been overthrown in a military coup, accused of 'weakness' by his former allies.

Papadopoulos was one of the engineers of Greece's last military coup by which the army seized power in 1967. In June this year, in a dramatic, unilateral move, he appointed himself president of a new 'presidential parliamentary republic'. Today's events, which follow weeks of unrest, have exposed the divisions within the ruling junta, although the new military government, headed by Brigadier Dimitrios Ionanides, claims that the coup is simply a 'continuation of the revolution of April 21 1967'.

Arab oil embargo brings Europe to its knees

SOLD OUT Motorists are among the hardest hit by the rising prices and petrol shortage.

17 DECEMBER, LONDON
The British government today announced a number of measures to try to combat the most worrying economic situation that Britain has faced since the end of World War II. The measures include a speed limit of 50 miles per hour (80 km/h), thanks to the oil shortage that is one of the key factors in the current crisis.

Oil provides much of Europe's and the USA's energy, and most of it comes from the Middle East. In what is the first time that oil has been used as a political weapon, Arab countries have responded to the West's support for Israel in this year's Arab–Israeli war by raising the price of crude oil to $6 a barrel – four times its previous price.

Motorists across Europe are now used to the frustrating business of queueing at petrol stations, while in Britain the situation is made worse by grievances in other areas of the power industry; overtime bans have drastically reduced coal supplies to power stations. The dramatic oil-price rise will destabilise economies around the world and could signal the end of the postwar boom.

··· 10 PER CENT OF AMERICANS CLAIM TO HAVE SEEN A UFO AND MORE THAN 50 PER CENT BELIEVE THEY EXIST ···

Chile's president commits suicide after rebel coup

11 SEPTEMBER, SANTIAGO
Salvador Allende Gossens, the president of Chile, committed suicide today rather than bow to demands for his resignation as his presidential palace went up in flames and his government was overthrown by a right-wing military coup. The new leader of Chile is General Augusto Pinochet, who masterminded the air and ground assault on the palace.

Pinochet heads a military junta which has pledged to deliver the country from the 'Marxist yoke' that it claims was imposed when Allende was elected president in 1970. World leaders have expressed their dismay that one of the few South American countries with a distinguished history of stable constitutional government and the rule of law has succumbed to dictatorship. Yet many believe such a coup to have been inevitable in the face of increasing public unrest, economic problems, and the CIA's support of right-wing factions.

HAPPIER DAYS Allende, the world's first elected Marxist president, meets workers a month before the coup.

Glam rock: singers in sequins, men in make-up

GET DOWN Dave Hill (left), Noddy Holder and the rest of Slade bash out a hit.

Glam rock, with its sequins, heavy make-up and bell-bottom trousers, burst on to the music scene in a shower of glitter and has reached new peaks this year. As much about dressing up as about rock, the style started as a reaction against the dull jeans-and-T-shirt uniform of rock music. It is spearheaded by the likes of David Bowie, who dressed up for his 'Ziggy Stardust' tour in a futuristic, androgynous style complete with silver platform boots and bright orange hair. Soon a clutch of bands sprang onto the British music scene wearing sequins and glittery eye-shadow. The sight of men wearing make-up was yet another shock for the British and American establishments, and the style of the new music movement has received acres of news coverage.

Although the image is new, the music is often a predictable formula of hard rock with commercial top notes. Some groups have produced memorable songs, such as T Rex's 'Telegram Sam' and 'Children of the Revolution', fusing strong melodies with lots of electric guitar. The Sweet use glam rock to give their commercial sound a glamorous gloss; anthems like 'Blockbuster' and 'Ball Room Blitz' have inspired a whole generation of boys to put on blue eye-shadow – for the band's concerts, if nothing else.

Glam rock seems to be at its height in 1973, but it will soon begin to look dated. Some groups, such as Mott the Hoople, begin to cut back on the sequins and concentrate on the music. Others, like Gary Glitter who has had a string of hits this year, including 'I'm the Leader of the Gang (I Am)' and 'I Love You Love Me Love', are resorting to ever more outrageous costumes. Gary Glitter's platform boots are becoming ever higher; for one of his stage costumes they were nearly 2 metres (6 ft) tall. Some say that this sort of spectacle means that glam has lost any sense of cool it started out with and descended into pantomime.

STARMAN David Bowie is a serious musician with an extraordinary and much-imitated sense of style.

··· PICASSO'S *FEMME ASSISE* FETCHES £340 000 AT AUCTION – A RECORD PRICE FOR A 20TH-CENTURY PAINTING ···

US HITS OF THE YEAR

1	KILLING ME SOFTLY WITH HIS SONG	*Roberta Flack*
2	TIE A YELLOW RIBBON ROUND THE OLD OAK TREE	*Dawn*
3	MY LOVE	*Paul McCartney*
4	YOU'RE SO VAIN	*Carly Simon*
5	CROCODILE ROCK	*Elton John*

US TV HITS

1	*All in the Family*
2	*Sanford & Son*
3	*Hawaii Five-O*
4	*Maude*
5	*Bridget Loves Bernie*

M*A*S*H comes to the small screen

Three years ago the movie *M*A*S*H* was a surprise box office hit for 20th Century Fox. The black comedy, set in a Mobile Army Surgical Hospital unit during the Korean War, showed little respect for the US military machine – an attitude deliberately intended to appeal to an American public disillusioned with the then current war in Vietnam. Now there is a television spin-off, written by Larry Gelbart and directed by Gene Reynolds, which premiered in the United States last year to enormous success. Screened in Britain this year, the series has proved just as successful as its movie predecessor.

At the same time as it reflects the tragedy of the war, the programme wrings comedy out of everyday events. Cynical, irreverent 'Hawkeye' Pierce, his room-mate 'Trapper John' McIntyre, irascible blonde Major 'Hot Lips' Houlihan and their colleagues play out their comic exploits against a background of desperation. The human cost of the war is never forgotten, and the anarchic humour serves to underline the poignancy of the situation.

DROWNING THEIR SORROWS Trapper (left) and Hawkeye, masters of downbeat humour, share a toast.

Sears Tower is the world's tallest by far

The incessant struggle to build the world's tallest building reached a new stage this year with the completion of the Sears Tower in Chicago. The tower was designed by the Chicago offices of Skidmore, Owings and Merrill as the headquarters of the Sears Roebuck mail-order company. The 110-storey structure soars 443 metres (1454 ft) into the sky, beating the twin towers of the World Trade Center in New York City by about 30 metres (100 ft). A television mast on top takes its total height to 549 metres (1800 ft).

The Sears Tower, prominently situated in the centre of the city, is constructed of strengthened steel and clad in black aluminium and bronze-tinted glare-reducing glass. About 16 500 people will use the building every day.

CON MEN OF FILM

HAVING A BALL Woody Allen, in the guise of a robot butler, juggles with the future.

In the year of the Watergate scandal, con men were surprising heroes. *The Sting* reunited Robert Redford and Paul Newman as two con artists out to swindle a gangster in 1920s Chicago. The ragtime soundtrack did wonders for Scott Joplin's reputation. *Paper Moon* had Ryan O'Neal and his daughter Tatum conning their way across the Midwest in the 1930s; 12-year-old Tatum became the youngest actor to win an Oscar.

Young girls weren't always so appealing: in *The Exorcist* Linda Blair spewed on priests, croaked blasphemies, defiled a crucifix and generally behaved badly, owing to demonic possession. *American Graffiti*, famous mostly for its soundtrack, nostalgically harked back to the innocence of teen life in pre-Vietnam America; *Sleeper* looked forwards, to a glossy future where sex is provided by machines – Woody Allen was hilarious as the 20th-century man failing to come to grips with technology.

Mean Streets, set among petty gangsters in New York, introduced three major talents: director Martin Scorsese and actors Harvey Keitel and Robert de Niro. Another important talent seems to be signalled with *Badlands*, the debut of director Terence Malick.

··· FRANCE: THE DISPOSABLE LIGHTER IS INVENTED BY THE BIC COMPANY ···

1974

BORN
6 Jan: Alanis Morissette, Canadian pop musician
16 Jan: Kate Moss, British model
11 Nov: Leonardo DiCaprio, US actor

DIED
31 Jan: Samuel Goldwyn, US film producer
24 May: Duke Ellington, jazz musician and composer
26 Aug: Charles Lindbergh, US aviator

Evel Knievel, the American daredevil cycle stuntman, gets ready for a leap on his V-twin Harley-Davidson. His spectacular shows attract huge audiences – he recently earned $6 million for an abortive attempt to leap the Snake River Canyon in Idaho.

ELECTED
10 Oct, UK: Harold Wilson, as prime minister
24 May, France: Giscard d'Estaing, as president

KIDNAPPED
4 Feb: Patty Hearst, 19-year-old newspaper heiress, by Symbionese Liberation Army; she later serves four years in jail for helping them to carry out an armed bank raid

ATTEMPTED
20 Mar, London: kidnapping of Princess Anne in the Mall, by 26-year-old Ian Ball, which leaves four guards wounded

DISCOVERED
Xian, China: terracotta army – 6000 life-size figures and 10000 valuable objects, in the 3rd-century BC burial mound of Emperor Qin
UK: oil fields in the North Sea

BANNED
USA: discrimination against gay job applicants, by American Telephone and Telegraph Corporation, biggest US private employer
Zaire: Christmas, wigs and Christian names of Western origin, in order to revive African culture

INVENTED
Boston, USA: disposable lightweight plastic razors, by Gillette

Kojak, the New York police television series, is launched and quickly gains a cult following. Played by Telly Savalas, Kojak is a cop with a difference – he sucks lollipops, calls people 'pussycat' and has a startlingly bald head underneath his trilby. Kojak's catchphrase – 'Who loves ya, baby?' – catches on quickly.

ANNOUNCED
12 May: Italy says 'yes' to divorce in a referendum, by 59.1 per cent
10 July: India has the nuclear bomb

DEPOSED
12 Sept, Ethiopia: Emperor Haile Selassie – he spends the rest of his life under house arrest

RIOTED
13 Sept, Boston: students opposed to desegregation, who boycott classes and attack black students

INTRODUCED
2 Jan, UK: three-day working week, owing to power shortages caused by miners' strike and oil embargo
UK: free family planning on the NHS
USA: first catalytic converter, by General Motors

DEVASTATED
20 Apr, USA: Kentucky and Ohio, as 100 tornadoes rage at speeds of 800 km/h (500 mph) and heights of 305 m (1000 ft), killing 300 people

EXHIBITED
Japan: the *Mona Lisa* in Tokyo – one million people pay to see it in 50 days; each person is allowed no more than 10 seconds' viewing time

RECORD
8 Feb: 89 days in space spent by *Skylab* space station – astronauts suffered no ill-effects, but came back 2–3 cm (1–1½ in) taller

NEW WORD
page-turner *n*: a book with a compelling storyline, often a bestseller

On 3 February, Om Kalsoum, the Arab world's best-loved singer, dies at the age of 77. Kalsoum began her career singing religious songs in the village in Egypt where she was born, until her first solo concert in Cairo in 1930. She quickly rose to fame ,and was soon performing in concert and, via broadcasts, all over the world.

PRESIDENT AVOIDS IMPEACHMENT BY QUITTING

9 AUGUST, WASHINGTON DC

'Dear Mr Secretary of State, I hereby resign the office of President of the United States. Sincerely, Richard Nixon.' With this terse note, delivered today to Henry Kissinger, Richard Nixon achieved the dubious distinction of being the first American President to step down from office before the end of his term. Resignation was the only way for Nixon to avoid impeachment by Congress for 'high crimes and misdemeanours' related to the Watergate affair.

As investigations into the scandal continued, evidence mounted that while Nixon did not actually order the break-in at the Democrat headquarters in 1972, he became embroiled in a top-level cover-up to hide the tracks of senior aides who had masterminded the burglary. Several were convicted earlier this year, and others have been indicted. Announcing last night that he intended to resign, Nixon, 61, stated that he was reluctant to go: 'I have never been a quitter,' he said. He went on to express sorrow for 'any injury that may have been done'.

Nixon is succeeded by Gerald Ford, also aged 61, who became vice-president last year after the resignation of Spiro Agnew, who was himself forced to step down following

SAD FAREWELL Gerald Ford (left) escorts the Nixons to a waiting helicopter.

charges of tax evasion. Ford now has the unenviable uphill struggle of restoring credit to the most thoroughly disgraced administration in American history.

··· SCIENTISTS PROVE THAT CHLOROFLUOROCARBONS (CFCs) DESTROY THE EARTH'S OZONE LAYER ···

Soldier's solo war is over

I SURRENDER Lieutenant Onoda (left) hands over his sword to Major General Jose Rancudo of the Philippines Air Force.

9 MARCH, PHILIPPINES

Lieutenant Hiroo Onoda has surrendered, finally convinced that the war is over – 29 years late.

Onoda arrived on the island of Lubang in 1944 with orders to fight until the Japanese army came back for him. He stuck literally to his orders for three decades, living in the jungle, making raids on villages, and evading all attempts to contact him. Waging a solo guerrilla war, he killed at least 30 Filipinos.

Last month Onoda stumbled across a Japanese member of a search party, Norio Suzuki, who attempted to persuade him that the war was over. Suspecting an Allied trap, Onoda insisted he would only surrender on the order of his superior officer, Major Taniguchi. Suzuki contacted Japan, and the elderly Mr Taniguchi – now a bookseller – agreed to come and give the order that would finally end Lieutenant Onoda's war.

Ali wins the 'rumble in the jungle'

VICTORY BLOW Fans chanted 'Ali, kill him!' during the match.

29 OCTOBER, ZAIRE

In the much-hyped 'rumble in the jungle', Muhammad Ali, aged 32, has beaten George Foreman to regain the world heavyweight title. He won the title in 1964 and is only the second person ever to regain it. A crowd of 60000 fans cheered him on. Ali used his famous 'rope-a-dope' tactics, luring Foreman into punching himself out without landing telling blows. He won the match with a knockout in the eighth round of what was to have been a 15-round bout.

Naked ambition runs riot

10 MARCH, NEWARK, DELAWARE
The craze for running about without clothes on that has gripped the United States – it has been given the tag of 'streaking' – turned nasty yesterday, when rioting at the University of Delaware between police and streakers injured 11 police officers and 11 students.

Since the beginning of the year thousands of students on American campuses have been bitten by the bug to undress, and the wheeze has spread to Europe. In Belgium a streaking cyclist won a bet with his mate, but was fined 3000 francs and jailed for one month. In Paris two days ago 11 streakers circled round and round the Eiffel Tower. In Britain, sports events have become a focus for streaking.

Psychologists in the United States have attempted to explain the fad as a reaction to boredom – students having a last fling before taking on adult responsibilies – or as a quest for instant fame. The phenomenon shows no sign of abating, but a philosophy don from the University of Missouri commented: 'One good blizzard and the whole thing will come to an end.'

SOMETHING TO HIDE Police do their best to spare the public's blushes as they arrest a streaker who ran on to the pitch during a Twickenham rugby match.

··· UK: HELEN MORGAN RESIGNS AS MISS WORLD WHEN IT IS REVEALED THAT SHE HAS AN ILLEGITIMATE CHILD ···

Love-all for Wimbledon pair

MIXED DOUBLES Connors (centre) and Evert show off their trophies.

8 JULY, WIMBLEDON
Two fresh-faced American youngsters have carried off the singles titles at the Wimbledon championships.
Jimmy Connors, 21, beat Ken Rosewall – the crowd's favourite – in a one-sided show of baseline power, 6–1, 6–1, 6–4; and 19-year-old

Chris Evert, also a driving baseliner, saw off the Russian Olga Morozova 6–0, 6–4.

For both of the pair – who are famously involved in an off-court romance – it is their first Wimbledon title. Their hard-hitting style is certain to be copied by thousands of budding players.

The search is on for vanished aristocrat and murder suspect

10 NOVEMBER, NEWHAVEN, SUSSEX
Detectives searching for the vanished peer, Lord Lucan, who is wanted in connection with the murder of his children's nanny three days ago, have made their first significant breakthrough.

A blue Ford Corsair, which the suspect is known to have borrowed from a friend, has been found at Newhaven on the Sussex coast. The interior is heavily bloodstained. Police have recovered from the boot a piece of lead piping bound with adhesive tape, which matches another length of piping that was left at the scene of the crime and is presumed to be the murder

weapon. Local trawlermen also reported sighting a figure that could have been Lucan walking pensively along the jetty in the early hours of 8 November.

Twenty-nine-year-old Sandra Rivett was battered to death at the plush Belgravia home of Lucan's estranged wife, where she was working as a nanny. Lucan, a professional gambler, is known to have been bitter about the break-up of his marriage and the loss of his children. This has led to speculation that he killed Rivett by mistake on the evening of 7 November, believing her to be Lady Lucan. His wife was also injured in his frenzied attack.

Soviets expel voice of dissidence

13 FEBRUARY, MOSCOW
Alexander Solzhenitsyn was
expelled from the Soviet
Union today, the first
Russian citizen to suffer this
indignity since Leon Trotsky
in 1929. The dissident author
is no stranger to conflict; in
1945 he was sent to a labour
camp for criticising Stalin,
and in 1963 his books were
banned in the Soviet Union.
Cancer Ward and *The First*
Circle were published abroad,
and in 1970 he won the
Nobel Prize for literature.

Official hostility towards
Solzhenitsyn has increased
following publication of *The*
Gulag Archipelago, an account
of life in the Russian camps.
The manuscript, smuggled to
the West, appeared in print

FACE IN THE CROWD Solzhenitsyn (centre) makes his way to freedom in exile.

last year. For the Soviets this
was the final straw. In January
the newspaper *Pravda*

launched a tirade against
Solzhenitsyn, giving an early
hint of today's deportation.

Aaron hits his way to baseball history

8 APRIL, ATLANTA,
GEORGIA
Atlanta was the scene of
boisterous rejoicing tonight
as Hank Aaron became the
greatest hitter of home runs
in baseball history. The
40-year-old star of the
home-town Braves achieved
this status with the greatest of
ease when he knocked a
pitch over the left centrefield
wall. That homer was number
715 in Aaron's career, and
one more than the record
established 40 years ago by
the immortal Babe Ruth –
and not all baseball fans are
happy that the great Yankee
has been eclipsed.

Aaron himself, a quiet,
unassuming outfielder, took
the historic moment in his
stride, telling the crowd after
the game that he was 'just
glad it's all over'. Only, as
everyone knows, it isn't all
over. There are many more
home runs still to come from
Aaron's bat.

US HITS OF THE YEAR		US TV HITS	
1 THE WAY WE WERE	*Barbra Streisand*	1 *All in the Family*	
2 THE STREAK	*Ray Stevens*	2 *The Waltons*	
3 SEASONS IN THE SUN	*Terry Jacks*	3 *Sanford & Son*	
4 (YOU'RE) HAVING MY BABY	*Paul Anka with Odia Coates*	4 *M*A*S*H*	
5 KUNG FU FIGHTING	*Carl Douglas*	5 *Hawaii Five-O*	

The world watches Geller's mindbending powers

Throughout 1974, newspapers and
journals focused on the controversial
phenomenon of Uri Geller. This
extraordinary 28-year-old Israeli seems
to possess extrasensory powers, such as
the ability to bend spoons and mend
watches at will.

In October the British scientific
journal *Nature* published the results of a
series of controlled experiments by
Geller at the Stanford Research Institute
in the United States. *New Scientist*
published an article, also in its October
issue, that was highly critical of the

Stanford tests. The article claimed that
Geller had a miniature radio implanted
in his teeth – a charge he denied. In
December he asked his New York
dentist to testify that 'no foreign objects'
were implanted in his mouth.

One of the most bizarre allegations
against Geller came earlier in the year,
when a Swedish woman sued the
psychic for making her contraceptive
loop ineffective.

KEY TO SUCCESS One of Geller's party turns is to
bend keys with sheer 'mind power'.

1975

BORN

22 Feb: Drew Barrymore, US actress
5 Oct: Kate Winslet, British actress
30 Dec: Tiger Woods, US golfer

DIED

11 Apr: Josephine Baker, US entertainer
27 Aug: Haile Selassie, former Emperor of Ethiopia
20 Nov: General Francisco Franco, Spanish dictator

INTRODUCED

2 June: first road-pricing measures, in Singapore; £25 rush-hour travel permits cut traffic congestion by 40 per cent
Japan: the Betamax video system by Sony and the VHS by JVC
USA: the laser printer, IBM 3800

On 25 March, *King Feisal of Saudi Arabia is assassinated at his palace in the capital, Riyadh. The killer is his nephew, who has a history of mental illness. King Feisal was seen as a political opponent of Israel but nevertheless worked for peace in the Middle East. He will be succeeded by Crown Prince Khalid.*

On 11 February, *Margaret Thatcher is elected as the first female leader of the Conservative Party in Britain, replacing Edward Heath. Thatcher was elected as MP for Finchley in 1959, having originally qualified as a research chemist in 1947 before studying law.*

FIRSTS

16 May, Nepal: woman to climb Everest, Junko Tabei of Japan, leader of 15-strong female expedition
18 June, UK: North Sea oil is piped ashore, at the Isle of Grain refinery
5 July, UK: black man to win Wimbledon, American Arthur Ashe
17 July: link-up in space, as Soviet spacecraft *Soyuz 19* docks with US craft *Apollo 18*, 224 km (140 miles) above Earth, signalling the end of the 'space race'
20 Dec, UK: pop video is shown on BBC's *Top of the Pops*, Queen's 'Bohemian Rhapsody'

SENTENCED

4 July: Gestapo chief in Warsaw, Ludwig Hahn, to life imprisonment for the murder of at least 230 000 Jews during World War II

REOPENED

5 June, Egypt: the Suez Canal, after eight years, to shipping of all nations except Israel

KILLED

7 Apr: 40 people by avalanches, caused by freak weather conditions, in the Swiss, Italian and Austrian Alps
UK: about 6.5 million trees, by Dutch elm disease

DISBANDED

22 Feb, USSR: the Soviet national football team after a run of poor results; replaced by top club side Kiev Dynamo

DONATED

USA: 2000 acres of land in California, by Marlon Brando, to Native American Indians

WORST

28 Feb, UK: accident on the London Underground, when a train goes down a dead-end tunnel at Moorgate, killing 50 people

SURVIVED

5 and 23 Sept, California: two separate assassination attempts, by President Ford

ANNOUNCED

5 June: Britain says 'Yes' to EEC membership in referendum, by 17 378 581 votes to 8 470 073

AWARDED

World Chess Championship to Anatoly Karpov, because Bobby Fischer does not defend his title in permitted time

BANNED

16 June, USA: the sale of aerosols containing CFC gases in Oregon – first place to do so

MARRIED

2 June: Richard Burton and Elizabeth Taylor, for the second time, after a divorce two years earlier

REQUESTED

9 Sept, USA: political asylum, by Czech tennis player Martina Navratilova

Tammy Wynette, Nashville country singer, releases 'Stand by Your Man', which becomes a number one hit. Wynette has enjoyed ten years as the most famous female country performer in the world.

SURRENDERED

30 Apr: South Vietnam, to North Vietnamese Communist forces

NEW WORDS

punk rock *n*: rock music characterised by aggressive lyrics and performance
Sloane Ranger *n*: (British) young upper-class person with a home in London and in the country, who wears expensive but casual clothes

Khmer Rouge sweeps to power, vowing retribution

17 APRIL, PHNOM PENH
Half a decade of war which has killed 250 000 people came to an end today when Cambodian government forces surrendered the capital, Phnom Penh, to the communist guerrillas of the Khmer Rouge. The black-uniformed rebels swept into the city after a devastating four-month siege, during which the North Vietnamese army has cut a swathe through the rest of the country in support of its communist comrades.

Confusion reigns over who is in charge following the fall of the corrupt regime of General Lon Nol, the American-backed right-wing dictator who drove the former head of state, Prince Norodom Sihanouk, into exile five years ago. Although Sihanouk is the nominal head of the coalition against Lon Nol, power now seems to lie in the hands of the Khmer Rouge leader, Pol

MASTER PLANNER Pro-Chinese Khmer Rouge leader Pol Pot is interviewed in the Cambodian jungle.

Pot. Many Cambodians are worried that Pol Pot, a strongly Maoist former schoolmaster who inspires fanatical loyalty, will not be forgiving towards his

former foes. Already the signs are ominous – a Khmer Rouge spokesman has promised a grim fate for 'the traitors of Phnom Penh'.

··· 18 JAN, CHINA: THE PEOPLE'S CONGRESS BANS ALL PRIVATE PROPERTY ···

Lebanon torn apart by civil war

WAR ZONE A slogan protesting at Syria's military support for the Christians adorns a Beirut building.

17 SEPTEMBER, BEIRUT
Rashid Karami, the prime minister of Lebanon, narrowly avoided death when a missile smashed into his car late last night in an Arab suburb of Beirut. This divided city is now in the grip of full-scale civil war as Muslim and Christian

groups fight it out on the streets with rockets and machine-guns.

This is the first outbreak of violence since 1973. It erupted on 13 April, when Christian militants attacked a bus in Beirut, killing 27 Palestinians. This led to intense fighting, resulting in 90 dead in three days. Street battles broke out again in June, leaving 40 dead.

Tensions between the ruling Maronite Christians and the leftist Muslim group led by Kamal Jumblatt escalated into full-scale war when the Palestine Liberation Organisation, based in camps in the south of the country, allied itself with the Muslims. Syria has shown conflicting allegiance; after initially backing the Muslim private militias, President Hafez Assad, fearing Israeli intervention in the crisis, now seems to be preparing to send Syrian troops to aid the Christians.

Jackal may slip away after hostage crisis

23 DECEMBER, ALGIERS
Six pro-Palestinian commandos, led by the notorious Venezuelan terrorist Carlos the Jackal, have surrendered to the Algerian authorities and released their hostages unharmed. All eyes have been on Carlos since the militants burst into a meeting of the Organisation of Petroleum Exporting Countries (OPEC) in Vienna two days ago and took 70 hostages, including 11 oil ministers. The Austrian government gave them safe passage to Algeria.

The kidnapping will net the Popular Front for the Liberation of Palestine several million dollars, and it is believed that Carlos will soon be a free man. It is rumoured that he and his group of militants acted with the support of the Algerian government.

Linking the rough and the smooth

This year a prominent surgeon took some of the shine off the processed foods on which so many people have come to rely. Denis Burkitt, a British doctor, announced that he had discovered a link between low-fibre diets and cancer of the colon. Foodstuffs such as white bread, sugar and rice have become a significant part of the family diet in the West – but Dr Burkitt realised that refined foods had all their natural 'roughage' removed and were very low in fibre.

A press campaign has informed the public that roughage, otherwise known as 'dietary fibre', appears to be crucial for a healthy diet. People have been advised to go back to natural, unrefined foods, because the insoluble fibre that is found in cereals such as wheat and brown rice helps the digestive system to speed food through the body and eases digestive ailments like constipation. Soluble fibre, found in fruit and vegetables, oats and beans, is linked to the reduction of cholesterol in the blood, and eating it can decrease the risk of heart problems.

BACK TO BASICS Brown rice and pulses are back on the dinner table.

··· ALASKAN SUPREME COURT RULES THAT THE POSSESSION OF MARIJUANA FOR PERSONAL USE IS LEGAL ···

Victory for Viet Cong as Saigon is captured

FINAL RETREAT Desperate South Vietnamese try to force their way into the US Embassy in Saigon.

30 APRIL, SAIGON
Saigon has fallen and the war in Vietnam is over, leaving the Viet Cong masters of both the north and the south of the country. The end has been inevitable since January, when the North Vietnamese army succeeded in taking the whole of Phuoc Long province, north of Saigon. It was then that the United States, which withdrew its army from Vietnam two years ago, suspended aid to President Nguyen Van Thieu's government.

On 21 April, after a last stand by South Vietnamese forces at Zuan Loc, the president resigned in the hope that his departure would lead to a ceasefire and thus prevent a bloody last battle in the streets of Saigon. But the ceasefire did not come until today when Viet Cong tanks rolled into Saigon.

Refugees are desperately attempting to flee the city, but so far the Viet Cong have been able to hem them in. All American citizens have been evacuated from Saigon in a dramatic helicopter airlift, leaving the embassy to be sacked by jubilant Viet Cong soldiers.

It is estimated that more than two million Vietnamese have died since 1965; for those who have survived, the future is grim. Many civilians have been maimed or are ill because of pesticides that US forces sprayed on crops to deprive the Viet Cong of sustenance and cover. Even the resumption of farming will be difficult, as the country is riddled with land mines and bomb craters.

Hanging loose in free-form fashion

BOLD LINES Hems dropped with the maxi skirt.

Halfway through the decade, the 1970s have certainly made their sartorial mark on the century. Bell-bottoms, platform shoes, big collars, kipper ties, smocks, loon pants, crochet, suede and the wrinkled look: elegance has not been much in evidence lately – even on the international catwalks.

It looks as if it's going to be a decade of excess. Not since the Middle Ages have people chosen to wear such thoroughly impractical footwear, and platform shoes just seem to get higher and higher. As for the width of flared trousers, the wider the better. Bodies have disappeared under layers of free-form clothes. Following James Laver's theory of fashion, hemlines have followed the stock market on its downward course. Some mourn the passing of the miniskirt, but a great many women are relieved that they no longer have to dress like Lolitas. The unstructured look goes right down to underwear: bras went out at the beginning of the decade.

The biggest fashion statements these days seem to be made by men, who are sporting more facial hair than they have had since before World War I. And to match the sideburns, they're growing flowing locks. Skinny hipster trousers and turtlenecks have had a feminising effect – sometimes it's hard to tell the men from the girls. They're calling it unisex.

··· EX-BEATLE PAUL McCARTNEY IS FINED FOR GROWING MARIJUANA PLANTS ON HIS FARM IN BRITAIN ···

IRA gunmen take London couple hostage

12 DECEMBER, LONDON

John and Sheila Matthews are recovering in hospital tonight after a six-day hostage ordeal at the hands of four Irish Republican Army (IRA) men. The gunmen – wanted for questioning about two IRA murders – stormed into the middle-aged couple's central London flat following a dramatic police chase.

Holding the Matthews as hostages, the gunmen demanded a passage to Ireland. Police surrounded the house with marksmen, resolving to starve the terrorists out. Today this tactic paid off, and the gunmen surrendered.

THE TERROR THAT STALKS FROM THE DEEP

The blockbuster of the year was *Jaws*, a horror movie that was a record box office hit. A gripping story about a man-eating shark that terrorises a small resort, it went all out for shocks and thrills, and director Steven Spielberg – in his first big success – showed that he really knew how to build up the tension.

One Flew Over the Cuckoo's Nest was not a huge commercial hit, but it was lavishly praised by critics and won four Oscars, including best picture and best actor (Jack Nicholson, in what some admirers consider his best ever performance). Directed by Milos Forman, the film is set in a mental hospital and contains some brilliant and subtle acting in the portrayal of the patients.

Subtlety was the last thing on offer in *The Rocky Horror Picture Show*, an outrageous musical spoof of monster movies, with Tim

HELPLESS Jaws claims a victim.

Curry contributing an over-the-top performance as Frank N Furter. The film became a cult hit, with audiences dressing in horror costumes and joining in the songs.

US HITS OF THE YEAR	
1 LOVE WILL KEEP US TOGETHER	*Captain & Tennille*
2 ISLAND GIRL	*Elton John*
3 FLY ROBIN FLY	*Silver Convention*
4 HE DON'T LOVE YOU (LIKE I LOVE YOU)	*Tony Orlando & Dawn*
5 BAD BLOOD	*Neil Sedaka*

US TV HITS
1 *All in the Family*
2 *Sanford & Son*
3 *Chico and the Man*
4 *The Jeffersons*
5 *M*A*S*H*

1976

DIED

12 Jan: Agatha Christie, British author
14 Mar: Busby Berkeley, US choreographer and film director
2 Aug: Fritz Lang, German film director
18 Nov: Man Ray, US photographer and artist

OPENED

2 Feb, Birmingham, UK: National Exhibition Centre
26 Oct, London: National Theatre, on the South Bank

ABOLISHED

14 July, Canada: the death penalty

INDEPENDENT

October, South Africa: the Republic of Transkei

Robert Redford stars in one of this year's box office successes, All the President's Men, *which brought the Watergate scandal to the screen. Redford got his lucky break in* Butch Cassidy and the Sundance Kid *in 1969 and has been one of Hollywood's top names since then.*

On 4 July, US citizens pour into the streets to celebrate the bicentenary of the US Declaration of Independence. There has never been such an Independence Day extravaganza, with a 16-km (10-mile) long international parade, a fleet of tall ships, a new museum, and an unending sea of stars and stripes in the streets.

FIRSTS

21 Jan: commercial flights by the supersonic airliner Concorde (Paris–Rio and London–Bahrain)
Female news anchor on a US network evening news programme; Barbara Walters joins ABC
New York: women admitted to the US Military Academy at West Point
Philadelphia, Pennsylvania: outbreak of Legionnaires' disease, at a hotel convention of the American Legion; disease produces pneumonia-like symptoms and is spread by air-conditioning systems

PASSED

UK: the Race Relations Act, making the incitement of racial hatred a criminal offence
USA: law allowing terminally ill patients to have life-support machines switched off

FOUNDED

USA: Apple computer company, by Steven Jobs and Stephen Wozniak

SEPARATED

19 Mar, London: Princess Margaret and Lord Snowdon, after 15 years of marriage

QUIT

16 Mar, London: Harold Wilson, British prime minister, in a surprise announcement; he is succeeded by James Callaghan

PUBLISHED

Alex Haley, *Roots*
Shere Hite, *The Hite Report: A Nationwide Study on Female Sexuality*
Anne Rice, *Interview with the Vampire*
Leon Uris, *Trinity*
Patrick White, *A Fringe of Leaves*

AWARDED:

Nobel Prize for peace: Mairead Corrigan and Betty Williams, as co-founders of the Ulster Peace Movement

APPROVED

16 Sept, USA: Ordination of women priests by Episcopalian Church

INJURED

1 Aug, West Germany: Niki Lauda, racing driver, burnt in Grand Prix

The phrase 'junk food' enters the English language, denoting processed food with a high calorific content but low nutritional value. A diet of junk food, such as hamburgers and french fries, is the result of an speeded-up urban lifestyle, in which people eat while on the go.

NEW WORDS

photo opportunity *n*: organised opportunity for news photographers to take pictures of a public figure
slam dunk *n*: basketball term describing vigorous overhand shot
soundbite *n*: brief excerpt from a recorded interview, suitable for inclusion in news bulletins

A close-up look at the red planet

ALIEN WORLD The *Viking 1* lander's robot arms stretch out into a hostile landscape of iron-rich sand and rocks.

20 JULY, HOUSTON
Seconds after landing near the equator of Mars, the USA's *Viking 1* probe began to transmit the first pictures of the planet's surface. NASA scientists received them minutes later – views of a barren red landscape, strewn with rocks.

The Viking project consists of two spacecraft, *Viking 1* and *Viking 2*, launched in August and September last year. Each one comprises two parts, an orbiter and a lander, which between them will send back thousands of photographs and important data about Mars's atmosphere, weather systems and soil structure.

··· TANGSHAN, CHINA: THE BIGGEST EARTHQUAKE OF THE CENTURY KILLS 250000 PEOPLE ···

SKYJACKERS FOILED

HERO'S WELCOME One of the Israeli pilots is mobbed on return to Tel Aviv.

4 JULY, UGANDA
A crack team of Israeli commandos today landed at Entebbe airport and rescued 106 mostly Israeli and Jewish travellers held hostage by Palestinian hijackers. Against all odds, 'Operation Jonathan' succeeded in killing the skyjackers and airlifting the hostages to safety.

Israeli paratroops led by 30-year-old Yonatan Netanyahu took off yesterday in three Hercules C-130 cargo planes. They landed at Entebbe in the dead of night, throwing guards into confusion by emerging from the craft in a limousine identical to that of Uganda's president, Idi Amin. The hit squad stormed the airport lounge in which the hostages were being held, and quickly overwhelmed the terrorists. As the hostages ran for the planes, Ugandan guards attacked; the retreating Israelis killed 20 of them, and destroyed 11 MiG fighter jets. There were four Israeli casualties – three hostages and Netanyahu himself, shot in the back by a Ugandan sniper as he headed for the aircraft. Just 53 minutes after the raid had begun, the hostages were in the air.

Street fighting flares in South Africa

AUGUST, SOUTH AFRICA

In the worst sustained violence since South Africa was created in 1910, at least 176 people have been killed and over 1200 injured in riots between police and protesters. The trouble started in mid-June following a government order that Afrikaans – seen by blacks as the language of colonial oppression – must be used for teaching in all secondary schools. The death of a 13-year-old on a protest march in the Soweto township, near Johannesburg, sparked rioting and looting, fuelled by years of oppression and frustration with South Africa's brutal race laws.

Following a command from Prime Minister John Vorster to end the riots 'at all costs', police threw a cordon around Soweto and dropped tear gas from helicopters. Around 100 people were killed. The Afrikaans law was withdrawn in July, but by then the protests were

FREEDOM FIGHT Rifles at the ready, South African police struggle to contain rioting in Soweto.

against apartheid in general. Rioting and lawlessness spread to Pretoria and Cape Town, and to black universities in Zululand and the Transvaal.

Foreign leaders have roundly condemned South Africa. The United Nations called apartheid 'a crime against the conscience and dignity of mankind'.

··· 4 MAY, ENGLAND: LIVERPOOL FOOTBALL CLUB WINS LEAGUE CHAMPIONSHIP FOR RECORD NINTH TIME ···

Mao, China's revered leader, is dead

ALL POWERFUL Mao was leader of a quarter of the world's population.

9 SEPTEMBER, BEIJING
Mao Zedong, Chairman of the Communist Party of China, has died aged 82.

Minutes after his death was announced on Chinese State Radio, sobbing mourners started to arrive in Beijing's

Tiananmen Square to pay a final tribute to the man they revered above all others.

Mao led the Communists to victory against Chiang Kai-shek's Nationalists in 1949, and founded the People's Republic of China. With his right-hand man, Zhou Enlai, who died in January this year, Mao embarked on a series of radical reforms, including the Great Leap Forward in 1958 and the Cultural Revolution in 1966, when millions were tortured, jailed and executed.

China's future is uncertain. Moderate Communists, led by Hua Guofeng, are now manoeuvring for power.

US Democrats back in power

2 NOVEMBER, WASHINGTON DC
Georgian peanut farmer Jimmy Carter has defeated incumbent President Gerald Ford to win back the White House for the Democrats. In a close-run poll, Carter won the South and the key states of New York and Pennsylvania. The West held firm for the Republicans.

The Watergate affair of 1973 is still fresh in people's minds, and Ford's electoral chances were damaged by his decision to pardon former President Richard Nixon for his role in that scandal.

Blue skies bring drought to Europe

A relentless heatwave hovered over Europe this year, bringing Britain its driest summer since 1727 and drying up rivers and reservoirs from Denmark to Italy. As forest fires raged, several countries introduced emergency water rationing. The British, who usually complain of the cold and damp, took advantage of the rare opportunity to moan about how hot it was.

Women demand peace in Ulster

PROTEST SINGERS Ewart-Biggs, Corrigan, Baez and Williams (left to right) lead singing in London.

27 NOVEMBER, LONDON
A march for peace in Northern Ireland today drew 30 000 marchers to the centre of London. The peace movement grew out of the death of three children, the youngest a boy of six months in a pram, who were crushed by a car careering out of control after its terrorist driver had been shot and killed by the army. The women of Ulster – who have seen too many of their children, lovers and husbands slaughtered – rebelled. Spontaneous protests against this senseless tragedy grew into the Ulster Peace Movement.

At the head of the march today were the movement's co-founders, Mairead Corrigan (the dead children's aunt) and Betty Williams, and Jane Ewart-Biggs, wife of the British ambassador who was murdered by the IRA in Dublin. A large contingent from Europe and from the USA – including 1960s folk singer Joan Baez – helped to put the march on the international map.

Grot versus glamour as punk attacks disco

ROUGH STUFF The Sex Pistols, punk rock's finest.

Elton John and Kiki Dee dominated the US and British charts this year with 'Don't Go Breaking My Heart'; Abba had three massive hits with 'Mamma Mia', 'Fernando' and 'Dancing Queen'; and the Eagles became the first group to go platinum, with a million sales of their soft rock album *Greatest Hits 1971–75*. But the story of the year in pop has come from Britain's run-down inner city areas where punk, rock's newest baby, was born. Early heroes are the Sex Pistols, four brash London lads who first played live in November 1975; the Damned, formed in July this year; and the Clash, who played as support band for the Sex Pistols this summer.

The Sex Pistols exploded into public consciousness in December when they appeared on a British current affairs television programme. Goaded by host Bill Grundy, the Pistols swore like troopers. Amid press uproar the band have been sacked by their record label EMI and had tour dates cancelled. Their only single, 'Anarchy in the UK', which begins with singer Johnny Rotten yelling 'I am an antichrist', has been withdrawn, but other record labels are ready to sign them up.

The publicity is fuelling the punk explosion. In London a punk venue, the Roxy Club, opened in December. The Ramones, among the leaders of an earlier punk scene in New York City, brought their intense high-speed rock to London. The Damned are at work on an LP which should be ready for release early next year.

MAMMA MIA Agnetha Faltskog of Swedish group Abba, the most successful pop band since the Beatles.

Sweden's 'Iceborg' wows Wimbledon Centre Court tennis fans

3 JULY, WIMBLEDON

His long blond hair held back by a headband, 20-year-old Bjorn Borg today beat Ilie Nastase of Romania 6–4, 6–2, 9–7 to become the youngest Wimbledon champion for 45 years and the first Swede to win the title. Borg's graceful crafting of strength and technique – and his beautifully conditioned hair – thrilled spectators on Centre Court and delighted hordes of teenage girls, who mob him wherever he goes.

Borg's ability to stay cool under pressure has earned him the nickname of 'the Iceborg'. Two years ago, at 18, he became the youngest ever winner of the French Open. Last year he led the Swedish team to its first ever victory in the Davis Cup.

CHAMPION Borg returning a shot against Raul Ramires of Mexico in the Tennis World Championship Tournament in Dallas, before his Wimbledon victory.

Romanian gymnast is just perfect

1 AUGUST, MONTREAL
The boycott by 22 African nations, angered by the presence of New Zealand – a country that still has sporting links with South Africa – cost the Montreal Olympics dear. The long-distance races and the boxing seemed flat without them.

But as always there was plenty of excitement – and none was more supercharged than that supplied by 14-year-old Nadia Comaneci. On the very first day of the gymnastics performances, judges awarded the Romanian the first perfect score of ten in Olympic history for her performance on the asymmetric bars. She bagged five further tens on her way to three gold medals. Comaneci,

spotted at the age of seven by Romanian coach Bela Karolyi, had been trained by him for years before being set loose on the world stage. She has already been dubbed 'Little Miss Perfect'.

Other headliners included the US men's swimming team, whose stars Bruce Jenner and John Naber led the way to victory in all the events except the high dive. Lasse Viren of Finland repeated the 5000 and 10 000 metres double he achieved in Munich four years ago, and the USSR's Victor Sanayev triple-jumped his way to a third Olympic gold in a row.

WELL BALANCED Romanian athlete Nadia Comaneci displays poise on the parallel bars.

US HITS OF THE YEAR

1	TONIGHT'S THE NIGHT (GONNA BE ALRIGHT)	*Rod Stewart*
2	SILLY LOVE SONGS	*Paul McCartney*
3	DISCO LADY	*Johnnie Taylor*
4	DON'T GO BREAKING MY HEART	*Elton John & Kiki Dee*
5	PLAY THAT FUNKY MUSIC	*Wild Cherry*

US TV HITS

1	*All in the Family*
2	*Rich Man, Poor Man*
3	*Laverne & Shirley*
4	*Maude*
5	*The Bionic Woman*

··· ANITA RODDICK OPENS THE BODY SHOP IN BRIGHTON, ENGLAND, WITH A £4000 LOAN ···

Volkswagen spices up the hatchback

The oil crisis of 1973 changed the way in which people viewed cars. Economy, especially high mileage per litre, became the priority, and vehicles became smaller. The Volkswagen Golf, launched in 1974, revolutionised the modern car, with its radical hatchback design that fused the rear window with the boot door.

With fuel prices easing, this year Volkswagen introduced the Golf GTi. It keeps all the model's popular features – practical design, good handling, safety and reliability – but adds a punchy 1.6-litre fuel-injection engine.

The Volkswagen GTi soon becomes popular. The car is capable of accelerating from 0–22 kilometres per hour (0–10 mph) in just eight seconds, and its top speed is a very respectable 180 kilometres per hour (112 mph).

BLACK BEAUTY The sleek Golf GTi brought sporty driving to the hatchback classes, and spawned a new generation of boy racers.

A TAXI DRIVE TO MAYHEM

Based on the true story of the Watergate scandal, *All the President's Men* played to packed houses against the background of a real-life presidential election. Incisive performances by Dustin Hoffman and Robert Redford, and a gripping tale of investigative journalism and intrigue, made this the outstanding film of the year.

Elsewhere three very different newcomers set the screen alight. The magnificently muscled Sylvester Stallone wrote and starred in the brilliantly choreographed *Rocky* – one of the best boxing movies ever. Robert de Niro, by contrast, was skinnily neurotic in *Taxi Driver*, directed by Martin Scorsese. De Niro shone as the misfit driver of the title, who befriends a teenage prostitute played knowingly by 14-year-old starlet Jodie Foster.

CITY SLEAZE Foster and De Niro the Taxi Driver walk the streets.

··· THE FIRST AUTOMATIC-FOCUS CAMERA IS DEVELOPED IN JAPAN BY KONICA ···

1977

DIED

10 May: Joan Crawford, US actress
12 Sept: Steve Biko, black South African activist
16 Sept: Maria Callas, Greek opera singer
16 Sept: Marc Bolan, British rock musician
14 Oct: Bing Crosby, US actor

QUIT

22 Apr, Israel: President Rabin
1 Oct, New Jersey: Pelé, world's greatest footballer, after exhibition match between his Brazilian former club, Santos, and his current club, New York Cosmos

FOUNDED

29 Apr, UK: British Aerospace
11 Nov, UK: Anti-Nazi League

FREED

9 May, USA: Patty Hearst, US newspaper heiress, jailed for seven years last September for armed robbery; on probation

STORMED

11 June, Netherlands: hijacked train, by Dutch marines; terrorists had kept passengers hostage for 20 days; six terrorists and two hostages are killed in the raid
18 Oct, Mogadishu: hijacked Lufthansa airliner, by German anti-terrorist officers; three of the four Palestinian terrorists die, but none of the 86 passengers is hurt

ELECTED

17 May, Israel: Menachem Begin, as prime minister
15 June, Spain: Adolfo Suarez, as prime minister

On 4 December, *Jean Bedel Bokassa is crowned Emperor of the newly declared Central African Empire. Bokassa, a former captain in the French army, has been criticised for the lavish cost of his coronation ceremony; his country, which has only just gained independence from France, is one of the poorest in the world.*

FLEW

13 Aug: the US Space Shuttle prototype *Enterprise*
26 Sept: British entrepreneur Freddie Laker's first 'Skytrain', cut-price London–New York air service

CHAMPIONS

25 May, Rome: Liverpool football team, winners of top European club competition the European Cup, beating Germany's Borussia Mönchengladbach 3–1

29 May, Indianapolis: veteran racing driver A J Foyt, who wins record fourth Indy 500 race
29 Sept, New York City: Muhammad Ali, who wins world heavyweight boxing crown, defeating Ernie Shavers in 15 rounds

OPENED

July, London: Central London Mosque in Regent's Park

LAUNCHED

10 Jan, UK: miniature television set with 5-cm (2-in) screen

DISCOVERED

4 Feb, Liverpool: IRA bomb factory, by police
Rings around the planet Uranus, by several groups of astronomers

CELEBRATED

2 July, London: Centenary of the Wimbledon tennis championships; men's winner is Bjorn Borg, and women's is Virginia Wade
11 Aug, Yorkshire: English cricketer Geoff Boycott, who scores his 100th century in a Test match, against Australia

POLLUTED

23–30 Apr: North Sea, after blowout at drilling platform; 31.8 million litres (7 million gallons) of crude oil escape

NEW WORD

pogo *n*: dance consisting of jumping on the spot, popular with punk rockers (from the pogo stick, a toy with side-mounted footrests and a spring in the bottom, used for jumping high into the air)

South African leader Biko killed

DEMAND FOR JUSTICE A demonstrator holds up a wreath and a portrait of Steve Biko in Pretoria.

25 SEPTEMBER, SOUTH AFRICA Fifteen thousand mourners attended the funeral today of the South African anti-apartheid activist Steve Biko in his native King William's Town. Diplomats from 12 Western countries were among those paying their respects to the young Black Consciousness leader, whose sudden and suspicious death in police custody shocked the world.

Biko, aged 30, died in a Pretorian police hospital on 12 September from brain injuries. He had been detained by the police in Port Elizabeth on 18 August, and interrogated and allegedly beaten for the next 25 days. On 11 September, Biko was thrown naked, shackled and unconscious into the back of a police van, and driven 1130 kilometres (700 miles) to Pretoria, where he died the next day, without receiving any medical attention. The official police version of what happened is that Biko died from banging his head on the floor of the van.

Biko was seen by the South African government and police as a threat to national security. His call to 'black pride' is thought to have helped to fuel the Soweto riots of June last year, precursor of the nationwide rebellion which has brought about the current state of emergency. Biko's arrest and death have come at a time of extreme tension in South Africa.

Paris building has nothing to hide

The Pompidou Centre in Paris, opened this year, has turned preconceived ideas about architecture inside out – literally. The building was commissioned in 1968 by the then prime minister, Georges Pompidou, to give Paris a new cultural focus. It includes a public library, a centre for experimental music, a cinema and a stunning art collection. But its outer appearance has grabbed all the attention.

To match the ambitious plans for the inside, British architect Richard Rogers and his Italian colleague Renzo Piano had the novel idea of putting all the building's services – pipes, ducts, even the lifts – around the outside of the building. Critics say that it makes the arts centre look like a sewage works. But the public appears to love the building's high-tech industrial appearance, and it is rapidly becoming one of Paris's biggest tourist attractions.

··· THE APPLE II, THE FIRST MASS-PRODUCED PERSONAL COMPUTER, IS LAUNCHED ON THE MARKET ···

Hundreds die in runway collision

28 MARCH, TENERIFE The worst disaster in airline history happened yesterday at Los Rodeos airport when two Boeing 747 jumbo jets, one American and one Dutch, collided on the ground. All passengers and crew on the KLM (Royal Dutch Airlines) jet died – 248 people in all; 70 people, including the cockpit crew, escaped from the Pan Am jet, but the remaining 326 died, making a total of 574 deaths. Several of the survivors are in a critical condition, and it is feared that the final death toll will be higher.

The accident was caused by poor visibility. Fog covered the runway as the KLM jet opened its throttle and built up speed in order to become airborne. It drove straight into the Pan Am jet, which was taxiing for take-off.

It has not yet been established who was to blame for the tragedy. Both jumbos were on chartered flights, with full loads of holidaymakers. Normally neither would have been at Los Rodeos; they were diverted there because of a bomb incident at Las Palmas yesterday morning.

AFTERMATH Spanish soldiers help to clear the wreckage of the Pan Am jet.

Murderer Gilmore chooses death

Indochina's 'boat people' make bid for new life in Asia

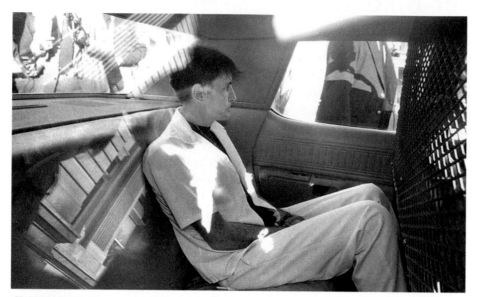

STATE PROPERTY Gilmore goes to another hearing in the long legal wrangle that led to his execution.

17 JANUARY, SALT LAKE CITY
At 8.07 this morning, double murderer Gary Gilmore became the first criminal to be executed in the United States for ten years. He was strapped into a chair and shot by a five-man firing squad in a makeshift execution chamber – a disused cannery inside the compound at Utah State Prison.

Gilmore killed two men on successive nights last year while conducting a series of armed robberies. Although he was sentenced to death at his trial, the sentence was not carried out because the Supreme Court called a halt to all executions in 1967. After spending half of his 36 years behind bars, Gilmore found the prospect of decades in prison worse than death and fought a unique legal battle for the right to die. While the legal arguments raged he made two suicide attempts.

Gilmore was allowed to choose whether he died by hanging or shooting. His last words to the firing squad were simply: 'Let's do it.'

DECEMBER, BANGKOK
In one of this century's biggest mass migrations, thousands of people from Laos, Cambodia and Vietnam are fleeing their war-torn countries and pouring into nearby states. The governments of Thailand, Hong Kong, Indonesia, Malaysia and the Philippines say that they can no longer cope with the influx of refugees, and have begged Western nations to help.

Middlemen are extorting large amounts of money from the refugees. Those who go overland to Thailand are stripped of their valuables at the border, but most go by sea, and are charged enormous sums to be stuffed into dangerous, leaky pirate ships. Observers estimate that 10000 refugees are fleeing Vietnam every month, while Thailand is already coping with a grand total of about 100000 refugees.

The United States has taken 165000 Indochinese refugees since pulling out of South-East Asia in 1975, but this year Congress has passed a bill that limits numbers to 15000 a year.

··· 1 OCT, SOMALIA: THE LAST RECORDED CASE OF SMALLPOX IN THE WILD OCCURS ···

Midnight coup puts military in charge of Pakistan

5 JULY, ISLAMABAD
The army has intervened in the political turmoil in Pakistan and its chief of staff, General Muhammad Zia ul-Haq, has taken over the government. President Zulfikar Ali Bhutto, leader of the left-wing Pakistan People's Party, has been interned, together with other leading politicians from both the government and the opposition.

Bhutto is widely believed to have rigged his party's victory in the recent general election, and opposition parties joined forces and took to the streets to demand new elections. Zia responded by imposing martial law, and in the last three months 200 people have died in the political violence. General Zia has pledged to check 'the drift towards political chaos' and to hold fresh elections.

A NEW DICTATOR Zia's coup gives him absolute power to rule the country.

ELVIS FANS MOB FUNERAL OF 'THE KING'

23 AUGUST, MEMPHIS, TENNESSEE The king of rock-and-roll, Elvis Presley, was buried today. Grieving fans are still coming to terms with the loss of their idol, who was found dead at his Memphis home on 16 August, aged 42.

The funeral sparked off scenes of fanatical hero-worship, the likes of which have not been witnessed in the United States since the death of Italian-born film star Rudolf Valentino in 1926. Crash barriers had to be erected around Presley's Graceland mansion as more than 80 000 mourners arrived to pay their last respects to 'the King'. Dozens fainted, either from the heat or from the pressure of the crowd, and two fans were killed when a drunk ran his car into the throng – but in the end 30 000 people were able to file into the house to see the singer lying in state. Thousands more lined Elvis Presley Boulevard to watch the funeral procession of white Cadillacs. The cemetery was decked out with wreaths in the shape of hound dogs and guitars.

Elvis shot to fame in 1956 and made 14 million-selling records before being called up to the US Army in a blaze of publicity in 1958. His early fame was propelled by his hip-thrusting dance when singing live, which won him the nickname 'Elvis the Pelvis'. He quit performing live shows in 1961 but returned to them in 1968, after which his act was gradually transformed from rock-and-roll rebel to lounge crooner.

But in the 1970s the singer's live performances and studio albums became increasingly erratic, and his girth ballooned. Many ascribed this to Presley's dependence upon barbiturates, and there is speculation that his death – officially blamed on an irregular heartbeat – was drug-related.

His decline never dimmed the devotion of his fans. In the days since his death eight million of the King's records have been sold. Some fans are unable to accept their loss, and are suggesting that Elvis is not really dead but has only gone into hiding.

GONE, BUT STILL GREAT Presley's records – 106 top 40 hits – keep him alive for his adoring fans.

··· THERE ARE 120 MILLION KNOWN CASES OF MALARIA WORLDWIDE ···

FENCE MASTER Red Rum gracefully glides over the Grand National course.

A record-breaking hat-trick

1 APRIL, LIVERPOOL The British nation has taken a racehorse to its heart. Red Rum has won the Grand National for the third time, repeating the triumphs of 1973 and 1974 and leaving his jockey, Tommy Stark, in tears as he trotted into the winner's circle.

There were scenes of unparalleled enthusiasm at the Aintree track outside Liverpool. A director of the betting empire Ladbroke's burst into the press room, startling journalists by shouting: 'We've lost a quarter of a million and I don't care!' Red Rum's purse of £100 000 was the largest ever won by a jumper.

Winning the Grand National – the hardest race over fences in the world – was supposed to be beyond a horse that was run into the ground as a two-year-old. But in five consecutive appearances in the National, Red Rum has never finished lower than second. Today he finished 25 lengths ahead of the runner-up, Churchtown Boy, leaving the 51 000 fans present hoping that they have not seen the 12-year-old gelding race for the last time.

Street parties and bonfires mark Royal Jubilee

7 JUNE, LONDON

In scenes reminiscent of VE night and the Festival of Britain, the nation has been celebrating the twenty-fifth anniversary of Queen Elizabeth II's accession. Events have been taking place throughout the year, but the past 24 hours have witnessed the climax of the festivities. Last night a chain of beacons was lit on hillsides up and down the country, and today the Queen and Prince Philip took part in a grand procession from Buckingham Palace to St Paul's Cathedral for a service of thanksgiving. Prince Charles rode along behind the royal coach, just as the future Edward VII had done at Queen Victoria's jubilee; at one stage he almost ran into the back of it, when the procession halted at Temple Bar for the Queen to receive the Sword of the City from the Lord Mayor.

Throughout the day, revellers have enjoyed thousands of street parties – in London alone, an estimated 6000 took place. In the evening a huge fireworks display on the bank of the Thames lit up the capital, and the Queen and Prince Philip appeared on the balcony of Buckingham Palace to greet cheering crowds.

So far the Silver Jubilee has proved more popular than anyone dared to hope. Some were sceptical about putting on such displays of patriotism and pageantry at a time of economic crisis, but – apart from those who bought 'Sod the Jubilee' T-shirts or the Sex Pistols' ironic tribute single 'God Save the Queen' – public reaction has been generally positive.

ROYAL TRIUMPH Popular enthusiasm has made the Royal Jubilee celebrations a resounding success.

··· USA: PRESIDENT JIMMY CARTER PARDONS ALL US CITIZENS WHO DODGED THE VIETNAM DRAFT ···

Jiving Americans hit the floor

The coolest, most happening club in the whole world is Studio 54 in New York City. The disco has a frightening door policy: only the rich, the beautiful and the famous are allowed in. If you make it past the bouncers, you arrive at the centre of the disco inferno that is burning across the United States.

New York's fashion and art aristocracy are always whisked in straight past the doormen. Andy Warhol and Bianca Jagger rarely miss a night, and half of Hollywood is in permanent residence there – Jeff Bridges and Liza Minnelli are regulars.

If, by any chance, you are turned away from New York's most talked-about club, you can do the next best thing and go to the cinema to watch *Saturday Night Fever*. Newcomer John Travolta plays a New Jersey shop clerk who comes alive once a week on the dancefloor of New York's clubs. With the film's electric dance routines set to a soundtrack of disco classics by artists such as the Bee Gees, cinema has never been so funky.

EXPRESS YOURSELF Disco dancers make an art form of their Saturday nights.

SPACE DREAMS, CITY ANGST

FUTURE COWBOYS The heroes of *Star Wars*, a kind of space western.

George Lucas's science fiction adventure *Star Wars* broke all records at the box office this year. Estimates suggest that it may eventually gross as much as $350 million worldwide, making it the biggest earner in cinema history. The final tally will also be boosted by toys and other merchandising – an increasingly important part of the film industry. Hot on its heels came *Close Encounters of the Third Kind*, Steven Spielberg's blend of mysticism and special effects.

Those two films garnered most of the technical awards at the Oscars, but the main prizes went to Woody Allen's

Annie Hall. It won best picture and best director, and many reckon it Allen's finest work to date. The plot-line has genuine emotional depth – apparently drawn from his real-life relationship with leading lady Diane Keaton.

1977 has also been a good year for European and art-house movies. Luis Buñuel was in typically mischievous form in *That Obscure Object of Desire*, while Bernardo Bertolucci's five-hour epic *1900* charted the rise of fascism. Plaudits for the most original newcomer go to David Lynch, who conjured up a nightmare world in *Eraserhead*.

Home truths for TV drama

Two television series that topped the ratings in the USA this year were *Roots* and *The Waltons*. A powerful 12-hour drama, *Roots* follows the fortunes of Kunta Kinte and his family over several generations. Born in Africa, Kunta is taken into slavery in the United States at the age of 17 and set to work in the southern plantations. The series tells the story of Kunta and his descendants through the horrors of slavery, survival during the American Civil War, and into a 'freedom' of poverty and racial discrimination. More than half the entire US

population watched the final episode of the series.

Also telling tales of life in the American countryside – though considerably more gentle – was *The Waltons*, the story of a down-to-earth family in Virginia in the Great Depression of the 1930s. Mom, Dad, Grandma, Grandpa, seven children and a dog called Reckless live in the town of Walton's Mountain, where they run a sawmill. At times the series seems innocent almost to the point of parody in an age which takes such sentimentality with a liberal pinch of salt.

HISTORY LESSON *Roots* shows how black Americans are bound to their past.

US HITS OF THE YEAR		
1	YOU LIGHT UP MY LIFE	*Debby Boone*
2	BEST OF MY LOVE	*Emotions*
3	I JUST WANT TO BE YOUR EVERYTHING	*Andy Gibb*
4	HOW DEEP IS YOUR LOVE	*Bee Gees*
5	EVERGREEN (LOVE THEME FROM 'A STAR IS BORN')	*Barbra Streisand*

US TV HITS	
1	*Happy Days*
2	*Laverne & Shirley*
3	*ABC Monday Night Movie*
4	*M*A*S*H*
5	*Charlie's Angels*

··· USSR: A YOUNG MAMMOTH, FROM AROUND 38 000 BC, IS FOUND PRESERVED IN ICE ···

1978

DIED

15 Sept: Wilhelm Messerschmitt, German aircraft designer

8 Dec: Golda Meir, former prime minister of Israel

KILLED

11 Mar, Israel: 37 Israelis, in Palestinian terrorist attack on three buses near Haifa

24 June, Rhodesia: British missionaries and their families, by Robert Mugabe's Zimbabwe African National Liberation Army; 12 dead

24 June, North Yemen: President Ahmed al-Ghashmi, by parcel bomb

20 Sept, UK: newspaper delivery boy Carl Bridgewater

25 Sept, San Diego: 135 passengers, when a light aircraft and a Southwest Airlines 727 collide; at least 15 others on ground killed by falling wreckage

DECLARED

8 Sept, Iran: martial law, by the Shah

ON SHOW

25 Aug, Italy: 'Turin shroud', cloth bearing imprint of a bearded man said by some to be Jesus Christ, at Cathedral of San Giovanni, Turin

The Magimix food processor, designed in France and manufactured out of a lightweight, durable plastic called lexan, causes a sensation in the kitchen. A range of attachments enables this new kitchen machine to do the work of a blender, a food mixer, a potato peeler and more.

ELECTED

28 Sept, South Africa: Pieter Willem Botha, as prime minister

JAILED

18 May, USSR: human-rights activist Yuri Orlov, for seven years

14 July, USSR: human-rights activists Anatoli Shcharansky, for 13 years, and Alexander Ginsberg, for 8 years

The Smurfs appear on television, and rapidly become some of the most popular children's characters ever created. Children enjoy collecting plastic Smurf models, including Papa Smurf, Moon Smurf and Smurfette – the only girl Smurf.

EXILED

6 Oct, France: Iranian religious leader Ayatollah Ruhollah Khomeini, opponent of Shah of Iran, from Iraq, where he has lived since 1964; Iraq aims to win favour with the Shah

EXPLODED

11 July, Spain: gas tanker on Spanish campsite at San Carlos de la Rapita; almost 200 killed

QUIT

31 Mar, UK: Grand National champion racehorse Red Rum

8 July, Italy: President Giovanni Leone, accused of corruption

5 Nov, Teheran: Iranian prime minister, Jaffer Sharif-Emami, following two days of rioting

7 Nov, South Africa: Connie Mulder, South African information minister, in wake of 'Muldergate' scandal over misuse of funds

INVADED

25 Dec: Cambodia, by Vietnam

BANNED

Feb, UK: 'Glad to be Gay', singer Tom Robinson's pop record, by the BBC

CHAMPIONS

July, London: Martina Navratilova, who wins the Wimbledon women's tennis championship, defeating Chris Evert; and Bjorn Borg, who wins the men's championship for the third year running, defeating Jimmy Connors

19 Oct: Soviet chess player Anatoly Karpov, who beats challenger Victor Korchnoi to retain world chess championship

FIRST

17 Aug: balloon crossing of Atlantic Ocean, by Ben Abruzzo, Max Anderson and Larry Newman in *Double Eagle II*; 138 hrs, 6 mins aloft

FIRST NIGHT

21 June, London: *Evita*, musical written by Andrew Lloyd Webber (score) and Tim Rice (lyrics)

On 12 June, *serial killer David Berkowitz, known as 'Son of Sam', receives six life sentences for the murders of six young women over the course of a year in New York City. Berkowitz, a postal worker, claimed that the spirit of a black labrador dog told him to carry out the shootings. When lawmen came to arrest him, he asked: 'What took you so long?'*

SEIZED POWER

27 Apr, Afghanistan: People's Democratic Party of Afghanistan, in coup; President Mohammed Daoud is killed

NEW WORDS

trainer *n*: shoe worn for athletic training; increasingly, a leisure shoe

twelve-inch *n*: a pop or dance record, usually an extended single track

Mass suicide in Jones's mad jungle town

29 NOVEMBER, GUYANA

Troops have come across a macabre scene of death deep in the Guyanan jungle. At the remote settlement of Jonestown, home to a cult called the People's Temple, the corpses of more than 900 men, women and children, linked arm in arm and dressed in brightly coloured clothes, were found strewn on the ground, giving the area the appearance of a battlefield. The people had apparently all killed themselves.

There was, however, little bloodshed. The leader of the cult – the self-styled 'Reverend' Jim Jones – had shot himself in the head, but his fanatical followers died from drinking or injecting a poisonous cocktail of a soft drink, Kool Aid, and cyanide. The lethal solution had been mixed in large vats, which were found at the site of the tragedy, surrounded by syringes. Many of the bodies were wearing identification tags.

Among the dead are five US investigators who, led by Congressman Leo Ryan, had gone to the settlement to look into complaints that some members of the cult were being held there against their will. The American team was shot dead by cult members before Jones ordered the mass suicide.

Jim Jones has been described as a sex-mad megalomaniac who believed that he was God. He incited his followers to commit suicide by saying: 'The time has come to meet in another place.' A note in his handwriting described the deaths as 'revolutionary suicide'.

DEADLY POTION Bodies flank one of the vats containing the cyanide mixture.

··· LAETOLI, TANZANIA: FOOTPRINTS MADE BY A HUMAN ANCESTOR 3.6 MILLION YEARS AGO ARE DISCOVERED ···

Bond-style death of Bulgarian dissident

14 SEPTEMBER, LONDON

In a bizarre episode reminiscent of a James Bond film, a Bulgarian defector has been murdered with a pellet-gun hidden inside an umbrella. Georgi Markov was stabbed, apparently accidentally, with the point of an umbrella in broad daylight in central London; after developing a fever, he died four days later. The post-mortem revealed he had been poisoned by a tiny capsule of the lethal poison ricin.

Granted asylum in Britain ten years ago, Markov had consistently infuriated the Communist government in Bulgaria with his outspoken broadcasts on the BBC World Service.

Polish Pope to lead world's Catholics

HOLY FATHER John Paul II on a visit to Britain – he became the first Pope to travel abroad extensively.

16 OCTOBER, ROME

The Roman Catholic Church has its first non-Italian pope for four and a half centuries with the election today of Polish cardinal Karol Wojtyla – at 58 the century's youngest pontiff. Wojtyla will be known as John Paul II, after the last pope, who died suddenly in September after barely a month in office.

John Paul I was keen to root out corruption, and it is said that he had already uncovered links between Vatican financiers and businessmen with Mafia connections. The eyes of the world are now on the new man. The election of anti-Communist Wojtyla has received an ecstatic welcome in his native Poland – although not from the country's Communist leaders.

HISTORIC ARAB–ISRAELI PEACE ACCORDS SIGNED

18 SEPTEMBER, CAMP DAVID, MARYLAND
The peace initiative mediated by President Jimmy Carter has achieved a historic breakthrough in the Arab–Israeli conflict. After 12 days of talks at the President's country retreat, Anwar Sadat of Egypt and Menachem Begin of Israel have signed a peace treaty between their two countries. The accord makes Egypt the first Arab country to enter into official relations with Israel, and thus tacitly recognise the Jewish state's national sovereignty.

Last November, President Sadat paid a symbolic visit to Jerusalem and addressed the Israeli parliament. Now Israel has agreed to withdraw troops from Sinai, and the two countries have pledged to seek a solution to the problem of Palestinian refugees. However, Yasser Arafat's Palestine Liberation Organisation has denounced the agreement.

FRESH START Carter worked hard to dispel Begin and Sadat's mutual hostility.

··· *LOVE SUBLIME*, STARRING SHASHI KAPOOR AND ZEENAT AMIN, FEATURES THE FIRST KISS IN INDIAN CINEMA ···

World's first 'test-tube baby' is born

26 JULY, BRITAIN
The world's first ever 'test-tube baby' was born today at Oldham District Hospital, weighing in at 2.6 kilos (5 lbs 12 oz). Named Louise Brown, she was pronounced 'quite normal' by Patrick Steptoe, the obstetrician responsible for the birth. Steptoe has spent more than 12 years developing his in vitro fertilisation techniques in collaboration with a Cambridge physiologist, Dr Robert Edwards.

Louise's mother Lesley had been unable to conceive normally because a lack of Fallopian tubes prevented any eggs from her ovaries from reaching her uterus.

Steptoe removed some eggs from her ovaries using an instrument called a laparoscope, and then fertilised them with her husband John's sperm in a shallow glass dish – not

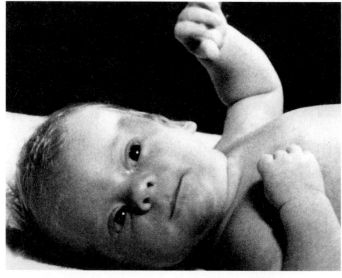

THE LUCKY ONE The in vitro technique that enabled Louise to be born will become widely available; it results in a baby in up to 25 per cent of cases.

actually a test tube. Finally the embryo was implanted in Mrs Brown's womb.

The world's media have been so excited by the story that newspaper rights have been sold for £300 000. The Church and some moralists have attacked test-tube babies as unethical and unnatural.

However, the controversy that surrounds the treatment has not deterred the many couples, desperate for a child, who have already applied for treatment – despite the long and complicated process that it involves and the fact that the techniques are so far relatively untested.

Giant oil spill harms sea life

18 MARCH, PORTSALL, BRITTANY
The supertanker *Amoco Cadiz* ran aground off the Brittany coast last night, threatening French beaches and fishing grounds with devastation. The ship was experiencing steering difficulties when it ran into a force 10 gale yesterday. A West German tug set out to help, but high seas snapped the tow-rope three times, and the *Amoco Cadiz* ran aground at midnight.

By 9.00 am the tanker had split in two, spilling more than a third of its 230 000-ton load. The British and French navies are struggling to check the spread of the oil, but damage to marine life and beaches is already high. The spill is believed to be the worst in history, and the captains of both tanker and tug are being held by police.

No crying for Argentina as they win World Cup

25 JUNE, BUENOS AIRES Amid a sea of blue-and-white streamers in the stands of the River Plate stadium, Argentina has made its home fans delirious by winning football's World Cup for the first time ever.

It won by a score of 3–1 after two goals in extra time sank the Netherlands, who were playing without the gifted Johann Cruyff. This is now the second time in a row that the Dutch side has lost the World Cup final.

The Argentinian victory represents a tribute to the high-attacking style which their chain-smoking manager, Cesar Luis Menotti, has instilled into his side.

Free-running Mario Kempes – the star of this year's tournament – gave Argentina a half-time lead, but with just nine minutes until the final whistle the Dutch substitute, Nanninga, brought the Netherlands level. Looking far less tired than its opponents, Argentina claimed the Jules Rimet trophy with goals at the last minute from Kempes and Daniel Bertoni.

PLAY TO WIN Daniel Passerella clutches the World Cup after the final whistle.

US HITS OF THE YEAR

1	NIGHT FEVER	Bee Gees
2	SHADOW DANCING	Andy Gibb
3	LE FREAK	Chic
4	STAYIN' ALIVE	Bee Gees
5	KISS YOU ALL OVER	Exile

US TV HITS

1	Laverne & Shirley
2	Happy Days
3	Three's Company
4	Charlie's Angels
5	All in the Family

AUDIENCES BELIEVE A MAN CAN FLY

SUPER STAR Reeve is the hero from Krypton.

Marlon Brando was paid a record-breaking $2 million for a cameo appearance in *Superman*. Fine special effects and a straight-faced central performance by Christopher Reeve tempted audiences large enough to outweigh the extravagance. The public also flocked to *Grease*, a slab of 1950s teen nostalgia, starring John Travolta and Olivia Newton-John. While *Grease* collared the receipts, the Oscars went to Michael Cimino's *The Deer Hunter*, a stately drama about the effects of the Vietnam War on a group of Pennsylvania steelworkers, Christopher Walken and Robert de Niro among them – although some said its portrayal of the Viet Cong bordered on xenophobia. There were similar criticisms of *Midnight Express*, a harrowing account of the experiences of an American imprisoned in Turkey for smuggling heroin.

Space Invaders have the whole world in their power

The minds of young people around the world have been seized by Space Invaders – the first ever arcade video game. The aim of the game is for players to shoot down incoming hordes of green alien spacecraft as they rain down the screen, accompanied by an irritatingly catchy tune. Compared with some of the games being developed by electronics manufacturers it is primitive – but it is certainly addictive. In Japan, where the game was created by the Taito Corporation, the game has been held responsible for a minor crime wave and a shortage of small change.

1979

DIED

13 Feb: Jean Renoir, French movie director

29 May: Mary Pickford, Canadian actress

11 June: John Wayne, US actor

27 Sept: Gracie Fields, British music-hall entertainer and actress

ON STRIKE

Jan–Mar, UK: lorry drivers, rail workers, hospital workers, teachers, and other public sector workers and local authority staff

FIRSTS

21 May, Leningrad: Western rock star to perform in the USSR, Elton John

9 Aug, Brighton: official British nudist beach, a 200-m (660-ft) stretch of land

29 Sept, Dublin: papal visit to Ireland, by Pope John Paul II

On **4 May**, *Margaret Thatcher, above, with her husband, Denis, enters 10 Downing Street as Britain's first female prime minister. Thatcher, who has been leader of the Conservatives since 1975, begins her term of office with an overall majority of 43 seats.*

UK: soccer player transferred for £1 million, 24-year-old Trevor Francis, moved to Nottingham Forest from Birmingham City

DEFEATED

28 Mar, UK: Prime Minister James Callaghan, in 'no confidence' vote in parliament, by a single vote; he calls a general election

APPOINTED

1 June, Zimbabwe-Rhodesia: Bishop Abel Muzorewa, as prime minister

SIGNED

26 Mar, Washington DC: Arab-Israeli peace treaty, by Egyptian president, Anwar Sadat, and Israeli prime minister, Menachem Begin

21 Dec, London: ceasefire agreement, to end guerrilla war in Zimbabwe-Rhodesia

ELECTED

31 Jan, Algeria: Colonel Benjedid, as president

7 Dec, Ireland: Charles Haughey, as prime minister

FLED

29 Mar, Uganda: President Idi Amin, from troops of Uganda Liberation Front

17 July, Nicaragua: dictator Anastasio Somoza Debayle

RETURNED

13 Apr, Uganda: Yusuf Lulu, from exile, to become president of Uganda, following collapse of Idi Amin's regime

12 Nov, UK: *The Times* newspaper, first printing since November 1978, following ending of industrial dispute

Japanese firm Sony launches the personal stereo with headphones, called the Walkman in Japan, the Soundabout in the USA and the Stowaway in Britain. The portable cassette player was devised by Sony's chairman, Akio Morita, so that his children could listen to loud rock music without disturbing him.

SEIZED

8 Jan, Cambodia: capital, Phnom Penh, by invading Vietnamese forces; Khmer Rouge regime ousted

12 Mar, West Indies: power in Grenada, by Maurice Bishop, leader of the New Jewel movement

21 Nov, Pakistan: US Embassy in Islamabad, by Islamic militants; Pakistani troops free 110 trapped US citizens, and one US marine is killed

SENTENCED TO DEATH

29 Sept, Equatorial Guinea: overthrown dictator Francisco Nguema

QUIT

4 June, South Africa: President John Vorster, in wake of 'Muldergate' scandal of misappropriation of funds

KILLED

3 Nov, North Carolina: four protesters on anti-Ku Klux Klan march, shot by 12 Klan supporters

REVEALED

21 Nov, UK: art historian Anthony Blunt, keeper of the Queen's pictures, as a former Soviet spy

VOTED

30 Jan, Rhodesia: Majority of white Rhodesians endorse multiracial elections

1 Mar, UK: Scottish and Welsh, on whether their countries should have separate parliaments; majority of Scots who vote say 'yes', but too few vote for result to stand; Welsh say 'no'

FASTEST

21 Oct, New York City: Norwegian female runner Grete Waitz, sets record 2 hrs 27 mins 32.6 secs for New York marathon, 42 km (26 miles)

LAUNCHED

Europe: the EEC's European Monetary System (EMS) and Exchange Rate Mechanism (ERM)

INDEPENDENT

22 Feb: St Lucia, of Britain

27 Oct: St Vincent and Grenada, of Britain

NEW WORDS

heavy metal *n:* loud, crashing rock music

winter of discontent *phrase:* the winter of 1978–79 in Britain, when the country suffered a wave of strikes; from Shakespeare's 'Now is the winter of our discontent ...' in the play *Richard III*

Red Army invades Afghanistan

HATED OCCUPATION A Soviet soldier guards the refugee route out of Kabul.

27 DECEMBER, KABUL KGB gunmen shot dead Hafizullah Amin, the Afghan president, today and are preparing to install a new head of state. Meanwhile the Soviet military machine continues to roll into Afghanistan to consolidate the invasion begun late on Christmas Eve, when a Soviet squad took control of Kabul airport and a fleet of Antonov transport aeroplanes began flying in military equipment and troops.

Ground troops crossed the border while fighters gained control of the skies.

The Soviets have invaded in order to pre-empt a revolt against Afghanistan's government. There has been widespread opposition to the regime, which took power in a coup in April 1978. Many Afghans are unhappy with the government's relentless modernisation programmes and close links to Moscow.

Opposition to the invasion, which is the first deployment of Soviet troops outside Eastern Europe since World War II, is sure to be fierce. If the rebels choose to fight a guerrilla resistance war in the mountainous Afghan countryside, Soviet troops will face a difficult task in pinning them down.

Mountbatten assassinated

27 AUGUST, COUNTY SLIGO, IRELAND Lord Mountbatten was killed today when his holiday boat was destroyed by an Irish Republican Army (IRA) bomb. His 14-year-old grandson, Nicholas, and a 15-year-old boatboy were also killed. Three other passengers – Mountbatten's daughter and her husband and mother-in-law – are fighting for their lives in hospital.

Lord Mountbatten, 79, a cousin of the Queen and the last viceroy of India, holidayed in Ireland every year. Tonight the Irish government expressed sorrow at the deaths but the IRA proudly claimed responsibility for what they call an 'execution'.

··· PETRA KELLY FOUNDS WORLD'S FIRST POLITICAL 'GREEN PARTY', IN WEST GERMANY ···

Nuclear accident at Three Mile Island plant

30 MARCH, PENNSYLVANIA The authorities have admitted that there is a danger of a nuclear meltdown at a power plant only 16 kilometres (10 miles) south-east of the Pennsylvania state capital, Harrisburg. The first sign that something was wrong occurred two days ago, when radioactive steam escaped into the atmosphere after a cooling pump broke down at the nuclear plant on Three Mile Island in the Susquehanna River.

A state of general emergency was immediately declared inside the plant, but residents of the island are furious that they were not warned of the accident until five hours later. The fission process in the reactor was shut down automatically when the cooling system failed, but it now seems that the

uranium rods may already have overheated and begun to break down.

No one yet has been evacuated from the area, but the latest radiation level measurements suggest that radioactive material is still escaping into the environment. All pregnant women and children under the age of five have been advised to leave the island. Nearly a million people in surrounding Pennsylvania counties have been put on evacuation alert, in case the unthinkable happens and the reactor melts down.

While the plant battles to contain the toxic gas leak, critics of nuclear power feel that their fears of catastrophe have been vindicated. Already there are suggestions the government will impose a moratorium on new plants while an investigation is being conducted.

CHECKING UP Plant workers use specialised equipment to measure radiation in the area.

AYATOLLAH RETURNS TO TAKE POWER IN IRAN

KHOMEINI FEVER A youthful supporter clenches her fist to salute the ayatollah.

1 FEBRUARY, TEHERAN
Islamic cleric Ruhollah
Khomeini, spokesman for
the opposition to the Shah
of Iran, returned in triumph
to Teheran today. The rule of the Shah, Mohammad Reza Pahlavi, is over; he fled to Egypt on 16 January following months of strikes and demonstrations by Islamic fundamentalists.

Khomeini – who is an ayatollah, or Muslim religious leader – was greeted by ecstatic crowds shouting 'God is Great'. The way is open for him to set up a new Islamic republic.

Khomeini was expelled by the Shah in November 1964 after making outspoken attacks on the government's secular reforms, such as greater freedom for women. He has been in exile ever since, taking refuge in Paris last year after Iraqi premier Saddam Hussein expelled him from Qom in Iraq.

The headlong pace of the Shah's reforms and the repressive nature of his regime united conservatives, radicals and liberals against him. Khomeini led the opposition movement in exile, recording messages on cassette tapes and sending them back to Iran, where they were widely circulated without the knowledge of the press or the Shah's dreaded secret police.

Khomeini has promised to set up a new Shi'ite government and impose strict Islamic laws. Although the ayatollah is not expected to become prime minister, observers believe he will be all powerful. The United States has lost a Cold War ally. Khomeini's view that the USA is the 'great Satan' is widespread among Iranians resentful of the way the Americans backed the Shah.

··· OVER A MILLION PEOPLE VISIT THE PICASSO RETROSPECTIVE AT THE MUSEUM OF MODERN ART, NEW YORK ···

Kampuchea's legacy of death

The full story of Khmer Rouge leader Pol Pot's four-year reign of terror is coming to light after his regime was overthrown by Vietnamese troops in January this year. In April 2000 corpses, weighed down with stones, were found in a lake near the town of Stung Trengin in Kampuchea (Cambodia). This is only one example of the Khmer Rouge's mass execution of those considered to be its enemies.

The world has been shocked to find that political purges have taken the lives of perhaps one million people – about one-fifth of the nation's population. In a concerted attack on religion, the regime reduced the number of Buddhist monks in the country from 30000 four years ago to about 6000 today. In line with Pol Pot's wish to reorientate the population towards agriculture, whole cities have been evacuated.

An international relief operation has been mounted to send food and medical supplies to the hundreds of thousands of displaced people, many of whom have fled to Thailand. There are, however, indications that aid is being diverted to the Khmer Rouge, which has taken to the jungle.

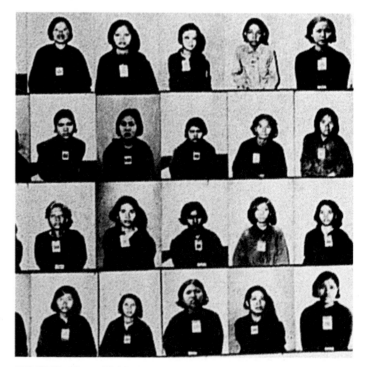

MEMORIAL Many of Pol Pot's victims were photographed before being killed.

Nicaragua falls to populist Sandinista rebels

20 JULY, MANAGUA

Nicaraguan President Anastasio Somoza Debayle has been driven from office by Sandinista rebels and today fled into exile. Months of fierce fighting between government troops and rebels have killed thousands and made around 20 per cent of Nicaraguans homeless. The Sandinistas are now in control of the capital, Managua, and will form a new government.

Reports last September indicated that Somoza was willing to step down in a deal brokered by US President Jimmy Carter's special envoy, William Jordan. The USA was keen to avoid a takeover by the socialist Sandinistas, but Somoza clung on to power as long as he could, and the USA broke off relations with his government on 8 February this year.

Somoza's departure ends more than 40 years of rule by his family. His father Anastasio Somoza García seized power in 1930. The Sandinista National Liberation Front – named in honour of the 1930s Nicaraguan freedom fighter César Augusto Sandino – was founded in 1962 to oust the Somoza dynasty. The impetus for serious opposition came with the killing of a Managua newspaper editor in 1978. From bases in Honduras and Costa Rica, the Sandinistas fought an effective guerrilla campaign against the repressive Somoza government.

The Sandinistas have won the broad support of peasants, students and the business community. The new regime's radical plans include the confiscation of Somoza's lands and the nationalisation of Nicaraguan industry.

SHOW OF ARMS A young Sandinista and his older comrades wave their guns.

··· THE NIKE 'TAILWIND', DEVELOPED BY ENGINEER FRANK RUDY, IS THE FIRST AIR-CUSHIONED TRAINER ···

Superpowers slow the arms race

18 JUNE, VIENNA

'A victory in the battle for peace' is US President Jimmy Carter's verdict on the new arms limitation treaty that he signed with Soviet leader Leonid Brezhnev today. Both sides have agreed to limit their armouries to 2250 strategic nuclear missiles by 1981, with no more than 1320 of these fitted with multiple warheads. There are other limits on bombers fitted with inter-continental ballistic missiles such as Cruise.

In real terms the agreement means that the USA will be able to increase its arsenal by a small degree, while the Soviet Union cuts back slightly. The treaty – the second Strategic Arms Limitation Talks agreement (SALT II) – caps almost seven years of negotiations

following the first SALT agreement, signed by President Nixon and Brezhnev on 26 May 1972. Carter faces the difficult task of winning US Senate approval for SALT II, which still has to ratified by both countries. Many senators have criticised the treaty for being too soft on the Soviets and Carter for being too idealistic.

In Europe some critics are complaining that the agreement covers only long-range missiles and does not offer any protection against Soviet intermediate-range attack. Others say that the arms limitation treaty is futile, since both superpowers still have the firepower to destroy each other. Observers also noted that Brezhnev, now 72, seems to be in very poor health.

Punk rocker found dead after overdose

1 FEBRUARY, NEW YORK CITY
The punk-rock star Sid Vicious was found dead in his Greenwich Village apartment this morning, apparently from a heroin overdose. The former Sex Pistols bass guitarist – real name John Simon Ritchie – was on bail awaiting trial for the murder of his girlfriend, Nancy Spungen, who was found stabbed to death in Vicious's hotel room in October last year.

Following his arrest Sid attempted to commit suicide, and he had recently been rearrested for allegedly using a broken glass to attack a man in a nightclub. He had been undergoing treatment for heroin addiction.

The world gazes at Saturn in wonder

SEPTEMBER, PASADENA

The world is marvelling at photographs of Saturn being sent back by the *Pioneer 11* space probe, which was launched in 1973, passed by Jupiter in December 1974, and this month flew within 20 900 kilometres (13 000 miles) of Saturn. Meanwhile scientists at the Jet Propulsion Laboratory in Pasadena, California, have been excited to identify two more rings around Saturn, and the pictures also reveal that the rings – first observed by Galileo in 1610 – comprise particles ranging from grains of dust to ice-covered rocks the size of moons.

These astonishing photographs follow the data transmitted to Earth from the *Voyager I* and *Voyager II* probes earlier this year. The Voyager missions, which were launched in 1977, revealed that Jupiter was encircled by a ring of rocky debris which was estimated to be 29 kilometres (18 miles) thick. Unusually, both space probes are carrying long-playing records called 'Sounds of Earth', to serve as humanity's introduction to any alien civilisations they might encounter when they leave our solar system.

HEAVENLY SIGHT The probes revealed that Saturn's rings contain a wide variety of cosmic debris.

··· 10 JULY, USA: ROCK-AND-ROLL STAR CHUCK BERRY IS JAILED FOR THREE MONTHS FOR TAX EVASION ···

Nobel Peace Prize given to angel of Calcutta

RECOGNITION Mother Teresa accepts the award.

10 DECEMBER, OSLO

Mother Teresa, tireless champion of the world's poor, received the Nobel Prize for peace in Oslo tonight. The award came as recognition of a lifetime's devotion to the destitute and dying.

At first sight it is hard to believe that this 69-year-old nun can have had such a huge influence on attitudes towards the poor. Mother Teresa is of humble origin and was born in Albania (now Macedonia), and baptised Agnes Gonxha Bojazhui. At the age of 12 she felt a calling to spend her life working for God, and at 18 she joined the Catholic Order of the Sisters of Our Lady of Loreto, arriving in India in 1929.

In August 1948 she received permission to leave the relative security of her Calcutta convent, and after receiving medical training in Patna she began work in the slums of Calcutta. Soon she was joined by sisters who shared her vocation, and the Missionaries of Charity society was founded. Word of their work spread fast throughout and there are now 700 shelters and clinics run by the society in India, and Mother Teresa's charitable movement is active in many countries around the world.

Coe races to a record hat-trick

15 AUGUST, ZURICH

Great Britain's resurgence in middle-distance running, led by Sebastian Coe, goes on and on. In only 41 days the diminutive Coe has taken the athletics world by storm by setting new international records in the 800 metres, the 1500 metres and 1 mile races. This unprecedented hat-trick was completed tonight in Zurich, where the 22-year-old Coe ran a stunning last lap in the 1500 metres race to break the tape in 3 minutes 32.1 seconds.

On 5 July Coe completed the 800 metres in 1 minute 42.33 seconds at Oslo. Twelve days later he ran the mile in 3 minutes 48.95 seconds, becoming the first person to hold both world records at the same time since Peter Snell of New Zealand in the 1960s.

The mechanic and the Orkian steal the limelight

Two comedy shows became established favourites this year – *Happy Days* and *Mork and Mindy*. The top-rated comedy since the mid-1970s, *Happy Days* began as an innocuous sitcom set in 1950s middle America, based on the everyday life of the Cunningham family – but it rapidly became apparent that the main attraction for viewers was a minor character, the Fonz, an ultra-cool garage mechanic played by Henry Winkler. He was allowed to take over the show, and by 1977 *Happy Days* was the most popular series on American television.

The Fonz's black leather jacket even went on display in the Smithsonian Institute in Washington DC.

In 1978 the Fonz met and duelled with Mork from Ork, a cheerful alien played by young comedian Robin Williams. Mork's catchphrase '*Na nu, na nu*' (Orkian for 'hello' and 'goodbye') was so popular that he was given his own series almost immediately, and Williams's quick-fire, quirky delivery of Mork's topsy-turvy views (he lived upside down in a cupboard) made *Mork and Mindy* another massive hit.

CRAZY NAME, CRAZY GUY Mindy reassures Mork after another puzzling encounter with humanity.

ALIEN AT THE HEART OF DARKNESS

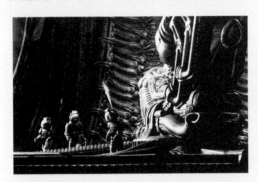

THE MONSTER AWAITS The crew of the *Nostromo* search an ominously abandoned spacecraft.

The Vietnam War was the background for Francis Ford Coppola's disturbing *Apocalypse Now*, starring Martin Sheen and Marlon Brando. It burst onto the screen and forever associated Wagner's 'Ride of the Valkyries' with machine-gun-toting helicopters. An ambitious film, it was praised for its contemporary interpretation of Joseph Conrad's classic novel *Heart of Darkness*.

Meanwhile audiences leapt out of their seats at screenings of *Alien*, Ridley Scott's unbeatable action thriller. Sigourney Weaver revelled in the strong, no-nonsense female character who heads the crew of the space cruiser *Nostromo* as they stumble across a derelict spacecraft with a terrifying space alien on board. Even the advertising slogan – 'In space no one can hear you scream!' – passed into common usage.

Blake Edwards's vapid but popular sex comedy *10*, starring Bo Derek and Dudley Moore, turned Ravel's 'Bolero' into an unexpected hit. Monty Python's *Life of Brian* caused ecclesiastical outrage when it was released in October, and Woody Allen's latest movie, *Manhattan*, featured Diane Keaton again playing opposite the director. This was also the year that comedian Bette Midler made her debut in *The Rose*, and that screen legend John Wayne died after battling cancer.

Court awards 'palimony' to Marvin's girl

20 APRIL, CALIFORNIA Michelle Triola Marvin has been reflecting bitterly on the failure of her lawsuit against the actor Lee Marvin. Two days ago Judge Arthur Marshall ruled that she was not entitled to half the estimated $1.8 million earnings of her former live-in lover; instead, he granted her just $104000 in 'rehabilitation costs' so that she could learn new skills.

The ruling comes seven years after 46-year-old Michelle pressed her original claim. 'In future,' she said, 'if a man wants to leave a toothbrush at my house, he can bloody well marry me.'

Yet the judge's award establishes a legal precedent for unmarried people to claim compensation from their cohabitees. It has been dubbed 'palimony' by reporters, who have been riveted by the case.

US HITS OF THE YEAR	
1 MY SHARONA	Knack
2 BAD GIRLS	Donna Summer
3 DA YA THINK I'M SEXY	Rod Stewart
4 REUNITED	Peaches & Herb
5 HOT STUFF	Donna Summer

US TV HITS
1 *Laverne & Shirley*
2 *Three's Company*
3 *Mork & Mindy*
4 *Happy Days*
5 *Angie*

1980

DIED
31 Mar: Jesse Owens, US athlete
15 Apr: Jean-Paul Sartre, French writer and philosopher
29 Apr: Alfred Hitchcock, British film director
7 June: Henry Miller, US author
24 July: Peter Sellers, British comedian and actor
7 Nov: Steve McQueen, US film actor

On 4 November, *Republican candidate Ronald Reagan defeats Jimmy Carter to become President of the United States. A Hollywood veteran, the star of such B-movie classics as* Bedtime for Bonzo *and* The Killers *has been governor of California since 1966.*

DEFEATED
2 Oct, Las Vegas: Muhammad Ali, aged 38, exhausted and outfought by reigning world heavyweight boxing champion Larry Holmes, aged 30

COMMITTED SUICIDE
18 May, UK: Ian Curtis, singer with British band Joy Division

Italian climber Reinhold Messner becomes the first explorer to make a solo ascent of Mount Everest, the Himalayan peak that marks the highest place on Earth. Two years ago Messner and Austrian Peter Habeler were the first climbers to scale Everest without bottled oxygen.

TRIUMPHED
5 July, London: Bjorn Borg, Wimbledon men's singles tennis championship, for fifth time, beating John McEnroe

QUIT
15 Oct, UK: James Callaghan as leader of the British Labour Party; replaced by Michael Foot

KILLED
11 Oct, Algeria; 20000 people, in major earthquake
23 Nov, Italy: 3000 people in earthquake in the south

ARRESTED
16 Jan, Japan: ex-Beatle Paul McCartney, for cannabis possession; he is later freed and deported
22 Jan, Soviet Union: dissident Andrei Sakharov, for his criticism of the Soviet invasion of Afghanistan

OPENED
5 Sept, Switzerland: world's longest road tunnel, from Goschenen to Airolo, covering 16 km (10 miles)

PRIVATISED
1 May: British aerospace industry
13 Nov: British Airways

VOTED
20 May, Canada: Quebec on whether the province should separate from Canada; 59.9 per cent vote against

RIOTED
3–4 Feb, USA: prisoners at New Mexico state penitentiary; 50 inmates are killed
17–19 May, Miami: black residents, after all-white jury acquits white policemen of murder of black businessmen; 18 people killed
12 June, Turin: English soccer fans, during European Championship match between England and Belgium

PROTESTED
21 Sept, UK: supporters of CND (Campaign for Nuclear Disarmament), at Greenham Common in Berkshire, the planned site for US Cruise missiles
27 Oct–18 Dec, Belfast: seven IRA prisoners in the Maze prison, who hunger-strike to promote their claim to be treated as political prisoners

FIRST NIGHT
17 Sept, Paris: *Les Misérables*, musical by Claude-Michel Schönberg (score) and Herbert Kretzmer (lyrics)

NEW WORDS
car-boot sale *n*: display and sale of small items, often junk, from the back of a family car
ghetto-blaster *n*: portable but powerful radio-cassette player, also known as beat-box or boom-box
phonecard *n*: a special credit card used to operate a public telephone instead of coins

Composer Andrew Lloyd Webber is inspired by T S Eliot's Old Possum's Book of Practical Cats *to write the musical* Cats. *The production, directed by Trevor Nunn, launches the stage careers of Bonnie Langford (left) and Elaine Paige (centre), as well as singer Sarah Brightman and dancer Wayne Sleep.*

War in the Gulf as Iraq invades Iran

23 SEPTEMBER, BAGHDAD
The festering hostility between Iran and Iraq exploded into open warfare yesterday when Saddam Hussein, the recently installed Iraqi dictator, ordered his tanks to roll across the border and set fire to the oil refinery at Abadan – the world's largest.

The Islamic fundamentalist government of Iran, led since last year by Ayatollah Khomeini, has repeatedly incensed Saddam by calling for his overthrow; but the real motive for the invasion is to seize control of the border province of Khuzestan. The absorption of this mainly Arab area into Iraq would not only satisfy Iraqi nationalist opinion but also provide a buffer zone between the countries and give Saddam the access to the Persian Gulf which Iraqi economy so badly needs.

Saddam has been encouraged by the United States' attitude towards him. Alarmed by the growth of Islamic

OPEN WARFARE An Iranian mullah walks across land near Ahwaz, now under Iraqi military control.

fundamentalism, the Pentagon appears to look upon him as a lesser evil than Khomeini. At this early date there is no

sign that either the Americans or the Soviets – who supply arms to Iran – will intervene in the war.

··· A GOLD RUSH IN THE AMAZON FOREST, BRAZIL, YIELDS $50 MILLION WORTH OF GOLD ···

Zimbabwe wins freedom, and Mugabe is first prime minister

4 MARCH, HARARE
The people of Zimbabwe, the former British colony of Rhodesia, have elected their first parliament, bringing to power a black majority and installing Robert Mugabe as prime minister. Victory is all the sweeter for the Mugabe, coming as it does after a lifetime devoted to liberating Zimbabwe from white rule, including 11 years' imprisonment for terrorism from 1964 to 1974. He will also derive great pleasure from defeating his great rival Joshua Nkomo, whose party won 20 seats against Mugabe's 57. The parliament contains 20 seats reserved for white members, and Mugabe has promised fair treatment of people of all

NEW LEADER Robert Mugabe (centre) holds his first press conference after being elected.

WHO declares the end of smallpox

19 DECEMBER, GENEVA
Smallpox, the scourge of humankind for centuries, has at last been eradicated, the World Health Organisation declared in a statement signed by the 20-member Global Commission for the Certification of Smallpox Eradication.

A mass vaccination programme launched by WHO in 1966 overcame all obstacles, and the vaccination of millions of people finally halted the disease. The last person to catch it naturally was a three-year-old Indian girl, Rahima Banu, in October 1975. The last person to die from it was Janet Parker, a laboratory worker at Birmingham University, in 1978.

The first free trade union behind the Iron Curtain

22 SEPTEMBER, GDANSK
The independent Polish trade union Solidarity was formed today after a summer of strikes that won major concessions from Poland's Communist government. Solidarity – in Polish *Solidarnosc* – is the first independent trade union in any country in the Soviet sphere of influence.

On 14 August Lech Walesa, an electrician at the Lenin shipyards in Gdansk, led 17 000 fellow workers at the yards out on strike. They were protesting at food price rises and the dismissal of trade union activists. Unrest began to spread. The workers called a general strike and presented the government with a series of demands.

An agreement signed by Walesa and the Polish deputy prime minister Mieczyslaw Jagielski on 30 August gave Polish workers the right to strike and recognised trade unions as legal. It was unprecedented in a Communist country.

This summer's historic events grew out of the activities of KOR (Komitet

UNITED WE STAND Lech Walesa and Anna Walentynowicz answer questions on behalf of Solidarity.

Obrony Robotnikow), a Polish workers' committee formed in 1976, which last September published a

charter of workers' rights. Lech Walesa, the heroic shipyard worker, is to be the chairman of Solidarity.

··· 50 PER CENT OF MARRIED BRITISH WOMEN HAVE JOBS OUTSIDE THE HOME ···

US hostage rescue bid ends in disaster

HELPLESS Officials at the US Embassy in Teheran sleep beside an Iranian Revolutionary Guard.

25 APRIL, TEHERAN
A dramatic bid to rescue the 53 hostages in the American Embassy ended in humiliating fiasco this morning before it had even begun.

The mission, code-named Operation Eagle Claw and undertaken by the Delta Force, encountered a host of technical failures, including a shortage of helicopters to carry the hostages to safety. The operation had already been cancelled, and the planes were refuelling in the desert for their return flight, when a helicopter crashed into a tanker aircraft, burst into flames and left eight Americans dead.

President Carter has taken full responsibility for the disaster, which leaves the hostages with little hope of release nearly six months after the storming of the embassy by Iranian troops. The Islamic revolutionaries are demanding the return of the Shah, deposed last year, to face justice in Iran.

Washington volcano blows its top

18 MAY, WASHINGTON STATE
A massive eruption of Mount St Helen's, a long-dormant volcano in the north-western United States, has caused widespread destruction. At least seven people are believed to have been killed, mainly in the Toutle River Valley, which was thought to be out of danger and therefore had not been evacuated. Most of the surrounding area had already been cleared.

The force of the explosion made the entire northern side of the volcano collapse and flow downhill on a river of lava. The mountain, 2975 metres (9760 ft) high before the eruption, is now 375 metres (1235 ft) shorter.

Gang of Four verdict awaited

**30 DECEMBER, BEIJING
The show trial of China's
Gang of Four is finally
drawing to a close,** and few
people doubt that they will
eventually be found guilty of
treason and crimes against
the revolution.

The so-called 'Gang'
consists of Jiang Qing (Mao's
widow), Zhang Chungqiao,
Yao Wenyuan and Wang
Hongwen. Having helped to
implement some of the most
extreme measures of the
Cultural Revolution, they
effectively ruled China
during Mao's declining years.
After his death in 1976,
however, they were ousted
by Hua Guofeng. Few
mourned their going and
people celebrated when
news spread of their arrest.

MANIAC SHOOTS LENNON

**9 DECEMBER, NEW YORK
John Lennon is dead. The
former Beatle was gunned
down outside his Manhattan
apartment late last night.**

His killer, a deranged fan,
is now in police custody; he
has been identified as Mark
Chapman, a 25-year-old
security guard with a history
of mental illness.

In October, Chapman
quit his job in Hawaii and
purchased a .38 calibre snub-
nosed revolver. Then he flew
to New York and began
staking out the Dakota
apartment building, where
Lennon lived with his wife,
Yoko Ono. It seems that, in
his twisted mind, he was
acting out a war against
'phoneys', as waged by a
character in J D Salinger's
The Catcher in the Rye.

STUNNED Over 50000 fans stand vigil outside Lennon's apartment building.

At 5.00 pm yesterday
Chapman approached
Lennon and asked him to
sign his latest record, the new
LP *Double Fantasy*.

Six hours later the pair
met again. This time
Chapman was carrying his
gun, and he called out as the
singer walked towards the
apartment building. Then
Chapman dropped to one
knee, held the gun with both
hands, just as he had been
taught, and fired five times.
Lennon staggered into the
building, fatally injured.
Chapman simply dropped his
revolver and waited to be
arrested.

··· IN-LINE ROLLER SKATES ARE DEVELOPED BY US ICE-HOCKEY PLAYER SCOTT OLSON ···

75 dead in Bologna station terror blast

**2 AUGUST, BOLOGNA
Police are today hunting terrorists who
planted a bomb in Bologna's central
station yesterday, killing at least 75
people and injuring hundreds more.**
The attack deliberately targeted Italian
holidaymakers travelling on one of the
busiest weekends of the year.

The suitcase device, containing
40 kilos (198 lbs) of high explosive, was
left in a second-class waiting room. It
exploded at 10.25 am, destroying the
room and an adjoining restaurant. Four
coaches of the Basle–Ancona express
were also damaged.

Responsibility has been claimed by
the Armed Revolutionary Nuclei, the

STATION TERROR Experts sift through the ruins of the station and express train destroyed by the bomb.

same neo-fascist group that bombed the
Italicus express in August 1974. Many
people believe that the latest outrage

was planned as a dramatic protest against
the forthcoming trial of terrorists from
the organisation.

The world waits to see who shot JR

Throughout the summer, millions of people around the world have been obsessed with the cliff-hanger of the year: who shot JR?

Dallas, a shamelessly melodramatic soap opera of greed, lust and feuding among the super-rich oil families of Texas, has become the most popular television series in the world, offering an endless parade of beautiful women, rugged, square-jawed men and sprawling emotions.

The plot revolves around the rivalry between the two Ewing brothers – nice, happily married Bobby (Patrick Duffy) and ruthless, scheming adulterer JR (Larry Hagman), who was shot by an unseen assailant at the end of the 1979–80 season. Viewers spent the summer debating whether he would survive – this question was

OIL FOLK The cast of *Dallas* outside their palatial family home, Southfork.

genuinely undecided, pending pay negotiations with actor Larry Hagman – and who had done the deed. Practically everybody had a motive.

The opening episode of the subsequent series had the

highest rating of any television programme yet broadcast. Viewers found out that JR lived, and that the would-be assassin was his mistress, and sister-in-law, Kristin.

New laser discs will outlast vinyl records

APRIL, SALZBURG
The conductor Herbert von Karajan gave his blessing this month to a new kind of record, developed by the Dutch firm Philips: the compact disc. 'All else is gaslight,' von Karajan declared of the 12-centimetre (4 $^3/_4$-in) discs.

Compact discs store the music digitally as a series of microscopic 'pits' and play it back with a laser beam. The new discs have a wider frequency range than traditional vinyl discs, and can be played for ever without wear since nothing is in physical contact with the playing surface. Philips signed a deal with Sony to launch compact disc players.

··· IRISH ROCK BAND U2 RELEASE THEIR FIRST ALBUM, *BOY* ···

WINNER TAKES ALL Coe is overwhelmed after coming first in the 1500 metres.

Russia scoops up golds

3 AUGUST, MOSCOW
The Olympic Games, disrupted by the American-led boycott, have nevertheless ended successfully, with more new world records being set than in 1976. The Soviet invasion and continuing occupation of Afghanistan prompted President Carter to bar American participation in the Games and call for a general boycott. Every European country except Great Britain refused to take part.

The eagerly anticipated duel between the British middle-distance runners Steve Ovett and Sebastian Coe ended in a draw. Ovett beat Coe into second place in the 800 metres, but could only finish third in the 1500 metres, which was won by Coe with a typical burst of speed off the last bend. Benefiting from the absence of crack American sprinters, Alan Wells of Scotland brought gold home in the 100 metres.

As expected, athletes from the Soviet Union dominated the medals table, winning 80 golds against the 47 won by their closest rivals, East Germany.

Office workers drawn to manual labour in the gym

The start of the new decade has seen a boom in the fitness industry. It is no longer only a good idea to keep fit – it is also very trendy. Aerobics is perhaps the number one fitness craze of the year. This sustained rhythmical exercise, usually carried out to the regular beat of pop music, involves the whole body in movement. Health clubs and gyms are opening in many towns and cities to promote a variety of health-related exercise.

Dr Kenneth Cooper, whose 1968 bestseller *Aerobics* introduced the concept of aerobic exercise to the world, is at last seeing his healthy-living suggestions taken up on a huge scale.

The goal of aerobic exercise – which makes the heart beat faster and thus oxygenate the blood – is to make the body stronger, more efficient and less prone to heart disease. Aerobic exercise does not, of course, have to be performed to music – other

STRETCH IT Aerobic exercise classes aim to make keeping fit fun.

forms of steady physical exertion, such as jogging, cycling and swimming, also fall into this category, and are consequently becoming increasingly popular.

US HITS OF THE YEAR		US TV HITS	
1 LADY	*Kenny Rogers*	1 *60 Minutes*	
2 CALL ME	*Blondie*	2 *Three's Company*	
3 (JUST LIKE) STARTING OVER	*John Lennon*	3 *M*A*S*H*	
4 UPSIDE DOWN	*Diana Ross*	4 *Alice*	
5 ANOTHER BRICK IN THE WALL	*Pink Floyd*	5 *Dallas*	

Rubik's toy is a brain teaser

One of the most popular toys ever, Rubik's Cube, was this year voted Britain's 'Toy of the Year'. It has sold 100 million units throughout the world.

THE AMERICAN GIGOLO TOUCHES A NERVE

JUST A GIGOLO Richard Gere as a male prostitute.

This was a year in which Richard Gere touched on the risky subject of male prostitution in *American Gigolo*. Gere was perfectly cast as the suave stud who does the rounds of rich LA women before finding happiness with Lauren Hutton. More brutally, Jack Nicholson played a homicidal psychopath in Stanley Kubrick's *The*

Shining, and Brian de Palma caused controversy with the 'slasher' movie *Dressed To Kill*. Martin Scorsese's *Raging Bull* saw Robert de Niro as middleweight boxing champion Jake La Motta. For the later scenes, when La Motta has become an obese layabout, de Niro went on an eating binge and gained 25 kilos (55 lb).

The year's most expensive flop was Michael Cimino's *Heaven's Gate*, which came in at $35 million and was immediately panned by the critics. George Lucas released the second film of the *Star Wars* trilogy: *The Empire Strikes Back*. Bob Guccione's soft-porn *Caligula*, starring – surprisingly – Helen Mirren, Malcolm McDowell and John Gielgud, opened in the United States with a record high admission price of $7.50. *Cruising*, starring Al Pacino, was attacked by gay rights activists for its stereotypical portrayal of homosexuals.

ABSORBED The cube is a real puzzle.

The cube consists of 26 smaller coloured cubes that rotate on a central axis. When the cubes are twisted out of alignment, the player must then return them to the original pattern, one of billions.

Its inventor, Erno Rubik, a Hungarian professor of design, took a month to solve his first cube. He never patented his design, so made no money at all from it.

1981

DIED
9 Feb: Bill Haley, US rock and roller
12 Apr: Joe Louis, US boxer
7 Sept: Christy Brown, Irish author
29 Nov: Natalie Wood, US actress

PUBLISHED
Salman Rushdie, *Midnight's Children*

ELECTED
18 Oct, Greece: Andreas Papandreou and Pasok Socialist Party
10 Nov, Cairo: Hosni Mubarak, as president of Egypt, by members of People's Assembly

EXHUMED
4 Oct, USA: Lee Harvey Oswald, held to have been the killer of President John F Kennedy in 1963; body confirmed to be that of Oswald

LAUNCHED
26 Mar, UK: the Social Democratic Party, by former Labour cabinet ministers Shirley Williams, Roy Jenkins, David Owen and Bill Rodgers

FREED
21 Jan, Teheran: 52 US hostages, held for 444 days by Iranians

1 Sept, UK:
petrol sold by litre rather than gallon in British garages
25 Sept, USA: woman appointed to US Supreme Court, Sandra Day O'Connor
China: Western pop musician to play in China, Jean-Michel Jarre

JAILED
25 Aug, USA: Mark Chapman, for 25 years to life, for murder of John Lennon
14 Sept, London: Marcus Serjeant, who fired six blanks at the Queen on 30 June, for five years
30 Oct, London: Mark Lyons, leader of Exit, the voluntary euthanasia group, convicted of abetting suicide; for two and a half years

FIRED
6 Aug, USA: 2000 striking US air traffic controllers, by President Reagan

INDEPENDENT
20 Sept: Belize, of Britain
1 Nov: Antigua and Barbuda, of Britain

SWORN IN
22 June, Los Angeles: 9700 new US citizens in a single ceremony in Memorial Stadium

CHAMPIONS
6 Feb: British pair Jayne Torvill and Christopher Dean, who win European ice-dancing championship
20 Apr, UK: Steve Davis, who wins world snooker championship, beating Doug Mountjoy 18–12 at Sheffield

APPOINTED
9 Feb, Warsaw: General Wojciech Jaruzelski, as prime minister of Poland

On 30 September, *France abolishes the death penalty and with it the guillotine – used in Europe since the Middle Ages. The design of the guillotine was improved in 1789 by French physician Joseph Guillotin, and it was used for countless executions during the French Revolution.*

COUPS
23 Feb, Madrid: led by Spanish soldier Lt-Col Tejero de Molina; fails
30–31 Dec, Ghana: led by former leader Jerry Rawlings against President Hilla Limann; succeeds

BROKEN
18–28 Aug: world record for the mile, three times in ten days by Sebastian Coe and Steve Ovett; Coe: 3 mins 48.53 secs; Ovett: 3 mins 48.40; Coe: 3 mins 47.53

NEW WORD
loony left *n*: derisory phrase invented by British tabloid press to describe far-left members of British Labour Party or local government; eventually used loosely to describe almost any left initiative with which the writer or speaker disagreed

On 11 May, *Bob Marley, Jamaican reggae singer, dies of cancer at the age of 36. Marley left Jamaica for the USA in 1976 following an assassination attempt, but he was buried in Jamaica. He will be remembered for his revolutionary lyrics and charismatic performances, and for taking reggae to audiences worldwide.*

BOMBED
8 June, Iraq: nuclear reactor being built near Baghdad, by Israeli jets
17 July: Lebanon, by Israeli aircraft in response to attacks by Palestinian terrorists

PROTESTED
24 Oct, London: 150000 marchers against positioning of US Cruise missiles in UK

CLEARED
27 Jan, UK: Rupert Murdoch's plan to buy *The Times* and the *Sunday Times*, by John Biffen, British secretary of state for trade

FIRSTS
15 Feb, UK: British Football League games played on Sunday
29 Mar, London: London Marathon; 7055 runners enter

REAGAN SHOT IN ASSASSINATION ATTEMPT

30 MARCH, WASHINGTON DC
President Ronald Reagan was shot in the chest at close range today as he left a trade union conference at the Washington Hilton hotel. Six shots rang out as the President was waving to crowds. Press secretary Jim Brady fell to the pavement with blood pouring from a head wound, while the President was pushed by his bodyguard into the back of his car, which then sped away to George Washington Memorial hospital. The would-be assassin, 25-year-old John Hinckley Jr, was immediately jumped on and pinned against a wall.

At the hospital Reagan quipped 'Honey, I forgot to duck' when his wife Nancy came to his bedside, and jokingly asked his surgeons whether they were Republicans. Although a bullet pierced his ribcage and lodged in his left lung, his life is not said to be in danger.

In the aftermath of the assassination attempt, the government has gone into a state of panic. Secretary of State Alexander Haig gaffed when he claimed that, after Vice-President George Bush, he was in charge of the country. In fact it is the speaker of the House of Representatives who stands next in line, and the current speaker, Tip O'Neill, is reported as being singularly displeased.

NEAR MISS Agents tend James Brady and a policeman, both wounded in the attack on the President.

··· AIDS IS OFFICIALLY RECOGNISED BY THE US CENTRE FOR DISEASE CONTROL ···

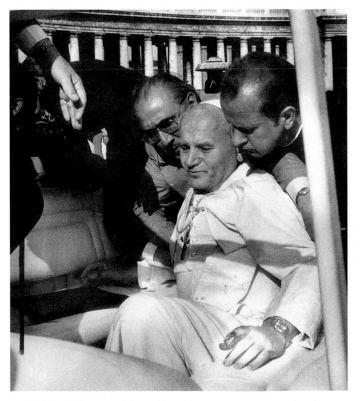

LUCKY ESCAPE The Pope is helped into his vehicle just after the shooting.

Turkish jailbreaker shoots Pope

13 MAY, ROME
Pope John Paul II was shot today by a Turkish gunman during his weekly audience in St Peter's Square. The Pope was travelling through the square in his open-topped 'pope-mobile', blessing members of the 20000-strong crowd, when 23-year-old Mehmet Ali Agca opened fire, hitting him twice in the abdomen and seriously injuring two bystanders. A witness said: 'It was awful. There was blood on the Pope's cassock.'

The Pope was rushed to Gemelli Hospital, where he underwent a five-hour operation. A hospital spokesman has said that he is confident that 'the pontiff will recover soon'.

Police had to surround the gunman to stop him being lynched by the crowd. They later found a letter that Agca had written, claiming: 'I am killing the Pope as a protest against the imperialism of the Soviet Union and the United States.' He said he was protesting at what he called Soviet and American 'genocide' in Afghanistan and El Salvador. It has emerged that he recently escaped from a Turkish jail after being convicted of the murder of a newspaper editor in 1979. Agca arrived in Rome three days ago, posing as a student at the Italian University for Foreigners in Perugia.

Wedding of the century watched by millions

DREAM WEDDING Lady Diana Spencer sits beside her groom, Prince Charles.

29 JULY, LONDON
Amid a glittering show of pageantry, the nation has been celebrating the marriage of Prince Charles and Lady Diana Spencer, which has been called the wedding of the century.

The festivities started at 10.00 pm yesterday, when Charles lit a chain of beacons, followed by a spectacular fireworks display in Hyde Park. Afterwards many revellers borrowed deckchairs from St James's Park and camped out overnight in order to gain the best possible view of today's procession.

One of the main points of interest was Diana's wedding gown of ivory silk taffeta, designed by the Emanuels, which had been a closely guarded secret. At St Paul's Cathedral the service was attended by more than 160 heads of state, although room was also found for Diana's three former flat-mates. During the ceremony the couple showed their nerves by fluffing their lines – hardly surprising, since they were being watched by a television audience of around 750 million worldwide. Most must have nodded agreement when Archbishop Runcie began his address with the words: 'Here is the stuff of which fairy-tales are made.'

After the wedding breakfast at Buckingham Palace, the couple made an appearance on the balcony and kissed before the cheering crowds. The couple then left for Waterloo Station in an open landau, with a 'Just Married' sign pinned to the back. There they boarded a train for Romsey, where they will be spending the first part of their honeymoon.

··· WEST GERMANY: BMW DEVELOPS THE FIRST IN-CAR COMPUTER, TO MONITOR ENGINE PERFORMANCE ···

Rebel troops kill Egyptian leader at parade

6 OCTOBER, CAIRO
Egyptian President Anwar Sadat was assassinated today as he was watching a military parade in Cairo. Ten others, including foreign envoys attending the parade, were also killed, and more than 40 people were injured.

Thousands of spectators looked on in shock as four soldiers in an armoured car turned out of the parade formation and showered the review stand with a hail of bullets and grenades. Sadat collapsed in a pool of blood. Guards immediately returned fire, and one of the assassins was shot dead; the others were arrested. Vice-President Hosni Mubarak moved swiftly to declare a state of emergency and stationed troops and riot police throughout the capital.

It is thought that the assassins belonged to an extremist Islamic group and that the killing was a protest against Sadat's controversial peace deal with

MURDERED FOR PEACE Under Sadat, Egypt was the first Arab state to sign a treaty with Israel.

Israel, which has angered many Arabs. Mubarak, who takes over the presidency, has promised to honour the treaty.

Police and youths clash across Britain

In early April the streets of Brixton, an area of south London with a large black community, erupted into rioting. Trouble began when police attempted to arrest a youth and a crowd gathered in an effort to free him. The ensuing rioting in which police fought battles against local youths – black and white – continued sporadically for many days.

In mid-July riots broke out across the provinces, with the worst violence occurring in the Toxteth district of Liverpool. One of the more bizarre images was the sight of rioters forming orderly queues in front of the stores they were looting. Police used CS gas on mainland Britain for the first time and – although many of the rioters were white – the home secretary, William Whitelaw, has been urged by Tory right-wingers to institute curbs on immigration.

Yorkshire Ripper sentenced to life

23 MAY, LONDON
Following a sensational trial at the Old Bailey, Peter Sutcliffe, the so-called 'Yorkshire Ripper', has been found guilty on 13 counts of murder and seven of attempted murder. Sutcliffe pleaded guilty to manslaughter on grounds of diminished responsibility, but the jury found him guilty of murder. Mr Justice Boreham duly sentenced him to life, with a recommended minimum term of 30 years. Sutcliffe was removed to the top security unit at Parkhurst jail on the Isle of Wight.

With these formalities, the public hopes that it has seen the last of one of Britain's most notorious serial killers. Sutcliffe, a lorry driver from Bradford, committed his first murder in October 1975 and continued his reign of terror until his arrest in January 1981. Many of the atrocities, all on young women, took place around the red-light district of Chapeltown in Leeds.

During the police operation more than 175000 people were interviewed. Sutcliffe was among the suspects, but he slipped through the net. He was finally detained for a motoring offence.

IRA claims terrorist martyr

BURNING PASSION Irish-Americans burn a Union Jack and an effigy of Margaret Thatcher in New York.

5 MAY, BELFAST
IRA terrorist and hunger-striker Bobby Sands died today in Belfast's Maze prison after refusing food for more than two months. The protest was part of a campaign to win the IRA internees special status as prisoners of war.

Sands, serving a 14-year sentence for a firearms offence, was a leading figure among the Maze's Republican prisoners.

His death today delivers him a kind of immortality as a martyr for the Irish Republican cause.

The IRA prisoners' special status was taken away in 1976. A hunger strike late last year – also aimed at winning back that status – ended on 12 December. Several Maze Republicans remain on hunger strike, and Sands's death is sure to fan unrest in Ulster.

··· PICASSO'S *GUERNICA* RETURNS TO SPAIN FOLLOWING THE RESTORATION OF A DEMOCRACY ···

Socialism comes to France with election of Mitterrand

CASTING VOTE François Mitterrand poses at the ballot box in the presidential election yesterday.

10 MAY, PARIS
Parisians sounded their car horns and danced in the streets tonight at the news that François Mitterrand, leader of the Socialist Party, had won the French presidency from right-winger Valéry Giscard d'Estaing.

The shock result opens a new era in French politics. Mitterrand, who won 52 per cent of the vote, is the first Socialist president to be elected since the French Fifth Republic was established in 1958.

In a radical departure from the style of government to which France is accustomed, the new president has promised to nationalise banks and key industries, to increase the minimum wage and social security benefits, and to fight France's high unemployment with a programme of job creation.

Mitterrand has been the figurehead for France's left wing since the late 1950s and has worked hard to make the Socialists electable, often allying them with the Communists on a common platform. He has stood twice before, losing to Charles de Gaulle in 1965 and to Giscard d'Estaing in 1974.

PacMan fever hits the arcades

In the wake of the Space Invaders phenomenon a new video game dominated amusement arcades this year: PacMan. The object is to steer the PacMan – a round, gobbling head – around a maze, swallowing (life-enhancing) energy pills and dodging (life-depleting) blobby ghosts. Despite its simplicity, PacMania has become the single most popular video game ever, inspiring unprecedented devotion from fans. The game has even given rise to a minor hit record, Buckman and Garcia's 'PacMan Fever'.

HUNGRY HERO The object of devotion for PacMan fans is this insatiable little mouth on legs.

Space shuttle's maiden flight

PIGGYBACK The space shuttle *Columbia* rides a converted 747 jumbo jet in its early flight trials.

16 APRIL, FLORIDA
The NASA shuttle *Columbia* has become the first vehicle ever to go into space like a rocket and come back to Earth like an aeroplane. *Columbia* took longer to build than the entire Apollo project took to put a man on the Moon. It was finally launched from Cape Canaveral two days ago – more than three years late and over its original $5 billion budget.

When 50-year-old astronaut John Young shot into the skies on a 200-metre (600-ft) tail of fire and became the first man to go five times into space, he and his co-pilot Bob Crippen were riding in a vehicle that had never been flown, powered by engines that had never been flight-tested, riding piggy-back on a giant fuel tank containing 23 million litres (5 million gallons) of explosive liquid oxygen and nitrogen. But in little more than two minutes, at an altitude of 50 kilometres (30 miles), *Columbia* was in orbit, while its rockets and fuel tank were falling back to Earth, where they were picked up by the US Navy from the Indian Ocean.

This morning, flying it like an enormous, partially powered glider, Young successfully piloted the world's first reusable spaceship home.

··· 1 AUG, USA: THE POP MUSIC VIDEO TELEVISION STATION MTV IS LAUNCHED ···

IBM challenges Apple's desktop computer

12 AUGUST, NEW YORK CITY
The computer giant IBM has broken the mould by marketing a personal computer to challenge the success of the Apple corporation. The company, nicknamed 'Big Blue' for its huge, blue-painted mainframe computers, has thought small for the first time. Its PC, available at the affordable price of $1365, will convince many buyers that micro-computers which will fit on a desktop

are more than just a passing fad. IBM has even borrowed techniques from the likes of Apple, buying its operating system for the PC from Microsoft, a small Seattle company run by a Harvard dropout called Bill Gates.

In a move to expand the available software tools, IBM will also abandon its secretive ways and publish the design of the PC, enabling other companies to write software compatible with it.

SLEEPING GIANT IBM's first desktop computer marks a change of direction for the manufacturer.

'Bad boy' takes trophy

4 JULY, WIMBLEDON

John McEnroe, the bad boy of tennis, has finally loosened Swede Bjorn Borg's stranglehold on the men's singles title at the Wimbledon championships. Borg had won five titles in succession, beating McEnroe in last year's final, but today his service deserted him and, after winning the opening set, he succumbed to the left-handed American 4–6, 7–6, 7–6, 6–4.

Within two hours of his victory, McEnroe was fined £5000 by the International Professional Tennis Council for his tantrums on court and abusive language to court officials during the tournament; he will appeal against the punishment. In today's championship match, however, he exhibited not a trace of bad behaviour – though at times he held his head in despair and looked close to tears. As much as beating Borg he beat his own temper. The All England Club has still to decide whether to extend membership of the club to McEnroe, an honour that is usually awarded automatically to champions.

NOT CRICKET McEnroe, angered by a line call, kicks his racquet in fury.

FIERY CHARIOTS, LOST ARKS, GOLDEN PONDS

RAID ON Harrison Ford as Indiana Jones.

Britain led the film world when *Chariots of Fire*, starring Ian Charleson and Ben Cross, won Oscars for best picture, best screenplay, best original score and best costume design. This stirring, sentimental portrayal of two British athletes – one Jewish, one Christian – preparing for the 1924 Paris Olympics captured movie-goers' hearts with its nostalgia for classically English bygone days.

Steven Spielberg went back to the days of comic-book adventure with *Raiders of the Lost Ark*, which introduced Indiana Jones to movie fans young and old. Tom Selleck had been first choice for the leading role, but Harrison Ford seized his chance and has become a widely loved hero. *On Golden Pond* saw an emotional reunion between Jane Fonda and her father Henry; the two had become distant over Jane's anti-Vietnam and pro-abortion stance, and *On Golden Pond* was the perfect opportunity for both father and daughter – on screen and in real life – to embrace and make up.

Endless success for hit duo

Two giants of the music industry came together this year to perform the duet 'Endless Love', released to promote the motion picture of the same title. Diana Ross, who shot to fame during the 1960s with her girl group the Supremes, joined her singing talents with those of Lionel Richie, singer and saxophonist with the band the Commodores.

Endless Love the film featured Brooke Shields and Martin Hewitt as high-school sweethearts thwarted by circumstance and accident. The title song was nominated for a best song Oscar.

The single 'Endless Love' has been a huge success for the veteran Motown label, breaking all previous sales records. The emotional love song remained at the number one position for nine weeks on the US *Billboard* chart, from August to October.

US TV HITS	
1	*Dallas*
2	*The Dukes of Hazzard*
3	*60 Minutes*
4	*The Love Boat*
5	*Private Benjamin*

US HITS OF THE YEAR		
1	PHYSICAL	*Olivia Newton-John*
2	BETTE DAVIS EYES	*Kim Carnes*
3	ENDLESS LOVE	*Diana Ross & Lionel Richie*
4	ARTHUR'S THEME	*Christopher Cross*
5	KISS ON MY LIST	*Daryl Hall & John Oates*

1982

BORN

21 June, UK: William Arthur Philip Louis, first son of the Prince and Princess of Wales

DIED

17 Feb: Thelonious Monk, US jazz pianist
10 June: Rainer Werner Fassbinder, German film director
12 Aug: Henry Fonda, US actor
29 Aug: Ingrid Bergman, Swedish actress
14 Sept: Princess Grace of Monaco (Grace Kelly)

NOT GUILTY

21 June, Washington DC: John Hinckley, who tried to kill President Ronald Reagan in March 1981; because of insanity

On 13 December, *the Vietnam War Memorial is dedicated in Washington DC. Designed by Maya Ying Lin, a 21-year-old architecture student at Yale University, the monument is a black granite wall inscribed with the names of the 60 000 soldiers killed in the war or declared missing in action.*

On 1 October, *Helmut Kohl, leader of the Christian Democrats, forms a new coalition government in West Germany after the collapse of the existing coalition. Kohl, now the interim chancellor until the next election, heads an alliance of his own party and the Free Democrats.*

GUILTY

18 May, USA: Reverend Sun Myung Moon, founder of the Unification Church of America, of tax fraud

OPENED

4 Mar, London: Barbican Arts Centre
7 June, Memphis: Graceland, luxurious home of the late Elvis Presley, as tourist attraction
June, Manchester: Hacienda nightclub
15 Dec: Spanish border with Gibraltar, closed for 13 years

SOLD

28 May, Spain: Argentinian soccer player Diego Maradona, by Boca Juniors to FC Barcelona, for £5 million

ELECTED

28 Oct, Spain: Socialist Party, led by Felipe González

EXECUTED

15 Apr, Cairo: five men found guilty of murdering President Anwar Sadat

HONOURED

Aug, Liverpool: the Beatles, as four streets are renamed – John Lennon Drive, Paul McCartney Way, George Harrison Close, Ringo Starr Drive

QUIT

October: rock bands the Jam and Blondie; both split; the Jam's Paul Weller forms the Style Council
9 Nov, USA: welterweight Sugar Ray Leonard, because of eye trouble

TRESPASSED

7 July, London: Michael Fagan, who broke into Buckingham Palace, stole a bottle of wine, sat on the Queen's bed and asked her for a cigarette

LAUNCHED

15 Sept, Virginia: new full-colour newspaper, *USA Today*
2 Nov, UK: fourth television channel, Channel Four

BANNED

19 Mar, UK: 15 cricketers, from Test cricket for three years, because of their unofficial tour of South Africa
19 Apr, Washington DC: tourists from visiting Cuba
8 Dec, London: Irish Sinn Fein politicians Gerry Adams and Danny Morrison, from entering UK

On 1 July, *the Reverend Sun Myung Moon, leader of the Unification Church, presides over a mass wedding ceremony, marrying 2075 couples in New York's Madison Square Garden. All the brides wore identical dresses and the grooms identical blue suits. The ceremony also ordained the couples as missionaries.*

PUBLISHED

Isabel Allende, *The House of the Spirits*
Thomas Keneally, *Schindler's Ark*
Alice Walker, *The Color Purple*

PROTESTED

12 June, New York City: 550 000 people, against nuclear weapons

FIRST

29 May, UK: papal visit to Britain for 450 years; last was in 1531

NEW WORDS

airhead *n*: unintelligent person
back up *vb*: to copy computer data, for example onto a floppy disk in case original is corrupted or lost

ARGENTINIAN SURRENDER ENDS FALKLANDS WAR

14 JUNE, LONDON
Crowds gathered in Downing Street tonight to hail Margaret Thatcher, the British prime minister, after she had announced to the House of Commons that Argentina's surrender had brought an end to the war for the Falkland Islands. 'Great Britain is great again,' the jubilant Tory leader told her admirers, who treated her to a rousing rendition of 'For She's A Jolly Good Fellow'.

The war began on 2 April, when the Argentinian president, General Galtieri, believing that Great Britain would not fight to retain the disputed South Atlantic islands, ordered an invasion. A force of 2000 easily captured the token Royal Marine garrison in Port Stanley, the capital, and reinforcements soon bolstered the occupation to 20 000 troops. The Falklands have only 1800 inhabitants, and the economy is based on sheep-farming. The British government, backed by the Labour opposition, resolved to defend British sovereignty.

A task force of some 70 ships, including the requisitioned *QE2* and led by the warships HMS *Hermes* and *Invincible*, left Portsmouth on 5–6 April. During the force's two-week passage to the islands, US attempts at mediation failed. On 25 April marine commandos, meeting little Argentinian resistance, recaptured the island of South Georgia without a single casualty. 'Rejoice, rejoice!' Mrs Thatcher urged the nation.

There followed a month of classic struggle reminiscent of the Pacific war of World War II, involving land-based air power and an amphibious assault force. The British sinking of the *General Belgrano* on 2 May, costing 321 Argentinian lives, was followed two days later by the loss of HMS *Sheffield* and 20 British lives, but after British forces landed on the Falklands on 21 May the outcome was inevitable.

The British government has made it clear that the sovereignty of the Falklands is not negotiable. Meanwhile Conservatives are heartened by the great boost in public support that the government has received by its successful campaign so far away from home.

SUNK The British frigate HMS *Antelope* explodes in San Carlos Water, Falklands.

CAUGHT A Royal Marine guards a group of captured Argentinian soldiers.

··· ASTRONOMERS IN PENNSYLVANIA DISCOVER RINGS AROUND THE PLANET NEPTUNE ···

Polish government bans Solidarity trade union

8 OCTOBER, WARSAW
Deputies in the Polish parliament tonight voted to dissolve the Solidarity trade union, which has been illegal since Polish leader General Wojciech Jaruzelski declared martial law on 13 December last year. The government has promised to set up a new trade union controlled by the Communist Party. Riot police patrol the streets, ready to enforce the will of the ruling party.

After its formation in 1980 Solidarity grew quickly, to around ten million. The union pressed the government hard throughout 1981, demanding free elections and economic reforms. At the year's end Jaruzelski arrested Solidarity leaders and 14 000 members. On 13 August tear gas and cannons were used to stop a workers' protest in Gdansk.

Solidarity chairman Lech Walesa has been in prison for the last ten months, but the banned movement will be kept alive underground.

ISRAELI AIR RAIDS FLATTEN LEBANON

EYE FOR AN EYE A Palestinian woman is led from a Beirut apartment building targeted by Israeli planes.

On 6 June the Israeli prime minister, Menachem Begin, angered by the terrorist shooting of the Israeli ambassador to Britain two days before, announced an end to Israeli restraint after a year of 'constant terrorist provocations'. He ordered extensive air raids on Palestinian refugee camps in Beirut, the headquarters of the PLO.

That assault has now been followed up by a ground and naval attack to bolster the continuing aerial assaults on Palestinian positions. The Israeli forces outnumber the Palestinians by ten to one and, despite determined resistance from the *fedayeen* (anti-Israeli commando fighters), the towns of Tyre and Sidon have fallen after massive bombardment. In Sidon 1000 buildings are reported to have been flattened, and another 1500 are severely damaged.

The situation in west Beirut, the last enclave of Palestinian resistance, is, if anything, even worse. The Israelis are avoiding face-to-face fighting and relying upon a deadly mix of devastating bombs. Suction bombs are causing whole buildings to collapse inwards; cluster bombs are doing incalculable damage; and phosphorous shells are inflicting agonising internal burning and slow death on their victims.

11 JUNE, BEIRUT
Five days after launching 'Operation Peace in Galilee', Israel has begun to bombard Beirut with terrible force, combining air raids, naval bombardment and heavy artillery barrages in an attempt to destroy the Palestine Liberation Organisation (PLO).

··· BRITAIN AND THE VATICAN RESUME FULL DIPLOMATIC RELATIONS AFTER A 400-YEAR BREAK ···

Verdict on banker's death is suicide

23 JULY, LONDON
An inquest today returned a verdict of suicide on the death of the Italian banker Roberto Calvi, who was discovered hanging from Blackfriars Bridge in central London on 19 June.

Dubbed 'the Vatican banker', Calvi was the former head of Milan's Banco Ambrosiano and one of the leading financiers of the Holy See. He was deeply involved in a corruption scandal that ended in the collapse of the bank, and was linked with P-2, a secretive Masonic lodge thought to be little more than a cover for the Mafia.

This group wielded influence at the highest levels of Italian society – one government resigned last year after a number of ministers were revealed to have P-2 connections.

It is rumoured that Calvi was in dispute with the lodge, which is why many Italians are greeting the 'suicide' verdict with derision. P-2 just happens to have the nickname 'Fratelli Neri' – Italian for 'Black Friars'.

RISKY BUSINESS Roberto Calvi, banker to the Pope, was found hanging from Blackfriars Bridge.

KGB hardliner is chosen to succeed Brezhnev

12 NOVEMBER, MOSCOW Two days after the death of the Soviet leader Leonid Brezhnev, his successor has been chosen by the Communist Party Central Committee. He is 68-year-old Yuri Andropov, who until recently was head of the country's intelligence agency, the KGB.

Andropov resigned from the KGB in May, already manoeuvring himself into line for succession as the health of the 75-year-old Brezhnev declined. Brezhnev had led the Soviet Union for the past 18 years, during which he concentrated on foreign relations – he pursued a policy of détente – and on modernising the country's armed forces.

LAST JOURNEY Thousands watch as Brezhnev's coffin is drawn on a gun-carriage through the streets of Moscow.

Judging by his past record, Andropov is likely to pursue a hard line in foreign affairs. As ambassador to Hungary he helped to coordinate the Soviet invasion of the country in 1956, and as head of the KGB he helped to plan the invasion of Czechoslovakia in 1968. Last year he put pressure on the Polish authorities to impose martial law in their country and to ban the Solidarity union.

··· SCIENTISTS TRANSFER A GENE CONTROLLING GROWTH FROM A RAT TO A MOUSE, WHICH DOUBLES IN SIZE ···

Artificial heart used on first human

2 DECEMBER, SALT LAKE CITY Barney Clark, a 61-year-old dentist, has become the first person to have an artificial heart inserted into his body. The pioneering surgery was performed at the University of Utah Medical Centre by Dr William de Vries, who used a heart made of plastic and glass-fibre reinforced fabric. The artificial heart was the result of 12 years' research by Dr Robert Jarvik, also of the University of Utah.

Like millions of others in the developed world, Clark was the victim of heart disease. Since there was nothing further that doctors could do for him, Dr de Vries thought that using the experimental device, which had been tested by Jarvik on animals, was justified.

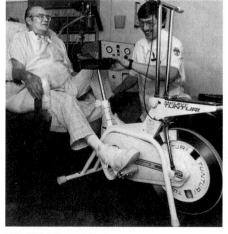

LIFE CYCLE Barney Clark exercises for a doctor.

The Jarvik-7, the model used, is driven by compressed air, requiring tubes to run through the patient's skin. In calves it has worked for up to 66 days. The Jarvik-7 is not a permanent solution for patients with heart failure, more a temporary measure while they wait for a suitable donor heart.

Surgery could work where diets fail

European surgeons are offering a new surgical technique for people who have tried diets and exercise, but still cannot lose bulging thighs or other areas of stubborn fat. Liposuction involves mechanically sucking away fat cells through a blunt, hollow probe-like tool, or cannula, inserted through a small incision in the skin. Developed in the late 1970s for the removal of diet-resistant fat cells, the technique is also known variously as suction lipectomy, lipoplasty, lipodissection, or lipolysis.

The operation sounds an extreme measure, but is said to be safe and effective. Doctors say, however, that it is not an alternative to sensible eating, and should be carried out in conjunction with traditional weight-loss methods.

Italian squad sweeps aside all opposition

11 JULY, MADRID

Italy, captained by the veteran goalkeeper Dino Zoff and managed by Enzo Bearzot, has won football's World Cup for the third time, thus equalling Brazil's record. Before an estimated worldwide television audience of more than a billion, the Italian side swept aside a formidable team from West Germany by three goals to one.

Italy had to overcome adversity, starting without its key midfield player, Giancarlo Antognoni. After only ten minutes Francesco Graziani limped off with a shoulder injury. Worse still, Cabrini missed a penalty in the first half, shooting wide of the goal – the first time that a penalty has been missed in a World Cup final.

But in the second half the Italians rallied, running rings around the Germans. Paolo Rossi, controversially selected for the World Cup side just after returning from a two-year suspension for his part in a football betting scandal, opened the scoring in the fifty-sixth minute, and Tardelli and Altobelli put the result beyond doubt. Italy is a worthy champion, having earlier put out the favourites, Brazil, before beating Poland in the semi-final, courtesy of two goals from Rossi, who has become an instant national hero. He finished the final as the tournament's top scorer with a tally of six goals.

SAVOURING VICTORY The winning team lifts the World Cup trophy in Madrid.

··· COCA-COLA LAUNCHES DIET COKE, 30 YEARS AFTER THE FIRST DIET SOFT DRINK BECAME AVAILABLE ···

Navratilova wins Wimbledon for the third time

TOP WOMAN Martina Navratilova, now a US citizen, proudly brandishes the Ladies' Shield.

3 JULY, WIMBLEDON

Martina Navratilova, whose displays of temper have not always endeared her to Wimbledon fans, today beat the darling of the Centre Court crowd, Chris Evert Lloyd, 6–1, 3–6, 6–2, to claim her third Wimbledon title. It follows her victory in the French championships last month and is her first Wimbledon title since becoming an American citizen last year.

Navratilova, only the second left-handed woman to win the Wimbledon crown (Ann Jones was the first, in 1969, is the most powerful exponent of the all-court, serve-and-volley game since the heyday of Margaret Court and Billie-Jean King in the 1960s and early 1970s. Her style demonstrates that the two-handed baseline game made immensely popular by Chris Evert is not the only route to success. And she herself, by her rigorous training,

carefully controlled diet and ever-present entourage of assistants, is leading professional tennis into a new era.

Ranked number one in Czechoslovakia from 1972 to 1975, Navratilova came to international prominence when she led her team to victory in the 1975 Federation Cup. In that year she went into exile in the United States, and she took American citizenship in 1981.

Since 1975 Navratilova has consistently been one of the world's top five women players. She made her first claim to the number one position in 1978, winning the Virginia Slims championship and the Wimbledon Ladies' singles final. In 1979 she again won the Wimbledon Ladies' singles as well as the Ladies' doubles, and was ranked the undisputed top player.

Michael Jackson releases thrilling new album

Michael Jackson, probably the most gifted of the famous Jackson brothers, released his latest LP, intriguingly entitled *Thriller*, in December this year. It is promoted with a ten-minute feature film directed by John Landis.

Three years on from the phenomenal *Off the Wall*, this follow-up looks likely to enjoy similar, if not greater, commercial success. *Off the Wall*, released just days after the pop star's twenty-first birthday, sold more than ten million copies worldwide,

and four singles released from the album quickly became smash hits. *Off the Wall* was produced by Quincy Jones, and Jackson has continued this collaboration in the making of *Thriller*.

Work on the album, originally to be called *Starlight,* began early this year in Los Angeles. Jackson invited a number of guest performers to work with him on the record – Eddie van Halen contributes an electric guitar riff and solo on 'Beat It', Paul McCartney sings

with Jackson in the duet 'The Girl is Mine', and the title track features a tongue-in-cheek voiceover by the horror-movie actor Vincent Price. The smash hit single of the album is 'Billie Jean'.

Thriller sees Jackson in meaner mood than previously; while it is as full of catchy dance tunes as ever, there is definitely a harder edge to the sound. The mix of styles will appeal to a broad audience, and sales of this album could well make music industry history.

GHOST WRITER Jackson in John Landis's promotional film *Thriller.*

··· USA: *TIME* MAGAZINE'S 'MAN OF THE YEAR AWARD' IS GIVEN TO PACMAN ···

Rap music makes it into the big time

US rock critics voted 'The Message', by Grandmaster Flash and the Furious Five, single of the year. This is the first record featuring rap – rhymed speech chanted over a disco beat – to receive such an accolade, and it underlines the breakthrough of rap into mainstream pop.

Flash – born Joseph Saddler – grew up in New York and studied electronics before starting work as a mobile disc jockey playing in parks and clubs. He creates a montage effect on his records by 'scratching' the disc with the stylus and mixing in his streetwise rap vocals – a style that he claims to have invented as a DJ because he was 'too fidgety' to wait for records to end.

CROSS-DRESSING BECOMES BIG BOX OFFICE

PAINTED LADY Hoffman (right) and Jessica Lange.

Dustin Hoffman gave one of the best drag acts in cinema when he played the lead in *Tootsie,* a movie about a failed actor who pretends to be a

woman to get a part in a television soap. In similar vein, Julie Andrews also triumphed as a woman playing a man playing a woman in Blake Edwards's *Victor/Victoria.*

Spielberg scored again with *ET: The Extra-Terrestrial,* in which a fatherless ten-year-old boy finds a friend in an alien who has been left stranded on Earth. At the other end of the sci-fi spectrum, Ridley Scott directed *Blade Runner* – a dreamlike exploration of the future which starred Harrison Ford. *Gandhi* won eight Oscars including best picture, best director and best actor. Lee Strasberg, the director, actor and teacher of greats such as Marlon Brando, Paul Newman and Joanne Woodward, died aged 81.

US TV HITS

1 *Dallas*
2 *60 Minutes*
3 *The Jeffersons*
4 *Joanie Loves Chachi*
5 *Three's Company*

US HITS OF THE YEAR

1	I LOVE ROCK 'N' ROLL	*Joan Jett & The Blackhearts*
2	EBONY AND IVORY	*Paul McCartney & Stevie Wonder*
3	EYE OF THE TIGER	*Survivor*
4	CENTERFOLD	*J Geils Band*
5	MANEATER	*Daryl Hall & John Oates*

1983

DIED

25 Feb: Tennessee Williams, US playwright

29 July: David Niven, British actor

KIDNAPPED

9 Feb, Ireland: Shergar, champion race horse and winner of 1981 Derby; a £2 million ransom is demanded

30 Nov, Amsterdam: Dutch beer magnate Alfred Heineken; freed after a $14 million ransom is paid

On 17 December, an IRA car bomb explodes outside Harrods department store in London at the height of the Christmas shopping rush, killing six people. Around 90 other people are injured in the blast. The bombing is part of the IRA's terrorist campaign on the British mainland.

CELEBRATED

27 Sept, New York City: longest-running Broadway show, *A Chorus Line*, which reaches 3389th performance

Raunchy new pop singer Madonna releases her first album, entitled Madonna, *which includes the disco-influenced singles 'Everybody', 'Borderline', 'Lucky Star' and 'Holiday'. Her voice has been compared to Minnie Mouse on helium.*

RECORD

4 Oct, Nevada: Briton Richard Noble establishes a new world land-speed record of 950 km/h (633 mph) in his jet-car at Black Rock desert

FIRSTS

13 June: man-made object to travel beyond the solar system, the US space probe *Pioneer 10*, launched in 1972

24 June: US woman in space, 32-year-old astrophysicist Sally Ride, on space shuttle *Challenger*

Aug: World Athletics Championships, held in Helsinki

26 Sept: loss of the America's Cup yacht race by the USA in 132 years – the US competitor *Liberty* is beaten by *Australia II*

11 Nov, UK: US Cruise missiles arrive at Greenham Common airbase, despite protests

CONVICTED

23 Nov, London: Dennis Nilsen, of murdering and dismembering 17 young men at two north London flats – Britain's worst mass murderer

RE-ELECTED

9 June, UK: Conservative Party, under Prime Minister Margaret Thatcher

AWARDED

Nobel Prize for peace to Lech Walesa, leader of independent Polish trade union Solidarity

MARRIED

29 Dec: Italian industrialist Stephano Casiraghi and Princess Caroline of Monaco

EXPELLED

5 May: 47 Soviet diplomats from France, on charges of spying

18 June: three million foreign workers from Nigeria, as falling oil prices hit the economy – all must leave within two weeks

BIGGEST

24 Mar, UK: robbery ever in Britain – three tons of gold bullion and diamonds, worth £26 million, stolen from the Brink's-Mat security warehouse at Heathrow

PUBLISHED

John le Carré, *The Little Drummer Girl*

Gabriel García Márquez, *Chronicle of a Death Foretold*

Norman Mailer, *Ancient Evenings*

LAST

2 Mar: episode of *M*A*S*H*, watched by largest ever worldwide television audience of 125 million viewers

KILLED

13 Feb, Italy: 63 people, in a theatre fire in Turin

25 May, Egypt: 500 people, when a Nile steamer sinks in crocodile-infested waters

NEW WORDS

chatline *n*: premium-rate telephone service which connects the caller to a group of other callers, supposedly to discuss shared interests

premenstrual tension *n*: symptoms such as nervous tension, caused by hormonal changes and experienced by some women before a menstrual period begins

toy boy *n*: the much younger male lover of an older woman

On 21 August, the opposition leader in the Philippines, Benigno Aquino, is assassinated at Manila airport. Rumours are rife that the killing was arranged by President Ferdinand Marcos or one of his agents. Aquino was returning home from the USA after three years spent in exile because of death threats.

Soviets shoot down civilian airliner

AIR TRAGEDY Distraught relatives of the victims of flight 007 show their grief at a memorial service.

1 SEPTEMBER, SIBERIA
A Soviet Sukhoi fighter plane tonight shot down a Korean Airlines Boeing **747 bound for Seoul, killing all 269 passengers and crew.** The airliner, flight 007 from New York City, was in Soviet airspace and had flown over the high-security military base at Sakhalin Island off the Siberian coast. The Sukhoi unleashed an air-to-air missile which hit the airliner at 10 500 metres (35 000 ft), throwing it into a terrifying 12-minute plunge to the sea. Among the passengers were 81 South Koreans, 61 American citizens and 28 Japanese.

The Soviets believe that the Boeing was on a spying mission, and claim that it was flying without navigation lights and that it ignored several warnings. It is certainly difficult to believe that the airliner, which had three navigational computers on board, could have gone off course in error. But the Soviets' claims are being treated with suspicion, and the action has been widely condemned all around the world. US President Reagan called it 'a horrifying act of violence'.

··· 21 AUGUST, USA: COMPUTER HACKERS BREAK INTO THE COUNTRY'S TOP DEFENCE COMPUTER ···

Suicide bombers attack peacekeepers

23 OCTOBER, BEIRUT
The future of US policy in Lebanon lies in grave doubt tonight after the suicide bombing early this morning by Islamic Jihad of the headquarters of both the American and French peace-keeping forces in Beirut.

Only seconds after a bomb-laden lorry hurtled into the US Marines' housing complex, another exploded at the quarters of the French paratroopers. According to the latest reports, 241 American and 59 French servicemen have died. Rescue workers continue to search among the rubble in the faint hope of finding more survivors.

BOMBED OUT A rescue party searches the wreckage of the French base.

The tragedy has shocked Paris and Washington. No French soldier has lost his life in combat since the Algerian war of the 1950s, and the Americans never took such severe losses from a single strike throughout the whole Vietnam War. US public opinion, never happy with the country's involvement in Lebanon, may now force President Reagan to withdraw the troops.

Reagan aims to wage 'Star Wars' in space

23 MARCH, WASHINGTON
President Ronald Reagan today announced a new Cold War in space when he launched his Strategic Defense Initiative, or SDI, known as the 'Star Wars' project. Over the next decade the United States intends to pump billions of dollars into a plan to erect a 'nuclear umbrella' in space. Orbiting satellites will use high-power laser beams to intercept and destroy Russian nuclear missiles before they are able to enter American, or even Western, airspace.

Hopes raised for AIDS cure as HIV virus identified

French scientist Dr Luc Montagnier has discovered the cause of Acquired Immune Deficiency Syndrome (AIDS), the deadly disease that was first identified less than three years ago by the Centre for Disease Control in Atlanta, Georgia.

Dr Montagnier, of the Institut Pasteur, reported in the American journal *Science* that the mystery disease is caused by a retrovirus which he called LAV, or lymphadenopathy-associated virus. But, in the same issue of the journal, Dr Robert Gallo of the US National Institute of Health suggested that a different virus is responsible. Later, however, Dr Gallo realised that his virus was identical to Montagnier's, and it was renamed Human Immunodeficiency Virus, or HIV. The discovery of the virus has led to hopes that treatment for AIDS may be found.

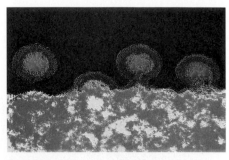

MICRO KILLER Electron micrograph of the HIV virus budding from a human white blood cell.

··· 28 JUNE: WILLEM DE KOONING'S *TWO WOMEN* SELLS FOR $1.2 MILLION, A RECORD SUM FOR A LIVING ARTIST ···

US troops invade Grenada

STRONG ARM American troops run a security check on a handcuffed Grenadan citizen.

27 OCTOBER, GRENADA
The Cuban-backed military regime that seized power in Grenada last week has crumbled in the face of an American-led invasion of the tiny Caribbean island. American troops landed five days after Prime Minister Maurice Bishop was ousted and murdered in a coup sparked by faction fighting within the left-wing ruling party, the New Jewel Movement. Bishop, who came to power four years ago, had been a popular premier, and the new regime had to declare martial law in the face of an uprising.

President Reagan claims that the troops were sent in to defend the 1000 Americans who live on the island, but many say that in reality he has used the coup as an excuse to rid America's backyard of 'another Cuba'. There has been widespread international criticism of the operation, which has left 17 Americans and many more Grenadans and Cubans dead. Forty-seven mental patients died in a mistaken American attack on a hospital.

Condemnation has been quick to come from both the Soviet Union and many Latin American states, which denounced the attack as an 'American imperialist intervention'. Criticism also came from the European Allies and from the UN Security Council, which called the invasion a 'flagrant violation of international law'.

There was also much anger among journalists as President Reagan barred reporters from Grenada and placed restrictions on press coverage. A *Washington Post* journalist commented: 'A secret war, like a secret government, is … absolutely outrageous.'

'Hitler's diaries' an elaborate hoax

5 MAY, BONN
The diaries of the century – the journals claimed to be the diaries of Adolf Hitler – have been revealed as a brilliant fake. Their 'discovery' by a reporter on the magazine *Stern* caused a sensation. A leading British historian, Lord Dacre, backed the diaries' authenticity, and the *Sunday Times* is rumoured to have paid £1 million for serialisation rights. Now experts have proved that they are modern forgeries.

SECRET UNVEILED *Stern* announces its discovery, unaware that the diaries were forged.

LOST IDEALS AND PRODUCT PLACEMENT

PAIRED OFF Nicholson and MacLaine falling in love.

The idealistic 1960s met the pragmatic 1980s in Lawrence Kasdan's *The Big Chill*. Tom Berenger, Glenn Close, Jeff Goldblum and William Hurt starred in this engaging comedy drama about a group of 1960s radicals who get together again at the funeral of a friend and rediscover their lost ideals. Best picture Oscar went to the weepie *Terms of Endearment*, which starred Jack Nicholson and Shirley MacLaine; Debra Winger is the young mother who dies of cancer. Barbra Streisand made her directing debut with *Yentl*, a tale about a traditional Jewish matchmaker.

This was also the year for Matt Dillon, who starred in two Francis Ford Coppola movies, *Rumble Fish* and *The Outsiders*. Both films portray life on the wrong side of the tracks and have launched Dillon as a new name to watch.

The third of the *Star Wars* trilogy, *Return of the Jedi*, hit the screens to a mixed critical response. 20th Century Fox launched 'product placement', in which manufacturers of anything from computers to breakfast cereals could have their products featured prominently in films.

US HITS OF THE YEAR

1	EVERY BREATH YOU TAKE	*Police*
2	BILLIE JEAN	*Michael Jackson*
3	FLASHDANCE	*Irene Cara*
4	SAY SAY SAY	*Paul McCartney & Michael Jackson*
5	ALL NIGHT LONG (ALL NIGHT)	*Lionel Richie*

US TV HITS

1	*60 Minutes*
2	*Dallas*
3	*M*A*S*H*
4	*Magnum, P I*
5	*Dynasty*

Cabbage dolls, plastic watches

The daftest consumer fad of the year, without question, was the Cabbage Patch Kids – large, ugly dolls with curly hair, pudgy faces and squidgy hands and bodies.

No two are quite alike, and every one comes with its personal 'adoption certificate'. Millions of the dolls have been sold, and there have been unpleasant scenes as stocks ran low and children, and some childish parents, refused to accept substitutes.

More practical is the Swatch, a cheap plastic battery-operated watch in which the mechanism is welded to the case. If it breaks, you simply buy another one. Designed to be an affordable, stylish accessory, it comes in a huge variety of styles and colours, and has helped Switzerland to dominate the watch market in a way it has not done for years.

··· 17 SEPT, USA: VANESSA WILLIAMS BECOMES THE FIRST BLACK MISS AMERICA ···

Motorists give the aerodynamic Sierra a chance

The future finally looks a little brighter for Ford's aerodynamically sleek Sierra, launched in 1982 as a replacement for the company's longstanding mid-range family car, the Cortina.

The Sierra's ultramodern design pleased the wind-tunnel technicians, but it was a rude departure for the public. The conventional, boxy Cortina which after all had transported a generation, had won a special and lasting place in the hearts of motorists, and in the Sierra's first months on the market drivers showed little interest in the 'all-new' arrival.

But car design and public taste move on. The lively and comfortable 1.6-litre Sierra is steadily winning admirers – and, much to Ford's relief, sales are picking up.

NEW KID IN TOWN The sleek new Ford Sierra is at last finding favour.

1984

BORN
15 Sept, UK: Prince Henry Charles Albert David, known as Harry

DIED
20 Jan: Johnny Weissmuller, US swimmer and 'Tarzan' actor
1 Apr: Marvin Gaye, US soul singer
26 Apr: William 'Count' Basie, US jazz musician
5 Aug: Richard Burton, British actor

On 10 December, *Bishop Desmond Tutu is awarded the Nobel Prize for peace. The South African clergyman has been a prominent anti-apartheid campaigner for many years, always advocating peaceful solutions to the violence and divisions in his country.*

RE-ELECTED
6 Nov, USA: Ronald Reagan, as President

ANNOUNCED
7 May: boycott of Los Angeles Olympics, by USSR, in retaliation for US boycott of Moscow Games in 1980

EXPLODED
12 Oct, UK: IRA bomb at the Grand Hotel, Brighton, during Conservative Party conference – four people are killed, but Prime Minister Margaret Thatcher and her cabinet escape

KILLED
21 July, USA: James F Fixx, jogging guru and author of bestselling *Complete Guide to Running*, by a heart attack while out running

EMBARRASSED
12 Aug, USA: President Reagan, after he jokingly orders a nuclear strike on Russia while testing a microphone before a speech and is picked up on live television

OPENED
8 May, London: Thames flood barrier, by the Queen

CELEBRATED
June, Florida: the 50th anniversary of Donald Duck, at Disney World

FIRSTS
6 Mar, West Germany: seat won in parliament by the Green Party
7 Feb: man to fly in space without a safety line; US astronaut Bruce McCandless roams 94 m (309 ft) from the spacecraft using a jet-pack
22 June, UK: Virgin Atlantic flight, flying from Gatwick to New York – a single fare costs £99
USA: credit cards with a hologram, as an anti-forgery device, issued by Visa, California
USA: operation on an unborn foetus; by William Clewall of the University of Colorado

BANNED
New Zealand: all US nuclear ships from New Zealand waters

AWARDED
USA: $325000 damages to Christine Craft, newsreader, who had been demoted for being 'too old' and 'unattractive'

MURDERED
17 Apr, UK: police officer Yvonne Fletcher by a shot fired from the Libyan Embassy, during an anti-Gadaffi demonstration – killer is never brought to trial
30 Oct, Poland: Catholic priest Father Jerzy Popieluszko, found dead in a reservoir after calling for democratic reforms in his sermons – four secret policemen are later convicted of his murder

ATTACKED
30 May, UK: modern architecture, by the Prince of Wales, in address to the Royal Institute of British Architects at Hampton Court, London

Boy George (George O'Dowd) is the gender-bending front man of pop group Culture Club. Despite the band's huge record sales, the British press is more interested in Boy George's unconventional style, including dresses and make-up.

On 31 October, *Indira Gandhi, Indian prime minister for four terms, is assassinated by her Sikh bodyguards. Gandhi made enemies in the Sikh community when she recently ordered a raid on a temple in Amritsar. Her son Rajiv will succeed her as prime minister.*

LARGEST
24 Mar, Rome: robbery in Italy, as Red Brigade terrorists rob a security company of $21.8 million
20 Nov, UK: share issue in the world, as British Telecom shares go on sale

CLOSED
San Francisco: bath houses in the city, because they are believed to contribute to the spread of AIDS

PUBLISHED
Milan Kundera, *The Unbearable Lightness of Being*
Sue Townsend, *Secret Diary of Adrian Mole, Aged 13¾*

NEW WORDS
break-dancing *n*: acrobatic style of dance often performed on the street
compassion fatigue *n*: loss of ability to be moved by other people's distress, due to bombardment of media appeals for 'good' causes
yuppie *n*: city-based young person with large income; acronym for young urban professional

Poison gas cloud kills thousands in India

4 DECEMBER, BHOPAL, INDIA
Hundreds of people – perhaps as many as 2000 – have died and thousands more been injured in the last 24 hours by a cloud of poison gas that escaped from a pesticide plant outside the city of Bhopal in central India.

More than 20 000 people have already been treated for swollen eyes, frothing mouths and breathing difficulties. Several thousand people are in a critical condition, and the death toll is expected to rise. Many survivors will go blind and face long-term lung disease and liver and kidney complications.

The most ghastly scenes occurred in the early hours of the morning, as thousands of people attempted to escape the gas by climbing to higher ground. One of them, Mrs Madhu Mishra, a professor at Bhopal University, spoke of the 'nightmare' of driving along through

THE HUMAN COST Relatives take away the bodies of family members killed by the chemical leak.

'eight or nine thousand people' who were blinded by fumes.

The methyl isocyanate gas escaped from an underground storage tank at the

American-owned Union Carbide plant, and the company is now steeling itself to face hundreds of millions of dollars' worth of lawsuits.

··· CALIFORNIA: A SECURITY GUARD SHOOTS DEAD 20 PEOPLE IN McDONALD'S BECAUSE HE 'HATES MONDAYS' ···

Stirling's new art gallery is hailed as a masterpiece

The new Staatsgalerie (State Gallery) unveiled this year in Stuttgart was praised as one of the most exciting pieces of museum architecture for many years. It was designed by the British architect James Stirling, who won the commission in an international competition.

Stirling's early work was mainly low-rise housing projects in the 'New Brutalist' style – dominated by glass and steel and heavy, rough concrete. But he has recently evolved a variant of the 'Postmodernist' style, creating buildings that express variety in a playful fashion. Postmodernist buildings blend styles,

HOME FOR ART The new State Gallery in Stuttgart – an 'urban landscape'.

materials and colours from many architectural eras.

The principal material of the Stuttgart gallery is stone, but it also uses glass and

strongly coloured metal. It is complex in form and has been admiringly described as 'more an urban landscape than a building'.

Fiction meets virtual reality

Latest developments suggest that computers can create an electronic world that users see and feel as real. Last year computer programmer Jaron Lanier coined the term 'virtual reality' to describe the experience simulated by the computer. This year Canadian writer William Gibson invented the word 'cyberspace' to describe the imaginary place in which computers and humans interact. In his novel *Neuromancer*, characters use goggles, gloves and earphones to combine the real world with the 'virtual' world in the computer.

1984

Torvill and Dean glide to gold

CAPTURING PERFECTION The king and queen of the ice-rink, during their perfect-scoring dance routine.

14 FEBRUARY, SARAJEVO
Tonight Christopher Dean and Jayne Torvill, the three-times world champions, raised ice-dancing to new heights with a sinuous, erotic performance to the music of Ravel's *Bolero*. The judges at this year's Winter Olympics awarded them 12 sixes for the final free-dance section and a perfect nine sixes for artistic impression.

Apple unveils 'Mac'

23 JANUARY, CALIFORNIA
Apple Computer has launched a revolutionary new product, the Macintosh, designed to change the face of personal computing. The Macintosh – or 'Mac' – relies on a user-friendly graphical interface with icons and pull-down menus, originally developed by Xerox. Apple claims that the Mac is 'as easy to use as a telephone'.

EASY PC The Macintosh is designed to make computers easier to use and understand.

··· 1 APR: AN OIL SLICK THE SIZE OF BELGIUM FORMS IN THE PERSIAN GULF ···

Iglesias sets hearts and charts alight

This was an incredible year for Spanish crooner Julio Iglesias. The former Real Madrid soccer player is already an established international superstar, performing romantic ballads in at least seven different languages, including Japanese. Iglesias has finally conquered the English language, with the release of his all-English album, *1100 Bel Air Place*. This, remarkably his fifty-sixth album, was a successful attempt to crack the American market, and sold more than three million copies. Four further albums released this year were simultaneously in the US *Billboard* charts – an achievement shared only with the Beatles and Elvis Presley.

CROONER Julio's live shows were a big hit.

US TV HITS

1 *Dallas*
2 *60 Minutes*
3 *Dynasty*
4 *The A Team*
5 *Simon & Simon*

US HITS OF THE YEAR

1	LIKE A VIRGIN	Madonna
2	WHEN DOVES CRY	Prince & The Revolution
3	JUMP	Van Halen
4	FOOTLOOSE	Kenny Loggins
5	AGAINST ALL ODDS (TAKE A LOOK AT ME NOW)	Phil Collins

Striking miners hit back at government

16 AUGUST, BIRMINGHAM

In the most recent episode of the long-running miners' strike, protesters have occupied the offices of the accountants charged with sequestrating union funds. The miners' strike, which began on 15 March, has resulted in scenes of violence as working miners cross picket lines, in pitched battles between police and strikers, and in several deaths.

Today's action stems from the fines imposed on the miners' union following its refusal to abandon 'secondary picketing' – when workers picket premises not directly connected to the dispute. It is another blow in the war of attrition between the Conservative government and the miners.

Lewis is an Olympic speed sensation

JUMP TO IT Carl Lewis on the run-up to the winning long jump that added a fourth Olympic gold medal to his tally.

12 AUGUST, LOS ANGELES
Los Angeles has shrugged aside a revenge boycott by Iron Curtain countries and staged a spectacular Olympic Games. The razzmatazz of the Games' opening ceremonies has been matched by the performance of American athletes, who won more than four times as many golds as their nearest competitors, Romania.

Pride of place goes to sprinter and jumper Carl Lewis, who lived up to Jesse Owens's 1936 achievement by winning gold medals at 100 metres, 200 metres, the long jump and the 4 x 100 metres relay. His margin of victory in the 100 metres –

2.44 metres (8 ft) – was the largest in Olympic history.

The hot favourite for the women's 3000 metres gold, Mary Decker of the United States, was controversially tripped by the young barefooted South African Zola Budd, who was running for Britain. Decker left the arena in a flood of tears.

··· 15 NOV, USA: A ONE-MONTH-OLD INFANT HAS A HEART TRANSPLANT FROM A BABOON AND SURVIVES 20 DAYS ···

PURE HOKUM Dan Akroyd and Bill Murray hit the phantoms where it hurt in *Ghostbusters*.

GHOSTBUSTERS STRIKE A FUNNY CHORD

The trend for movie merchandising tie-ins scaled new heights with the success of Ivan Reitman's *Ghostbusters*, a fun film which combined the comedy talents of *Saturday Night Live* stalwarts Bill Murray and Dan Akroyd with spectacular special effects. The film took more than $120 million, making it the highest-grossing film of the year. Hot on its heels came *Beverly Hills Cop*, which catapulted stand-up comedian Eddie Murphy – who took over the role after Sylvester Stallone had turned it down – to screen stardom.

Amadeus took Peter Shaffer's successful stage play and turned it into a lavish musical feast which won Oscars for best picture, best director and best actor. James Cameron's *The Terminator*, starring Arnold Schwarzenegger, and Wes Craven's *A Nightmare on Elm Street* added fuel to the debate over screen violence. On a lighter note, Donald Duck, who celebrated his fiftieth birthday, was made a member of the Screen Actors Guild. Ironically *the* big-screen version of George Orwell's novel *1984* made little impact at the box office.

1985

DIED
28 Mar: Marc Chagall, Russian-born French painter
17 Sept: Laura Ashley, British fashion designer
10 Oct: Orson Welles and Yul Brynner, US actors

The compact disc is replacing the vinyl record in more and more homes, as equipment becomes more affordable. The music CD has a brother in the CD-ROM, which can store pictures, text and sound and can be run on a special player or a computer. It can store up to 1000 times more information than a floppy disk.

LAUNCHED
23 Apr: new, sweeter recipe for Coca-Cola; but after poor sales and consumer protests, the company has to revert to the original recipe

ARRESTED
USA: Amy Carter, aged 17, daughter of former President Jimmy Carter, at an anti-apartheid demonstration outside the South African Embassy in Washington DC

On 18 January, Gary Kasparov beats reigning champion Anatoly Karpov in one of the longest matches in the history of chess. Kasparov, aged 22, is the youngest ever world chess champion. The two Russian players met for 48 games over a period of six months in Moscow.

KILLED
21 Mar, South Africa: 21 people, by police, during demonstrations to mark the 25th anniversary of the Sharpeville massacre
23 June: 329 people when Air India jet explodes off the Irish coast; there is speculation that a bomb was planted by Sikh terrorists
19 July, northern Italy: 261 people, when a dam bursts, causing a tidal wave that envelopes the tourist resort of Tésero
13 Aug, Japan: 520 people, in an air crash, as a Tokyo to Osaka shuttle flight plummets into forest; worst air crash to date in civil aviation history
7 Oct, UK: PC Keith Blakelock, during riots by youths on the Broadwater Farm estate, Tottenham, London

DENIED
29 Jan, Oxford: an honorary degree to Margaret Thatcher

FIRST
20 Feb, Ireland: legal contraceptives sold in Ireland

AWARDED
4 July, Oxford: first-class mathematics degree to child prodigy Ruth Lawrence, aged 13

INTRODUCED
10 Jan, UK: the C5, a battery-operated car by Clive Sinclair – it has a 36-km (20-mile) range and costs £399

On 16 December, actor Rock Hudson dies of AIDS, after becoming the first public figure in the USA to admit to suffering from the disease. Hudson's revelation stops America's moral panic in its tracks, if only briefly. As the country mourns the death of a popular star, the realisation dawns that the fatal illness strikes indiscriminately.

ELECTED
11 Mar, USSR: Mikhail Gorbachev, as general secretary of Communist Party

APPOINTED
UK: Ted Hughes as Poet Laureate

DISCOVERED
7 Mar, UK: a system of genetic fingerprinting, using DNA from blood, semen and saliva, by Dr Alec Jeffreys at Leicester University
19 July: large quantities of Austrian wine to contain antifreeze, added to make it sweeter – 50 arrests follow and an international ban on sales of Austrian wine
1 Sept: the wreck of the *Titanic* off Newfoundland, at a depth of 4000 m (13 200 ft); many objects are salvaged

ENDED
3 June, Italy: compulsory Roman Catholic instruction in schools

NEW WORDS
brat pack *n:* a group of popular young Hollywood actors
wannabe *n:* someone who aspires to be like his or her idol, or to have a particular lifestyle

DOUBLE TRAGEDY FOR FOOTBALL

DEATH IN BRADFORD Flames leap from the stricken stand at Bradford City.

DEATH IN BRUSSELS Juventus fans tend to injured fellow fans at Heysel.

12 MAY, BRADFORD

The Valley Parade football ground, home of third-division Bradford City, went up in flames today and now lies a skeletal ruin. What started as a small fire in a corner of the ground swept through the old timber structure in a blazing torrent and within four minutes 52 fans lay dead. Hundreds more are being treated in hospital.

Fans described the horror of seeing people on fire and children being hurled on to the pitch for safety, and were quick to blame officials for locking the gates to the ground. Several charred bodies were found pressed against the turnstiles, where the frantic effort to escape ended in tragedy for many. At least there were no

barriers against hooligans between stands and pitch; had that avenue of escape been cut off the numbers who would have died is unimaginable. According to the Bradford fire chief, the club had been warned of the fire risk, but had taken no action to reduce it.

In one of European football's worst ever months, football fans were killed in an incident at the Heysel stadium in Brussels on 29 May. Rioting English football supporters lived up to their worst reputation, scarring the European season's greatest night, the final of the European Champions' Cup, between Liverpool and Juventus.

The trouble started before the kick-off, apparently sparked off by Juventus

supporters who threw fireworks at the Belgian police. Hundreds of English fans then charged into the Italian section of the crowd and a full-scale riot erupted in which both sides hurled slabs of concrete, bottles and any other missile to hand at each other. Tragedy struck when a wall and a safety fence collapsed, crushing 41 people to death and injuring more than 200 others.

Officials decided that the match should go ahead. It began 85 minutes late and, not surprisingly, lacked sparkle. Juventus won by a second-half penalty taken by Michele Platini. Liverpool may have lost more than this match: a possible ban from European competition now hangs over all English clubs.

··· BECAUSE OF HOOLIGANISM, ALL ENGLISH FOOTBALL CLUBS ARE BANNED FROM EUROPEAN COMPETITIONS ···

French suspected in sinking of Greenpeace boat

10 JULY, AUCKLAND

Rainbow Warrior, **the converted Scottish fishing trawler that has become the flagship of the environmental group Greenpeace, was blown up in Auckland Harbour today.** Eleven of the 12 people who were aboard the 160-foot boat at the time escaped with their lives, but Fernando Pereira, a Portuguese photographer who was trying to rescue his equipment, was killed.

The two explosions that sank the trawler were caused by bombs expertly planted below the waterline. Witnesses reported seeing a man in a wetsuit pulling a rubber raft up a nearby beach a few hours before the blast. Police say that there could be 'political or terrorist' implications, and are waiting to interview the crew of the French ship *La Rochelle*, which left Auckland harbour shortly after the bombing. *Rainbow*

Warrior was in the South Pacific to stage a Bastille Day protest, leading a small flotilla against French nuclear testing in the Muroroa Atoll.

Over the past eight years, the *Rainbow Warrior* has travelled the globe for Greenpeace, carrying environmental protesters to engage in peaceful civil disobedience against nuclear weapons testing, radioactive waste dumping and the slaughter of marine animals.

Ethiopian war victims starving to death

20 MAY, ETHIOPIA
Reports from Ethiopia have revealed one of the worst humanitarian disasters of the century. The scandal concerns the refugee camp at Ibnet where, it is said, government officials have expelled some 30000 famine victims, ordering them to make the impossible journey back to their homes. Once again, Western leaders have taken issue with President Mengistu Haile Mariam for paying more attention to the rebel war than to the needs of his beleaguered people.

It is six months since the West first became aware of the disaster, caused by a decade of civil war and drought. In November 1984, cameraman Mohamed Amin filmed graphic evidence of a catastrophe of 'biblical proportions'. The footage showed skeletal figures so starved that they could barely move, fly-covered corpses wrapped in sacking and aid

ONE OF MILLIONS A severely malnourished woman lies on the ground at a feeding station in Ethiopia.

workers forced to make decisions about whom they should try to save. The shocking pictures were circulated throughout the West, causing widespread shock and eliciting promises of support from all the major powers. Even so, it is thought that a million Ethiopians may die this year alone.

··· THE CHURCH OF ENGLAND APPROVES THE ORDINATION OF WOMEN AS DEACONS ···

Pop superstars unite to feed the world

LIVE AID Bob Geldof and fellow rock stars make another appeal for cash.

13 JULY, LONDON
Crowds in London's Wembley stadium have been enjoying the star-studded Live Aid concert, staged for the benefit of Ethiopia's famine victims. The event,

the most ambitious of its kind ever produced, ran for a full 16 hours and was broadcast to 152 countries. In total, almost two billion viewers are thought to have tuned in.

The Prince and Princess of Wales attended the start of the concert which kicked off with Status Quo singing, appropriately enough, 'Rocking All Over the World'. Half-way through the event, satellite link-ups switched the action to the JFK stadium in Philadelphia, where the second half of the concert was held. The line-up included Madonna, Queen, David Bowie, Led Zeppelin, U2, Duran Duran and Phil Collins, who played at both concerts, using Concorde to jet between the two. Amazingly, the concert adhered to its strict schedule and, with a red light to indicate when the performers

had to leave the stage, the entire show over-ran by a mere two minutes.

The Live Aid project was the brainchild of Bob Geldof, lead singer of the Irish new wave band the Boomtown Rats. After seeing news reports of the famine last November, Geldof was determined to galvanise the aid process, circumventing the traditional aid charities with their high overheads.

The project came to life when Geldof organised the Band Aid single 'Do They Know it's Christmas?', which raised £8 million for the cause. He hopes that the present concert will net a further £60 million.

Terrorists release TWA hijack hostages

30 JUNE, BEIRUT
Lebanese Shia terrorists who hijacked a TWA jet and held 39 US citizens hostage for 16 days today boasted to the watching world's press that they had humiliated the US government. Earlier they had handed the hostages flowers as they released them.

The Americans' 16 days of terror began on 14 June, when the terrorists diverted a TWA Boeing 727 bound for Damascus. One American, US Navy diver Robert Stethem, was shot during the hijacking. After their release today, the hostages were driven from Beirut, where they had been held in a slum after being taken off the aircraft, to Damascus and then flew on to West Germany.

The terrorists had demanded the release of 700 Shias imprisoned in Israel. The US and Israel deny coming to an agreement with the hostage-takers, but Israel is set to release many of the Shia prisoners tomorrow. In the USA, President Reagan said 'we will not rest until justice has been done' and promised terrorists that the US would 'fight back against your cowardly attacks'.

Earthquake hits Mexico City

AFTER EFFECTS The earthquake left more than 7000 dead and 50000 homeless in Mexico City.

20 SEPTEMBER, MEXICO CITY
Following the earthquake that struck Mexico yesterday further tremors hit the capital today, hampering the efforts of rescue workers. The main quake, which measured 7.8 on the Richter scale, shook the country just before the start of the morning rush hour, causing widespread devastation. Its epicentre was in the resort of Acapulco, but it has left a trail of devastation right across the country, and the shock waves were felt as far away as Houston, Texas.

The worst damage is in Mexico City, where about 450 buildings, including skyscrapers purported to be quake proof, have been destroyed. A makeshift morgue has been set up in the city's baseball stadium, and the president of Mexico has appealed for blood donors.

··· USA: LASERS ARE FIRST USED IN SURGERY, TO CLEAN OUT CLOGGED ARTERIES···

New York's self-appointed 'Dirty Harry' shoots subway youths

7 JANUARY, NEW YORK CITY
Amid a storm of controversy, Bernhard Goetz, the New York subway vigilante, has been granted bail of $50000. On 22 December the white, 37-year-old electrical engineer shot four black youths who approached him on the subway and demanded money. Later Goetz admitted that, when he noticed that one of the teenagers was not bleeding, he said, 'You seem to be alright – here's another,' and shot him again.

When Goetz, the victim of a vicious mugging in 1981, turned himself in to police five days ago he gained instant notoriety as the East Coast's answer to 'Dirty Harry', the film vigilante played by Clint Eastwood. Many New Yorkers, weary of their crime-ridden subway, are supporting Goetz, hoping that he will be acquitted of attempted murder.

UNLIKELY HERO Bernhard Goetz, who took the law into his own hands.

Coffee cups blamed for 'hole' over Antarctica

A British scientist, Dr Joe Farman, announced the existence of a 'hole' in the atmosphere over Antarctica, where ozone appears to have almost completely disappeared. Farman, a member of the British Antarctic Survey, began measuring the amount of ozone in the air over Halley Bay, in the eastern portion of the Weddell Sea, in 1982.

Ozone is chemically a very active form of oxygen and is important because it forms a layer in the high atmosphere that filters out ultraviolet light from the Sun. Without the ozone layer, it is unlikely that life on Earth would have evolved, and if higher than normal amounts of ultraviolet light reach the Earth, they could cause skin cancers and eye cataracts, as well as damaging plants and plankton. According to the British Antarctic Survey, ozone levels over Halley Bay have decreased every spring since 1975, and are now half what they were in the early 1970s. It is possible that this ozone hole covers millions of square kilometres, and that it is growing.

Some scientists claim that the ozone hole is seasonal and no cause for alarm. Most, though, blame its growth on chlorofluorocarbon gases, or CFCs. These were invented in 1928 for use in fridges and air conditioners, and gradually they also became popular solvents and aerosol propellants. They are even used to puff up polystyrene foam to make coffee cups and hamburger cartons. They do not degrade, but simply stay floating in the atmosphere, so their concentration has been increasing by 4.5 per cent each year since 1970. These gases are thought to interfere with the chemical process that allows the formation of ozone.

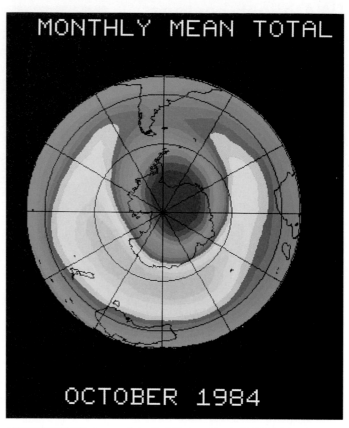

MONTHLY MEAN TOTAL

OCTOBER 1984

VIEW FROM SPACE A map of the Earth's atmosphere, obtained from the American *Nimbus-7* weather satellite, shows the severe depletion in the ozone layer over Antarctica. The 'hole', represented by the purplish/blue oval covering most of Antarctica, is largest in October, the Antarctic spring.

··· THE INTERNATIONAL WHALING COMMISSION BANS COMMERCIAL WHALING ···

A decade on, fighting factions contrive to tear the heart out of Beirut

FIGHTING ON A jubilant member of the Ibaath Party in downtown Beirut.

31 OCTOBER, BEIRUT
Renewed fighting in the war-scarred streets of Beirut **this month – killing at least 200 people – has dashed the hopes of a settlement** raised by Syrian mediators in the summer, and doomed the Lebanese capital to a continuation of the bloody faction-fighting that has now been going on for a decade.

The shape of this complex conflict is almost impossible to discern. The recent battles have been primarily between Muslim militias and leftist Syrian forces. At the heart of the struggle is the irreconcilable opposition of Shiite Islamic fundamentalists to the traditional Sunni control of government. Last May Shiite militias unleashed an onslaught of rocket-propelled grenades, mortar and artillery against three camps of Palestinian, mostly Sunni, refugees in west Beirut. In January they almost forced the Maronite Christian president, Amin Gemayel, to abandon his Sunni prime minister, Rashid Karami.

After a decade in which more than 100 000 militia and civilians have lost their lives, no end to the fighting appears to be in sight.

Parisian bridge is turned into a work of art

Following nine years of negotiations, the artist Christo achieved a long-standing ambition when he added the Pont Neuf, one of the main bridges across the Seine in Paris, to the list of structures he has temporarily wrapped.

Christo, who dropped his surname, Javacheff, is Bulgarian by birth and American by adoption. He began wrapping objects as a form of art about 25 years ago when he was living in Paris, starting with things that were at hand in his studio, such as paint tins, and working his way up to whole buildings.

His monumental later projects included *Valley Curtain,* a great net hung between two Colorado mountains about 300 m (1000 ft) apart and *Surrounded Islands* in 1983, when he ringed 11 small islands in Biscayne Bay, Florida, with bright pink material. The artist called his Florida masterpiece 'my water lilies'.

Christo uses synthetic fibres and ropes and employs construction workers and sometimes rock-climbers to carry out his massive projects, financing them by the sale of his smaller works.

Some people deny that what he does is art, but Christo has become world-famous for his work and won much praise. For his next big project he plans to wrap the Reichstag in Berlin, for which he started lobbying the German parliament 14 years ago.

IT'S A WRAP The Pont Neuf, covered in fabric.

··· AUSTRALIAN MEDIA TYCOON RUPERT MURDOCH BECOMES A US CITIZEN FOR BUSINESS REASONS ···

BACK TO THE FUTURE DELIVERS FUN FAMILY ENTERTAINMENT

GOOD TIMES Michael J Fox and friend.

This was the year of the brat pack. Director Joel Schumacher reunited Emilio Estevez, Judd Nelson and Ally Sheedy from last year's *The Breakfast Club,* added Rob Lowe, Andrew McCarthy and Demi Moore and came up with *St Elmo's Fire,* a tale of young graduates which perfectly captured yuppie dreams and anxieties. Teen hero Michael J Fox took to time travel in one of the few remaining De Lorean handmade sports cars in the sci-fi drama *Back To The Future,* directed by Robert Zemeckis. The special effects and charming collision between 1980s gadgetry and 1950s innocence ensured a huge box office success.

In Peter Weir's film *Witness,* a street-smart cop hid out in a traditional Amish community when an eight-year-old boy was witness to a murder, with predictably disturbing effect. The not-too-distant future was depicted in *Mad Max: Beyond Thunderdome* as a post-apocalyptic outback overrun with savage warlords. Swedish director Lasse Hallström received huge acclaim for *My Life As A Dog,* as did Stephen Frears for *My Beautiful Laundrette,* which was originally made for Channel Four television and brought talented actor Daniel Day Lewis to the attention of the British film industry.

US HITS OF THE YEAR

1	SAY YOU, SAY ME	*Lionel Richie*
2	WE ARE THE WORLD	*USA For Africa*
3	CARELESS WHISPER	*Wham! featuring George Michael*
4	CAN'T FIGHT THIS FEELING	*Reo Speedwagon*
5	MONEY FOR NOTHING	*Dire Straits*

US TV HITS

1	*Dynasty*
2	*Dallas*
3	*The Cosby Show*
4	*60 Minutes*
5	*Family Ties*

1986

DIED

30 Mar: James Cagney, US actor
14 Apr: Simone de Beauvoir, French writer and feminist
13 June: Benny Goodman, US jazz musician
24 Apr: Duchess of Windsor, widow of ex-King of England, Edward VIII

MARRIED

23 July, London: Prince Andrew and Sarah Ferguson

ELECTED

8 Apr, USA: Clint Eastwood, as mayor of his native city, Carmel, California

BANNED

29 May, UK: cricketer Ian Botham, from playing for two months, after admitting he smoked cannabis

On 28 February, the Swedish prime minister, Olof Palme, is assassinated in Stockholm while walking home with his wife after an evening at the cinema. During his first premiership, between 1971 and 1976, Palme introduced key constitutional reforms. A highly popular leader, he was re-elected twice after that.

On 27 February, Ferdinand and Imelda Marcos are toppled from power in the Philippines and forced to flee to Hawaii after Corazon Aquino, wife of murdered opposition leader Benigno Aquino, is swept to power at the polls. The press seizes on Imelda Marcos's vast shoe collection as a symbol of the couple's corruption.

FIRSTS

20 Feb: staffed space station, *Mir*, which is launched by Soviet Union
16 Apr, USA : surrogate birth of a test-tube baby, in Cleveland, Ohio
Japan: disposable camera, the Fuji 24-shot camera in a cardboard box, with plastic lens

ABOLISHED

UK: corporal punishment in schools

RELEASED

3 June, Italy: 8000 prisoners, including suspected terrorists, to celebrate the 40th anniversary of the republic

CONVICTED

29 July, UK: pop star Boy George, of possessing heroin

ADMITTED

21 Sept, UK: by Prince Charles, on television, that he talks to plants

KILLED

17 Nov, France: George Besse, head of state-owned car company Renault, who is murdered by terrorist group *Action Directe*
Italy: 20 people, after drinking wine that has been adulterated with ethanol to make it stronger

DISAPPOINTED

29 June: Richard Branson, after crossing the Atlantic in record time; he was refused the Blue Riband because his specially designed boat, *Challenger II*, was ruled ineligible

LAUNCHED

25 May: Sport Aid by Bob Geldof – 30 million people worldwide take part in sponsored runs for famine relief
27 Oct: London Stock Exchange reforms, known as 'Big Bang'; new computerised systems allow share-dealing to go on around the clock

DEVASTATED

31 Mar, UK: Hampton Court Palace, by a fire started by a bedside candle
France: 10000 hectares of forest, as the mistral wind fans a forest fire for more than five weeks

REJECTED

27 June, Ireland: proposal to allow divorce, by a referendum

CELEBRATED

4 July, USA: the 100th anniversary of the Statue of Liberty

US cop series Cagney and Lacey *is a landmark show in television portrayals of police and of women. The no-nonsense New York detectives, played by Tyne Daly and Sharon Gless, battle against sexism in the police force and violence on the streets while managing tough personal lives.*

ARRESTED

2 June, India: 1000 Sikh protesters, on the second anniversary of attack by Indian army on the Sikh Golden Temple in Punjab

NEW WORDS

bonk *vb*: to have sex
cardboard city *n*: urban area with large homeless population dwelling in cardboard boxes on the streets
Yardie *n*: member of a black criminal syndicate originally based in Jamaica

CHERNOBYL NUCLEAR PLANT EXPLODES

28 APRIL, CHERNOBYL, UKRAINE
One of the reactor fuel piles at the Chernobyl nuclear power plant exploded two days ago and is spewing tons of radioactive gas and debris into the air, causing what looks set to be the worst nuclear accident in history – but the Soviet authorities are denying that there is any cause for concern. It was only after Finland and Denmark reported radiation levels up to six times higher than normal that the Soviet news agency Tass finally admitted that there had been an accident at the Chernobyl plant 96 kilometres (60 miles) north of Kiev.

The Soviet Council of Ministers claims that two people have died, but the real number is likely to be much higher. The authorities have evacuated 15000 people from Pripyat, the city built near the plant to house its workers. If the fire continues, the plant will have to be sealed and an area of several hundred square kilometres turned into an exclusion zone. Levels of radiation in the Baltic are so high that 600 workers have been evacuated from a nuclear power station at Forsmark on the Swedish coast, after fears that the radioactive leak was theirs.

The Chernobyl plant has been in service since 1977. Only two months ago it was described in the state magazine *Soviet Life* as a model of nuclear safety, and the Ukrainian Minister of Power was quoted as saying: 'The odds of a meltdown happening are one in 10000.'

FALLOUT Investigators measure the radiation over Chernobyl from a helicopter.

··· THE DUTCH REFORMED CHURCH OF SOUTH AFRICA DECLARES THAT RACISM IS A SIN ···

Tragedy as shuttle explodes over Cape Canaveral

BLOW-UP The *Challenger* explosion was the worst disaster in the history of the US space programme.

28 JANUARY, CAPE CANAVERAL, FLORIDA
The space shuttle *Challenger* exploded in mid-air today, 90 seconds after lift-off, killing its crew of seven. After an apparently perfect launch, a rocket booster exploded, turning *Challenger* into a spinning, cartwheeling ball of fire 16 kilometres (10 miles) above the Earth. The wreckage plunged into the ocean a few kilometres off Cape Canaveral, followed by burning debris which continued to rain down for almost an hour after the explosion, preventing rescue teams from entering the area to hunt for survivors. Among the dead was the first schoolteacher to go into space, Christa McAuliffe.

The Soviet Embassy in Washington called the accident 'an enormous tragedy', and President Ronald Reagan gave a five-minute television address to a shocked nation, in which he promised that 'there will be more shuttle flights … more teachers in space.'

It was Reagan's idea to send a teacher up in the shuttle. McAuliffe, a mother of two, was chosen from more than 11000 applicants. She was to give two televised lessons in orbit. Before the flight she said that her hope was to 'humanise the technology of the Space Age'.

Investigators believe that freezing conditions may have played a part in the tragedy. The mission – which was the 25th space shuttle flight – had already been postponed twice because of the weather, and there were 60-centimetre (2-ft) icicles visible around *Challenger* not long before the launch.

1986

Villages poisoned by toxic gas

25 AUGUST, CAMEROON

News is reaching the West of a freak geological accident which may have killed up to 1200 people, including one entire village. The tragedy occurred three days ago, when poisonous gas seeped out of Lake Nyos near Wum, some 320 kilometres (200 miles) north-west of Cameroon's capital, Yaoundé.

The lake is on a volcanic crater, and it is thought that vapours leaked out from a fissure at its base. Vulcanologists are still uncertain about the precise make-up of the gases, although they were probably hydrogen sulphide or carbon monoxide, or a combination of the two.

President Paul Biya has been quick to visit the region and declare it a

POISONED EARTH North-west Cameroon is littered with dead cattle, legacy of the toxic gas escape.

disaster area. The accident, while unusual, is not unprecedented in Cameroon. Two years ago, 36 people died when a similar leakage occurred at Djindoum.

Dissident Sakharov is released from exile

23 DECEMBER, MOSCOW

Crowds in Moscow welcomed Soviet dissident Andrei Sakharov and his wife Yelena tonight after their internal exile in the city of Gorky was lifted.

Sakharov, a nuclear physicist who helped develop the Soviet hydrogen bomb, became a critic of the Kremlin's hard line against dissidents.

In 1980 Sakharov was sent to Gorky, 400 kilometres (250 miles) east of Moscow, for criticising the Soviet invasion of Afghanistan. His wife Yelena was sent to Gorky in 1984. Their release shows how far the thaw in Soviet politics has gone under Mikhail Gorbachev.

··· THE WORLD HEALTH ORGANISATION ESTIMATES THAT THERE ARE 100 000 CASES OF AIDS WORLDWIDE ···

Hong Kong building mixes ultra-modern with ancient tradition

Hong Kong's reputation as a dynamic, forward-looking economy was given a further boost this year with the opening of the colony's new Hongkong and Shanghai Bank building, designed by the innovative British architect Norman Foster.

Foster's design stresses the structural and technological aspects of a building, celebrating them rather than hiding them under the surface. The architect is renowned for his use of new technology, and borrows techniques from engineering disciplines such as bridge construction and the aerospace industry.

Instead of the conventional 'stack' of storeys, the bank is arranged like a system of ladders, with the floors suspended from steel pylons around a huge central space. Three towers of different heights support a tall atrium containing offices and a central banking hall, and natural light is maximised by a complex system of reflectors in the roof, which move to follow the Sun throughout the day.

For all its hi-tech extravagance, Chinese tradition played a key role in the building's design. Before starting work, Foster consulted a feng-shui expert. Hong Kong Chinese attach special importance to this ancient art, which seeks to create harmony between people and their surroundings. The expert's advice meant costly changes to Foster's design – the bank's location in front of a hillside rock representing a dragon caused problems as it symbolically 'blocked' access to water. This was overcome by making parts of the building transparent.

OLD AND NEW Foster incorporated Chinese designs into the building's detail.

Libya bombed as USA exacts its revenge

15 APRIL, TRIPOLI
US bombers flying from Britain and carriers in the Mediterranean pounded Libyan targets in a surprise attack early this morning. As many as 130 Libyans have been killed, including the adopted baby daughter of Libyan leader Colonel Gaddafi. The United States has lost two pilots and one F-111 bomber.

President Reagan ordered the attack to punish Libya for its support of international terrorism, most recently the bomb attack early this month on a West Berlin nightclub frequented by US servicemen. Spokesman Larry Speakes said that 'the US has chosen to exercise its rights of self defence'.

The raid used 18 F-111 bombers which had set off from British bases in Oxfordshire and Suffolk. The USA also used 15 other attack aircraft as well as mid-air refuelling tankers. In Tripoli the bombers hit the airport, the harbour, army barracks and airfields.

AVENGED A Libyan aircraft in pieces after the US raids, which focused primarily on military targets.

In Britain controversy is brewing over the use of the British-based F-111s. Prime Minister Thatcher must have given permission. By contrast, France did not back the US action. It refused permission for aircraft to fly through French airspace, forcing them 4000 kilometres (2400 miles) out of their way.

··· SINGER STOPS PRODUCING SEWING MACHINES AND CONCENTRATES ON AEROSPACE PRODUCTS ···

Superpowers clash at Reykjavik

FRIEND OR FOE Though talks in Iceland were fruitless, Reagan later softened his hard-line stance.

12 OCTOBER, REYKJAVIK
Nuclear arms limitation talks between Soviet leader Mikhail Gorbachev and US President Ronald Reagan broke up abruptly tonight without agreement.

Earlier the two leaders were reportedly ready to agree to significant cuts in long- and intermediate-range nuclear weapons. But Gorbachev said that any deal was dependent on Reagan abandoning the US Strategic Defense Initiative, or 'Star Wars' – the proposed creation of a shield of weapons in space. Reagan refused, and the men reached an impasse, with Gorbachev saying 'only a madman' would carry on with arms control if the USA developed Star Wars.

A six-hour meeting held in Geneva in November 1985 was surprisingly successful, and resulted in a mutual commitment to reduce the number of nuclear weapons, inspiring Gorbachev to proclaim that 'the world has become a safer place'. But tonight US–Soviet relations have cooled significantly.

Chewing gum helps to beat the evil weed

Growing public awareness of the hazards of smoking was emphasised this year by the arrival of nicotine chewing gum. Nicoret, developed by a Swedish pharmaceutical company, is designed to help smokers quit by satisfying their craving for nicotine – hence helping them to avoid the undesirable side-effects of giving up, such as tension and food binges.

Greeted by doctors as a useful step forward, the new gum was initially derided by many smokers, but it is gradually coming to gain more widespread acceptance. Other ways of delivering nicotine into the bloodstream, including patches and nasal sprays, are also being developed.

Divine victory for Argentina

29 JUNE, MEXICO

The highly fancied team from Argentina has lifted football's World Cup for the second time in eight years. In an all-action final that sparkled right from the opening kick-off, they defeated West Germany 3–2 at the Azteca Stadium in Mexico City.

The star of the tournament was Argentina's midfield dynamo, Diego Maradona, whose tight ball-control and powerful bursts of speed helped to make all three of Argentina's goals in the final. Maradona finished the tournament with five goals, one behind the leader, Gary Lineker of England, who scored six – including a hat-trick against Poland.

But Maradona was also the villain of the piece. In the tense quarter-final match with England, he scored the crucial opening goal for Argentina with what looked to be an impressive header, but television replays established beyond doubt that Maradona had deliberately

HAND BALL Maradona tips the ball into the net despite efforts from England's Peter Shilton.

directed the ball into the net with his hand – the 'hand of God', as he was to describe it to journalists later.

Round the world nonstop in nine days

23 DECEMBER, CALIFORNIA

A crowd of 50 000 excitedly watched as Dick Rutan and Jeana Yeagar made history when they landed their light-weight aircraft, *Voyager*, at Edwards Air Force Base this morning, completing the first ever nonstop round-the-world flight achieved on a single tank of fuel.

The hi-tech $2-million aeroplane, which was designed by Rutan's brother Burt, took off on 14 December carrying 4540 litres (1200 gallons) of aviation gas. For nine days Yeagar and Rutan lived side by side in a cabin that was only 60 centimetres (2 ft) wide. Their diet consisted of pre-packaged food and they took it in turns to sleep.

Rutan and Yeagar were cutting it fine. When *Voyager* finally touched down in California after a flight of 40 000 kilometres (25 000 miles) there were only 140 litres (37 gallons) of fuel left in the tank.

··· UK: HEALTH MINISTER EDWINA CURRIE BLAMES POOR HEALTH OF NORTHERN BRITONS ON 'IGNORANCE' ···

Experience wins the day

13 APRIL, GEORGIA

Jack Nicklaus has added yet another jewel to his golfing crown by becoming, at the age of 46, the oldest player ever to win one of the four grand slam titles.

At Augusta today the US golfer, nicknamed 'Golden Bear', finished a stroke ahead of rivals Greg Norman and Tom Watson to win his sixth Masters title – itself another golfing record.

At the start of the final day's play few pundits would have thought that Nicklaus stood a chance. He was lying four shots behind Norman, and eight other star golfers

were ahead of him. At one point Seve Ballesteros of Spain looked certain to don the famous Augusta green jacket, but he dumped a four-iron into the water before the fifteenth green and relinquished the lead.

By contrast, Nicklaus played the last nine holes with imperial sang-froid and panache, coming home in 30 with five birdies and an eagle.

Nicklaus will now without doubt be remembered as the finest golfer in history. He has amassed 18 grand slam titles – the six Masters, five PGAs, four US Opens and three British Opens.

DRIVING HOME Nicklaus's ability to be cool under pressure helped him to win.

Tyson knocks them out with his boxing prowess

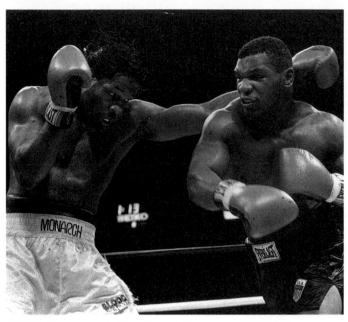

HIT MAN Tyson pummels Mitch Green in the run-up to his WBC title.

22 NOVEMBER, LAS VEGAS
Mike Tyson, a 20-year-old New Yorker, has become the youngest world heavyweight boxing champion in history.

He is a bruising brawler of a fighter with a devastating punch. Reigning champion Trevor Berbick was sent sprawling on to the canvas two minutes into the second round by a vicious left hook.

The champion had been on the attack against his shorter opponent but flailed around on the floor as Tyson's arms were raised in victory by the referee.

Tyson, who came to the ring undefeated in 27 bouts, said that his ambition was to be like John L Sullivan, champion in a bygone age. In the confused world of boxing, Tyson, the new WBC (World Boxing Council) champion, has to share the 'world champion' title with the IBF (International Boxing Federation) and WBA (World Boxing Association) champions.

There is no doubt he will seek to win all three crowns. 'I am the youngest champion,' he bragged last night, 'and I will also be the oldest.'

Music for the global village

Paul Simon has jumped on the World Music bandwagon to produce a chart-topping album. *Graceland* was recorded in South Africa, where Simon worked with local musicians Ladysmith Black Mambazo to create African-inspired pop tunes.

Simon was blacklisted for breaking the United Nations boycott of South Africa. He defended himself by saying that his motivations were musical rather than political.

Graceland is the latest and most successful to date in a series of collaborations between non-Western musicians and rock stars, notably David Byrne and Peter Gabriel, whose WOMAD (World of Music, Arts and Dance) festival has brought music from around the world to the attention of Western audiences.

CRUISE IS GUNNING FOR SUCCESS

TOP CLASS Tom Cruise had to stand on a box for some of his scenes with tall Kelly McGillis in *Top Gun*.

Paul Newman won his first Academy Award for *The Color of Money* – a sequel to *The Hustler*, made in 1961. He played the same character

25 years on – and most thought he should have got the Oscar first time around. This time he was overshadowed by his co-star, Tom Cruise, possibly the biggest star in the world after this and the aerobatic high-jinks of the patriotic naval adventure *Top Gun*. Cruise was rivalled by Paul Hogan, playing a good-natured Aussie transported from the Outback to New York City, in *Crocodile Dundee*. Oliver Stone made a huge impact with *Platoon*, a graphic, brutal film about the Vietnam War. The world looked much prettier in *A Room with a View*, another lush Merchant-Ivory adaptation of an E M Forster novel, with accomplished performances from Helena Bonham Carter, Julian Sands and Maggie Smith, among others.

US HITS OF THE YEAR	
1 THAT'S WHAT FRIENDS ARE FOR	Dionne Warwick & Friends
2 WALK LIKE AN EGYPTIAN	Bangles
3 ON MY OWN	Patti Labelle & Michael McDonald
4 GREATEST LOVE OF ALL	Whitney Houston
5 ROCK ME AMADEUS	Falco

US TV HITS
1 The Cosby Show
2 Family Ties
3 Murder, She Wrote
4 60 Minutes
5 Cheers

1987

DIED
4 Feb: Wladziu Valentino Liberace, US pianist
21 Feb: Andy Warhol, US artist
14 May: Rita Hayworth, US actress
22 June: Fred Astaire, US actor and dancer

OPENED
Egypt: Cairo underground system, built by the French

Hungarian-born Italian porn star Ilona Staller ('La Cicciolina') is elected to the Italian parliament, campaigning on ecological issues and sexual liberation. Staller says that her concern for the environment persuaded her to abandon pornography for politics.

RE-ELECTED
11 June, UK: Conservative Party, led by Margaret Thatcher – first prime minister this century to win three successive elections

RECORD
20 Dec: Soviet cosmonaut Yuri Romanenko returns to Earth after spending 11 months in space

SOLD
11 Nov: Van Gogh's *Irises*, for $53.9 million – most expensive painting ever
3 Apr: Duchess of Windsor's jewellery at auction in Geneva for $50 million – money goes to the Pasteur Institute in Paris

FIRSTS
16 Jan, USA: television commercial for condoms, shown on KRON in San Francisco
1 Feb, Japan: digital audio tapes (DAT), introduced by Aiwa
USA: musical newspaper advertisement for Absolut vodka – it plays 'Jingle Bells' when opened
UK: driverless, computer-run public railway, Docklands Light Railway, in London

INVENTED
UK: active suspension, by General Motors, for Lotus Formula 1 racing cars – it moves wheels up or down according to the curve of the track

BANNED
2 Jan: black golliwogs in Enid Blyton's 'Noddy' stories; replaced with politically correct gnomes
10 Mar: conception by artificial methods, by the Catholic Church
1 Sept: smoking in all public buildings in Belgium
6 Oct: all foreign visitors to Tibet, by the Chinese government

CONVICTED
23 Oct: jockey Lester Piggott, of evading £3.1 million tax – he is jailed for three years
21 Dec, Italy: 338 people, in the biggest ever trial of Mafia criminals

MURDERED
20 Aug, UK: 14 people by Michael Ryan in Hungerford in Britain's worst shooting incident to date; he later turns the gun on himself
2 Oct, Tibet: six Buddhist monks demonstrating against the Chinese occupation
8 Nov, Northern Ireland: 11 people attending a Remembrance Day parade at Enniskillen, by IRA bombs

US pop musician Whitney Houston collects a host of trophies at the American Music Awards, following the phenomenal success of her second album, Whitney. *She becomes the first female artist in history to have an album enter the* Billboard *charts at number one. Houston comes from a family of soul and gospel singers.*

REFUSED
USSR: US diplomats, to enter their new Moscow Embassy, after finding hundreds of bugging devices hidden around the building

KILLED
19 Nov, London: 34 people at King's Cross underground station, when a rubbish build-up underneath an escalator catches fire

ROCKED
1 Oct, USA: Los Angeles, by an earthquake which measures 6.1 on the Richter scale; only seven people are killed, because many buildings have been designed to withstand the shockwaves

DEVASTATED
16 Oct, UK: southern England, by hurricanes in the 'storm of the century'; hours before, the Met Office had predicted calm weather

PUBLISHED
Margaret Atwood, *The Handmaid's Tale*
Bruce Chatwin, *Songlines*
Kazuo Ishiguro, *An Artist of the Floating World*
Toni Morrison, *Beloved*
Tom Wolfe, *Bonfire of the Vanities*

NEW WORDS
glasnost *n*: a policy of political frankness and accountability developed by Soviet leader Mikhail Gorbachev
executive *adj*: relating to an executive; very expensive or exclusive
thirtysomething *n*: a person in their 30s – an important consumer group

Hundreds feared dead in ferry disaster

WATERY GRAVE The *Herald of Free Enterprise* keeled over less than a kilometre outside Zeebrugge.

6 MARCH, ZEEBRUGGE
Wet and exhausted, the shocked survivors of the sinking of a cross-channel car ferry gathered today in the harbour of Belgium's biggest port.

Pulled from the wreckage of the half-submerged *Herald of Free Enterprise*, most of them were too bewildered to weep. Some desperately sought loved ones among the other survivors.

Divers have already rescued some 200 people, and 26 bodies have been recovered. At least 300 people are still trapped in the crippled vessel.

The boat left the harbour at 7.00 pm today, bound for Dover. Tragedy struck within minutes of the ferry's departure. The 7951-ton vessel simply keeled over, too fast for an SOS message to be sent. Almost immediately, the lights failed, icy water rushed through passages and cabins, and screaming, panicked passengers started to scramble to the top of the capsized ship.

Tales have already begun to be told of incidents of outstanding heroism from passengers and crew. One man turned himself into a human bridge to help other people escape.

Doubts are being expressed about safety procedures on board the *Herald of Free Enterprise*, which is owned by Townsend Thoresen. It appears that the bow doors may have been left open when the ship set sail.

··· 31 JULY, SAUDI ARABIA: 400 IRANIAN PILGRIMS DIE IN A STAMPEDE AT MECCA ···

World stock exchanges collapse on 'Black Monday'

20 OCTOBER,
NEW YORK CITY
World financial markets are still trying to come to terms with the massive losses suffered yesterday, as the New York Stock Exchange suffered a frenzy of selling that has already been dubbed 'Black Monday'.

The Dow Jones share index plummeted 22.6 per cent – almost double the record 12.8 per cent fall at the time of the Wall Street Crash in 1929. Stock markets around the world soon followed Wall Street's lead. The crash has come after months of unprecedented stock market rises.

When brokers arrived at their desks yesterday morning, early results from the markets in Europe and the Far East already showed a sizeable downturn; as trading commenced on Wall Street the market went into freefall. Stock values plunged – wiping out all the gains that had been made in the previous months. Panicky brokers stayed glued to their monitors all day, by the end of which some $500 billion in stock values had vanished into the ether.

Worries have been voiced that the United States is about to enter a new depression, but economists

SELL, SELL, SELL Frenzied traders try to make the best of a bad day.

have been swift to deny this. Instead, they point out that stocks had been overvalued for some time, and that some form of adjustment was inevitable. Many old hands also consider that the problem has been aggravated by the recent rapid growth of computerised trading.

President 'should have known' of secret arms deals

19 NOVEMBER, WASHINGTON DC
According to the report from the recent Congressional hearings, responsibility for the Iran–Contra debacle lies with the President. The affair involved the funding of right-wing Nicaraguan Contra rebels by renegade CIA men, using money made from secret arms sales to Iran. It seemed impossible that the President was unaware, but Reagan denied all knowledge.

In July this year Reagan's national security adviser, Rear Admiral John Poindexter, took the stand during the hearings and accepted full responsibility for the affair, saying 'the buck stops with me'. He died not long afterwards.

Poindexter's assistant and the key man in the operation, Lieutenant-Colonel Oliver North, said he had assumed that he had the President's approval in diverting the funds. North made a forthright defence of his actions in terms of patriotism, and many Americans warmed to him during the televised hearings. The United States began the secret Iranian arms sales – against US law and official government policy – in 1980, hoping to win the freedom of the American hostages then held in Iran.

JUST A PATRIOT? Oliver North, a key organiser of the Iran–Contra operation.

··· WORLD POPULATION REACHES FIVE BILLION, DOUBLE THE NUMBER IN 1950 ···

Lebanon hostages still held

31 DECEMBER, BEIRUT
As the year ends, 17 Western hostages, captured in a spate of kidnappings in the war-torn Lebanese capital of Beirut, are still missing. Another three hostages have reportedly been executed.

The only good news of the hostage crisis has been the release of two French hostages, which was successfully negotiated between France, Syria and the kidnappers. Despite French denials, suspicions remain in many Western capitals that the French government paid ransom money.

Among those still held is Terry Waite, the Archbishop of Canterbury's special envoy to the Middle East, who has in the past been a skilful negotiator for the release of hostages. Mr Waite, who was about to enter into talks with Shi'a Muslims, disappeared after leaving his Beirut hotel on 20 January. Despite strenuous inquiries there has been no reliable news of his whereabouts or condition since then, and fears for his safety are growing.

WHERE ANGELS FEAR Anglican special envoy Terry Waite has been missing for almost a year.

'Baby M' mother denied custody

31 MARCH, NEW JERSEY
In a shock decision in the controversial 'Baby M' surrogacy case, a judge has stripped the biological mother of all rights to her child. The judge awarded custody to Baby M's biological father, William Stern, and his wife Elizabeth, a paediatrician.

Mary Beth Whitehead was promised a fee of $10000 to bear a child – known only as 'Baby M' – for Mrs Stern, who has mild multiple sclerosis and was advised that pregnancy would worsen her condition. After giving birth last year, Mrs Whitehead – already a mother of two – reneged on the surrogacy contract, refusing to give the baby up and taking it with her to Florida. The Sterns hired a private detective to track her down and then sued for custody.

The case has caused controversy in the United States, with many people arguing that the affluent Sterns simply rented a womb.

Superpowers' historic arms treaty

FRIENDLY SMILES The new spirit of entente has led to greater cooperation.

8 DECEMBER, WASHINGTON DC
The Soviet leader Mikhail Gorbachev and US President Ronald Reagan have signed the first treaty in history to cut nuclear strength. Under today's Intermediate Nuclear Forces Treaty (INF), 10 per cent of the world's stock of nuclear warheads will be decommissioned. All Soviet and US nuclear missiles with ranges of between 480 kilometres (300 miles) and 5500 kilometres (3400 miles) must be withdrawn and made inactive within three years. The agreement requires the destruction of 1752 Soviet and 859 US missiles.

To ensure that these promises are kept, American observers will be stationed in the Soviet Union and Soviet observers in the United States. They will be able to carry out both unannounced and scheduled checks on the other side's facilities.

The treaty has yet to be ratified in both countries; there may be opposition from right-wingers in the US Senate, but the government is expected to carry the day.

After the failed summit of October 1986 at Reykjavik in Iceland, this meeting has seen a return to more cordial relations between the leaders of the world's superpowers. They also began talks about future cuts of up to 50 per cent in both countries' long-range missiles.

··· RICHARD BRANSON AND PER LINDSTRAND MAKE FIRST TRANSATLANTIC HOT-AIR BALLOON CROSSING ···

Hess, last inmate of Spandau, kills himself

17 AUGUST, BERLIN
Former Nazi leader Rudolf Hess died today in Spandau prison, where he had been the sole prisoner since 1966. Hess, who was 93, is said to have hanged himself with electrical flex.

Hess became Adolf Hitler's political secretary in 1920, and was a close confidant during his rise to power. In 1934 he was appointed deputy leader of the Nazi Party, and in 1941 he caused a sensation when he flew to Scotland on his own initiative to try to negotiate peace with Britain. He was held prisoner in Britain, and in 1946 was sentenced to life imprisonment at the Nuremberg trials of war criminals. In his old age the American, British and French governments proposed he should be released, but the Russians – the fourth power controlling Spandau – insisted that he remain incarcerated until death.

Nazi Butcher of Lyons gets life

4 JULY, LYONS
Klaus Barbie, a former Gestapo leader, was sentenced to life imprisonment yesterday after being convicted of the deaths of about 4000 people and the deportation of many more during World War II. Barbie, now aged 73, was head of the Gestapo in Lyons from 1942 to 1944, when his brutality earned him a grim reputation as 'Butcher of Lyons'.

After the war Barbie and his family escaped to South America, aided by the US authorities, who had briefly used him for intelligence work against the Soviet Union; the Americans later officially apologised to France for helping him. Four years ago France succeeded in getting Bolivia to deport Barbie, who had been living under the name Klaus Altmann. His lawyers argued that he had been illegally abducted from Bolivia, and that as he was now a Bolivian national the country had no authority to deport or expel him.

SINS OF THE PAST Barbie's war crimes included torturing hundreds of people to death.

At his trial, Barbie said he was innocent of all crimes. St Joseph prison where he is being held is, ironically, a stone's throw from his former Gestapo headquarters.

TV evangelist caught with his pants down

19 MARCH, SOUTH CAROLINA
The Reverend Jim Bakker, leader of the multi-million dollar religious empire 'Heritage USA', resigned today after admitting he had committed adultery. This morning the US national press broke the scandal of his illicit relations with Jessica Hahn, a church secretary from New York. Hahn said that they had a sexual encounter in a Florida motel room in December 1980.

Bakker is married to Tammy Faye, his co-presenter on a popular Christian chat show produced by PTL, Bakker's religious satellite television network. As a 'TV

evangelist' Bakker has enjoyed prestige, power and mass adulation – and an extravagant lifestyle.

Preaching an upbeat message of health and prosperity, he has persuaded millions of Americans to donate their money to him and his wealthy organisation. Heritage USA, a theme park based at an 890-hectare (2200-acre) Christian retreat centre in Fort Mill, South Carolina, became an extremely successful outfit. Last year Heritage USA drew more than six million visitors, making it the third most popular American tourist attraction after Disneyland and Disney World.

FAILURE Tammy and Jim Bakker presented themselves as an ideal couple.

··· THE FIRST GLASS-FIBRE OPTIC CABLE IS LAID ACROSS THE ATLANTIC OCEAN ···

Lone flyer lands in Red Square

29 MAY, MOSCOW
The Soviet Union's air defence systems may be effective against a massed airborne onslaught by NATO, but they have proved no match for a greenhorn flyer in a tiny Cessna. As Muscovites gaped in astonishment, Matthias Rust, a 19-year-old West German with just 25 hours' flying experience, casually touched down in Red Square and calmly brought his hired aeroplane to a halt right next to the Kremlin walls.

No one is sure why Rust – now under arrest – performed his epic flight from Helsinki to the Russian capital. But the Soviet authorities are more interested in knowing how a civilian could pilot a light aircraft unchallenged through 640 kilometres (400 miles) of airspace supposedly bristling with early-warning defence technology.

CROWD PULLER Excited Muscovites greet the arrival of daredevil flyer Matthias Rust.

In the circumstances, heads were bound to roll, and the government today gave the Soviet military an unheard-of public rebuke. This was followed by the sacking of defence minister Marshal Sergei Sokolov. He has been replaced by Dmitri Yasov, an ally of the Soviet leader Mikhail Gorbachev.

Rapist convicted by genetic fingerprint

13 NOVEMBER, BRISTOL
Robert Melias was found guilty of rape by Bristol Crown Court on the basis of DNA testing. His is the first criminal conviction using the new means of identification known as 'genetic fingerprinting' developed by Dr Alec Jeffreys of Leicester University.

Melias raped a polio victim after breaking into her house in Avonmouth and was convicted from the genetic fingerprint obtained from a semen stain on his victim's petticoat.

The technique, first described in 1985, uses an analysis of DNA samples from bodily fluids or tissues to identify individuals. It depends on the fact that the likelihood of two people having exactly the same genetic fingerprint is virtually nonexistent – unless they happen to be identical twins.

HOLLYWOOD MORALITY TALES

DANGEROUS GAME Michael Douglas looks after destructive Glenn Close.

The movie business produced a bumper harvest this year, the most productive ever. *Fatal Attraction*, a chilling tale of adultery and obsession, starring Glenn Close and Michael Douglas, had filmgoers rushing home to check on their pet rabbits. Douglas also gave us the memorably repellent character of Gordon Gekko in *Wall Street*, Oliver Stone's indictment of financial greed. There were period pieces too, such as Bernardo Bertolucci's sumptuous Chinese epic *The Last Emperor*, about the life of Pu Yi, who started life as an emperor and ended it as a humble gardener. The Mob movie *The Untouchables* told the story of legendary cop Eliot Ness and his defeat of Al Capone in the 1930s. Closer to our own time was Richard Attenborough's *Cry Freedom*, the true story of the murder in 1977 of South African hero Steve Biko. Stanley Kubrick's *Full Metal Jacket* – shot in Britain – and Oliver Stone's *Platoon* were the best of a crop of films that re-examined America's involvement in the Vietnam War.

Prince proves his pop stamina

Multi-talented pop musician Prince's impressive double album, *Sign O' The Times*, marks a new chapter in the career of Minneapolis's most famous son. He has disbanded the Revolution, the band that played with him on his last three albums, to produce this release as a solo artist: the Purple One has written, arranged, mixed and performed the whole lot himself.

Originally intended as a triple album with the working title *Crystal Ball*, *Sign O' The Times* contains the raunchy power-funk we have come to expect ('U Got the Look' and 'Strange Relationship') as well as sophisticated songs exploring Prince's favourite themes of love, sex and God. The title track, the sensuous 'If I Was Your Girlfriend' and the ballad 'Dorothy Parker Says' are standout tracks.

Prince himself cuts quite a dash. A minute, eccentric and reclusive figure, he dresses in peach and purple and wears stiletto heels.

SMALL GUY, BIG TALENT Minneapolis's most famous son gets sexy.

··· A SOUTH AFRICAN WOMAN GIVES BIRTH TO TRIPLETS FORMED FROM HER DAUGHTER'S TRANSPLANTED EMBRYOS ···

US TV HITS

1 *The Cosby Show*
2 *Family Ties*
3 *Cheers*
4 *Murder, She Wrote*
5 *The Golden Girls*

US HITS OF THE YEAR

1	FAITH	George Michael
2	LIVIN' ON A PRAYER	Bon Jovi
3	ALONE	Heart
4	WITH OR WITHOUT YOU	U2
5	LA BAMBA	Los Lobos

1988

DIED
15 Apr: Kenneth Williams, British comic actor
13 May: Chet Baker, US jazz trumpeter
6 Dec: Roy Orbison, US singer

PUBLISHED
Margaret Atwood, *Cat's Eye*
Stephen Hawking, *A Brief History of Time*
Salman Rushdie, *The Satanic Verses*

FIRSTS
5 Feb: British 'Comic Relief' fundraising day
Moscow: McDonald's restaurant opens

RE-ELECTED
8 May, France: President Mitterrand

In December, *Francisco 'Chico' Mendes, Brazilian environmentalist, is gunned down in his own backyard by a rancher's son. Mendes led the battle to protect Brazil's rainforests against ranchers, loggers and international developers. His death helped to focus world attention on the need to save the rainforests from the electric saw.*

On 13 October, *the Bishop of Turin announces that the Turin Shroud, a piece of cloth believed to bear the imprint of Jesus Christ's face, is a medieval fake. Carbon dating science locates the religious artefact in the 13th or 14th century.*

CHAMPIONS
25 June, Munich: Holland, winners of soccer European Championship, beating USSR 2–0 in final
27 June, Atlantic City: Mike Tyson, who knocks out Michael Spinks to retain world heavyweight boxing championship
10 Sept, US: West German tennis star Steffi Graf, who wins US Open tennis championship to complete 'Grand Slam' of Australian, French, Wimbledon and US tournaments

OPEN ALL DAY
22 Aug, England and Wales: pubs, as licensing restrictions are lifted

PROMISING
9 Apr, UK: British footballer Alan Shearer, aged 17, who is youngest scorer of a First Division hat-trick; in Southampton's 4–2 win over Arsenal

BLEW UP
6 July, North Sea: Piper Alpha oil rig; 170 killed

CRASHED
26 June, France: Airbus A320 airliner during airshow demonstration
27 June, Paris: trains at Gare de Lyon; 57 killed
28 Aug, West Germany: Italian aerobatic aircraft, in airshow; three pilots and 30 spectators die
12 Dec, London: three trains, which collide at Clapham Junction station; 36 killed

ELECTED
1 Oct, USSR: Mikhail Gorbachev, as president
8 Nov, USA: George Bush, as President
21 Nov: Brian Mulroney, as Canadian prime minister

KILLED
7 Mar, Gibraltar: IRA members Danny McCann, Mairéad Farrell and Sean Savage, by British SAS agents

ATTACKED
Aug, USA: *The Last Temptation of Christ*, movie directed by Martin Scorsese, as blasphemous

SOLD
Pablo Picasso's painting *Acrobat and Young Harlequin* at auction for $38 million
Jasper Johns's sculpture *False Start*, for $17.05 million, a record price for a living artist

CEASED FIRE
24 Mar, Nicaragua: Sandinista government and Contra rebels
8 Aug: Iran and Iraq

FOUND
New York City: three giant turtles, inside sewage system; each weighs about 22 kg (50 lbs) and was probably flushed down the lavatory when smaller as an unwanted pet

CELEBRATED
10 June, USSR: 1000 years of Christianity in Russia

On 2 December, *Benazir Bhutto, head of the Pakistan People's Party, is sworn in as prime minister of Pakistan, becoming the first woman to head a Muslim state. Bhutto's victory restores democracy to Pakistan after the death of dictator Mohammad Zia ul-Haq in a plane crash earlier this year.*

NEW WORDS
bum bag *n*: small bag attached to belt and worn around the waist
desktop publishing *n*: using computer software and equipment that allows user to design own pages
global warming *n*: rising temperatures in Earth's atmosphere because of build-up of pollutants

'Storm of flames' falls on Scottish village

21 DECEMBER, SCOTLAND
A Pan Am 747 jumbo jet heading for New York City tonight disappeared from radar screens and crashed in the small town of Lockerbie in southern Scotland. All the aeroplane's 259 passengers and crew died, and 11 others were killed on the ground by falling wreckage. Eyewitnesses described a storm of flames as more than 40 homes in Lockerbie, including two complete rows of houses, were crushed. Debris was strewn over a radius of more than 16 kilometres (10 miles).

The jet – flight 103 – began its journey in Frankfurt, Germany, stopping at London's Heathrow airport. It left London at 6.25 pm for New York's John F Kennedy airport and followed a normal flight path. But at 7.19 pm, flying at 880 kilometres per hour (550 mph) at an altitude of around 9300 metres (31 000 ft), the jet fell apart.

Experts cannot yet be sure what caused the tragedy. Among the passengers were US diplomats, servicemen and

LOCKERBIE'S HORROR Policemen carry one of the victims past the shattered cockpit of flight 103.

students heading home for Christmas. Some suggest a bomb may have been planted on the aircraft by terrorists in retaliation for the incident last July in which an American cruiser mistakenly shot down an Iranian airliner over the Persian Gulf, killing 290. There are also reports that anonymous warnings of an impending bomb attack on a Pan Am flight were sent to US embassies.

··· A FRENCH COMPANY LAUNCHES AN ABORTION-INDUCING DRUG, RV486 ···

UPRISING BRINGS NEW HOPE TO PALESTINIANS

TROUBLED YOUTH Palestinian children display their guns and their support for the PLO.

All year – sometimes it has seemed every night – television pictures have carried the Palestinian uprising, or Intifada (literally, 'shaking off'), against Israel into living rooms around the world.

The fight has been uneven. On the Palestinian side women and youngsters, some of them hardly into their teens, shout slogans, set fire to cars and hurl stones – their chief weapons – at Israeli forces. The Israeli troops return rounds of live ammunition and rubber bullets. Children are being killed, but the Palestinians are gaining their objectives – self-esteem and sympathy abroad for the cause of Palestinian nationalism. Their hope is that the Intifada will raise the issue that has bedevilled the Middle East

for 40 years to the top of the international agenda.

The violence began over a year ago, on 6 December 1987, following the killing of several Arabs in retaliation for the murder of an Israeli plastics salesman in Gaza. Yitzhak Shamir, the Israeli prime minister, has called the Palestinians' action 'terrorism'.

But Israeli opinion is now deeply divided. On one side are those who believe the Intifada proves that there is no point in making peace; on the other, people who are, perhaps reluctantly, coming to the conclusion that a political solution to the conflict must be found – and that it will have to include the exchange of land for peace.

New anti-depressant brings high hopes

The search for a safe and effective anti-depressant drug has been littered with false hopes, but early indications are that Prozac, launched this year, might be a significant breakthrough.

Prozac seems to cause less sedation than other drugs of its type and to have fewer side-effects (which usually take such forms as sweating and an irregular heart rhythm). In certain cases, however, it has caused headaches and nausea. An interesting feature of the drug is that it tends to act as an appetite suppressant. In the United States application has been made to use it as an aid to dieting, but in Britain its only approved use is in the treatment of depression.

Spaniards tried for poisoning oil

28 JUNE, MADRID
The longest trial in Spanish history ended today, but the verdict is not expected for several months because the judges have a mountain of evidence to review. The 38 defendants are charged with causing the deaths of more than 600 people with contaminated cooking oil. The prosecution alleges that the product sold as olive oil was in fact industrial-grade rapeseed oil that had been reprocessed and mixed with other oils.

The defence lawyers argue that the 'toxic syndrome' that caused so many painful deaths and serious disabilities was brought about by pesticides or by chemical weapons tests at an American airbase. The poisonings occurred in 1981 and the trial began 15 months ago.

ADULTERATED EVIDENCE Hundreds of bottles of contaminated oil were presented at the trial.

During the court proceedings, relatives of the oil victims screamed 'Killers!' at the defendants.

··· SNOW FALLS ON THE SYRIAN CAPITAL, DAMASCUS, FOR THE FIRST TIME IN 50 YEARS ···

US warship downs airliner

GRAPHIC COMMENT The USA's act of aggression is vividly depicted at the victims' funeral in Teheran.

3 JULY, PERSIAN GULF
A US cruiser guarding oil tankers in the Gulf today shot down an Iranian airliner, killing all 290 people on board. The USS *Vincennes* reportedly mistook the Iran Air Airbus for an Iranian F14 fighter and sent warnings on both military and civilian radio airwaves before bringing it down.

At a press conference in Washington DC, Admiral William Crowe, the US Joint Chiefs of Staff chairman, said it was difficult to identify a radar signal from a head-on target. He insists that the *Vincennes* cannot be blamed and that the Airbus, which was flying at only 2250 metres (7500 ft), was not following the normal route for civil air traffic and should have been transmitting a radar signal to identify itself as a civilian aircraft. He added that the *Vincennes'* captain 'acted with good judgment in a very trying period'. President Reagan says that the United States 'deeply regrets' the loss of life in a 'terrible human tragedy' and has ordered an inquiry into the affair.

Whatever the full explanation of the incident, it is sure to inflame further the already hostile relations between the United States and Iran. In a troubling broadcast, Teheran Radio described the episode as a 'barbaric massacre' and made a gruesome pledge to meet violence with violence: 'We will resist the plots of the great Satan [the US] and avenge the blood of our martyrs.'

Royal couple met by boos in Australia

11 MAY, CANBERRA
The Queen and the Duke of Edinburgh yesterday left Australia, after a controversial three-week tour as part of the country's bicentenary celebrations. This was the eleventh time the royal couple had visited Australia, but the usual cheering crowds were this time often replaced by booing protesters.

At the opening of Canberra's New Parliament House, the Queen was met by a show of hostility that shocked her loyal supporters. The protests come both from Australians who want complete constitutional independence, resenting the idea of owing allegiance to a far distant sovereign, and from Aboriginals who have been thwarted in their attempts to achieve a treaty on land rights.

Although most of the protests have been verbal, one Aboriginal used the now fashionable method of 'mooning' – exposing his bare bottom to the Queen as a mark of disrespect.

USA breaks new ground in technology to unveil 'invisible' aircraft

10 NOVEMBER, NEVADA
After years of rumours and clandestine testing, the US Air Force has unveiled its latest secret weapon: the Lockheed F-117A Nighthawk 'stealth' aircraft, designed to be invisible to radar. The futuristic aircraft – which has the sharp, jutting angles of a handmade paper plane – is made of a top-secret material capable of absorbing radar signals. The hot air produced by its non-afterburning engines is mixed with cold air and expelled through large slots so that the Nighthawk does not even leave an infrared trace of its passing, making its detection by enemies very hard indeed.

The Nighthawk – created at Lockheed's 'Skunk Works', where the U-2 and SR-71 Blackbird reconnaissance aircraft were developed – first flew in June 1981. It entered USAF service in 1983 and pilots have been flying it for five years – but only at night. The security surrounding the project could not stop rumours circulating and the aviation world has been alive with talk of the secret aeroplane.

There are 52 Nighthawks in USAF service with the 4450 Tactical Group in Tonopah, Nevada. In a war, their role would be not to fight other aircraft but to steal undetected into enemy

TOMORROW'S BOMBER The F-117A, designed for laser-guided bombing attacks.

airspace and hit strategic targets. The aircraft can carry two 900-kilo (2000-lb)

bombs and is equipped to track and identify its targets with pinpoint accuracy.

··· GENETIC ENGINEERS CLONE CATTLE EMBRYOS TO PRODUCE DAIRY CATTLE ···

Earthquake shakes Armenia

9 DECEMBER, YEREVAN
The Soviet Union was in shock and mourning yesterday following one of the greatest natural disasters in living memory – a huge earthquake in the small southern republic of Armenia, which borders Turkey. Several towns and villages are said to have been destroyed completely, and according to eye-witness reports, whole buildings simply disappeared into immense fissures which opened up in the ground. The death toll is estimated to be at least 50000 and could be much higher.

A massive rescue operation has been launched, with thousands of troops helping to clear the debris. Donations of blood have been collected in Moscow and other major cities and these and other medical supplies are being rushed to the region. Messages of sympathy and offers of aid have come from all over the world. A team from the London Fire Brigade is

SOMBRE TRIBUTE Vodka glasses are raised in a toast to those lost in the tragic Armenian earthquake.

leaving for Armenia today, taking special infrared equipment designed to locate people trapped under rubble. President Gorbachev has cut short his visit to the United States and returned to Moscow because of the tragedy.

Reagans see their future in the stars

3 MAY, WASHINGTON DC
Decisions that affect the future of the entire free world are in the hands of an astrologer, according to one of Ronald Reagan's former right-hand men.
Donald Regan, ex-chief of staff at the White House, claims in a new book that the President consulted his wife's astrologer before almost every important event. The stars and planets even dictated the date of the nuclear arms talks with the Soviet leader, Mikhail Gorbachev, held at the end of last year.

Apparently the astrologer, who lives in California, advised the Reagans whether the timing was right for major summits. If it was not, Regan alleges, the President would insist that meetings be moved to a more auspicious time. In the USA, responses to the revelations range from shock to ridicule.

Racing champion passes his last winning post

STYLISH FINISH Bill 'the Shoe' Shoemaker, veteran of 21 Kentucky Derbies, won his fourth in 1986.

27 APRIL, NEW YORK CITY

The American jockey William Lee Shoemaker, who started racing back in 1949, has announced his retirement at the age of 56, after a glittering career that leaves all his rivals in the shade.

No one else has come close to his lifetime total of nearly 9000 wins, and his record of 485 winners in a single season of flat racing in 1953 still stands. Shoemaker was the least flamboyant of jockeys. He seemed to do little to his horses, indulging in no acrobatics in the saddle and rarely using the whip. But he won the Kentucky Derby four times, the Preakness Stakes five times and the Belmont twice – a record in the USA's classic races that will be hard to beat.

··· COMPUTER SYSTEMS WORLDWIDE ARE RENDERED USELESS BY VIRUSES IMPLANTED BY HACKERS ···

Games tarnished by drugs scandal

2 OCTOBER, SEOUL

Despite the twin triumphs of the sisters Jackie Joyner-Kersee and Florence Griffith-Joyner, the Seoul Olympics have proved a great disappointment for the United States. Joyner-Kersee won the gold medal in the long jump, while Griffith-Joyner won both the 100 metres and the 200 metres – and was equally celebrated for her flashy tracksuits and long, painted fingernails. But the American team lagged well behind the Soviet Union.

The most sensational turn of events was the disqualification of Ben Johnson, the Canadian world-record holder at 100 metres, who was stripped of his gold medal after he failed a drugs test. The likelihood is that Johnson will also have his world record taken from him.

Almost as startling were events in the pool. The American diver Greg Louganis bled profusely after hitting his head on the board in the springboard diving. Temporary sutures were applied to the wound and he went on to retain the gold medal he had won in Los Angeles.

SPORTING ATTRACTION Florence Griffith-Joyner at the USA's Olympic athletic trials in Indianapolis.

People have often insisted that politics should be kept out of sport. Here the tables have been turned. The Games were held in Seoul only after the dictatorship in South Korea bowed to international pressure and held democratic elections.

Moral guardian falls from grace and begs flock's forgiveness

21 FEBRUARY, BATON ROUGE, LOUISIANA

Jimmy Swaggart, a firebrand right-wing television evangelist – who last year denounced a fellow preacher for his adultery – confessed today to seeing a prostitute. In a televised service, the Reverend Swaggart sobbed as he admitted his 'past sin' to his congregation and begged forgiveness.

Swaggart announced his withdrawal from his hugely successful television ministry, where his particular style of showbiz evangelism has netted millions of dollars in donations. When the Reverend Jim Bakker, who peddled a similar brand of fundamentalist Christianity and political conservatism, admitted an affair last year, Swaggart, Bakker's main 'televangelical' rival, called him 'a cancer on the body of Christ'. Now Swaggart, too, is exposed as nothing more than a hypocrite.

WOMEN RETURN TO STEAL THE SCENE

TOON TOWN Bob Hoskins has his work cut out keeping up with animated co-star Roger Rabbit.

Is the 'women's picture' – dead since Doris Day's heyday – making a comeback? The phenomenal success of the Spanish film *Women on the Verge of a Nervous Breakdown* points that way. Directed by the flamboyant Pedro Almodóvar and starring Carmen Maura it deals with the battle of the sexes. On a darker note, the year's most harrowing performance came from 26-year-old Jodie Foster, who played the victim of a gang rape in *The Accused*. The movie controversially showed the rape in all its disturbing detail. Michelle Pfeiffer proved she wasn't just a pretty face by turning in a moving performance as a wronged woman in love in Stephen Frears' spectacular costume drama *Dangerous Liaisons.* The prize for this year's femme fatale is a close-run thing. Should it go to Jamie Lee Curtis as the tough, sexy con artist who scares the pants off John Cleese in the comedy hit *A Fish Called Wanda*? Or to curvaceous cartoon redhead Jessica Rabbit who creates havoc for her fellow stars in *Who Framed Roger Rabbit?* She explained it herself: 'I'm not bad, I'm just drawn that way.'

Roseanne – the tarnished star

There has never been a sitcom heroine like her: loud, overweight and working-class. Roseanne is the antithesis of the typical television housewife. She and her family live in a town in the American Midwest, are constantly worrying about money, bickering and making snide comments – and, perhaps seeing their own lives reflected, television audiences everywhere love them.

Roseanne's creator, the stand-up comedian Roseanne Barr, was touted as broadcasting's most powerful woman. Her turbulent private life, including divorce and public confessions of childhood abuse, was reflected in backstage rows and daring story-lines, including American television's first prime-time lesbian kiss. Later, she underwent extensive plastic surgery; as she was prettified, so was the show, losing its edge and its audience.

ABRASIVE WIT Roseanne, her husband Dan, and two of her three children take time out.

··· AN ESTIMATED 70 000 DEALERS ARE SELLING CRACK COCAINE AND OTHER DRUGS IN LOS ANGELES ···

US HITS OF THE YEAR

1	ROLL WITH IT	*Steve Winwood*
2	EVERY ROSE HAS ITS THORN	*Poison*
3	ONE MORE TRY	*George Michael*
4	LOOK AWAY	*Chicago*
5	NEVER GONNA GIVE YOU UP	*Rick Astley*

US TV HITS

1	*The Cosby Show*
2	*A Different World*
3	*Cheers*
4	*The Golden Girls*
5	*Growing Pains*

1989

DIED

7 Jan: Michinomiya Hirohito, Emperor of Japan
23 Jan: Salvador Dali, Spanish artist
26 Apr: Lucille Ball, US comedian
11 July: Laurence Olivier, British actor
6 Oct: Bette Davis, US actress
22 Dec: Samuel Beckett, Irish playwright and novelist

BOUGHT

28 Sept, USA: Hollywood studio Colombia Pictures, by Japanese electronics firm Sony; for $3.4 billion

BURNT

18 July, Nairobi: 12 tons of elephant tusks, worth $3 million, in ceremony to demonstrate Kenya's commitment to stamping out trade in ivory

On 19 October, the British court of appeal takes just 30 minutes to overturn the convictions of four Irish citizens jailed in 1975 for the Guildford pub bombings. Gerard Conlon (shown above as he walked free), Carole Richardson, Patrick Armstrong and Paul Hill were found to be victims of a miscarriage of justice, in which police officers had forged confessions and fabricated evidence.

PUBLISHED

Martin Amis, *London Fields*
Kazuo Ishiguro, *The Remains of the Day*
Alice Walker, *The Temple of My Familiar*

ON STRIKE

June–Aug, London: Underground staff, in series of one-day actions
July: Soviet coal miners
27 Nov: Czech workers, on two-hour general stoppage organised by the Civic Forum political opposition

CELEBRATED

14 July, Paris: 200th anniversary of the French Revolution

INVADED

28 Sept, Czechoslovakia: West German Embassy in Prague, by East Germans desperate to escape to the West
19 Dec: Panama, by US troops

WITHDRAWN

26 Sept, Cambodia: last Vietnamese soldiers, ending 11-year occupation

On 25 August, the US spacecraft Voyager 2 sends back pictures of the planet Neptune (above) and one of its moons, Triton. Neptune, the eighth planet from the Sun, is seen to have five rings and a stormy climate, as well as clouds that throw shadows.

THREATENED

Mar, USA: US singer Madonna, with excommunication from the Roman Catholic Church, following video for her song 'Like A Prayer' which suggests sexual attraction between the singer and a vision of Jesus

KILLED

9 Jan, UK: 30 passengers, when British Midland Boeing 737 crashes into M1 motorway embankment
23 Jan, USSR: more than 1000 people, in Tajikistan earthquake
20 Aug, London: 26 partygoers, on pleasure cruiser the *Marchioness*, which collides with dredger *Bowbelle* at night on river Thames
28 Dec, New South Wales: 11 people, in Australia's first fatal earthquake

BEATEN

25 Feb, Las Vegas: British boxer Frank Bruno, by US fighter Mike Tyson in world heavyweight championship bout

QUIT

3 Feb, South Africa: P W Botha, as leader of National Party, due to poor health; he is replaced by F W de Klerk

ELECTED

10 Feb, Jamaica: Michael Manley, as prime minister

PROTESTED

Apr: British rock musician Sting, who tours to publicise ecological disaster threatening Brazilian rainforests

NEW WORDS

karaoke *n*: machine that plays songs without the vocals, enabling user to sing the words; popular in bars, exported from Japan to USA and Europe

On 19 October, the San Andreas fault triggers a series of earth tremors and San Francisco is hit by a major earthquake, measuring 6.9 on the Richter scale: 273 people are killed and a further 650 are injured. Most of the deaths occur when a section of highway collapses and crushes traffic underneath.

CHINESE ARMY MASSACRES STUDENTS

FACE-OFF The near-carnival atmosphere evaporated as students and soldiers clashed in Tiananmen Square.

4 JUNE, BEIJING
In the early hours of this morning, the Chinese government clamped down on pro-democracy protesters gathered in Beijing's Tiananmen Square. It is estimated that as many as 3000 people have been killed and 10000 injured. Over the past seven weeks, since the death of liberal reformer Hu Yaobang, the square has become the symbol and focus of China's fledgling democratic movement. Support has been growing into what looked like a popular revolution in the making. Until yesterday the Chinese government were divided in its reaction to the protesters.

However, last night the People's Liberation Army swept through the streets of the capital, firing automatic weapons indiscriminately into the crowds. It is believed that 26 people died on the ironically named Avenue of Eternal Peace as the 300000-strong army advanced towards Tiananmen Square. Armoured vehicles smashed their way through burning barricades into the square to confront the students. Troops lined up for their final assault, and up to a thousand protesters were massacred as the soldiers opened fire. The city's hospitals are tonight filled to overflowing with the victims.

··· THE EUROPEAN COMMISSION ORDERS A TOTAL BAN ON CFC GASES BY THE END OF THE CENTURY ···

Russia quits Afghanistan

15 FEBRUARY, AFGHANISTAN
The last Soviet soldier of the occupying force in Afghanistan left today. He was General Boris Gromov, the army commander.

The Soviets invaded Afghanistan in 1979 to keep in place a pro-Moscow regime, but the army has been unable to quell the rebels who waged a guerrilla war in the rugged Afghan countryside. About 16000 Soviet soldiers and more than a million Afghans have died during the occupation.

Death sentence for British novelist

15 FEBRUARY, TEHERAN
Iranian leader Ayatollah Khomeini imposed a death sentence yesterday on Salman Rushdie, author of *The Satanic Verses*. Khomeini claims that the book blasphemes Islam – in one light-hearted passage, prostitutes play-act as wives of the prophet Mohammed. Thousands of Iranians marched on the British embassy in Teheran today in support of the decree – or *fatwa* – chanting 'Death to England, death to America'.

Indian-born Rushdie, 42, has dismissed the charge, saying that he doubts anyone

INCITING ANGER Rushdie's book is destroyed at a demonstration in Bradford.

in Iran has read the book. But he has gone into hiding under police protection. *The Satanic Verses* has already been banned in India. In Bradford today crowds burned copies of the book. An Islamic charity has offered $1 million to any non-Muslim who carries out the decree.

BERLIN REJOICES AS THE WALL COMES DOWN

FREEDOM Berliners stand on the wall that has divided them for 28 years.

10 NOVEMBER, BERLIN

East and West Berliners let out a raucous cheer at midnight last night as the once fiercely guarded checkpoints of the Berlin Wall were thrown open. The opening of the gates in the wall – so long the hated symbol of the Cold War – follows the opening of East Germany's other borders.

Last night, as the gathering crowd rushed through the checkpoints and clambered jubilantly onto the wall, many Berliners could hardly believe what they were witnessing. Some have smashed off pieces of the wall and there are reports throughout Eastern Europe that people are heading to Berlin carrying sledgehammers, pick-axes and any other tools they can find. While most Germans are stunned at the recent developments, West German politicians will already be looking forward to a new era of German unification.

When dawn broke over Berlin, the party was still going on. Millions around the world watched on television. President Bush said he was 'elated', while British prime minister Margaret Thatcher called it a 'great day for freedom'. Walter Momper, the mayor of West Berlin, said: 'The Germans are the happiest people in the world today.'

··· THE US SUPREME COURT RULES THAT THE RIGHT TO FREE SPEECH INCLUDES BURNING THE US FLAG ···

How the East was won

The pressure for reform in East Germany had built almost to boiling point by the end of the year. Mass demonstrations in East Berlin, Leipzig and other cities called on the Communist government to relax border controls and allow free movement to the West. After the increasingly liberal Hungary opened its border to Austria in May, tens of thousands of East Germans emigrated through Austria to West Germany where they gained automatic citizenship. Many more sought refuge in West German embassies in Poland and Czechoslovakia.

Soviet leader Mikhail Gorbachev, who had assumed power in 1985 preparing to dismantle Stalin's empire, visited East Germany on 7 October and backed reform, sparking further protests. The East German Communist Party leader Erich Honecker seemed determined to hold on to power and was considering using force to bolster the party's position. But on 18 October he was forced to resign by the politburo and the younger hardliner Egon Krenz took power. He proceeded to sack members of the ruling politburo and the demonstrations continued. Ultimately it was the sheer flood of East Germans to the West that turned the tide. The government had little choice but to relax travel restrictions on 4 November and at midnight on 9 November, after the resignation of Krenz's politburo, all the checkpoints on the Berlin Wall were opened.

TURNING TIDE A rally in Hungary demands democratic reforms.

Tens of thousands of refugees flowed into the West after the collapse of Europe's most closely guarded frontier. Now the challenge for Germany is to fulfil the hopes of its new residents by finding them homes and jobs.

Beat around the broccoli

Dissidents' hero is new Czech premier

PEOPLE'S PLAYWRIGHT Havel greets the public after being elected president.

22 MARCH, WASHINGTON DC
President Bush upset the nation's broccoli farmers at a news conference this morning, when he vowed never to eat broccoli again: 'I do not like broccoli … I'm President of the United States, and I'm not going to eat any more broccoli.'

The question of the President's broccoli consumption arose after a report revealed that Bush had banned the offending vegetable from meals on the presidential plane. Yesterday the California Broccoli Shippers Association protested by sending boxes of broccoli to the White House, along with some gourmet recipes.

29 DECEMBER, PRAGUE
Vaclav Havel, the Czech playwright who earlier this year was jailed for inciting demonstrations against the Communist government, was today voted president of Czechoslovakia. This unanimous vote of confidence in Havel by parliament is the culmination of months of campaigning and popular protests.

The pivotal moment came when Communist president Gustav Husak's successor, Milos Jakeš, was forced to resign on 24 November along with the ruling politburo. Triumphant crowds thronged the streets of Prague shouting out the name of Alexander Dubček, whose moderate government was crushed by the notorious Soviet invasion in 1968, and of Havel.

Prague-born Havel, the dissidents' hero, was jailed in 1979 for four years when his plays were declared subversive. After his three-month spell in prison this year he was appointed head of the Civic Forum, a coordinating body for various groups which have been vocal opponents of the repressive regime – testimony to his enormous popularity. General elections are expected to be held in the country next year.

··· MIKHAIL GORBACHEV IS THE FIRST SOVIET LEADER TO VISIT THE VATICAN ···

Mass hysteria at Khomeini's burial

Bloody end for hated Romanian dictator

8 JUNE, TEHERAN
There were scenes of mayhem yesterday as the body of Ayatollah Khomeini made its last journey to the cemetery for 'martyrs of the revolution' 22 kilometres (15 miles) south of the city. Khomeini died two days ago, aged 86.

Originally, Teheran officials had planned to transport his coffin through the streets in a funeral procession, but more than two million mourners had massed along the funeral route since dawn. Instead the coffin was flown to the site by helicopter, but even then chaos ensued as mourners, in a fury of mass hysteria, pushed towards the bearers, grabbed at the coffin and tore at Khomeini's shroud. In the melee, the body was exposed and the coffin was

OUTBURST OF GRIEF The burial was postponed after the jostling crowd burst open the coffin.

almost lost to the crowd. Revolutionary Guards moved in to restore order and returned the coffin to the helicopter.

When the body was brought back to the graveside it was in a metal coffin and only senior officials and army personnel were allowed near it.

30 DECEMBER, BUCHAREST
Five days after hated Romanian dictator Nicolae Ceausescu and his wife, Elena, were shot, his Communist regime has fallen apart. The couple were executed after a military tribunal found them guilty of 'crimes against the people'. Today the Communist Party was abolished. The army-backed National Salvation Front is in control and has declared its intention to hold elections in April next year.

On 21 December the army turned against Ceausescu and took on his secret police. It has taken a week of bloody street battles for the army to gain the upper hand – and thousands of Romanians have been killed.

Hillsborough football ground turns into death crush

15 APRIL, SHEFFIELD
Liverpool was in a state of shock today after 94 football fans were crushed to death at the FA Cup semi-final between Liverpool and Nottingham Forest. The match at the Hillsborough ground was abandoned after just six minutes amid horrifying scenes of congestion in which another 200 people were injured.

The late arrival of hundreds of Liverpool supporters cramming to get into the stadium caused such a crush that the police opened an exit gate to relieve the pressure. But it only made things worse. Fans spilled onto terraces which were already filled to capacity, pushing those ahead of them into the barrier fence separating the crowd from the pitch.

The police have been accused of making a sluggish response to the build-up of fans and of failing to maintain efficient communications between officers inside and outside the ground. There will now be a full inquiry into the tragedy, and the demand for all-seater stadiums will gain urgency.

RESCUED Fans are hauled onto the balconies from the packed terraces.

··· NEW YORK'S GUARDIAN ANGELS ARRIVE IN LONDON TO PATROL THE UNDERGROUND SYSTEM ···

Devastating oil spill hits pristine Alaskan coastline

BLACK ROCKS The clean-up crew hose down the oil-covered coastline of Green Island, Alaska.

24 MARCH, ALASKA
One of the last unspoiled areas on Earth is threatened with destruction by the worst crude oil spill in American history. The 320-metre (990-ft) tanker *Exxon Valdez* ran aground on Bligh Island in Prince William Sound, spilling nearly 50 million litres (11 million gal) of oil onto the surface of the water. Winds and currents spread the oil over 2300 sq km (900 sq miles), suffocating the coastline and endangering the lives of seals, birds and other marine life.

The accident is being blamed on human error. The tanker's captain, Joseph Hazlewood, admits that he went to his cabin leaving the third mate, who was not licensed to pilot a vessel through the Sound, in charge. The Exxon Shipping Company has sent three aeroplane loads of clean-up crew to start containing and mopping up the spill. However, environmentalists estimate that it will take more than a year to remove all the oil, which is floating in a layer up to 10 centimetres (4 in) thick on the water at some parts of the shoreline.

British teenagers are all loved-up with everywhere to rave

Ecstasy, or 'E', began to have a profound effect on youth culture this year. The drug goes hand in hand with a new movement in music known as 'acid house' and all-night parties or 'raves'. In Britain raves were held over the summer in abandoned warehouses, private houses and even in the middle of fields. The police watched from the sidelines, powerless to stop the gatherings of young people dancing till dawn, fuelled by ecstasy and drinking water.

Behind the 'E' culture is a revival of the hippy philosophy of peace, love and togetherness, influenced by the feelings of euphoria and affection induced by the drug. In the clubs, fashion changed from the style-conscious formality of the 'new romantic' look to baggy, casual sportswear – often given a psychedelic twist with luminous colours and the yellow smiley-face logo that has come to be synonymous with acid house.

Worries have begun to be expressed that such wide-scale drug-taking is dangerous. The long-term psychological and physiological side-effects of ecstasy are not yet known.

HAPPY SMILEY A raver loses himself in the beat.

··· IT IS REVEALED THAT POP GROUP MILLI VANILLI DID NOT SING ON ANY OF THEIR HITS ···

'Cold fusion' does not work

At a press conference on 23 March at the University of Utah, Martin Fleischmann and Stanley Pons announced that they had found a simple, cheap method for taming the power of the Sun. They passed electric current through a beaker of heavy water, a coolant used in some nuclear reactors. The process generated large amounts of heat and the only logical conclusion was that deuterium (isotopes of hydrogen) were fusing in a process known as nuclear fusion. Fusion – the opposite of nuclear fission, in which the atomic nuclei split – takes place at high temperatures in the Sun, but had occurred at low temperatures in the trial.

Most physicists were openly sceptical of 'cold fusion' and when tested the experiment did not work. Fleischmann and Pons had been in error.

WHEN SALLY FAKED HER WAY INTO A CLASSIC

BROTHERS Cruise and Hoffman, whose role won him a Golden Globe and an Oscar in 1989.

Meg Ryan's faked orgasm helped *When Harry Met Sally*, a film that used cynical humour to camouflage old-fashioned romance, to become an instant comedy classic. A darker take on relationships was offered by *sex, lies and videotape* – writer-director Steven Soderbergh's clever study of voyeurism made him and most of his cast hot property. Handicap was a popular theme: cerebral palsy in *My Left Foot*, based on the autobiography of the Irish poet Christy Brown – Daniel Day-Lewis won an Oscar; and autism in *Rain Man*, released towards the end of 1988. The film saw egotist Tom Cruise learning the value of human relationships from autistic brother Dustin Hoffman. A popular series came to an end, as Harrison Ford picked up the bullwhip for the last time in *Indiana Jones and the Last Crusade*.

US HITS OF THE YEAR	
1 ANOTHER DAY IN PARADISE	*Phil Collins*
2 MISS YOU MUCH	*Janet Jackson*
3 RIGHT HERE WAITING	*Richard Marx*
4 LIKE A PRAYER	*Madonna*
5 STRAIGHT UP	*Paula Abdul*

US TV HITS
1 *The Cosby Show*
2 *Roseanne*
3 *A Different World*
4 *Cheers*
5 *60 Minutes*

1990

DIED
3 Apr: Sarah Vaughan, US jazz singer
15 Apr: Greta Garbo, Swedish actress
16 May: Sammy Davis Jr, US comedian
22 May: Rocky Graziano, US boxer (born Rocco Barbella)
23 Nov: Roald Dahl, British author

PUBLISHED
A S Byatt, *Possession*
Thomas Pynchon, *Vineland*
Derek Walcott, *Omeros*

CHAMPIONS
11 Feb, Tokyo: US boxer James 'Buster' Douglas, who shocks boxing world by knocking out world heavyweight champion Mike Tyson
9 Apr, Georgia, USA: British golfer Nick Faldo, who wins the US Masters for second year running at Augusta

CHAMPIONS (cont.)
7 July, London: US tennis player Martina Navratilova, who wins Wimbledon women's tennis singles for a record ninth time, beating Zina Garrison 6–4, 6–1

JAILED
20 Dec, Thailand: British woman Karyn Smith, for 25 years, guilty of attempted heroin smuggling

BANNED
21 July, UK: Pakistani-produced movie *International Guerrillas*, in which Salman Rushdie is portrayed as a murderer who is struck down by a bolt of lightning

SACKED
8 Aug, Pakistan: Benazir Bhutto, as prime minister, by President Gulam Ishaq Khan

Game Boy, the hand-held computer games console, is launched by Japanese computer company Nintendo. Although portable computer games have long been available, the programmable Game Boy introduces a new level of sophistication.

DECLARED INDEPENDENCE
11 Mar: Lithuania, from USSR
12 June: Russian Federation, from USSR
20 June: Uzbekistan, from USSR

FREED
24 Aug, Beirut: Irish hostage Brian Keenan, after being held captive for four years and four months by Islamic Dawn terrorists

TRIUMPHED
28 Jan, New Orleans: US football team San Francisco 49ers, who beat Denver Broncos 55–10 in biggest ever Super Bowl win
4 Feb, New Zealand: New Zealand cricketer Richard Hadlee, who is the first bowler to take 400 Test wickets

8 July, Rome: West Germany, in football World Cup, beating Argentina

ELECTED
29 May, Russian Federation: Boris Yeltsin, as president
9 Dec, Poland: Lech Walesa, as president
9 Dec, Serbia: Slobodan Milošević, as president
16 Dec, Haiti: Jean-Baptiste Aristide, as president

NEW WORDS
out *vb*: to publicise another person's homosexuality without his or her consent; from the phrase 'to come out of the closet', meaning to declare one's own homosexuality
yuppie flu *n*: chronic fatigue experienced by people in highly pressured professions

On 26 October, *Washington mayor Marion Barry receives a six-month prison sentence for possession of cocaine. Barry was arrested in January after being secretly filmed smoking crack cocaine in a hotel room by the FBI. Black leaders in the USA are worried that the incident may damage the credibility of other black politicians.*

On 1 December, *French and British workers in the Channel Tunnel make the final breakthrough. Graham Fagg (left) exchanges national flags with his French counterpart Philippe Cozette before construction work continues.*

MANDELA IS FREE AT LAST

TRIUMPHANT RETURN An exuberant Mandela and his wife Winnie greet a crowd of well-wishers.

11 FEBRUARY, CAPE TOWN
The world's most famous prisoner of conscience, Nelson Mandela, became a free man today. The South African government unconditionally released 71-year-old Mandela after keeping him locked up for most of the last 26 years on the notorious Robben Island. The news has been rapturously received by black and many white South Africans.

Mandela will no doubt reassume the active leadership of the ANC, and take a prominent place in the country's political life. De Klerk's government is clearly paving the way for a new constitution, which will allow non-whites to participate in national politics. This new direction looks set to anger right-wing politicians and strain the ruling National Party to near breaking-point.

Dignified step from prisoner to leader

The serenity, dignity and apparent lack of bitterness with which Nelson Rolihlahla Mandela has re-entered political life have deeply impressed the world, which has embraced him as an international statesman.

He was sentenced in 1964 to life imprisonment for his membership of the armed wing of the ANC, which carried out a sabotage campaign against the apartheid regime. From then on he lived in solitary confinement on Robben Island, reserved for political prisoners. His quarters were a tiny concrete cell with one 40-watt bulb for light.

In 1985 the government offered to release Mandela if he renounced violence – an offer that he rejected, insisting on unconditional release. During his long spell in prison, Mandela became a powerful symbol of the ANC's continued defiance and a focus for international protest against the injustices of apartheid.

Despite his harsh treatment by the South African regime, Mandela has emerged from isolation eager to return to the political arena and work with those who imprisoned him.

··· 28 FEB, USSR: SOVIET CITIZENS ARE PERMITTED TO OWN LAND FOR THE FIRST TIME SINCE 1922 ···

Germany reunites on a wave of popular enthusiasm

3 OCTOBER, GERMANY
West and East Germany died at midnight last night and were reborn as a united nation. Less than a year after the Berlin Wall was made redundant by the opening of East German borders, fireworks lit up the sky over Berlin and the city's streets were once again filled with tearful, celebrating Germans.

Talks on reunification began in March this year, shortly before the conservative Alliance for Germany was elected in East Germany's first free elections. Alliance leader Lothar de

END OF AN ERA The whole of Berlin is a party as fireworks light up the Brandenburg Gate.

Maizière, appointed prime minister on 12 April, agreed terms for economic union with West Germany. On 1 July the West German Deutschmark became the currency of the whole of Germany, replacing the East German Ostmark, and on 12 September the Allied victors of World War II signed a treaty in Moscow giving full sovereignty to the future united Germany.

The new country faces a difficult time dealing with East Germany's economic problems, but today a long and dearly held dream has been realised.

Iraqi troops overrun oil-rich Kuwait

MILITARY MIGHT The Iraqi invasion of Kuwait City was captured on security cameras.

3 AUGUST, BAGHDAD
Iraqi armies have swept into Kuwait and, in what one US military officer has called 'a cake walk', seized control of the entire country in just 24 hours.

It took only five hours for 100 000 troops – some of them arriving in buses – to ring the capital, but their apparent effort to capture the Kuwaiti royal family has failed. The Emir and several other members of the Sabah family have escaped in a limousine convoy across the border into Saudi Arabia.

Kuwait is little more than a city state, but its vast oil resources have made it fabulously wealthy. In contrast, Iraq is one of the poorest countries in the region, crippled by war debt, with a burgeoning population and lacking the natural resources of its neighbours.

Iraq has always regarded Kuwait as part of its nation, torn from it by Western powers after World War I. But disputed border claims as well as the beleaguered Iraqi economy lie behind yesterday's swoop. Since 1988, when hostilities ceased in the Iran–Iraq War, Iraqi dictator Saddam Hussein has been asking countries to cancel $70 billion in war debts. Some, such as Saudi Arabia, have complied; Kuwait refused. Yesterday the tiny but immensely rich country on the Persian Gulf paid the price of that refusal.

··· BRITAIN PUMPS 300 MILLION TONS OF SEWAGE INTO THE SEA EVERY YEAR ···

Iraq plans to build nuclear 'supergun'

12 APRIL, LONDON
Evidence is mounting that Iraq has the capacity to make nuclear weapons and is busy trying to construct a 'supergun' capable of carrying both nuclear and chemical warheads.

Two weeks ago British customs officials confiscated 40 American-made electrical components designed for use as nuclear triggers. Yesterday a consignment of high-precision steel tubing, manufactured by the British firm Sheffield Forgemasters, was seized. Taken together these components suggest that the Iraqis are planning to manufacture a gun larger than any the world has ever seen.

These events have brought to the fore the murder of Dr Gerald Bull in Brussels on 28 March, which at the time went virtually unnoticed. The Canadian ballistics expert has been linked to the design of a 'supergun'. Mystery surrounds his death; it is not known who was responsible, although there are persistent rumours that American undercover agents from the CIA may be involved.

USA sends troops to Saudi Arabia

DESERT SHIELD Nearly 250 000 troops and 2.5 million tons of equipment are being sent to Saudi Arabia.

31 DECEMBER, BAGHDAD
Saddam Hussein has two weeks to get his troops out of Kuwait. If he fails to do so by 15 January, the United Nations has sanctioned member states 'to use all necessary' means to liberate Kuwait.

Saddam undoubtedly feels hard-done-by. His invasion of Kuwait took place only a few days after he was informed by US officials that the United States had no view on 'inter-Arab disputes such as your border dispute with Kuwait'. Yet on 4 August, only two days after the Iraqi strike, President Bush committed troops to the defence of Saudi Arabia and the rescue of Kuwait. King Fahd invited the troops into Saudi Arabia, and within days the 82nd Airborne Division had secured Saudi airports, ports and oilfields, clearing the way for allied forces – what the Americans have dubbed the 'Desert Shield'.

Saddam uses civilians as 'human shield'

28 AUGUST, BAGHDAD

In a move designed to appease the international forces lining up against him, Saddam Hussein has released all the women and children taken as hostages after the occupation of Kuwait.

The action has undoubtedly come too late to reverse the revulsion felt throughout the West when Saddam announced that all foreign 'guests' in Iraq and Kuwait would be detained in order to ensure the good conduct of their native countries.

The creation of a 'human shield' to protect vital sites began within hours of the capitulation of Kuwait on 2 August. A British Airways plane, en route to India, landed in Kuwait just as the invasion began and the crew and passengers were taken prisoner and transferred to the Iraqi capital, Baghdad.

CAMERA SHY Saddam forces six-year-old Briton Stuart Lockwood to appear on TV as a 'hero for peace'.

About 4000 Britons and 2500 Americans were in Kuwait at the time of the invasion, most working in the oil industry. Those who stayed behind are now either being held captive by Saddam's troops or hiding in fear.

··· AFTER A TV COMMERCIAL IMITATES HIS VOICE, SINGER TOM WAITS IS AWARDED £2.5 MILLION DAMAGES ···

Thatcher's party stabs 'Iron Lady' in the back

THE NEXT STEP Thatcher considers her options after Downing Street.

27 NOVEMBER, LONDON

Today, only seven days after Margaret Thatcher lost a key ballot of her own MPs, the relatively unknown contender John Major has taken over at 10 Downing Street. The spectacular coup that ended Thatcher's 11-year reign as Britain's first woman prime minister has brought the youngest Conservative leader this century to power.

Thatcher, a grocer's daughter from Lincolnshire, was first elected in 1979. She won again at the polls in 1983, riding a wave of patriotism created by the Falklands War, and even appalling unemployment figures did not prevent her re-election in 1987. Thatcher's political philosophy, which became known as 'Thatcherism', was based on a firm belief in the efficiency of free market forces. It stressed individualism and promoted the economic policies of privatisation and monetarism. For years, the Iron Lady seemed invincible – but her fierce anti-European stance and nationwide anger at her poll tax policy have scared the party into dumping her.

Her successor John Major, aged 47, has had a meteoric political career, entering the cabinet for the first time only three years ago. He has received Thatcher's warm endorsement – today she said she was 'thrilled' by his success in the brief leadership contest following her resignation.

ISRAELIS KILL 21 RIOTERS IN JERUSALEM

8 OCTOBER, JERUSALEM

An uneasy calm between Palestinians and Israeli forces was shattered yesterday when Israeli police opened fire on Palestinian rioters, shooting 21 dead. The incident took place around the Jewish and Muslim shrines on the Temple Mount – the Western Wall and the Dome of the Rock, among Jerusalem's holiest places.

The trouble began when a fundamentalist Jewish sect tried to lay a foundation stone for a new Jewish Temple on the site. They were stopped by a crowd of Palestinians, who then threw stones at Jews praying at the Wailing Wall. Police opened fire with plastic bullets, tear gas and live ammunition – and rioting ensued. As well as the 21 dead, hundreds of rioters were wounded and many others arrested and taken away.

UNHOLY RIOT The Temple Mount, sacred to both Muslims and Jews, is desecrated by violence.

Since the Palestinian Intifada broke out in 1987, both sides have become more hard-line. Yitzhak Shamir, Israel's right-wing prime minister, this year dismissed his Labour allies in government, while Palestinian leader Yasser Arafat's 'two-state' proposals were overshadowed by hard-line calls from within the PLO.

··· 14 FEB: PERRIER WITHDRAWS 160 MILLION BOTTLES OF WATER AFTER SUSPECTED POISONING ···

Hubble Telescope goes into orbit

SCIENTIFIC GIANT The space telescope is named after the man who discovered galaxies.

25 APRIL, CAPE CANAVERAL, FLORIDA

A telescope as big as a railway carriage was launched into space on board a space shuttle from Kennedy Space

Center today. The Hubble Space Telescope, named after astronomer Edwin Hubble, is designed to see the heavens more clearly than any ground-based instrument can do. Orbiting at an altitude of 600 kilometres (375 miles) above the Earth, the telescope avoids the distorting effects of the atmosphere which limit the sharpness of telescopes on the ground.

The Hubble has a 240-centimetre (95-in) mirror, curved so as to focus the light falling on it on to a smaller secondary mirror and then on to five scientific instruments, including two cameras. The images are supposed to be so sharp that the telescope can detect a penny at a distance of 1000 kilometres (622 miles), but it was only when it reached orbit that a mistake was discovered: the main mirror had been cut to the wrong curvature. A rescue mission is now planned to put it right.

Namibia wins its independence

21 MARCH, WINDHOEK

After decades of white colonial rule and 23 years of armed struggle, Namibia has at last broken free of South Africa and become an independent nation.

The victory is a triumph for SWAPO – the South West Africa People's Organisation – and its leaders, Sam Nujoma and Toivoja Toiva, whose long war of attrition has finally brought apartheid and the illegal rule by South Africa to an end.

The die was cast last November, when elections returned a majority of SWAPO candidates to the legislature, which promptly drew up a new constitution. Namibia now has to find a way of living under the shadow of South Africa's much greater military and economic power.

Television viewers discover a passion for crime

The dominance of detective shows in television schedules has been much commented upon this year. In Britain, the top TV sleuth was, without a doubt, Inspector Morse, the crusty, beer-swilling intellectual of Colin Dexter's novels. Glossy photography, scores lavishly borrowed from opera, attractive Oxford locations and John Thaw's polished performance all contributed to the series' success.

Far less high-falutin' was fatherly Detective Inspector Wexford, star of the *Ruth Rendell Mysteries*. Unlike the solitary Morse, Wexford was married and led a comfortable home life – but behind the façade of a slow-speaking country copper lay a razor-sharp mind.

Both British creations looked pretty orthodox next to the American offering, *Twin Peaks,* with its hero Special Agent Dale Cooper. A spellbindingly weird concoction of murder and satanism set in a lumber town in the Pacific Northwest, David Lynch's series had buffs on both sides of the Atlantic waiting eagerly for the next instalment, eating quantities of cherry pie and chanting Cooper's catchphrase: 'Damn fine cup of coffee.'

The combination of sex, violence, intriguing characters and a fine score by Angelo Badalamenti kept viewers watching, but interest began to wane when it became clear that the answer to the central question, 'Who killed Laura Palmer?' would be a long time coming.

COFFEE BREAK Sherilyn Fenn and Kyle McLachlan in *Twin Peaks*, a kinky tale of small-town America.

Crowds jeer Gorbachev

1 MAY, MOSCOW
Protesters interrupted the May Day parade on Red Square today, directing whistles and catcalls at Soviet leader Mikhail Gorbachev. The display of hostility was unprecedented – traditionally the parade is scrupulously stage-managed.

At times this year the Soviet Union of 15 republics has seemed on the verge of collapse. In January Gorbachev sent troops into Azerbaijan to restore order after ethnic conflict and nationalist uprisings there. On 11 March Lithuania declared itself independent from the Union and has since defied Moscow pressure to reintegrate. Closer to home, severe economic difficulties have taken the shine off Gorbachev's political reputation.

SCHLOCKBUSTERS MAKE BIG BUCKS

GHOSTLY LOVE AFFAIR Patrick Swayze and Demi Moore get in touch with their emotions.

Ghost, the surprise hit of the year, is a romantic thriller with a supernatural theme – with the help of a medium, a murdered man returns to warn his wife that she's in danger. Just to show that this was not a one-off, another slushy romance pulled in the audiences: *Pretty Woman*, a modern *Cinderella*, had Richard Gere making an honest woman out of hooker Julia Roberts – the film made her Hollywood's biggest female star. Macaulay Culkin, meanwhile, became the world's biggest child star in *Home Alone*, playing a small boy accidentally left at home by his parents, to fight off burglars and learn the meaning of Christmas. Family values were also celebrated in two Mafia pictures: *The Godfather Part III* – a disappointment, with Francis Ford Coppola criticised for casting his own daughter in a central role – and Martin Scorsese's realistic, hyper-energetic *Goodfellas*.

US HITS OF THE YEAR	
1 BECAUSE I LOVE YOU (THE POSTMAN SONG)	*Stevie B*
2 NOTHING COMPARES 2 U	*Sinead O'Connor*
3 VISION OF LOVE	*Mariah Carey*
4 VOGUE	*Madonna*
5 ESCAPADE	*Janet Jackson*

US TV HITS
1 *Roseanne*
2 *The Cosby Show*
3 *Cheers*
4 *A Different World*
5 *America's Funniest Home Videos*

1991

DIED
21 Feb: Margot Fonteyn, British ballet dancer
3 Apr: Graham Greene, British author
28 Sept: Miles Davis, US jazz musician

ATTACKED
7 Feb, London: British prime minister's residence, 10 Downing Street, by IRA mortar bomb
20 Nov, Croatia: Osijek, by Serbian-controlled Yugoslav Federal Army

PROTESTED
20 Jan, Moscow: 100 000 Soviet citizens, over military action against rebel republics Lithuania and Latvia

TRIUMPHED
15 May, Rotterdam: Manchester United, in football's European Cup Winners' Cup, beating Barcelona 2–1
2 Nov, London: Australia, in rugby union World Cup, beating England 12–6

QUIT
24 Aug, USSR: Mikhail Gorbachev, as first secretary of the Soviet Communist Party
20 Dec, Yugoslavia: Ante Markovich, as Yugoslav federal prime minister

BANNED
17 Mar, Italy: soccer star Diego Maradona, of Napoli, after testing positive for cocaine; for 15 months

FIRST
18 May: British astronaut; Helen Sharman, aged 27, leaves on an eight-day space mission with Soviet *Soyuz TM-12*

PUBLISHED
Angela Carter, *Wise Children*
Bret Easton Ellis, *American Psycho*

JAILED
21 May, Bangkok: British woman Patricia Cahill, for 18 years, guilty of attempted heroin smuggling

On 6 July, *the Bank of Commerce and Credit International (BCCI) is ordered to stop trading in Britain. The bank is found guilty of laundering $32 million of drug money in Florida, and is at the centre of a scandal in Panama over funds deposited by General Manuel Noriega.*

FREED
14 Mar, London: the 'Birmingham Six', prisoners jailed for IRA pub bombing in Birmingham in 1974, after their conviction is rejected by the Court of Appeal
4 Apr, UK: children taken from their families in Orkney following claims of sexual abuse; they are sent home and social workers are criticised

DECLARED INDEPENDENCE
20 Aug: Estonia, from USSR
21 Aug: Latvia, from USSR
30 Aug: Azerbaijan, from USSR
22 Sept: Armenia, from USSR

WOUND UP
5 Sept, USSR: the Union of Soviet Socialist Republics, following spate of declarations of independence by member countries

KILLED
30 Apr, Bangladesh: around 100 000 people by a cyclone
21 May, India: Rajiv Gandhi, former prime minister, by suicide bomber

TRANSPORTED
25 May, Ethiopia: 15 000 black Jews (Falashas), to Israel, because of political turmoil in Ethiopia

LIFTED
15 Apr: EC sanctions against South Africa, imposed in protest at apartheid
10 July, Washington DC: US sanctions against South Africa

SIGNED
31 July, Moscow: Strategic Arms Reduction Treaty, to cut nuclear weapons by one-third, by Mikhail Gorbachev and George Bush

NEW WORD
eco-terrorism *n*: acts of violence or obstruction by green activists, also applied during the Gulf War to Iraq's deliberate release of oil slicks

On 18 January, *Iraq fires Scud missiles at civilian targets in Tel Aviv and Haifa. Israeli citizens are urged to wear gas masks in case the Scuds contain germ or chemical weapons. The bombardment was part of an attempt to divide the Arab-American alliance against Iraq in the Gulf War.*

On 15 June, *Mount Pinatubo erupts in the Philippines, showering surrounding regions with ash, rock, dust and mud. Earthquakes follow, triggered by fissures in the volcano, and more than half a million people are evacuated from their homes. Some abandoned villages have already been buried in mud.*

IRAQI FORCES EXPELLED FROM KUWAIT

28 FEBRUARY, WASHINGTON DC
The war in the Gulf is over and Kuwait has been liberated. President George Bush announced a suspension of fighting today, two days after Saddam Hussein caved in. Saddam has agreed to withdraw his forces from Kuwait, but he saved face by announcing to his subjects that he has won the war.

After six weeks of Operation Desert Storm – the intense aerial bombardment of military targets and communications centres in Iraq and Kuwait – the end came surprisingly swiftly, after only 100 hours of the ground war launched on 24 February. Iraq, which had the world's fifth largest army, lined up nearly a million soldiers along the Saudi border to face the 500 000 soldiers of the US-led coalition of 28 nations. But Iraqi soldiers, battle-weary after the long war against Iran and accustomed to defensive infantry warfare, were no match for the

DESERT WARFARE A soldier from the 101st Airborne Division takes up his position behind Iraqi lines.

two-pronged assault devised by US Commander Norman Schwarzkopf. There were few casualties on the Allied side, but Iraqi losses have been heavy.

Although the war was fought to keep Kuwaiti oil out of Saddam's hands, President Bush has hailed the victory as one for 'a new world order'.

··· CHILE: MOUNT HUDSON ERUPTS, WIPING OUT 15 PER CENT OF THE OZONE LAYER OVER THE ANTARCTIC ···

Saddam takes ecological revenge

1 AUGUST, BAGHDAD
Following Kuwait's liberation, the full scope of the environmental vandalism that Saddam Hussein has wreaked on the country is becoming evident. Months after the ceasefire hundreds of oil wells that were deliberately set on fire by Iraq are still burning out of control, despite the best efforts of Texan fire specialist Red Adair to bring a halt to the desert inferno.

Huge columns of flames, some rising as high as a 20-storey building, have left a dense pall of smoke hanging over the countryside, so thick that it blocks out the sunlight, turning day into night. The coastal waters of the Gulf itself have been fouled by an oil slick that stretches for mile after mile – the result of Saddam's command that thousands of gallons of oil be released into the sea.

BURN OUT The heavy pollution caused by oil wells burning cost Kuwait billions of dollars.

Great damage has also been done to Kuwait's desalination plants, which are essential for the country's agricultural irrigation. The toll on wildlife in the region has been incalculable. Experts believe that it may take more than 20 years for some areas to recover fully.

Hi-tech war was won on computer screens

The Gulf War will be remembered as the first major 'hi-tech' conflict of the 20th century. Television screens carried live images of the fighting into rooms across the Western world. Audiences watched as Iraqi missiles were shot from the sky by Patriot anti-ballistic missiles and laser-guided bombs exploded on their targets.

An important Allied weapon was the A10, an airborne tank-buster nicknamed the 'Brute', which was armoured to absorb damage that would bring other aircraft down and had a cannon that fired 3000 shells a minute.

Iraqi soldiers were bombed by a 'fuel-air explosive', which creates a fireball that incinerates or asphyxiates everything, and everyone, near it.

Yeltsin stops Russian coup

POPULAR HERO Boris Yeltsin rallies support against the military coup in Lubianka Square in Moscow.

21 AUGUST, MOSCOW
Mikhail Gorbachev is tonight back in power in the Soviet Union after a coup against him was seen off by popular protest coordinated by Boris Yeltsin, president of Russia.

The coup was launched on 18 August by leading Communists including the Soviet vice-president, Gennady Yanayev, the prime minister, Valentin Pavlov, and the KGB chief, Vladimir Kryuchkov. The men declared a state of emergency and sent the army to keep order in Moscow and Leningrad. They put Gorbachev, who was on holiday in the Crimea, under house arrest, claiming that he was unwell.

Yeltsin moved quickly in support of Gorbachev, calling the development 'a cynical attempt at a right-wing coup', and urging strikes and army mutinies to bring it to an end. Thousands set up street barricades. This morning the coup's leaders sent tanks to attack the Russian parliament where Yeltsin had taken refuge, but found it surrounded by his supporters. Three civilians were killed but the tanks did not force their way through. The defence ministry ordered troops to leave Moscow this afternoon.

The men behind the coup face prosecution. Gorbachev is back, but his position is weaker. The winner is Yeltsin, whose authority received a huge boost.

End of an era as Soviet reformer Gorbachev resigns

25 DECEMBER, MOSCOW
Just over four months after the failed coup this summer, Mikhail Gorbachev, architect of the Soviet Union's reforms, has quit his post as president and the Soviet Union has ceased to exist.

In the aftermath of the coup it became clear there was no future for the USSR as Moldavia, Georgia and Armenia declared that they would seek independence from the union. The Soviet parliament voted to dissolve the USSR on 5 September, and a Commonwealth of Independent States (CIS) was founded on 21 December by all the Soviet republics except Georgia, Estonia, Latvia and Lithuania. Gorbachev was opposed to the CIS.

FALLEN HERO The USSR's collapse saw Russians turning their backs on Communist iconography.

··· 25 AUG, TOKYO: CARL LEWIS SETS WORLD RECORD FOR 100-METRE SPRINT, 9.85 SECONDS ···

Mystery surrounds death of tycoon Maxwell

5 DECEMBER, LONDON
After weeks of speculation, the truth has been confirmed – the late Robert Maxwell's financial empire lies in ruins and the fraud squad is investigating alleged misconduct by the tycoon.

The problems had just come to light when Maxwell died under mysterious circumstances on 5 November. At the

end of October, several of Maxwell's creditors had started to recover the money that was owed to them by selling their shares in the Maxwell Communications Corporation.

News of these transactions reached the London Stock Exchange on the day Maxwell died. He was sailing in the Canaries on his yacht, *Lady Ghislaine*,

when he toppled overboard. The official cause of death was a heart attack, before or after the fall, but the timing sparked rumours of suicide or murder, and shares in his companies plummeted.

Details of financial irregularities have since leaked out – the most serious being £300 million missing from the Mirror Group pension fund.

Ordeal is finally over for hostages held in Lebanon

4 DECEMBER, LEBANON
Terry Anderson, the last US citizen to be held hostage in Lebanon by Islamic Jihad terrorists, was freed today, leaving only two German hostages still held by the terrorist organisation. Two other hostages, Alann Steen and Joseph Cicippio, were given their freedom earlier this month.

Anderson's homecoming will be made even more emotional by his first sight of his six-year-old daughter, Sulome, who was born just after he was taken prisoner.

The latest release of hostages is believed to be a direct result of Israel's setting free 25 Lebanese prisoners who had been held in custody on terrorist charges. Hopes for the hostages were first raised in August when the British journalist John McCarthy was released bearing a letter from the Islamic Jihad to the UN secretary-general Javier Perez de Cuellar. It appeared to offer promises of further releases but reiterated Islamic Jihad's demands for Israel to release Arab prisoners including Sheikh Obeid, an important Muslim cleric.

In September another Briton, Jackie Mann, was freed by Islamic Jihad, but it was only last month that perhaps the most symbolically important hostage was released. Terry Waite, who was the Archbishop of Canterbury's special envoy to the Lebanon, arrived back home on 19 November.

As Waite stepped off the plane in Britain, he spoke emotionally about how his Christian faith had given him the strength to carry on during nearly five years held in captivity. He said that for four years he had not been allowed to speak to anyone except the people who were guarding him.

FREE AT LAST British journalist John McCarthy returns home after his release by Islamic Jihad.

··· 15 MAY, FRANCE: EDITH CRESSON IS ELECTED THE FIRST FEMALE PRIME MINISTER OF FRANCE ···

Glacier reveals Bronze Age secret

24 SEPTEMBER, INNSBRUCK
A corpse believed to be more than 5000 years old has been found high up in the Austrian Alps in a remarkable state of preservation. The discovery was made five days ago by a holidaying couple from Nuremburg in Germany who were on a mountaineering trip to the Tyrol.

When they had climbed to a height of 3200 metres (10500 ft) they found the upper part of a mummified, frozen corpse protruding from a glacier. They reported their discovery to the authorities and 'Ötzi', as scientists have called the body, became a star.

Forensic scientists working at the Innsbruck University Department of Anatomy have identified the body as an important prehistoric find, probably dating back to around 3350 BC. Ötzi is approximately 158 centimetres (62 in) tall and weighs a little over

ICEMAN Ötzi's body had been preserved by the natural deep-freezing effect of an alpine glacier.

13 kilos (29 lbs). The Bronze Age man was found with a bow and a quiver of arrows slung over his shoulder, and an autopsy later revealed that shortly before his death he had eaten nuts and berries.

Many features of his well preserved body are clearly visible. Perhaps most fascinating and mysterious are the tattoos found on his back, knees and ankles.

Yugoslavia in crisis as Dubrovnik is attacked

1 NOVEMBER, CROATIA
The Yugoslav National Army today intensified its assault on the Croatian-held port of Dubrovnik as civil war continued to rage in Yugoslavia. For weeks the army has besieged Dubrovnik, an historic city known as the 'pearl of the Adriatic', and in the last few days it has begun shelling the city's medieval walled Old Town.

Conflict flared over Croatia's declaration of independence from the Yugoslav federation on 25 June. Serbia, the largest republic, controls the National Army and dispatched troops following clashes between Croatians and some of the 600 000 Serbs who live in Croatia. EC-backed peace talks have failed and the war, fuelled by centuries-old racial differences, is building up a terrible momentum.

Crop circles keep the world guessing

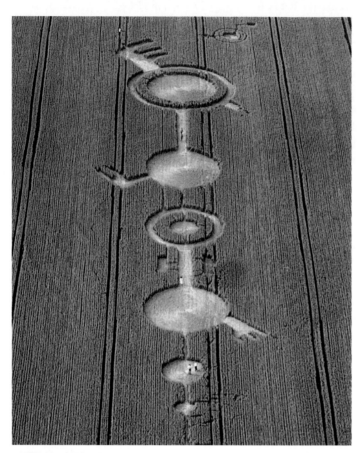

BETTER BY DESIGN Some farmers charged admission to view crop circles.

Crop circles – geometric patterns found in fields – were reported across Britain, and soon became a worldwide phenomenon, especially common in the USA and Germany. The shapes were formed of flattened areas of crops such as wheat or barley to form impressive, often intricate designs of interlocking circles, triangles and other complex patterns.

A variety of theories soon developed as to what caused the circles. Predictably, the less exciting views that they were the product of freak local weather conditions or a wave of copycat hoaxes were swept aside by some sections of the media, which preferred to speculate that they were the result of aliens at work. Enthusiasts found a historical basis for the phenomenon, pointing to an 18th-century pamphlet produced in England which warned of a 'Mowing Devil' that wreaked havoc on cornfields. Crop circles also fitted neatly into the burgeoning New Age movement, which embraced a wide variety of 'alternative' philosophies.

Eventually, in September, two retired artists from Southampton confessed that they had made many of the first circles by means of a wooden pole and a piece of rope. But many enthusiasts were not convinced, pointing out that not all of the thousands of circles worldwide could have been hoaxes. Conspiracy theorists argued the Southampton artists' statement was simply part of a misinformation plot launched by the British government, reputedly afraid of the mysterious signs being delivered by a higher alien intelligence.

··· 4 DEC, USA: PAN AMERICAN AIRLINES HAS TO CLOSE BECAUSE OF MASSIVE DEBTS ···

Awareness growing as HIV marches relentlessly on

AIDS came to the centre of public attention this year when one of the United States's most famous basketball stars, Earvin 'Magic' Johnson, revealed that he had become HIV-positive and announced his retirement from the game. Johnson, aged 32, said that from now on he wanted to focus his energies on campaigning for greater AIDS awareness among heterosexuals.

Johnson's statement on 8 November was a watershed in the USA – up until now the public's perception has tended to be that AIDS was a disease that only affected drug-users and homosexuals. Media coverage was sympathetic towards Johnson, although some commentators questioned whether public reaction

would have been so sympathetic had he caught the virus through homosexual sex or drug use.

The AIDS debate intensified when two weeks later, on 23 November, rock star Freddie Mercury of the rock group Queen died of an AIDS-related illness. Unlike Johnson, Mercury had been secretive about having the condition until shortly before he died.

Some sections of the gay community criticised the singer for being secretive about his homosexuality and HIV status. But the general public did not seem to be adversely affected by his behaviour – the re-release of Queen's single _Bohemian Rhapsody_ went straight to the top of the British charts.

FALLEN STAR Flamboyant Freddie Mercury, the latest victim of a disease that can affect anyone.

Powell breaks 22-year-old record

30 AUGUST, TOKYO

The greatest duel in the history of the long jump took place at the world athletics championships in Tokyo tonight between the two US athletes Carl Lewis and Mike Powell. Anticipation gripped the packed stadium in Tokyo when the crowd sensed that the record leap of 8.9 metres (29 ft 2½ in) set by Bob Beamon of the United States on 18 October 1968 was in jeopardy.

In the fourth round Lewis soared to Beamon's record, benefiting from maximum wind assistance. Powell responded to the challenge by smashing the record convincingly with a distance of 8.95 metres (29 ft 4½ in).

Lewis finished with two more jumps over 8.84 metres (29 ft), the greatest sequence of jumps ever recorded, but was stunned when he discovered that the record he had sought to break for so long had fallen to his little-known compatriot.

NOW THE BEST Powell stretches to break Beamon's long-standing record.

HOPKINS IS A WOLF IN SHEEP'S CLOTHING

WHAT'S COOKING? Anthony Hopkins (right) and Anthony Heald in *The Silence of the Lambs*.

Kevin Costner's politically correct western *Dances with Wolves* swept up seven Academy Awards in February, including best picture and best director for Costner, who had fought for many years to raise money for his unfashionable project. Success was sweet for Costner, who was able to confound the critics who had mocked the 'simplistic' vision of his three-hour epic. The dark, disturbing thriller *The Silence of the Lambs* was a strong candidate for an Academy Award after bringing new levels of horror to mainstream cinema. The intelligent script was imaginatively directed and outstandingly acted, with Jodie Foster impressive as a rookie FBI agent. Anthony Hopkins's subtle portrayal of the psychopathic killer Hannibal 'the Cannibal' Lecter had been highly controversial, but contributed much to the thriller's spellbinding effect. The makers of the $100-million sci-fi blockbuster *Terminator 2: Judgment Day* were also hopeful of Oscar success. Computer-generated special effects were used with breathtaking results in this action movie starring the Austrian strongman Arnold Schwarzenegger.

Accused judge is innocent

27 OCTOBER, WASHINGTON DC

A real-life courtroom drama mixing sex, race and politics has kept Americans glued to their TV screens. The focus of attention is Supreme Court nominee Judge Clarence Thomas. A former colleague, Professor Anita Hill, alleges that Clarence sexually harassed her.

Both are successful, middle-aged – and black. Clarence was nominated by President George Bush for the Supreme Court in July, seemingly an ideal choice – black, ultra-right-wing and from a poor background.

Then Ms Hill's allegations prompted a hearing. She said Clarence boasted about his penis, propositioned her and talked about pornography. In the event, the Senate – which is 98 per cent male – found in Clarence's favour. He could serve on the court until well into the 2030s.

US HITS OF THE YEAR

1	(EVERYTHING I DO) I DO IT FOR YOU	*Bryan Adams*
2	BLACK OR WHITE	*Michael Jackson*
3	RUSH RUSH	*Paula Abdul*
4	EMOTIONS	*Mariah Carey*
5	GONNA MAKE YOU SWEAT	*C & C Music Factory*

US TV HITS

1	*Cheers*
2	*60 Minutes*
3	*Roseanne*
4	*A Different World*
5	*The Cosby Show*

1992

DIED
9 Mar: Menachem Begin, former prime minister of Israel
20 Apr: Benny Hill, British comedian
28 Apr: Francis Bacon, British artist
6 May: Marlene Dietrich, German film actress

LAUNCHED
15 Aug, UK: new Premier League of elite English football clubs
7 Sept, UK: Classic FM, new national radio station playing classical music

RECORD
July, Italy: football transfer fee, for Gianluigi Lentini, who signs for AC Milan from Torino for £13 million

On 3 November, *Democrat candidate Bill Clinton is elected President of the USA with a clear majority. However, public attention soon focuses on the Clintons' cat, Socks, shortly to become a White House resident.*

On 20 April, *Expo '92, the first universal exposition since 1970, opens in Seville, Spain. Millions of visitors are expected to flock to the capital of Andalucia province for the event. Nations from all over the world are displaying their finest achievements and inventions in industry, science and the arts.*

PUBLISHED
Madonna, *Sex*
Toni Morrison, *Jazz*
Michael Ondaatje, *The English Patient*
Donna Tartt, *The Secret History*

FOUGHT
6 Dec, India: Hindus and Muslims, after Hindus destroy mosque at Ayodhya, which is claimed as a holy place by both groups; 1200 die in ensuing violence

CAPTURED
25 Apr, Afghanistan: Kabul, by Muslim Mujahidin forces, following overthrow of President Najibullah on 16 April
13 Sept, Peru: terrorist leader Abimael Guzman, leader of Shining Path group, after 12 years as a wanted man

RIOTED
25 Feb: Albanians, protesting over food shortages

DEVASTATED
13 Mar: eastern Turkey, by earthquake; at least 376 are killed
10–16 Sept: northern Pakistan, by heavy floods; 2000 die and two million lose their homes
12 Oct, Egypt: Cairo, by earthquake; 540 die
12 Dec: eastern Indonesia, by earthquake; more than 1500 die

MARRIED
Feb, Hawaii: rock musicians Kurt Cobain and Courtney Love
29 Apr, USA: film actor Emilio Estevez and pop singer Paula Abdul
May, USA: rock musician David Bowie and model Iman
June, USA: musicians Paul Simon and Edie Brickell

CHAMPIONS
26 June, Sweden: Denmark, surprise winners of football's European Championship, beating Germany 2–0

CONVICTED
10 Feb, Indianapolis: former world heavyweight boxing champion Mike Tyson, of raping beauty queen Desiree Washington; sentenced to six years
9 Apr, Miami: Mañuel Noriega, former president of Panama, of cocaine manufacturing and money laundering

ELECTED
9 Apr, UK: John Major, as prime minister
25 May, Italy: Oscar Scalfaro, as president

On 29 April, *rioting erupts in Los Angeles when four white policemen are acquitted of beating black motorist Rodney King, despite video evidence to the contrary. The outraged black community takes to the streets in protest. Several people die in the violence, and riots break out in other US cities.*

DIVORCED
23 Apr, UK: Princess Anne and Captain Mark Phillips

NEW WORDS
ethnic cleansing *n*: the extermination of an ethnic group; euphemism used for the genocide committed by Serbs against Croats and Bosnian Muslims.

Dodging the bullets in city under siege

30 AUGUST, SARAJEVO

As Serbian forces continued their five-month siege of the city, an artillery shell today killed 15 citizens of Sarajevo queuing for bread in a marketplace. Bitter fighting broke out in Bosnia-Herzegovina, one of the six republics of the former Yugoslav federation, following its declaration of independence on 3 March. The Yugoslav National Army, controlled by Serbian leader Slobodan Milošević, backed Bosnian Serbs in clashes with Bosnian Croats and Muslims. Serb troops closed in on the capital, Sarajevo, and imposed a blockade on 10 April.

In Sarajevo many buildings have been reduced to rubble. People attempt to carry on with their lives while knowing that they face death at any time from a shell or a sniper's bullet. For months the only food on sale has been bread and, on occasion, vegetables. United Nations peacekeeping troops have brought in some supplies by land

UNDER FIRE A woman runs for cover from snipers amid the bodies that lie in Sarajevo's streets.

and air, but they too have come under fire from the besieging army.

Each week the war seems to grow more brutal. On 22 June a group of Muslim women and children arrived in the centre of Sarajevo, telling of

executions carried out by Serbs in the suburbs. Elsewhere in former Yugoslavia atrocities are committed by all sides. It is estimated that 1.4 million Muslims, Croats and Serbs have fled their homes this year trying to escape the genocide.

··· EVERY YEAR ITALIANS CONSUME AN AVERAGE OF 70 LITRES OF WINE EACH ···

Negotiators fashion a South African miracle

CLAIMING THE COUNTRY Marchers sing and dance in support of the ANC.

Momentous strides towards democracy have been taken this year in South Africa, where the multi-party Convention for a Democratic South Africa (Codesa) has brought all races together to thrash out a constitution for the nation. The negotiations have not always run smoothly. They were suspended in May, when the National Party government, headed by F W de Klerk, insisted on a veto over Codesa decisions. The African National Congress (ANC) responded by calling for marches and national strikes, which succeeded in paralysing the nation.

In October consensus was finally reached on the constitution as well as on amnesty for perpetrators of politically motivated violence committed before 1 October.

The promise made by De Klerk in 1990 when the ANC was unbanned and Nelson Mandela was released from prison – to provide equal citizenship for all, guaranteed by an independent judiciary – is being fulfilled. In the past two years many apartheid laws – designed to keep the races segregated – have been scrapped. Since the lifting of the state of emergency blacks and whites mingle on beaches, in hospital wards, on railway carriages and in restaurants. The desegregation of schools has also begun.

1992

Big talk but little commitment at Earth Summit

14 MARCH, RIO DE JANEIRO
The Earth Summit ended today with the world's leaders in agreement that the planet needs saving, but less certain about how to do it, how quickly it should be done, or how much each country should pay.

The United States emerged as the villain of the conference, refusing to sign the biodiversity treaty to protect rare and endangered species because, in the words of President George Bush, it 'threatened to retard biotechnology and undermine the protection of ideas'. The leaders of 152 other countries disagreed

with him, and signed the document. However, the USA was one of 150 countries that signed a treaty on climate change, aimed at reducing the emission of gases that are believed to damage the ozone layer and cause global warming. Delegates also agreed on a system of environmental aid, to help developing countries to avoid the over-exploitation of natural resources.

Environmentalists have expressed disappointment that the summit made only limited progress towards a world forestry convention, without which climate control will be almost impossible.

WE ARE THE WORLD A group of children show their support for a healthier environment.

··· THE USA HAS THE HIGHEST RATE OF CAR OWNERSHIP IN THE WORLD – 56 CARS PER 100 PERSONS ···

Famine takes its toll in lawless Somalia

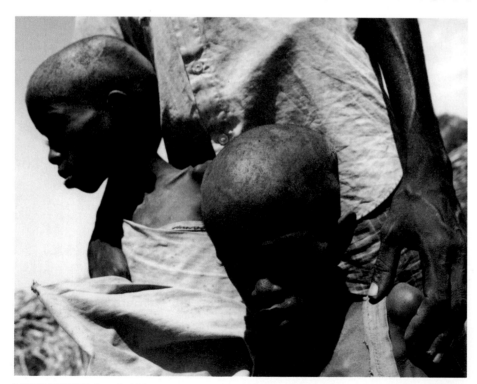

DESPERATE DAYS Somali children are among the hardest hit as malnutrition and disease takes hold.

A year of brutal warfare and banditry has wreaked havoc in the lives of the people of Somalia. Now the year-long drought has produced a famine so widespread that it has become the United Nations' most pressing crisis. Somalia, in north-eastern Africa, is

one of the world's poorest countries and has a population of just under eight million. Amid the anarchy that has gripped the nation there are no official figures for victims of the famine, but it was estimated in August that there were 1.5 million starving people in Somalia.

There has also been a mass exodus of more than a million refugees to Ethiopia, Djibouti, Kenya and Yemen.

Somalia is a divided, unstable nation in which separate regions are each ruled by the warlord of a clan or alliance of clans. The north-western part of the country, controlled by the Somali National Movement, has failed to win international recognition as the independent state of 'Somaliland'. In 1991 a guerrilla war began in the south when an army coup, led by General Mohamed Farah Aidid, ousted Somalia's dictator Mohamed Siad Barre. This sparked fighting between the rival clans of Aidid and Barre, as well as a split within Aidid's own clan.

A United Nations ceasefire brokered in March was largely ignored, and by August calls for food relief became widespread as the international press focused attention on the famine. The UN began sending shipments of food and aid, which often failed to reach the people most in need as they were hijacked by militiamen. By the end of the year the UN and the United States had sent in troops although expectations of their effectiveness were not high.

Two serial killers that shocked the world

Amid scenes of pandemonium in the courtroom, Russia's most notorious serial killer was sentenced to death in October. Throughout the six-month trial in Rostov, north-east of Moscow, 56-year-old Andrei Chikatilo had resembled a wild animal as he sat in his metal cage, glaring out at witnesses and interrupting the proceedings with screams and shouts. He was accused of killing 53 people over a 12-year period. Most of the victims were prostitutes, tramps or children, apparently chosen because they were easier to lure to deserted spots. Their bodies were cruelly mutilated by the killer. During the trial doctors were on hand to tend to any relatives who were overcome by the gruesome details.

Amongst the evidence was a police video showing the accused re-enacting the murders. The Russian police have been severely criticised for their handling of the case. An innocent man has already been executed for one of the murders. In their defence, detectives have pointed out that they were hampered by Chikatilo's rare blood condition, which caused his blood and semen samples to register as different groups when they were tested.

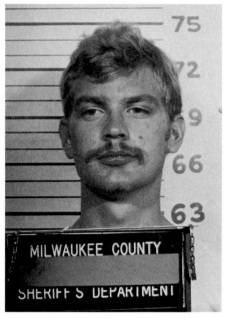

CANNIBAL The jury dismissed Dahmer's plea of insanity when they handed down a guilty verdict.

CAGED IN COURT Chikatilo's sentence was death by a single bullet in the back of the head.

The Russian trial came hot on the heels of an equally gruesome case in the United States. On 18 February, 31-year-old Jeffrey Dahmer was sentenced to life imprisonment – in the absence of the death penalty in Wisconsin – for the murders of 15 young men and boys. The crimes came to light after one of Dahmer's intended victims escaped wearing handcuffs.

When detectives called on Dahmer in his tiny Milwaukee apartment, they discovered a severed human head in the fridge. A search revealed body parts from ten other corpses. Some of the skulls had been defleshed and painted, and were displayed in a grisly shrine – a filing cabinet next to the killer's bed. Dahmer later admitted that he had eaten the flesh of some of his victims.

··· SYDNEY: THE WORLD'S FIRST DAMAGES AWARD IS MADE FOR ILLNESS BROUGHT ON BY PASSIVE SMOKING ···

The law catches up with mob boss 'Teflon Don'

23 JUNE, NEW YORK CITY
Two months after a jury convicted the notorious Mafia godfather John Gotti of 13 charges of murder and racketeering, he was sentenced today to life imprisonment without parole. As Judge Leo Glasser handed down the sentence, a crowd of Gotti supporters gathered outside the courthouse to demonstrate against the proceedings.

The 51-year-old Gotti, dubbed the 'Teflon Don' because he managed to escape conviction in three previous trials, grew up in the slums of Brooklyn,

and rose through the Mafia ranks with gambling rackets and lorry-hijacking escapades. It emerged in one of the most highly publicised US trials to date that the young mobster graduated to murder and gained control of the Gambino 'family' by having its previous boss, Paul Castellano, ambushed outside a Manhattan restaurant. This is one of the murders for which the jury found him guilty on 2 April.

As the new godfather, Gotti revelled in the high life, modelling himself on former Chicago Mafia boss Al Capone,

with his fondness for fine suits. Gotti became known as the best dressed gangster in New York.

All this came to an end when he was betrayed by one of his most trusted lieutenants, Salvatore 'Sammy the Bull' Gravano, whose nine-day testimony dramatically swung the trial. The mobster's conviction marks the end of an era. At his home in the Ozone Park district of New York, Gotti's daughter wept as she told reporters: 'My father is the last of the Mohicans. They don't make men like him any more.'

It was a horrible year for royalty, says the Queen

It has been an 'annus horribilis', announced Queen Elizabeth in a speech at the end of the year. And frankly, she did have a point.

First, there was Charles and Diana – and Camilla. Although there have long been rumours that the Prince and Princess of Wales were not the happiest of couples, it came as a shock to the British public to find that the marriage had been a sham from the beginning. According to Andrew Morton's sensational biography of the princess, 19-year-old Diana was hand-picked by Charles's long-term mistress, Mrs Camilla Parker Bowles. After Diana dutifully produced an heir, the book claimed, Charles returned to the arms of Mrs Parker Bowles. A devastated and isolated Diana then developed an eating disorder and made five suicide attempts.

The transcript of a private telephone conversation between the prince and Mrs Parker Bowles, in which he proclaimed among other things his desire to become her tampon, served to confirm the whole sordid story.

Then there was Prince Andrew's wife, Fergie – and her 'financial adviser'.

Pictures of a fleshily topless Duchess of York having her toes sucked by balding American millionaire John Bryan were splashed all over the *Daily Mirror*. Clearly, the Yorks' marriage was over.

Finally, there was the fire at Windsor Palace, and instead of sympathy there was dissent about who was to foot the bill. The call for the richest woman in the world to pay income tax like most

of her loyal subjects has become deafening, and it looks likely that the Queen will soon capitulate.

As of this November, Charles and Diana are separating and divorce could well be on the cards. Little William and Harry will come from a broken home. No wonder the Queen is wondering what went wrong. Some people might even blame Charles's parents.

BEHIND THE SCENES The Duchess of York with her friendly financial adviser, John Bryan.

THE OTHER CHEEK The tension between the prince and princess started to show in public.

··· AT 39 MINUTES, 'THE BLUE ROOM', BY BRITISH BAND THE ORB, IS THE LONGEST EVER SINGLE ···

Olympic Games enjoy rare political harmony

AGILE STRENGTH Belorussian gymnast Vitaly Scherbo, who won four individual gold medals at the Barcelona Games, on the pommel horse.

9 AUGUST, BARCELONA After the political turmoil that afflicted the Olympic Games for two decades, the Barcelona Games have ended amid renewed optimism. South Africa was back in the Games after 32 years, while Cuba, North Korea and Ethiopia ended their boycotts. Estonia, Latvia and Lithuania, liberated from Soviet rule, competed as independent nations.

No individual competitor dominated the headlines.

British athlete Linford Christie won the 100 metres at the age of 32. Carl Lewis beat the world-record holder, Mike Powell, to retain his Olympic long-jump title; while in the 1500 metres the overwhelming favourite, Noureddine Morceli of Algeria, was trapped in the pack and finished seventh. The highlight for the home crowd was cheering Spaniard Fermin Cacho Ruiz on to victory in the same race.

The ripples that led to the beginning of time

23 APRIL, USA
Astronomers have announced that they have discovered the seeds from which the Sun, the stars and the planets evolved.
At a meeting in Washington DC of the American Physical Society, the team responsible for NASA's Cosmic Background Explorer satellite (COBE) reported the existence of 'ripples' in the microwave background radiation which bathes the universe. This radiation is believed to be the dying echo of the Big Bang with which the cosmos is believed to have begun between 10 and 20 billion years ago.

Before COBE, the radiation appeared to be the same in whichever direction you looked – a perfectly smooth hum, with no hint of variation. This has long puzzled scientists because the universe is actually very lumpy, consisting of large areas of empty space dotted with stars and other bodies such as planets.

The COBE data shows for the first time that the microwave radiation is not perfectly smooth but contains ripples representing extremely wispy clouds of matter – 'the largest and most ancient structures in the universe', according to Dr George Smoot of the University of California at Berkeley. Smoot proudly announced: 'What we have found is evidence for the birth of the universe.'

SPACE ECHOES A computer-enhanced microwave map of the sky reveals the all-important fluctuations in cosmic background radiation.

WAYNE AND GARTH'S EXCELLENT MISADVENTURES

PARTY ON, DUDES Mike Myers and Dana Carvey in *Wayne's World*.

Debate raged over the serial killer thriller *Basic Instinct* – just how much did Sharon Stone reveal when she crossed her legs? Enough to make it pretty clear she wasn't wearing any underwear. Another taboo-breaking film was *The Crying Game*, which started as a straightforward thriller about the IRA but included a clever twist, ending up as a playful look at sexual identity. The world also gained a new batch of catchphrases from Mike Myers' comedy about two nerdy teenagers, *Wayne's World*, a serious, thought-provoking and ultimately moving work – NOT!

Clint Eastwood revived and subverted an old Hollywood genre, the western, directing and starring in the violent but brilliant *Unforgiven*. It earned Eastwood an Oscar nomination for best actor and the film got the best picture award. And Hollywood subverted itself in Robert Altman's *The Player*, a murder story and satire of the film industry rolled into one. It became the smart film to be in – it contains more celebrity cameos than you can shake a stick at.

US HITS OF THE YEAR

1	I WILL ALWAYS LOVE YOU	*Whitney Houston*
2	END OF THE ROAD	*Boyz II Men*
3	JUMP	*Kris Kross*
4	BABY GOT BACK	*Sir Mix-A-Lot*
5	SAVE THE BEST FOR LAST	*Vanessa Williams*

US TV HITS

1	*60 Minutes*
2	*Roseanne*
3	*Murphy Brown*
4	*Cheers*
5	*Home Improvement*

1993

DIED

6 Jan: Rudolf Nureyev, Russian ballet dancer
6 Jan: Dizzy Gillespie, US jazz musician
20 Jan: Audrey Hepburn, US actress
24 Feb: Bobby Moore, British football player
31 Oct: River Phoenix, US actor
4 Dec: Frank Zappa, US rock musician

On 27 May, *a terrorist bombing wrecks the Uffizi Gallery in Florence, Italy, killing five people and injuring 26. Several works of art are also destroyed in the blast. No one has claimed responsibility, but the bomb is thought to be the work of terrorists trying to block a government campaign against political corruption.*

STRANDED

24 Nov, London: more than 20000 passengers, in underground train tunnels during power failure

PROTESTED

6 July, London: 15 women, who climb into Buckingham Palace to oppose nuclear tests

KILLED

10 Mar, Florida: gynaecologist Dr David Gunn, by anti-abortion campaigner
28 Apr, Gabon: most of the Zambian national football side, when the aircraft taking them to a World Cup match crashes
29 May, Germany: five Turkish women, by neo-Nazi arsonists
2 July, Turkey: around 40 people, when Muslim campaigners set fire to hotel in which a translator of Salman Rushdie's *The Satanic Verses* is staying

CONVICTED

17 May, UK: nurse Beverley Allitt, of killing four babies in Grantham and Kesteven hospital in 1991
24 Nov, Preston, UK: Robert Thompson and Jon Venables, both aged 11, of murder of two-year-old Jamie Bulger in Liverpool in February

PARDONED

20 July, Thailand: Karyn Smith and Patricia Cahill, British women jailed for heroin smuggling in 1990

MADE TO PAY

24 Mar, Los Angeles: US actress Kim Basinger, $8.9 million to Main Line Pictures because she pulled out of movie *Boxing Helena* a month before the start of filming
4 Nov, UK: the *Sunday Mirror*, damages of £350000 to rock musician Elton John for an article alleging he had an eating disorder

BANNED

5 Mar: Canadian sprinter Ben Johnson, for life, after failing drugs test; in 1988 he was banned for two years for using steroids at the Olympics

Following an increase in the number of satellite-linked cellular networks, companies offer competitive discounts on mobile phone services, making them hugely popular. No longer the symbol of the yuppie elite, mobile phones start to be thought of as essential, instead of a luxury.

FIRSTS

12 Mar, USA: female attorney-general in USA, Janet Reno
6 Aug, London: public tours of Buckingham Palace
1 Sept, UK: multi-channel satellite television in UK, British Sky Broadcasting

SIGNED

3 Jan: second Strategic Arms Reduction Treaty by USA and Russia

COIFFED

22 May, Los Angeles: President Clinton's hair, by Beverly Hills stylist, on board presidential aircraft while it sits on the runway for 40 minutes holding up all other traffic; scandal dubbed 'Hairgate'

DEVASTATED

1–31 July: Nepal and parts of India after monsoon rains; 1750 killed and 250000 made homeless
4–31 July, USA: Midwest, after Mississippi and Missouri rivers burst their banks following heavy rains; 50 die and 70000 made homeless
30 Sept, India: Maharashtra state, by earthquake; 22000 die and 130000 made homeless

RENAMED

7 June: US rock musician Prince, who drops his name and replaces it with a symbol, becoming the Artist Formerly Known as Prince

PUBLISHED

Roddy Doyle, *Paddy Clarke Ha Ha Ha*

On 2 December, *Columbian drug boss Pablo Escobar Gaviria is shot dead by police. Gaviria, who ran the Medellín cocaine-trafficking cartel, handed himself in in 1991 on condition that he live in a luxury jail. When he was transferred to a more modest prison, he went on the run.*

NEW WORD

stalk *vb*: to spy on, harrass and follow someone, usually famous, in a threatening and obsessive fashion

Old foes shake hands on new peace accord

MOMENTOUS DAY Clinton embraces Arafat and Rabin's symbolic gesture.

13 SEPTEMBER, WASHINGTON DC
It was 'Shalom' and 'Salaam' today as Yasser Arafat and Yitzhak Rabin, once sworn enemies, shook hands on the White House lawn and heralded a new accord **between Israel and the Palestinians.** Minutes earlier, the Israeli foreign secretary, Shimon Peres, and PLO official Mahmoud Abbas, had signed a historic peace agreement giving Palestinians limited autonomy in the Gaza Strip and West Bank.

The chairman of the PLO and the Israeli prime minister had been brought together by US President Bill Clinton in much the same way as his predecessor Jimmy Carter brokered the peace treaty between Israel and Egypt in 1979. It also emerged that the Norwegian government had been working secretly for months to organise talks between the PLO and Israel.

The deal means that the Palestinians will gain control over most of the Gaza Strip and West Bank territories, although the regions will still be part of the state of Israel. An elected Palestinian Council will be established and the Palestinians will have their own police force and internal security organisations.

The ultimate objective is a permanent peace accord, to come into operation in 1998. Amid the euphoria, however, extremists on both sides who find the proposed solution unacceptable are threatening to sabotage the agreement.

··· AT 1000 PAGES, VIKRAM SETH'S *A SUITABLE BOY* IS THE LONGEST NOVEL IN ENGLISH FOR 245 YEARS ···

One step closer to an integrated Europe

1 NOVEMBER, BRUSSELS
After months of wrangling, the Maastricht Treaty came into force today, opening the way for further European integration and setting a detailed schedule for achieving it. The treaty, which was signed on 9–10 December 1991, has proved controversial in many European countries; in Denmark it was initially rejected by a referendum, while in France a referendum accepted it by the slimmest of margins.

At the top of the agenda is the prospect of a single currency. However, memories of the recent collapse of the Exchange Rate Mechanism are still painful and, in an interview in the *Economist*, the British prime minister John Major remarked that talk of monetary union had 'the quaintness of a rain dance and about as much potency'.

Israeli court lets 'Ivan the Terrible' walk free

29 JULY, JERUSALEM
In a move that has angered Holocaust survivors around the world, John Demjanjuk was today found not guilty of being a Nazi war criminal. He was immediately freed.

A retired car mechanic from Ohio who was born in the Ukraine, Demjanjuk worked as a guard in the Treblinka extermination camps. Following his extradition from the United States in 1986, he was convicted by an Israeli court in 1988 of being 'Ivan the Terrible', the brutal guard who helped to operate the gas chamber where almost 900 000 Jews were murdered. However, he appealed against the conviction and, in today's ruling, the Israeli Supreme Court said there were serious doubts about his identity. In accordance with the age-old Jewish legal system, they refused to condemn Demjanjuk, overturning the guilty verdict.

MAN OR MONSTER? After appealing against his conviction, Demjanjuk waits to clear his name.

Very few perpetrators of the Holocaust have been brought to justice, even though it is believed that many of them are living openly in Europe and the former Soviet Union. Survivors of the Holocaust are campaigning for tighter laws which would enable the prosecution of former Nazi collaborators on war crimes charges.

Eighty-four die as Waco siege comes to bloody end

20 APRIL, WACO, TEXAS A two-month siege ended in dozens of deaths yesterday as the headquarters of the Branch Davidian cult became an inferno. Of the 95 people believed to have been inside the sect's compound, only nine have survived the blaze, which the FBI say was started deliberately as a form of mass suicide. Among the dead was David Koresh, the cult's leader.

The siege began on 28 February, when about 200 agents of the Bureau of Alcohol, Tobacco and Firearms attempted to raid the compound to search it for illegally held weapons. Cult members opened fire with high-powered rifles, killing four federal agents and wounding 16 others.

The community was completely dominated by the charismatic Koresh, whose bizarre doctrines blended apocalyptic Christianity with psychological manipulation and violence. Koresh had promised to surrender if the FBI broadcast one of his sermons, but he broke his word. The fire started after the FBI – tired of playing a waiting game – rammed the

REAL-LIFE DRAMA Television brought the events at Waco into people's homes.

compound with tanks and fired tear gas into it. One of the survivors is reported as saying that Koresh told his followers: 'Just sit back and wait until you see God.'

BOMB ROCKS THE WORLD TRADE CENTER

SHOCKED SURVIVOR Officials lead a traumatised victim away from the scene.

26 FEBRUARY, NEW YORK CITY At least seven people were killed and more than 300 injured when a bomb exploded in a car park underneath the twin towers of the World Trade Center yesterday.

Thousands of other people were trapped in the upper storeys of the building, and several hundred were stuck in the building's lifts after the power was cut off. Many people who tried to walk down the stairs were forced back by thick smoke.

Every day up to 100 000 people pass through the building, either to work or to visit it as a tourist attraction. Completed in 1973, the World Trade Center was designed to bring together more than 1000 businesses and government agencies involved in international trade. It is the tallest building in New York City and the second tallest in the world, after the Sears Tower in Chicago; yesterday two parties of schoolchildren were on the observation deck on the 107th storey (three floors from the top) when the bomb exploded. The car park in which the explosion occurred was used by the secret service for a fleet of 100 automobiles.

According to the New York Police Department, several calls have been received claiming responsibility for the bombing, but no one has yet been accused of the crime.

Experts on terrorism are saying that the culprits could be members of a Croat, Muslim or Serb group angered at US policy in Yugoslavia, Haitians protesting against curbs on immigration, or Palestinians.

Gene study could lead to cures for human diseases

1 OCTOBER, CALIFORNIA
A plan to map and sequence the entire genetic structure of humankind, the Human Genome Project, was launched at a conference in San Diego today.

The overall nature of the human species, and the individual characteristics that make each person different from others, are determined by a set of some 100 000 genes. Each gene consists of a length of DNA, a 'coded' molecule comprising complex sequences of four protein 'bases'. Some three million of these bases make up the full complement – or genome – of a human being. The aim of the Human Genome Project, which has been planned for many years, is twofold: to draw up maps of the genome, pinpointing where the key genes lie; and to work out the sequence of all the bases, including the ones that seem to have no function ('junk' DNA).

The task is to be undertaken by the US Department of Energy, but scientists

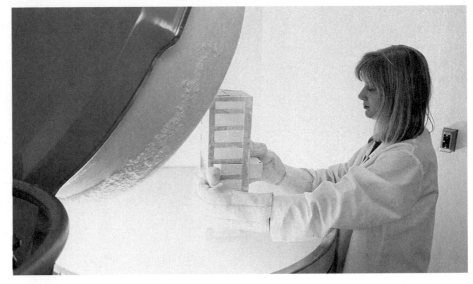

GENOME RESEARCH A scientist removes samples of human cancer cells from storage to conduct tests.

in other countries will also contribute. Dr James Watson, one of the scientists who discovered the structure of DNA in 1953, has been appointed to run the programme, which is expected to cost billions of dollars and last at least ten years. The results could transform our knowledge of how the human body functions, leading to a greater understanding of the basis of disease and heredity, and enable the development of gene therapies for inherited diseases.

··· QUEEN ELIZABETH II BECOMES THE FIRST BRITISH MONARCH TO PAY INCOME TAX ···

Woody loses custody battle with Mia Farrow

7 JUNE, NEW YORK CITY
Veteran film director Woody Allen today lost his month-long court battle for custody of his three children, Dylan, Moses and Satchel. The children will remain with their mother, Allen's ex-partner Mia Farrow.

The celebrity couple broke off their 13-year relationship in January last year, when Farrow discovered that Allen was having an affair with her 21-year-old adopted daughter Soon-Yi. The split has been acrimonious – Farrow has accused Allen of sexually abusing his adopted daughter Dylan, and Allen accused Farrow of fabricating the charge because of his relationship with Soon-Yi. Although a psychological report found no evidence to support Farrow's allegations, Judge Eliot Wilk has now questioned this report and found Allen to be an 'unfit father'.

ODD MATCH Korean-born Soon-Yi found romance with Woody Allen, her adoptive mother's partner.

Czechoslovakia is dissolved

1 JANUARY, CZECHOSLOVAKIA
The central European federation of Czechoslovakia today split to form the separate Czech and Slovak republics. The change will bring economic difficulties for both countries.

In a general election in June 1992, voters returned a right-wing government favouring free-market economics to the Czech parliament, while in the Slovak republic they elected a nationalist government supporting state intervention in the economy. Talks to dissolve the Czech–Slovak federation began shortly after the election. President Havel, who refused to preside over the country's dissolution, quit over the plans, but moves are already afoot to bring him back as leader of the new Czech Republic.

Internet weaves its magic Web

The National Center for Supercomputer Applications at the University of Illinois has created a program that can scour thousands of computers around the world in its search for a piece of information. The results are presented in a graphic form with pictures.

Mosaic, as the program is called, is a 'browser' – it allows its user to navigate the bewildering oceans of information available on the worldwide systems of computer networks known as the Internet. It manages this by using the World Wide Web, a program developed at CERN, the European Particle Physics Laboratory in Switzerland. Tim Berners-Lee, one of the CERN scientists, started to develop the Web in 1989 because he believed that physicists around the world were in need of an instantaneous way to exchange research information.

Mosaic, together with the Web, is sure to swell the millions already surfing the information superhighway.

The rise and rise of fashion's supermodel stars

BEAUTY SPOT Cindy Crawford: 'I'm rich, independent and successful'.

CATWALK QUEEN Christy Turlington models Christian Lacroix in Paris.

The fashion industry has created its very own Frankenstein's monsters – but these ones are beautiful, young, and oh-so-rich. The term 'supermodel' was coined in the late 1980s to help revive waning interest in couture clothes. It worked: in 1990 *Vogue* put them on its cover and now the whole world knows who Cindy, Naomi, Linda, Christy and friends are.

They're seen at the chicest parties, they date film stars, they give interviews to *Hello!* magazine, they hire bodyguards: in short the supermodels are stars in their own right, no longer owned by an agency or dependent on the goodwill of magazine editors. Canadian-born model Linda Evangelista states: 'We don't get out of bed for less than $10000 a day.'

And there's the rub. Having made them, all the fashion industry can do is complain. 'The most famous woman in the world,' said Paco Rabanne of Cindy Crawford, 'and she's just a coathanger.'

··· USA: ALMOST ONE MILLION PEOPLE ARE SERVING TIME IN PRISON ···

Two false starts – and the Grand National is off

3 APRIL, LIVERPOOL
After two false starts the 150th Grand National, the world's most famous steeplechase, was abandoned today and will not be re-run.

Twice the non-elasticated fibre tape holding in the horses at the start failed to fly upwards at the pull of a lever, entangling runners and riders in its coil.

At the second attempt the red flag used by the starter to indicate a false start would not unfurl. As a result only nine horses responded to the signal; the remainder charged off as if the race were on. While most riders eventually realised the problem and pulled up their horses, seven actually completed the course. A crestfallen John White, who crossed the finishing line first on Esha Ness, held his head in his hands on discovering the truth. The bookies will have to return nearly £60 million to punters.

The fiasco at the famous Aintree course will surely be the outstanding memory of the 1993 British horse-racing season for both bookies and race enthusiasts everywhere.

From street to store, grubby grunge is in style

Grunge is the music that the disillusioned youth dubbed 'Generation X', or 'slackers', listen to, and grunge is the clothes they wear.

The grunge movement began around 1987 in Seattle, USA, when bands such as Nirvana, Pearl Jam and Mudhoney started experimenting with new sounds based on wildly distorted, heavily amplified guitar. A string of similar bands followed suit, tying in with the Riot Grrl rock movement – a politicised, feminist version of grunge – and reinventing punk rock for the nineties.

Nirvana, the biggest grunge phenomenon of all, sold ten million copies of their album *Nevermind* last year – and angst-ridden songwriter Kurt Cobain has become a cult figure all over the world.

The grunge look is deliberately anti-chic and draws heavily on 'working-class' imagery – torn jeans, heavy boots, flannel shirts and unkempt hair make up the slacker uniform. Desperate to keep hip, high-fashion houses are trying to market ready-ripped sweatshirts for £350 – a snip. Hollywood has also jumped on the grunge bandwagon, making films about the slacker generation.

SLACKER CHIC Whether the 'real thing' or a cleaner look, grunge is in.

··· THE WORLD'S BEST-KNOWN PHOTOGRAPH OF THE LOCH NESS MONSTER IS PROVED TO BE A FAKE ···

MONSTERS, MALADIES AND MELODIES

PREHISTORIC RAMPAGE Special effects steal the show in *Jurassic Park*.

Voracious dinosaurs ran amok in Steven Spielberg's *Jurassic Park*, which was something of a monster itself, breaking every box office record, along with several laws of nature. No other movie was built on anything like the same scale.

In *Philadelphia*, the first mainstream Hollywood film to deal with AIDS, Tom Hanks won an Oscar playing a gay lawyer sacked for having the disease. The low-key *Groundhog Day* was set in a sleepy Pennsylvania town on a single day – but that day is repeated over and over again for Bill Murray, a cynical television weatherman, until he learns to be a better person. And on a more complex note was *The Piano*, Jane Campion's finely worked tale of sexual frustration and fixation set in 19th-century New Zealand, with a haunting score by Michael Nyman.

Exhausted end to epic trek

19 FEBRUARY, LONDON Back in London after their attempt to cross Antarctica on foot, intrepid explorers Sir Ranulph Fiennes and Dr Mike Stroud today described their experiences. When they were picked up from the Ross ice-shelf, they were badly frostbitten, close to starvation and too exhausted to cover the last 560 kilometres (350 miles) to open water. They had, however, realised their ambition of being the first to cross the frozen continent unassisted by people, animals or machines.

For 95 days they walked for up to 13 hours a day with wind-chill temperatures as low as −85° C (−121° F), resting for just one day, when a raging blizzard forced them to a halt. Each man pulled nearly 227 kilos (500 lbs) of essential food and fuel on sledges over a total distance of 2167 kilometres (1347 miles).

US HITS OF THE YEAR	
1 DREAMLOVER	*Mariah Carey*
2 THAT'S THE WAY LOVE GOES	*Janet Jackson*
3 CAN'T HELP FALLING IN LOVE	*UB40*
4 INFORMER	*Snow*
5 I'D DO ANYTHING FOR LOVE	*Meat Loaf*

US TV HITS
1 *60 Minutes*
2 *Roseanne*
3 *Home Improvement*
4 *Murphy Brown*
5 *Murder, She Wrote*

1994

DIED
22 Apr: Richard Nixon, former US President
12 May: John Smith, British Labour Party leader
7 June: Dennis Potter, British television writer
20 Oct: Burt Lancaster, US film actor

FOUND DEAD
7 Feb, London: Tory MP Stephen Milligan at home, killed by self-strangulation
4–6 Oct, Switzerland and Canada: 53 members of international religious cult Order of the Solar Temple

ELECTED
26–27 Mar, Italy: businessman Silvio Berlusconi as prime minister, leading right-wing Italian Freedom Alliance
21 July, London: Tony Blair, as Labour Party leader
3 Oct, Brazil: Fernando Henrique Cardoso, as president

On **1 May,** *Brazilian Formula 1 driver Ayrton Senna is killed in a crash during the San Marino Grand Prix in Bologna, Italy. Senna began his career in karting championships in the late 1970s before going on to compete as a racing driver. The car racing community is mourning the loss of a legendary sportsman.*

On **19 September,** *the US army invades Haiti, restoring the democratically elected president Jean-Bertrand Aristide to power. Aristide has been in exile for three years since being overthrown by a coup. The military government led a reign of terror and is believed to have murdered 3000 opponents of its regime.*

QUIT
26 Apr, USA: US boxer Evander Holyfield, because of heart condition
28 Dec, USA: James Woolsey, director of the CIA, following allegations that the intelligence agency is vulnerable to double-agent 'moles'

RETURNED HOME
27 May, Russia: Alexander Solzhenitsyn, novelist and dissident, after 20-year exile
1 July, Gaza: Yasser Arafat, leader of Palestine Liberation Organisation, first visit to Palestinian territory since 1969.

CAPTURED
14 Aug, Khartoum: international terrorist 'Carlos the Jackal' (real name Illich Ramirez Sanchez)

AGREED
21 Feb, UK: by MPs to cut age of consent for gay sex from 21 to 18

CHAMPIONS
17 July, Los Angeles: Brazil, winners of football World Cup, beating Italy on penalties after a 0–0 final
6 Nov, Las Vegas: George Foreman, world heavyweight boxing champion at age 45, beating Michael Moorer
13 Nov, Australia: German racing driver Michael Schumacher, winner of world drivers' championship

KILLED
2 July, Colombia: Andrès Escobar, Colombian soccer star whose own-goal eliminated his country from the World Cup in the USA; shot on his return home to Medellín

DEVASTATED
7 June: S-W Colombia by earthquake that triggers avalanche; 1000 die and thousands are left homeless
23 Aug, China: Zhejiang province, by typhoon; around 700 are killed

LAUNCHED
8 Nov, The Hague: United Nations tribunal for war crimes in the former Yugoslavia, first public hearings

FIRST
12 Mar, UK: female priests ordained by the Church of England

OCCUPIED
11 Dec: Chechnya, by Russian troops

On **8 April,** *Kurt Cobain, lead singer of US rock band Nirvana, is found dead after he shot himself at his Seattle home. Credited with founding the grunge music movement, Cobain was a brilliant songwriter, a fine performer and an idol to millions. But his extreme lifestyle, exacerbated by chronic illness, led to his untimely end.*

CEASED FIRE
10 Feb, Bosnia: Bosnian-Serb forces around Sarajevo, under threat of NATO air strikes

NEW WORD
road rage *n*: state of anger and frustration induced by traffic conditions and the behaviour of other motorists

Mandela to lead reborn South Africa

6 MAY, PRETORIA

A week after the polls closed in South Africa's first multiracial elections, the African National Congress (ANC) have been declared the runaway winners. The ANC, led by Nelson Mandela, took nearly two-thirds of the vote; the predominantly white National Party, which has ruled South Africa since 1948 and is led by former president F W de Klerk, gained only 20 per cent.

The weeks leading up to the poll were fraught with tension and marred by acts of sabotage from white groups on the extreme right. Bombings killed 21 people and injured nearly 200 more but the intimidation tactics failed to work. Millions of people waited in long queues outside polling stations to cast their votes for the first time and the elections have been monitored and declared free and fair by an independent electoral commission.

Nelson Mandela will now become the republic's first black president and lead the Government of National Unity (GNU), a transitional administration from which cabinet ministers will be drawn from all parties lasting until the 1999 general elections. The real surprise in these election results is the fact that parties on the extreme right and left were marginalised.

END OF AN ERA Marike, wife of former president F W de Klerk, listens to Mandela's inaugural speech.

··· ROVER, BRITAIN'S ONLY REMAINING CAR MANUFACTURER, IS BOUGHT BY BMW FOR £800 MILLION ···

IRA CEASEFIRE RAISES HOPES

31 AUGUST, BELFAST

Leaders of the Irish Republican Army (IRA) have declared 'a complete cessation of military operations' from midnight tonight. Today relief swept the people of Northern Ireland, and MPs celebrated in Dublin's parliament. The Irish prime minister, Albert Reynolds, called it 'a historic opportunity to take the gun out of the war forever'.

The announcement raises hopes for an end to 25 years of conflict in Northern Ireland in which 3170 people have been killed. It comes eight months after the Downing Street Declaration, by Reynolds and the British prime minister, John Major, which offered Irish nationalist party Sinn Fein a role in talks

CHANCE FOR CHANGE Northern Ireland celebrates at the news of ceasefire.

on Northern Ireland's future, on condition that the IRA declared a ceasefire. Sinn Fein leader Gerry Adams said: 'The struggle is not over, it is in a new phase.'

Chunnel opens for business

6 MAY, LONDON

A dream first put forward by a French mining engineer in 1802 became reality today as the British Queen and France's President François Mitterrand opened a tunnel linking their countries beneath the English Channel. Eight years in the building, the Channel Tunnel is 50 kilometres (31 miles) long, with 38 kilometres (24 miles) under the sea bed.

The Queen opened the international terminal at London's Waterloo station before taking the passenger train through what has been dubbed the 'chunnel' to meet President Mitterrand at Calais. They travelled back together on the car shuttle in the Queen's Roll-Royce.

THOUSANDS MASSACRED IN RWANDAN CIVIL WAR

WAR BEHIND THEM Rwandan refugees stream across the border with Zaire.

31 AUGUST, RWANDA
The bitter war between the rival Hutu and Tutsi tribes which plunged Rwanda into bloody chaos last April may be at an end. The Tutsi-led Rwanda Patriotic Front (RPF), which gradually gained military ascendancy in June and July, is now in control of the majority of the central African country.

Since 1990 the RPF has been attempting to wrest control of the country from the Hutus, and the current round of bloodshed began as a deliberate attempt at the genocide of the minority Tutsi by Hutu extremists. It began in earnest after 6 April, the day of the assassination of President Habyarimana, whose plane was shot down; the next day, Prime Minister Agathe Uwilingiyimana was also gunned down. Those murders were the prelude to a mass slaughter. To date more than a million Rwandans have lost their lives in the conflict and nearly two million refugees, mainly Hutu, have fled to refugee camps in Zaire.

The USA and Europe have refused to contribute troops to a United Nations peacekeeping force and only a few of the 5500-strong all-African force have arrived in the country. French troops sent in June to establish a safe haven have been withdrawn.

All eyes are now turned on the refugee camps, where typhoid and cholera are flourishing in the crowded unsanitary conditions. There have also been reports of intimidation by Hutus who are hoarding food supplies.

The question hanging over Rwanda's future is whether, without international support, Hutus and Tutsis will ever be at peace with one another.

··· FORMER US PRESIDENT RONALD REAGAN ANNOUNCES THAT HE HAS ALZHEIMER'S DISEASE ···

Terror attacks threaten Middle East talks

Two bloody acts of violence perpetrated by extremists threatened to derail negotiations between Israelis and Palestinians this year. In February Baruch Goldstein, a Jewish extremist who had recently immigrated from the United States, opened fire with an automatic weapon in the Ibrahim Mosque in Hebron, killing 30 worshippers. When his ammunition ran out he was beaten to death by survivors. Many hard-line Jews are protesting about the proposed handing over of Hebron to Palestinian rule.

In October a suicide bomber blew up a bus in Tel Aviv, killing 21 people and wounding 45 others. The militant Islamic group Hamas claimed responsibility and threatened further attacks on Jewish targets.

The incidents are typical of hard-liners on both sides who feel that the treaty signed between Yasser Arafat and Yitzhak Rabin last year in Washington DC is too much of a compromise. In addition both sides endow their actions with deep religious significance. Goldstein is known to have considered the handing over of territories to the PLO as against the law of God in the Hebrew Scriptures, while Hamas suicide bombers see themselves as part of a *jihad*, or holy war, in which death leads to a saintly paradise.

WRECKED The suicide bombing claimed by Hamas ripped apart a city bus.

Simpson is the star of live court-room drama

IN THE LIMELIGHT A less glamorous new image for the football star, who also tried his hand at acting.

2 JULY, LOS ANGELES

Live media coverage of O J Simpson's pre-trial hearing has captivated the population of the United States. The hearing will decide whether the man whom many regard as the finest running-back in the history of American football will have to stand trial for the murder of his ex-wife, 35-year-old Nicole Brown Simpson, and her friend, 25-year-old Ronald Goldman.

The pair were stabbed to death on the evening of 12 June and detectives claim to have built up a formidable case against the athlete. In particular, the court heard of a bloodstained glove found in Simpson's home that allegedly matched another at the murder scene.

The case is already dividing the USA along racial lines; African-Americans claim Simpson is being victimised and will not receive a fair trial from the white-dominated legal system. The case has already become a media circus: a bizarre car chase, in which police followed Simpson and a friend as they cruised slowly along a California freeway on 17 June, received blanket television coverage. Eventually O J gave himself up to the police.

Since then, the three main networks have cleared their schedules, even sidelining the Wimbledon semi-finals. Not everyone is pleased. One company received death threats from viewers angered at missing their favourite soaps.

··· ASTEROID PASSES EARTH AT ONLY 160 000 KM (100 000 MILES) – ON A COSMIC SCALE, A NEAR-MISS ···

Skating Association bans US champion

30 JUNE, COLORADO SPRINGS
The US Figure Skating Association today banned Tonya Harding, the 1994 national figure-skating champion, and stripped her of her title. Following an attack on Nancy Kerrigan, the former national ice-skating champion, at the national championships in January, Harding was implicated in the incident.

Greed and malicious envy prompted the assault, planned by Harding, her ex-husband and her former bodyguard. As Kerrigan completed a perfect routine, a masked man leapt into the rink and hit one of her knees with a metal baton. Kerrigan collapsed and her attacker disappeared in the confusion.

Both women were due to have joined the US team for the Winter Olympics in February. With her rival out of the way, Harding would have had a chance of winning gold. At the two-day hearing, a member of the association said Harding had shown a 'disrespect for fairness, good sportsmanship and ethical behaviour'.

Munch's masterpiece found intact

7 MAY, AASGAARDSTRAND, NORWAY
Eighty-four days after the disappearance of Edvard Munch's celebrated work *The Scream* from Oslo's National Art Museum, the painting has been found in a hotel 65 kilometres (40 miles) south of the capital. Three men have been arrested for handling stolen goods.

A motive for the crime emerged shortly after the theft, when a church minister declared that the action was part of an anti-abortion campaign. He told the press that the painting would be returned if Norwegian television would broadcast a film showing a foetus being aborted. Significantly, the film was entitled *The Silent Scream*.

In public, police showed little interest either in the minister's request or in an offer made in March by a Norwegian lawyer on behalf of an unidentified client who was prepared to return the masterpiece in exchange for $1 million. However, this ransom attempt was foiled and the painting was recovered virtually unharmed.

EXISTENTIAL PAIN *The Scream* has become an emblem of the spiritual void of urban life.

Painted in 1893 as Munch, Norway's greatest Impressionist, was nearing a mental breakdown, *The Scream* is one of Norway's greatest treasures — a scene of panic under a blood-red sky that has come to symbolize the angst of the modern world.

Hubble Telescope reveals the secrets of the universe

For the first time, the impact of a comet on a planet was observed this July as fragments of Shoemaker-Levy smashed into Jupiter. The event was photographed by the Hubble Space Telescope, which was successfully repaired by the crew of the shuttle *Endeavour,* launched in December 1993. In a series of five space walks, the astronauts carried out repairs and corrected faults in its mirror, at last enabling it to fulfill its potential.

The impacts, estimated at speeds of around 210000 kilometres per hour (130000 mph), took place on the 'dark side' of Jupiter, but the planet's rapid rotation soon brought the area into view. The most impressive collision occurred on 18 July; 'Fragment G' –

measuring up to 4 kilometres (2½ miles) across – created a fireball 3000 kilometres (1875 miles) high, and left a scar on Jupiter. The fragment would have left a crater 60 kilometres (40 miles) across had it hit Earth.

The Hubble has also produced the clearest evidence yet that black holes – objects with so much gravitational pull that not even light can escape – are real. Images of the centre of galaxy M87 in the constellation of Virgo showed gas whirling at more than 1.6 million kilometres per hour (1 million mph). Without a hugely dense object at its centre, the galaxy would fly apart. Most astronomers believe that this object must be a black hole.

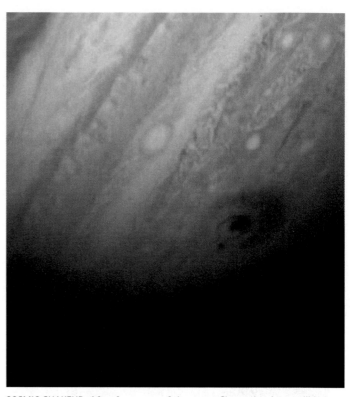

COSMIC SHAKEUP After fragments of the comet Shoemaker-Levy collided with Jupiter, black and brown patches appeared on the planet's red surface.

··· ETHIOPIA: SKULL OF THE EARLIEST HUMAN, THOUGHT TO BE 3–3.9 MILLION YEARS OLD, IS FOUND ···

A sharp lesson for John Bobbit

SNAP HAPPY Mrs Bobbit was the focus of global media attention following her act of revenge.

15 JANUARY, MANASSASS, VIRGINIA Lorena Bobbit could not remember the moment she cut off her husband's penis, she told a packed court today. Charged with malicious wounding, Mrs Bobbit is pleading temporary insanity.

The 24-year-old manicurist said that she remembered going into the kitchen

to fetch a knife after she was allegedly raped by John Wayne Bobbit. Then, she says, her memory is a blank. She recalls driving away from home and looking down at herself to see that she was covered in blood and holding Mr Bobbit's severed penis. She threw the mangled member out the car window.

'I just wanted to get rid of it,' she reportedly told police who retrieved the penis from the roadside. Mr Bobbit had it reattached during a nine-and-a-half-hour operation. Apparently it is now back in working order.

John Bobbit may have suddenly become the butt of many new jokes but he looks set to make a lot of money from his ordeal. His lawyers are said to be negotiating lucrative book and film deals and this week he was seen shopping for a luxury car.

Jacko's private life under police scrutiny

Pop star Michael Jackson's reputation was badly tarnished this year when it emerged that he was being investigated by the Los Angeles Police Department over allegations of sexual abuse. The musician was accused of making sexual advances on a 13-year-old boy whom he had befriended and invited to his Los Angeles home, Neverland. After raids on Jackson's mansion and the cancellation of tour dates in the Far East, the matter was settled out of court for an undisclosed sum.

Within months Jackson had another surprise for his fans with the announcement that he had married Lisa-Marie Presley, Elvis's daughter. Immediately there was speculation that it was a marriage of convenience.

Lara's spectacular 501 puts him in the record books

3 JUNE, BIRMINGHAM
The sustained brilliance of the left-handed Trinidadian Brian Lara has carried him to another peak of sporting achievement. Forty-nine days after he eclipsed the Test record score for a single innings, the remarkable young Warwickshire batsman today became the first cricketer to score more than 500 runs in a first-class innings.

As his team's match with Durham was reaching its close, the umpire told Lara – on 497 – that he had only two more balls in which to break Hanif

Mohammed's 1959 record of 499 runs. On the stroke of 5.30 pm Lara drove the next delivery from John Morris to the extra-cover boundary to reach 501 not out. Stumps were drawn and the match ended in a draw.

This was Lara's seventh century in eight innings, a sequence that began with his record-breaking triumph in Antigua, where he broke Gary Sobers's long-held Test record of 365 with an almost chanceless 375. Sobers witnessed the event and was first out on the pitch to congratulate him.

BIG INNINGS Brian Lara gets a hug from a team mate after his record-breaking performance.

SPIELBERG TRIUMPHS WITH NEW TAKE ON COMMERCIAL SUCCESS

FLAWED HERO Neeson's role as Schindler earned him an Oscar nomination.

After years as the world's most commercially successful film-maker, Steven Spielberg finally won an Oscar – in fact, several of them – with his most serious film yet: *Schindler's List*, the true story of a German factory owner who saved thousands of Jews from concentration camps. The cast (Liam Neeson as Schindler, Ralph Fiennes as a Nazi commandant) was excellent, as was the

script, taken from the prize-winning book by Australian novelist Thomas Keneally. A film of unquestionable sincerity and intelligence, it was regarded as the finest non-documentary film yet to deal with the Holocaust.

Equally powerful was the New Zealand film *Once Were Warriors*. Following the trials of a Maori family in a city ghetto, the film investigates the violence, alcohol abuse and hopelessness that prey on a community stripped of its traditional lands and culture. It also earned the lead actress Rena Owen, who played the gutsy mother, a best actress Award at the Montreal Film Festival. Such a level of intelligence didn't show elsewhere: *Forrest Gump* was a potted history of America through the eyes of a simpleton who always managed to come out on top. A bigger box office draw than *Schindler's List*, it contributed to the debate about the 'dumbing down' of arts in the USA. Most impressive was the weaving together of historical footage with the dramatic action.

The rejuvenated Disney Studios had a smash hit with *The Lion King*, which became the highest grossing film in the company's history. It was also the first Disney film to be based on an original story. Children loved the winning combination of animal characters, stunning animation and entertaining songs.

US HITS OF THE YEAR

1	I'LL MAKE LOVE TO YOU	*Boyz II Men*
2	I SWEAR	*All-4-One*
3	THE SIGN	*Ace Of Base*
4	ON BENDED KNEE	*Boyz II Men*
5	THE POWER OF LOVE	*Celine Dion*

US TV HITS

1	*60 Minutes*
2	*Home Improvement*
3	*Seinfeld*
4	*Roseanne*
5	*These Friends of Mine (Ellen)*

1995

DIED

17 Mar: Ronnie Kray, British criminal
4 Apr: Kenny Everett, British comedian
25 Apr: Ginger Rogers, US dancer and actress
29 June: Lana Turner, US actress
22 Oct: Kingsley Amis, British author

APOLOGISED

15 Aug, Japan: Tomiichi Murayama, prime minister, for the suffering caused by Japan in World War II

On 27 June, *British film actor Hugh Grant is arrested in Los Angeles after being caught with a local prostitute, Divine Brown. Grant issues a statement saying how much he regrets his behaviour, while the newspapers vie to offer Brown large sums of money to 'kiss and tell'.*

ELECTED

7 May, France: Jacques Chirac, as president
14 May, Argentina: Carlos Menem, as president
17 Dec, Haiti: Rene Préval, as president

KILLED

29 June, South Korea: 640 people, when a shopping centre collapses
18 July, France: Italian cyclist Fabio Casartelli, in accident during Tour de France cycle race
10 Sept, Nigeria: Ken Saro-Wiwa, Nigerian writer and human rights activist, executed in public for political dissidence

DISGRACED

25 Jan, London: Manchester United soccer player Eric Cantona, who launches a kung-fu kick at a fan in the crowd after being sent off in a match against Crystal Palace

CHARGED

25 July, The Hague: Bosnian-Serb leaders Radovan Karadzić and Ratko Mladić, and Croatian-Serb president, Milan Martić, with crimes against humanity, by the International War Crimes Tribunal for the former Yugoslavia

OPEN

6 Aug, England and Wales: pubs on Sunday afternoons, as licensing laws are relaxed

PRACTICAL JOKER

26 Oct: chat show host on Canadian radio, who poses as Canadian prime minister in telephone talk with Queen Elizabeth about Quebec independence vote, then broadcasts part of their discussion on radio

STOPPED

19 Jan, UK: export of live animals from Shoreham harbour, West Sussex, following protests by animal rights activists

On 17 January, *the 'Great Hanshin' earthquake devastates the city of Kobe in Japan. 6000 people are killed and 30000 injured. At least 100000 buildings are destroyed and the region lies in ruins, with no electricity or infrastructure left.*

ARRESTED

14 Mar, UK: Bruce Grobbelaar, Hans Segars and John Fashanu, British football stars, during inquiry into alleged match-fixing
2 June, London: British Conservative MP Sir Nicholas Scott, after road accident involving three-year-old child

CHAMPIONS

30 Apr, UK: British snooker player Stephen Hendry, winner of world championship for fourth year running
21 May, UK: British rugby league club Wigan, winners of grand slam of Premiership, Challenge Cup, League Championship and Regal Trophy titles
24 June, South Africa: South Africa, winners of rugby union World Cup
18 July: British athlete Jonathan Edwards, who sets new world triple-jump record of 17.98 metres

FIRSTS

10 Apr, Birmingham, UK: national computer database of DNA records in the world
30 Nov, Northern Ireland: visit by a US President

SUSPENDED

13 Nov, Auckland: Nigeria's membership of Commonwealth, because of human rights abuses

REBELLED

14–15 June, Iraq: Iraqi soldiers against President Saddam Hussein; they are defeated by loyal troops, and 150 rebels are executed

NEW WORD

gangsta *n*: style of US rap music accompanied by violent culture and lifestyle

When the Shell Oil company proposed to sink the defunct Brent Spar oil rig in the North Sea, environmental group Greenpeace occupied the platform in protest at the threat to marine life. Shell backed down in June; in October, Greenpeace admits that it was wrong - and that sinking the rig was the safest option.

Hundreds injured in Oklahoma bombing

20 APRIL, OKLAHOMA CITY
Dozens of people were killed and hundreds injured when a government office building was devastated by a huge bomb blast yesterday. Many of the victims were children aged between one and seven who were in a day-care centre on the second floor of the nine-storey Alfred Murrah Building. Some of the bodies recovered from the rubble were burned beyond recognition.

The building is so badly damaged that it is expected to take days to finish searching for corpses and trapped survivors. Authorities believe that the bomb was planted in a car parked outside the building.

No one has claimed responsibility for the atrocity, but the FBI is said to be following up leads linking it with Middle Eastern terrorists. Another line of inquiry is suggested by the fact that

BOMB DAMAGE The building is wrecked, making the rescue job an extremely dangerous one.

the bombing occurred on the second anniversary of the destruction of the headquarters of the Branch Davidian cult in Waco, Texas; members of the cult have denied responsibility. President Clinton has vowed that the culprits will be found, and that 'justice will be swift, certain and severe'.

··· JAPAN HAS THE HIGHEST LIFE EXPECTANCY IN THE WORLD: 81.6 YEARS FOR MEN AND 75.9 FOR WOMEN ···

Cult leader accused of murder

16 MAY, TOKYO
Eight weeks after the horrific nerve gas attacks on the Tokyo underground that left 12 people dead and 5000 injured, police made a series of dramatic arrests today. The 41 suspects detained are all members of the fanatical Aum Shinrikyo religious cult and include 40-year-old Shoko Asahara, the sect's leader.

Raids on several of the sect's premises started simultaneously at dawn today, and in one house police found 40 lorry-loads of chemicals for making the nerve gas sarin. Asahara himself was barricaded in a secret compartment at the group's headquarters near Mount Fuji; when he was discovered, he gave himself up without resistance.

In the weeks following the gas attacks, Asahara released several videos in which he denied his involvement, saying he was too ill to plan such an attack.

WANTED MAN Prior to his arrest, partially sighted Asahara asserts his innocence.

However, cult members have told police that he gave orders to make and release the poison gas. His cult, an apocalyptic blend of Buddhism and Hinduism, has about 2000 full-time members who call themselves monks and nuns, and some 30000 lay members.

Rogue trader brings down British bank

27 FEBRUARY, LONDON
Barings, Britain's oldest bank, collapsed last night after the Bank of England admitted defeat in its efforts to put together a rescue package. Amazingly, one employee has single-handedly brought about the collapse of what had previously been a flourishing financial institution. He is 26-year-old Nick Leeson, a high-flying trader for the bank in Singapore who ran up losses of £620 million in the futures market. Leeson managed to conceal the losses from his employers, who turned a blind eye to what they thought was a risky, but profitable, trading operation.

A search is now on for Leeson, who disappeared five days ago, before the bank was forced into receivership. He is believed to be hiding in Germany.

DEADLY VIRUS SPREADS IN ZAIRE

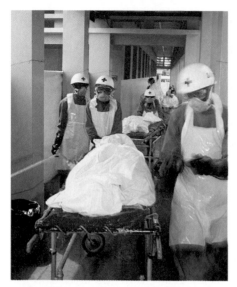

HELPING HAND Red Cross nurses in protective clothing tend to the Ebola victims in Kikwit.

16 MAY, KIKWIT, ZAIRE
At least 77 people have died in the past week of a deadly viral infection in this swampy town in central Africa. The epidemic started in the local hospital. Panic is spreading and thousands of people have taken to the roads to escape the scourge.

A member of the same family which includes the measles virus, the Ebola microbe is transmitted via body fluids and kills by destroying internal organs. The disease tends not to cause massive epidemics because it kills its victims so fast that they do not have time to pass it on to others. Ebola was first identified in 1976, after an outbreak near the Ebola River in Zaire, from

which it took its name. Between outbreaks it lies low, presumably in an animal host that is immune to its effects.

Like the virus, the notoriously corrupt government of Mobutu Sese Seko is making a killing. The province in which the disease started has been quarantined – throwing up plenty of opportunities for bribery. Hundreds of journalists, medical experts and aid workers who have flocked to Zaire have been forced to pay up.

Meanwhile, the half a million people left in Kikwit are rallying to stop the virus. Student volunteers on bicycles are alerting people to the dangers, and doctors at the hospital are struggling to spread the word on hygiene.

··· 3 FEB: THE DUTCH PARLIAMENT MAKES IT A CRIMINAL OFFENCE TO DENY THE HOLOCAUST ···

Hopes of peace for Bosnia

14 DECEMBER, PARIS
Beneath the chandeliers of the Elysée Palace, leaders of the Serb, Muslim and Croat factions in the Bosnian war signed a peace treaty today. The deal, agreed in talks at Dayton, Ohio, in November, is the best hope for an end to a war that in three and a half years has left 200 000 missing or dead.

Bosnian Muslim leader Alija Izetbegović, Franjo Tudjman, president of Croatia, and Slobodan Milošević, president of Serbia, shook hands after signing the treaty. Izetbegović said, 'I feel like a man swallowing a bitter but useful medicine.'

Under the agreement, there will be a single Bosnian state, the Union of Bosnia-Herzegovina, with 51 per cent held by a Muslim–Croat alliance and the remaining 49 per cent by Serbs. Reports from Bosnia indicate that local people are treating the agreement with cynicism, but 60 000 NATO-led troops will be sent to enforce its terms.

Rose West guilty of serial killing

22 NOVEMBER, WINCHESTER
Amid a blaze of publicity, housewife and mother Rosemary West has been found guilty on ten counts of murder and sentenced to life imprisonment.
For weeks the court has listened to the mind-numbing details of how she and her husband, Fred West, subjected their victims to depraved sexual abuse before killing them. The case, which has been the focus of public attention for more than a year, has profoundly shocked the country.

Detectives began making their grisly discoveries in February 1994, when a police team was sent to 25 Cromwell Street, Gloucester, the home of Fred and Rosemary West, hoping to find some trace of their eldest daughter, Heather.

Sophisticated scanning equipment was used, and a round-the-clock guard was kept on the premises. Eventually Heather's corpse was found buried in the back garden, and the remains of other victims were discovered in the cellar and under the patio. Further bodies were also unearthed at the Wests'

SUBURBAN KILLERS Fred and Rosemary West, who neighbours said were just an ordinary couple.

previous homes. The victims included Fred's first wife and a series of young girls, some of whom had been lodgers at Cromwell Street.

Fred West eventually made a full confession to the police, but he cheated justice by hanging himself in his cell on New Year's Day this year.

Rabin assassinated at peace rally

A NATION MOURNS Hundreds of shocked Israelis laid flowers at the spot where Rabin was killed.

4 NOVEMBER, TEL AVIV
Israeli prime minister Yitzhak Rabin was shot dead today after speaking at a rally intended to counter right-wing opposition to the Israeli–Palestinian peace deal. More than 100000 people had heard him deliver an impassioned speech reassuring the world that Israel wanted peace when a 25-year-old Jewish student pushed through the crowd and shot him twice at close range. Security officers jumped on the assassin, Yigal Amir, and bundled him away, and Rabin was rushed to hospital, where he died an hour later.

Amir freely confessed to the crime, admitting that he had planned for more than a year to assassinate Rabin and his deputy Shimon Peres. He said he was protesting about the recent Israeli agreement with the Palestine Liberation Organisation (PLO) and the handing over of territories to Palestinian control. Amir said he had twice attended events where Rabin was expected but his plans had been thwarted each time. He told police: 'I acted alone on God's orders and I have no regrets.'

Shimon Peres, one of the chief architects of the peace process, now becomes prime minister. Meanwhile, Israelis are coming to terms with the idea of a Jew killing another Jew.

France condemned for nuclear tests

5 SEPTEMBER, MURUROA, SOUTH PACIFIC
French forces exploded a 10-kiloton nuclear weapon under the tiny Pacific atoll of Mururoa, the first of eight proposed tests of France's new nuclear deterrent. Within hours of the explosion anti-French riots had broken out in Papeete, the capital of Tahiti, and French paratroopers were being flown in to control the situation.

World opinion has been against the French since June, when President Chirac announced the resumption of nuclear testing. The Australian government called for a boycott of French companies, and the New Zealand government attempted to take the French to the International Court of Justice. A recent poll in France revealed that 60 per cent of the population believe that the tests are wrong. Many are afraid of the consequences as millions of people worldwide boycott French products.

··· SWEDEN: CUSTOMS OFFICERS CATCH A WOMAN TRYING TO SMUGGLE IN 65 BABY SNAKES IN HER BRA ···

Hindu pilgrims flock to satisfy divine thirst for fresh milk

23 SEPTEMBER
Holy statues that seem to drink milk are being hailed by Hindus around the world as a miracle. Two days ago, worshippers at several temples in New Delhi said that statues of the elephant god Ganesh began to drink milk with their trunks; since then, there have been similar reports from Hindu temples across the world. In Hong Kong, one silver statue of Ganesh reportedly drank 20 litres. Other deities, including the god Krishna, his bull Nandi and the cobra deity Shash Naagall also discovered a penchant for milk.

In London, devotees queued up for hours to make their offerings for offerings at the Vishwa Hindu temple in Southall, and stores in the area are selling out of milk as soon as they take delivery. Sceptics are dismissing the reports as religious hysteria, and scientists say that the milk-drinking effect is simply the natural capillary action of porous stone. However, today the gods' thirst seems to be quenched, for fewer reports of drinking statues are coming in.

THIRSTY GOD A Hindu worshipper makes an offering of milk to Ganesh.

Cow carcass wins prestigious British art prize

28 NOVEMBER, LONDON
Britain's Turner Prize for contemporary art was tonight awarded to 30-year-old Damien Hirst, the best-known and most controversial artist of his generation. The annual competition, worth £20 000 to the winner of the prize, regularly attracts criticism on the grounds that it ignores mainstream art and artists, instead showcasing all that is most pretentious in today's overhyped art market. This year is no exception.

The main work by Hirst currently on show at the Tate's annual Turner Prize exhibition is *Mother and Child*

SHEEP AHOY *Away from the Flock* is one of Hirst's more accessible pieces.

Divided – four glass tanks containing the neatly-divided halves of a cow and her calf

preserved in formaldehyde. The Tate catalogue says that by revealing the innards of

the cow and its offspring 'Hirst strips the closest of bonds between living creatures to its starkest reality'. Hirst himself says, perhaps with a hint of irony: 'It's amazing what you can do with an E in A-level art, a twisted imagination and a chainsaw.'

He is regarded as the leading figure of the 'brat pack' of young British artists who – like pop stars – attract attention for their trendy lifestyles as much as for what they create. Much of their work is intended to shock or provoke rather than to produce something that is visually pleasing.

··· IRAN: THE GOVERNMENT BANS SATELLITE TELEVISION DISHES ···

Gates goes graphic

24 AUGUST, SEATTLE
After months of delay and speculation Microsoft, the firm that makes the operating software used by four out of five desktop computers, today launched Windows 95. The new system promises to make computers easier to use, faster and more reliable than its predecessor, Windows 3.x, which brought icons and menus to Microsoft's text-based DOS operating software. New features include multi-tasking, which allows the computer to do several jobs simultaneously, and instant access to the Microsoft Network on-line service.

Critics say that Windows 95 is still slower, less reliable and less user-friendly than the system that Microsoft's rival, Apple, has had on the market since the 1980s. Windows 95 also requires more powerful computers, with much more memory, to run successfully. Nevertheless, Microsoft confidently expects to sell 20 million copies of Windows 95 in the first year.

Bill Gates, co-founder and chief executive of Microsoft, is the richest man in the world, with a personal fortune of $12.9 billion, according to *Forbes* magazine. Fascinated by computers since he was a child, Gates became rich by striking a series of brilliant licensing deals that put the DOS program into millions of computers around the world. Since then he has run Microsoft with tremendous energy and acumen.

BIG BUDGET Gates's Microsoft spent £124 million launching Windows 95.

Oasis win the battle of the bands

1 OCTOBER, LONDON
Record stores throughout the United Kingdom opened at midnight last night to sell the first copies of *(What's the Story) Morning Glory?***, the second album from Oasis.** This long-awaited new release comes after the much-hyped 'battle of the bands' between the Manchester group and rivals Blur, from Essex, for the number one position in the singles chart. Blur's 'Country House' won by a whisker over the Oasis song

'Roll With It'. In the album stakes, however, Oasis win hands down – the raucous 90s rock 'n roll of *What's the Story* is predicted to sell 350 000 copies in the UK in the next two days.

The headline-grabbing antics and laddish reputations of the group's front men, brothers Noel and Liam Gallagher have helped to generate further sales. Recently Noel apologised for saying that he hoped Damon Albarn, Blur's lead singer, would die of AIDS.

NEW LAD Liam Gallagher's devil-may-care blokeishness has won him millions of fans.

··· AUSTRALIA: WORLD'S FIRST VOLUNTARY EUTHANASIA LAW IS PASSED ···

HOLLYWOOD EXPOSES AMERICA'S SEEDY UNDERBELLY

DEATH ROW Penn played a heartless killer in *Dead Man Walking*.

Underworld stories pulled in audiences at the cinema this year. Quentin Tarantino's *Pulp Fiction* – a mosaic of gory stories – gave John Travolta back his street cred. *The Usual Suspects*, directed by newcomer Bryan Singer, showed that audiences can follow even the most complicated heist. Meanwhile, with *Léon*, French director Luc Besson proved that foreigners can direct Hollywood movies – especially if they're about a French hitman in America. Susan Sarandon and Sean Penn turned in searing performances in *Dead Man Walking*, which was about the spiritual redemption of a murderer on the way to the electric chair.

British films did well, with *Shallow Grave*, *The Madness of King George* and *Four Weddings and a Funeral*. The last made its foppish lead Hugh Grant a hot property overnight. His beautiful girlfriend Liz Hurley, and an illicit rendezvous with a certain Ms Divine Brown, made him a tabloid sensation as well. But the real star of 1995 was, of course, a piglet called *Babe*. The Australian kiddie flick, based on Dick King-Smith's book *The Sheep-Pig*, was a masterful technical achievement, using a combination of computers, puppets and farm animals to create a thoroughly entertaining story about a porker who thinks he's a dog.

US HITS OF THE YEAR

1	ONE SWEET DAY	*Mariah Carey & Boyz II Men*
2	FANTASY	*Mariah Carey*
3	WATERFALLS	*TLC*
4	TAKE A BOW	*Madonna*
5	THIS IS HOW WE DO IT	*Montell Jordan*

US TV HITS

1	*Seinfeld*
2	*ER*
3	*Home Improvement*
4	*Grace Under Fire*
5	*NFL Monday Night Football*

1996

DIED

8 Jan: François Mitterrand, former French president

28 Jan: Joseph Brodsky, Russian poet

15 June: Ella Fitzgerald, US jazz singer

12 Dec: William Rushton, British humourist and cartoonist

DIVORCED

30 May, London: the Duke and Duchess of York

28 Aug, London: the Prince and Princess of Wales

PROHIBITED

21 Sept, USA: same-sex marriages, under new Defence of Marriage Act

EXPLODED

18 July, New York City: TWA jet, all 230 people on board are killed

On 29 July, *England striker Alan Shearer is transferred from Blackburn to Newcastle United for a record £15-million fee, making him the world's most expensive football player. Shearer was signed to Blackburn in 1992 for what was then a British record of £3.2 million.*

On 4 May, *the European Space Agency rocket Ariane-5 is blown up one minute after takeoff from Kourou, French Guiana. The rocket, which carries four spacecraft, veers off course immediately after lift-off and has to be destroyed. The Ariane project, which cost £500 million to develop, is not insured.*

ELECTED

31 May, Israel: Benjamin Netanyahu, as prime minister

20 Oct, Nicaragua: Arnoldo Alemán Lacayo, as president

RE-ELECTED

17 Mar, Zimbabwe: Robert Mugabe, as president

11 May, Uganda: Yoweri Kaguta Museveni, as president

5 Nov, USA: Bill Clinton, as president

CLEARED

25 Mar, UK: British athlete Diane Modahl, banned in 1994 after drugs test wrongly showed positive

SACKED

5 Nov, Pakistan: Benazir Bhutto, as prime minister, by President Farooq Ahmed Leghari

FOUND GUILTY

28 May, USA: Jim and Susan McDougal, former business associates of President Clinton, of fraud and conspiracy in 'Whitewater' scandal over property deals in Arkansas

JAILED

27 Mar, Israel: Yigal Amir, assassin of Israeli prime minister Yitzhak Rabin, for life

29 Nov, The Hague: Drazen Erdemović, Bosnian Croat who participated in Bosnian-Serb killing of Muslims at Srebrenica in 1995; for ten years, by United Nations Tribunal for the former Yugoslavia

RIOTED

24–25 Oct, Florida: black youths, after teenager Tyron Lewis was shot dead by police

KILLED

14 July, Libya: around 50 football fans, when police open fire because the crowd is chanting slogans against President Muammar Gaddafi

16 Oct, Guatemala: 82 people, in stampede during football World Cup qualifying game between Guatemala and Costa Rica

SIGNED

6 June, UK: £743 million deal between British Premier League football clubs and BSkyB and the BBC, for four years' television coverage of League matches

EVICTED

29 Feb, UK: protesters against Newbury road bypass, who have been occupying the site since January

British dance act the Prodigy revitalise the pop charts with 'Firestarter' and 'Breathe' – two number one singles for which Keith Flint (right) provides vocals. The Prodigy fuse industrial techno with heavy rock guitar and a punk attitude.

NEW WORDS

cyberspace *n*: the virtual realm of the Internet

quality time *n*: leisure time to spend with friends and family, in contrast to the hectic pace of working life

Paris underground hit by bomb attack

3 DECEMBER, PARIS

Two people were killed and 50 others injured when a bomb exploded on a train in the Paris Métro underground rail system tonight. The device went off at 6.05 pm – the height of the rush hour – in the carriage of a train as it pulled into Port Royal station.

The bombing bears the hallmarks of Algerian Islamic fundamentalists, who carried out seven bomb attacks on the Paris Métro system last year. It is thought they were protesting at last week's referendum in Algeria which aimed to clamp down on Islamic fundamentalist political parties.

Speaking on national television, President Chirac described the incident as 'an attack on the innocent'.

Tunnel sparks confrontation

SECURITY ALERT Israeli soldiers take up positions on the West Bank in response to the unrest in the area.

27 SEPTEMBER, JERUSALEM

The opening of a tunnel in Jerusalem has led to renewed clashes between Israelis and Palestinians. Up to 70 are dead.

The violence started with Israel's decision to open a tunnel near the Dome of the Rock, a sacred site for Jews and Muslims. The site is also near the holy Al-Aqsa Mosque. The confrontation underlines the hostility between Palestinians and Jews that continues to undermine the peace process.

··· WORLD HEALTH ORGANISATION PREDICTS TUBERCULOSIS WILL KILL 30 MILLION PEOPLE IN NEXT TEN YEARS ···

Life on Mars is no longer sci-fi

7 AUGUST, HOUSTON

It's official – Earth may already have been invaded by Martians. It happened 13 000 years ago, and the 'invaders' were simple microscopic fossil bacteria. NASA scientists at the Johnson Space Centre in Houston, Texas, were thrilled as they unveiled what they believe is new evidence to support the theory.

The proof for their proposal lies in a meteorite called Allan Hills 84001, after the area of Antarctica where it was found. Chemical analysis suggests that it was blasted off the surface of Mars by an asteroid collision

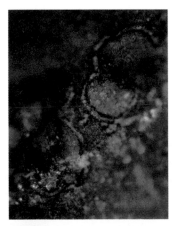

SIGN OF LIFE Orange carbon-based globules in the Allan Hills meteorite.

about 16 million years ago. It contains structures resembling worm casts, less than one-hundredth the diameter of a human hair, which may be the fossilised remains of Martian life forms.

NASA is not ruling out the possibility that primitive life still exists on Mars.

Islamic troops rule Afghanistan

28 OCTOBER, KABUL

The Taliban, a radical Islamic group of militiamen trained in Pakistan, have taken control of the Afghan capital Kabul, having swept through the rest of the country in less than a year. They have reiterated their intention to turn Afghanistan into a state under the rule of a pure Islamic law.

Hard-line religious decrees governing aspects of daily life are being broadcast from loudspeakers. Taliban troops mete out brutal punishments to those who are caught offending. Women have been forced back into the traditional black *burka*, which completely covers their body and face; those who fail to comply are beaten with rifle butts. Girls' schools have been closed, women have been forbidden to work and the death penalty for adulterers has been revived. Music and dancing have been banned.

The Taliban have also destroyed hundreds of television sets, hanging them from poles like criminals dangling from gallows.

Although thousands have fled Kabul since the Taliban onslaught began, others are welcoming the new laws, saying that they bring a welcome dose of law and order to a city that has been in turmoil since the end of the war with the Soviet Union in 1992.

Gunmen stage murder sprees

MEMORIAL FOR A MASSACRE Flowers honour the children who died for no reason at Dunblane.

29 APRIL, HOBART, TASMANIA
A gunman has killed at least 34 people in Australia's worst-ever mass murder. Michael Bryant, aged 28, systematically shot customers in a restaurant at Port Arthur, Tasmania, before going on a rampage around the island. The picturesque holiday resort, about 50 kilometres (30 miles) from Hobart, is the site of a former penal colony and a popular tourist attraction on the island.

Bryant began his killing spree on Sunday afternoon, pulling an automatic rife out of a sports bag in a packed café. He killed 20 there and then set off around the town, shooting at random. He has been arrested and charged with one of the murders.

With his long blond hair, Bryant looks more like a typical surfer than a mass murderer. He moved to Port Arthur several months ago and has no previous criminal record, although his behaviour had been worrying neighbours, who describe him as strange and withdrawn, with an unhealthy interest in firearms. He is said to have a history of psychological problems, but there were no indications that he would cause such destruction. His father, who emigrated from Britain to Australia, is believed to have committed suicide by shooting himself.

The Australian's terrifying spree has been linked with the mass murder of schoolchildren that took place in Dunblane, Scotland, last month. On 13 March, 43-year-old Thomas Hamilton walked into Dunblane Primary School carrying four guns, and killed 16 children, aged five and six, together with one of their teachers. He then shot himself dead.

Hamilton was a former scout leader who had a grievance against society, believing that he was being persecuted for his alleged sexual interest in young boys. The Dunblane shooting sent Britain into a state of shock, and pressure is building on the government to impose restrictions on the possession of firearms.

Speaking from California, the FBI's chief psychiatrist, Dr Park Deitz, made a connection between Bryant and Hamilton: 'Were it not for the experience of someone else's actions, such people would be more likely to just kill themselves. Bryant probably thought to himself: "I am as powerful as Hamilton is. The world needs to know my suffering and feel my rage."'

Rap star dies after drive-by shooting

13 SEPTEMBER, LAS VEGAS
Rapper Tupac Shakur died today, a week after being gunned down in Las Vegas. The 25-year-old star was being driven to a party for boxer Mike Tyson when a man in a white Cadillac drew up beside his vehicle and opened fire, injuring Shakur and his boss Suge Knight, head of Death Row Records. Police are examining the possibility that the star's murder may be gang-related. The public rivalry between West Coast rappers such as Shakur, Dr Dre and Snoop Doggy Dog and East Coast stars such as Notorious BIG has certainly resembled gang warfare.

Shakur's hardcore style of 'gangsta rap' earned him respect and record sales, especially among black American males. His last album, *All Eyez On Me*, went quintuple platinum in the United States.

His death focused the media's attention on the inherent brutality of the gangsta rap genre, in which singers boast of their violent crimes and sexual adventures. Shakur himself had been arrested for assault and battery, and in 1995 he served ten months for sexual assault. Detractors say Shakur and Snoop Doggy Dog are bad role models, but the fans continue to love what they see as a rappers' war against authority.

MARKED MAN Like many other gangsta rappers, Shakur made many enemies in his short life.

Meat from 'mad cows' may cause human disease

ROAST BEEF A scheme to destroy hundreds of thousands of cattle over a seven-year period kicks into action.

20 MARCH, LONDON
Scientists issued warnings last night of a new form of deadly brain disease which may be linked to eating beef from cattle infected with 'mad cow disease'. They said that ten cases had recently been diagnosed of a new variant of Creutzfeldt-Jakob Disease (CJD), a rare illness that usually attacks older people. The alarm was raised when it emerged that the latest CJD sufferers were all under 45 years of age. CJD, the human variant of bovine spongiform encephalopathy (BSE), attacks the central nervous system and causes dementia and seizures, eventually leading to a painful death.

BSE, first identified in the UK in 1986, was attributed to the practice of feeding dairy cows with animal protein from sheep infected with scrapie – a common nervous disease. BSE causes erratic behaviour and staggering in cattle – hence the name 'mad cow disease'.

Although scrapie seems to have moved from sheep to cows, there is no proof that BSE can be transferred to humans, and many scientists have backed government reassurances that there is no health threat to the public. To show his confidence the agriculture minister, John Gummer, publicly fed his young daughter Cordelia with a hamburger.

But last night's shocking warning overturns eight years of complacency. European countries have demanded that the entire British herd should be slaughtered, and Britons – who have already curbed their consumption of beef – now expect a Europe-wide ban on the export of British cattle, beef and related products.

··· 1000 PEOPLE DROWN WHEN FERRY *MV BUKOBA* CAPSIZES IN LAKE VICTORIA, TANZANIA ···

British cities are bombed as IRA abandons ceasefire

15 JUNE, MANCHESTER
Shoppers fled for their lives after a bomb exploded in Manchester's busy city centre this afternoon, creating a terrifying hail of glass as shop windows were blown out. The attack happened at 12.40 pm, three hours after a coded warning had been received from the IRA. Police evacuated the immediate area, but the blast was so powerful that glass was hurled up to 800 metres (2600 feet) into crowds of shoppers. Around 228 people have been injured, four seriously, and insurance experts estimate the damage at £50 million.

The IRA had kept to their ceasefire, announced in August 1994, for 17 months. On 9 February this year a 225-kilo (500-lb) IRA bomb exploded in the Canary Wharf office complex in London's Docklands area, signalling a return to violence. Two people were killed and more than 100 injured.

Further attacks followed. On 18 February a bomb exploded while IRA terrorist Edward O'Brien was carrying it on a bus in London, killing O'Brien and injuring four passengers.

The return to violence is linked to difficulties in peace talks between Irish parties and the British government. Last week politicians from Sinn Fein, the political wing of the IRA, were excluded from the talks.

BOMBSCAPE The blast was timed to coincide with the England-Scotland football clash in Euro '96.

Germans crush English hope of football glory

30 JUNE, LONDON
Football 'came home', as the England team song ran, in the form of the European Championships, but it was Germany, not England, who took the cup. The Germans beat the Czech Republic 2–1 tonight in the final at Wembley stadium.

At times it seemed as if the whole of England was caught up in the euphoria. Fears of violence proved to be unfounded. In the relaxed atmosphere, England appeared at last to have shaken off its reputation as the home of football hooliganism.

Hopes of a home victory were high, but in the semi-finals England went down to Germany – beaten in a penalty shootout after the match had drawn 1-1.

Basketball magician is back on court

**30 JANUARY,
LOS ANGELES**
Earvin 'Magic' Johnson, the basketball player who retired from the game because he was HIV positive, has made a sensational comeback with his old team, the Los Angeles Lakers.

Four-and-a-half years ago the 2.05-metre (6 ft 9 in) star quit the game and pledged to campaign for greater AIDS awareness among heterosexuals. He had led the Lakers to the NBA finals nine times in 12 years.

Now Johnson's condition is under control due to his taking 'combination therapy' – a cocktail of anti-AIDS drugs, which is proving useful to many sufferers.

The star also feels that knowledge about the virus has improved in recent years – there is now little talk of players being at risk from HIV through physical contact with him.

MAGIC TOUCH The Lakers stormed to a ten-point win on Johnson's return.

··· DURING A POWER BLACKOUT, FOUR MILLION HOMES IN THE USA ARE WITHOUT ELECTRICITY FOR FOUR HOURS ···

American athletes please home crowd in Atlanta

FALLEN VICTOR Kerri Strug is helped from the winner's podium.

**4 AUGUST, ATLANTA,
GEORGIA**
The crowd in Atlanta rose in a spontaneous standing ovation at the Olympic Games opening ceremony as former boxer Muhammad Ali, now debilitated by Parkinson's Disease, lit the Olympic Flame.

The Games were memorable for some notable firsts. Not only were they the first Games to have been entirely privately funded, but

also they were unique in being the first where every nation invited to send representatives did so. They were not unique, however, in being disappointing for Britain, which came way down the medals table with its lowest tally in years.

Notable individual achievements came from athlete Carl Lewis, who won his ninth Olympic gold, and his team mate Michael Johnson, who broke the

world record in the 200 metres as well as finishing first in the 400 metres.

However, the sentimental heroine of the Games had to be US gymnast Kerri Strug. In the final rotation of the team event – a nail-biting contest between the United States and Russia – she sprained her ankle on her first vault, but gritted her teeth to achieve a perfect second landing – securing another gold for the USA.

SPACE INVADERS STORM THE USA

WASHINGTON FIREBALL A space ship takes out the White House in *Independence Day*.

With the success of *Independence Day*, Hollywood was given further proof of the theory that the more money you spend on special effects, the more you make at the box office. The story of aliens invading Earth was flimsy, but the film featured some of the most spectacular computer-generated effects ever seen in cinema – including a convincing destruction of the White House. It went on to become one of the most financially successful movies of all time. Disney's live-action remake of *101 Dalmatians*, featuring real pups, computer-animated ones and an outrageous performance from Glenn Close as Cruella de Vil, was the other smash-hit of the year.

But the major studios were not having it all their own way. Independent productions started to make genuine inroads into the all-important American market. British director Mike Leigh's finely observed *Secrets and Lies* earned an Oscar nomination for Brenda Blethyn, who played a white mother coming to terms with finding her long-lost black daughter. *Shine*, an Australian film, movingly recounted the true-life story of pianist David Helfgott, who fought his way back from a debilitating mental illness to concert-hall success. The film catapulted the real-life Helfgott into the limelight, and led to a sell-out world tour for the pianist.

Fast-fingered addicts face their Doom

Two computer games developed by id software in Texas seem to have infested every computer on the planet. *Quake* and *Doom* drop players into familiar worlds of adventure. You may be running through endless creepy dark passages reminiscent of the film *Raiders of the Lost Ark*, or dodging attacks from a vicious alien as you try to reach a distant haven.

But unlike any previous computer game, *Quake* and *Doom* have spawned a brood of offspring. The company released the games' source code, so that real computer fiends have been able to go on adding more and more levels of difficulty to the games. Enthusiasts are now faced with the first generation of computer games that it is almost impossible to master.

CUTTING EDGE Duelling with other players on the Internet is a popular gaming pastime.

US HITS OF THE YEAR

1	MACARENA	*Los Del Rio*
2	UN-BREAK MY HEART	*Toni Braxton*
3	THA CROSSROADS	*Bone Thugs N Harmony*
4	BECAUSE YOU LOVED ME	*Celine Dion*
5	NO DIGGITY	*Blackstreet (featuring Dr Dre)*

US TV HITS

1	*ER*
2	*Seinfeld*
3	*Friends*
4	*Caroline in the City*
5	*NFL Monday Night Football*

1997

DIED

1 July: Robert Mitchum, US actor
2 July: James Stewart, US actor
15 July: Gianni Versace, Italian fashion designer

FIRSTS

8 Jan, USA: positive government health message, put on porridge oats
20 May: advertisement for trainee spies, placed by MI5, Britain's secret service, in *The Times* and *The Guardian* newspapers

DISCOVERED

14 Jan, Greece: the world's first university, in Athens, where Aristotle and Socrates taught philosophy

On 19 June, *the longest-running trial in English history, between fast food chain McDonald's and campaigners David Morris and Helen Steel, comes to an end. Morris and Steel were sued for distributing leaflets alleging that the burger chain damaged the environment. The court found for McDonald's, but agreed that some of the protesters' claims were true.*

ACCUSED

10 Jan: German prime minister, Helmut Kohl, of persecuting scientologists, in an open letter signed by 34 Hollywood stars, including John Travolta, Goldie Hawn, and Dustin Hoffman

On 4 July, *the US space probe* Pathfinder *lands safely on Mars after a journey of 624 million km (390 million miles) at speeds of 26 560 km/h (16 600 mph).* Pathfinder *sends back its first pictures of the Martian landscape before its small six-wheeled robot,* Sojourner, *sets off to examine nearby rocks.*

OVER

23 Apr, Peru: siege by Maoist group Tupac Amaru at Japanese Embassy, Lima; 72 people freed as police storm the building, only one hostage dies

KILLED

15 Apr, Saudi Arabia: 200 pilgrims burned and trampled to death, as fire surges through a campsite outside Mecca
July: more than 100 people and almost 70 000 made homeless, in flash floods in the Czech Republic, Germany and Poland
UK: 19 people, by contaminated meat containing *E. coli* bacteria; a further 400 people are poisoned but recover

COLLIDED

25 June: Russian space station *Mir*, with a supply craft 320 km (200 miles) above Earth, puncturing a hole in the side of the ship – cosmonauts have to flee to another part of the ship, as it quickly depressurises

HIGHEST

9 June, UK: salary in the world, £54 million per annum, paid to Briton Bernie Ecclestone, who negotiates television rights for Formula 1 motor-car racing

SURVIVED

8 Jan: round-the-world yachtsman Tony Bullimore, after spending five days trapped underneath his capsized boat, before his emergency beacon is spotted by the Australian Air Force
25 June: tandem skydiver Terry Griffiths, aged 27, after plunging 3658 m (12 000 ft) at 288 km/h (180 mph) when his parachute fails: his instructor, who cushioned his fall, dies on impact

CONVICTED

14 Jan, Germany: Peter Graf, father of tennis champion Steffi Graf, of defrauding German tax office out of £4.5 million; he is sentenced to four years imprisonment

4 Feb, USA: O J Simpson, of killing ex-wife Nicole and her friend Ronald Goldman, in a civil trial – he must pay $20 million compensation to the relatives of the deceased

ADMITTED

18 July: Hungary, Czech Republic and Poland to NATO

GUILTY

15 Aug, Denver: Oklahoma bomber Timothy McVeigh, sentenced to death by lethal injection for the explosion which killed 168 people

DEFEATED

May: Russian chess player Garry Kasparov, by IBM computer Deep Blue, in a six-game challenge match

NEW WORD

new lad *n*: a man with certain attitudes and lifestyle – combination of eighties 'lad' and nineties 'new man', joining new sensitivity with traditional male chauvinism

On February 10, *a state of emergency is declared in Albania to deal with mass rioting after the collapse of the country's pyramid savings schemes – which aim to pay investors with funds invested by others later on. More than half a million people lost their savings when the supply of new investors ran out.*

DIANA KILLED IN HIGH-SPEED CAR CHASE

1 SEPTEMBER, PARIS

Diana, Princess of Wales, died early yesterday morning when the armoured Mercedes she was travelling in crashed in a Paris underpass. Her companion, millionaire jet-setter Dodi Fayed, and the chauffeur, Henri Paul, were also killed.

A gang of paparazzi photographers on motorcycles had pursued the couple after they left the Ritz Hotel where they had enjoyed dinner. Initial reports blamed the accident on the attention of the photographers. However, French police said today that they believed the Mercedes might have been travelling at an excessive speed. Seven men are under investigation in connection with the accident.

At the age of 36, Diana leaves behind two sons: William, aged 15, who is second in line to the British throne, and Harry, 12. Tributes to the princess have poured in from around the world. South African premier Nelson Mandela praised her work with the poor, the sick and the disabled. President Bill Clinton said: 'Hillary and I knew Princess Diana and were very fond of her. We are profoundly saddened by this tragic event.' In Britain, Prime Minister Tony Blair said of the princess: 'She touched the lives of so many others in Britain and throughout the world with joy and with comfort.'

JEWEL IN THE CROWN Diana's glittering image brought style to the royal family.

··· THE UK PRESS WATCHDOG LAUNCHES AN INQUIRY INTO MEDIA INTRUSION FOLLOWING DIANA'S DEATH ···

World mourns the death of Diana, Queen of Hearts

PEOPLE'S PRINCESS Diana and her sons enjoy a ride in a British theme park.

2 SEPTEMBER, LONDON

Britain is slowly coming to terms with Diana's death. As the shock faded, the nation plunged into the greatest outpouring of grief since the death of Queen Victoria. Shops, pubs and banks will honour the princess by closing on the day of the funeral, and many sports events have been cancelled. People are queuing for up to 12 hours to sign a condolence book at St James's Palace.

When Lady Diana Spencer was plucked from obscurity at the age of 19 to marry Prince Charles, the heir to the British throne, few suspected that the shy nursery teacher would become the most photographed woman in the world.

Once the world's press realised that her image boosted sales she was hounded by photographers and journalists, with whom she had an ambiguous love-hate relationship. She realised that fame had one good use – bringing media attention to a variety of causes. In 1987, at a time when police dealing with AIDS sufferers wore gloves, she transformed public attitudes when she was photographed holding hands with an AIDS patient.

After her marriage collapsed in 1992, her private life was subject to even more media scrutiny and she toned down her public appearances. However this year the princess stated that she now felt ready to take on a fuller role on the international stage, so she could highlight the world's attention on causes which were close to her heart. In her visits to Bosnia and Angola she made a dramatic call for an international ban on landmines.

This summer saw the princess blossom; it seemed she had found love in her relationship with Dodi Fayed. But her story ended in tragedy yesterday, though her death is sure to turn her into one of the 20th century's most enduring and powerful icons.

LABOUR WINS BIGGEST LANDSLIDE THIS CENTURY

2 MAY, LONDON

In one of the most stunning general election results of the century, the Labour Party swept to victory by a huge margin early this morning.

It was a decisive rejection of the Conservative Party, which has held power for the last 18 years. Every opinion poll had predicted a victory for 'New Labour', as Tony Blair likes to call the party he leads, but the scale of the win has exceeded his wildest dreams.

New Labour's pre-election campaign promoted their party's efficiency, while challenging Tory sleaze and corruption. With almost all the results now in, Labour will have a majority of at least 170 seats; Tony Blair will be able to push through a raft of new legislation.

The Liberal Democrats also did very well, taking up to 40 seats – the best result since David Lloyd George in 1916.

The Conservatives, meanwhile, are shattered, having lost more than half the seats they previously held. Among their defeated MPs are former cabinet ministers whose seats had been regarded as Tory strongholds – including ex-defence secretary Michael Portillo and ex-foreign secretary Malcolm Rifkind. The party now does not now hold any seats in either Scotland or Wales.

Dignified in defeat, Conservative leader John Major telephoned Tony Blair at 2.30 am to concede he had lost the election and congratulate the new prime minister, who, at 43, is the youngest prime minister since Lord Liverpool in 1812.

VICTORY AT LAST Tony Blair takes a walkabout before entering his new home at No 10.

··· THE FIRST JOINT US-RUSSIAN SPACEWALK IS MADE BY ASTRONAUTS JERRY LINEGAR AND VASILY TSIBLIEV ···

Hong Kong is returned to China

1 JULY, HONG KONG

At midnight last night Hong Kong became a 'special administrative region' of China when it was handed back by Britain in accordance with the terms of the 99-year lease agreed between the two countries in 1898.

Dignitaries, led by the Prince of Wales and China's president Jiang Zemin, attended the ceremonies, which were accompanied by lavish celebrations, including spectacular firework displays, but there were also tension and rows over protocol.

Jiang Zemin has promised to safeguard the rights of Hong Kong's citizens, but there are fears that Chinese rule will prove repressive. As dawn broke, thousands of Chinese troops crossed over

NEW DAWN Hong Kong's new banner, and the red flag of China, fly together at the handover ceremony which marked the end of British rule.

the border and are now garrisoned in Hong Kong.

For the departing British there is a feeling of sad nostalgia. For the Chinese there is a sense of national pride at the recovery of what is now one of the most prosperous places on Earth. Some economists estimate

that up to four fifths of China's income will come via Hong Kong.

In the Chinese capital, Beijing, jubilant crowds thronged Tiananmen Square to watch a digital clock counting down the seconds to the moment of the historic handover.

Tallest building rises in Kuala Lumpur

For 20 years the Sears Tower in Chicago has been the world's tallest building. Now it has been elbowed aside by the Petronas Towers in Kuala Lumpur, Malaysia. The twin towers, designed for Malaysia's state oil company by the American firm Cesar Pelli and Associates, are 88 storeys high; their total height is 452 metres (1480 ft) – 10 metres (33 ft) higher than the Sears Tower. Some Americans grumble that without its 47-metre (155-ft) steel spires, the building would not break the record. But their pre-eminence will be short-lived – the unfinished Shanghai World Financial Centre will be even higher.

Fiery visitor lights the sky

PASSING THROUGH Amateur astronomers and the public alike were awestruck by Hale-Bopp's brilliance.

22 MARCH
People all over the world were gazing at the sky tonight to see the brightest comet in more than 400 years make its closest approach to the Earth.

Comet Hale-Bopp, a 32-kilometre (20-mile) wide lump of ice, frozen gas and sooty dust, passed by at a distance of 195 million kilometres (122 million miles) and a speed of 160000 kilometres per hour (100000 mph).

Two fiery tails of steam and dust, each millions of kilometres long – blasted off the comet's icy surface by the radiation of the Sun – make Hale-Bopp clearly

visible to the naked eye, even in brightly lit cities. In remote areas it dominates the sky like a big exclamation mark.

The ancient Egyptians record the last visit of Hale-Bopp, nearly 4000 years ago. On that visit to our solar system the comet's 57-billion-kilometre (36-billion-mile) orbit was gently tweaked by the gravitational pull of Jupiter, so it will return again in only 2400 years.

The comet is named after Alan Hale and Thomas Bopp, two American amateur astronomers who spotted it independently, but within a few hours of each other, in June 1995.

Scientists claim major genetic engineering breakthrough

27 FEBRUARY, EDINBURGH
Scientists have announced that they have successfully cloned a sheep. A lamb – known as Dolly – has been created from the tissue of an adult ewe: the first mammal ever to be cloned in this way.

Her creators at the Roslin Institute in Edinburgh took cells from a six year-old ewe and used them to fertilise an egg from another ewe whose own

ONE OF A KIND Dolly is unique, but at the same time a carbon copy of another living sheep – and oblivious to the controversy that surrounds her.

chromosomes had been removed. That meant that Dolly was a clone – a copy of the animal from which she came.

The news has sparked off worldwide debate. Many have voiced fears that the technique could be used in humans. But the scientists responsible said they have no such intention: their idea is to use the method to create genetically modified animals that will produce valuable human proteins in their milk, helping to treat human diseases.

Human cloning is already banned in Britain, while other countries are likely to move to introduce similar controls to prevent the nightmare of 'carbon-copy' humans being made to order.

Cult suicide aimed to win eternal life

26 MARCH, SAN DIEGO
The bodies of 39 people have been found in a secluded mansion today after a mass suicide linked to the appearance of Comet Hale-Bopp.

The 21 women and 18 men of the Heaven's Gate cult believed that a UFO was flying past the Earth, using the comet as a shield. According to the Heaven's Gate site on the World Wide Web, this was the last opportunity for the cult's members to rendezvous with the spaceship and fly off into eternity before the Earth was 'recycled'.

The leader of the group was 66-year-old Marshall Applewhite, who reinvented himself as King Do. He set up Heaven's Gate, which supported itself by designing websites. Members, crew-cut and celibate, addressed each other as 'brother' and 'sister'. According to one ex-member, some of the men had themselves castrated.

They killed themselves by drinking a cocktail of phenobarbitol and vodka, then putting their heads into black plastic bags. When discovered, their bodies were already starting to decay.

Murder sentence dropped for British au pair

IN THE SPOTLIGHT The Woodward case has created a media frenzy on both sides of the Atlantic.

10 NOVEMBER, CAMBRIDGE, MASSACHUSETTS

Louise Woodward, the 19-year-old British au pair at the centre of one of the USA's most controversial law cases, was today set free by a judge who overturned her conviction for murder.

Judge Hiller B Zobel, who delivered his verdict via the Internet, was 'morally certain' that Woodward's conviction for murdering Matthew Eappen, an eight-month-old baby in her care, represented a miscarriage of justice, and he replaced the life sentence he had given her 11 days earlier with one of 279 days – the period she had already spent in prison.

Woodward had been arrested on 5 February, after Matthew entered hospital; he died of a brain haemorrhage on 10 February. At the trial, which began on 7 October, the prosecution contended that the baby's death had been caused by Woodward shaking him, but the defence claimed that the fatal injury had been sustained weeks before he was taken to hospital.

On 30 October the jury returned a verdict of second-degree murder, and the following day Judge Zobel passed the mandatory life sentence. In reducing the verdict to one of involuntary manslaughter, he said he believed that Woodward's actions in trying to quiet a crying child 'were characterized by confusion, inexperience, frustration, immaturity and some anger, but not malice'. He said he hoped his judgement would bring 'this extraordinary matter to a compassionate conclusion', but neither side is satisfied. The prosecution plans to appeal for the original verdict to be reinstated; Woodward and her supporters want her declared innocent of any crime, rather than guilty of a lesser one.

··· 31 DECEMBER: FROM MIDNIGHT, SMOKING IS BANNED IN ALL CALIFORNIA BARS AND NIGHTCLUBS ···

India marks 50 years of independence

15 AUGUST, NEW DELHI

India's 50th anniversary of independence was celebrated today with parades and firework displays. However, the rejoicing was tempered by outbreaks of violence in Assam province and a call by Prime Minister Inder Kumar Gujral to combat the bribery and corruption that is so rampant in Indian politics.

Speaking from the ramparts of the 17th-century Red Fort, the prime minister asked citizens to drive out the 'curse on the country' by refusing to pay bribes and by reporting officials who demanded them. His speech followed a 21-gun salute and a fly-past by fighter jets trailing saffron, white and green smoke – the colours of the Indian flag. The ceremony ended with 7000 children singing the national anthem.

Earthquakes ravage central Italy

26 SEPTEMBER, ASSISI, ITALY

Two powerful earthquakes in Italy have killed at least ten people and inflicted catastrophic damage on some of the world's greatest art treasures.

The quakes, at 2.33 am and 11.42 am today, measured 5.5 and 5.7 respectively on the Richter scale. Their effects were felt as far north as the Alps and as far south as Rome, but the tragedy is centred on the Umbria region of central Italy, particularly the historic town of Assisi, the home of St Francis.

The church dedicated to him there is one of the world's great pilgrimage sites, containing 13th- and 14th-century frescoes that rank among the glories of Italian art. Some of these paintings are believed to be irreparably damaged. Four people died inside the church when the second quake brought down a vaulted ceiling. The death toll would have been higher had the building been open to the public after the first quake.

HOLY SMOKE TV cameras capture the first quake hitting the Basilica of St Francis in Assisi.

MOTHER TERESA DIES AGED 87

5 SEPTEMBER, CALCUTTA

In the week in which the world is in shock at the death of Diana, Princess of Wales, another icon of compassion, Mother Teresa, today died of heart failure at the age of 87.

Physically there could scarcely have been a greater contrast than that between the tall, young, supremely glamorous princess and the diminutive, aged nun, but the two women formed a bond and used their fame and personal magnetism to work for the humanitarian ideals in which they believed. Now, on different sides of the world, they will be buried within hours of each other.

Mother Teresa was born of Albanian parents in Skopje (now part of Macedonia) in 1910. Originally named Agnes Gonxha Bojazhui, she took the name Teresa in 1931 when she made her first vows as a nun. After training in Dublin (where she learnt English) and Darjeeling, India, she took her final vows in 1937. In 1948 she left her teaching post in Calcutta and after studying nursing began a ministry in the city's slums. Her organisation, the Missionaries of Charity, cares for thousands of sick and destitute people and has opened schools, orphanages and homes for the dying all over the world. These institutions depend on donations, and Mother Teresa became one of the world's greatest fundraisers. In 1979 she was awarded the Nobel Peace Prize. She was not without critics, particularly for her opposition to abortion and contraception, but she was regarded by many as a living saint.

SAINTLY FIGURE Mother Teresa remained humble and devout despite her fame.

··· IN A BID TO ERADICATE AVIAN FLU, ALL CHICKENS IN HONG KONG ARE DESTROYED ···

GREAT SCOT Film star Sean Connery is a high-profile campaigner for Scottish independence.

Devolution for Scotland and Wales

18 SEPTEMBER, CARDIFF

The people of Wales today followed the example set by Scotland a week ago by voting in a referendum in favour of a separate Welsh assembly. The margin of victory was narrow, only 50.3 per cent against 49.7 per cent, whereas in Scotland there was a massive 'Yes' vote for an independent parliament.

In both regions the Labour Party allied itself with the Liberal Democrats and the Scottish and Welsh Nationalists to defeat the Conservative-led 'No' campaign. Labour has thus delivered the goods on a major promise from last May's general-election manifesto.

The Welsh gain only an 'assembly' with no legislative or tax-levying powers. Scotland, where the demand for independence has been much more insistent, now has, for the first time since the Union with England in 1707, its own 'parliament', with authority over matters such as health and education, and with the power to raise or lower the basic rate of income tax set by the national government in London.

The Scottish Nationalist Party predicts that devolution will prove to be a stepping-stone to full independence. The Labour government argues that devolution will dampen the nationalist fires and so preserve the unity of the United Kingdom. It has promised that the new assemblies will be in place by the year 2000.

Girl Power rules the pop charts

CHOOSE YOUR FLAVOUR Left to right: Baby, Scary, Sporty, Posh or Ginger – all of them are spicy.

It's official: the Spice Girls are the most successful all-girl line up ever. Last year they made pop history by being the first band to reach number one with every one of their first four singles. 'Wannabe', the Girls' debut single, reached number one in the United States too, a feat unmatched even by the Beatles. This year they became the first band anyone can remember to have a number one in the USA and the UK simultaneously.

Those are the statistics, but they don't explain the phenomenal success of the feisty fivesome, who are especially popular with girls aged 8–14 years old. Probably not the greatest singers, the Girls don't play any instruments; and the tunes are just standard pop. But the group have tapped into the zeitgeist. Their slogan 'Girl Power!' has been adopted by millions of young women. And of course the marketing has been brilliant.

Mike Tyson bites off opponent's ear

29 JUNE, LAS VEGAS
Mike Tyson, the boxing star convicted of rape in 1992, last night blackened his name again by biting off part of Alabama fighter Evander Holyfield's ear in the third round of their heavyweight championship bout.

Holyfield leapt in the air, rushed frantically around the ring and retired to his corner, refusing to fight on. As his opponent dripped blood, Tyson was at once disqualified. Holyfield thus retains the title that he had won from Tyson last year. The severed part of his ear has been reattached by surgery.

Tyson's savagery was apparently premeditated – he left his corner without his gum shield. His future is in the hands of the Nevada State Commission. Many boxing devotees are calling for a lifetime ban.

Tyson was released from jail two years ago after serving time for the rape of beauty queen Desiree Washington. His publicists claimed that prison changed his character – while serving time he converted to Islam – but it seems he is still the wild man of America.

··· JUNE, UK: THE WORLD'S FIRST LESBIAN BEAUTY CONTEST IS HELD IN LONDON ···

Plenty of space for cosmic funeral

9 FEBRUARY, CANARY ISLANDS
The first-ever space funeral took place this morning when the ashes of 1960s icon Timothy Leary were launched into orbit from an airbase off the Spanish coast. Carrying Spain's first scientific satellite, the rocket also contained the ashes of *Star Trek* creator Gene Roddenberry and 22 other space enthusiasts.

The orbiting tomb, called *Pegasus*, is only temporary, however. It will circle the Earth before spiralling back into the atmosphere and burning up.

Leary, who died of cancer on 1 June last year, is mostly remembered as a

writer and an advocate of psychedelics and LSD, who advised people to 'turn on, tune in and drop out'. In the 1990s he reinvented himself as the spiritual leader of cyberspace, asserting that 'power to the people means personal technology available to the individual'. He originally intended to commit 'cybercide', allowing followers to experience his death live on his website. In the end, he died in his sleep.

Friends say that Leary was thrilled when told about the plans for the funeral, because it would give him the chance to 'ride the light into space'.

HIGH PRIEST OF LSD A former Harvard professor, Leary made a final request for 'one last far-out trip'.

Tiger proves that golf is cool

13 APRIL, AUGUSTA, GEORGIA
The world of golf is saluting its newest star, 21-year-old Eldrick 'Tiger' Woods, who over four days at the Augusta Masters has put on a show the like of which has never been seen before.

He is the youngest winner of the Masters title, his margin of victory – 12 strokes ahead of the field – is the greatest ever, and his final total of 270, or 18 under par, the lowest ever. He is also the first black player (he is of mixed African and Asian parentage) to win one of the grand slam championships. 'I hope my victory will make kids think that golf is cool,' Woods said.

Only a few months ago Woods was still an amateur. But he came to Augusta with three tour wins already behind him, and his sheer power – hitting greens on Augusta's par fives with a driver and an eight iron – has experts talking about golf entering a new era. In just 16 events on the pro tour Woods has already earned more than £1 million.

The proudest man in the USA today is Woods's father, Earl, who introduced him to the game as soon as he could walk and is still his coach and best friend. Home videos of Tiger show that his effortless, rhythmic swing has hardly altered since he was a toddler. At the age of six he scored his first hole-in-one; fifteen years on, he looks to have a chance of breaking Jack Nicklaus's record of 18 grand slam titles.

SMILING TIGER Golf's newest star brings a youthful ebullience to the professional golf links.

··· SWISS BANKS PUBLISH DETAILS OF 2000 DORMANT ACCOUNTS BELONGING TO VICTIMS OF THE HOLOCAUST ···

INVALID AND SUPERHERO MAKE HEARTS BEAT FASTER

NOVEL STORY Ralph Fiennes, the star attraction in *The English Patient*.

The revival of the British film industry was predicted yet again, following the success of *The English Patient*, a wartime adventure-cum-love story based on the Booker Prize-winning novel by Michael Ondaatje and directed by Anthony Minghella. Women, for the most part, went to see Ralph Fiennes, whose performance was delicious. *The English Patient* also heralded, supposedly, the return of the literary film. This didn't stop the release of *Batman and Robin*, the most ruthlessly hyped film of the year. George Clooney, star of the hospital television series *ER* and worldwide heart-throb, was the new man in the rubber suit; but the film won few fans, and was soundly trounced at the box office by *The Lost World*, the sequel to *Jurassic Park*. Still, it made more sense and more money than *The Fifth Element*, Luc Besson's spectacular bit of sci-fi nonsense about an alien trying to save the world, with a little help from Bruce Willis.

US HITS OF THE YEAR

1	CANDLE IN THE WIND 1997	*Elton John*
2	I'LL BE MISSING YOU	*Puff Daddy & Faith Evans (featuring 112)*
3	CAN'T NOBODY HOLD ME DOWN	*Puff Daddy (featuring Mase)*
4	WANNABE	*Spice Girls*
5	MMMBOP	*Hanson*

US TV HITS

1	*ER*
2	*Seinfeld*
3	*Suddenly Susan*
4	*Friends*
5	*Naked Truth*

1998

DIED

5 Jan: Sonny Bono, US singer and politician

6 Apr: Tammy Wynette, US singer

30 Oct: Ted Hughes, British Poet Laureate

AGREED

15 Jan, USA: by TV station NBC to pay £13 million to Warner Bros per episode of hit TV series *ER*

CELEBRATED

4 Feb, Sri Lanka: the nation's 50th birthday since independence

CLEARED

26 Feb, Texas, USA: TV presenter Oprah Winfrey of charges brought by a Texas cattlemen's group for remarks she made about beef and 'mad cow' disease. The group claimed that her comments had cost them $11 million

British designers are making their mark on the fashion world. Stella McCartney, John Galliano and Alexander McQueen, who created a bizarre new look for Icelandic pop star Björk (above), are at the forefront of so-called 'Cool Britannia'.

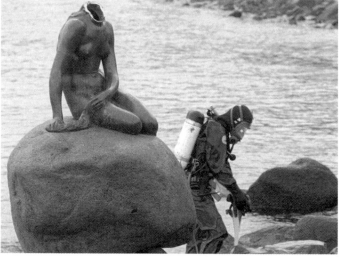

On 6 January, divers began a search for the head of Denmark's most famous landmark, the Little Mermaid statue, after morning joggers in Copenhagen reported that it had been decapitated. The head was found three days later outside a TV station 12 miles away, but the culprits were never caught.

BORN

13 Apr, UK: Bonnie, the first offspring of the first cloned mammal, Dolly the Sheep

SENTENCED

4 May, USA: 'Unabomber' Theodore J Kaczynski to four life terms for his 17-year bombing spree in the USA

4 Sept, Rwanda: former prime minister Jean Kambanda to life after being found guilty of genocide

CLOSED

24 June, Rome: Shroud of Turin exhibition; three million people have visited it since it opened on 18 April

MARRIED

18 July, Johannesburg: South African premier Nelson Mandela to Graça Machel, on the same day as he celebrates his 80th birthday

BANNED

6 Aug, Switzerland: Irish swimmer and Olympic medallist Michelle Smith de Bruin for allegedly tampering with a urine sample for drug-testing

FIRST

11 Aug: person to cross the South Atlantic in a balloon: American adventurer Steve Fossett flies from Mendoza, Argentina, to the southern tip of Africa

CRASHED

2 Sept, Canada: Swissair Flight 111 off the coast of Nova Scotia; all 229 people on board are killed

LIFTED

24 Sept, Iran: *fatwa* (death sentence) on British writer Salman Rushdie by Iranian government for his 1989 novel *The Satanic Verses*

APPOINTED

22 June, UK: Simon Lewis as the Queen's communications secretary, to improve the image of the royal family following the death of Diana, Princess of Wales

20 Oct, New York: former Spice Girl Geri Halliwell as cultural ambassador for the UN Population Fund

DISCOVERED

12 Nov, Niger: new species of dinosaur, *Suhcomimus tenerensis*, by US palaeontologist Paul Sereno

NEW WORDS

docu-soap *n*: a TV documentary that concentrates on characters and conflicts rather than facts

Disneyfication *n*: softening literary classics or historical facts for a 90s mass audience; often refers to Disney movies such as *Pocahontas*

On 12 January, Ronaldo of Brazil and Inter Milan won the FIFA World Player of the Year award for the second year in succession. He is tipped to be the most exciting player in this summer's World Cup.

Nobel Peace Prize for Hume and Trimble

10 DECEMBER, STOCKHOLM

Leaders from opposite sides of the political fence in Northern Ireland have been given this year's Nobel Peace Prize.

The award has gone to John Hume, the leader of the nationalist Social Democratic and Labour Party, and David Trimble, head of the loyalist Ulster Unionists. It caps a year in which hopes for peace have risen to new heights.

Protracted efforts to bring peace between the Protestant and Catholic communities received a boost in July 1997, when the IRA pledged itself to a ceasefire. In September, Trimble, in a surprise move, agreed to talks including representatives of Sinn Fein, the political wing of the IRA.

In April of this year the Irish and British governments signed an agreement at Stormont Castle in Belfast. A new assembly is to be elected in Northern Ireland, with power to be shared between Catholics and Protestants. Prisoners from paramilitary organisations are to be released within two years, and cross-border institutions will be established to improve relations between the North and the Republic.

The agreement was put to the people of both Northern Ireland and the Republic in a referendum in May. In the first all-Ireland ballot since 1918, Hume and Trimble campaigned

JOINT HONOURS David Trimble, left, and John Hume display their awards.

together for a 'Yes' vote. Trimble's stance was opposed by die-hard loyalists, but the 'Yes' vote was 71 per cent in Northern Ireland and 94 per cent south of the border. The new assembly met on 1 July and elected Trimble as president.

On 15 August the worst outrage for years occurred at Omagh, County Tyrone, when 28 people were killed by a bomb planted by a Republican splinter group called the 'Real IRA'. The attack seems only to have fortified the people of the province in their determination to make peace work. The Stockholm committee has honoured them as much as their two leaders.

··· THE WORLD'S LONGEST SUSPENSION BRIDGE, THE 3.9-KM (2.4-MILE) AKASHI KAIKYO BRIDGE, OPENS IN JAPAN ···

Panic grows over Y2K Bug

Predictions of global chaos as the change from 1999 to 2000 makes computer systems crash are the latest take on millennial anxiety.

The 'Millennium Bug' or 'Y2K' (Year 2000) has arisen because, in the early days of computers, programmers saved on memory space by using just six digits for each date – December 31 1999 will be 123199. When 010100 arrives, experts fear that systems will either interpret the year as 1900 or shut down altogether.

Scenarios include meltdown of air-traffic control, financial chaos, widespread power shutdowns and rioting when food supplies fail. The Bug has gripped public imagination because even the experts cannot predict how computer systems will respond.

CRASH COURSE Japanese programmers attempt to find a solution to the Millennium Bug.

Programs have been launched to make computers 'compliant' – or able to cope with the date change. Some companies are making big profits from selling dried foods and water filters to the nervous.

School's out

1 JULY, KABUL, AFGHANISTAN

The Taliban Islamic Movement, which effectively seized control of Afghanistan two years ago, has banned home-based schools for girls in the capital, Kabul.

Girls have been barred from official schools since September 1996, but the Taliban authorities had turned a blind eye to the classes that people set up in their homes to teach literacy and numeracy. Religious police are now said to have closed more than 100 schools.

Mawlawi Qalamuddin, the minister responsible for the promotion of virtue and the suppression of vice, said that the schools were contrary to Islamic principles. Earlier this year the regime claimed that Afghan women (who must be completely covered in public) retained their dignity, unlike Western women, who 'are prey to an animal way of life'.

Serbian forces strike at KLA strongholds

31 JULY, BELGRADE

In the space of just a week, Serbian forces have struck three blows against the Kosovo Liberation Army. The KLA, which is fighting for the independence of the southern province of Yugoslavia, Kosovo, has been forced to surrender its stronghold villages of Orahovac, Lapusnik and Malisevo. The Serbian assault has dimmed hopes of peace in the region.

Almost 90 per cent of Kosovo's two million inhabitants are ethnic Albanians, but Slobodan Milosevic, the president of Yugoslavia, rose to prominence a decade ago by pledging to protect the Serbian minority there. The current troubles flared in February, when four Serbian police officers were shot dead in Likosane by the recently emerged KLA. A Serbian retaliatory raid left 80 Albanian Kosovars dead. The Yugoslav government claimed that the dead were members of the KLA; the Albanians protested that they were civilian villagers.

Amid fears that the violence might result in greater destabilisation of the entire Balkans area, the USA and the European Union denounced Serbian aggression and threatened sanctions against Yugoslavia. Russia and China distanced themselves from the West, but in the spring Western governments froze Yugoslavian financial assets held abroad and banned foreign investment in Yugoslavia. When, in May,

TAKING COVER Serbian police seek protection from the KLA and the sun.

President Milosevic agreed to accept external mediation of the dispute in Kosovo, sanctions were suspended. The renewed outbreak of violence, however, brings Yugoslavia to the brink of another civil war and raises the possibility that the West may intervene militarily to restore order.

··· 18 AUGUST: KAREN THORNDIKE (USA) BECOMES THE FIRST WOMAN TO SAIL SOLO AROUND THE WORLD ···

India and Pakistan test nuclear weapons

31 MAY, NEW DELHI

Global efforts to curb the proliferation of nuclear weapons received a major setback this month when India and Pakistan conducted a series of nuclear tests. India detonated five nuclear devices on 11 and 13 May; Pakistan responded by setting off six devices on 28 and 30 May. The two countries have thus graduated from 'threshold' to fully fledged nuclear powers. The Indian prime minister, Atal Behari Vajpayee, has stated that no radioactivity has been released into the atmosphere.

The tests have provoked strong condemnation from the world's great powers, who fear the destabilising effects of what appears to be an arms race in

FLAG DAY Crowds gather in Lahore, Pakistan, to celebrate the detonation of nuclear devices.

southern Asia. On 28 May, President Bill Clinton of the USA announced a package of sanctions between the two countries. But in Pakistan and India the tests have been greeted with wild scenes of popular rejoicing, while opinion polls

show almost universal backing for them. Since exploding a nuclear device in 1974, India has been unwilling to sign non-proliferation and test-ban treaties, and the Indian people have never accepted what they refer to as nuclear 'apartheid'. They believe that nuclear capability wins them international respect.

The Indian government has justified its action by pointing out that China has been supplying Pakistan with nuclear missiles and technology and has also been siting nuclear weapons on the Tibetan border with India. Pakistani authorities have defended their tests as a response to 'Indian provocation'. Pakistan claims it has now 'settled the score' with India.

BANKS COMPENSATE HOLOCAUST VICTIMS

**12 AUGUST,
BROOKLYN, NEW YORK**
**Three Swiss banks today agreed
a settlement of $1.25 billion (£800
million) with Jewish survivors of the
World War II Nazi Holocaust in
compensation for the lost contents
of deposit boxes and bank accounts.**

Crédit Suisse, the Swiss Bank
Corporation and the Union Bank of
Switzerland admitted errors in handling
wartime deposits made by thousands of
Jews, but denied deliberate attempts to
misappropriate the funds. The settlement
is to be paid in four instalments: $250
million (£151 million) within 90 days,
followed by three annual payments of
$333 million (£201 million).

STILL FIGHTING Holocaust survivors Ruth
Abraham and Michael Schonberger, who are suing
two German banks for $18 million (£12 million).

The agreement ended a class action
against the three banks in Brooklyn filed
by Holocaust survivors and their heirs
on 3 October 1996. On 19 June this year
the banks had offered $600 million
(£364 million) to settle the case, but the
World Jewish Congress and other groups
denounced the sum as 'humiliating'.

The court case did not address the
problem of 'victim gold': the coins,
watches, jewellery and even gold teeth
that the Nazis stole from their Jewish
victims in concentration camps, some of
which were allegedly bought by Swiss
banks. A report by nine US, Swiss,
Israeli, Polish and British historians
published in Zürich in May this year
suggested that the Swiss central bank
unknowingly bought at least 118 kg
(263 lb) of concentration-camp gold,
worth $1.2 million (£0.8 million) at
late 20th-century prices.

··· JANUARY: ICE STORMS LEAVE THREE MILLION PEOPLE IN THE USA AND CANADA WITHOUT ELECTRICITY FOR WEEKS ···

Silicone implant women sue

8 JULY, BAY CITY, MICHIGAN
**A group of US women today won
$3.2 billion (£1.9 billion) in
compensation for health problems
they reportedly suffered after silicone-
implant breast enlargements.**

Dow Corning Inc, manufacturer
of silicone implants, has agreed to pay
the compensation to around 170000
women who claim that their implants
ruptured or leaked, causing a range of
diseases including rheumatoid arthritis.
Today's agreement is part of a settlement
allowing Dow Corning to emerge from
bankruptcy, which it declared in May
1995 when faced with thousands of
legal claims. Despite the controversy,
many body-conscious women in the
USA continue to flock to plastic
surgeons for breast enlargements. The
use of silicone gel has been banned
since 1991, and the latest implants
use a saline gel.

Hurricane Mitch devastates Central America

**3 NOVEMBER,
MANAGUA, NICARAGUA**
**More than 7000 people are thought to
have died in the devastating floods and
mudslides unleashed by Hurricane
Mitch, which has been sweeping
through Central America.**

After a week of relentless rain
the storm is at last abating, and relief
workers are beginning to count the
cost. Honduras and Nicaragua are the
countries that have suffered the most,
but many deaths are also reported in
Guatemala and El Salvador. Many of the
places that have been worst hit are in
remote areas, and dozens of villages have
been cut off, with bridges destroyed and
roads impassable. Some communities
have been completely swept away.

Shanty towns around the capital,
Managua, are partly submerged, and

THE MISERY OF MITCH Children in Honduras
wait as the hurricane hovers out at sea.

Lake Managua, to the north of the
city, has become so swollen that it
has linked with Lake Nicaragua to
the southwest, creating a vast inland
sea. About 80 kilometres (50 miles)
northwest of Managua, the town of
Posoltega has been submerged in mud
after the lip of a volcano broke away;
rescue workers have already recovered
hundreds of bodies, and the death
toll may rise to more than 1000.

The International Red Cross has
announced that it will triple its relief
package to £4.5 million, and pledges
from other nations are pouring in.

BILL CLINTON IMPEACHED

A TOUCH TOO MUCH Monica Lewinsky embraces President Clinton at a White House lawn party in 1996.

**19 DECEMBER,
WASHINGTON DC**

In a day of high drama on Capitol Hill, the US Congress today voted to impeach President Bill Clinton on charges of lying under oath to a federal grand jury and obstructing justice.

Counts of perjury and abuse of high office were rejected. The proceedings centred on Clinton's alleged attempts to cover up sexual encounters with Monica Lewinsky, a former White House intern. Today's votes were in the House of Representatives, the lower house of Congress, and the president now faces trial early next year before the upper house, the Senate.

The controversy has dominated US politics since January. An investigation by special prosecutor Kenneth Starr into President and Mrs Clinton's roles in the Whitewater affair – a 1980s property deal in Arkansas, where Clinton was governor – was expanded to cover a sexual harassment case brought by Arkansas state worker Paula Jones, and then the involvement with Lewinsky. On 17 January, Clinton, giving

testimony in the Paula Jones case, was surprised to face questions about Lewinsky and denied under oath having had sexual relations with her.

In July, Lewinsky, offered immunity from prosecution, agreed to co-operate with Starr and handed over a dress stained with the president's semen. Testifying on 17 August, the president admitted 'inappropriate intimate contact' with Lewinsky.

The process paraded details of the president and Ms Lewinsky's sexual behaviour before global audiences. Comedians made much of Clinton's distinction between 'sexual relations', which he denied, and 'intimate contact'. His domestic popularity did not wilt, while around the world the affair variously provoked mirth, disgust and concern that the US government might be distracted from international affairs.

Clinton, who under US rules must stand down in any case in November 2000, dismissed calls that he should resign, promising that he would fight on and stay in office 'until the last hour of the last day of my term'.

Desert Fox bombs Iraq

**20 DECEMBER,
WASHINGTON DC**

President Clinton last night announced the successful end of Operation Desert Fox, a four-night US-British onslaught of air strikes on Iraq.

The Pentagon today says that it hit 100 military and political targets and degraded Iraq's nuclear capacity. The action resulted from Iraqi leader Saddam Hussein's refusal to co-operate with United Nations inspections of weapon-production sites that were agreed in the 1991 ceasefire to the Gulf War.

Desert Fox ended months of tension between the West and Iraq, which blocked the inspections in protest at UN sanctions imposed in 1990. Under the terms of the ceasefire, the sanctions would not be lifted until inspections proved that Iraq no longer held weapons of mass destruction.

A report by the United Nations' chief weapons inspector, Richard Butler, said that Iraq had not honoured its commitment to work with the inspectors. The attack launched earlier this week went ahead without the backing of the UN Security Council.

A WATCHFUL EYE Iraqis read about the recent air strikes in front of a poster of Saddam Hussein.

French jubilation at World Cup victory

13 JULY, PARIS

In a surprisingly one-sided final, the host nation, France, last night defeated the defending champions, Brazil, 3-0 to win football's World Cup for the first time.

The match took place amid rumours and wild speculation about the fitness of Brazilian striker Ronaldo, the world's most marketable player. Brazil were the pre-tournament favourites, but they were unimpressive in reaching the final, losing to Norway in the preliminary round and winning the semi-final against Holland on a penalty shoot-out after the match itself had finished 1-1.

The French team, on the other hand, had played consistently but not spectacularly well throughout the tournament, with a tight defence that

MON BRAVE President Chirac congratulates French captain Didier Deschamps on his team's win.

conceded only two goals in the seven matches played and a creative and combative midfield. Only in attack did France lack truly outstanding players, but this mattered little; their 15 goals in the tournament came from nine different players. The goals in the final were all scored by midfielders; Zinedine Zidane, the man of the match, got two headers in the first half, and Emmanuel Petit added the third just before the final whistle.

Excitement had steadily mounted in France as the national team progressed to the final, and there were scenes of mass jubilation in the streets of Paris and other cities last night as the World Cup at last came to the country of its creator – Jules Rimet.

··· 17 JANUARY, FRANCE: MASS DEMONSTRATIONS ARE HELD TO PROTEST AGAINST UNEMPLOYMENT ···

Smart designs brighten up future

Not since the 1960s has product design been so important. Consumers today require the optimum balance of form and function, beauty and ease of use – or so the designers would have us believe.

Some radical reworkings of consumer goods have won over the most conservative of shoppers. Apple's iMac computer, designed by Briton Jonathan Ives, has been a huge

success: not simply because the user can just take it out of the box and plug it in, but because its fruity colour schemes transform the computer from a dull office tool to a stylish furniture item. The iMac also has the shortest-ever manual for a home computer, with just 36 words and six pictures.

Mercedes-Benz is also pioneering design and hopes that its new MCC Smart will revolutionize the small-car market in the same way that the Mini did 40 years ago. With fuel consumption of 70 mpg, and being small enough to park perpendicular to the pavement, the Smart is seen by many as an answer to the pollution and congestion that plague the

streets of so many big cities. The Smart is a joint venture with the watch company Swatch, whose eye for fun fashion should win over any drivers who are nervous of being seen in such an unconventional vehicle.

Other recent design success stories include the Dyson vacuum-cleaner, which dispenses with the conventional waste bag in favour of a transparent drum. After British inventor James Dyson spent many fruitless years trying to persuade investors of the advantages of his design, his company has achieved worldwide sales of £2 billion ($3.3 billion).

TANGERINE DREAM The iMac has turned Apple's fortunes around.

But design innovation doesn't just benefit the developed world. Trevor Bayliss's BayGen clockwork radio is increasingly popular in areas where electricity sources can be scarce.

SMALL BUT SMART The MCC Smart.

Ol' Blue Eyes bids farewell

HIS WAY Sinatra's life may not have been perfect, but nobody could deny his talent or charisma.

14 MAY, BEVERLY HILLS
Frank Sinatra, one of the giants of popular music, died today at the age of 82. His 60-year career brought him success and fame in a host of different ways. In his youth he virtually invented the modern image of the idolized pop star, and in his prime he created an enduring legacy of great recordings as well as forging a distinguished career as a movie actor. In old age he was almost a parody of himself, but still attracted sell-out audiences whenever he performed – now as a living legend rather than a mere singer.

His private life, with its four marriages (his wives included the actresses Ava Gardner and Mia Farrow), love affairs, nightclub brawls and alleged links with gangsters, generated millions of words of newspaper gossip.

Sinatra, the son of Italian immigrants, was born in Hoboken, New Jersey, in 1915. He became a sensational success with teenage fans in the USA in the early 1940s, and world fame quickly followed. In the 1950s his singing career temporarily declined, but he achieved acclaim as a serious actor, winning an Oscar for his role in *From Here to Eternity* (1953). He originally announced his retirement in 1971, but continued to make new recordings and 'final' concert appearances into the 1990s. In stylishness of phrasing and subtlety of emotional shading of a lyric, he ranks as one of the greatest singers of all time.

··· TEN YEARS' RENOVATION OF THE GREAT SPHINX IS COMPLETED ···

FIRST DIGITAL TV BROADCAST

1 NOVEMBER, USA
Hi-tech images of Disney's arch-villainess Cruella DeVil were beamed into US homes tonight in the world's first digital television broadcast. ABC inaugurated its digital service with the cartoon *101 Dalmatians*.

Digital broadcasting involves compressing signals using the latest computer processors, then transmitting them in the computer code of binary digits. The signals are decoded in people's homes by special receivers. Many different channels of TV or radio can be transmitted on a single frequency, doing away with competition for space on the airwaves. At present, few homes possess digital TV sets, which cost more then $5000 (£3030) each in the USA, but cheap decoder boxes that can be plugged into existing sets are already on the market.

Wonder drug Viagra gives men a lift

Throughout the year the drug Viagra – a pill to combat male impotence – was rarely out of the news. It was developed by the pharmaceuticals company Pfizer, which originally saw the drug as a medicine for angina.

During tests, men discovered that it had remarkable 'side effects', and Pfizer realized that it had stumbled on a wonder drug. Last year the company's shares rose by 74 per cent in anticipation of its launch, and there was a stampede to obtain it in the USA after it was approved by the Food and Drug Administration. It was licensed in Britain in September, but NHS doctors were told not to prescribe it for patients until proper guidelines had been prepared. The government feared a massive bill if every impotent man were given the drug.

Viagra generated countless stories about old men turning into rampant studs and scares about men dying through sexual exertion (the death of Sani Abacha, dictator of Nigeria, on 8 June was attributed by local gossip to Viagra, although the official cause was a heart attack). In Paris, a restaurant served food with Viagra sauce.

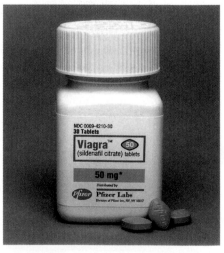

BLUE WONDER Viagra's high rate of success has given many men a new lease of lust.

Titanic proves unsinkable

13 MARCH, USA

Titanic, James Cameron's $200-million (£121-million), 194-minute feature film, which many predicted would be as ill-fated as its subject matter, this week becomes the most successful movie of all time as its US box office takings reach $477,349,092 (£288 million), finally knocking the 21-year-old *Star Wars* off the top spot.

While the 'ship of dreams' and its frozen nemesis were to became part of contemporary legend and folklore, so the movie has sailed into the cinema history books with a similar impact. When Cameron had the character of Jack Dawson gleefully shouting 'I'm the king of the world', he was perhaps anticipating his own success. There has been much speculation as to the factors contributing to this watery phenomenon. Critics originally saw the film as a conventional action blockbuster, its appeal centring on the big-budget dazzling special effects. However it soon became apparent that most of the diehard fans rewatching the film dozens of times were teenage girls, entranced by the love story played out by the young stars Leonardo DiCaprio and Kate Winslet. Was this the spirit of the old-fashioned Hollywood weepie triumphing over the technical trickery that has come to dominate the industry in recent years? Whatever the reason, there has never been an impact like this in movie history.

KING AND QUEEN Leo and Kate set sail together.

··· ELIZABETH TAYLOR IS RECOGNIZED BY THE US COUNCIL OF FASHION DESIGNERS FOR A LIFETIME OF GLAMOUR ···

MOVIELAND SURVIVES COLOSSAL *TITANIC* IMPACT

SPLIT SECOND Gwyneth Paltrow makes a life-changing decision in *Sliding Doors*.

The year opened with Captain James Cameron steering the not-so-unlucky *Titanic* into an iceberg of monumental box-office proportions, not to mention 11 Oscars, including Best Film. Roland Emmerich, director of the hugely successful *Independence Day*, must have thought that big special effects equalled big-box office returns. However, his monster of a movie *Godzilla* proved to be a giant, green, scaly turkey and the big flop of the summer. Eddie Murphy wooed young audiences as *Doctor Dolittle*, while rising star Gwyneth Paltrow wooed the grown-ups in the time-twisting romantic comedy *Sliding Doors*.

End-of-the-millennium jitters surfaced for Mimi Leder and Michael Bay when they respectively directed the big-bang disaster movies *Deep Impact* and *Armageddon*. Vincent Gallo's manic talent was showcased in the quirky *Buffalo '66*. He not only starred with Cristina Ricci but also directed, produced and composed the score. Shekhar Kapur's *Elizabeth* was both a visually sumptuous period drama and a gripping vehicle for the eminently talented Cate Blanchett. A surprise success for first-time director Guy Ritchie was *Lock, Stock and Two Smoking Barrels*, a punchy comedy about Cockney wide-boys in an East End gangster caper.

US HITS OF THE YEAR

1	THE BOY IS MINE	*Brandy & Monica*
2	I'M YOUR ANGEL	*R Kelly & Celine Dion*
3	TOO CLOSE	*Next*
4	THE FIRST NIGHT	*Monica*
5	I DON'T WANT TO MISS A THING	*Aerosmith*

US TV HITS

1	*Seinfeld*
2	*ER*
3	*Veronica's Closet*
4	*Friends*
5	*NFL Monday Night Football*

1999

DIED

2 Mar: Dusty Springfield, British singer

7 Mar: Stanley Kubrick, US-born film director

8 Mar: Joe DiMaggio, US baseball icon

8 May: Dirk Bogarde, British film star

17 June: Cardinal Basil Hume, leader of the Roman Catholic Church in England and Wales

ARRESTED

2 Apr, New Jersey: David Smith, accused of originating the highly destructive Melissa computer virus

SACKED

2 Feb, London: Glenn Hoddle, as England football manager, after he reportedly said that disabled people were paying the price for sins they had committed in a past life

*In the wake of the Spice Girls, a new wave of manufactured pop groups is wresting control of the charts from guitar bands. B*Witched (above), Steps, Boyzone and S Club 7 alarm rock purists but delight young fans.*

On 4 August, *Queen Elizabeth the Queen Mother celebrates her 99th birthday. 'The Queen Mum', as old as the century, is held in particular affection by the British people and supporters of the royal family worldwide. As late as 1997 she was still carrying out more than 50 public engagements per year.*

ELECTED

27 Feb, Nigeria: Olusegan Obasanjo as president

17 May, Israel: Ehud Barak, Labour Party leader, as prime minister

SENTENCED TO DEATH

29 June, Istanbul: Kurdish separatist leader Abdullah Ocalan, convicted of treason against the Turkish state

SOLD

8 June, Italy: Striker Christian Vieri, by Lazio football club of Rome to Inter Milan for record £28 million

CHAMPION

4 July, London: Pete Sampras, winner of the Wimbledon men's singles for the sixth time; he beats Andre Agassi 6-3, 6-4, 7-5

Diamond launch the Rio, the first portable music player for the MPEG Layer 3 (MP3) format, which consists of compressed digital files that can be downloaded from a computer and the Internet. Some experts are forecasting the death of the music industry.

IMPRISONED

8 June, London: Jonathan Aitken, former British Conservative government minister, for perjury

CLEARED

12 Feb, Washington DC: President Clinton, of perjury and obstruction of justice, by the US Senate

PUBLISHED

8 June: *Hannibal* by Thomas Harris, the latest adventures of Dr Hannibal Lecter, the world's favourite psychopath

NEW WORDS

cyberstress *n*: information overload from hi-tech sources including pagers, faxes and emails

digitopia *n*: state in which viewers will be able to choose from a huge range of digital TV channels

NATO launches humanitarian war

THE HARD MAN A bogeyman in the West, Milosevic is a heroic figure to many Serbs.

24 MARCH, BELGRADE
NATO bombs are falling on Belgrade tonight after last-ditch attempts to stave off war in the Balkans came to nothing. The US envoy to Kosovo, Richard Holbrooke, announced that he had failed to strike a peace deal with the president of Yugoslavia, Slobodan Milosevic, who has repeatedly ignored an agreement reached last autumn to end his offensive against the Kosovo Liberation Army and to reduce the levels of Serbian police and army personnel in the troubled province.

Western governments hope that a bombing campaign, without the use of ground troops, will be enough to bring Milosevic to his knees, thus protecting the ethnic Albanian population in Kosovo from 'ethnic cleansing' and guaranteeing Kosovo's autonomy within the Yugoslav federation. Spokespersons for NATO and the USA, who are acting without approval from the United Nations, have stressed that the decision to make war on the Yugoslavian government is a strictly 'humanitarian' one. Bombs will be targeted at strategic sites only, with the objective of destroying Milosevic's military capability.

The British prime minister, Tony Blair, said: 'We cannot contemplate, on the doorstep of the European Union, a disintegration into chaos and disorder.' In recent weeks Mr Blair has been the most persistent advocate of a military strike.

Refugees fleeing Kosovo in increasing numbers – 250 000 Albanians have so far been made homeless during the conflict – have welcomed the intervention. But the withdrawal of international monitors from the province has raised fears that, unless ground troops are deployed, the Kosovar Albanians will suffer severe reprisals from Serbian forces.

··· 1 AUGUST: THE WORLDWIDE BAN ON BRITISH BEEF EXPORTS ENDS AFTER THREE AND A HALF YEARS ···

Pinochet to appeal extradition ruling

16 APRIL, LONDON
Former Chilean dictator General Augusto Pinochet has been denied the right to return to his homeland. British Home Secretary Jack Straw has upheld the latest ruling of the Law Lords that Pinochet has no immunity against extradition to Spain, where he faces charges of crimes against humanity.

Chilean supporters of the general regard Straw's decision as an affront to Chilean democracy; but Straw's statement has cheered all those, including many Chileans, who want world leaders to be accountable to world opinion. Pinochet's lawyers say that they will take an appeal to the High Court, and even if that fails, extradition hearings have still to take place, dragging the case out yet further.

Kennedy Curse claims JFK Jr

21 JULY, MASSACHUSETTS
The bodies of John F Kennedy Jr, his wife Carolyn and her sister Lauren Bessette were brought ashore tonight, four days after the plane Kennedy was piloting was reported missing off Martha's Vineyard.

The son of legendary US president John F Kennedy, famous for saluting his father's coffin as a three-year-old, established the current affairs magazine *George* in 1995 but denied he had political ambitions. His death is now being seen as the latest evidence for a so-called 'Curse of the Kennedys'. Previous family 'victims' include his father, who was assassinated in 1963, and his uncle Bobby, shot in 1968. Bobby's son David died of a drug overdose in 1984, and another son, Michael, was killed in a skiing accident only last year.

THE LOST SON JFK Jr, seen here with his wife, appeared to have ruled out a political career.

Lawrence report highlights institutional racism

24 FEBRUARY, LONDON
The report of a public enquiry into the 1993 murder of black British teenager Stephen Lawrence has accused London's Metropolitan Police of 'professional incompetence' and 'institutional racism'.

However, the enquiry, under former High Court judge Sir William Macpherson, cleared the force of 'overt racism or discrimination'. After Lawrence – an 18-year-old student – was stabbed to death in Eltham, south London, on 22 April 1993, the Metropolitan Police arrested five white youths as suspects. Two of them were charged, but government prosecutors dropped the case in July of that year,

NEVER FORGET Neville and Doreen Lawrence campaign in front of an image of their son.

claiming insufficient evidence. Stephen's parents, Neville and Doreen, later failed in a private prosecution against the five youths, and in 1997 the British home

secretary, Jack Straw, ordered the Macpherson Enquiry in the light of accusations that officers had been motivated by racism and had acted slowly and inefficiently.

Today Mr Straw said that he would accept the enquiry's recommendations to extend existing race discrimination laws to cover the police and government departments, including the immigration service, and to allow appeal judges to order suspects to be tried a second time for offences when they have already been cleared. Metropolitan Police Commissioner Sir Paul Condon said he felt a sense of shame and admitted that his force had failed in many areas, but rejected calls for his resignation.

··· 22 JULY, USA: EILEEN COLLINS BECOMES THE FIRST WOMAN TO COMMAND A SPACE SHUTTLE MISSION ···

Shaky start for single currency

The new single European currency, the Euro, has had mixed fortunes since its launch on 1 January.

At its launch the Euro was valued at $1.16, but after only four months it had lost 10 per cent of its value. By 26 July, however, it had recovered strongly, reaching $1.724. The currency's slow start was a boon to British Eurosceptics,

such as the Conservative Party leader William Hague, who oppose abandoning sterling and giving up to the Central European Bank the UK's power to set interest rates. The low turnout in the European elections on 10 June has also been blamed on voters' disillusionment with the EU, but the currency's improved performance may change matters.

SYMBOL OF SUCCESS Guests celebrate the launch of the Euro at a party in the Paris Bourse in January.

Mobile phone scare on hold

8 APRIL, BRISTOL
Research findings published today will be music to the ears of mobile phone manufacturers. Recent studies have suggested that long-term use of mobiles could be linked to cancer and memory loss because microwave radiation from the phones has detrimental effects on the human brain.

However, a government-funded study rejects these claims and even reports that exposure to microwave radiation improved short-term memory in tests with 39 volunteers. Nevertheless the scientists did find that phone radiation produced mysterious warming in the brain.

About 500 million people around the world use mobile phones. Some consumers who became ill have tried to sue employers or manufacturers, but all have failed due to lack of hard evidence. Today's reassuring report is certainly not the final word on the subject.

12 KILLED IN HIGH-SCHOOL BLOODBATH

21 APRIL, DENVER, COLORADO

Two teenage students yesterday ran amok with automatic handguns at Columbine High School in the Denver suburb of Littleton, slaughtering 12 of their classmates and one teacher before turning their guns on themselves. More than 20 people were wounded.

The killers – Eric Harris (18) and Dylan Klebold (17) – laughed as they taunted and killed their victims and booby-trapped the premises with more than 50 home-made pipe-bombs. Police and SWAT gunmen surrounded the site while television crews, quickly on the scene, broadcast live footage of the incident and desperate parents raced to the school. The SWAT teams fired no shots, and when they moved into the buildings they found Harris and Klebold dead in the library.

The killers were members of a group known as the Trenchcoat Mafia and were said by surviving students to be obsessed with the Nazis and the occult. They had a special animosity towards athletes and African-American and Hispanic students; Harris left a note in which he said the attack was in revenge for being ridiculed. The outrage is again provoking debate over US gun laws. The National Rifle Association is due to hold its annual convention in Denver early next month and seemingly has no intention of calling it off. The NRA president, Charlton Heston, has called on Association members to 'stand in sombre but unshakeable unity'.

TEARS ARE NOT ENOUGH A mother and son mourn the Columbine dead.

··· APRIL, USA: SCIENTISTS DISCOVER A DNA VACCINE THAT CAN PROTECT MONKEYS AGAINST AIDS ···

Kosovo bombs stop but problems remain

11 JUNE, BELGRADE

It took longer than expected, but Yugoslav president Slobodan Milosevic has at last accepted the peace terms set out by NATO, and the bombing of Yugoslavia has come to an end. In a tent on Kosovo's border with Macedonia, the NATO commander, General Sir Michael Jackson, and generals from the Serbian army signed an agreement that requires Yugoslavia to move all of its 40 000 troops out of Kosovo within the next 11 days. A five-mile buffer zone is to be established between Serbia and Kosovo.

In 79 days of air bombardment Yugoslavia offered almost no resistance to NATO's superior power. The greatest embarrassment to the Western powers arose from a number of 'accidents', most

notably the bombing of a refugee convoy in April and an attack on the Chinese Embassy in Belgrade in May, when four people died and more than 20 were injured. A few days later an assault on the village of Korisa killed 87 Albanian Kosovar civilians. The total number of Yugoslavian casualties in the war is not known, but the real toll has been borne by the Albanians in Kosovo. Thousands have died as a result of 'ethnic cleansing' by Serbian forces, and almost one million homeless have taken refuge in Macedonia and Albania.

A 50 000-strong peace-keeping force of NATO and Russian troops now has the task of resettling refugees and protecting them from renewed Serbian assault. Meanwhile President Milosevic,

regarded as the architect of this crisis, is still in power despite war crimes indictments and growing opposition in his own country.

WARM WELCOME Ethnic Albanians in the town of Gnjilane celebrate the arrival of NATO troops.

TV presenter shot dead

26 APRIL, LONDON
Jill Dando, presenter of the popular BBC show *Crimewatch*, was shot dead today outside her home in west London by a mystery gunman.

Just after 11.30 am Dando's neighbours in Fulham found her in a pool of blood on her doorstep. Doctors and paramedics rushed to the scene and tried to resuscitate the 37-year-old presenter where she lay. She was then taken to nearby Charing Cross Hospital but pronounced dead at 1.03 pm. Police later announced that she had been killed by a single gunshot to the head.

Initial reports were that witnesses heard a car alarm and a scream and then saw a man with a mobile phone walking away calmly. Another witness, however, saw a suspicious-looking man who had been running and who escaped towards the adjacent Putney area on a bus. No motive for the attack is apparent, and there is speculation that it was the act of a stalker attracted by Dando's fame, or the result of a robbery that went wrong. Police have also not ruled out the possibility that it was a contract killing.

GOLDEN GIRL Jill Dando had been planning to anchor the BBC's Millennium coverage.

This afternoon flags were flown at half-mast at the BBC, and the Queen and prime minister both paid tributes. Dando's apparently motiveless murder has provoked widespread grief.

Barbie doll hits 40

9 MARCH, CALIFORNIA
Barbie, the world's best-selling doll, hit middle age today – but she is refusing to grow old gracefully. One of the new models for 1999, 'Butterfly Art Barbie', has a butterfly tattoo on her stomach and is going on sale with a set of removeable stick-on tattoos for her young (or not so young) owner.

The doll's manufacturer, Mattel, sells two Barbies every second around the world and has designated today as her 40th birthday because she was unleashed on the market on 9 March 1959. Ruth Handler, who founded the company with her husband Elliot and named the doll she created after her daughter Barbara, rang the opening bell at the New York Stock Exchange this morning.

Several more conventional Barbies have been released to mark the anniversary, including 'Crystal Jubilee Barbie', with a white chiffon gown decorated with minute coloured crystals, and 'Le Papillon Barbie', who wears a strapless black dress with dramatic butterfly wings. In her 40 years, Barbie has had 500 new looks.

··· 4 JULY: NOSTRADAMUS PREDICTED THAT THE WORLD WOULD END TODAY. IT DOESN'T ···

No go for human cloning

24 JUNE, LONDON
The British government has rejected the advice of its scientific advisers and refused to give the go-ahead to the cloning of human cells for medical research and treatment.

Two advisory bodies had recommended allowing cloning for research as long as the embryos were destroyed within 14 days. Now a committee of experts has been created to report on the pros and cons of this area of cutting-edge science.

Attempts to clone human embryos are under way in the USA, although President Clinton has blocked government funding while the ethics of such research are considered.

Geron Corporation of California recently bought the Scottish laboratory where Dolly the Sheep was cloned in 1997 and is carrying out top-secret research. In December last year, researchers at Kyunghee University in Seoul, South Korea, announced that they had achieved the breakthrough, cloning a human embryo using an unfertilized egg and cells from a woman in her 30s, but scientists have since cast doubt on this claim.

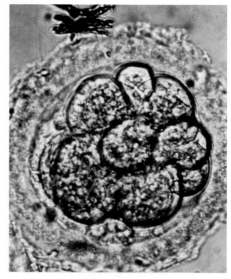

CELL SHOCK In a survey, almost 50 per cent of people say they don't trust scientists on cloning.

Nail-bomb suspect arrested

THE POWER OF HATE Victims of the nail-bomb receive treatment outside the Admiral Duncan pub in Soho.

3 MAY, LONDON

A 22-year-old engineer from Farnborough, Hampshire, has been arrested and charged with the 'nail-bomb' pub murders in the West End of London. The Soho outrage, which took place three days ago, followed two other bombings in April, the first on Brixton High Road and the second on Brick Lane. Saturation coverage in the media of a photograph of a young man in a baseball cap, caught by security cameras in Brixton, led to a tip-off. Materials to make the bombs were found when police entered the home of David Copeland.

More than 200 people have been injured in the attacks, and in the most recent one, three people have died, including a pregnant woman, Andrea Dykes, and the best man at her wedding. Her husband is still unconscious and remains in a critical condition in hospital.

It was thought that the perpetrator of the crimes was likely to be a member of a neo-Nazi organisation. The bomb in Brixton, where there is a big Afro-Caribbean population, and the one on Brick Lane, a centre of the Bangladeshi community, were directed at minority racial groups. The Soho bomb was planted in the Admiral Duncan pub, one of many gay venues in the area. However, police now believe that the accused man was operating on his own.

GM food row

20 JUNE, COLOGNE
Leaders of the major nations at the G7 summit agreed today to set up international research groups to study the safety of genetically modified (GM) food – crops whose genetic make-up has been changed by scientists.

The agreement comes after controversy in Britain over the safety of GM food. Last year researchers claimed that modified potatoes had caused stunted growth in rats, but the findings were dismissed by many scientists. On 15 March this year Marks & Spencer food stores banned GM produce, and on 27 April Tesco followed Iceland, Sainsbury's, Asda and Safeway in banning GM ingredients from its own-brand products.

HEALTH WARNING A Greenpeace activist carries stalks of genetically-modified corn.

THE LONG WALK TO RETIREMENT

3 JUNE, CAPE TOWN, S AFRICA
Nelson Mandela has handed the torch of multicultural nation-building in post-apartheid South Africa to his successor as leader of the African National Congress party, Thabo Mbeki.

In South Africa's election yesterday the ANC scored a landslide victory, taking almost two-thirds of the votes cast. The former ruling white National Party saw its vote fall to just 7 per cent, from 20 per cent in 1994.

The biggest task ahead of the new

FAREWELL Mandela, now 80 years old, hopes for a peaceful retirement in his Transkei birthplace.

president is to stem South Africa's soaring crime rates – perhaps the highest in the world. He is expected to initiate a campaign to drive out corruption in the police force, and to introduce tougher laws for gun crimes.

He has a tough act to follow. Whatever failings Mandela had as a president were balanced by his status as an international icon for reconciliation, showing no resentment to the architects of apartheid after his 26 years in captivity, which ended in 1990.

'Bloody hell!' United's treble triumph

27 MAY, BARCELONA

Last night, in the Nou Camp stadium, Manchester United won the European Cup for the first time in 31 years.

Mario Basler's sixth-minute free kick appeared to have handed victory to Bayern Munich, but, in one of the most dramatic reversals of fortune in football history, Teddy Sheringham equalized in injury time and then Ole Gunnar Solskjaer stabbed a Sheringham flick into the roof of the net, making United the first English club to seize the treble. Earlier this month they won the League Championship and the FA Cup.

Bayern players wept as the United fans went wild. 'Football, bloody hell!' was manager Alex Ferguson's succinct post-match comment.

THE BIG RED ONE The record-breaking United team make a triumphant bus-top tour of Manchester.

For Ferguson, the victory crowns what must be the greatest coaching career in British history. In addition to three Scottish championships, four FA Cups and one League Cup with Aberdeen in the 1980s, he has now led United to five English league titles, four FA Cups, one League Cup, two Cup-Winners' Cups and, not before time, the European Cup itself.

SABRES, SHAKESPEARE AND SOBS TAKE OVER HOLLYWOOD

QUEEN OF SPACE Natalie Portman plays Queen Amidala in *The Phantom Menace*.

The year of the second coming was nigh. George Lucas wielded his directorial light-sabre again for *Star Wars Episode I – The Phantom Menace*, but the movie's publicity campaign probably deserved the most honours. *Shakespeare in Love* swept seven Oscars; Joseph Fiennes starred as the playwright-in-tights, and co-star Gwyneth Paltrow was dramatically moved to tears by her Best Actress award. *The Matrix* was a hit for the Wachowski brothers, with Keanu Reeves leaping into the realms of virtual disbelief. The feel-good *Notting Hill* starred a terribly English Hugh Grant and an awfully American Julia Roberts. Mike Myers returned to spoof 007 as dentist's nightmare Austin Powers, but Pierce Brosnan proved that the real James Bond is still fit for the next millennium in *The World Is Not Enough*.

Real royals put in the shade by Spice Girl nuptials

5 JULY, DUBLIN

Traditionally, the marriage of Prince Edward and Sophie Rhys-Jones at Windsor Castle on 19 June would have been the unchallenged 'Wedding of the Year'. The newly-created Earl and Countess of Wessex are seen as the last chance for the troubled Royal Family to regain its place in the hearts of the British people. But it was Victoria Adams (aka Posh Spice) and Manchester United footballer David Beckham whose match created the bigger media frenzy.

The ceremony took place yesterday in a huge marquee at Luttrellstown Castle in Dublin. The reception was a lavish affair, featuring an 18-piece orchestra, 125 security staff, a firework show and, to add to the royal overtones, a pair of red velvet thrones. The couple sold exclusive picture rights of the day to *OK!* magazine, a deal that will add to their £30-million ($50-million) combined fortune. They were previously the focus of attention in March with the arrival of their baby boy, Brooklyn.

NEW ROYALTY Becks and Posh, media monarchs.

FUN AND FIREWORKS AS CENTURY ENDS

A century marked by the bloodiest conflicts in human history ended on a note of unity and celebration as people around the world marked the arrival of the third millennium.

Kiribati in the south Pacific was the first place to see in the new era and television audiences watched as the wonder of satellite broadcasting followed the celebrations as they moved westwards.

One million people massed on the shores of Sydney Harbour as performers abseiled from the sloping roofs of the Opera House and fireworks erupted in the skies behind them. It was the first event in a year of celebrations as the biggest city in Australia counts down to the Olympic Games.

The Pyramids of Egypt were serenaded by the French musician Jean-Michel Jarre, whose 'electronic opera' *Twelve Dreams Of The Sun* was accompanied by his customary dazzling display of laser effects.

NO PLACE LIKE DOME London's Millennium Experience is on a 181-acre site in North Greenwich.

OOH LA LA! The Eiffel Tower in a blaze of glory.

Although the original meaning behind the celebrations – the 2,000th anniversary of the birth of Jesus Christ – seemed to be forgotten by many revellers, the Vatican celebrated with a concert attended by 60,000 people in St Peter's Square and a special midnight blessing by Pope John Paul.

The people of France needed cheering up, after devastating storms left much of the country without electricity. Troubles were forgotten as fireworks erupted from the Eiffel Tower and 11 ferris wheels lit up along the Champs Elysées.

Britain also had a big wheel, the largest in the world, but a last-minute hitch meant that the 136.1-m (446-ft 7-in) tall London Eye failed to turn as planned. Nevertheless, the River Thames was lit up with dazzling pyrotechnics, and celebrations in the £758-million ($1,256-million) Millennium Dome went on until the early hours. Londoners woke up to 150 tonnes of rubbish – much of which consisted of empty champagne bottles.

New York City's traditional dropping of the glass ball was even more spectacular than usual, as over 500 strobe lights and halogen bulbs lit up a massive '2000' above Times Square. A bar in California was so keen to get in on the act that the owner applied for it to become part of New York State so customers could celebrate three hours early.

Best of all, despite the predictions, the fabled Y2K bug failed to bite. The most pressing question as the 20th century faded was whether the next 100 years could be as eventful.

US HITS OF THE YEAR

1	SMOOTH	*Santana featuring Rob Thomas*
2	IF YOU HAD MY LOVE	*Jennifer Lopez*
3	GENIE IN A BOTTLE	*Christina Aguilera*
4	LIVIN' LA VIDA LOCA	*Ricky Martin*
5	NO SCRUBS	*TLC*

US TV HITS

1	*ER*
2	*Friends*
3	*Frasier*
4	*NFL Monday Night Football*
5	*Jesse/Veronica's Closet*

Worldwide Fund for Nature

Picture Acknowledgements

86cl Readers Digest Association
86cr Library of Congress/Corbis
86, 87t Hulton Deutsch Collection/Corbis
87b The National Archives/Corbis
88t Corbis
88b UPI/Bettmann/Corbis
89c Everett/Corbis
89l UPI/Bettmann/Corbis
89r Erich Lessing/AKG London
90l ET Archive
90r AKG London
91t Jerry Lordiguss/Science Photo Library
91b Hulton Getty
92t/bl AKG London
92br, 93t Hulton Deutsch Collection/Corbis
93b AKG London
94l Hulton Getty
94c Erich Lessing/AKG London
94r Everett/Corbis
95 Hulton Getty
96l John Reader/Science Photo Library
96c AKG London
96r E O Hoppé/Corbis
97t Bettmann/Corbis
97b Hulton Getty
98l Everett/Corbis
98c Bettmann/Corbis
98r UPI/Bettmann/Corbis
99t Corbis
99b, 100 Hulton Getty
101t AKG London
101c Hulton Getty
101b Bettmann/Corbis
102l Hulton Getty
102r Michael Nicholson/Corbis
103t Library of Congress/Corbis
103c Bettmann/Corbis
103b Bettmann/Corbis
104t AKG London
104b Hulton Getty
105t Bettmann/Corbis
105b Museum of Flight/Corbis
106t AKG London
106b Bettmann/Corbis
107t Hulton Getty
107b AKG London
108l The Robert Opie Collection
108c ©1997 King Features Syndicate Inc
108r Everett/Corbis
109t Range/Bettmann/Corbis
109c Bettmann/Corbis
110l The Robert Opie Collection
110c Science Photo Library
110, 111t UPI/Bettmann/Corbis
111b Hulton Getty
112t Hulton Deutsch Collection/Corbis
112bl Hulton Getty
112br Antonio M Rosario/The Image Bank
113t AKG London
113b UPI/Bettmann/Corbis
114c Hulton Getty
114l Bayer Plc
114r Hulton Getty
115l Jack Fields/Corbis
115r The Robert Opie Collection
116t Library of Congress/Corbis
116b UPI/Bettmann/Corbis
117t UPI/Bettmann/Corbis
117b Hulton Getty
118l UPI/Bettmann/Corbis
118c The Robert Opie Collection
118r Illustrated London News
119t Bettmann/Corbis
119b Hulton Deutsch Collection/Corbis
120t Hulton Getty

120b E O Hoppé/Corbis
121t Corbis
121b AKG London
122l Hulton Deutsch Collection/Corbis
122c Everett/Corbis
122r UPI/Bettmann/Corbis
123t Franklin D Roosevelt Library/Corbis
123t Christel Gerstenberg/Corbis
123b Hulton Deutsch Collection/Corbis
124b The Science Museum/Science & Society Picture Library
125t The Robert Opie Collection
125b Bettmann/Corbis
126t NMPFT/Science & Society Picture Library
126b, 127t UPI/Bettmann/Corbis
127b Al Hamdan/The Image Bank
128t N Wright/National Motor Museum/Nicky Wright
128b, 129t The Robert Opie Collection
129b UPI/Bettmann/Corbis
130l Corbis/Bettmann/UPI/Corbis
130c UPI/Bettmann/Corbis
130r The Robert Opie Collection
131t UPI/Bettmann/Corbis
131b Bettman/Corbis
132t Hulton Deutsch Collection/Corbis
132b Dean Conger/Corbis
133t The Robert Opie Collection
133c Everett/Corbis
134t Stiftung Automuseum Volkswagen
134cl UPI/Bettmann/Corbis
134l The Robert Opie Collection
134r Hulton Getty
135t AKG London
135bl Polaroid
135br Hulton Deutsch Collection/Corbis
136 Hulton Getty
137t AKG London
137b Bettmann/Corbis
138l BBC Picture Archives
138c UPI/Bettmann/Corbis
138r Hulton Getty
139 Bettmann/Corbis
140c UPI/Bettmann/Corbis
140l Hulton Getty
140r W A Sharman/Milepost
141t Illustrated London News
141b Central Press Photos/Hulton Getty
142 AKG London
143t Bettmann/Corbis
143b UPI/Bettmann/Corbis
144l Hulton Getty
144c The Robert Opie Collection
144r, 145t Hulton Deutsch Collection/Corbis
145b, 146t UPI/Bettmann/Corbis
146b Hulton Getty
147t Hulton Deutsch Collection/Corbis
147b, 148t UPI/Bettmann/Corbis
149 Bettmann/Corbis
149b, 150 Corbis
151 Imperial War Museum
152t, 153t The National Archives/Corbis
153c Imperial War Museum
153b Illustrated London News
154t AKG London
154b Corbis
155t AKG London
155b UPI/Bettmann/Corbis
156l Everett/Corbis
156c The Robert Opie Collection

156r Hulton Getty
157t Imperial War Museum
157b The National Archives/Corbis
158t Corbis
158c The National Archives/Corbis
159 AKG London
160, 161t UPI/Bettmann/Corbis
161b AKG London
162l AKG London
162c The Science Museum/Science & Society Picture Library
162r The Robert Opie Collection
163t Hulton Getty
163b Hulton Deutsch Collection/Corbis
164t The National Archives/Corbis
164b UPI/Bettmann/Corbis
165 AKG London
166, 167t Imperial War Museum
167b UPI/Bettmann/Corbis
168t The Robert Opie Collection
168b AKG London
169t UPI/Bettmann/Corbis
169b AKG London
170 UPI/Bettmann/Corbis
171t Imperial War Museum
171b Corbis
172t The Science Museum/Science & Society Picture Library
172b UPI/Bettmann/Corbis
173 Hulton Getty
174c The Robert Opie Collection
174 Hulton Getty
175t Keystone/Hulton Getty
175b UPI/Bettmann/Corbis
176t Imperial War Museum
176b Bettmann/Corbis
177t Imperial War Museum
177b, 178b UPI/Bettmann/Corbis
179t Tate Gallery Publications
179b Everett/Corbis
180l/c UPI/Bettmann/Corbis
180r Hulton Getty
181t Bettmann/Corbis
181b, 182t AKG London
182b UPI/Bettmann/Corbis
183t Bettmann/Corbis
183b UPI/Bettmann/Corbis
184t UPI/Bettmann/Corbis
184b Library of Congress/Corbis
185t Hulton Getty
185b UPI/Bettmann/Corbis
186l Hulton Getty
186c John Hill/The Image Bank
186r The Robert Opie Collection
187t Bettmann/Corbis
187b UPI/Bettmann/Corbis
188t UPI/Bettmann/Corbis
188b Everett/Corbis
189t Hulton Getty
189b David Sparrow
190l The Robert Opie Collection
190c Kai-Uwe Franz (K&K)/Redferns
190r Hulton Getty
191t AKG London
191b, 192t Hulton Getty
192b Polaroid
193 UPI/Bettmann/Corbis
194c Merlyn Soyern/Hulton Getty
194 Hulton Deutsch Collection/Corbis
195, 196l UPI/Bettmann/Corbis
196tr Hulton Getty
196br National Motor Museum
197t Franz Cancellare/UPI/Bettmann/Corbis
197b, 198b UPI/Bettmann/Corbis

199t AKG London
199b Everett/Corbis
200l Bettmann/Corbis
200c Adidas
200r, 201t UPI/Bettmann/Corbis
201b Hulton Getty
202t Bettmann/Corbis
202b UPI/Bettmann/Corbis
203t Hulton Getty
203b Everett/Corbis
204t Hulton Getty
204b ©1950 United Feature Syndicate, Inc
205t UPI/Bettmann/Corbis
205b AKG London
206t Silkeborg Museum/Science Photo Library
206b, 207t UPI/Bettmann/Corbis
207b Everett/Corbis
208l UPI/Bettmann/Corbis
208c Michael Ochs Archive/Redferns
208r Keystone/Hulton Getty
209 Hulton Deutsch Collection/Corbis
210t Keystone/Hulton Getty
210b The Robert Opie Collection
211t UPI/Bettmann/Corbis
211b Hulton Getty
212t Bettmann/Corbis
212b Hulton Getty
213t UPI/Bettmann/Corbis
213b, 214t Hulton Getty
214c Stephen Marks/The Image Bank
214b UPI/Bettmann/Corbis
215t AKG London
216b, 216t Everett/Corbis
216c Hulton Getty
216b The National Archives/Corbis
217t Hulton Getty
217b A Barrington Brown/Science Photo Library
218t Hulton Getty
218b, 219t UPI/Bettmann/Corbis
219b, 220t Keystone/Hulton Getty
220c Kurt Hutton/Hulton Getty
221t AKG London
221b UPI/Bettmann/Corbis
222t Library of Congress/Corbis
222b Hulton Getty
223 Everett/Corbis
224c The Robert Opie Collection
224 UPI/Bettmann/Corbis
225t Hulton Getty
225b, 226t UPI/Bettmann/Corbis
226b AKG London
227t Hulton Getty
227b AKG London
228l Science Photo Library
228c Hulton Getty
228r Corbis
229t Hulton Deutsch Collection/Corbis
229b Corbis
230t Hewitt/Hulton Getty
230b Joseph McKeown/Hulton Getty
231t UPI/Bettmann/Corbis
231b The Kobal Collection
232l Novosti/Science Photo Library
232c Hulton Getty
232r Science Photo Library
233 UPI/Bettmann/Corbis
234t Hulton Getty
234b UPI/Bettmann/Corbis
235 Everett/Corbis
236l UPI/Bettmann/Corbis
236c Peter Newark's Pictures
236r Science & Society Picture Library
237t Key Sports/Hulton Getty
237b Hulton Deutsch Collection/Corbis
238 UPI/Bettmann/Corbis
239l Keystone/Hulton Getty
239r Peter Newark's Pictures

240l Hulton Getty
240c Hulton Getty
240r Mattel UK
241 UPI/Bettmann/Corbis
242t Library of Congress/Corbis
242b Hulton Getty
243t Roger Wood/Corbis
243b Peter Newark's Pictures
244 NASA/Science & Society Picture Library
245t UPI/Bettmann/Corbis
245b Hulton Getty
246t The Kobal Collection
246b National Motor Museum
247t Hulton Getty
247b The Robert Opie Collection
248cl Science & Society Picture Library
248cr The Robert Opie Collection
248l UPI/Bettmann/Corbis
248r Hulton Getty
249t Novosti/Science Photo Library
249b Hulton Getty
250t UPI/Bettmann/Corbis
250b Peter Newark's Pictures
251l The Kobal Collection
251r Evening Standard/Hulton Getty
252l Science & Society Picture Library
252c Corbis
252r, 253t Hulton Getty
253b Corbis
254t UPI/Bettmann/Corbis
254b Bridgeman Art Library/©ARS, NY and DACS, London 1997
255t Hulton Getty
255b The Kobal Collection
256l Novosti/Science & Society Picture Library
256c Adam Hart-Davis/Science Picture Library
256r Evening Standard/Hulton Getty
257t Hulton Deutsch Collection/Corbis
257b Evening Standard/Hulton Getty
258t UPI/Bettmann/Corbis
258b Keystone/Hulton Getty
259t Peter Newark's Pictures
259b, 260t Hulton Getty
260b Hulton Deutsch Collection/Corbis
261t Evening Standard/Hulton Getty
261b Corbis
262l UPI/Bettmann/Corbis
262c The Robert Opie Collection
262r Everett/Corbis
263t UPI/Bettmann/Corbis
263b Evening Standard/Hulton Getty
264t UPI/Bettmann/Corbis
264b Hulton Getty
265t Express Newspapers
265b The Kobal Collection
266c Hulton Getty
266l UPI/Bettmann/Corbis
266r AKG London
267b UPI/Bettmann/Corbis
268tl Hulton Getty
268tr,b Hulton Deutsch Collection/Corbis
269t UPI/Bettmann/Corbis
269b Peter Newark's Pictures
270 Hulton Getty
271t Hulton Deutsch Collection/Corbis
271c UPI/Bettmann/Corbis
271b The Kobal Collection
272l The Kobal Collection
272c Hulton Getty
273 Hulton Getty
274 Hulton Getty

275t The Kobal Collection
275b Hulton Getty
276l,c UPI/Bettmann/Corbis
276r Frank Edwards
277 UPI/Bettmann/Corbis
278 Hulton Getty
279 UPI/Bettmann/Corbis
280t Henry Diltz/Corbis
280b Hulton Getty
281t Redferns
281b Everett/Corbis
282c The Kobal Collection
282l UPI/Bettmann/Corbis
282r NASA/Corbis
283 Hulton Deutsch Collection/Corbis
284t Hulton Getty
284b Corbis
285t UPI/Bettmann/Corbis
285b Everett/Corbis
286l Hulton Getty
286c The Robert Opie Collection
286r UPI/Bettmann/Corbis
287t Bettmann/Corbis
287b NASA/Zooid Pictures
288t UPI/Bettmann/Corbis
288b Evening Standard/Hulton Getty
289t Museum of Flight/Corbis
289b Hulton Getty
290t AKG London
290b UPI/Bettmann/Corbis
291t Hulton Getty
291c UPI/Bettmann/Corbis
291b Everett/Corbis
292l Hulton Getty
292c Allsport
292r Elliot & Landy/Redferns
293t Hulton Getty
293b UPI/Bettmann/Corbis
294t Roger Clifford
294b UPI/Bettmann/Corbis
295t Keystone/Hulton Getty
295bl Everett/Corbis
295br IBM
296l Hulton Getty
296c National Motor Museum
296r Science Photo Library
297t Keystone/Hulton Getty
297b UPI/Bettmann/Corbis
298t UPI/Bettmann/Corbis
298b Central Press Photos/Hulton Getty
299t Ian Dickson/Redferns
299b Everett/Corbis
300c UPI/Bettmann/Corbis
300l Hulton Getty
300r Hulton Deutsch Collection/Corbis
301t UPI/Bettmann/Corbis
301b, 302t Hulton Getty
302b National Archives/Corbis
303 UPI/Bettmann/Corbis
304tl David Redfern/Redferns
304tr Michael Ochs Archives/Redferns
304b, 305t UPI/Bettmann/Corbis
305b Everett/Corbis
306l Invicta Plastics Ltd
306c/307t Hulton Getty
307b Dept of Defence/Corbis
308t AKG London
308b UPI/Bettmann/Corbis
309 AKG London
310l Redferns
310r Michael Ochs Archives/Redferns
311 Everett/Corbis
312l Hulton Getty
312c Everett/Corbis
312r Hulton Getty
313t National Archives/Corbis
313b UPI/Bettmann/Corbis
314t Mirror Syndication International
314b Hulton Deutsch Collection/Corbis
315 Hulton Getty
316l UPI/Bettmann/Corbis
316c Hulton Getty

316r Redferns
317t Popperfoto
317b Hulton Getty
318t James Meyer/The Image Bank
318b UPI/Bettmann/Corbis
319t AKG London
319b Everett/Corbis
320l UPI/Bettmann/Corbis
320c Corbis
320r, 321t Corbis
321b Telegraph group Ltd, London 1976
322t, 323t Hulton Deutsch Collection/Corbis
323bl Denis O'Regan/Corbis
323br Hulton Deutsch Collection/Corbis
324l Bettmann/Corbis
324r Corbis
325t National Motor Museum
325b Everett/Corbis
326t Rex Features
327, 328 UPI/Bettmann/Corbis
329t Sipa Press/Rex Features
329b, 330t Hulton Getty
330b David Redfern/Redferns
331 Everett/Corbis
332l The Robert Opie Collection
332c Magimix
332r, 333t UPI/Bettmann/Corbis
333b, 334 Hulton Getty
335t Allsport
335b, 336t AKG London
336t Sony
336b UPI/Bettmann/Corbis
337t Rex Features
337b Sipa Press/Rex Features
338, 339 UPI/Bettmann/Corbis
340 NASA/Science Photo Library
341 Everett/Corbis
342l UPI/Bettmann/Corbis
342c Reinhold Messner
342r Rex Features
343t Sipa Press/Rex Features
343b Arthur Rackham Collection/Mary Evans Picture Library
343b, 344t Hulton Getty
344b Sipa Press/Rex Features
345t UPI/Bettmann/Corbis
345b Sipa Press/Rex Features
346t Everett/Corbis
346b Central Press Photos/Hulton Getty
347t Richard Hamilton Smith/Corbis
347bl The Kobal Collection
347br Hulton Getty
348 Sipa Press/Rex Features
349 UPI/Bettmann/Corbis
350t Corbis
350b, 351t UPI/Bettmann/Corbis
351b Keystone/Hulton Getty
352t NASA/Corbis
352c Namco Ltd
352b IBM
353t UPI/Bettmann/Corbis
353b Everett/Corbis
354l Robert Trippett/Rex Features
354c Rex Features
354r Sipa Press/Rex Features
355 Rex Features
356 UPI/Bettmann/Corbis
357t Sipa Press/Rex Features
357b UPI/Bettmann/Corbis
358 Steve Powell/Allsport
359t Pacific Group International
359b Everett/Corbis
360l Today/Rex Features
360c Richie Aaron/Redferns

360r UPI/Bettmann/Corbis
361 Sipa Press/Rex Features
362t Science Photo Library
362c Sipa Press/Rex Features
362r AKG London
363t Everett/Corbis
363b National Motor Museum
364l Ron Tussy/Sipa Press/Rex Features
364c Redferns
364r Sipa Press/Rex Features
365t Mahendra Singh/Sipa Press/Rex Features
365b AKG London
366t Corbis
366c Bite Communications
366b Redferns
367t David Cannon/Allsport
367b Everett/Corbis
368l Stephen Marks/The Image Bank
368c UPI/Bettmann/Corbis
368r Sipa Press/Rex Features
369l Alain Schroder/Sipa Press/Rex Features
369r Rex Features
370t UPI/Bettmann/Corbis
370b Rex Features
371 UPI/Bettmann/Corbis
372t Science Photo Library
372b Sipa Press/Rex Features
373t D Stevens/Rex Features
373b Everett/Corbis
374c Sipa Press/Rex Features
374l Erich Lessing/AKG London
374r Everett/Corbis
375t Bettmann/Corbis
375b NASA/Corbis
376t Reuters/Bettmann/Corbis
376b Martin Jones/Ecoscene/Corbis
377t Rex Features
377b UPI/Bettmann/Corbis
378t Bob Thomas Sports/Popperfoto
378b Allsport
379t UPI/Bettmann/Corbis
379b The Kobal Collection
380l Media Press International/Rex Features
380r UPI/Bettmann/Corbis
381t Sipa Press/Rex Features
381b-384t UPI/Bettmann/Corbis
384b Sipa Press/Rex Features
385t Everett/Corbis
385b Glenn A Baker/Redferns
386l Sipa Press/Rex Features
386c Corbis
386r Rex Features
387t Bettmann/Reuters/Corbis
387b Rex Features
388 Sipa Press/Rex Features
389t Rex Features
389b David Turnley/Corbis
390t UPI/Bettmann/Corbis
390b David Boe Colour Photography/Corbis
391 Everett/Corbis
392l Today/Rex Features
392c/r Rex Features
393t Bettmann/Corbis
393b Guzelian/Sipa Press/Rex Features
394t Jacques Witt/Rex Features
394b Rex Features
395t Chesnot/Sipa Press/Rex Features
395b Sipa Press/Rex Features
396t Rex Features
396b Corbis

397t Rex Features
397b Everett/Corbis
398l Q A Photos Ltd
398c Harvard PR
398r Trippett/Sipa Press/Rex Features
399t UPI/Bettmann/Corbis
399b Action Press/Rex Features
400t Rex Features
400b Jacques Witt/Sipa Press/Rex Features
401t Rex Features
401b Kevin Harvey/Sipa Press/Rex Features
402t Sipa Press/Rex Features
402b NASA/Corbis
403t Everett/Corbis
403b, 404l Sipa Press/Rex Features
404c Rex Features
404r Dennis Cameron/Rex Features
405t Rex Features
405b Sipa Press/Rex Features
406t East News/Sipa Press/Rex Features
406b Robert Wallis/Sipa Press/Rex Features
407t Rex Features
407b Paul Hanny/Gamma/Frank Spooner Pictures
408 Rex Features
409t G Vandystadt/Allsport
409b Image Press/Rex Features
410l Dakota/Rex Features
410c Corbis
410r Mantel/Rex Features
411t Delahaye/Sipa Press/Rex Features
411b Johan Koos/Sipa Press/Rex Features
412t Sipa Press/Rex Features
412b Corbis
413 Sipa Press/Rex Features
414tl Mirror Syndication International
414tr Allsport
414b Mirror Syndication International
415t NASA/Science Photo Library
415b Everett/Corbis
416l Action Press/Rex Features
416c Larry Gatz/The Image Bank
416r Gilbert Blecken/SIN
417t Rex Features
417b Sipa Press/Rex Features
418t Rex Features
418b Sipa Press/Rex Features
419t Hank Morgan/Science Photo Library
419b Richard Young/Rex Features
420l Rex Features
420r Sipa Press/Rex Features
421t Rex Features
421b Everett/Corbis
422l Sipa Press/Rex Features
422c Leon Schadberg/Rex Features
422r Sipa Press/Rex Features
423t Corbis
423b Alan Lewis/Rex Features
424t Corbis
424b Rex Features
425t Sipa Press/Rex Features
425b AKG London/©The Munch Museum/The Munch-Ellingsen Group/DACS 1997
426t NASA/Corbis
426b Rex Features
427t Shaun Boterill/Allsport
427b, 428l Rex Features

428c Sipa Press/Rex Features
428r Action Press/Rex Features
429t Sipa Press/Rex Features
429b, 430 Rex Features
431t Chris Harris/Rex Features
431b Rex Features
432t Saatchi Collection
432b, 433t Rex Features
433b Everett/Corbis
434t David Parker/Science Photo Library
434c Stu Forster/Allsport
434b Rex Features
435t Heidi Levine/Sipa Press/Rex Features
435b NASA
436t Drew Farrell/Rex Features
436b J Lash/Sipa Press/Rex Features
437t Greg Williams/Rex Features
437b AKG London
438t Allsport
438b Sipa Press/Rex Features
439t Everett/Corbis
439b GT Interactive Software Corp
440l Reuter/Popperfoto
440c NASA
440r Bertal/Sipa Press/Rex Features
441t Tim Rooke/Rex Features
441b Rex Features
442t Tim Rooke/Jorgensen/Rex Features
442b Sipa Press/Rex Features
443t Tony & Daphne Hallas/Science Photo Library
443b J Sutton-Hibbert/Rex Features
444t Associated Press
444b Popperfoto
445t Popperfoto
445b Rex Features
446t Richard Young/Rex Features
446b D Berkowitz/Sipa Press/Rex Features
447t David Cannon/Allsport
447b Rex Features
448t Associated Press
448bl One Little Indian
448br Popperfoto
449t, b Associated Press
450t Popperfoto
450b Associated Press
451t, b Associated Press
452t Associated Press
452b Popperfoto
453t Popperfoto
453bl Rex Features
453br Apple Macintosh
454t, b Associated Press
455t, b image.net
456b Epic Records
456tl Press Association
456tr Diamond Multimedia
457tl Associated Press
457br Rex Features
458t Popperfoto
458b Associated Press
460t Press Association
460b Popperfoto
461t Popperfoto
461r Popperfoto
461b Rex Features
462t Press Association
462c image.net
462b Press Association
463t Rex Features
463b PA News Photo Library

50 51 52 53 54
60 61 62 63 64
70 71 72 73 74
80 81 82 83 84
90 91 92 93 94